BRASENOSE

The Biography of an Oxford College

Old Quad, 1814 (R. Ackermann, *Oxford*, 1813–14)

BRASENOSE

The Biography of an Oxford College

J. MORDAUNT CROOK

OXFORD

UNIVERSITY PRESS

OXFORD
UNIVERSITY PRESS

Great Clarendon Street, Oxford OX2 6DP

Oxford University Press is a department of the University of Oxford.
It furthers the University's objective of excellence in research, scholarship,
and education by publishing worldwide in

Oxford New York

Auckland Cape Town Dar es Salaam Hong Kong Karachi
Kuala Lumpur Madrid Melbourne Mexico City Nairobi
New Delhi Shanghai Taipei Toronto

With offices in

Argentina Austria Brazil Chile Czech Republic France Greece
Guatemala Hungary Italy Japan Poland Portugal Singapore
South Korea Switzerland Thailand Turkey Ukraine Vietnam

Oxford is a registered trade mark of Oxford University Press
in the UK and in certain other countries

Published in the United States
by Oxford University Press Inc., New York

British Library Cataloguing in Publication Data
Data available

Library of Congress Cataloging in Publication Data
Data available

Typeset by SPI Publisher Services, Pondicherry, India
Printed in Italy by Rotolito Lombarda S.p.A.

ISBN 978-0-19-954486-8

1 3 5 7 9 10 8 6 4 2

ACKNOWLEDGEMENTS

This book was written over a period of five years, between 2002 and 2007. It was commissioned during the Principalship of Lord Windlesham; begun during the Acting Principalship of Professor Vernon Bogdanor; and completed during the Principalship of Professor Roger Cashmore. From all three I received encouragement and help. Prompt and handsome publication was facilitated by the generosity of the Delafield Trust. Thanks to Mr. Algernon Heber-Percy, I was given access to the family archives at Hodnet, Shropshire. As a Supernumerary Fellow I received timely aid from a number of allies, inside and outside Brasenose. In particular from the following: Professor Caroline Barron, Professor John Blair, Mrs Elizabeth Boardman, Ms Sarah Boada, Dr. Carole Bourne-Taylor; Mr Geoffrey Bourne-Taylor, Dr. Jeremy Catto, Professor Richard Cooper, Dr. Jim Daniel, Mr. John Davies, Dr. Robin Darwall-Smith, Professor Robert Evans, Dr. I.D. Fallows, Mr. Stephen Green, the Revd. Dr. Peter Groves, Dr. Harry Judge, The Hon. Christopher Lennox-Boyd, Dr. Robert Peberdey, Dr. Bernard Richards, the Revd. Richard Smail, Dr. Andrew Stockley, the Revd. Dr. William Whyte, and last, but certainly not least, my wife Susan Mayor.

J.M.C.

28 *October* 2007

CONTENTS

LIST OF ILLUSTRATIONS   viii

LIST OF BLACK AND WHITE PLATES   ix

PRINCIPAL ABBREVIATIONS   xv

INTRODUCTION   I

1. 1509–1688: Martyrs and King's Men: Reformation, War, and Revolution   6

2. 1688–1785: Georgian Brasenose: Tories and Jacobites, Methodists and Freemasons   95

3. 1785–1822: 'The First College in Oxford': Cleaver, Hodson, and the Hebers   159

4. 1822–1853: Religion and Reform: The Brasenose of Gilbert and Harington   201

5. 1853–1886: The Age of Athletic Prizemen: Walter Pater and 'the Chief'   246

6. 1886–1918: Officers and Gentlemen: The Days of Haig and Buchan   290

7. 1918–1948: Brideshead Suspended: The Legacy of Stallybrass   324

8. 1948 onwards: All Change: Towards a Global Elite   385

PLANS: COLLEGE SITE AND BUILDINGS   434

APPENDICES

    A. List of Principals   436

    B. List of Major Benefactors   437

    C. Members of the Phoenix Common Room   442

    D. List of Rhodes Scholars   477

    E. Presidents of the Brasenose Society   485

    F. The College Grace   487

INDEX OF NAMES   489

EPITOME   530

LIST OF ILLUSTRATIONS

Frontispiece:

Old Quad, 1814. R. Ackermann, *Oxford* (1813–14)

Colour Plates (Between pages 14 and 15)

  I. Lord Grenville's installation as Chancellor, 3 July 1810
Author's collection.

 II. Fancy dress, 1897
Uncat. album.

III. Fancy dress, 1898
Uncat. album.

IV. 'Bacon Faced Fellows of Brazen Nose Broke Loose' (1810)
Author's collection.

BLACK AND WHITE PLATES

(1–16 between pages 78 and 79)

1. Lady Margaret Beaufort, Countess of Richmond and
   Derby (1443–1509)
   QM7 A14/3.

2. William Smith, Bishop of Lincoln (1460–1514)
   QM7 A2/2.

3. Sir Richard Sutton (c.1460–1524)
   QM7 A3/2.

4. The Brazen Nose (12th century)
   QM2/13.

5. A. The Brazen Nose over the college gateway (c.1520)
   QM2/4.
   B. Caricature Nose in hall (c.1635)
   QM2/2.

6. Bird's-eye view of Brasenose, 1578
   QM3/A6/2.

7. Brasenose College, 1674
   D. Loggan, *Oxonia Illustrata* (1675).

8. Pair of chalices and patens, silver-gilt (1498/9)

9. Alexander Nowell (1507–1601)
   QM7 A6/2.

10. Joyce Frankland (née Trappes; 1531–87)
    QM7 A9/3.

11. John, 2nd Baron Mordaunt (1508–71)
    QM7 A8/2.

12. Samuel Radcliffe (1580–1648)
    QM7 A11/3.

13. Thomas Yate (c.1603–1681)
    QM7 A12/3.

14. Robert Burton (1577–1640)
    QM7 A10/3.

15. Sir William Petty, FRS (1623–87)
    N.P.G. 2924.

16. The Radcliffe Cup (1610)

    (17–32 between pages 142 and 143)

17. Robert Shippen (1675–1745)

18. Nicholas Hawksmoor: Baroque design for reconstructing
    Brasenose (1719–20)
    QM3 A17/2.

19. *Samson and the Philistine* (known as 'Cain and Abel')
    T. Wright, *Walter Pater*, ii (1907), pl. 14.

20. A. [Sir] John Soane: Gothic design for enlarging
    the Old Quad (1804)
    QM3 A21/2.
    B. Philip Hardwick: Gothic design for a new
    High Street front (1810)
    QM3 A25/2.

21. A. [Sir] John Soane: Roman design for a new
    High Street front (1807)
    QM3 A24/2.
    B. [Sir] John Soane: Grecian design for a new
    High Street front (1807)
    QM3 A23/2.

22. Sarah Alston, Duchess of Somerset (*c.* 1642–1692)
    QM7 A13/3.

23. Old Quad in 1861

24. William Cleaver (1742–1815)
    PRI 17A1.

25. Frodsham Hodson (1771–1822)
    QM14.2, 12.

26. Henry Halliwell (1765–1835)
    Author's collection.

27. John Napleton (?1738–1817)
    Hereford Cathedral.

28. Francis Yarborough (1696–1770)
    QM 13/1.

29. The library, in 1935
    Country Life.

30. Reginald Heber (1783–1826)
    QM 14/2/3.

31. Henry Hart Milman (1791–1868)
QM 14/2/5.

32. The Ante-Chapel and Organ Screen, in 1935
Country Life.

(33–48 between pages 206 and 207)

33. Edward Tindal Turner (1822–1911)
Private collection.

34. Ashurst Turner Gilbert (1786–1870)
Punch, 25 Oct. 1868.

35. Richard Harington (1800–53)
9PIC. Uncat.

36. Edward Hartopp Cradock [formerly Grove] (1810–86)
MPP 41 A2.

37. Walter Pater, in 1872
The Bookman, Aug. 1906.

38. The Fellows, in 1861

39. A. 'Brasenose Ale', 1886
PR I, 22. A1.
B. Walter Pater: in Oxford and in London
H 144.

40. John Bossum (d. 1861)
MPP 42 A1.

41. Brasenose servants, 1861
MPP 42 A1.

42. Undergraduate lodgings, *c.*1862
A. Above Standen's outfitters in Catte Street (later part
of Hertford College)
B. Interior
Both MPP 41 A2.

43. The Prince of Wales, in residence at Frewin Hall, 1859–60
B1064/19.

44. Walter Bradford Woodgate and Weldon Champneys
MPP 42 A1.

45. C. J. Ottaway (1850–78)
MPP 46 D1.

46. The Brasenose Coach, *c.*1863

47. A. The Octagon, 1867
SL 11 B 8/2.

B. Old Quad, *c.*1891
Uncat. album.

48. The Phoenix, chapel steps, 1861
MPP 41 A2.

(49–64 between pages 270 and 271)

49. Walter Pater (1839–94)
MPP 134 B3.

50. Albert Watson (1828–1904)
MPP 41 A2.

51. Hartwell de la Garde Grissell (1839–1907)
MPP 42 A1.

52. A. Vincent's Club Room, 23 The High, *c.*1892
B. St Mary's Chambers, *c.*1892
Both uncat. album.

53. A. Brasenose: Radcliffe Square front, *c.*1887
B. The old High Street frontage in 1887, prior to reconstruction
QM3 A27/3.

54. The chapel, in 1935
Country Life.

55. Nine Brasenose cricketers, 19th–20th centuries

56. The Torpid, Hilary term 1861
MPP 41 A2.

57. The Eight, Trinity term 1862
MPP 42 A1.

58. The Vampires, 1882
MPP 80 E1.

59. The Vampires, 1886
SL 9 A2/2.

60. Dr Frederick William Bussell (1862–1944)
PP 1 C3/1.

61. Walter Pater, in 1894
PP 1 C3/2.

62. Entrance from Cloister to Chapel, 1935
Country Life.

63. The Cloister from the Chapel, 1935
Country Life.

64. The Childe of Hale's nose (*c.*1850)
QM14, 1, A11.

(65–80 between pages 334 and 335)

65. W. T. S. Sonnenschein ('Sonners'; later Stallybrass)
PRI 25 G5/1/1.

66. The Ingoldsby Club, 1898
SL 14 A5/1.

67. The Fellows, June 1907
MEM 1, E1.

68. Brasenose JCR, *c.*1892
Uncat. album.

69. Brasenose hall, in 1891
Uncat. album.

70. T. G. Jackson: design for a new High Street front
with 'Crowned Spire'
QM 3/30.

71. T. G. Jackson: the New Quadrangle
QM 3/33.

72. The second Torpid, Hilary term, 1914
SL 7 C5/8.

73. Officer Training Corps, BNC section, 1915
MEM 2 DS/2/4.

74. The Pater Society, 1911
SL 7 C5/7.

75. The Phoenix, Trinity term 1914
SL 7 C5/8.

76. Eights Week, 1901
SL 7 C5/5.

77. Eights Week, 1931
SL 8 B9/2/13.

78. Bump supper in hall, 1922
SL 7 C5/9.

79. The Wanderers at the Imperial Hotel, Eastbourne, 1924
PRI 25 G5/4/5.

80. Arnold Strode Jackson (d. 1972)
PRI 25 h 1/2/A 566. Photo: W. T. S. Stallybrass.

(81–96 between pages 398 and 399)

81. Principal Stallybrass (1883–1948)
PRI 25 H3/3/2. Photo: J. L. Halstead.

82. Albert Thomas, *c.*1944
    T 50.

83. A. Christopher William Dawson, CMG
    PRI 25 G5/3/17.
    B. Reginald Jeffery (1876–1956) and Mrs Jeffery
    PRI 25 H1/2/A5 11. Photo: W. T. S. Stallybrass.

84. Jimmy Halstead (d. 1941)
    PRI 25 H3/3/1. Photo: W. T. S. Stallybrass.

85. Dick Holdsworth (d. 1942)
    PRI 25 H3/3/24. Photo: W. T. S. Stallybrass.

86. Tony Tisdall (d. 1940)
    PRI 25 H1/2/A772. Photo: W. T. S. Stallybrass.

87. Conrad Cherry (d. 1943)
    PRI 25 H1/2/A778. Photo: W. T. S. Stallybrass.

88. Carl von Ruperti (d. 1943)

89. Alan Bulmer (d. 1940) and Ken Millar (d. 1940)
    PRI 25 H1/3, no. 3032. Photo: W. T. S. Stallybrass.

90. Edmund King (1872–1963)

91. Edgard Stanley Cohn (1899–1963)
    Photo: D. Lomax.

92. Dinner in hall, Trinity term 1958
    SL 7 A6/1.

93. Collections in hall, Trinity term 1958
    SL 7 A6/1.

94. Revd Leslie Styler (1908–90)

95. Three Principals, 1972
    SL 7 A6/1. Photo: L. Styler.

96. Lord Windlesham (1932–)

PRINCIPAL ABBREVIATIONS

Asquith Commn.	*Report of Royal Commission on Oxford and Cambridge Universities*, 2 vols., 1922 (*Parliamentary Papers* (1922), x).
BL Add. MS	British Library, Additional Manuscript.
Boase	F. Boase, *Modern English Biography*, 6 vols. (1892–1921; reprinted 1965).
Bodl.	Bodleian Library, Oxford.
Brasenose Reg.	[C. B. Heberden], *Brasenose College Register* 1509–1909, 2 vols. in 1 (OHS lv, 1910).
Cleveland Commn.	*Royal Commission Appointed to Inquire into the Property and Income of the Universities of Oxford and Cambridge*, 2 vols., 1874 (*Parliamentary Papers* (1873), xxxvii).
CUF	Common University Fund.
Franks Report	*Report of the Commission of Enquiry*, 2 vols. (Oxford, 1966).
Gent's Mag.	*Gentleman's Magazine.*
Hearne's Collections	*Remarks and Collections of Thomas Hearne*, 11 vols. (OHS, ii, vii, xiii, xxxiv, xlii–iii, xlviii, l, lxv, lxvii, lxxii 1884–1918).
Heber MSS	Heber Manuscripts, Hodnet Hall, Shropshire.
Hist. Parl.	*History of Parliament* (H.M.S.O., 1964 onwards).
HMC	Historical Manuscripts Commission.
HUO	*History of the University of Oxford*, ed. T. H. Aston, et al., 8 vols. (Oxford, 1984–94).
North Report	*Commission of Inquiry*, 2 vols. (Oxford, 1997).
ODNB	*Oxford Dictionary of National Biography*, 60 vols. (Oxford, 2004).
OHS	Oxford Historical Society.
OU Commn.	*Royal Commission Appointed to Inquire into the State, Discipline, Studies and Revenues of the University of Oxford*, 1852 (*Parliamentary Papers* (1852), xxii).
Parl. Debates	*Parliamentary Debates.*
PP	*Parliamentary Papers.*

Quat. Mon.	*Brasenose College Quatercentenary Monographs* [ed. F. Madan], 2 vols. in 3 (O.H.S. lii–liv, Oxford, 1909).
Robbins Report	*Higher Education* (Committee of Higher Education (1963), Cmnd. 2145).
RCHM	Royal Commission on Historic Monuments.
Selborne Commn.	*University of Oxford Commission*, 1881 (*Parliamentary Papers* (1881), lvi).
UCCA	Universities' Central Council for Admissions.
UFC	Universities' Funding Council.
UGC	University Grants Committee.
VCH	*Victoria County History.*
Visitors' Register	*Register of the Visitors of the University of Oxford*, ed. M. Burrows (Camden Soc., NS 29, 1881).
V.-P.'s Reg.	Vice-Principal's Register, Brasenose College Archives.
Wood, *Fasti*	Anthony Wood, *Athenae* [*Fasti*] *Oxonienses*, ed. P. Bliss, 4 vols. (1813–20).
Wood, *City of Oxford*	'Survey of the Antiquities of the City of Oxford'... 1661–6, by Anthony Wood, ed. A. Clark, 3 vols. (OHS, xv, xvii, xxxvii, 1889–9).
Wood, *Colleges and Halls*	Anthony Wood, *The History and Antiquities of the Colleges and Halls in the University of Oxford*, [*Fasti Oxonienses*], ed. J. Gutch (Oxford, 1786–90).
Wood, *Annals*	Anthony Wood, *The History and Antiquities of the University of Oxford*, [*Annals*] ed. J. Gutch, 2 vols. in 3 parts (Oxford, 1792–6).
Wood, *Life and Times*	The Life and Times of Anthony Wood... 1632–95, *ed. A. Clark,* 5 vols. (O.H.S., xix, xxi, xxvi, xxxv, xl, 1891–5).

Note:
Dates: New Style throughout.
Manuscript references: Brasenose College Archives, unless otherwise stated.
Place of publication: London unless otherwise stated.

History...is the biography of a society...histories of universities [explore]...the biography of their common life.

(Dr Thomas Arnold, *Lectures on Modern History* (1842), 4–5)

History is the essence of innumerable Biographies.

(Thomas Carlyle, 'Thoughts on History', *Fraser's Mag.* 2 (1830), 414)

Read no history, nothing but biography, for that is life without theory.

(Benjamin Disraeli, *Contarini Fleming* (1832; 1927), 110)

INTRODUCTION

Brasenose—with all her virtues and her foibles, her surface Philistinism, her
very real culture, her physical robustness, her intellectual vitality, her rich
generosity...there is nothing in England more intimately English than
Brasenose.

(John Buchan, 1935; *Brazen Nose* vi. 88)

Centenaries are an achievement. Quincentenaries are a triumph. Even so,
college histories need not necessarily be triumphalist. Their tone tends to be
dictated by circumstance. Around 1809, when Brasenose was 300 years old, it
marked the occasion by publishing two pious biographical studies devoted to
three of its founding fathers: William Smith, Richard Sutton, and Alexander
Nowell. Their author was the college's first historian, the Revd Ralph Churton.[1]
One hundred years after that, we celebrated our quatercentenary rather more
lavishly. In 1909 there appeared not only a full-scale *Register* of Brasenose men
edited by C. B. Heberden, but fourteen *Monographs*—masterminded by Falconer
Madan—dealing in detail with the history, fabric, and personnel of the college.[2]
The *Register* is heroic in scale but inevitably defective, and it has never been
revised, let alone completed. As for the *Monographs*, they vary in quality. They are
strongest in the chronicling of sporting triumphs and in transcriptions of early
documents. Despite omissions they remain a vital quarry. By comparison, John
Buchan's *Brasenose College* (1898) was simply a *jeu d'esprit*.[3]

By 1909, however, the groundwork of research had indeed been laid.
'Brasenose', noted Sir Charles Mallet in 1927, 'has given itself a history such
as few Colleges possess.'[4] In 1954—and again in 1974—that verdict could still
legitimately be repeated.[5] But since then the historiographical temperature has

[1] R. Churton, *The Lives of William Smythe, Bishop of Lincoln, and Sir Richard Sutton, Knight, Founders
of Brazen Nose College* (1800); idem, *The Life of Alexander Nowell, Dean of St. Paul's* (1809). For the
Churton family, see G. Baker, *History and Antiquities of the County of Northampton* (1822–41), s.v.
Middleton Cheney, and *The Guardian*, 22 July 1874, 929–30.

[2] *Brasenose Reg.*; *Quat. Mon.*; MS. additions by M.L. Walker: MPP 75 A1.

[3] J. Buchan, *Brasenose College* (College Histories Series, 1898).

[4] C. E. Mallet, *A History of the University of Oxford*, iii (1927), 408 n. 2.

[5] 'No other college in the University has produced any work of comparable scale' (Lady de
Villiers in *VCH Oxfordshire*, iii (1954), 213). 'No college has ever recorded its historic past

risen. The new *History of the University of Oxford* (1984–94), in eight magisterial volumes, has lifted Oxonian studies to an altogether higher level.[6] Over the same period Brasenose itself has radically changed. Two hundred years after Churton's memoirs, one hundred years after Buchan's essay and Madan's monographs, the college is a rather different place. It faces its quincentenary in very different circumstances. A new history is called for, and a new approach.

Brasenose was a hall before it was a college, and a lodging before it was a hall. But it has always occupied the same site, halfway between the Bodleian Library and St Mary's Church, a site at the very heart of Oxford. This new account of Brasenose—or 'BNC', as it has been called since the later eighteenth century—sets out an essentially collegiate story, academic, social, and architectural. The book is based on private and public archives, in collegiate and national libraries, and on the printed papers, letters, and diaries that supplement those archives as documents of corporate memory. It is not a conventional narrative. Its pulse is episodic rather than chronological. Its method is impressionistic and its structure is informal, as befits a college which has seldom stood on ceremony.

Unlike most college histories this study concentrates as much upon the lives of undergraduates as it does upon the careers of successive generations of dons. Again, unlike many histories, the emphasis here is not on the origins of the college but on its period of greatest reputation: between the mid-eighteenth century and the mid-twentieth century. The earlier decades appear, of course; but the narrative expands as the quantity of evidence increases. It is only in the eighteenth century that Brasenose emerges as a defining force within the University. It is not until the nineteenth century that the process of institutional change quickens into structural reform. And it is only in the twentieth century that reform accelerates into revolution. Brasenose entered the nineteenth century as an Anglican monopoly, a male preserve, independently financed, largely governed by bachelor Fellows in holy orders. The curriculum was narrow—mostly classics, mathematics, and divinity—and the basis of recruitment narrower still. We enter the twenty-first century larger and poorer, exercising only an illusory independence; secularized, bureaucratized, state regulated; but with an integrated intake— male and female, undergraduate and postgraduate, national and inter-national—and a syllabus diversified beyond the dreams of our predecessors.

Many of these changes have been the result of wider economic shifts. But this is not an economic history. Estate management plays only a small part in

more impressively' (A. B. Emden, *A Biographical Register of the University of Oxford,* 1501–1540 (Oxford, 1974), p. xx).

[6] HUO.

the story.[7] I deal mostly with people and buildings; but not in a prosopo-graphical or archaeological way. Rather I have tried to recreate the texture, the social politics, of college life: the learning, the conversation, the sport; the physical setting; the architecture, inside and out; the food and drink; the quirks of personality, the little dramas and absurdities that make up the small change of corporate living. I have not avoided anecdote. But I have avoided current affairs. There is little here about the living: a historian is happier with the dead. In any case, a history that tries too hard to be up to date will itself be very soon outdated. So this study ends with trends rather than topicalities; in particular with two triumphs of optimism over tradition: the admission of women and the globalizing of recruitment and research.

An Oxford college is a permanent set of buildings and an impermanent set of people. Its context is multifarious. As an institution, its history is a micro-cosm of the history of England. National and international events—the Reformation, the civil war, the age of reform, the First and Second World Wars, the emergence of mass democracy—each left its imprint on the lives of individual dons and students. It is the duty of a college historian to explain the way in which these external events interact with the internal circumstan-ces of college life. Hence the emphasis on context. I have tried to relate the college to the University, and the University to the wider world of politics. And I have tried to let the participants speak for themselves. The result is a plain story, unencumbered by theory. But its scope is ambitious. It treats college living as more than an insulated experience. Rightly or wrongly, I have gone for the bigger picture. Biography is never easy; collective biography is almost impossible. But here at least the rewards of narrative are fairly evenly distributed. The Whigs are the winners; the Tories have most of the fun.

Soldiers and novelists; priests and politicians; lawyers and sportsmen; eccentrics, tycoons, and travellers—Brasenose has seen them all, and their variety is bewildering. Once we had martyrs and theologians; then we had landowners and manufacturers; then clerics and schoolmasters, barristers and judges; now we have managers aplenty and executives galore. The obvious establishment trophies are here: we have a Prime Minister (Henry Addington, Viscount Sidmouth), a Lord Chancellor (Thomas Egerton, Baron Ellesmere), a Commander in Chief (Earl Haig), and an Archbishop of Canterbury (Lord Runcie). Over the years, we have produced six arch-bishops and more than fifty bishops. And our tally of judges is almost too numerous to count. We have the physicist who discovered the fuel cell, and

---

[7] For a historical survey of college estates and advowsons, see A. J. Butler, in *Quat. Mon.* VI, 1–64. A table of financial returns was prepared in 1871 for the Cleveland Commission (*PP* (1873), xxxvii, pt. i, summary: 91–5; pt. ii, details: 579–613).

the barrister who defended 'Poisoner Palmer' (the same man: Sir William Grove). We have a Prime Minister of Australia (John Gorton). We have Shakespeare's tutor (John Cottam). We have the great-grandfather of the first President of the United States (Laurence Washington), as well as the grandfather of the second and great-grandfather of the sixth (Thomas Adams). There are traces of Brasenose the world over, from Brazen Nose Street, Manchester, and Brazenose Street, Liverpool, to far away in the Antipodes: Brasenose Point, New Zealand.

As for literary stars, our own are as bright as any. In the early days we find John Foxe, compiler of *The Book of Martyrs*; Robert Burton, author of *The Anatomy of Melancholy*; and Thomas Traherne, the poet of *Thanksgivings and Meditations*. Then there is Jeremy Taylor, that euphuistic divine, whose time at Brasenose was as short as his sentences were long. In the modern period, our list of authors has multiplied: we have Walter Pater, John Buchan, Middleton Murry, Charles Morgan, William Golding, John Mortimer, and J. G. Farrell. It is an impressive list. Our roster of sportsmen since the eighteenth century is legendary: Sir Tatton Sykes and Squire Osbaldeston, 'Guts' Woodgate and 'Jacker' Strode Jackson, Ottaway and Obolensky, Boobbyer and Cowdrey. No wonder Vincent's Club was founded in BNC. But there is more to Brasenose than athletics. Here *Brideshead Revisited* was born: Sebastian was a Brasenose man. Here Oxford's first Masonic Lodges were inaugurated: the Alfred and the Apollo. Here C. S. Lewis looked into a chapel wardrobe and emerged in the kingdom of Narnia. In Thackeray we are 'St Boniface'; in Kipling 'Brazenface'. And in the wider world we have no shortage of idols. Among churchmen—in the modern period alone—we have Heber of Calcutta, Robertson of Brighton, and Forbes of Brechin, as well as Runcie of Cuddesdon. Among antiquaries, we have Elias Ashmole, founder of the Ashmolean Museum, and Richard Heber, the greatest of English book collectors. Among historians and archaeologists we can boast the heaviest of heavyweights: Henry Hart Milman, Sir Arthur Evans, F. J. Haverfield, and Sir Ronald Syme. By contrast, among figures of controversy and figures of fun, we have John Profumo and Jeffrey Archer, and the irrepressible Michael Palin. Finally—or rather currently—we have the rising hope of liberal Tories: David Cameron.

Over the centuries, we have often surprised. Brasenose was the first Oxford college to admit undergraduates on a statutory basis; and the first to agree to change its statutes so as to grant admission to women. We may boast the oldest dining club in Oxford or Cambridge (the Phoenix). But we were also the first college in either university to admit a candidate from a comprehensive school (Paul Barker). Our intake has been extraordinarily diverse. How many colleges can claim the lyricist of 'Danny Boy' (Fred Weatherley), the anthologist of 'Widdecombe Fair' (F. W. Bussell), the founder of *The Eagle* (Marcus Morris), and the begetter of *Private Eye* (Andrew Osmond)? How many can claim the first authenticated English Freemason (Elias Ashmole), and the first to call himself a Methodist (John Clayton), as well as the inventor of garden gnomes (Sir Charles Isham) and the father of political economy (Sir William Petty)? How many can claim the originator of rugby football (William Webb Ellis), the doctor who cured George III (Francis Willis), the instigator of modern income tax (Addington again), and the inventor of bottled beer (Alexander Nowell)? The story of the college is the story of all these lives; all these and many more.

The mythology of a college can sometimes be more potent than its history. Image, in the long run, trumps every sort of reality. 'Sending another athlete to BNC', noted the Dean of Christ Church in 1948, is like 'sending coals to Newcastle, and sending a Christian there is almost cruelty'.[8] Amusing enough. But the truth about Brasenose has always been rather more complex. Explaining that complexity—its curiously contradictory culture—has to be counted one of the primary purposes of this book.

In the later 1950s, the Principal of BNC was Maurice Platnauer: bachelor, classicist, gourmet, benefactor; the quintessential college man. According to legend, one unusually solemn Rhodes Scholar emerged from an interview with him and addressed a waiting queue of undergraduates: 'when you enter that room you will encounter civilisation.'[9] That was pitching it a little high. But any college worth its salt is ultimately engaged in some sort of civilizing process. Each generation will define that elusive goal of civility in a different way, sometimes in a radically different way. Such is the nature of historical change. All we can do is to judge our predecessors by standards they might have recognized as their own. Their customs are not ours; our values are seldom theirs. But memories of their living here encrust the very fabric of the place. Their history is the history of the college.

---

[8] John Lowe to Sir Edgar Williams, 10 Jan. 1948, quoted in P. Ziegler, *Legacy: Cecil Rhodes, the Rhodes Trust and Rhodes Scholarships* (2008), 182.

[9] L. Styler, Address, 22 Feb. 1975 (*Brazen Nose*, xvi/1. 25).

I

1509–1688

Martyrs and King's Men: Reformation, War, and Revolution

Over the hall doorway at Brasenose—'The King's Hall and College of Brasenose'—stand two crumbling lumps of stone. Once they took the form of matching heads, twin icons of collegiate legend. Underneath were Latin inscriptions, translatable as follows:

'Alfred the Great, King, founder of the King's Hall'.

'John Scotus Erigena, first lecturer in the same place about the year 882'.[1]

Almost every word is false. King Alfred may well have been a patron of art and learning. But he did not found the University of Oxford, still less the house which bears today the title Brasenose and its accompanying presumption of royal patronage. That legend dates only from the 1380s. As for John Scotus— 'Erigena' means 'born in Ireland'—his connection is equally spurious. It was not he whom Alfred summoned to Malmesbury and then sent on to Oxford. Once that was thought to be Grimbald of St Bertin.[2] Now even Grimbald has been banished from college history. Again—to shoot down another brace of myths—the John Scotus commemorated here had nothing at all to do

---

[1] A. Wood, *History and Antiquities of the Colleges and Halls in … Oxford*, ed. J. Gutch (Oxford, 1786; 1790), 371. Engravings of these busts—Alfred left, Scotus right: 'super portam Refectory'—appear in J. Spelman, *Aelfredi Magni … Vita* (Oxford, 1678), tab.1 and in F. Wise, *Annales Rerum Gestarum Aelfredi Magni* (Oxford, 1722). Spelman was briefly a Brasenose man. For the legend of Erigena's bronzed or 'reddish beard', see J. R. McGrath, *The Flemings in Oxford*, ii (OHS lxii), 62: 25 July 1682. The porch was restored by J. C. Buckler *c*.1865.

[2] For Grimbald, Alfred, etc., see J. Parker, *The Early History of Oxford*, 727–1100 (OHS iii), ch. ii and *ODNB*. In *De Aelfredi Rebus Gestis* (1602), William Camden seems to have been misled by what E. A. Freeman called a 'shameless' interpolation in the text of Asser's biography of Alfred. See also *Asser's Life of King Alfred*, ed. W. H. Stevenson (Oxford, 1904); ed. and trans. S. Keynes and M. Lapidge (1983). When University College held a millenary dinner in 1872, Freeman sent the Master 'a small box … containing some burnt cakes' purportedly dug up at Athelney (F. Madan, *Oxford Outside the Guide Books* (Oxford, 1923), 104).

with Duns Scotus (the thirteenth-century metaphysician), and even less to do with Friar Bacon (the thirteenth-century polymath who legendarily constructed a brazen head capable of speech).[3] None of these men—King Alfred, John Scotus, Duns Scotus, or Roger Bacon; not even the shadowy Grimbald—can be shown to have had any link with Brasenose. They are part of college mythology. And yet their legends persist. For here we stand on classic ground, 'the very eye and centre of this our Athens!'[4] On this spot—between the old University Schools and the University Church: the site of modern Brasenose—scholars have studied continuously for eight centuries or more.

The time-span of this book is rather less than that: a mere 500 years. For Brasenose was not founded as a college until 1509. Before that date its site was occupied by a series of academic halls. And only one of these bore the name of Brasenose. Its story as an independent hall can be traced back to 1381, when a lease was obtained from the proprietor of the site, University College. Halls such as these began as lodging houses and schools for students of the University, living under the direction of a regent or teaching master. In 1313 there were more than 120 of them. In 1436 there were still as many as seventy. But by 1552 there were only eight. Their numerical decline has disguised the fact of their educational significance. For in the operation of these halls lay the germ of future collegiate teaching. Here residence and instruction coexisted, both graduate and undergraduate. Here University lectures were supplemented by tuition in hall. And the two systems could operate on contiguous or even identical sites.

Why then did their numbers dwindle? Academically speaking, the halls of Oxford did not decline. They were not even superseded. They simply changed their spots. In their new guise they emerged as colleges. Now there were several advantages to collegiate status. Colleges were chartered bodies with rights of perpetual succession. Like the University, they were dedicated to godly learning. But thanks to the practice of corporate inheritance, they became increasingly independent of University control. And they rejoiced in the fact that this independence was hedged about with legally guaranteed immunities, stemming ultimately from the protection of the Crown.

---

[3] The magical head of brass—which could 'yeelde forth strange and uncouth aphorisms'—appears in Robert Greene's play *Friar Bacon and Friar Bungay* (1588). Several of these legends are confused in a description by one French visitor of 1663: 'There is one College where I saw a great bronze nose over the gate, as if it were a Polichinello's mask. They told me it was also called the College of the Nose, and that a nose had been placed over the gate as a likeness of John Duns Scotus, who had taught there' (S. Sorbieres, *Relations d'un voyage en Angleterre* (Cologne, 1666); trans. 1707). As late as 1831, Thomas Love Peacock could still conjure up memories of Friar Bacon and his 'immortal nose...resplendent over the portals of its cognominal college' (*Crotchet Castle*, ch. ix). See also *Notes and Queries*, ser. 9/12, 361; *Brazen Nose*, iv. 55–63 and xiii. 121.

[4] R. Churton, *The Lives of William Smyth, Bishop of Lincoln and Sir Richard Sutton, Knight, Founders of Brasen Nose College* (1800), 284.

The process by which Brasenose expanded from a mere lodging house into a kind of 'superhall'—on its way to maturity as a fully fledged college—has been tracked by Jeremy Catto to its origins in the fourteenth and fifteenth centuries; and in particular to the efforts of two individuals: John Legh and William Sutton. As Principals of Brasenose Hall they were responsible for annexing as many as six near-neighbouring halls. Legh it was who began this expansionist process. And it is Legh therefore—at the end of the fourteenth century—who can claim to be regarded as 'the true founder of Brasenose'.[5] His example was followed by several of his successors. By the early sixteenth century, Brasenose had absorbed no fewer than ten contiguous halls. The roll-call of expansion runs as follows: Brasenose Hall, Little University Hall, St Thomas's Hall, Shield Hall, Ivy Hall, St Mary's Entry, Salissury Hall, Little St Edmund Hall, Haberdasher Hall, and Broadgates Hall.[6]

The first two on this list are of particular significance. Little University Hall, at the corner of Brasenose Lane, had been owned by the University since 1253. It was in fact the first corporate property held by the University for educational purposes. As such it became first site of University College; and then—from about 1450—a satellite of Brasenose Hall. And it was this Brasenose Hall, immediately adjacent—recorded as early as 1244, bought by the University in 1262, mentioned by its distinctive name in 1279, and independently leased in 1381—that eventually gave the new foundation its ever-memorable title.[7] As halls went, it was fairly large. Its buildings included four schools or lecture rooms, and it cost the University £55 6s. 8d.; more than twice as much as Little University Hall. Apart from the names of its Principals—recorded from 1435 onwards—we also know something of its personnel and practice. Most of its members would have been studying canon or civil law. The names of some twenty-seven scholars survive. Their learning, their worship, their recreation, were all corporately controlled. This was a prospering place, not an institution

---

[5] J. I. Catto, 'The Triumph of the Hall in 15th Century Oxford', in *Lordship and Learning: Studies in Memory of Trevor Aston* (2004), 217–8 (site plan, fig. 4).

[6] Details in F. Madan, *Quat. Mon.* I, 2–18 and I. S. Leadam, *Quat. Mon.* IX, 8–11. Also W. A. Pantin, in OHS, NS xvi. 31–100 and J. I. Catto and T. A. R. Evans (eds.), *HUO* i (Oxford, 1984), map 3.

[7] Wood, *Colleges and Halls*, appendix, 222–3; Madan, *Quat. Mon.* I, 12–14; H. E. Salter, *Survey of Oxford*, i (OHS xiv), 67–8, NE 92–3. On one side Little University Hall was bounded by Brasenose Lane, originally known as St Mildred's Lane; on the other by the west side of Radcliffe Square, then known as School Street. Wood traces Brasenose Hall back to 1239, as the house of Jeffry Jussell (A. Wood, *History and Antiquities of the University of Oxford: Annals*, ed. J. Gutch (1792–6), ii. 755–7), from whom it passed to Simon de Balindon, who sold it to the University in 1262. The name also occurs in a forged charter professing the date 1219 (Madan, in A. Clark (ed.), *The Colleges of Oxford* (1891), 253 n. 2). When the masters of University College migrated from School Street to High Street *c.*1332, they leased out Brasenose Hall first as University schools, and then in 1381 as an independent hall.

in decline. Most of its story is now lost to history. But details of the occasional incident survive. In 1438, for example, Principal Roger Grey was charged with throwing Robert Brown, under-park-keeper at Beckley, into the water below Magdalen Bridge.[8] Poaching, no doubt, lay at the root of this altercation. But old Brasenose Hall did fulfil a serious academic role. And from it the new college inherited distinctive pedagogic traditions. It also inherited its own eponymous totem: a sanctuary knocker—a leopard's head of brass and iron—probably dating from the twelfth century and treasured today as the Brazen Nose (pl. 4).[9]

From before 1279 it was this knocker that marked the entrance to Brasenose Hall.[10] In 1333—so Brasenose loyalists believe—it was removed to Stamford in Lincolnshire by a band of migrating students. Stamford at that time was host to a group of Carmelite schools. It was 'an university in all but name'.[11] Hence its selection by these wandering scholars. Their origins were northern, and it seems to have been a battle between North and South that drove them from their Oxford home. Be that as it may, in Stamford the nose remained, long after its bearers had returned to Oxford in 1335 at the command of Edward III.[12] Not until 1890 was it retrieved and set up in

[8] *Cal. Chancery Proceedings* 16 Henry VI, 1437–8, Bundle 75, no. 11. For names of Principals etc., see Registrum Cancellarii, in Wood, *City of Oxford*, 588–9. An inventory of the furniture of one member, Thomas Cooper (d. 1438), is printed in H. Anstey, *Munimenta Academica*, ii (1868), 515.

[9] Sir John and Sir Arthur Evans suggested 1120–30 (*Quat. Mon.* II, 13–14). The knocker—shown at a meeting of the British Archaeological Assocn. in June 1889—may have come originally from an ancient sanctuary in St Edward's parish. Laboratory tests in 1979 concluded that the lead content (10%) was 'not incompatible' with its reputed date (*Brazen Nose*, xvii/1. 9). Two caricature noses (pl. 5B) in the north bay window of the hall probably date from the 1630s. The legend that the name 'Brasenose' descends from the brew house of King Alfred's Palace or Hall [low Latin *bracinum*+Teutonic *haus* or *huis=brasinhuse* or *brausenhaus*] goes back no further than J. Ingram, *Memorials of Oxford*, ii (1837), 2. For all this see H. Hurst, *The Four Noses of Brasenose College* (Oxford, 1904).

[10] 'Eadem Universitas habet quandam aliam domum quae vocatur Brasenose cum quatuor Scolis in eadem parochia, et taxantur ad octo marcas, et fuit illa domus aliquo tempore Galfridi Jussell' (Survey or Inquisition of 1279, quoted in Wood, *Annals*, ii. 756).

[11] H. H. Henson, in *Collectanea*, i (OHS v), 3 ff.

[12] Madan, in *Quat. Mon.* II, 12–20; *Brazen Nose*, iv. 75–84. In July 1335 'Philippus obsonator [Manciple] Eneanasensis [of Brasenose]' is listed among the Stamford residents (Madan, in Clark (ed.), *Colleges*, 254). 'The Brazen-nose College Gate at Stamford' survived until 1688, when it was rebuilt, incorporating old masonry. After further changes it eventually became the property of Stamford School in 1929 (F. Peck, *Academia Tertia Anglicana* (i.e. Stamford) (1727), lib. xi, 6–27; Wood, *Annals*, i. 425–31; *VCH Lincs.*, ii (1906), 468–74; B. L. Deed, *A History of Stamford School* (Stamford, 1982), 1–8, 100–2). In 1961 Maurice Platnauer presented the school with a reproduction of the knocker. Until 1827 every Oxford graduate took an oath: 'Tu jurabis, quod non leges nec audies [deliver or attend lectures] Stamfordiae' (quoted by Madan in Clark (ed.), *Colleges*, 254 n. 3).

hall, in a place of honour over high table.[13] Meanwhile—and here at last we move to stronger ground—another nose of brass (pl. 5A) had been fixed to the new-built college gate. As early as 1534—perhaps as early as 1513—this second nose was noted as already existing by Polydore Vergil.[14] Since then, for nearly 500 years, its rude proboscis has greeted freshman and Fellow alike. And there it stands to this very day, the object of many a priapic pun.

So hall and college overlap. Seen in its wider context, 1509 does not mark a new foundation so much as one more step in a process of succession. The last Principal of Brasenose Hall—Matthew Smyth—becomes the first Principal of Brasenose College. Confusingly, in 1514 he is referred to—in the registers of the Vice-Chancellor's Court—as 'Principal of the College or Hall of Brasen Nose'.[15] While the new college was actually being built, parts of the old hall remained in use. Hence the confusion, and hence the continuity. In terms of chronological seniority, it might even be argued that Brasenose is actually older than Balliol and Merton, and second only to University College. But that would be to ignore a fundamental distinction. Constitutionally speaking, a hall and a college are very different things. When Brasenose received its royal charter in 1512 it emerged in reincarnate form. Without chartered legal status, independent of the University; without in particular some title to corporate endowment, a college remains no more than a hall of residence with pedagogic functions. So 1512 is definitive. But 1509—the date of the new foundation stone—is symbolic. Hence this volume's starting date.

Just below the hall battlement of Brasenose today stand two more heads, sculpted in 1635 and partly renewed in the mid-eighteenth century.[16] They are almost as shapeless as those of Alfred and Scotus. But, historically speaking, they carry rather more conviction. For these are the images of William Smith and Richard Sutton. And they are the founders of Brasenose College. Below them—and now invisible—were once the arms of Samuel Radcliffe, effectively the third founder of the college. To Dr Radcliffe we will return. Meanwhile, what of Smith and Sutton? Their intentions seem to have been clear as early as January 1508. That was the moment when Edmund

---

[13] A. J. B[utler] in *The Guardian*, 23 July 1890, 1175; F. Madan, in *Proceedings of the Oxford Architectural and Historical Soc*, NS 5 (1890), 298–304: this 'Palladium of the traditions of Brasenose . . . this monument of its ancient pluck and solidarity'.

[14] P. Vergil, *Anglica Historia* (written 1513; 1st edn. 1534), ed. and trans. D. Hay (Camden Soc. 3rd ser. 74, 1950), 146; *Notes and Queries* (1888), 426. Perhaps originally this also incorporated a brass ring.

[15] Churton, *Smyth and Sutton*, 291; *Brazen Nose*, iii. 107.

[16] Hugh Davies, 'Statuarist', received £6 in 1635 'for 2 statues of ye Founders' (Clennell A3.20, tipped in). 'A new Gothick head' was installed in 1752–3, and 'a New Head of the Founder against the Hall' at a cost of £2 2s. 0d. in 1769 (Hurst Bursarial: Tradesmen's Bills 27, cited by E. Boardman in *Brazen Nose*, xxxv. 28). The decayed busts were kept for some years in the antechapel (Madan, in Clark (ed.), *Colleges*, 270).

Croston, twice Principal of Brasenose Hall, left £6 13s. 4d. towards 'the building of Brasynnose in Oxford'.[17] Thanks to their determination, the foundation stone was laid on 1 June 1509.[18] Thanks to their initiative, the college acquired its royal charter, authorized by Henry VIII, on 15 January 1512.[19] Its title was tactically ambiguous, combining prestige from the myth of old King Alfred with the immediate potency of young King Hal. From this date forward its official name would be 'The King's Hall and College of Brasen Nose'.[20] Not until the later eighteenth century would the title be shortened, more familiarly, to 'BNC'.

William Smith (pl. 2)—Smyth is an alternative spelling—had made his way from Prescot in Lancashire to the highest offices in Church and state. Perhaps it was at Brasenose Hall that he learned his canon and civil law. We do not know for certain. But it was through the influence of the Stanley family, and in particular through Lady Margaret Beaufort (pl. 1), mother of Henry VII, that he became Bishop of Lichfield and Coventry in 1493, and Bishop of Lincoln in 1496; then Chancellor of Oxford in 1500; and finally Lord President of the Marches in 1501. Smith was essentially an administrator. The Protestant Hugh Latimer doubtless regarded him as an 'unpreaching prelate'.[21] His religious aims were in one sense reformist: he hoped for a better-educated clergy. Not all his attitudes, however, were so enlightened. He burned at the stake a number of dissentient Lollards, and he manipulated the levers of patronage with undisguised enthusiasm.[22] But within the

[17] Will dated 23 Jan. 1508 (Churton, *Smyth and Sutton*, 242 n.). He was Principal of Brasenose Hall in 1501 and 1503. For his memorial brass in St Mary's, now in the tower porch over the door to the organ gallery, see ibid. 244–6; Bodl. MS Top. Oxon. e. 286, fos. 18–19 [10ᵛ–11ʳ]. For his arms in hall, see Wood, *Colleges and Halls*, 368.

[18] Long since accepted as the canonical date; though Churton admitted he had not 'been able to satisfy [himself] as to the real date of the foundation of the college' (Churton, *Smyth and Sutton*, 273). The inscribed foundation stone, above the entrance to the old chapel on staircase I, was recut in 1853. For a squeeze taken in 1851, see *Quat. Mon.* III, pl. iv. Building at Corpus was similarly begun before a charter was obtained.

[19] *Cal. Patent Rolls*, 15 Jan. 1512; Hurst College: Charter 1; BL Add. MS 25239, fos. 10–12 (16th c. transcript); A.3.19: 'Principal Yate's Book' (1668), transcript, pp. 1–4; printed in T. Rymer (ed.), *Foedera*, xiii (1727), 320–2 (Latin), and *Statutes of the Colleges of Oxford*, ii (1853), pt. 9: Brasenose, iii–vi (English).

[20] 'Aula Regia et Collegium de Brasen-nose' (*Statutes of Colleges*, ii, pt. 9: Brasenose, xxxii. 93).

[21] H. Latimer, *Sermons*, ed. G. E. Corrie (Parker Soc. 16, i. 1844), 67. For a selection of Smith's correspondence as Chancellor, see H. Anstey, *Epistolae Academicae Oxon.* (OHS xxxv–xxxvi). For his palaces at Buckden, Huntingdonshire, and Lyddington, Rutland, see P. Hembry, in E. W. Ives et al. (eds.), *Wealth and Power in Tudor England* (1978); N. Pevsner, *Leicestershire and Rutland* (1984 edn.), 483; H. Avray Tipping, *English Homes: Early Tudor* (1924), 295–310.

[22] Foxe noted: 'Although he was somewhat eager and sharp against the poor simple flock of Christ's servants;... yet he was nothing so bloody or cruel as was [his successor, Bishop] Longland' (J. Foxe, *Acts and Monuments*, iv (1856 edn.), 219). Smith's memorial brass in the nave of Lincoln Cathedral, destroyed in 1642 (drawing by W. Dugdale, in W. Stukeley, *Itinerarium*

parameters of pre-Reformation politics Smith must be counted far-seeing, conscientious, even pious. One thing he learned from Lady Margaret was the importance of scholastic institutions. His foundation of Brasenose—like her foundation of St John's and Christ's College Cambridge—shines brightly in the firmament of Tudor educational patronage. Whether or not he owed his own education to the same patroness remains unclear. Whether he shared her concern for humanistic piety *per se* is equally uncertain. What is clear is that for many years Lady Margaret was his mentor. In Polydore Vergil's words, he was 'Margaritae exemplo ductus'.[23] Henry Hornby, her secretary and dean of chapel, must certainly have been his ally. Appropriately, thanks to George Hornby—a nineteenth-century Fellow of Brasenose—her portrait presides today above the chimneypiece in the Senior Common Room. The painting bears a legend with the date of her death, the same year as the date of the college foundation: 1509.[24]

But Smith was nearing the end of his life. 'Now in myself', he wrote in 1501, 'being old and full of sickness and aches in my bones . . . [I] cannot do such service to the king's grace as I could if I were able and in good health.'[25] In setting up a new college he needed a coadjutor. He found one in the person of Richard Sutton (pl. 3), a successful Inner Temple lawyer. Now Sutton was the son of a Cheshire landowner. He probably began his career at Macclesfield Grammar School. Several of his family had been at Brasenose Hall. And his friendship with Smith had ripened during their years in the service of Henry VII. It was Sutton who on 20 October 1508 took the initiative in acquiring the leases of Brasenose Hall and Little University Hall from University College.[26] The following June a quarry was leased at Headington, and construction of the new college began. The two founders had

Curiosum (1724), table xvi), was replaced with a copy of the original in 1927. His stained glass portrait in hall (pl. 2) has been dated *c.*1635; his portrait, on canvas, *c.*1632 or *c.*1670–80: there is another version of the latter in the Bodleian (*Quat. Mon.* VII, 5–10, 33–4; R. L. Poole, *Catalogue of Oxford Portraits*, II, pt. i (OHS lxxxi), 244–5).

[23] Vergil, *Anglica Historia*, ed. Hay, 146. Smith also endowed Lincoln and Oriel, and founded schools at Banbury, Leicester, and Farnworth, nr. Prescot, Lancs. (his birthplace). For humanistic piety in the circle of Lady Margaret, see J. K. McConica, *English Humanists and Reformation Politics* (Oxford, 1965), 56 *et seq.*

[24] *Quat. Mon.* VII, 23–4; *Oxford Portraits*, II, pt. i (OHS lxxxi), 243. Hornby acted, with Bishop Fisher, as executor to Lady Margaret's will. The painting, on canvas, is a posthumous copy, perhaps mid-17th century; there are several earlier versions, in the National Portrait Gallery and at St John's College, Cambridge. See also M. K. Jones and M. G. Underwood, *The King's Mother: Lady Margaret Beaufort, Countess of Richmond and Derby* (1992) and *ODNB*.

[25] Westminster Abbey Muniments, no. 16038: Smith to Sir Reginald Bray (transcribed in Churton, *Smyth and Sutton*, supp., p. 15 and modernized by Margaret Bowker in *ODNB*).

[26] A3. 19: transcripts of leases in 'Principal Yate's Book', 83–4; Churton, *Smyth and Sutton*, 270–2.

much in common. Both were northerners, bred up in the law, worldly men with powerful allies at court. But Smith was an episcopal careerist, suspicious of monastic orders. What he had in mind was a college for the education of secular clergy; that is clergy operating outside the orbit of the monastic system. Sutton's emphasis was rather different. He was a practising lawyer, pious beyond his calling; a bachelor with a partiality for the cloister.[27] Smith was apparently determined to keep the new college out of monkish hands. Sutton had no such inhibitions. Paradoxically for the first lay founder of any college in Oxford or Cambridge, he seems to have thought of his creation as a quasi-monastic foundation. Not for nothing was he Squire Steward of the Brigettine monastery at Sion, the wealthiest nunnery in England and later one of the last outposts of opposition to Henry VIII. Several of his grants of property to the college were tied to the performance of daily services for the souls of the founders, to be conducted by the Principal and Fellows or by stipendiary priests and choristers.[28] Something of these differences emerges in the drafting and redrafting of the college statutes, and in the spasmodic construction of the King's Hall and College of Brasenose.

It was Smith who drew up the earliest statutes, some time before 1512. It was Sutton who first amended and then reissued them in 1522.[29] These statutes would govern the college until the ordinances of 1855–7. Smith had envisaged a Principal and sixty unmarried scholars, soberly clad, 'as

[27] His portrait in martial dress is testament merely to his knightly standing: 'His countenance breathes the sweetness of benevolence; his aspect is clothed with the serenity of peace' (ibid. 461). His stained glass image in the north-east window of the hall (pl. 3) dates from *c.*1635, later restored (*Oxford Portraits*, II, pt. i (OHS lxxxi), 244, 246). In 1519 Sutton sponsored the printing by Wynkyn de Worde of *The Orcherd of Syon*, an early 15th-century translation of *The Dialogue* of St Catherine of Siena (ed. P. Hodgson and G. M. Liegey, 1966). He was probably buried at the Brigettine monastery, and his memorial destroyed in the Edwardian Reformation (Churton, *Smyth and Sutton*, 452; *ODNB*). He appears as Squire Steward in a MS miniature of 1520 (*Quat. Mon.* VII, pl. v), and in 16th-century glass in the east window of St James, Gawsworth, Cheshire (noted by Ashmole, 1663: C. H. Joston, *Elias Ashmole*, iii (Oxford, 1996), 967).

[28] I. S. Leadam in *Quat. Mon.* IX, 165–7, citing Sutton's 'Composition' of 1519. Goldwin Smith would later describe these provisions as 'devotions of a peculiarly Roman Catholic character' (*OU Commission Report* (1852), 129). They are in fact typical of pre-Reformation piety. Scholars funded by Humphrey Ogle (1543), for example, were to 'say *placebo* and *dirige*' (Matins and Vespers for the dead), every Sunday in chapel, 'the one being on the one side of the Choir, the other on the other' (*Quat. Mon.* IV, 14). The bequests of Elizabeth Morley (1516), John Cox (1520), William Porter (1531), and William Clifton (1538) were similarly tied to masses and priestly prayers.

[29] The statutes originally drafted by Smith have not survived. They were revised by his executors between 1514 and 1519 (A 2.1, fo. 1), and then amended by Sutton in 1522 (*Statutes of Colleges*, ii (1853), pt. 9: Brasenose: Latin text). Caps. xii, xxii, xxiv, xxxvii, and xxxviii, and much of viii and xxiii, can be assigned to Sutton's revision. For summaries, see Leadam, in *Quat. Mon.* IX, 13 *et seq.*

lamps burning before the people'. Sutton reduced that number to twelve. In return for their commons and lodging, plus an annual stipend, these 'Scholar-Fellows' were to study 'philosophy and sacred theology', as well as the sophistry and logic already specified by Smith. These men were to be chosen from the diocese of Coventry and Lichfield, with preference for the products of Lancashire and Cheshire, especially the natives of Prestbury and Prescot (birthplaces respectively of Sutton and Smith). In this way the loyalties of Brasenose men were circumscribed from the start. So too was the governance of the college. Power resided with the Principal (stipend £5 p.a.) and the six senior Fellows (20s. p.a. each, excluding lecturers' allowances). It was they who monitored tuition; they who appointed the Vice-Principal (26s. 8d., later 31s. 8d. p.a.), as well as the Lecturer in hall or Lector Scholarium (£4 p.a.), the two Bursars (13s. 4d. p.a. each) and, eventually, the Lecturer in Greek (£4 p.a.).[30] And it was they who administered discipline. This last responsibility reads curiously today. Misbehaviour, even by junior Fellows—absence, intemperance, swearing, speaking English rather than Latin—all these were punished by fining or beating. Brawling and violence in particular incurred both financial and physical penalties. 'The Statutes of Brasenose', Rashdall reminds us, 'are the first which exhibit the undergraduate completely stripped of all his medieval dignity, tamed and reduced to schoolboy level.'[31] Schoolboys indeed: entrants to the University at this time could be as young as 11 or 12 years of age. 'In 16th century Oxford', Mallet concludes, 'the rod came into its own.'[32] Finally, the wielding of all these powers was to be subject to the authority of successive Visitors: that is, the bishops of Lincoln in perpetuity. Except in the formal awarding of degrees, the senior Fellows were now effectively autonomous. Such privileges were soon translated into monetary reward. It was to the Principal and senior Fellows alone that the bulk of surplus income—as an addition to stipend and allowances—was eventually directed.[33]

In the long perspective of Oxford scholarship, Brasenose has sometimes been seen as the last of the medieval colleges: 'the expiring cry of the Middle Ages'. Its foundation has been regarded as a scholastic buttress against the humanistic teaching of the Renaissance. By contrast, Corpus (founded 1517) is portrayed as a beacon of progress, an engine of new learning. Certainly, in the early Brasenose curriculum, scholastic philosophy—the apex of medieval

---

[30] *Quat. Mon.* IX, 150 and X, 39, citing Bursar's rolls of account.

[31] H. Rashdall, *The Universities of Europe in the Middle Ages*, ed. F. M. Powicke and A. B. Emden iii (Oxford, 1936), 371. Statutes (1521), cap. xv.

[32] C. E. Mallet, *A History of the University of Oxford*, ii (1924), 7.

[33] For stipends, excluding lodging and commons, see *Quat. Mon.* X, 39. In the early 17th century only one-ninth of entry fines for leases went to the college rather than to the senior Fellows (G. E. Aylmer, in *HUO* iii. 528).

I. **Lord Grenville's Installation as Chancellor, 3 July 1810.**

Cartoon by James Gillray, parodying the ascent of James Sadler in a balloon above Christ Church Meadows. Frodsham Hodson's hot-air balloon floats the triumphant Grenville high above the ranks of dons, massing below in Radcliffe Square. Grenville's relatives – Buckingham and Temple: supporters of Catholic Emancipation – cheer from the windows of the Camera. Prominent on the left are the Bishops of Oxford, London and St. Asaph; on the right Sheridan – déshabillé – and the Public Orator, Dr. Crowe. A rare pirate cartoon, published in August 1810 by Humphrey Bachelor, of 'Broadbum College'; and sold by Clinch of 20 Princes Street, Soho.

II. **Fancy Dress, 1897.**

    Dr. Bussell sits in the centre, in scarlet robe and judicial wig. Prince Meerza (son of the Nawab of Bengal) is on the far right.

III. Fancy Dress, 1898.

Bussell, in the centre, wears scarlet as a Dr. of Music.
The Minister of the Kirk, at Bussell's feet, is John Buchan.
The bearded man on Bussell's left is H. Le B. Lightfoot, Bursar of Corpus.

BACON FACED FELLOWS OF BRASEN NOSE, BROKE LOOSE.

IV. 'Bacon Faced Fellows of Brasen Nose Broke Loose'.

A fanciful caricature by Thomas Rowlandson (1811). It would be many years before the Fellows actually broke loose from the College's constricting site. Published by Thomas Tegg, III Cheapside; price 1 shilling.

studies—was predominant. Undergraduates continued to attend sophistry lectures in college, and disputations in grammar and logic in St Mary's Church. Postgraduates continued to dispute in the Schools. In college, BAs debated in chapel the abstractions of natural and moral philosophy; MAs the higher meaning of theology. But there was nothing unusual in any of this. On the whole, colleges retained their medieval arts curriculum—and their traditional lectures and disputations—well into the seventeenth century. Even so, there were portents of change. College teaching was beginning to shift, away from scholastic theology towards the study of classical and patristic texts; from logic to grammar and rhetoric; from Peter Lombard and Duns Scotus to Augustine and Jerome, Origen and Ambrose. One symptom of this new approach was the growing practice of declamation in hall; that is, declamation rather than disputation. In its earliest days Brasenose showed little sign of following these trends. Not until the 1540s did the college go out of its way to purchase nearly thirty volumes of patristic theology.[34] A certain conservatism in those early years—or perhaps an understandable loyalty to the older traditions of Brasenose Hall—may well have given one or two patrons pause for thought. Hugh Oldham, for example—another protégé of Lady Margaret Beaufort—may have diverted some of his benevolence to Corpus, rather than subscribe to the old-fashioned curriculum at Brasenose.[35] And when in 1538 John Claymond endowed six Brasenose scholarships, he took care to specify that their holders should attend lectures in Greek and Literae Humaniores, not at Brasenose but at his own college Corpus.[36] Clearly, in its early years, Brasenose could or would not supply the necessary teaching. It was not until 1572 that Richard Harpur endowed the college with a Lectureship in Greek.[37] Writing in 1909, I. S. Leadam concluded that a comparison between the early statutes of Brasenose and the near-contemporary statutes of Corpus 'exhibits the contrast of medieval and modern scholarship'.[38] That

[34] N. R. Ker, ibid. 459. See the catalogue probably prepared for the Marian Visitors of 1556 (LIB 1 A1/1). For Brasenose as 'medieval', see I. S. Leadam in *Quat. Mon.* IX, 134–5.

[35] Wood, *City of Oxford* (OHS xv), 542 and *Colleges and Halls*, 393. Oldham, however, must also have been a patron of Brasenose: his arms appeared in the old library (*Quat. Mon.* IX, 154 n. 2). Sutton's arms similarly adorned the gate at Corpus (Churton, *Smyth and Sutton*, 440).

[36] *Collectanea*, ii (OHS xvi), 372. The six Claymond Scholars each received 13s. 4d. per quarter (*Quat. Mon.* X, 39).

[37] *Quat. Mon.* IV, 19–20 and X, 31. This provided for Greek grammar and literature, three days per week, in hall. The Lectureship was funded by property in Derby and Warwick (Harpur-Crewe MSS, Derbyshire RO: D 2375 M/28/10). Peter Lombard's *Sentences* were not replaced, as part of the theology syllabus, with scriptural texts in Greek until the University statutes of 1565 (J. McConica, in *HUO*, iii. 707 n. 6). Apart from lodging and commons, the Greek Lecturer received £4 p.a.: the same salary as the college coachman or 'custos equorum' (*Quat. Mon.* X, 47).

[38] *Quat. Mon.* IX, 24.

was a statement too far; in fact it was a false antithesis. The statutes of Brasenose recall the statutes of Christ's College, Cambridge, rather than those of Lincoln College, Oxford.[39] Brasenose was not a particularly reactionary place; it simply remained in the conservative mainstream of sixteenth-century Oxford learning. When we look at the library of one Brasenose student of the later 1560s—William Napper—we find as much new learning as old: Melanchthon and Erasmus are just as prominent as Cicero and Aristotle.[40]

What is clear, however, is that a certain rivalry did exist in their earliest days between the colleges of Corpus and Brasenose. Their respective workmen even came to blows in 1512 and 1514.[41] This rivalry grew out of an initial difference of approach. Thomas More summed it up in 1518 with his celebrated epistle concerning Greeks (humanists) versus Trojans (scholastics).[42] At Corpus, Bishop Fox made no bones about his interest in Renaissance studies. Not so Richard Sutton. And that put Brasenose on the wrong foot in the run-up to the Henrician reformation. When the Royal Visitation of 1535 arrived in Oxford—bent on 'the abolishment of sophistry', and the suppression of 'Dunce' Scotus and 'such like stuff'—it found acquiescence, even support, among colleges already committed to the new learning.[43] The University, in any case, could sense the way of the wind. The old learning had been associated with monastic institutions, and the days of monasteries were numbered.[44] As it happened, Brasenose lacked the resources to alter quickly. It did adapt, but slowly. It was not until the final quarter of the sixteenth century that the college could boast a full range of endowed lectureships, or 'public readerships', covering both old and new learning: in logic, humane letters, Greek, and natural philosophy.[45]

---

[39] McConica, in *HUO* iii. 10.

[40] Ibid. 705, citing OU Archives c.c. invents. vol. M–O, Hyp./B/16.

[41] Churton, *Smyth and Sutton*, 289–90; *Quat. Mon.* IX, 154–5.

[42] *Correspondence of Sir Thomas More*, ed. E. F. Rogers (Princeton, 1947), 111–20.

[43] 'We have sette Dunce [Scotus] in Bocardo [jail], and have utterly banisshede hym [from] Oxforde for ever, with all his blind glosses, and [he] is now made a common servant to evere man, faste nailede up upon postes in all common howses of easement: *id quod oculis meis vidi*' (T. Wright (ed.), *Letters Relating to the Suppression of Monasteries* (Camden Soc. 26, 1843), 71: Layton to Cromwell). For details, see *Cal. Letters and Papers... Henry VIII*, IX, no. 312: 9 Sept. 1535 (Magdalen) and F. D. Logan, 'The First Royal Visitation of the English Universities, 1535', *English Hist. Rev.* 106 (1991), 861–88.

[44] 'What, my lord, shall we build houses and provide livelihoods for a company of bussing monks, whose end and fall we may live to see?' (Oldham to Fox, recalled in *Holinshed's Chronicles of England, Scotland and Ireland*, ed. H. Ellis, iii (1808), 617). Oxford lost a sizeable proportion of its senior membership with the abolition of canon law teaching in 1538 and the suppression of religious orders between 1536 and 1540.

[45] McConica, in *HUO* iii. 17.

This slow emergence of a fuller curriculum—a mingling of old and new—can be paralleled in the hesitant progress of the college towards architectural completion. In effect, fulfilment of the ultimate plan had to be postponed for several generations. When Queen Elizabeth visited the University in 1566, she was presented with a visual survey of Oxford, complete with woodcut vignettes by John Bereblock.[46] His view of Brasenose showed the college complete; but complete only in its primary incarnation.

This first stage in the construction of the new college took only a decade to build. At the earliest opportunity came the foundation stone, over the entrance to the first chapel, in the south-west corner of the site. As it stands—fragmented and recut—the inscription is a jumble of contractions and revisions. Anthony Wood is the best guide:

> Anno Christi 1509 et Regis Henrici VIII primo
> Nomine divino Lyncoln Presul quoque Sutton
> Hanc posuere petram regis ad imperium
> Primo die Junii.[47]

The old chapel staircase (now rearranged as staircase I) was begun first. Then came a series of residential chambers, disposed around an irregular quadrangle; eight in the west range, six in the north range (where the library occupied part of an upper floor), four in the east range (where the Principal's Lodgings occupied most of the space), and three more in the south range (on the western flank of hall and chapel). Each lower chamber was designed—according to the statutes—for four occupants; each upper chamber for three. And each set was arranged—following precedents at New College—to incorporate separate studies opening off communal bedrooms in which masters shared or 'chummed' with their pupils.[48] Scarcely any documents survive to date the progress of these works; no drawings, no letters, and very few accounts. Only one sequence of bills remains, for part payments due for leading, presumably of the tower and its adjoining roofs. But at least these provide us with the probable date of the gate tower's completion: 1520. In Bereblock's view — and more accurately in a drawing by Radulph Agas of 1578 (pl. 6) — it rises up to dominate its setting; flanked by two-storey ranges of rooms and by chimneystacks of ribbed and moulded brick.[49]

---

[46] H. Dodwell, *De Parma Equestri Woodwardiana Dissertatio*, ed. T. Hearne (1713), appendix; *Collegiarum Scholarumque Publicarum Academiae Oxoniensis Topographica Delineatio, Auctore Thoma Nelo, cum Figuris Johannis Berebloci*, introd. F. Madan (Oxford, 1882); C. Plummer (ed.), *Elizabethan Oxford* (OHS viii); H. Hurst (ed.), *Oxford Topography* (OHS xxxix).

[47] Wood, *Colleges and Halls*, 367.

[48] The ground-floor layout, as altered in the 17th century, is indicated in W. Williams, *Oxonia Depicta* (1730–3), pl. xxxv.

[49] *Quat. Mon.* III, pl.ii; six payments totalling £23 8s. to 'Wm Thos plumar', from 'Ric. Shirwood, bursar of ye King's College of Brasenose' (Bursar's rolls of account 1517–20,

While the new Brasenose was being built, the Principal and perhaps some of the Fellows lived opposite the future entrance to the college in Staple Hall, rented from Lincoln, on the other side of School Street.[50] Some of the students continued to live in 'lodging rooms' in Little St Edmund Hall on the site of the eventual chapel. Of the original building of Brasenose Hall only the late fifteenth-century kitchen survived this first building programme. And even that seems to have been a temporary expedient. The founders had in mind something rather more grand.

Much of this early work must have been given only rudimentary finishing. The exterior was faced in local Headington stone: fine enough in the short run, though it would certainly pose problems before long. But the interiors of quite a number of rooms must have been economical in the extreme. Several ground-floor chambers are described as 'unboarded...dampish and un-wholesome'. Not until 1572 did Alexander Nowell's donation of 'above £40' make it possible for 'them thoroughly to be boarded'.[51] A century later the college was still reusing wainscoting from the hall to decorate several private rooms. Only in 1691 was III, 1 properly panelled; and the dining room in the Lodgings (later the Tower Bursary) had to wait until 1699.[52] As we shall see, it was not until almost the end of the seventeenth century that Brasenose acquired a hall that was worthy of its collegiate status.

On only one feature of the early college was no expense apparently spared. The gate lodge and tower, overlooking the jumbled buildings of School Street, must originally have appeared striking in scale and profuse in orna-ment. Above the gateway was a grand dining room; above that a vaulted apartment; and above that the treasury: home to the college chest, triple locked and shod in iron. Three hundred years later the tower's decorations—mullions and mouldings, panelling and battlements—would be admired as prototypes for the Gothic Revival.[53] On either side of the tower were situated the better rooms in college, in particular those assigned to the Principal.

misquoted in *Quat. Mon.* III, 5–6 and IX, 151). When the attic storey was added at different dates during the 17th century, the old brick chimneys were not removed. They were built into the new structure on grounds, presumably, of economy and strength (A. J. B[utler], in *Brazen Nose*, i. 234, photo).

[50] *Brazen Nose*, iii. 106–7, citing Lincoln Bursar's accounts, 1512.

[51] R. Churton, *Life of Alexander Nowell* (Oxford, 1809), 205–6, 422.

[52] 'Davy' was paid £42 10s. od. for this (*Brazen Nose*, iv. 23, citing Senior Bursar's accounts, 3 Jan. 1699). The panelling in III, 1 hides an earlier college arms above the chimneypiece (ibid., i. 323–4).

[53] A. Pugin, *Specimens of Gothic Architecture*, ii (1823), pl. xxx: 'richly panelled fronts...bar-barously broken into, and the original windows displaced by wooden frames'. The oak doors are original (c.1520); the wicket gate an addition (c.1680). The statues—St Hugh and St Chad; and the Virgin and Child—date from Buckler's restoration in the 1860s, as does the gateway vaulting (R.C.H.M., *City of Oxford* (1929), 25). Smith's central niche remains empty.

These were entered from the quadrangle, on the southern side of the tower, via a telling symbol of continuity. Remember, Smyth was last Principal of Brasenose Hall as well as first Principal of Brasenose College. Appropriately, one surviving doorway from Brasenose Hall became the entrance portal to the new Principal's Lodgings.[54]

So the old buildings of the hall gave way gradually to the new buildings of the college. Of the original chapel—there must surely have been one on site—there is now no trace.[55] The first chapel of the new college—in a space now occupied by the Senior Common Room—only came into use in 1520. That was probably the year of its consecration.[56] Liturgically aligned, east and west, it was situated on the first floor of staircase I. Its traceried windows looked north across a formal parterre and south towards offices and orchards. In 1521 vestments were bought; in 1525 service books. The sumptuous accoutrements bequeathed by Bishop Smith seem never to have arrived: they were probably intercepted by the first Visitor, Cardinal Wolsey.[57] Even allowing for the diminutive size of the college in those early days, this first chapel can never have been commodious. Anthony Wood calls it—chapel as well as antechapel—no more than 'a little Chapel, or rather Oratory, over the Buttery'.[58] It was a tiny sanctuary. But it did possess a set of three chalices and patens, almost certainly presented by Smith. Two of each have survived, rarities from a world before the Reformation (pl. 8).[59] With these the Latin mass was said each day; the sanctus sounding, occasional incense wafting out across the gardens. Later, under Queen Elizabeth, services would be said

---

[54] *Quat. Mon.* III, pl. 5. The door may well be late 15th century (*ex inf.* Dr. W. Rodwell); but it has been enlarged to fit a broader arch.

[55] Sometimes confused with the King's hall and chapel at Woodstock. See *Cal. Close Rolls*, 3 Henry III, part 2, m. 14: 7 Nov. 1218 (repairs to King's hall); 49 Henry III m. 12 (oaks for forms and tables in King's hall, chapel chamber, and kitchen; 51 and 53 Henry III (King's chapel and kitchen, chamber for chaplains); 56 Henry III m. 3 (oaks from Woodstock Park for rafters of King's hall).

[56] *Quat. Mon.* IX, 151, citing Plate Book 1520, fo. 4. Churton suggests Oct. 1512 (Churton, *Smyth and Sutton*, 295–6).

[57] A.3.19: 'Principal Yate's Book', 'Chappell stuffe...bequeathed...to the Kinges Colledge of Brasen-Nose', transcript of will, pp. 77–9 (including 'a paire of Orgaynes bought at London of the facion of a Counting borde or low-table'). See also Browne Willis, *Survey of Cathedrals*, v. iii. 59; *Quat. Mon.* III, 8; V, 8–9; IX, 151–2, 164; Churton, *Smyth and Sutton*, 349.

[58] Wood, *Colleges and Halls*, 373.

[59] Their hallmark—maker's mark 'M.W.' in monogram—was identified in 1882 by A. J. Butler as 1498–9; older therefore than those of Corpus (1511) and Trinity (1527). They were regilded in 1676 and 1749. See *Quat. Mon.* V, 3–5, 11, 14, 28; Butler in *Athenaeum*, 25 Nov. and 9 Dec. 1882; *Oxford and Cambridge Undergraduates Jnl.* 30 Nov. 1882, 131; *A Treasured Inheritance: 600 Years of Oxford College Silver* (Oxford, 2004), no. 12, fig. 34.

here in accordance with the new Prayer Book, but still in Latin, in a version prepared specifically for the universities.[60]

Like the first chapel, the first college library (now IV, 4) can never have been regarded as more than temporary. Still, when it was finished in 1520–1, glazed and boarded and fitted with reading stands, it must have been handsome.[61] Its ceiling glinted with gilded panels. Its south-facing windows glowed with the arms of its first benefactor, Hugh Oldham, Bishop of Exeter.[62] Here books were chained, catalogued, and well kept.[63] Croston's were there, and John Booth's; and a little later Thomas Allen's: Bellarmine and Pliny, Fagius and Aldrovandi.[64] And Alexander Nowell's bequest was eventually kept there too: 'the Centuries of Magdeburg, Henry Stephen's Greek Lexicon, in three volumes, strongly bound and armed, and all the History of Martyrs written by Mr. John Fox, in two volumes of the best paper and fair bound'.[65] Most valuable of all were the volumes presented in the reign of James I by Henry Mason. Wood thought they were worth £1,000.[66] Here the library would remain until 1663.

But a college is inevitably judged by its hall; and in this respect the new Brasenose must long have seemed deficient. Not until the 1680s was there a dining hall of appropriate grandeur. For its first one and a half centuries it must have seemed almost humble. Outside, its buttresses, oriel, and lantern were little more than domestic. Inside, the walls were wainscoted at low level in squared oak; the floor was planked; the ceiling roughly beamed. Heating took the form of an open fire in the centre, supplemented by movable braziers. At some point in the early seventeenth century the hall must have acquired a chimneypiece, apparently with arcaded panelling. But there is no clear documentation.[67] The only distinctive feature was a single bay or 'compass'd window' at the north-east end; its casements bright with the armorial bearings of early benefactors.[68] Here dined the senior Fellows at

---

[60] W. K. Clay (ed.), *Occasional Forms of Prayers set Forth in the Reign of Queen Elizabeth* (Parker Soc., Cambridge, 1847), 299–434.

[61] Churton, *Smyth and Sutton*, 320; *Quat. Mon.* II, 37–8.

[62] Wood, *Colleges and Halls*, 371: 1511; *Quat. Mon.* IV, 8 and IX, 154 n. 2.

[63] *Quat. Mon.* XI, 22. A new catalogue was made in 1635.

[64] *Quat. Mon.* IV, 5, 14, 22 (quoting old Plate Book). Booth was Archdeacon and Canon of Hereford (G. Ormerod, *History of Cheshire*, ii (1882), 380). Allen became Fellow of Merton and Fellow of Eton.

[65] Churton, *Nowell*, 354.

[66] Wood, *Colleges and Halls*, 371; Senior Bursar's accounts 8 July 1635, cited by Jeffery in *Brazen Nose*, iv. 24. Other bequests of books included those from John Haster, the first Vice-Principal, and Ralph Colton, Fellow.

[67] Sketch by Augustus Hare (P Mellon Colln., Yale, B 1977.14.3139–3184: 22 Mar. 1854).

[68] The surviving arms of Smith could be early 16th century; those of Thomas Piggot and William Fermor—lawyer friends of Richard Sutton—are probably late 17th century. Glass

their 'High Mess' table, accompanied by gentlemen commoners who took their places next to the tutors. In the early years at least, they could enter via a private corner doorway from what is now lecture room VII.[69] At the other end of the hall commoners and battellers had their own tables, approached via the screens passage next to the buttery. Also at the west end stood the only other feature of note: a minstrels' gallery, entered from a tiny doorway halfway up staircase VIII.[70] In hall Fellows, commoners, and scholars were served dinner every day. Battellers took their commons from the buttery. Servitors were content with broken meats.

So there it was. Chapel and library, hall and tower; chambers, lodgings, quadrangle, and garden: the work of Smith and Sutton—architecturally, the first phase of the college—and now provisionally complete.

> Begun by one but finish'd by another,
> SUTTON he was my NURSE, but SMITH my mother;
> Or if the Phrase more proper seem, say rather,
> That SUTTON was my GUARDIAN, SMITH my FATHER.[71]

In most respects the new Brasenose followed traditional collegiate norms. But in one way its first statutes did establish a precedent that would transform Oxford. The early colleges were not primarily undergraduate societies. The business of the Fellows was scholarship not teaching. Colleges were essentially graduate seminaries, even if their Fellows did instruct undergraduates living in University halls. From the beginning, however, Smith envisaged the presence in his college of up to six noblemen's sons; non-Fellows who could pay their own way in return for tuition. In this Smith was developing precedents set by Waynflete at Magdalen. But Sutton turned these nobles into scholars. Brasenose might now admit scholars who were not Fellows, so far as the capacity of the buildings allowed.[72] And these scholars 'on the foundation' did not need to be poor. Like Smith's young nobles they retained immunity from regulation; and they gained—however meagrely—the benefit of collegiate largesse. In return they had to submit to the control of a tutor.

relating to the following benefactors was removed some time after 1786: Sir Thomas Brudenell, Edmund Bury, Sir John Port, and William Greville. For the glass portraits of Smith and Sutton, see nn. 22 and 27 (*VCH Oxon.*, iii. 215; 'A.C.C.' [Sir Colin Cole, Garter King of Arms], in *Brazen Nose*, ix. 63–7, 103–7, 199, 207). The northern bay window's external battlements were removed in 1958 (V-P's Reg. 19 Feb. 1958, fo. 99 and 28 May 1958, fo. 116).

[69] Not the present central door, which was inserted in 1901. The original door was discovered—and then covered up—while the hall floor was being relaid with oak in 1909 (B 272–80).

[70] *Quat. Mon.* XI, 12; *Brazen Nose*, i. 42–3.

[71] T. Fuller, *The Worthies of England*, i (1662; ed. P. A. Nuttall, 1840), 279.

[72] *Statutes of Colleges*, ii, pt. 9: Brasenose, 12, cap. viii.

Here was an innovation. The title 'tutor' in this context is itself new.[73] So is the very notion of gentlemen undergraduates admitted to a community of indigent clerics. This innovation was quickly regularized. From 1576 a tutor had to be one of the Fellows.[74] By 1579 Edward Stanley, aged 16, could arrive at Brasenose with no fewer than three servants, all Lancashire men.[75] He expected, and received, tuition. And where Brasenose led, Christ Church followed. From the start, Wolsey's foundation admitted commoners. The Oxford scene was thus set for a twofold takeover: of the college by the undergraduate (as the paying recipient of tuition), and of the University by the colleges (as autonomous controllers of entry).[76] These undergraduate gentry in the early years of Brasenose—installed in privileged accommodation: inside and above the future lecture room VII—turned out to be progenitors of a new order of University governance. Here we can trace the genesis of the tutorial system; a system sufficiently flexible to accommodate the new humanism, sufficiently resilient to absorb the new puritanism. Its development enabled colleges to set their own academic standards, prior to supplication for a degree. By 1567 John Foster of Brasenose, in effect Fellow and Tutor, could expect to be paid twenty shillings a year for 'reading' with one pupil, a young man named Richard Marckland.[77] That was as much as a Fellow received for lecturing on sophistry and logic. Even so those twenty shillings represented a bargain: in 1538 it had been established that this new breed of tutor was entitled to three times as much.[78] The notion—if not the title—of 'Fellow and Tutor' was beginning to take hold. By the early seventeenth century an average of four Fellows of Brasenose habitually acted in this dual capacity.

At least part of their salaries could be funded out of fee income. But for capital endowment the college depended upon bequests. From the beginning, Brasenose was rich, but not especially rich, in endowments. Smith and Sutton each contributed lands with a capital value of perhaps £2,000. By any standards, these are sizeable sums; though considerably less than those available, for instance, to St John's, Cambridge, or St John's, Oxford.[79] College income in

[73] Rashdall, *Universities of Europe in the Middle Ages*, iii. 231 n. 3 and 375 n. 1; *Quat. Mon.* IX, 32–3 and 42–3. The word 'tutor' corresponds to 'creancer' or 'creditor' in the Magdalen statutes, a term which Smith himself had used. A tutor's duties were at first financial and disciplinary rather than didactic: they were to 'answer for their [pupils'] expenses and fines'.

[74] V-P's Reg. 18 Aug. 1576, fo. 40.

[75] A. Clark (ed.) *Register of the University of Oxford*, II, pt. i (OHS x), 391.

[76] In this process, Brasenose was a leader. Exeter, for example, did not take undergraduates on the foundation until 1566; University College did not organize undergraduate teaching until 1583 (E. Russell, in *English Hist. Rev.* 92 (1977), 727, 736).

[77] *Brazen Nose*, vi. 168–9, citing *Reports of Chancery Proceedings*, ser. ii, 63/52.

[78] McConica, in *HUO* iii. 694, citing OU Archives, Chancellor's Reg. 1527–43, fo. 233.

[79] W. K. Jordan, *The Charities of London* (1960), 256, 399 n. 183, citing wills. For discussion of Jordan's figures see *Econ. Hist. Rev.* 29 (1976), 203–10 and 31 (1978) 105–28, and *Hist. of Education*, viii (1979), 257–73.

those early years was however precarious. Bishop Smith died in 1515, but Brasenose received no profit from his bequests until 1543–4.[80] Much, therefore, depended on Smith's co-founder, Sutton. It seems to have been Sir Richard Sutton—belatedly knighted between 1521 and 1523—who drew a third key patron into the orbit of the new college: Elizabeth Morley. Her husband, who probably died in 1508, had been a prosperous draper and vintner of London. She herself may well have been related to Sutton. And the terms of her bequest—tied to prayers and exequies for her soul—reflect the piety of Sutton's circle. Before Mrs Morley's benefaction in 1515, the total income of the college stood at £47 1s. 8 ¼d. p.a.[81] By 1535 the figure was £113 9s. 2d.[82] By 1547 it was £198 2s. 9 ¾d.[83] The picture was actually not quite as rosy as this might suggest. Expenditure exceeded income in that final year by £12 13s. 9d.[84] Even so, Brasenose was now, in terms of endowment, mid-way in the league table of Oxford colleges.[85] In the first century of its existence, the college received twenty-eight significant benefactions.[86] Claymond Scholars, Mordaunt Scholars, Nowell Scholars, Ogle Scholars, Walker Scholars, Palin Scholars, even scholarships—for Middleton School, Lancashire—sponsored by Queen Elizabeth herself; Cox, Harpur, and Morley Lectureships; Williamson and Port Fellowships; Clifton and Porter Fellowships; Baker, Darbie, and Higden Fellowships—all these helped to swell the numbers of Brasenose recruits. Several of these bequests were indeed considerable; but none quite matched the legacy of Joyce Frankland (pl. 10). In 1586 Mrs Frankland, daughter of Robert Trappes, a great London goldsmith, gave lands which included numbers 39–53 Kensington High Street. Childless and twice widowed, she resolved—'in lieu of her most loving son [deceased]'—'to rayse and begett unto her selfe in virtue and learnyng manye Children'. The Trappes family came from Lancashire; her executor was Dean Nowell. Hence

---

[80] *Quat. Mon.* IX, 136, 157.

[81] *Quat. Mon.* IX, 79. For the terms of her bequest see *Quat. Mon.* IV, 8.

[82] *Valor Ecclesiasticus* (1535), ii (Record Commission, 1814), 271–3 (recalculated by Leadam in *Quat. Mon.* IX, 209–10 and followed in *VCH Oxon.*, iii. 208).

[83] Leadam, in *Quat. Mon.* IX, 162, citing the *Valor* of 1547, made for the chantry commissioners of 1546 (Augmentation Office Miscell. Books, vol. 441; reprinted in *Quat. Mon.* IX, 188–206), and based on the Bursar's Roll of 1545–6 (reprinted, *Quat. Mon.* IX, 177–87).

[84] For Leadam's analysis of the Bursar's rolls of account, 1515–47, see *Quat. Mon.* IX, 173–6.

[85] G. E. Aylmer, in *HUO* iii. 556. In a list of ecclesiastical patronage drawn up before 1550, giving the yearly value of 'spiritual promotions', Brasenose is credited with £111 0s. 3¼d. University College, Lincoln, Exeter, and Balliol have less; Merton, Queen's, All Souls, Corpus, Christ Church, New College, and Magdalen have more (*Cal. State Papers Domestic . . . Edward VI* (rev. edn. 1992), no. 431).

[86] See A. J. Butler in *Quat. Mon.* IV, 7–23, for full details of these bequests. For the Nowell, Walker, Morley, Cox, and Mordaunt Trusts, see *Property and Income of Oxford and Cambridge* (Cleveland Commission), ii (1874), 605–6. Mostly sold, 1870–1970.

the benefaction. At the time her Kensington property alone was worth £7 p.a.; by the 1920s its value had multiplied to more than £3,000 p.a. In all, Mrs Frankland's capital endowment of Brasenose totalled £1,840 in money of that day.[87] That was impressive. So too, to a lesser degree, were the bequests of Morley, Nowell, and Mordaunt (pl. 11). And as benefactions grew, collegiate numbers increased significantly.

Counting heads in this period is a hazardous operation. The records, both at college and University level, are imperfect. If we examine the annual Brasenose intake, the years of greatest increase would seem to be 1553–6, 1564–5, and 1578–81. But that is to ignore the statistical distortions created by the matriculation statutes of 1565 and 1581.[88] It is safer to take a series of snapshots. The *Valor* of 1535 suggests ten Fellows apart from the Principal and four servants; the *Valor* of 1547 indicates fourteen Fellows besides the Principal, seven scholars, and eight servants.[89] In 1552 the Chancellor's census lists nearly seventy names: 9 *magistri*, 12 *domini*, 47 *subgraduati*; perhaps 40 per cent of these being undergraduate commoners.[90] That made Brasenose fourth in order of magnitude, after Christ Church, Magdalen, and New College. By 1566 the University's matriculation register records thirty-one graduates, fifty-seven undergraduates, eight poor scholars, and five matriculated servants.[91] By 1578, the same register lists seventy undergraduates at matriculation stage, varying in age from 12 to 24.[92] Different figures; different systems of counting. But whatever the basis of calculation, the expansion of numbers had been swift; and it continued. The census of 1612 suggests no fewer than 145 commoners at Brasenose. That would be an astonishing

[87] Jordan, *Charities of London*, 402 n. 223; Mallet, *Hist. Oxford*, ii. 10. For the history of this Kensington property, see R. W. Jeffery, in *Brazen Nose*, iv. 404–22. As a goldsmith, Trappes began taking apprentices in 1509; he profited much from sales of monastic property; and he was twice Warden of the Goldsmiths Company. Mrs Frankland's arms were formerly in one of the windows of the hall, with her motto: 'Suffer and Serve' (Wood, *Colleges and Halls*, 368). By her will of 1586 (revoking that of 1585), she also benefited Lincoln College Oxford, and Emmanuel and Caius College, Cambridge (J. Venn, *Biog. Hist. of Gonville and Caius College* iii (1901), 229–30). But Brasenose was the principal beneficiary (*Quat. Mon.* IV, 20–1; VI, 33 and VII, 15). She lived at the Rye House, Stansted Abbotts, Herts. (later scene of the celebrated plot), and at a 'great house' in Philip Lane, Aldermanbury, which she bequeathed to Caius (Churton, *Nowell*, 341). Her memorial in St Leonard's, Foster Lane, was destroyed in the Great Fire, 1666 (Wood, *Colleges and Halls*, 358; *Quat. Mon.* X, 16–17). Her portrait in hall—by Gilbert Jackson, 1629— was engraved by Fittler in 1810 (*Quat. Mon.* VII, pl. ix; *Brazen Nose*, vii. 2).

[88] E. Russell, in *English Hist. Rev.* 17 (1977), 721–45.

[89] Cited by Leadam in *Quat. Mon.* IX, 145, 149, 159–60. For details of the *Valor* of 1535 and 1547 as regards Brasenose, see ibid. 188–210.

[90] C. W. Boase (ed.), *University Register*, I (OHS i), xxiii; McConica, in *HUO* iii. 11–12.

[91] *University Register*, II, pt. ii, 25–7; Mallett, *Hist. Oxford*, ii, 12. Servants like the manciple and porter often matriculated and drew commons.

[92] *University Register*, II, pt. ii, 412; *Quat. Mon.* X, 34–5.

number, if it were accurate. The truer figure is more likely to be 133.[93] Even so, this is an impressive total; at a time—in the 1590s for example—when many college rolls were static or even declining. The catchment area, however, was largely unchanged. During the reigns of Henry VIII, Edward VI, and Mary, for example, at least sixty entrants came from Lancashire; during the reign of Elizabeth perhaps 200. The names of those recruited remained rich in regional resonance: Heywood, Radcliffe, Leigh, Watson, Latham, Brooke, Byrom, Blundell, Moseley, Egerton, Singleton, and Shuttleworth. In social terms, too, there is little discernible movement. The *embourgeoisement* of sixteenth-century Oxford was a very slow process.[94]

How then should we characterize mid-Tudor Brasenose? It was northern, it was conservative, its roots were in the yeomanry—parish rather than county gentry—and it was comparatively under-endowed. But its numbers were growing, and its status was starting to rise. First and foremost—like any college at this date—it was a religious foundation. The rhythms of its existence followed the diurnal pattern of traditional religious observance. Daily mass at dawn; weekly sermons in St Mary's Church; Latin grace before and after every meal, with Latin spoken in hall; a meagre breakfast followed by private study and lectures until dinner at 11 a.m.; then reading and tuition until supper and more prayers at 5 p.m.; and after that disputations or further lessons, then sleep at last at 10 p.m. To these exercises we must add, year by year, the multitudinous obligations of the ecclesiastical calendar. Clothing was strictly regulated: no fur, silk, or velvet; no padded hose; no lace of gold or silver; no 'dublet of any light colour, as white, green, yellow etc.'[95] Food was plain, heating negligible, and sanitation primitive. Damp, cold, and undernourished, the poorer scholars might even be reduced—with authority—to begging.[96] No wonder there were at least six outbreaks of plague or pestilence between the 1550s and the 1590s.[97] In an almost physical sense, Tudor education was not just a discipline for life; it was a preparation for death.

Because much of the menial work was done by poor scholars, there were very few college servants. Only seven appear regularly on the Bursar's Roll: the Bible Clerk (£2 p.a.), the manciple (£2 p.a.), the butler (£1 10s. p.a.), the

[93] J. Gutch, *Collectanea Curiosa*, i (Oxford, 1781), 197; *Quat. Mon.* XI, 7. Compare Aylmer, in *HUO* iii. 556, with S. Porter, ibid., iv. 40.

[94] 'The argument about what class was profiting from the growth in higher education is...a largely meaningless one. So great was the boom...that all classes above a certain level took their part' (L. Stone, in *Past and Present*, 28 (1964), 68). For some cautionary advice on this subject, see McConica, in *Jnl. of Interdisciplinary Hist.* 3 (1973), 543–54.

[95] Wood, *Annals*, ii. 153.

[96] Clark (ed.), *University Register*, II, pt. ii, 1–3; 14 Eliz. c. v.

[97] Wood, *Annals*, ii. 138, 170–1, 179, 189–91; *Quat. Mon.* X, 45–6. One Fellow, Thomas Standley, died in the outbreak of 1577; he left forty-one books (N. R. Kerr, in *H. U. O.* iii. 473).

cook (£4 3s. 4d. p.a.), the porter who also acted as 'tonsor' or 'barbitonsor' (£2 p.a.), the Clerk of Accounts (£1 6s. 8d. p.a.), and the laundress (the only woman, incidentally, and she was not admitted within the gates; she dried her washing nearby in the University School of Arts).[98] Gentlemen scholars, of course, lived a slightly easier life: they had their own attendants. As for the Principal and Fellows, they fared rather better than their pupils. The total bill for their commons regularly came to £50 or £60 p.a.[99] Apart from daily meals and lodging, they enjoyed special feasts and anniversary gaudies. One bill, listing the cost of dinner and supper for all the Fellows in what is now the Tower Bursary, has been preserved:[100]

Laid out for dinner in the Tower, 14th of November 1597.

Inprimis for a cabbagde	...	2d.
Item for a p[iece] of beefe	...	1s. od.
Item for a legge of porcke	...	1s. 6d.
Item for 2 coople of rabbets	...	2s. 8d.
Item for a quarte of wyne and sugar	...	1s. 1d.
Item for ale, apples & cheese	...	1od.
Item for table cloath and napkins	...	6d.
ffor supper dod[o]		
Item for a loyne of mutton	...	1s. 6d.
Item for [a couple of rabbits]	...	1s. 4d.
Item for a quarte of sacke	...	1od.
Item for ale, apples & cheese	...	1od.
Sum	12s. 3d. ita est.	

The wch. sum of 12s. 3d. I have received of Mr. Dalton [Bursar] on the day above written [signed] Rich. Billingsley [M.A.].

By later standards, all this seems fairly modest.

And what of recreation? Organized games were still generations away. Relaxation in Oxford was haphazard, and often disorderly. In 1582, according to Anthony Wood, there was much 'tipling, dicing, carding, tabling' in alehouses, 'all day and much of the night'. Brasenose students were statutorily forbidden to play at dice, or ball, or cards; though the latter were permitted—not for money—in hall at Christmas; and in 1608 there was even some hope of building a court (*sphaeristerium*) for playing hand ball (*ludo pilae palmariae*).[101] Then there was football and fives, drama and singing, and for the better off,

---

[98] *Quat. Mon.* IX, 145–50 and X, 38–9, citing Bursar's Rolls.

[99] *Quat. Mon.* IX, 146, 150 and X, 40, citing Bursar's Rolls.

[100] *Quat. Mon.* X, 44.

[101] V-P's Reg. 20 Sept. 1608, fo. 24ʳ and 24ᵛ (correspondence with the Visitor). For gaming etc. see Wood, *Annals*, ii. 213. For sports and pastimes see P. Manning in *Oxford Hist. Soc.* 75 (1923), 85–135.

riding, hunting, and coursing. But all these were peripheral. A college was still a species of monastery; and collegians, in the majority, were still prospective priests. Not that religious observance guaranteed piety. The Visitation of John Longland, Bishop of Lincoln, in 1530 had uncovered a good deal of laxity. William Sutton, lecturer in hall, for example, was found to spend too much time in taverns. Worse still, when the college retreated to Cold Norton because of the plague, he somehow managed to keep the wife of a local tradesman in a house situated next to the chapel. When neighbours denounced him, he rounded on them as 'horesons churls and knaves'. And when challenged by the constables of Chipping Norton he raised a gang of twenty men and put the objectors to flight with bows and arrows. Not surprisingly, he stayed a Fellow no longer.[102]

Such behaviour can hardly have been typical. Brasenose men in fact, in those early years at least, seem to have been only too serious; thoroughly committed to religious practices, sometimes puritan, more often Catholic. Of the sixty Lancastrians, for example, who went up to Brasenose between the death of Henry VII and the death of Mary, more than half went into holy orders. Such commitment required delicate negotiation as regards college politics. The first two Principals, Matthew Smyth and John Hawarden, had to tread a cautious path. In the 1530s Smyth appears as a conservative conformist in a college reluctantly agreeing to gainsay the authority of the Pope. First came the University's grudging acceptance of the royal divorce in 1530.[103] Then came the crucial question of ecclesiastical supremacy. With seven senior Fellows, Smyth agreed to repudiate papal supremacy in June 1534; and in July of the same year he formally acknowledged the ecclesiastical supremacy of the King.[104] In both matters he was following resolutions already passed in Congregation. The University valued the protection of the Crown too much to put up any serious resistance. Inside Brasenose, however, things were rather less clear-cut. On 9 June 1534 a royal proclamation had ordered the removal of the Pope's name from all service books. Four and a half years later that had still to be done. The Dean of Chapel, Thomas Hawarden, found himself reported to the Chancellor by a member of his own college, George Munson. Unabashed, Hawarden brazened out his culpability with rough language. 'Hawarden', so Anthony Wood suggests, 'was a great stickler

---

[102] Citations in *VCH Oxon.*, iii. 209.

[103] *Cal. Letters and Papers... Henry VIII*, IV, pt. 3, nos. 6308, 6320, and app. no. 254.

[104] *Cal. Letters and Papers... Henry VIII*, VII, no. 891: 27 June 1534 and IX, no. 306: 9 Sept. 1535 (formal declaration from Corpus), no. 351: 12 Sept. 1535; *7th Report, Deputy Keeper Public Records* (1846), app. ii, no. 9, 297: 31 July 1534 (signed by Simon Starkey, Robert Cotton, John Leche, Robert More, George Bruch, Thomas Hawarden, and Robert Holmes, with two votes from Principal Smyth).

for the Pope.' And when questioned by the Chancellor he 'appeared so foul by some rash expressions dropt from his mouth, that he was cited soon after to appear before the King's [Privy] Council, to answer for what he had said and done'.[105] That tells us something about the religious temper of the college. So does the fact that in 1537 one of the very few matriculands was William Constable, son of a leading figure in the Pilgrimage of Grace, Sir Robert Constable.[106] That tragic uprising—a grass-roots reaction to the dissolution of the monasteries—resulted in the execution of one notable college benefactor: Lord Hussey. As the King veered away from Rome, Hussey transferred his loyalty to the future Queen Mary. Such opportunism proved premature.[107] But Brasenose has reason to be grateful to him. It would not be the last occasion when the college acted as a focus for forlorn hopes.

Thereafter Brasenose seems to have pursued a route of minimal conformity. Principal Smyth had accepted the implications of Henrician supremacy. But he could still preside, in cope or chasuble, over traditional services in chapel. In this he was aided by the survival until 1547 of the Visitor, Longland, Bishop of Lincoln. Like Smyth Longland was a conservative conformist. The next Principal, John Hawarden, was however in an even trickier position. He had to implement the new Order of Communion in 1548, as well as the Injunctions of 1549 and the rubrics of the First and Second Prayer Books in 1549 and 1552. The use of Latin, Greek, and Hebrew was still permitted in Oxford by the Act of Uniformity (1549), for 'matins, evensong, litany and all other prayers ... the mass [alone] excepted'. But the framework of services in chapel was now dictated by the Book of Common Prayer. That left little room for manoeuvre. Even so, Hawarden followed the great majority of heads in opposing—albeit passively—the doctrinal drift of the Edwardian reformation.[108]

Passivity, however, could have unforeseen consequences. It certainly did so during the reaction under Mary. The University—as Thomas Reynolds assured Cardinal Pole—was now to have 'a new face ... as well in life as learning'. It was, once again, to be Catholic. But Brasenose seems to have moved slowly; too slowly for several zealots among the Fellowship. In the summer of 1556, Hawarden expelled—or forced the resignations of—no

---

[105] Wood, *Annals*, ii. 60: 'what became of the matter I find not.' These orders were reinforced in 1542 (ibid. 71–2). See also B 2a 42: Madan's extract from Bodl. MS Twyne 24, fo. 384, citing OU Archives, Chancellor's Reg. 1527–43, fo. 327ᵛ as in J. Loach, in *HUO* iii. 367.

[106] *Cal. Letters and Papers ... Henry VIII*, XII, pt. 1, no. 30: 6 Jan. 1537.

[107] *Quat. Mon.* IX, 135, 171, citing Bursar's Rolls; *ODNB*.

[108] G. D. Duncan, in *Oxoniensia*, 45 (1980), 226–34. For the first Act of Uniformity (1549), see *Statutes of the Realm*,. iv. 37–49. For the Oxford Visitation, Statutes, and Injunctions (or Ordinances) of 1549, see *Cal. State Papers Domestic: Edward VI*, vii, no. 6: 8 May 1549; Rymer, *Foedera*, xv (1728), 183–5; and Wood, *Annals*, ii. 92–106.

fewer than five Fellows: William Eley, Christopher Cary, Patrick Sacheverell, Morgan Carr, and John Hodgson. They had 'absented theym selfes' from 'dyvyne service' at Christmas 1555, presumably because the college had yet to reinstate the full apparatus of the mass. The details of this episode are by no means clear: at a crucial point two leaves have been cut out of the Vice-Principal's Register, after composition but prior to foliation. On the face of it, the authority of the Principal (Hawarden) seems to have been pitted against the powers of the Chancellor (Pole), the Vice-Chancellor (Marshall), and the Visitor (White). But religion was surely at the root of the matter. And in this respect Brasenose was by no means unique. The Marian Injunctions of 1554–5 were in many places implemented slowly. It took over a year, for example, to re-establish Catholic ceremonial in St Paul's Cathedral, London. This must have made it quite possible for Hawarden—liturgically speaking— to drag his feet. With the Injunctions of autumn 1556, however, he was quickly forced to comply. When it came to church politics, he seems consistently to have played it by the book. The Bursar's Roll for 1557 shows an unusually high bill (£4 19s. 3d.) for 'chapel necessaries'. The mass had returned to staircase I; and Brasenose—'this troubleous house', as the Visitor described it—had survived yet another revolution.[109] But there was one more turn of the wheel to come. Hawarden did not resign; he stayed on. In surplice and square cap—grudgingly or happily, we know not which—he was still there to administer the compromise formularies of Elizabeth.[110]

So John Hawarden remains an enigma: he survived. First he tutored the arch-Protestant John Foxe; somehow he negotiated the reaction under Mary; then he managed to avoid being one of the nine heads of house removed under Elizabeth. He attended Cranmer's trial in 1556, and he accepted the Oath of Supremacy in 1559. And all along he was able to preside over a college that remained—like Exeter and St John's—obstinately Catholic in its sympathies. Only with his successors Thomas Blanchard and Richard Harris—Principals in 1564–74 and 1574–95—did Brasenose swing belatedly

---

[109] V-P's Reg. 10 Jan. 1556 and 14 Aug. 1556, fos. 85–7; T. Yate, 'Schedula & Abstracta' (1668), fos. 416–17; *Cal. State Papers Domestic, Addenda* 1547–65, 446: 24 Nov. 1556; *Quat. Mon.* X, 40, 49–51; *Brasenose Reg.* 12, 14, 18, 19; Wood, *Annals,* ii. 117–22, 135–8; D. M. Loades, in *Jnl. Eccles. Hist.* 16 (1965), 60, 64. For the Latin text of Pole's statutes, see S. Gibson, *Statuta Antiqua Universitatis Oxoniensis* (Oxford, 1931), 363–75. Brasenose may have been mollified by Marian largesse: see a warrant granting lands to 'the Kinges [Hall and] Colledge of [Brasenose] Oxford, for such wantes as the lack their foundation requireth' (*Cal. Acts of Privy Council* 1554–6, 45). See also *Cal. State Papers Domestic, Mary I*, no. 119: 28 June 1554.

[110] Compare Bishop Horne's Injunctions for Corpus, New College, and Magdalen (1566–7), and Bishop Parker's Orders for Merton (1567), in W. H. Frere (ed.), *Visitation Articles and Injunctions of the...Reformation*, iii (Alcuin Club Collections 16, 1910), 59–73. Between 1536 and 1578 Hawarden also held the college living of Steeple Aston.

behind the Elizabethan settlement.[111] In that, it could be argued, the college typified the evolution of religious attitudes nationwide.

Under Hawarden Brasenose did include a number of young puritans who would one day have dramatic parts to play in Protestant politics. One was Christopher Goodman, another was William Whittingham. Goodman was a protégé of Peter Martyr who became an ally of John Knox. Whittingham travelled a similar route, from Cheshire to Brasenose, from Brasenose to Christ Church, and then from Oxford to Geneva and Scotland. Both men were thorns in the side of church hierarchy; both were creatively involved in the translation of the Geneva Bible; and both made permanent contributions to the quality of Anglo-Scottish Protestant culture.[112] A third member of this group was not an Oxford matriculand at all, but a Cambridge man named Nicholas Grimald who migrated briefly to Brasenose. At Easter 1542 he produced a satirical drama with subversive overtones, entitled *Christus Redivivus*. It may actually have been performed in Latin in Brasenose hall.[113] He went on to support, and betray, both sides in the doctrinal debates of the 1540s. Today Grimald's significance is difficult to assess. Catholic, Protestant, poet, spy, he could be said to have played an equivocal role throughout his life, and in death he has been forgotten. But two of his near contemporaries still remain important figures. Their names are Nowell and Foxe.

As an undergraduate, Alexander Nowell (pl. 9) seems to have shared rooms with John Foxe.[114] That conjunction is intriguing; but Principal Smyth surely knew what he was doing. In a conservative college potential firebrands must have been in a minority. Anyway these two young men— Foxe from Lincolnshire; Nowell from Lancashire—turned out to be appropriately matched. The future martyrologist remembered the future Dean of St Paul's as 'a man earnestly bent on the true worshipping of God'.[115] And

---

[111] After resigning the Principalship in 1574, Blanchard was Rector of Quainton and Vicar of Aston Abbotts, both in Bucks., until his death in February 1595. Harris combined his Principalship with a prebendal stall at Hereford until his resignation in 1595 (V-P's Reg. 21 Feb. 1573, fo. 84).

[112] For both Goodman and Whittingham see C. H. Garrett, *The Marian Exiles* (Cambridge, 1938), 162–4, 327–30 and *ODNB*. Goodman—Lady Margaret Professor, 1548–54—was deprived of his Fellowship, on grounds of absence, in 1515 (C. M. Dent, *Protestant Reformers in Elizabethan Oxford* (Oxford, 1983), 15).

[113] L. R. Merrill, *Nicholas Grimald, the Judas of the Reformation* (PMLA, Baltimore, 1922); R. H. Blackburn, *Biblical Drama under the Tudors* (The Hague, 1971), 91. Grimald—'the first Oxford playwright of mark whom we are able to identify'—was encouraged by Junior Bursar Matthew Smith and Senior Bursar Richard Caldwell, 'vir per honestus, & insigniter doctus' (F. S. Boas, *University Drama in the Tudor Age* (Oxford, 1914). 26–32, 42; *ODNB*). In 1549 Grimald supplied Sir William Cecil with Latinized lists of Oxford clerics with idle lifestyles and pro-Catholic sympathies (L. R. Merrill, *Life and Poems of Nicholas Grimald* (1925), 38–43).

[114] This story goes back at least to T. Tanner, *Bibliotheca Britannico-Hibernica* (1748), s.v. Nowell.

[115] *Hist. Parl.: Commons* 1509–58, iii. 28.

their friendship endured. Years later, in 1572, it was Nowell and Foxe whom the condemned Duke of Norfolk summoned to hear his last prayers on the scaffold. And years after that, in 1602, the dying Dean made a point of leaving his own copy of Foxe's *Martyrs* to the college library. But Nowell and Foxe were not at Brasenose together for long. After graduating in 1537 Foxe departed for Magdalen. He had before him a noisy career as England's leading Protestant publicist. His *Acts and Monuments* (1563 onwards)—universally known as *Foxe's Martyrs*—became a veritable cyclopaedia of anti-popery. It made him, in effect, 'England's first literary celebrity'.[116] Nowell, on the other hand, seems to have been sprung of subtler material. After graduation, he stayed on at Brasenose; then moved steadily up the church hierarchy, eventually rising via the mastership of Westminster School to the deanery of St Paul's. In the process, he survived all the doctrinal changes of Henry VIII, Edward VI, Mary, and Elizabeth, emerging in the end as one of the key architects of the future Anglican settlement. Nowell's instincts were consistently reformist; but temperament made him moderate. In Churton's phrase, he became 'one of the best mirrors to discern the true spirit and temper of the . . . Reformation'.[117] During the Marian interlude, he prudently withdrew to Frankfurt. It is said that Bishop Bonner, the heresy hunter, one day saw him fishing in the Thames and vowed to 'catch' this piscatorial radical. That threat he survived; and he returned to England with his reputation enhanced. The young Elizabeth promoted him Dean, while famously curbing his radicalism: 'to your text Mr. Dean . . . we have heard enough of that.'[118] Her judgement was soon amply justified. Nowell's *Catechism*—published in scores of editions, English, Greek, and Latin, from 1570 onwards—could be said to rival the Thirty-Nine Articles as the didactic bedrock of Anglican faith.[119]

All these men—Goodman and Whittingham, Grimald, Foxe, and Nowell—belonged to a generation of reformers who went up to Oxford under Henry VIII, came to prominence under Edward VI, went into exile under Mary, and reappeared at different times and in different ways to make their mark under Elizabeth. Each had been at Brasenose towards the end of

---

[116] T. S. Freeman in *ODNB*.

[117] Churton, *Nowell*, p. viii. In 1553 he was elected MP, but was refused by the House of Commons as being in holy orders (*Commons Jnls*. i. 27: 13 Oct. 1553).

[118] Fuller, *Worthies*, i (1811 edn.), 547; J. Strype, *The Life and Acts of Matthew Parker* (1711), i. 318–19.

[119] For Latin and English editions, see *A Catechism by Alexander Nowell*, ed. G. E. Corrie (Cambridge, Parker Soc., 1853). For context, see I. M. Green, *The Christian's A.B.C.: Catechisms and Catechising in England, c.*1530–1740 (Oxford, 1996). Nowell's *Catechism* went through forty-four editions before 1647 (J. R. Mulder, *The Temple of the Mind* (New York, 1969), 107). In 1795 a new edition was produced by Principal Cleaver.

Principal Smyth's regime. Each developed there a set of radical attitudes that
seem curiously at odds with the college's conservative leadership. And yet we
need assume no contradiction. At a time of fast-changing doctrinal norms,
collective consistency in any college would be most unlikely. The politics of
religion involved stakes which were dangerously high. Thomas Fane, for
example, who went up in 1552, narrowly escaped execution for backing the
'Protestant' side in Wyatt's rebellion of 1554.[120] It must often have seemed
wiser to bend a little with the wind. Take, for example, the career of Henry
Pendleton. He was a Lancastrian who went up to Brasenose about 1538, and
stayed on to become Vice-Principal and Bursar. Anti-Lutheran under Henry
VIII, anti-papal under Edward VI, Catholic under Mary—'Bloody' Bonner's
chaplain, no less—Pendleton, doctrinally speaking, was everything and nothing. No wonder, when preaching at St Paul's Cross in 1554, he narrowly
escaped assassination. Strype tells us it was not clear whether the shot was
fired 'out of detestation of Pendleton's doctrine, or his person'.[121]

To this group of religious radicals we should no doubt add two more with
pronounced evangelical sympathies: John Coxe, an able translator; and
Richard Barnes, who would one day be Bishop of Durham.[122] But half a
dozen radicals do not add up to a puritan college. In the early sixteenth
century Brasenose never rivalled Magdalen or Corpus as a centre of religious
radicalism.[123] In fact, until the 1580s—like the majority of Oxford colleges—
Brasenose remained residually loyal to the old faith.[124] The number of
lifetime recusants—those who refused to accept the sacraments of the
reformed Church—is considerable.

Take first those appearing in the college registers during a single decade,
1543–53. The Edwardian Acts of Uniformity (1549 and 1552) altered the
forms of service but not the loyalties of many college men. Here we find at
least eleven whose lives were spent in open opposition to Protestantism:
Henry Henshaw, William and Humphrey Eley, Laurence Vaux, Edmund
Ansley, John Bridgewater, John Ashbroke, Sampson Erdeswick, Robert
Dymocke, William Stock, and Thomas Palmer. Each paid the penalty of
deprivation, or worse. Of course they were just the bolder spirits: less than a
twelfth of the total intake during those years. They were the ones who took a
public stand. They all, however, managed to avoid the scaffold. Henshaw
became Rector of Lincoln, but was compelled to resign in 1559; he fled to

[120] *Brasenose Reg.*; *ODNB*; M. R. Thorp, in *Church History*, 47 (1978), 363–80.
[121] J. Strype, *Ecclesiastical Memorials*, iii (1822), pt. i, 213, cited in *ODNB*.
[122] *Quat. Mon.* X, 7; *ODNB*.
[123] Dent, *Protestant Reformers, passim*; P. Collinson, *The Elizabethan Puritan Movement* (1967), 129.
[124] C. M. J. F. Swan, 'The Introduction of the Elizabethan Settlement into the Universities
of Oxford and Cambridge, with Particular Reference to Roman Catholics, 1558–1603' (Ph.D.,
Cambridge, 1955).

Rome and ended up at Douai.[125] William Eley became President of St John's, but resigned rather than take the Oath of Supremacy in 1563; he died obscurely, perhaps in Hereford jail, in 1609. His brother Humphrey, also of St John's, left for Douai in 1577.[126] Vaux became Warden of Manchester Collegiate Church, but was deprived under the Act of Uniformity in 1559 and fled to Louvain.[127] Ansley, who became a Jesuit, was expelled from Merton in 1558 and then imprisoned in 1573 for corresponding with Mary Queen of Scots.[128] Bridgewater was nominated Rector of Lincoln in 1563, but had to escape to Reims eleven years later where he also became a Jesuit.[129] Ashbroke resigned as Vice-Principal of Brasenose in 1558, and spent some years as a recusant priest in the Prescot area of Lancashire.[130] As for Erdeswick, a Staffordshire landowner, he comes down to us as the classic provincial recusant; an antiquary and a gentleman; breathing defiance all his life at the intrusions of the Privy Council.[131] Others matched his constancy—Robert Dymocke, for example, who was born into the family of the King's Champion, and eventually died in Lincoln jail in 1580.[132] Finally two more, Stock and Palmer, were successive Principals of that nest of Oxford Catholics, Gloucester Hall.[133] All these men—college entrants of a single decade—remained, in the language of the day, 'notorious papists'. And William Eley—so soon to be expelled by Hawarden—achieved at this point his own sad niche in history. He was one of those who hectored Cranmer as the frail Archbishop was hustled to his death up Brasenose Lane in 1556. He refused in the end even to shake the doomed man's hand.[134]

Now look at the careers of Brasenose Catholics in the later part of Elizabeth's reign. Here we enter the age of the Brasenose martyrs. In 1559 the Acts of Supremacy and Uniformity had re-established by law not only the spiritual authority of Henry VIII, but much of the Protestant practice of

---

[125] *Brasenose Reg.* The seminary at Douai was founded in 1568, moved to Reims in 1578, and returned to Douai in 1593.

[126] *ODNB.*

[127] Ibid.

[128] *Brasenose Reg.*; G. C. Brodrick, *Memorials of Merton College* (OHS iv), 263. He became Professor of Canon Law at Pont-à-Mousson, Lorraine.

[129] *ODNB.* He published a Catholic equivalent of *Foxe's Martyrs*, entitled *Concertatio Ecclesiae Catholicae in Anglia adversus Calvino-papistas et Puritanos sub Elizabetha Regina* (Treves, 1589).

[130] C. Haigh, *Reformation and Resistance in Tudor Lancashire* (1975), 255. He received a 40s. payment from Brasenose, on resignation (*Brasenose Reg.*).

[131] *ODNB.* His monument in Sandon church is 'a magnificent pile to a magnificent man' (W. Dyott, *Diary*, ed. R. W. Jeffery, i (1907), 352–3).

[132] *Brasenose Reg.*

[133] M. Foster, in *Oxoniensia*, 46 (1981), 106–7.

[134] J. Strype, *Memorials of Archbishop Cranmer*, ed. P. E. Barnes, ii (1853), 128; Foxe, *Acts and Monuments*, viii (1868 edn.), 89; Wood, *Annals*, ii. 126–7.

Edward VI. Even so, not until 1581 was formal acceptance of either Act obligatory for undergraduates. Between the Visitation of 1561 and the matriculation statutes of 1565 and 1581, quite a number of Catholic students escaped the pressure to conform by living outside college, in lodgings.[135] After that loophole was closed, not once but twice, they were at the mercy of collegiate custom. In a sympathetic college, like St John's, the rules might be weakly enforced. Between 1578 and 1581, for example, subscription to the Thirty-Nine Articles might be enjoined but not imposed. Students had to attend chapel, of course, with its services now conducted according to the Book of Common Prayer. And in Brasenose, at any rate, from 1578 onwards, all scholars over 16 who failed to subscribe to the Thirty-Nine Articles of 1562 were technically liable to 'expulsion and perpetual exclusion'.[136] But prior to 1581, public subscription to the oaths was compulsory only for Principal and Fellows. After that date there was no escape: for all those over the age of 16, subscription to both the royal supremacy and the Articles were conditions of matriculation.[137] Chancellor Leicester made it known that the University would tolerate no more 'secret and lurking Papists'.[138] More important, in the nation at large, it became high treason after 1581 to convert or be converted to Rome. From 1585 it was also treason to be a Jesuit or missionary priest. In Sir Francis Walsingham's view, these penalties involved a simple matter of loyalty. Catholicism implied obedience to a foreign power: 'priest, ergo traitor'.[139]

That was the rationale behind the years of terror. Between 1581 and 1603, at least 123 priests and 56 laymen were put to death in England. In addition there were considerable numbers who died in prison. Of those who died upon the scaffold—hanged, drawn, and quartered; that is throttled, disembowelled, and dismembered—six were from Brasenose: more than from any other Oxford college except St John's.[140] Their names deserve to be recorded: John Shert, Thomas Cottam, and Laurence Johnson (alias Richardson), all executed at Tyburn in 1582; Robert Anderton, executed on the Isle

---

[135] Clark, in *University Register* (OHS x–xi), II, pt. ii, 5.

[136] V-P's Reg. 14 June 1578, fo. 41ᵛ. Attendance at reformed (or 'schismatical') services was condemned by seminary priests from abroad, but often condoned by local Catholic confessors (A. Morey, *The Catholic Subjects of Elizabeth I* (1978), 176; P. Milward, *Religious Controversies of the Elizabethan Age* (1978), 50–2).

[137] For records of the Subscription Books, see *University Register*, II, pts. i–ii.

[138] *University Register*, II, pt. i (OHS x), 5, 47, 151–7; Gibson, *Statuta Antiqua*, 416, 421; Wood, *Annals*, ii. 212–13: 25 Jan. 1582; P. Williams, in *H.U.O.* iii. 413.

[139] Walsingham, in R. Challoner, *Memoirs of Missionary Priests*, ed. J. Hungerford Pollen (1924), 156.

[140] P. McGrath, *Brasenose Priests and Martyrs under Elizabeth I* (Oxford, 1985), 2, 23 n. 1 and *Papists and Puritans under Elizabeth I* (1967); G. Anstruther, *The Seminary Priests*, i: *Elizabethan, 1558–1603* (Ware, 1968).

of Wight in 1586; Francis Ingleby, executed at York in 1586; and George Nichols, executed at Oxford in 1589. Cottam, Johnson, and Anderton were Lancastrians; Ingleby was a Yorkshireman; and Shert and Nichols were from Cheshire and Oxford respectively. It is not easy now to decode the mind of the martyr. So let John Shert speak for all of them. At Tyburn he was asked, for the last time, to recant and submit. He replied that the Queen might be his sovereign but she could never be head of his church.

> 'Should I for saving this carcase condemn my soul?
> God forbid!...I will give to Caesar that which is his,
> and to God that which belongeth to God. She is not,
> nor cannot be [Head or Supreme Governor], nor any other,
> but only the supreme pastor. [Nor can I recant, for]
> whosoever dieth out of the Catholic Church dieth in
> the state of damnation.'[141]

We do not know the exact number of Brasenose men who remained overtly Catholic during the reign of Elizabeth. But we do know that twenty of them became priests. Apart from those already mentioned, these included Richard Barrett and Thomas Worthington, successive Presidents at Douai; and Arthur and Robert Pitts, William Holt, Hugh Charnock, and Edward Rishton, all of whom narrowly escaped execution in England.[142] At least five became Jesuits: Holt, Ansley, Bridgewater, Cottam, and Leech. The career of Thomas Lister, who matriculated in 1577, was not untypical: first Lancashire, then Oxford, then a wandering life in Europe. Six years in Rome, ten years in Lorraine, teaching philosophy and theology at Pont-à-Mousson; priesthood in Germany and illness 'through overstudy'; hunted in England; betrayed in Holland; imprisoned at Middelburg and 'spoiled of all [his] goods': Lister's life was fraught indeed, and in 'all things full of fears'.[143] Brasenose never matched New College in its number of Catholic Fellows. But its catalogue of priests and martyrs is striking. Records are insufficiently precise to establish accurate percentages. But the number of men emerging from Brasenose with openly Catholic sympathies— like the numbers in Oxford and Oxfordshire generally[144]—remained significant

---

[141] Challoner, *Missionary Priests*, 48–9. For George Nichols's arrest at the Catherine Wheel public house in Oxford, and subsequent trial, see *Cal. Acts of the Privy Council*, xvii. 329: 1589.

[142] Details in McGrath, *Brasenose Priests and Martyrs*, 14–21 and J. B. Wainewright, in *Downside Rev.*, NS 13 (1913), 41–68. Arthur Pitts became chaplain to the Stonors of Blount's Court, 1603–35.

[143] HMC, *De Lisle MSS*, ii. 229: [1596].

[144] A. Davidson, 'Roman Catholics in Oxfordshire, c.1580–1640' (Ph.D., Bristol, 1970). In 1561 the Mayor of Oxford informed the Privy Council that there were 'not three houses in [the city] wherein there were not papists' (*Cal. State Papers...Spanish*, i. 217–18).

between the 1540s and the 1570s. However the figures do taper off in the last
two decades of the century. Repressive measures eventually had their effect.

As ever, it is unwise to generalize. The pressures of doctrinal hatred during
these years produced traitors as well as martyrs. John Nicholls, for example, who
briefly became a Jesuit, seems to have been a serial apostate. Protestant, Catholic,
Protestant, and Catholic again, he changed sides with bewildering rapidity, 'either
through vain-glory, envy, fear or hopes of reward'.[145] And accidents of chronology sometimes brought together strange bedfellows. In 1568 there were only
four entrants into college. Two emerged as leaders, one on each side of the
sectarian divide. One lived to be a chronicler of Oxford recusancy: Edward
Rishton. Another became Bishop of Gloucester and wrote the preface to the
Authorized Version of the Bible: Miles Smith.[146] In 1570—the very year of Pius
V's Bull, *Regnans in excelsis,* which 'deposed' and excommunicated the Queen—
there were, not surprisingly, only ten entrants into college. Nicholls the apostate
was one of them; the martyr Laurence Johnson was another; and Thomas
Worthington, editor of the Douai Bible, was another.[147] Traitor, martyr, scholar:
the destinies of these three men were strangely linked and would one day be torn
apart. By the end of the century, thanks to the operation of the penal laws, there
can have been few Catholics, overt or covert, actually residing in college.
Humphrey Leech[148], who became a Jesuit, and Ralph Antrobus,[149] who became
a monk, appear to have been late vocations. By about 1580, in Rishton's words,
'the very flower of... Oxford ... [had been] carried away, as it were, by a storm,
and scattered in foreign lands'.[150]

And what—intellectually speaking—did they take with them? The Oxford
curriculum at this date had changed little since the fifteenth century. The
statutes of 1564–5, for instance, prescribed traditional texts—conventionally
updated—for the *trivium* and *quadrivium;* that is for the seven liberal arts at
lower degree level. For grammar Linacre or Virgil; for rhetoric Aristotle or
Cicero; for logic Porphyry or Aristotle; for arithmetic Tunstall or Gemma
Frisius; for music Boethius; for geometry Euclid; for astronomy Ptolemy.
These would have been the authors studied at Brasenose from 1561 to 1564,

[145] *ODNB*; F. Edwards, *Robert Persons: The Biography of an Elizabethan Jesuit, 1546–1610*
(1998), 52–3, 62.
[146] For both Rishton and Smith, see *ODNB*.
[147] Ibid.
[148] Ibid.
[149] Ormerod, *Cheshire*, i. 658.
[150] N. Sander, *Rise and Growth of the Anglican Schism* (1585), continued by E. Rishton, trans.
and ed. D. Lewis (1877), 261. One Catholic, who matriculated in 1610 and became a Divinity
Reader at Douai, was Christopher Phippes, a Nowell Scholar from Middleton School, Lancs.
(*Quat. Mon.* V, 17, 25).

for example, by Henry Savile, the future Warden of Merton and Provost of Eton. Already something of a prodigy in mathematics and astronomy—even when matriculating at the age of 12—Savile was at the same time firmly grounded in classical scholarship and patristic theology. He would have recognized no conceptual gulf between arts and sciences.[151] Postgraduate studies remained similarly traditional and similarly omnivorous. The long ascent to MA status was still punctuated by Aristotelian hurdles: the *Ethics*, the *Politics*, the *Metaphysics*, and the *Physics*. In 1887 Andrew Clark, master of early Oxford records, explained the value of all this:

> The student of Grammar learned to use language, the common instrument of thought; in Logic he learned to think correctly; and in Rhetoric, he learned to convey his thought persuasively.... [In] Mathematics... he exercised his capacity for abstract reasoning; [in] Natural Philosophy... he studied the laws of nature; [in] Moral Philosophy... he studied the laws of human nature and human society; and [in] Metaphysics... he studied the nature of being.[152]

It was a demanding course: seven long years—twenty-eight terms at four terms per year—all the way from matriculation to MA. And despite the reformers its content changed slowly. Unlike Cambridge, for example, Oxford was little influenced by Ramist radicalism.[153] Not that there was no movement at all. The royal Visitation of 1535 had accelerated the progress of new learning, by abolishing the study of canon law and by diluting the teaching of scholastic theology. That left a little space for the growth of humanistic studies. Despite the Marian Visitation of 1556—with its brief encouragement of canon law—the new humanism managed to adjust the balance of what was actually taught, making room for a development of arts scholarship in its own right. Literae Humaniores emerged as a training in civility; not just a prelude to metaphysics and theology. Then came a pedagogic revolution. As undergraduate instruction increased in importance, the higher faculties began to wither away. Lectures and disputations at university level became increasingly formulaic. And there were good practical reasons for that. As the accessibility of printed books increased, so the need for general oral instruction diminished. By the end of the sixteenth century, the old system was already approaching atrophy. The future lay in collegiate tuition. And therewith came a new set of conventions. Notes on Aristotle's

---

[151] For Oxford teaching, see J. M. Fletcher, in *HUO* iii. 172. For Savile and his scholastic context, see M. Feingold, *The Mathematicians' Apprenticeship: Science, Universities and Society in England,* 1560–1640 (Cambridge, 1984). The Saviles were Protestant rather than puritan (*ODNB*).

[152] Clark, in *University Register*, II, pt. i, 226.

[153] H. Kearney, *Scholars and Gentlemen: Universities and Society in Pre-industrial Britain,* 1500–1700 (1970), 63–4.

Ethics, for example, compiled by Edward Brerewood as a tutor at Brasenose in the 1590s, continued to be used in several colleges for decades before their eventual publication in 1640.[154] Meanwhile, far away in Catholic Lancashire—in the Stanley kingdom of Knowsley and Prescot—a Brasenose recusant named John Cottam, brother of the Jesuit martyr, was handing on the fruits of Brasenose learning to a crypto-Catholic schoolmaster named William Shakespeare. That at least is one interpretation of Shakespeare's 'missing years'. And who from Brasenose would dare to doubt it?[155]

If the curriculum changed slowly, the social composition of the University changed fast. Throughout the sixteenth century senior college positions in Oxford remained firmly in the hands of the clergy. Not so the junior membership. The numbers of undergraduate gentry not intending to enter the church increased significantly. In 1549 the Protestant Hugh Latimer had famously lamented: 'There be none now but great men's sons in colleges'.[156] That was an exaggeration. Even by the end of the century, nearly half the intake came from non-gentry backgrounds. What had changed however—in terms of educational perspective—was the balance between clerical and secular. An Oxford degree was becoming, for the first time, a hallmark of gentility. And through these changes pressure developed to make the syllabus reflect the demands of its new audience. Hence the advance of humane studies. And hence the emergence of a novel educational construct: the gentlemanly ideal.

All this was a gradual process. It was not always accelerated by the continuing pressure of theological debate. Most of the young men matriculating at Brasenose in the latter half of Elizabeth's reign had been brought up within the framework of the reformed Church. Not surprisingly, several became 'resolute puritans'—William Leigh, Robert Eaton, and Ellis Sanderson, for instance, all Lancastrians. Quite a number were scholars from Manchester Grammar School, on the foundation of Robert Nowell, brother of the Dean of St Paul's: Edward Rilston, William Massey, and Thomas

---

[154] E. Brerewood, *Commentarii in Ethica Aristotelis*, ed. T. Sixsmith (1640). See R. M. H. Curtis, *Oxford and Cambridge in Transition 1558–1642* (Oxford, 1959), 96–100.

[155] John Cottam was schoolmaster at Stratford from 1579 to 1581, when he was succeeded by another Brasenose Lancastrian, Alexander Aspinall. But it is Cottam's Lancashire connections rather than his Stratford years which are crucial to the argument. For the whole debate see E. A. J. Honingmann, *Shakespeare: 'The Lost Years'* (Manchester, 1985). There is some evidence that *Richard III* and *Love's Labour's Lost* were first staged at Knowsley Hall or nearby Prescot. Through Cottam, Shakespeare may have worked as a tutor for recusant or crypto-recusant families like the Hoghtons, the Heskeths, and the Stanleys. Hence the Prescot Playhouse, built in the 1590s: the only Elizabethan theatre outside London; hence too its re-creation in the form of Inigo Jones's Cockpit-in-Court: built in London in 1629 and reprojected for Prescot in 2010.

[156] Latimer, *Sermons*, 179.

Sorocold, for example. Such men could be relied on to preach a good Protestant sermon. Most of all Rilston: 'He was a pious man…whose preaching was of such life and power and in such evidences and demonstration of the Spirit that his hearers were ordinarily struck with fear and reverence, if not with terror.'[157]

From the time of James Bateson, who went up in 1554 and became High Master soon after graduating in 1558, the succession of pupils from Manchester to Brasenose is significant. Quite a few returned home in the end to Lancashire and Cheshire, to Protestantize the parishes of the north-west. Brasenose produced as many as fourteen puritan ministers who worked in Lancashire in the run-up to the civil war.[158] But that lay a little in the future. Towards the end of the sixteenth century the tenor of the college is probably best characterized as tactically establishmentarian. Protestant scholarship, however, had clearly gained ground. The library of one Fellow—Edward Higgins, another Lancastrian—indicates that during the mid-1580s, the college was well acquainted with the writings of later Calvinist authors.[159] By the 1590s Brasenose had evidently decided not only to accept, but to celebrate the patronage of the Queen. When Principal Harris welcomed Elizabeth in 1592, the college made a point of proclaiming its rising status in the University. A considerable amount of money was spent in feasting and ceremony. Harris, Singleton, and Leech—Principal, Vice-Principal, and chaplain—were all active in staging entertainments.[160]

By this date Richard Harris had long been noted for his hot temper and 'high spirit'. In 1580 he had embarked upon 'a public quarrel' with Dean Matthew of Christ Church which set off a 'feud' between their respective colleges. Anthony Wood's description of this intercollegiate saga is a curiosity worth repeating. In his capacity as Vice-Chancellor, Matthew had apparently prevented Harris from taking his rightful seat, among the other heads of houses in St Mary's Church, during the ceremony of Act Monday (the predecessor of Encaenia). This affront rankled. So much so that on the

---

[157] Quoted in A. A. Mumford, *Manchester Grammar School, 1515–1915* (1919), 26. For scholars on the Nowell foundation, see A. B. Grosart (ed.), *The Townley Hall MSS: The Spending of the Money of Robert Nowell* (Manchester, 1877). Eaton was chaplain to the Protestant 4th Earl of Derby; Leigh became tutor to Prince Henry, the Protestant elder son of James I (*ODNB*).

[158] e.g. Christopher Harvey, Anthony Calcott, Robert Eaton (R.C. Richardson, *Puritanism in North West England* (Manchester, 1972), 58–63, 186–7). In the later Tudor period, however, few returned to their native county (Haigh, *Reformation and Resistance in Tudor Lancashire*, 39, 297).

[159] e.g. works by H. Zanchi, J. Rainolds, J. Prime, A. Kingsmill. See Dent, *Protestant Reformers*, 98.

[160] *Quat. Mon.* X, 19, citing bakers' and brewers' bills in Bursar's Roll, 1592. For the programme of events, see Clark, in *University Register*, II, pt. i, 228–32. As the author of a much-used Latin grammar (*Certaine Grammar Questions*, 1590 onwards), Leech had a reputation as a pedagogue (*ODNB*). He was followed as chaplain by Richard Taylor and James Dalton in 1603, and then by John Pickering in 1613.

following Wednesday, 13 July—again in St Mary's—at the very moment when Matthew stepped down from office, Harris caused consternation in Convocation by stage-whispering in his enemy's ear: 'remember how you kept me down from the Stage...[and] showed your vile despite...[well, I wish you] the Devil's turd in thy teeth.' Matthew, 'being much startled at this, could not at [that moment] make any reply, but taking it as a great contempt upon authority, sent his complaints to the Chancellor'. Harris was thereupon ordered to apologize publicly, so that he and the Dean of Christ Church 'and their [respective] Colleges now should be friends'. But the Principal of Brasenose remained obdurate. In fact for several years after, 'nothing but affronts and scuffles passed between [the two colleges], coursing in the Schools followed with blows, denying of Graces and I know not what'. By 1590 seven Fellows of Brasenose were complaining to the Visitor about persistent debt and disorder.[161]

Brasenose clearly needed a Principal with rather more finesse. So when Harris at last resigned in 1595, the obvious candidate was Alexander Nowell. And when Nowell—now in extreme old age—succeeded, Brasenose could at last be said to have made its peace with the reformed establishment. Like Exeter and Queen's, it was now a Protestant college. Nowell remained Principal for less than four months. It was almost a symbolic appointment: 'the last surviving Father of the English Reformation'. Symbolic perhaps in other ways too. The records are by no means clear, but he seems to have been the first married Principal. When he moved into the Lodgings, his second wife—Elizabeth, widow of Thomas Bowyer—presumably moved in with him. Queen Elizabeth did not care for married dons. Her Injunctions of 1561 discouraged academic procreation: 'the quiet and orderly profession of study and learning...[indeed] the very rooms and buildings be not answerable for such families.'[162] Fellows with matrimony in mind could aspire to a college living. Heads of houses, however, were rather different. Their status was almost episcopal. And in this respect Dean Nowell fitted the bill admirably.

---

[161] Matthew seems to have been 'a most excellent Scholar, yet being too young for the office of Vice-Chancellor, showed himself a little too busy and pragmatical' (Wood, *Annals*, ii. 202–3). This was not the only occasion when fisticuffs involving Brasenose Fellows occurred. On 4 July 1574 Ralph Tompson, Vice-Principal, and Clement Colmore, Lecturer in Logic, apparently came to blows (V-P's Reg. 4 July 1574, fo. 67ᵛ). 'Coursing' had once involved 'a fair trial of learning and skill in logic, metaphysics, and school divinity'; but by this date had degenerated into 'affronts, confusion and very often blows'; participants 'making a great noise with their feet, they hissed and shoved with their shoulders', driving their opponents out of the Schools (Anthony, 1st Earl of Shaftesbury, in L. N. Quiller-Couch (ed.), *Reminiscences of Oxford* (OHS xxii), 36). For complaints to the Visitor in 1559 and subsequent visitation, see Dent, *Protestant Reformers*, 167–8.

[162] Reprinted in C. Cross (ed.), *The Royal Supremacy in the Elizabethan Church* (1969), 184–5. For Nowell's appointment, see V-P's Reg. 14 Dec. 1595, fos. 25–6; Churton, *Nowell*, p. iv.

Coincidentally, around this time, the college began to attract recruits of wider range and greater distinction. It is always rash to generalize from a fragmentary statistical base. But towards the end of the 1580s four freshmen arrived at Brasenose who certainly represented a rather different level of sophistication: Barnabe Barnes, Richard Barnfield, John Marston, and Robert Burton (pl. 14). Barnes—son of the Bishop—was a dramatist and sonneteer whose work lent lustre to the court of James I. Barnfield was a poet whose lyrical talent has actually been mistaken for Shakespeare. Marston was a dramatic satirist worthy of his principal rival, Ben Jonson. And Burton was a polymath, whose reputation rests on a single gargantuan work; a work more quoted than read: *The Anatomy of Melancholy* (1621).[163]

Services in chapel had by now settled into an austere routine. In 1595 a 'vewe' revealed that there were hardly any vestments available: just '3 copes, [and] 1 pawle'.[164] A man like Nowell had no quarrel with such restraint. His inclinations were puritan, and his authority was already secure. He was the only Brasenose Principal in the whole of the sixteenth century with any claim to national reputation. Not one of the college's first five Principals became Vice-Chancellor. Only with Thomas Singleton's elections in 1598–9 and 1611–14 did Brasenose achieve that particular distinction.[165] Not that Singleton's churchmanship was wholly welcome at court. In 1601 the Bishop of London, Richard Bancroft—hammer of the puritans—warned Sir Robert Cecil that Singleton would be 'a very unmeet man' as a candidate for the deanery of Westminster. Indeed Bancroft had only kept him 'from being expelled out of Brasenose for [the] country['s] sake'.[166] Singleton, he knew, would always be too close to Nowell to be entirely acceptable to the Queen. Even so, as the new reign got under way,

[163] Barnes is chiefly remembered for *Parthenophil and Parthenope* (1593; ed. V. A. Doyno, Carbondale, Ill., 1971). See also P. E. Blank, *Lyric Forms in the Sonnet Sequences of B. Barnes* (The Hague, 1974). Two poems by Barnfield appeared as Shakespeare's in *The Passionate Pilgrim* (1599), but were omitted by E. Malone in his 1790 edn. of Shakespeare's *Complete Works*. In 1598 he dedicated two volumes of verse to Edward Lea and Nicholas Blackleech, with whom he had studied at Brasenose. Marston's plays—for which see P. J. Finkelpearl, *John Marston and the Inner Temple* (Cambridge, Mass., 1969)—include *The Malcontent* (1603–4), *The Dutch Courtesan* (1604–5), *The Fawn* (1606), *Sophinisba* (1606), and *The Insatiate Countess* (1613). Burton became a Student at Christ Church and is buried in the cathedral. His portrait at Brasenose is by Gilbert Jackson; a version was made for Christ Church in 1907 (*Quat. Mon.* VII, pl. x; *Brazen Nose*, xxv. 29–31). For all these, see *ODNB*.

[164] V-P's Reg. 10 Jan. 1595, cited in *Quat. Mon.* V, 13 n.5.

[165] A. Wood, *Fasti Oxonienses*, ed. J. Gutch (1790), 115, 119–20; *Quat. Mon.* XI, 8; V-P's Reg. 3 Oct. 1593, fo. 64ᵛ. Principal Harris retired to Worcester, and was probably buried in the cathedral there (Wood, *Colleges and Halls,* 365).

[166] HMC, *Hatfield House MSS*, xi. 407: Bancroft to Cecil, 5 Oct. 1601. Singleton was originally a Cambridge man. He was buried in St Mary's in 1614. For his recommendation of Thomas Elton of Brasenose as 'diligent in study, and sound and well affected in religion', see *Cal. State Papers Domestic,* 1598–1601, 335: 3 Nov. 1599.

the college was riding high. In 1611 there was not only a Brasenose Vice-Chancellor (Singleton), but a Brasenose Proctor (Samuel Radcliffe) and a Brasenose Chancellor too: Sir Thomas Egerton—Baron Ellesmere and Viscount Brackley—the grandest lawyer of his generation.[167]

Egerton's personal pilgrimage—from Catholic recusant in 1569 to reconciled Protestant in 1577—typified the evolution of Brasenose during the later sixteenth century: a progression towards the Calvinist centre, away from the religious periphery, popish or puritan.[168] As Attorney-General, it fell to Egerton to prosecute—or persecute—Campion, Arundel, and many other Catholics. His assimilation into the establishment could hardly have been more complete. He emerges as a pivotal figure in the Elizabethan regime. For a brief moment Brasenose seems to be almost at the centre of power. Then once again the kaleidoscope shifts, and the college finds itself on the sidelines. Long before Singleton's death in 1614, James I was already intriguing for the election of a Principal on whose churchmanship he could rely. His candidate was Henry Walmesley, 'who...deserved well of the College for his pains in reforming disorders'.[169] In the event, the next Principal proved to be a man with puritan instincts and very few friends at court. His name was Samuel Radcliffe. And his election was a straw in the wind. During the 1620s and 1630s, as Oxford veered towards the Arminianism of Archbishop Laud, Brasenose began to appear increasingly oppositional. In the meantime Nowell's brief Principalship might be taken to symbolize the late Tudor college's religious centrality. For this Dean of St Paul's—this 'dean of educationists'—with his catechism and his fishing rods, comes down to us as a markedly sympathetic figure. His resilience—and his longevity: he continued active into his mid-eighties at least—seems to have been the product of a distinctively personal buoyancy.[170] Not for nothing is he

---

[167] *ODNB*. His portrait in hall came by exchange from the Bodleian in 1817; other versions descended to St John's College, Cambridge, and Kirtlington Priory, Oxfordshire (*Quat. Mon.* VII, pl. vii).

[168] In 1577 Egerton, of Lincoln's Inn, was 'reconciled into our house' ('Diocesan Returns of Recusants, 1577', *Catholic Record Soc.* 22 (1921), 101).

[169] *Cal. State Papers Domestic, 1603–10*, 346 Jan. (?), 1607; Bodl. MS Ash. 1729, fo. 181ᵛ: 10 Oct. 1608. Walmesley's earlier expulsion from his Fellowship by Principal Harris had been reversed in 1591 (*Brasenose Reg.*).

[170] The inscription (Churton, *Nowell*, 83) on Nowell's portrait in hall—'Piscator Hominum': complete with rod and tackle—overestimates his age. This portrait (pl. 9), on panel, painted between 1601 and 1653 (*Quat. Mon.* VII, pl. vi) seems to be a version of a portrait on canvas originally at Read Hall, nr. Whalley, Lancs., owned in 1809 by Dr Sherson of London, and engraved in the same year for Alexander Nowell of Tirhoot, Bengal, and Underley Hall, Westmoreland (Churton, *Nowell*, frontispiece and 367–8). A copy was made for Westminster School in 1815; another was made for a descendant of Nowell—the Revd Mr Twopenny—in 1844; another version, also on canvas, was given to the Bodleian by the college in 1817 in exchange for a portrait of Lord Chancellor Ellesmere (V-P's Reg. 11 May 1844, fo. 20; *Oxford Portraits*, II, pt. i (OHS lxxxi), 249–50).

remembered as Izaak Walton's 'ideal angler': temperate and calm; author of 'that good, plain, unperplexed Catechism'; and the inventor, in the end, of one indispensable Brasenose boon, the miracle of bottled beer.[171]

As the college moved centre-stage, under Harris, Nowell, and Singleton, its religious temper began to echo the conventions of current church hierarchy: theologically Calvinist, institutionally episcopalian, and presentationally evangelical. It would be unwise to simplify these attitudes by plumping for the blanket label 'puritan'. The Brasenose clerics who went up to Oxford in the second half of Elizabeth's reign, and came to prominence under James I, differed in the extent of their commitment to parliamentary religion; that is in the strength of their loyalty to the Church by law established. But they accepted its organizational structure. They came in time to accept its liturgical apparatus: surplice and hood in church and chapel; Authorized Version for lesson and psalm; and generally of course the Book of Common Prayer. Few of this generation of collegians could be described as Presbyterians or non-conformists. Thomas Singleton might object to clerical non-residency. Richard Parkes might have unorthodox views about Hell. Thomas Peacock had deathbed doubts about salvation. William Crompton got into trouble for casting aspersions on the sign of the cross. Robert Bolton was uncertain about the validity of ceremonies. John Ball leant a little too far towards sectarian severity. Henry Mason was, quite rightly, suspected of Arminianism. But, in varying degrees, each might at some point have subscribed to Mason's credo: 'I am perswaded in my soule that [the Church of England] is the purest, best reformed Church in Europe.' And Bolton, in particular, seems to have been exemplary in his ministry: praying six times a day, preaching and catechizing thrice on Sunday.[172] Of course there were elements of careerism too. Several of these men were outsiders; poor scholars, mostly from Lancashire. They were not all as scrupulous as Ball and Bolton. Most had their living to make. And that led them towards accommodation with earthly powers. When Richard Mocket, successively chaplain to the Archbishop of Canterbury and Warden of All Souls, wrote a textbook on civil obedience—*God and the King* (1615)—it was highly praised. But when

---

[171] I. Walton, *The Compleat Angler* (1901 edn.), 35–6; Churton, *Nowell*, 80–3; A. L. Rowse, *The England of Elizabeth* (1950; 1957), 554. He discovered, accidentally, that the burial of a bottle of ale over some considerable time increased its gaseous properties: 'no bottle, but a gun, such [was] the sound at the opening thereof' (Fuller, *Worthies*, ed. Nuttall, ii. 204–5). For his memorial in old St Paul's Cathedral, see BL Lansdowne MS 983, fo. 13.

[172] For Bagshawe's studies of Peacock (1646) and Bolton (1632); and for Mason's *Christian Humiliation* (1627), see *ODNB*. Bolton's collected works appeared in 3 vols. (1638–41). Ball produced *A Catechism Shorter than the Short Catechism* (1649). For Ball, Parkes, Crompton, and Bolton, see also *ODNB*.

one of his later publications displeased James I, it was ordered to be publicly burned. Mocket was mortified. In fact he is said to have died of disappointment. At All Souls he is remembered as 'the roasted Warden'.[173]

Then came another change. The election of William Laud as Chancellor of Oxford University in 1630 marked a developing shift in religious temper: in shorthand terms, from Jacobean to Caroline; from Calvinist to Arminian; from sermon to ceremony; from beliefs which were largely predestinarian to rituals which were increasingly sacramentalist. These were the emerging attitudes— unclear then, and even less clear now—that seemed to underpin the King's proclamations of 1626 and 1628 as well as the Laudian statutes of 1636.[174] Of course not every college acquiesced. The new Chancellor's motto might be 'the beauty of holiness'. But his rise to power evoked reactions at Brasenose that were neither beautiful nor holy. He began to suspect that Brasenose beer might be a veritable agent of discord: the college, he believed, was becoming a 'Topick-place' of 'strong and unruly Argument'. There was more than a little truth in that view. Three Fellows of the puritan tendency—Atherton Bruch, Thomas Cook, and Richard Hill—were particular thorns in the Chancellor's side. The college had recently been home to Laud's inveterate enemy, Lord Chancellor Ellesmere. Its Visitor was now a greater enemy still, John Williams, Bishop of Lincoln. Even so, it was Laud who held most of the court cards.

> What do the Arminians hold?
> All the best bishoprics and deaneries in England.

Bishop Williams would soon find himself in the Tower of London. The future direction of ecclesiastical patronage began to seem only too clear. In 1636 a satire was published, couched in nautical terms, suggesting appropriate names for naval vessels financed by individual colleges. St John's—Laud's own college—would be the *Triumph* or *Speed-Well*; All Souls, under Gilbert Sheldon, the *Hope-Well*; Christ Church, under Brian Duppa, the *Prince Royal*; Queen's, under turncoat Christopher Potter, the *Convert*; and Merton—with its range of Laudians and anti-Laudians—the *Rainbow*. All these were colleges

---

[173] *ODNB*. He had been recommended for a Fellowship at All Souls, first by Elizabeth then by James I (*Cal. State Papers Domestic,* 1595–97, 496: 3 Sept. 1597 and 1603–10, 371: 25 Sept. 1607). The King had previously performed the same service for another Brasenose man: Matthew Anderton (ibid. 123: 22 June 1604). J. Doughtie was another Brasenose cleric who moved from Calvinism under James I to 'an ecclesiology defined by Erastian episcopacy' under Charles I (*ODNB*).

[174] S. R. Gardiner (ed.), *Constitutional Documents of the Puritan Revolution,* 1625–60 (Oxford, 1906), 75–6; J. P. Kenyon (ed.), *Stuart Constitution* (1966), 138–9; J. Griffiths (ed.), *Statutes of the University of Oxford* (1636), introd. C. L. Shadwell (Oxford, 1888). For differing contextual interpretations, see N. Tyacke, *Anti-Calvinists: The Rise of English Arminianism, c.*1590–1640 (Oxford, 1987) and J. Davies, *The Caroline Captivity of the Church: Charles I and the Remoulding of Anglicanism,* 1625–1641 (Oxford, 1992).

in favour. Outside this charmed circle were two colleges with no hope of preferment. Exeter would be the *Repulse*: that would be the fate of its Rector, John Prideaux, were he ever to apply for a bishopric. And Brasenose—with its Welsh Calvinist Visitor—would be known as the *Despair*. Its Principal had no hope whatever of promotion.[175]

To that Principal we must now turn, for Samuel Radcliffe (pl. 12) has some claim to be considered the third founder of Brasenose. Radcliffe came up from Middleton School, near Manchester—Nowell's *alma mater*—in 1597. As Fellow, Bursar, and Principal he spent his entire adult life in college. He never married; and in death he proved a munificent benefactor. His bequests we shall examine in due course. Meanwhile it is enough to note that apart from his involvement in two building programmes at Brasenose—the completion of an attic storey in the old quad (1635–7) and the eventual building of a new chapel and library (1656–66)—he was certainly active elsewhere. The school and almshouses at Steeple Aston were further products of his patronage. Radcliffe was not himself a major scholar. But he had the interests of scholarship at heart. In the year of his election as Principal four new Lectureships were created or recreated: philosophy, humanity, Greek, and Hebrew. In all he ruled the Fellowship for thirty-four years, 1614–48. During that time the college reached its highest peak of recruitment. Conversely, this was also the moment when Brasenose came closest to extinction and yet found the confidence to envisage its most arresting architectural development.

In the University as a whole, the 1630s were a boom decade for admissions. Early seventeenth-century England, 'at all levels', has been called 'the most literate society the world has ever known'.[176] The 1640s—the civil war years—saw a drastic contraction. Then in the 1650s came recovery under the Commonwealth, and boom again after the Restoration. Thereafter there was a steady decline—from the 1680s onwards—a decline that was not to be reversed until the later nineteenth century. Figures for Brasenose parallel these general trends, but mostly at the higher end of the register. By the first decade of the seventeenth century, the college was matriculating more students than any other college in Oxford. Thereafter there was some relative decline. But Brasenose held fourth place in terms of numbers, right through to the 1680s. Only Christ Church and Exeter were consistently ahead.

[175] K. Fincham, in *HUO* iv. 209, citing Nott. Univ. Lib. MS Cl. C84 b. For Laud's disputes with Brasenose see *Cal. State Papers Domestic*, 1631–33, 134: 23 Aug. 1631 and 135–6: 26 Aug. 1631; *Quat. Mon.* XI, 27–30 and *Works of … William Laud*, ed. W. Scott and J. Bliss (1847–60), ii. 16 and v. 101, 149, 261. It was Williams—'that unhappy casuist'—who organized opposition to Laud's election as Chancellor, and who advised Charles I that he could sign the Bill for Strafford's execution with an easy mind, since he had two consciences, public and private. The quip about Arminian tenets is attributed to George Morley of Christ Church.

[176] L. Stone, in *Past and Present*, 28 (1964), 68.

It would be a mistake to think that such figures simply show that Brasenose was now catering for growing numbers of the newly rich. Between 1670
and 1689, for example, 77 per cent of students holding exhibitions were
registered as plebeians or paupers, and 19 per cent as the sons of clergy.
Matriculation categories are open to all sorts of objections. Even so, a score
of 96 per cent for scholars below gentry status represents a striking contribution to social mobility. That figure, of course, excludes the far greater
number of commoners. Still, the number of scholarship entrants did increase
significantly as the century progressed. Only 9 per cent of entrants between
1610 and 1629 were scholarship holders; but the proportion for 1670–89 is
four times as high. Again, if we look at the Fellowship itself, we find a college
by no means genteel. During the seventeenth century as a whole, at least
43 per cent of Fellows had matriculated as plebeians or paupers; a higher
percentage than, for example, Exeter, Lincoln, or Wadham, and a much
higher percentage than Oriel or Magdalen. In addition, 21 per cent were the
sons of clergy; making a total of 64 per cent from outside the ranks of gentry,
squirearchy, and nobility. During the entire seventeenth century only 1 per cent
of Brasenose Fellowships went to scions of titled families.[177]

The rewards of Fellowship were not exactly lavish. Perquisites, in cash or
kind, are now difficult to quantify. The riding boots, for example, presented
to the Bursar each Christmas varied in value from 7s. to 13s. 4d. Others
received smaller monetary payments. Similarly, tutorial fees varied. So did
profits from fines on the renewal of leases. All but one-ninth of these, in any
case, were reserved for the Principal and six senior Fellows.[178] As a minimum, Fellows could rely on rooms and commons. Then there were statutory
allowances. In 1639 a Fellow's weekly allowance amounted to 8s. 5d. (corn-
rent 5s. 11d., founders' commons 1s. 2d., Frankland and Nowell augmenta-
tions 1s. 4d.).[179] But the bulk of any Fellow's emoluments derived from
established bequests. At Christmas 1634 quarterly payments to officers and
lecturers were recorded as follows.[180]

Edmund Leigh:	Vice-Principal and Chaplain:	31s. 8d.
Gabriel Richardson:	Palin Exhibitioner and Kertleton Lecturer:	30s. 8d.
Ralph Richardson:	Palin Exnr., Kertleton Lctr. and Chaplain:	46s. 0d.
William Hutchins:	Palin Exnr. and Bursar:	23s. 4d.

---

[177] Figures tabulated by S. Porter, in *HUO* iv. 82.

[178] *VCH Oxon.*, iii. 209. Junior Fellows protested in vain between 1621 and 1643 (Petition
to the Visitor: Visitor Uncatalogued: Treasury). For the 'Principal's Fine Book 1650–1705', see
B 1d 36. For payments in kind, see Jeffery in *Brazen Nose*, iv. 25.

[179] *Brazen Nose*, iv, 25, citing Bursar's rolls of account (Clennell UBS 21).

[180] *Quat. Mon.* XI, 67–8, conflated table. To this list should be added the annual wages of
servants: manciple £4 13s. 4d., barber £4 0s. 0d., porter £3 0s. 0d., and cook £2 0s. 0d. (*Brazen
Nose*, iv. 25 citing Bursar's account, 1634).

Richard Hill:	Bursar [dep. Edmund Leigh]:	3s. 4d.
John Trafford:	Palin Exhibitioner:	20s. 0d.
Thomas Cook:	Hebrew Lecturer:	30s. 0d.
Thomas Sixsmith:	Master [Lecturer] of the Hall:	20s. 0d.
John Newton:	Custos Jocalium [keeper, books & treasures]	3s. 4d.
Daniel Greenwood:	Greek Lecturer:	20s. 0d.
Robert Heywood:	Humanity Lecturer and Chaplain:	36s. 8d.
John Houghton:	Philosophy Lecturer:	20s. 0d.
Ralph Byrom:	Rudolph Lecturer:	16s. 8d.
Roger Porter:	Bible Clerk:	10s. 0d.
Nathaniel Bostock:	Morley Lecturer:	11s. 8d.

Sixsmith and Newton; Greenwood, Houghton, Byrom, and Porter: they would all have a part to play, just a few years later, when Brasenose broke apart in the civil wars.

Meanwhile, these are the men on whom the college depended for teaching and administration. On the administrative side, as we shall see, there was a distinct shortage of competence, at least until the appointment of Houghton as Bursar in 1641. One description, by the Revd Rowland Scudamore BCL— admittedly in a facetious letter—suggests that the Senior Common Room at this time was chiefly occupied in trivialities: gossiping, drinking, eating, and flirting. 'To be ever talkative', Scudamore explains in 1638, 'is as natural to [me], as for Mr. Richardson to drink, Mr. Houghton to eate, or Mr. Sixsmith to kisse [or to] read (as hee nick-names it) a virginitie lecture.'[181] The role of the tutor, at least as regards scholars, seems however to have been taken seriously. In 1622 Edward Andrews was singled out and recommended as 'a speciall good Tutor'.[182] And as regards teaching, there was certainly some serious talent. Picture good master Sixsmith in the run-up to civil war, tutoring daily in Old Quad; lecturing weekly in hall on logic, ethics, natural science, and mathematics; examining Aristotle through seventeenth-century eyes. We even know his preferred authorities. For logic, he recommends Brerewood, Smiglecius, Ruvio, Keckermann, and Crakanthorp. For ethics he suggests a brace of Aristotelian editors—Jean Buridan; Alessandro Piccolomini—as well as a pair of commentators on Aquinas: Domingo Banez and Bartolome de Medina. For astronomy, mathematics, anatomy, and physics, he offers the full Aristotelian canon with a battery of appropriate commentators: Sacrobosco, Maestlin, Zabarella, Mendoza, Spigelius, and Fernel.[183] Scholars at Brasenose did not get

---

[181] B 2a 38: R. Scudamore to Dr Thomas Legh, 29 July 1638 (Newton MSS, 1909 transcript). 'In eating [Houghton] has no fellow. The [greatest] part of his time is spent in ye Hall . . . not at disputations but at meales: for hee's only verst in that rule of grammar, whose verbes are of filling, emptying, loading, and unloading' (ibid. fo. 43).

[182] Ibid., William Gamull to T. Legh, 17 Oct. 1622.

[183] 'Directions for my Scholers, what books to buy and read' ('Commonplace Book of Thomas Sixsmith' [1638], MPP 158 A1, formerly MS 80). In 1614 Edward Brerewood's *Elementa*

off lightly. Here was scholarship with a formidably European dimension. Six-smith even supplied lectures in Hebrew.

As regards geographical recruitment, it is clear that during this period Brasenose was becoming still more north-western in its loyalties. When John Middleton, the Child of Hale, a legendary giant from Lancashire, called in at Brasenose in 1617—on his way back from London after trouncing the King's Wrestler—he left behind him in the Brasenose cellars an astonishing imprint of his hand. No doubt he enjoyed amazing his fellow countrymen.[184] There were certainly plenty of them in college. In the second quarter of the seventeenth century, thirty-nine of the fifty-nine Lancashire gentry who went to Oxford chose to go to Brasenose, 'the Lancashire college'. After all, it enjoyed 'many peculiar privileges in favour of Lancashire men'.[185] During the earlier part of the seventeenth century two-thirds of the entrants to Oxford from Lancashire and Cheshire went to Brasenose. By the end of the century that proportion had risen to three-quarters. Within Brasenose itself, by the same terminal date, entrants from Lancashire and Cheshire actually formed a majority of the college intake. And scholarships linked to the north-west inevitably acted as a magnet to undergraduates from other colleges. Between 1670 and 1689, 10 per cent of all holders of Brasenose scholarships had matriculated elsewhere.[186] As a Lancastrian and a former Nowell Scholar, Principal Radcliffe must have felt very much at home.

Logicae—composed in the 1580s while he was a tutor at Brasenose—was edited by his nephew Robert (1614 etc.). Brerewood's *Tractatus Quidam Logicae* (MS, Queen's Coll. Oxford) was later published by Sixsmith (1628; 1631; 1659), as was his *Commentarii in Ethica Aristotelis* (1640). Leading editions of some of Sixsmith's selected texts are as follows: R. Crakanthorp, *Logicae Libri Quinque* (1622); J. Fernel, *Universa Medicina* (Geneva, 1619); B. Keckermann, *Praecognitorum Logicorum Tractatus* (Hanau, 1606); M. Maestlin, *Epitome Astronomiae* (Tubingen, 1597); A. Picco-lomini (ed.), *Retorica d'Aristotele* (Venice, 1565); A. Ruvio, *Commentarii in Octo Libros Aristotelis de Physico* (1629); J. de Sacrabosco, *De Sphaera*, ed. C. Clavius (Rome, 1606; trans. L. Thorndike, Chicago 1949); M. Smiglecius, *Logica* . . . (2 vols., Oxford, 1634); A. Spigelius, *De Humani Corporis Fabrica* (Frankfurt, 1632). See also M. Feingold, in *HUO* iv. 294–5, 322, 378, 402–3.

[184] Samuel Pepys admired 'ye Hand' on 9 June 1668 (*Diary*, ed. R. Latham and W. Matthews, ix. 1976). The hand's outline, on one of the cellar doorposts, was repainted in 1680 (Bursar's Accounts, 12 Oct. 1680). Two versions survive in the antechapel, along with a portrait of the giant, copied by T. B. Banner, 1842, from an original in Hale Hall (*Quat. Mon.* VII, 28 and VIII, 19; *Brazen Nose*, iv. 7–8, 105–6). Middleton (1578–1623) is buried in the churchyard at Hale.

[185] T. Heywood (ed.), *The Moore Rental* (Chetham Soc. 12, 1847), 6–7; B. G. Blackwood, 'The Lancashire Gentry, 1625–1660' (D. Phil., Oxford, 1973), 76. 'If those born in the Parishes [of Prestbury and Prescot] were not *caeteris paribus* to those in the Counties [of Cheshire and Lancashire]—though those born in the Parishes were neither *inepti* nor *inhabiles*, yet if those born in the Counties were *aptiores et habiliores*, they ought to be preferr'd before those born in the Parishes' (A no 5 Visitor: Principal Yate to Visitor Fuller, 2 Mar. 1673, quoted in Churton, *Supplement to . . . Smyth and Sutton* (Oxford, 1803), 75–6).

[186] Porter, in *Hist. Univ.* iv. 60–1.

Perhaps too much at home. For some time, college finances had been less than secure. Debts to brewers and bakers, owing since 1588, had by 1592 accumulated to £178 8s. 0d. Legal action followed. As Junior Bursar, Edward Hutchins was held liable for the entire amount. He had to repay the college over a period of years.[187] But that was only the start of trouble. When one Fellow, James Mason, died in 1628 after lengthy illness, his debts were so great that his Fellowship had to be kept vacant until the bakers and brewers were paid.[188] There were still gaudies; still celebrations of past benefactions: Smith and Sutton; Morley and Frankland; Nowell, Mordaunt, Harpur, and Port. In 1635 there were still thirteen commemorative celebrations in a year. But eight years later, Brasenose was £1,750 in debt. A draconian Visitation ensued. One Fellow, William Aldersey, at his death in 1642, was found to owe £208 10s. 4d., for his own and his pupils' battels.[189] As newly appointed Junior Bursar, John Houghton uncovered a catalogue of misdeeds: non-payment of rents and battels, overspending on commons, and financial indiscipline above and below stairs. Ultimately, responsibility for all this had to lie with the Principal. As we shall see, Radcliffe was a man of courage and vision; and his fortune would one day transform the appearance of the college. But he favoured his relatives overmuch (two of his nephews were Clerks of Accounts); he seems to have found it impossible to delegate; and he played his cards very close to his chest. Above all, he stayed in office too long. The Fellows cannot have been far wrong in believing that only 'this most happy visitation' of 1643 saved the college from imminent ruin.[190]

During the eleven years of Charles I's personal rule, Radcliffe kept his head well below the political parapet. His sympathies were Calvinist not Arminian. In Holland Arminianism had been republican. In England it was monarchical. Its principles became the ritual adhesive holding together 'the Caroline synthesis of religion and politics'.[191] In his Lodgings at Brasenose Radcliffe would no doubt have preferred to ignore such things. He was certainly not a natural royalist.

---

[187] *VCH Oxon.*, iii. 210, citing Clennell UBS 15: Bursar's rolls of account, 1591–2. Similarly Visitor Barlow's agreement to keep void a Fellowship pending payment of the debt of a deceased Bursar (V-P's Reg. 16 Apr. 1684, fo. 127).

[188] 'Unless we should have suffered him, sick and weak in body as he was, without naturall compassion, and fellow-feeling, to have famished in Prison...' (V-P's Reg. 27 Apr. 1628, fos. 49–50). This was accepted by Visitor Williams (V-P's Reg., May 1628, fo. 49ᵛ).

[189] J. Twigg, in *HUO* iv. 774–5; *VCH Oxon.*, iii. 210 (corrected), citing Visitor uncatalogued: Treasury. Dates of commemorations are listed by Wood in Bodl. MS Wood F28. For costs in 1635, see *Quat. Mon.* XI, 68–9.

[190] Visitation records, 1643 (Visitor uncatalogued: Treasury). For legal action regarding Radcliffe's will, see *Quat. Mon.* XI, 61–2.

[191] H. R. Trevor-Roper, *Catholics, Anglicans and Puritans* (1987), 114; K. Sharpe, 'Archbishop Laud and the University of Oxford', in H. Lloyd-Jones, V. Pearl, and B. Worden (eds.), *History and Imagination: Essays Presented to H. R. Trevor-Roper* (1981), 146–64.

Anthony Wood considered him a puritan, albeit a church-puritan. He cannot have been happy with the Laudian ritual. Did altar rails reappear at Brasenose at this time? It seems most unlikely. The accoutrements of service were simple: 'three copes . . . foure cushions [and] a pulpite cloath'. Foxe's *Martyrs* remained in chapel, as well as old and new editions of the Prayer Book. Since 1615 there had been holy communion seven times a year. But it was distributed from a plain table which rested on a carpet and was simply covered with a cloth.[192] It took the pressure of a threatening Parliament to turn Radcliffe into a King's man. That threat materialized in the autumn of 1640 with the meeting of the Long Parliament.

Where then did Brasenose stand at the outbreak of civil war? It is difficult to be statistically precise. But one list survives which suggests that the loyalties of college members scarcely lay with the Presbyterian Commons. In the summer of 1641 the Long Parliament devised a test—an Oath or Protest-ation—designed to separate royalist sheep from parliamentary goats. In biblical terms, here was a 'Shibboleth to discover a true Israelite'. Those who signed it swore nominally to defend the protestant religion against the encroachments of popery. But there was, of course, a bigger dimension. This Protestation was a parliamentary stand against absolutist rule. As a test of Oxford loyalty, however, it turned out to be statistically meaningless. Half the student body were too young to sign; a third of those who were eligible were then marked up as absent; and a third of those remaining probably went unrecorded.[193] Even so, the figures deserve a moment's study. Early in 1642 Brasenose returned 120 names. Of these only seventy-eight are listed as present and signing. Eight are marked 'absent', and one 'aegrotat'. But the most significant section of the list is that giving thirty-three names marked 'Hi non sunt domi'. These men were simply 'not at home'. Brasenose was the only college to adopt this device. In all, nearly one-third of the college found some way of refusing to sign. More than one-quarter declined to reply. And even those who did accept Parliament's Protestation did so with stated reservations.[194] We can conclude that in 1642 Brasenose was still fundamen-tally loyal to Church and King. Six years later there would be a price to pay.

[192] V-P's Reg. 1615, fos. 34 and 89; receipt of Roger Porter, Bible Clerk, 1632, quoted in *Quat. Mon.* XI, 21–2. For the communion table, placed altar-wise at the east end—following Canon VII, 1640—as a 'metaphor of [royal] authority [and] . . . a visual and mnemonic means of [expressing] divine right', see Davies, *Caroline Captivity*, 206. Exeter was unusual in retaining the east–west arrangement as late as 1683 (R. A. Beddard, in *HUO* iv. 890). Rails and chancel steps in college chapels were mostly removed in 1641 (*Lords Jnls.* iv. 392, 395; HMC, *De Lisle and Dudley MSS*, vi. 364: W. Hawkins to Earl of Leicester, 24 Jan. 1641). For Radcliffe's previous puritan teaching, see Wood, *Athenae*, ii (1815), *Fasti*, 347.

[193] I. Roy and D. Reinhart, in *HUO* iv. 692–3. For returns nationwide, see 5th *Report of H.M.C.*, part i, appendix, 3 and 120–30 (University of Oxford: 130–1).

[194] C.S.H. Dobson (ed.), *Oxford Protestation Returns* (Oxfordshire Record Soc. 36, 1955), 100–19.

That is not to say that all products of Brasenose were King's men. Far from it. Quite a number—gentry mostly—who came up in the years before the civil war declared for Parliament: William Brereton, for example, a Cheshire baronet, army commander, and puritan MP. He was even appointed a Commissioner for the trial of Charles I. That honour he declined. So did Humphrey Salway, MP for Worcester, who had matriculated as long ago as 1590.[195] But another Brasenose man, James Chaloner, proved to be rather less scrupulous. Chaloner we will meet again. Meanwhile Brereton's exact contemporary, Thomas Croxton, was also a military commander. So was Thomas Blount, a colonel in the parliamentary army and later on an early Fellow of the Royal Society.[196] Another was William Jephson. He became a major general in Cromwell's army, Governor of Portsmouth, MP for Stockport, ambassador to Sweden, and lord of Mallow Castle, Co. Cork.[197] Two more parliamentarians were Henry Brooke, MP for Cheshire, and John Cartwright, a London barrister. Another was John Bingham of Melcombe, Dorset, commandant at the siege of Corfe Castle. He was a member of the Long Parliament in 1645, and a 'Rumper' in 1653. Others, of course, did not survive long enough to achieve high rank: William Shuttleworth of Lancashire and the Inner Temple, for instance, who died fighting for Parliament in the siege of Lancaster. These were all army men; parliamentarians, at least until the end of the war. Needless to say, the majority of those who graduated from Brasenose in the pre-civil-war period went straight into holy orders. But that did not prevent them from taking sides. James Bradshawe made very clear his support for Parliament. His sermons on a theme from Jeremiah 15: 14 urged on the siege of Lathom House, Lancashire. Equally vehement was Peter Ince: he was chaplain to the parliamentary garrison at Weymouth. In due course both of them would pay heavily for their allegiance. They were ejected from their livings in 1662. As we shall see, they were by no means alone.

It is hard, however, to recognize in all this any general pattern of resistance to the Crown. Brasenose was indeed a college of the north-west. But in Cheshire—even in Lancashire—Brasenose men operated on both sides of

---

[195] Salway was buried in Westminster Abbey, 1652; but disinterred 1661 by order of Parliament. He ended his days in the episcopal palace of Croydon, having converted its chapel into a kitchen to satisfy his 'prodigious stomach' (*ODNB*). For civil war loyalties in the north-west, see B. G. Blackwood, *The Lancashire Gentry and the Great Rebellion* (Manchester, 1978); J. S. Morrill, *Cheshire, 1630–1660: County Government and Society during the English Revolution* (1974) and *Revolt in the Provinces* (1999).

[196] 'A great stickler for the two houses of Parliament' (Sir Roger Twysden, quoted in *ODNB*).

[197] He 'moved in the house [of Commons] that Cromwell might be made king' (Edmund Ludlow, quoted in *ODNB*).

the battlefield. In early 1641 both MPs for the county of Cheshire were Brasenose graduates: Peter Venables and Sir William Brereton. Both had criticized the regime of Strafford and Laud. But Venables declared for the King and Brereton for Parliament. They took up different viewpoints at the start of the war; and then they found that the ground began to shift. As the momentum of conflict radicalized rebellion, Brereton was left politically exposed. By the middle of 1641, one of his supporters helpfully explained the predicament in which many local gentry found themselves: he 'loved Sir William Brereton well, but yet . . . loved decency, order and good discipline better'. If that were true for members of the established Church, it must have been truer still for northern recusants. So it was that the greater part of the north-west—actively or passively—eventually supported the King. After all, in 1642 one-third of gentry families in Lancashire were still Catholic. So were no fewer than thirty-one out of the forty-two Lancashire gentlemen on active service in the royalist army.[198]

Alexander Radcliffe, of Ordsall Hall, Lancashire, is one obvious example of soldierly Brasenose royalism. A knighted MP, he was wounded and captured at Edgehill, and imprisoned in the Tower of London until 1649. A fellow Lancastrian, William Ratcliffe of Foxenden, fought and died in the same battle. Also at Edgehill was Ratcliffe Gerard, another Lancastrian lieutenant colonel. Then there was Langdale Sunderland, a captain from Yorkshire, and Peter Leicester, a major from Cheshire; not to mention a veritable clutch of royalist colonels: Goddard Pemberton of Northampton-shire, Thomas Owen of Shropshire, John Pate of Leicestershire, Robert Freake of Somerset, Thomas Leigh of Cheshire, and Geoffrey Shakerley and Sir Thomas Prestwich of Lancashire. All these were Brasenose men, and King's men too. Sir Thomas Ashton, High Sheriff of Cheshire, was another royalist colonel: he was 'a mighty stickler for the prelates'. So was Thomas Ravenscroft, High Sheriff of Flintshire: initially, at any rate, he held Hawarden Castle for the King. Another royalist from Wales was Edward Stradling of Glamorgan: MP, colonel, and baronet. Soldierly royalism, in this Brasenose generation, must at times have seemed almost habitual.[199]

Edward Littleton, MP for Stafford, was among the most ardent of Brasenose King's men. Another was Edward Fisher: his *Appeal to the Conscience* (1643) was a powerful argument for loyalty to the Crown.[200] And King's men

---

[198] Morrill, *Cheshire 1630–1660*, 29–34 and 155–63; P. R. Newman, 'Catholic Royalists of Northern England, 1642–1645', *Northern Hist.* 15 (1979), 88–95 and 'Roman Catholic Royalists', *Recusant Hist.* 15 (1981), 396–405; Blackwood, 'Lancashire Gentry', 352–5.

[199] For Ratcliffe, Leigh, Freake, Owen, Pate, Prestwich, Ravenscroft, Pemberton, Leicester, and Sandys see P. R. Newman, *Royalist Officers . . . a Biographical Dictionary* (New York, 1981).

[200] For Stradling see *ODNB*. For Fisher, ditto. His tract, *The Marrow of Modern Divinity*, gained belated celebrity in 18th-century Scotland (A. Lang, *History of Scotland* (1907 etc.), iv. 284).

could be clergy too. While Bradshaw was encouraging the siege of Lathom from outside, inside was another Brasenose man, Ralph Brideoake, chaplain to the Earl of Derby.[201] Most Brasenose clergy, in fact, ended up as royalists. Gerard Browne, for instance, a Lancastrian; or Joseph Brooksbanke, a Yorkshireman. And clerics were by no means excluded from combat. Matthew Griffith, chaplain to the King, was actively present at the siege of Basing House: his daughter was murdered by the roundheads. Then there was Rowland Scudamore, by now prebendary of Hereford; facetious to the last, he was killed during the siege of that city in 1645. Another was Thomas Warmstrey: never a Laudian, but a middling Anglican through and through. And finally there was John Shaw of Newcastle, ejected from his living and placed in prison for four years: his tombstone bears the legend 'Deo, ecclesiae, patriae, regi, pie fidelis'.[202] That will serve as an epitaph for the bulk of this Brasenose generation.

Quite a number of Brasenose men who began as critics of Laud finished as defenders of the Stuarts. In this the college—as so often—mirrored in miniature the political nation at large. 'Idle Dick Norton' is one example: we shall encounter him again. Another is Sir Thomas Ashton. He began as a stout opponent of Laudian interference. He ended as a defender of Church and King, fighting fiercely against religious and political radicalism. For another example we can look to Edward Bagshaw. In Bagshaw's case, he had been drawn to the puritan side by the teaching of his tutor, Robert Bolton. As an MP however—Calvinist rather than Presbyterian—he became increasingly unhappy with the progress of the Long Parliament. In 1641 he had been a close associate of John Pym. By 1644 he found himself in the King's Bench Prison. Even Robert Holborne—counsel for Hampden in the Ship Money case of 1637—turned out to be a loyal supporter of the King. And when in 1642 Laud arranged for the arch-royalist Jeremy Taylor to take his DD from Brasenose, it cannot have seemed too incongruous. After all, this was the King's Hall and College of Brasenose. Francis Newman is a final, and perhaps extreme example of the same collegiate allegiance. From Brasenose he went to All Souls in 1639; from thence he was expelled by the parliamentary Visitors in 1648; in 1649 he is said to have died from shock at witnessing the execution of Charles I.[203]

Since 1641 the leaders of the Long Parliament had been determined 'to reform and purge [those] fountains of learning, the two Universities'; in particular to

---

[201] 'Busy, bustling, fawning, elbowing, grasping', he became high master of Manchester Grammar and eventually Bishop of Chichester. He is buried beneath a formidable Baroque tomb in St George's Chapel, Windsor (Mumford, *Manchester Grammar School*, 56: illus.; *ODNB*).
[202] For Griffith, Brooksbanke, and Warmstrey, and for Shaw's memorial, see *ODNB*.
[203] MPP 75 A1. For Bagshaw, Holborne, and Taylor see *ODNB*.

eliminate such 'great corruptions . . . [as] . . . Popish and Arminian . . . tenets . . . vestures, postures, ceremonies and administrations'.[204] The onset of hostilities in 1642 brought in more specific parliamentary action. Oxford became the King's headquarters. The University was an obvious target for reformers. In August 1643 came an Ordinance for the removal of all 'Monuments of Idolatry'. Henceforward there would be no altars, no altar rails, no candlesticks, no crucifixes, no images of any kind in any college chapel. And the head of each house was made responsible for their removal.[205] Principal Radcliffe's reaction is not known; but he must have guessed where such iconoclasm would lead. In any case the direction of these changes soon became clear. Step by step, the defeat of the King brought renewed demands 'for the reforming and regulating of both Universities'.[206]

Brasenose ended the war, in 1646, in a sorry state. Sacks of corn were stored above the gateway, in what is now the Tower Bursary; so were rations of bacon, salt butter, cheese, oatmeal, peas, and rice.[207] The college had been on siege alert for over three years. Primitive preparations had been made for defence: stakes for palisades were piled high in the quadrangle. During the emergency many rooms had been let out to royalist 'strangers'. Some of these were Brasenose men of earlier years: Thomas Gamul and Richard Church (royalist officers); Sir Thomas Manwaring (parliamentarian turned royalist) and Sir Henry Manwaring (pirate turned courtier). Similarly Sir Thomas Aston (apologist for bishops), Henry Mason (apologist for Arminians), and John Doughtie (apologist for divine right). Others can best be characterized as keepers of the Caroline flame: Sir William Le Neve (Clarenceaux King of Arms); Dr Edward Lake (he fought heroically at Edgehill, and defended the Crown with pen and sword); John Cleveland (satirist: 'a Notable High soaring Witty Loyalist', a veritable poet laureate in exile); and Richard Allestree (he read the Prayer Book publicly in Beam Hall, Merton Street, during the darker days of Interregnum). All these had good reason to take refuge in Brasenose. So too did other, more peripheral members of the court.

The Duchess of Buckingham, for example, was lodging in college in 1644, at the same time as Elias Ashmole. Apparently she left without paying her battels. Ashmole proved a better investment. Among many other treasures, he left to the museum of his own name a Van Dyck studio profile of the Royal Martyr. Today—by courtesy of the Ashmolean—it graces the Brasenose Senior

---

[204] For the texts of the Root and Branch Petition, Protestation, and Grand Remonstrance, see Gardiner, *Constitutional Documents*, 137–44, 155–6, 202–32.

[205] *Acts and Ordinances of the Interregnum*, i (1911), 265–6.

[206] Propositions of Uxbridge, 1644, and Newcastle, 1645 (Gardiner, *Constitutional Documents*, 277, 293).

[207] Bodl. MS Add. d.114, fo. 85; *Quat. Mon.* XI, 34–5, 39, 70 quoting Visitation papers (Visitor uncatalogued: Treasury).

Common Room. No doubt the Duchess could be classified as a bird of passage. But at least she was in college legitimately. Not so the 'concubine' of Lord Keeper Littleton. This lady—listed as 'Mris. Littleton' in the bursarial rolls of account—was 'kept... and lodged [with Littleton] in Brasenose... until his death [in 1645], after which... she was... tooke [by] Thomas Coke of Gray's Inn'.[208] And there were other random tenants too. Sir John Spelman, for example, theorist of mixed monarchy: he died of camp fever—typhus presumably—in college in 1643.[209] So too, in 1644, did Sir Henry St George, Garter King of Arms. Another who seems also to have been living there at this time—apparently *en famille*— was Sir William Campion. His son Edward was baptized in chapel on 15 August 1645. That was a very rare event: Brasenose has never owned a permanent font.[210]

These courtiers of Charles I must have appeared almost exotic to the few remaining undergraduates. Still, their quarters were not exactly luxurious. Overcrowded, insanitary, plague ridden, Brasenose at this time was hardly recognizable as a place of learning. Swords were more likely to be worn than gowns. And such scholars as did survive seem to have been 'much debauched' by the company of soldiers.[211] Chapel services continued, and no doubt their form was Laudian. But the war had cost the college dear. In August 1642, a loan of £500 was handed over to the King; and the following

[208] Clennell A8. 11* and A2.42; *Quat. Mon.* XI, 36; *Brazen Nose*, iii. 312 and xxxiii. 27 (Boardman); M. Toynbee and P. Young, *Strangers in Oxford... 1642–46* (1973), 182–3. Littleton was buried in Christ Church Cathedral. For his mistress, see letters of Thomas Heath, 1651, quoted in R. L. Hine, *The Cream of Curiosity* (1920), 107. Apparently, 'this Mr. Cook... for many years allowed her a plentiful revenue and by [him] she had three children. But it seems, intending to marry with a lady of good position, he thought to have shakt her off, withdrew his pension, and offered a composition of £1,000, which she refused and in revenge impeached him before the Council of State of having received a commission from the King of Scotts.' Coke managed to escape, despite a price of £100 on his head.

[209] The King made him a member of his Privy Council, and intended him to be Secretary of State (*ODNB*). He was buried in St Mary's (OHS xxxvii, 115). For wartime deaths and burials, see Wood, *Life and Times*, i. 104, 110, 125–6 and *City of Oxford*, iii. 198–264.

[210] A silver 'christening font' was eventually presented by Sir George Baker (V-P's Reg. 13 Oct. 1971, fo. 81). As many as thirty 'strangers' are listed for battelling purposes during wartime. Apart from those mentioned above, these included: Peter Venables, Baron Kinderton, Sir Edward Savage (like the Manwarings, a member of the Duke of Buckingham's circle); Dr Thomas Bispham, Mr Paget, Thomas Haywood, William Osbaldeston (who said he would cut his throat rather than contribute to the parliamentary cause), Mr Heyes, Robert Vernon, Henry Chiver, John Whitinge, Mr Bowden, Mr Backshaw, Edward Lloyd, Jasper Meyrick, Mr Manly, Arthur Wodenoth (a member of the Anglican circle at Little Gidding and patron of George Herbert), Mr Dirg and Mris Payton (Junior Bursar's Accounts 1644: Clennell A8.11*). Also *ODNB*.

[211] Wood, *Annals*, ii. 475, 487. For bad living conditions see also Toynbee and Young, *Strangers in Oxford*; R. and T. Kelly, *A City at War: Oxford 1642–46* (Cheltenham, 1987).

Christmas another £100.²¹² Neither sum—still less the interest at 8 per cent—was ever repaid. The following January Brasenose surrendered its stock of precious plate weighing more than 121lbs. Its value was £367 10*s.* 10*d.* in money of that day. But not everything went. The college's pre-Reformation chalices survived: they were excluded from the demands of the royal mint.²¹³ But by the end of the war any regular income from undergraduates had almost totally dried up. The number battelling each week fell from fifteen scholars and forty-two commoners in 1641 to three scholars and six commoners in 1644. In 1645 it was decided henceforth to elect Fellows without salary, 'till peace be restored to the Kingdom'. Even before the war—as we have already seen—Brasenose had been persistently insolvent. By 1646, the college was in debt to the tune of £1,214 8*s.* 0*d.*²¹⁴

The victorious parliamentarians of 1646 lost no time in announcing their intentions as regards Oxford's future: reformation by Visitation. That was a method with ample Tudor precedent. Since 1509 the Bishop of Lincoln had been Visitor, that is the statutory authority of last resort. Changes during the Reformation period, however, had as often as not been initiated by royal Visitation. Now it was the turn of Parliament. The Commons in particular had Oxford in its sights. But who would validate these parliamentary Visitors? Parliament itself was bitterly divided. For some time the Independent sectaries outside Westminster had been chafing at the Long Parliament's Presbyterian leadership. As early as 1643 Philip Nye—a free-spirited Independent from Brasenose—denounced the intolerance of Presbyterian rule. But that was as far as his independence took him. Years later he would end up as an apostle of conformity.²¹⁵ Others were more persistent. In 1646 William Earbury, an army chaplain turned Seeker—Glamorgan by origin, Brasenose by education—protested loudly in St Mary's against the whole Presbyterian programme.²¹⁶ He spoke out in vain. The Long Parliament hung on to power. The process of University reform was to be effected not by a clutch of free-range puritans but by a board of Westminster Visitors. They would be based in the University but answerable to a London body known as 'the Honourable Committee of Lords and Commons for the Reformation of

---

²¹² *Quat. Mon.* XI, 31–2, pl. i. Radcliffe was one of four heads—the others being Brent of Merton, Clayton of Pembroke, and Hood of Lincoln—who were 'too backward' in offering money, '[neither had they] stirred up their colleges' (Bodl. MS Clarendon 23, fo. 242).

²¹³ *Quat. Mon.* XI, 32–4 and V, pl. ii. One of the items sacrificed was a 'kan' of 16 oz given by Laurence Washington, the great-grandfather of George Washington.

²¹⁴ V-P's Reg. 1645, fo. 68ᵛ; *Quat. Mon.* XI, 33–6, 39–40, citing Houghton's rolls of account, 1642–6: Clennell UBS 22.

²¹⁵ *ODNB.*

²¹⁶ Ibid.

Oxford'. Only one active Visitor came from Brasenose; but his role turned out to be crucial. His name was James Chaloner. It was Chaloner who became the Visitors' secretary. His signature is prominent in their communications. An Etonian, an MP, a relative of Lord Fairfax, a judge at the trial of Charles I: Chaloner was implicated in rebellion at the highest possible level. He ended, in 1658, as Governor of the Isle of Man. His father had made a fortune from alum mining in Yorkshire, and the family held Charles I personally responsible for the loss of their monopoly. Hence their hostility; later they were tainted too with the republican thinking of Henry Marten and his 'gang'. Both James Chaloner and his brother Thomas—Exeter this time, not Brasenose—sat in judgement on the King, though only Thomas actually signed the death warrant. In 1660 Thomas Chaloner fled abroad. Brother James ended his life more dramatically. He is said to have committed suicide by taking poison.[217]

The Visitors' 'model' of University reform was drastic: the 'expulsion' of 'all ill affected and scandalouse persons'; the removal of 'impiouse, superstitiouse, or inconvenient' statutes; and the limitation of non-lecturing Fellowships, 'lest we should degenerate...and through retirement become droanes'.[218] That was a wide brief; in practice, too wide. The programme remained incomplete, despite the fact that—in terms of personnel—the Visitors became increasingly radical. Even so, the changes involved were drastic. The first Visitation (1647–52) was a Presbyterian board; the second (1652–3) and third (1654–58) were largely Independent.[219] With Cromwell as Chancellor from 1651 onwards—and with his former Irish chaplain, John Owen, as Vice-Chancellor from 1652 to 1657—the Oxford of the Interregnum veered between Independency and Calvinism. Either way, this was not a time for King's men. In all, ten out of eighteen heads of houses were ejected. Only Merton and Lincoln were wholeheartedly supportive of the new regime: Merton supplied the Visitors with their headquarters. Only New College, All Souls, and Jesus remained obdurately loyal. The remainder—including Brasenose—were largely purged of royalists, and settled down to restore their broken fortunes under a regime imposed from outside.

[217] *Cal. State Papers Domestic*, 1657–58, 60: 12 Aug. 1657; HMC, *7th Report* (1879), 147a; *Lords Jnls.* xi. 293–4; Wood, *Fasti*, iii. 502–4, 531; *Eton College Register*, 1 (1943), 67.

[218] M. Burrows (ed.), *Register of the Visitors of the University of Oxford* (Bodl. MS E. Museo 77), (Camden Soc., NS 29, 1881), pp. xciii–xciv and 264: 18 Sept. 1649; Wood, *Annals*, ii. 626–7; Gutch, *Collectanea Curiosa*.

[219] The parliamentary committee originated in July 1646 in the Commons' desire to undo Oxford appointments made during the time of the royalist garrison. For the composition and powers of the 1st and 3rd Commissions, see *Commons Jnls.* vi. 388; *Lords Jnls.* ix. 169–70; *Acts and Ordinances of the Interregnum*, i. 925–7, 1001–2 and ii (1911), 1026–7, 1139–40; *Cal. State Papers Domestic* 1645–47, 550–1, 1 May 1647. For the temporary 2nd Commission, see University Archives, NEP *supra* 50; *Commons Jnls.* vii. 124; Wood, *Annals*, ii. 650–2.

The sequence of events in this great Visitation, at least as regards Brasenose, can be studied in vivid detail. In September 1647 the college was asked to supply the names of one or two 'worthy . . . delegates' who could report to the Visitors regarding the allegiance of the Fellowship. That request was ignored. Unlike most colleges, Brasenose had not a single Fellow who would agree to act as a spy. A few weeks later, in October, the Fellows were ordered to hand over their 'statutes, registers, journals, Books of entrye, accompts, orders, and other writings'. Dr Radcliffe replied that they could not do so 'without perjury'.[220] One month later Radcliffe found himself summoned to Merton, along with several other heads of house. His demeanour seems to have been cautious. Anthony Wood thought him too pliable: 'he . . . showed himself false.' In fact 'stout' Radcliffe knew exactly what he was doing.[221] He placed the survival of Brasenose above all else. And so, in their way, did the Fellows. On 27 December 1647 the college Seniority met together and inscribed the following entry in the Vice-Principal's Register: 'Salva semper auctoritate Parliamentaria.' They were clearly playing for time. The following month Radcliffe received a summons to London, to the Painted Chamber, Westminster, no less; and then another summons to Merton, and then another after that. And then in January 1648, Radcliffe and several other heads were 'voted by the Committee to remove from their respective places, as being guilty of high contempt [of Parliament]'. That vote was simply ignored. The vote was repeated, and ignored again. 'Not a man', noted Wood, 'stirred from his place or removed.'[222] At this, 'the Visitation which had been for some time a sleeping Lion, began now to rouse itself'.[223] The 'outing' of heads began in earnest. But by this time the Principal of Brasenose had taken to his bed. The Visitors sent delegates to negotiate. Radcliffe's inactivity was masterly. In fact he epitomized the passive resistance of Oxford as a whole. But on 13 April the Visitors' patience snapped. First Magdalen, then Magdalen Hall, then All Souls, then Wadham, then Trinity, then St John's, then finally Brasenose: all on the same day, each college was subject to the abrupt imperative of military force.

While Principal Radcliffe lay dying in the Lodgings, Chancellor Pembroke arrived at nightfall with a guard of musketeers. Now the fourth Earl of Pembroke was not exactly an academic figure. Anthony Wood thought him 'foul-mouthed' and violent; 'more fit to preside over a Bedlam than a

---

[220] *Visitors' Register*, 3: 30 Sept. 1647 and 5: 6 Oct. 1647; *Quat. Mon.* XI, 45.

[221] Compare Wood, *Annals*, ii, pt. i, 522 with Bodl. MS Wood F 35, fo. 182^v: John Newton's diary, 5 Nov. 1647 ('Dr. Ratcliffe was stout'). See also *Quat. Mon.* XI, 46.

[222] V-P's Reg. 29 Feb. 1648, fos. 71^v and 72; Bodl. MS Wood F 35, fo. 215 (Newton's diary); *Quat. Mon.* XI, 547.

[223] Wood, *Annals*, ii, pt. i, 551.

learned academy'. Certainly he did not suffer dons gladly. On one occasion he told Samuel Fell to his face that he was a devil-made Vice-Chancellor, 'fit [to] . . . be whipped, nay hanged'.[224] That night he held the fate of the college in his hands. Sitting at high table, with the Visitors on either side—Francis Cheynell was there: 'the face of a fiery fury'; and the legendary ranter 'Marginal' Prynne—he simply declared Daniel Greenwood to be Principal. In 1637, when he was Greek Lecturer at Brasenose, Greenwood had been marked down by Laud as a 'verie peevish man', of puritan tendency.[225] Now he was head of a college that was confessedly Calvinist but never Presbyterian. An order appointing Greenwood—in English, for Pembroke's sake—was written by Cheynell in the Buttery Book and recorded in the Vice-Principal's Register.[226] Two days later a notice was nailed to the college gate, prohibiting all use of the Book of Common Prayer. Henceforward any services in Brasenose chapel were to be taken from the puritan Directory for Public Worship.[227] Instead of the Thirty-Nine Articles members of Brasenose would have to subscribe to the Confession of Faith. Oxford's former Chancellor, Archbishop Laud, had by now been struck down by process of parliamentary attainder. King Charles was soon to follow him. The majesty of Parliament—and thus the authority of the Visitors themselves—was absolute. That year, in the streets of Oxford, 'a mad woman [was] whipt for calling them "Roundheads and Rebels" '.[228]

But the Fellows of Brasenose were not easily cowed. When summoned to attend the Visitors at Merton—by an order 'put uppon ye wall on ye left hand going up ye stairs to ye chappell' [i.e. staircase I in its original position]—they proved remarkably composed. Their replies are worth studying. First to face the inquisitors was Robert King, Junior Bursar.

---

[224] *Visitors' Register*, lxx; Wood, *Fasti Oxonienses*, ed. P. Bliss, pt. 2 (1820), 113; *ODNB*.

[225] Wood, *Life and Times*, ii (OHS xxi), 238; Laud, *Works*, v, pt. i, 182.

[226] Bodl. MS Wood F35, fo. 215 and V-P's Reg. 13 Apr. 1648, fo. 71 (signed: Pembroke, William Prynne, William Cobbe, Robert Harris, Nathaniel Brent, Francis Cheynell, and John Cross); *Quat. Mon.* XI, 48–9. It may have been John Newton who wrote a pamphlet comparing Pembroke's actions to the gibbet law customary in Halifax, Yorks.: *Halifax Law Translated to Oxon: or the New Visitors' Justice* (1648). See F. Madan, *Oxford Books* (1895–1931), ii, 467, no. 1985.

[227] Wood, *Annals*, ii, pt. i, 572, 574. For details of the Directory (1645), and its enforcement in Oxford (1648), see *Acts and Ordinances of the Interregnum*, i. 582–607, 1143. Latin prayers continued at Christ Church until Christmas 1648; after that Dr Fell conducted services in Merton Street, until the Restoration (Wood, *Annals*, ii, pt. i, 613). Greenwood supported the Presbyterian party. Even so Brasenose was accused—by 'Sir Henry Vane's Advisor'—of superstitious practices in chapel (H. Stubbe, *A Light Shining out of Darknes: or Occasional Queries submitted to Judgment*, 1659). See Madan, *Oxford Books*, iii. 96, no. 2428.

[228] Wood, *Annals*, ii, pt. i, 574. For Pembroke's purge, see also *Commons Jnls.* v: 8 Mar. 1648 and 21 Apr. 1648.

Visitors. 'Have you brought the Rentalls, Books etc. of your College with you?'
King.   'No'.
Visitors. 'Why have you not?'
King.   'They are in the hands of the Senior Bursar, Mr. John Houghton'.
Visitors. 'Where is he?'
King.   'In the Country'.
Visitors. 'Do you say true?'
King.   'Yes, I speak the truth . . .'[229]

That did not satisfy the Visitors. Nor were they pleased, on 10 May, when eighteen members of Brasenose appeared and only two 'did directly submit'.[230] On 15 May it was deemed that Bursar King 'did not submit', and was therefore 'expelled'. With him went five more Fellows: Newton, Eaton, Rawson, Sixsmith, and Eaude.[231] Their answers were judged insufficient. Those of Byrom and Church were, however, quite clear. 'I dare not submit to this Visitation', Byrom explained, 'because whatsoever is not of faith is sin.' And Church was equally adamant: 'I can [not] submit to this Visitation, without incurring manifest perjury.'[232] Their thinking closely followed Convocation's official response to Parliament: *Reasons of the Present Judgment of the University of Oxford* (1647).[233] Oxford men, it was there explained, had sworn due loyalty to Church and Crown, to University and college. To break these oaths would be perjury. The replies of two Brasenose undergraduates, Thomas Readinge and Jasper Scoles, make the same point, though evasively. 'I submit to the Visitation', announced Readinge, 'soe farr as the Statutes of the Universitie and my owne particular Oathes can permit me.'[234] Scoles was equally cautious: 'I will actively or passively submit to the authoritie of Parliament in this Visitation soe farre as the Lawes of God, the Lawes of the land, the Statutes of the Universitie and my own conscience will give me leave.'[235]

It was not enough. They all had to go. So did the Bible Clerk, John Porter, and two more non-Fellows, William Burges and William Brewer.[236] More were to follow. They did not go willingly. The orders of expulsion for Eaton,

---

[229]   *Visitors' Register*, 26: 28 Apr. 1648.
[230]   Wood, *Annals*, ii, pt. i, 583.
[231]   *Visitors' Register*, 89–94: 15 May 1648.
[232]   Ibid. 152: 14 July 1648. For ambivalent replies by Sixsmith, Newton, Eaton, and Rawson, see ibid. 66: 10 May 1648.
[233]   See Wood, *Annals*, ii. 501 ff.; R. Sanderson, *Works*, ed. W. Jacobson, i (Oxford, 1854), p. xvii.
[234]   *Visitors' Register*, 123: 1 June 1648.
[235]   Ibid. 148: 14 July 1648.
[236]   Ibid. 144: 7 July 1648; 159, 166: 14 July 1648; Wood, *Annals*, ii, pt. i, 608–9. Other students expelled by the Visitors included Ralph Hulton, Walter Whitney, Peter Adams, Richard Furnivall, John Aston, John Smith, Thomas Jackson, Jasper Scoles, and John Broster (Bodl. MS Rawl. D 912, fo. 303ᵛ). Henry Dutton, once of Brasenose, later of Trinity and Corpus, George Halstead, later of Corpus, and Randle Domville, later of Merton, were also expelled.

Rawson, and Eaude had to be repeated twice.[237] So were those for Yate and Blackborne.[238] During the summer and autumn of 1648 as many as 200 Oxford men were expelled.[239] The number from Brasenose is not exactly clear. Only a handful of students were actually resident at that time. But, together with those Fellows who were recalcitrant, they must have brought the number of extruded Brasenose men to at least two dozen.

Meanwhile Dr Radcliffe was too ill to be moved. Right to the end he refused to cooperate. In particular he refused to surrender access to the college archive and treasury. On 21 March he had been ordered to 'give up his place and renounce all right to his Lodging'. Since he was 'not well', however, he had been granted permission to negotiate the date of his removal with his successor.[240] On 19 June a further order was delivered to the Lodgings:

> Ordered that Dr. Radcleiffe, now lodginge in Brasen Nose College, doe forthwith, upon sight hereof, deliver up to Mr. Daniell Greenewood, or his Assigne, all his keyes of the Treasury, the Corne Booke, Lease Booke, Rentalls, and what other Bookes or Keyes hee hath in his custody... And, in case the said Dr. Radcliffe shall refuse to obey this present Order, the souldiary are hereby desired to sett a Guard upon the said Dr. Radcliffe, which Guard is to be mayntayed at the proper cost and charges of Dr. Radcliffe aforesaid.[241]

No records seem to have been handed over; no key, no corn book, no rental. Radcliffe spent his last days under armed guard. And when he died at last on 26 June 1648, the Fellows had their own plan ready.

First came the funeral in St Mary's. This was held—to the annoyance of the Visitors—'with ye Common Prayer [Book], *more antiquo*'.[242] Then Vice-Principal Sixsmith—expelled but not removed—wrote out a notice of forth-coming election, to take place on 10 July, and pinned it to the chapel door. When that day dawned—almost literally in fact—the Visitors launched a pre-emptive strike. A guard of soldiers marched up to the gate lodge at seven in the morning, and barred the entrance to chapel and hall. Three senior Fellows were arrested: Sixsmith, Newton, and King. All three were kept together in one room until ten o'clock that night. Unabashed, next morning they called on Gilbert Sheldon, the royalist Warden of All Souls, and with his advice put the finishing touches to their plot. On 12 July six Fellows—all but

---

[237] *Visitors' Register*, 138: 29 June 1648.
[238] Ibid. 168: 17 July 1648.
[239] B. Worden, in *HUO* iv. 734 (correcting Burrows's higher figures in *Visitors' Register*, pp. lx–cvii). Preliminary lists in Bodl. MS Wood F35, fos. 241–2, 254–85.
[240] *Visitors' Register*, 11: 21 Mar. 1648.
[241] Ibid. 120: 1 June 1648; Wood, *Annals*, ii, pt. i, 589.
[242] The custom of funeral proclamation by the University bellman had been specifically forbidden by the Visitors on the day after Radcliffe's death (*Visitors' Register*, 136).

one of those resident in Oxford—gathered in Edmund Highfield's rooms, in the north-west corner of the old quad, probably III, 4 (later known as the White Room), overlooking Brasenose Lane. There they read out the relevant statute, intoned their oaths, and unanimously elected a new Principal. The chosen man was Thomas Yate (pl. 13). It was a bold gesture, and the names of these six men—the 'Yate Fellows'—deserve to be recorded: Sixsmith, Newton, Eaton, Highfield, Church, and Jones. It was Highfield who carried the news to London, where Yate—discreetly biding his time at 'Chilsey'—accepted election on 18 July. The election was declared valid by the Visitor.[243]

Not for twelve long years would Yate take up the Principalship. Until then he would remain 'the Fellows' Principal', not the Visitors'. Instead of Yate, the 'squint-eyed' Greenwood was installed by Visitatorial directive. He was to prove in fact a rather effective head of house. During his years of office (1648–60), finances steadied and recruitment improved: total numbers rose from 20 to 120.[244] And, as we shall see, the new chapel and library were at last begun. But the manner of his installation had been high-handed in the extreme. The Fellowship had been purged, and a new generation intruded. No fewer than thirteen out of sixteen Fellows were 'outed': Thomas Yate, Thomas Sixsmith, Richard Hill, John Newton, Robert King, Ralph Byrom, Edmund Highfield, Byrom Eaton, Richard Roberts, Thomas Church, Ralph Rawson, Richard Eaude, and John Blackborne. Three of these retired rather than face expulsion: Highfield, Blackborne, and Sixsmith.[245] Only two submitted outright to the parliamentary regime: Robert Jones, a junior Fellow, and Phillip Leycester—who was later expelled as 'homicida' and 'scandalouse'.[246] One Fellow, John Houghton—he who retreated to the country—somehow managed to evade the question and stay on. He would survive both revolution and restoration. But then he was Senior Bursar, and an ally of Oxford's military overlord, the city's Deputy Governor.[247] In October 1648 the list of expulsions was proclaimed at the college gate by beat of drum. Then the names of those removed were fixed for all to see upon the portal.

[243] The Visitor during the war years was Thomas Winniffe. Highfield's Latin narrative was inserted in V-P's Reg. 1647, fo. 69[r/v]. Yate's letter of acceptance is quoted in *Quat. Mon.* XI, 52.

[244] *Quat. Mon.* XI, 55 n. 2.

[245] Sixsmith and Highfield presented the college with a silver decanter, inscribed 1650 and 1652 (*Quat. Mon.* V, 30).

[246] Jones had received the living of Rotherfield Greys, Oxon., in 1645 (*Lords Jnls.* vii. 700). For Leycester, see *Visitors' Register*, 258: 8 Aug. 1649; V-P's Reg. 30 May 1649, fo. 72[v].

[247] The godly 'button-maker', Thomas Kelsey (Wood, *Annals*, ii, pt. i, 605; *Fasti*, ed. Bliss, pt. 2, 111). Houghton was reputed to have produced an illegitimate son, Richard Berry, a graduate of Brasenose and chaplain of Christ Church, 'one much given to the flesh and a great lover of Eliz. [an apple seller or 'huckster' at Carfax], the wife of Funcker and daughter of Woods of Bullock's [Bulwarks] lane' (Wood, *Life and Times*, i. 3, 195). Houghton also became a prebendary of Salisbury (V-P's Reg. 23 Oct. 1661, fo. 90). He was buried in the cloister in 1677.

Any who remained had already been threatened with execution as spies.[248] The revolution was complete.

And what became of those who were 'outed'? According to legend, this generation of dispossessed clergy—perhaps 200 Oxford Fellows in all— 'wandered to and fro like beggars', preserving in 'misery and poverty' their 'fidelity to the Church and the King'.[249] In fact, quite a number found places elsewhere—not least one or two of the King's men of Brasenose. Rawson found employment as a tutor: to Lady Ormond, to Sir George Savile, and to a young poet named Charles Cotton, of Beresford Hall, Derbyshire. None of this kept him entirely out of trouble: he was involved in the Booth Plot of 1659, a premature plan to restore the monarchy. And what of Yate? As ex-Principal he took a cautious line. He no longer had his rectory at Middleton Cheney to fall back on. In 1646 he had surrendered it to a parliamentary loyalist—perhaps a relative—named John Cave; and he seems not to have recovered it until after Cave's death in 1657. In the meantime he became a practising solicitor. Others also took up their former occupations. Not without difficulty, Blackborne found a curacy in Lancashire; Richard Eaude found livings in Herefordshire, Byrom Eaton in Oxfordshire and Berkshire.[250] Thomas Sixsmith certainly found compensation. In 1648 he was given the plum college living of Steeple Aston, Oxfordshire. At his death in 1650 this was passed on to another 'Yate Fellow', Edmund Highfield.[251] On Highfield's death in 1654 it was taken over by the Principal's nephew and namesake, Daniel Greenwood. One day Principal Greenwood himself would have need of it.

---

[248] Wood, *Annals*, ii, pt. i, 597; *Visitors' Register*, 143: 5 July 1648.

[249] J. Walker, *Sufferings of the Clergy during the Great Rebellion* (1862), 276.

[250] For Yate's clerical career, see Middleton Cheney parish register, cited by [George Ormerod], in Bras, C, 97: 'Collections relating to Brasenose', 'Compositions etc.', p. xix; A. G. Matthews, *Walker Revised* (Oxford, 1948), 287; Wood, *Life and Times*, ii. 62; *Topographer and Genealogist*, i (1846), 421–31; *ODNB*. Yate's legal expertise later proved useful in guiding the infant University Press (*Cal. State Papers Domestic*, 1672: correspondence with Sir L. Jenkins and 1675: correspondence with John Fell; Beddard, in *HUO* iv. 844, 846). For Rawson's conspiratorial and poetic career, see [B. Richards], in *Brazen Nose*, xvi. 55–9. For Rawson, Blackborne, and Eaton, see Matthews, *Walker Revised*, 24 (citing B L Harl. MS 6942, fo. 58), 228 and 296.

[251] V-P's Reg. 7 Dec. 1648, fo. 71^v and 13 Feb. 1650, fo. 75^v; *Lords Jnls*. x. 630. In his will of 1650 Sixsmith left ejected Fellows of Brasenose 50*s*. each and Fellows who voted for his appointment at Steeple Aston 20*s*. each (Matthews, *Walker Revised*, 24). Nathaniel Greenwood—another of the new Principal's nephews—eventually received the living of Cottingham, Northants, in 1680. Sixsmith's own theological position was always Calvinist rather than Arminian. In 1638 he described William Chillingworth's Laudian views as making him 'boggle . . . I conceive him to smell too much of the [rationalizing] Socinian' (B. 2 a. 38, p. 35, cited by Tyacke in *HUO* iv. 588–9).

By the autumn of 1648, therefore, Brasenose—like nearly every other college—had been reduced to a rump. Apart from Bursar Houghton, just three
of the old Fellows survived: 'squint-eyed' Greenwood, the pliable Jones, and
the 'scandalouse' Leycester. In place of those who had been expelled the
Visitors hastily recruited a generation of outsiders.

Who were these Oxford 'intruders'? Dr Fell famously called them 'an
illiterate rabble'. Anthony Wood dismissed them as nothing but the 'scum of
Cambridge'; 'a great rabble of new faces, scraped out of Cambridge and the
Country . . . a new plantation of Saints'. Even their hair had been shorn to suit
the newly fashionable 'committee cut'.[252] But at Brasenose the social origins
of these new men were in fact very similar to those of their predecessors. Of
those whose parentage is recorded, we find only one listed as armigerous; five
count as gentry; seven are noted as plebeian, one clerical, and one poor. Their
academic background, however, was varied. One thing only they did have in
common: loyalty to the parliamentary regime. Other than that, their provenance was diverse. Thomas Weston came from Oriel; Richard Duckworth and
William Williamson from New Inn Hall; William Coxe and Samuel Bruen
from the University of St Andrews; Robert Eaton and Nathaniel Hoyle from
Trinity College, Dublin; John Kershaw, Richard Adams, Thomas Higginson,
John Burscough, John Carpenter, John Glendole, Richard Farrand, and
Greenwood himself from Cambridge. Ithiel Walker's origins seem to defy
investigation. The Visitors did elect four men in the traditional Brasenose
mould: Thomas Deane, Charles Gerard, Robert Ridgway, and John Gilman.
Three of this group were from Cheshire, one from Lancashire. But none of
them lasted long. The same is true of several other intruders. Robert Eaton
stayed on just long enough to become vicar of two agreeable parishes:
Pangbourne and Cuddesdon.[253] Hoyle's Fellowship was declared void in
1650 when it was 'discovered' that he had refused to take the Engagement
of 1649 (an oath of allegiance to the Commonwealth). He was replaced by a
man with rather more influence—and greater claims on posterity—the future
Sir William Petty. Williamson resigned in 1650; Walker in 1652; Weston in
1655. Ashton was pensioned off in 1656. Walker, a year after his election, had
not even been incorporated as a senior member of the University.[254]

---

[252] J. Fell, *Life of Richard Allestree* (Oxford, 1684; 1848), 9; Wood, *Athenae*, ii. 106, 110–18.

[253] V-P's Reg. 18 Feb. 1649, fo. 73ᵛ; *Lords Jnls*. ix. 519 and x. 82.

[254] V-P's Reg. 12 Sept. 1650, fo. 74ᵛ (Petty) and 15 May 1650, fo. 73ᵛ (Williamson); *Visitors'
Register*, 278. For the appointment of this generation of Fellows, see Bodl. MS Raw. D 912, fo.
305ᵛ; V-P's Reg. 1648–9, fos. 72ᵛ and 73. In 1652 Farrand and Deane both received
extraordinary payments of £2 for their 'service to ye state and colledge' (Bursar's Accounts,
cited by Jeffery in *Brazen Nose*, iv. 30). Samuel Heskins was given a Claymond Scholarship by
the Visitors in 1648, as was James Purefoy in 1649; but Purefoy was expelled in 1652.

Of all those appointed by the Visitors only Greenwood made a significant, long-term career in Oxford. He actually became a Visitor himself; and as a stop-gap Vice-Chancellor in 1650–2, he won a general measure of approval. Cromwell admired his 'ability and zeal for Reformation'; even Anthony Wood admitted he was a 'severe and good governour'.[255] Of course there was some criticism. Two of those he recruited to the Fellowship were his own nephews, Nathaniel and Daniel Greenwood. Still, such nepotism was scarcely unexpected. As his puritanism faded, his college loyalty increased. But it took years for him to overcome the manner of his appointment. In 1648, when he asked to see the statutes, he was told by Bursar Houghton 'that the statute book was safe, and in such hands [Yate's presumably] as had more right to keep [it]'. Three years later he was still trying to recover that elusive volume.[256] In a way he could never be totally accepted: unlike Houghton he was not buried in the cloister, and no portrait of him survives in college. Even so, Principal Greenwood and Bursar Houghton would spend the 1650s side by side, working peaceably and constructively. They were building Brasenose anew. Thanks to their efforts, Radcliffe's architectural dreams were amply fulfilled by the very men who supplanted him. And both sides—intruders and extruded—contributed to the building fund. Perhaps the polarities of Oxford politics during the Interregnum were more apparent than real.

Anyway, after his removal in 1660 Greenwood retreated for the remaining fourteen years of his life, first to college property at Studley, Oxfordshire, and then to his nephew's rectory at Steeple Aston. There he was eventually buried. He died worth £9,000, of which £400 went to Brasenose.[257] During his Principalship—first under the direction of the Visitors; then, after 1650, on his own account—he did recruit a number of able people, John Howe for one. Imported from Cambridge as Bible Clerk in 1648, Howe later became a chaplain to Oliver Cromwell. Noted for his 'Rigide Calvinism in a Softer Dresse', he would end his days as an eirenic sage, a nonconformist pastor in London.[258] More prosaically, Ralph Eaton—Fellow from 1656 to 1663—will stand as a type of late seventeenth-century college man. Most unusually,

---

[255] Wood, *Fasti*, ed. Bliss, pt. 2 (1820), 157. Edward Calamy describes him as 'a profound scholar and divine, and a circumspect governor' (quoted in *Quat. Mon.* XII, 5). Greenwood restored the ceremony of the Act in 1651; but he had to call in the army to control 'raucus' scholars and prevent 'hummings and other clamorous noises' (M. Feingold in *HUO* iv. 304–5).

[256] Uncat. Bras. MSS, quoted by J. Twigg, in *HUO* iv. 797 n. 91.

[257] Wood, *Life and Times*, ii. 280 and iv. 74. His goods were nominally forfeit to the University; in the event, family members were the chief beneficiaries. In all, the Greenwood family supplied a Principal and four Fellows of Brasenose as well as a master at Charlbury School (ibid. i. 267).

[258] Wood, *Fasti*, pt. 2, 119; *ODNB*.

records survive of his teaching stint as Fellow: an average of nine students in his care, 1659–62; never more than fourteen in any one year; with full responsibility for each pupil's finances.[259] Apart from these men, only three of Greenwood's Fellows deserve particular mention. None of them could be described as an easy colleague. One was a rogue: Thomas Franckland. One was an oddity: Thomas Ashton. And one was a man of 'universal' genius: William Petty (pl. 15).

Franckland—'impostor and antiquary'—came up to Brasenose in 1649 and rose to be Vice-Principal in 1667. Anthony Wood found him 'a haughty, turbulent, and disagreeable man'. He was certainly not averse to self-promotion. He began by tricking his way into the Royal College of Physicians by means of a forged diploma. He then proceeded to claim bogus medical degrees from both Oxford and Cambridge. He even managed to inveigle himself onto a government secret service payroll before dying in the Fleet Prison in 1690. Along the way, however, he did publish anonymously one substantial piece of archival history: *The Annals of King James I and King Charles I* (1681).[260]

As for Ashton, his sanity must remain a matter of some doubt. A poor boy from Lancashire—plebeian, servitor, and Nowell Scholar—he found favour with the Visitors, and became a Fellow in 1652. In July 1654, according to Wood, he delivered 'a very offensive Sermon' at St Mary's on Job 37: 22: 'With God is terrible Majesty . . . there will be weeping and gnashing of teeth.' Taking 'a hint from the word *terribilis* (*terrae bilis* as he said) . . . among other conceits, [he announced] . . . that those in Hell that had no teeth to gnash should [simply] gnash their gums'. For this he was haled before the Vice-Chancellor and then expelled by the Principal. The Seniority were rather less censorious. The expulsion was declared void; an appeal was made to the Visitor; and a compromise was agreed. Ashton was given two *ex gratia* payments of £30 in successive years, plus a clerical office far away. He became chaplain to the military forces in Jersey.[261]

---

[259] Ralph Eaton's 'Pupill Booke of Accounts' (MPP 8 A1, formerly MS 85; ex Owston Hall, near Doncaster). See also Porter, in *HUO* iv. 66. For tutorial responsibilities in the previous generation, see also thirteen letters, 1608–12, from the Senior Bursar Richard Taylor to Sir Peter Legh regarding his two sons, Francis and Thomas Legh (MSS of W. J. Legh of Lyme Hall, Cheshire, HMC, *3rd Report*, 268b, quoted in *National Rev.* i. 620 and *Quat. Mon.* XI, 13 *et seq.* citing copies in B 2a 40, fos. 2–30). Taylor was particularly anxious that his pupils did not 'have money in their own custodie'; 'some yonge gentlemen can hardly be kept in any order, let them but have an angell or two in their purse.'

[260] *Brasenose Reg.*; *ODNB*.

[261] He was expelled under college statute cap. xxvi (V-P's Reg. 15 Sept. 1656, fo. 82 and 25 Dec. 1656, fo. 84; *Visitors' Register*, 417: 25 Dec. 1656; *Brasenose Reg.*; Wood, *Annals*, ii, pt. ii, 666–7).

Petty, by contrast, was a heavyweight intellect disguised as a Restoration *arriviste*. He was educated on the Continent in mathematics, anatomy, chemistry, and medicine. He was an early disciple of Pierre Gassendi, the French philosopher and mathematician. He was well read in Descartes and Hobbes. And he was a prominent member of the circle of empiricists who clustered round Samuel Hartlib. As early as 1646–7, he was practising medicine in Oxford. 'Being very poor', Thomas Hearne tells us, he 'came to Oxon., studied Physick, cut up doggs and taught Anatomy'. Then in 1650, 'after Oxon. was taken', he 'was made Fellow of Brasen-nose, the Visitors putting Loyal persons out, to put him and such others in'.[262] After that came the Vice-Principalship, and a University readership in anatomy in 1651. His lecture notes survive, and very conscientious they are too. But lecturing was not his only talent. The following year, by resuscitating the body of a woman named Anne Greene—cut down from an Oxford gallows and intended for dissection—he achieved an instant notoriety.[263] Appointed physician to the army in Ireland, he then proceeded to outmanoeuvre the Surveyor General by producing a radical programme for calculating forfeited estates. This, the celebrated Down Survey, laid the basis of his own fortune, and of his reputation as a statistical analyst. One day Keynes would call him the father of political economy.[264] And he had another claim to fame as well.

It was during the years 1648–50 that the earliest meetings were held of what would one day be known as the Royal Society. In 1662 Petty became one of its founders. The venue for some of the very first gatherings had been 'Mr. Pettie's Lodgings in an Apothecary's house against All Souls'. There he met up with a new generation of natural philosophers: Wilkins and Wallis,

[262] *Hearne's Collections*, i (OHS ii), 78. For the intellectual milieu which Petty encountered in Oxford, see Feingold, in *HUO* iii, ch. 6.

[263] The 'poor wench...had been hanged [for infanticide]...[But] he let blood, put to bed to a warme woman, & with spirits & other meanes recovered her to life; The Young Scholars joyn'd & made her a little portion, married her to a Man who had several children by her, living 15 yeares after, as I have ben assured' (J. Evelyn, *Diary*, iv (Oxford, 1955), 57: 22 Mar. 1675).

[264] For Petty in general, see C. Webster, *The Great Instauration: Science, Medicine and Reform, 1626–60* (1975); T. Aspromourgos, 'The Mind of an Oeconomist', *Hist. of Economic Ideas*, 9 (2001), 39–101; as well as *ODNB*. Petty's *Verbum Sapienti* (c.1655; 1691) contains the first estimate of English national income. His *Political Anatomy of Ireland* (c.1672; 1691) and *Political Arithmetick* (c.1671–6; 1690) were pioneering studies in economic geography and actuarial theory. 'His emphasis on the division of labour anticipates Adam Smith; his views on taxation anticipate Ricardo; and his macroeconomic outlook often anticipates Keynes' (P. Sinclair, *Brazen Nose*, xxi. 19). He was by no means a principled republican, and in 1685 produced a rationale of royal prerogatives; on the other hand he was an early advocate of parliamentary reform and national census. See *The Economic Writings of Sir William Petty*, ed. C. H. Hull (Cambridge, 1899), ii. 630–2 and *The Petty Papers*, ed. Marquess of Lansdowne, i (1927), 7–8, 258–60.

Bathurst and Boyle. Even in this company, Petty stood out. Pepys called him 'one of the most rational men that ever I heard speak with a tongue, having all his notions ... distinct and clear'.[265] 'If I were a Prince', noted Evelyn, 'I should make him my second Counselor at least.' He certainly had a talent to amuse.

facetious, and of Easy Conversation, friendly and Courteous [he] had such a faculty to imitate others, that he would take a Text, and preach now like a grave orthodox Divine, then fall into the Presbyterian way, thence to the Phanatical, the Quaker, the Moonk, and friar, the Popish Priest ... [even] an Enthusiast ... [all] very divertisant.

To cap it all there was 'not a better Latine poet living'.[266]

But young 'Mr. Pettie' was as much a politician as an academic. He had friends in high places. They ensured first his appointment at Brasenose and then a prolonged sabbatical. It was from Oxford, perhaps with his new colleague Samuel Bruen as assistant, that he set about planning the Plantation of Ireland. The mechanism for that ill-fated operation—the redistribution of nearly eight and a half million acres—involved a pioneering demographic and cartographic survey. By October 1653 Petty's work had the full backing of the Council of State. His Fellowship, Brasenose was informed, must in no way be endangered by his absence: 'Dr. Pettye's longer stay in Ireland is needed for the public service.'[267] All true, no doubt; but such government activity would mean, in the long run, that his influence in Oxford was limited. The University merely provided him with a useful base. Still, by 1658 he was back at Brasenose as Vice-Principal. Bruen meanwhile had been presented with the agreeable living of Cuddesdon. For Petty, however, London must always have seemed a rather more profitable field. In 1659 his Fellowship was declared void on grounds of unstatutable absence.[268] With that he could live: there was a world elsewhere. Backed first by Charles II, then by James II, he

---

[265] Pepys, *Diary*, v (1971), 27–8: 27 Jan. 1664; Wood, *Annals*, ii, pt. i, 633. For his work in Oxford as an anatomist, see R. G. Frank, *Harvey and the Oxford Physiologists* (Berkeley, 1998).

[266] Evelyn, *Diary*, iv (Oxford, 1955), 59: 22 Mar. 1675. In 1821 the Petty portrait at Bowood was copied for BNC by Ross of Bow St., London (V-P's Reg. 3 Sept. 1821, fo. 180ᵛ). Present location unknown.

[267] *Cal. State Papers Domestic*, 1653–54, 208; *Visitors' Register*, 335: 18 Apr. 1651 (Petty) and 364: 13 Sept. 1653 (Bruen). Petty's *Down Survey* (1655–6) was edited by Sir Thomas Larcom (Irish Archaeol. Soc. 1851). For Petty's denunciation by Sir Jerome Sankey, see *Commons Jnls.*, 24 Mar. 1658. For Petty's appointment at Brasenose, see V-P's Reg. 12 Sept. 1650, fo. 74ᵛ. For his battels account as Fellow in 1653, see BL Add. MS 72857, fo. 84; for his application for the Anatomy Lectureship founded by Richard Tomlins, 1650–1, see ibid., fos. 80–3; for his Oxford anatomy lectures and medical practice, see Add. MSS 72891–2. For his Irish estate, see T. C. Barnard, 'Sir William Petty, Irish Landowner', in Lloyd-Jones *et al.* (eds.), *History and Imagination*, 201–17; N. Everett, *A Landlord's Garden: Derreen Demesne, Co. Kerry* (Bantry, 2001).

[268] V-P's Reg. 18 Dec. 1657 and 9 Aug. 1659, fo. 86. 'Bruen's partie', which included the 'factious' Duckworth, had long 'opposed' Principal Greenwood (Houghton to Yate, 10 Sept. 1660, quoted in *Quat. Mon.* XII, 35).

floated easily upwards; through politics and finance, towards the higher realms of landownership and nobility. He would end as a political economist turned multi-acred magnate, founder of the dynasty of Shelburne.

Meanwhile, how was Brasenose faring in the final years of parliamentary rule? As Presbyterians gave way to Independents, the 'rule of the saints' had intensified. First came the Negative Oath of November 1648; then the puritan Engagement of October 1649. Henceforward 'none were to be admitted to a degree without subscribing' to both these oaths: against the King and for the Commonwealth.[269] Then, from 1650 onwards, the Visitors set out 'to reform reformation': in dress, speech, recreation, learning. There was to be no more 'powdering... haire, wearing knots of ribbands, [or] walking in boots and spures and bote-hose-tops'; no more avoidance of communal meals or of morning and evening chapel; no more keeping of 'hounds and horses'; no more casual study—not even by gentlemen commoners—without strict tutorial supervision.[270] Royalist sympathizers like Anthony Wood grudgingly welcomed this return to discipline. They began to look to Chancellor Cromwell as a guarantee of social order. Here—for those who cared to see—were the first faint hints of Restoration.[271]

Meanwhile, there were problems of finance.

By the end of the civil war, most colleges were financially distraught. They turned to government for rescue. In July 1649 the stipend of the Principal of Brasenose stood at £60 p.a., excluding allowances. This happened to be the same as St John's, but rather less than Wadham, Lincoln, or Queen's, and rather more than Exeter, Oriel, Trinity, Jesus, Pembroke, and Balliol. By the end of the century, Brasenose emoluments had risen somewhat. The Principal now received £80 p.a. Even so he continued to lag behind his compeers at Christ Church, New College, Magdalen, and Merton. Such payments were by no means generous. No head of house at this time received as much as an army colonel; and only four received the pay of a captain; while many scholars, exhibitioners, etc. earned little more than foot soldiers. And Brasenose was by no means prosperous compared with some other colleges. At £600 p.a., collegiate revenue in Brasenose ran at only half the level of Merton, only one-sixth that of Magdalen, and only one-tenth that of Christ Church.[272] That at least was one estimate. We cannot be certain of these figures. What

---

[269] *Cal. State Papers Domestic,* 1649–50, 339; *Visitors' Register,* 213 (Negative Oath), 274 (Engagement); Gardiner, *Constitutional Documents,* 289–90 (Negative Oath), 391 (Engagement).

[270] *Visitors' Register,* 294: 7 May 1650; 313: 5 Nov. 1650; 358–60: 27 June 1653; 366, 373–4: 10 Oct. 1653 and 29 Nov. 1653; 411–12: 22 Apr. 1656.

[271] Wood, *Annals,* ii, pt. i, 634.

[272] Compare *Visitors' Register,* 251: 26 July 1649 with Bodl. MS Tanner, vol. 338, fos. 203–6 (undated: ?1690), printed in Gutch, *Collectanea Curiosa.*

we do know is that in September 1649 two Fellowships had to be frozen: 'kept voyd for a tyme, untill the debts of the College be neere satisfied'. And in 1654 Brasenose was one of ten colleges whose heads petitioned the Lord Protector for more money: 'our places are so poor as not to afford a competent maintenance.' A grant was awarded of up to £100 p.a. to increase the salaries of these indigent heads.[273] Like most colleges, Brasenose had suffered serious disruption of income during the years of trouble. In 1643 there had even been an emergency levy on Fellows to pay for the cost of soldiers. Throughout the 1640s college accounts were repeatedly in deficit. After that, there is a marked improvement. Recruitment rises; rentals revive. Even so, Brasenose finances remained fragile until the eve of Restoration.[274]

By 1660 several of the Fellows removed in 1648 had died or accepted livings elsewhere. Six however survived to be reinstated: Yate, Newton, Church, Rawson, Blackborne, and Roberts.[275] For Thomas Yate in particular it must have been a moment to savour. In August 1660 a new set of Visitors, the Commissioners of Charles II—one of them the invincible Houghton— declared that Greenwood, the 'pretended Principal', had been 'illegally admitted'. His position was deemed 'unstatutable'. Henceforward Yate should be considered his legitimate successor (and predecessor).[276] He would go down to history as the only man to be twice Principal of Brasenose.

Yate's attitude to Greenwood is intriguing. Instead of banishing his predecessor like some discredited 'Moses', he allowed him—and Mrs Greenwood— to stay on for a while, using two Fellows' rooms in Staple Hall on the other side of School Street. Houghton thought this generosity unwise. 'It is much wondered at by many', he warned the incoming Principal, 'that he should desire such a courtesie, or that you should grant it to him.' Greenwood

is my friend [he adds obliquely] and I pray God he prove yours . . . onlie this lett me presume to whisper unto you . . . what doe you conceive may be [his] ayme in this? is

---

[273] *Visitors' Register*, 263: 18 Sept. 1649 and cx. 251–2: 26 July 1649; *Acts and Ordinances of the Interregnum*, ii. 373; *Cal. State Papers Domestic, 1653–4*, 423: 28 Feb. 1654. In 1656 Greenwood was awarded £112 10s. 0d. from First Fruits and Tenths (W. A. Shaw, *History of the English Church, 1640–60*, ii (1900), 575). Freezing a Fellowship continued to be an expedient way of settling debts, e.g. the debt of £54 12s. 2d. on the death of Gilbert Sherington (V-P's Reg. 5 Jan. 1684, fo. 127).

[274] Accounts tabulated by Twigg, in *HUO* iv. 781, 792 n. 63, 796 n. 88 (revising Burrows in *Visitors Reg.* pp. cxiii, cxxx).

[275] V-P's Reg. 18 Oct. 1662, fo. 93^{r–v}; HMC, *Leybourne–Popham MSS*, 186–7: 27 Dec. 1660.

[276] V-P's Reg. 10 Aug. 1660, fos. 87–8; F. J. Varley (ed.), *The Restoration Visitation of the University of Oxford and its Colleges* (Camden Soc. 3rd ser. 18, 1948), 21. Yate had by now recovered the living of Middleton Cheney, the advowson of which he had bought in 1639 and which in 1682 he bequeathed to the college; from 1661 it was occupied by his brother Samuel (Wood, *Fasti*, pt. 2 (1820), 238).

it to save chardges (and trulie that is a strong argument with him) or rather to be seated in such a convenient place, that he may have an Eye, and an eare, to heare and see, what ever is spoken or done in ye college...soe hee, his mistresse and his Presbyterian gang may att their gossopping conventicles pass their sencures uppon you...But I forget myselfe...and I owe a fayre respect to doctor Greenwood, and what I have spoken is meerely out of ye deep sense and care I have to preserve ye Coll. in united peace, which is too often interrupted by dilaters [i.e. temporisers], whisperers, and censurers.[277]

Be that as it may, collegiate amity prevailed. Dr and Mrs Yate moved into the Lodgings, and on 11 August 1660 the restored Principal was installed at last in the familiar chapel on staircase I. One of his first actions was to bring back his former colleague Newton in place of the intruded Bruen.[278] Soon afterwards Ridgway also was removed. He made way for the 'illegally ejected' Church.[279] Vice-Principal Burscough was less of a problem. He resigned his Fellowship in 1663. And Richard Duckworth seems to have made his peace with the restored regime. Houghton might suspect his 'morose, factious disposicon'. But he had at least one redeeming hobby: his *Tintinnalogia* (1668) was the first book ever published in English on the cheerful art of change ringing. So Duckworth remained for some time as Bursar and Vice-Principal before moving on to Steeple Aston and St Alban Hall.[280] When at last the new chapel was consecrated in 1666 it was Ralph Rawson—another 'outed' Fellow now happily restored—who delivered the Principalian sermon.[281] For another twenty-one years Yate would live on in the Lodgings. Much of his time must have been occupied in compiling 'Schedula & Abstracta' (1668), a manuscript register of primary sources indispensable for the history of Brasenose. He died at last in 1681, aged 78, honoured as a remarkable survivor, if not quite a third founder, and was buried in the new-built cloister.[282]

[277] Three letters—29 Aug., 30 Aug., and 10 Sept. 1660—from Houghton to Yate 'att his house by ye Plow stables in Lyncoln Inn ffields' (*Quat. Mon.* XI, 64 and XII, 33–6).

[278] V-P's Reg. 10 Aug. 1660, fo. 87ᵛ. Bruen had succeeded Robert Eaton in the living of Cuddesdon in 1657 (V-P's Reg. 17 Oct. 1648, fo. 72ᵛ; *Visitors' Register*, 435: 17 Dec. 1657). Newton 'died suddenly of an apoplexy at morning prayers in the College chapell...12 April 1664, and was buried in St. Marye's church' (Wood, *Life and Times*, ii. 9).

[279] V-P's Reg. 28 Aug. 1660. Church was buried in the cloister in 1677 (Wood, *Colleges and Halls*, 378).

[280] V-P's Reg. 18 Oct. 1662, fo. 92ᵛ; *Restoration Visitation*, 38; *ODNB*. Memorial in Steeple Aston church. In 1688 he refurbished the school established by Radcliffe in 1640.

[281] V-P's Reg. 13 Aug. 1660, fo. 87ᵛ. 'A very learned and orthodox divine who had been ejected by the rebels in 1648' (Wood, *Annals*, ii, pt. ii, 596). Rawson became Rector of Great Rollright in 1667, and died there in 1687 (Wood, *Life and Times*, iii. 216). See also Sir A. Cockayne, *Chain of Golden Poems* (1658), 207.

[282] 'A parricidis democraticis | Qui Academiam sub visitationis praetextu divastarunt | Exauctoratus...' (Wood, *Colleges and Halls*, 376). 'Principal Yate's Book' is now A3.19.

The Interregnum had been a traumatic time for Oxford, and of course for Brasenose. It is easy to forget the catastrophic nature of the civil war. More men were killed in Britain per head of population than in either the First or Second World Wars.[283] Oxford was never seriously besieged; the colleges emerged—apart from the loss of their plate—more or less intact. But the University had to endure all the disruption of military rule. Teaching had been interrupted if not suspended. Offices and degrees had been showered on parliamentary supporters. 'Brewers, tailors, goldsmiths, shoemakers': on one day in May 1649, seven regicides had been turned into Masters of Arts. Cromwell himself became a Doctor of Law. The following year he became Chancellor. All the old landmarks seemed to be crumbling away. In 1655–6, Vice-Chancellor Owen attempted to transfer teaching from college to University: that way it might be more easily controlled. He toyed with the idea of replacing episcopal Visitors with parliamentary nominees. He even tried to abolish cap and gown.[284]

Anthony Wood—whose memoirs throughout this period are indispensable—had little good to say about these years. He loathed his new masters, especially the Cambridge men, and he had no time for parvenu puritans.

instead of a cup of college beare and a stir'd machet [salad] which use to be the antient way of entertaining in a College at 3 or 4 in the afternoon, they would entertain with tarts, custards, cheescakes, or any other junkets that were in season...They encouraged instrumental musik...but [not] vocall musik...because used by the prelatical party in their devotions. They were great enimies to May-games...as May-poles, morrices, Whitson ales; nay, scarce wakes. They would not suffer any common players...nor scholars to act in privat...[nor] any swearing or cursing...[or] public drunkenness...Wee had no coffey houses then...Discipline [was] strict and severe; disputations and lectures often; catechising, frequent; prayers, in most tutors' chambers every night...[Altogether there was] Preaching and praying, too much...

And in the streets of Oxford he sensed the signs of something bigger still, a wholesale transfer of power and wealth.

---

[283] C. Carlton, *Going to the Wars: The Experience of Civil War in the British Isles,* 1638–1660 (1992), 214; S. Porter, *Destruction in the English Civil Wars* (Stroud, 1994). For the royalist Oxford garrison's treaty of surrender, guaranteeing 'all Churches Chapells Colleges Halls Librarys and Schooles', against 'defaceing or spoyle', see Bodl. MS Add. D 114, fo. 14: 22 May 1646.

[284] As 'reliques of popery'. See D. Holles, *Memoirs* (1699), 149; B. Worden, in *HUO* iv. 745. The Visitorship of Brasenose was to have been vested in Sir John Glynne and his successors at the King's Bench (Wood, *Annals*, ii, pt. ii, 680). For the awarding of degrees to 'great favourites of Cromwell', see Wood, *Fasti*, pt. 2, 129–38.

Many...that were the sons of upstart gentlemen, such that had got the good places into their hands...and had bought the lands of the clergy and gentry...bishops', deanes', and royallist lands...were generally very proud, saucy, impudent, and seldom gave respect to any but the leading person [of the new regime]. As for any of the old stock [i.e. pre-1641 Fellows], they laughed and flouted at them, scarse gave them the wall, much less the common civility of a hat: and so it was that the ancient gentry of the nation were dispised... [In short], money [was] then stirring, and comming from the new gentlemen.[285]

Still, the audit of war was by no means all one way. In the University, teaching and disputation had been reinvigorated. Foreign scholars arrived to study in the Bodleian. New talent had been recruited: Petty's career is testimony to that. A scientific revolution had been born. Petty's name will stand with those of Wren and Wilkins, Wallis, Boyle and Bathurst. Brasenose itself played only a small part in this renaissance. But the college was now in a position to attract students of quality. The poet Thomas Traherne came up in 1653; the same year as no fewer than three future bishops. Traherne's name survives in the Buttery Book, opposite that of William Petty. And while he was there it was Traherne who—in his own words—'received the taste and tincture of another education [altogether]'.

I saw there were things in this world of which I never dreamed; glorious secrets, and glorious persons past imagination. There I saw...logic, ethics, physics, metaphysics, geometry, astronomy, poesy, medicine, grammar, music, rhetoric, all kinds of arts, trades and mechanisms...[286]

As an undergraduate Traherne conformed to puritan attitudes. Only after the Restoration would he develop his lyrical vision of the Anglican ideal. Meanwhile, as a Herefordshire vicar, he was able to revisit the Bodleian, 'the Glory of Oxford, and this Nation'. Strolling in 'the New-Parks' he could still debate, with the occasional 'Grave Person', the persistent errors of popery. Such were the privileges of collegiate membership. In the evolving processes of higher learning—transcending the boundaries of knowing, galvanizing the mind of youth—Brasenose was now playing a significant part. And the setting for that performance—the architecture of the college—was about to be transformed.

[285] Wood, *Life and Times*, i. 298–301.
[286] T. Traherne, *Centuries, Poems and Thanksgivings*, ed. H. M. Margoliouth, i (Oxford, 1958), 132; *ODNB*. For his undergraduate reading see Bodl. MS Lat. misc., fo. 45. For foreign scholars in the Bodleian during the 1560s, see Wood, *Fasti*, pt. 2, *passim*. Interregnum scholarship was famously praised by Carlyle: 'Not easily before or since could the Two Universities give such an account of themselves to mankind, under all categories, human and divine, as during those Puritan years' (*Oliver Cromwell's Letters and Speeches*, ed. T. Carlyle, ii (1897), 286).

When asked to defend his record by the King's Visitors of 1660, Principal
Greenwood was justifiably proud. At his appointment in 1648, he claimed,
the college was between £12,000 and £13,000 in debt, 'all which I did fully
discharge in the space of two or three yeares; and have not onley provided a
sufficient stock to lay out beforehand for necessaries; but wee have beene
able to contribute and lend large summes toward the erecting and furnishing
of our new buildings'.[287] Quite so. In 1656 Brasenose began to build a new
chapel; in 1657–8 a new library and cloister.[288] Here, in effect, was a
new quadrangle, worthy of any of the smaller colleges of Oxford. Crucially,
it was an enterprise that brought together both sides in the civil war.
Collegiate loyalty came to count for more than the memory of political
animosities. It was Radcliffe who had begun to work towards this goal,
from the very start of his Principalship in 1614.[289] It was under Greenwood
that the first stone of the chapel was laid on 18 June 1656.[290] It was Yate who
presided over consecration on 17 November 1666.[291] Both sides in the war
contributed to the building fund. Radcliffe's benefaction, as we shall see, was
princely. Those of Yate and Greenwood were smaller, but symbolically
significant. John Cartwright (parliamentarian) gave £120: his arms still decorate the organ screen. Thomas Church (royalist) gave £300, as well as a
silver alms dish. Familiar Brasenose names fill up the list: Wilbraham and
Leigh, Cholmondeley and Shakerley, Manwaring, Stanley, and Moseley. By
1671 the total subscribed came to £4,775 4s. 4d.[292] Both sides in the recent
troubles must have recognized that the college had come very close to
collapse. Radcliffe, Greenwood, and Yate: parliamentarian, Presbyterian,
royalist; loyalty to Brasenose proved in the end more powerful than the
competing interests of all three. And yet each ended his days in very different
circumstances. Radcliffe was buried quietly in Holywell churchyard;[293] Yate
with collegiate ceremony at the entrance to the cloister.[294] But Greenwood
the intruder rests today in the chancel at Steeple Aston.

[287] PRI 1 A1/3, quoted by Twigg, in *HUO* iv. 799–800.

[288] Clennell A 3.20 [Houghton's] 'Booke of Accounts'; Bursarial—money 1.

[289] Contributions for the chapel date from 1613 onwards (*VCH Oxon.*, iii. 216).

[290] 'Foundacion of ye Chapple was layd on Wednesday ye 18. of June. 1656' (Clennell
A 3.19).

[291] Consecration by Walter Blandford, Bishop of Oxford; sermon by Ralph Rawson on
Exodus 20: 24 (Bodl. MS Wood F.28, fos. 158–60). Full details of the form of service are
printed in *Quat. Mon.* XII, 43–58 and *Collectanea*, iv (OHS 1905), 157–64. The party afterwards
must have been quite an event: bills include £14 6s. 0d. 'for wine', £1 17s. 0d. 'for a firkin of
Sturgeon', and 14s. 6d. 'for bottles lost and glasses broken up' (B 2a 42).

[292] Calculated in *Quat. Mon.* III, 15, from Clennell A 3.20, tipped in.

[293] *Collectanea*, iv. 110 n. 6; Wood, *City of Oxford*, iii. 246.

[294] V-P's Reg. 22 Apr. 1681, fos. 120–1.

It had long been Radcliffe's belief that fragments of irregular masonry on the south side of the former chapel clearly indicated expansionist intentions: a second quadrangle, containing a larger library and chapel, had presumably been planned from the start.[295] That supposition made sense. It explained the retention of the old kitchen as a temporary expedient prior to the building of a second quadrangle. The presumption that a new chapel would have to be built goes back at least to 1613, when James Lingham subscribed £140 for that purpose.[296] Principal Singleton made his own contribution the following year; and more might have been collected had not Radcliffe been diverted by a dispute with Christ Church over land. Only when this matter was settled in 1656—and the details of Radcliffe's will finally arranged—was it possible to start digging the foundations of the chapel.[297]

Meanwhile, other plans had for some time been in contemplation at University level. Radcliffe must certainly have been aware of these. Around the date of his appointment as Chancellor in 1630, Laud was already toying with the idea of a central square or piazza. As part of a master plan to rearrange the ceremonial operations of the University—removing from St Mary's, for example, all judicial, administrative, and celebratory functions—he 'had a design to open [a] great square ... between St. Marie's and the Schools [later Bodleian], Brasen-nose and All Souls'.[298] Whether the Chancellor actually took His Majesty up to the roof of the old schools' quadrangle, to examine the possibilities of the site, must probably remain uncertain. But Charles I undoubtedly warmed to the idea. In September 1629 we find him writing to the Vice-Chancellor regarding this warren of unprepossessing properties: 'Certain houses, situate betwixt All Souls and Brasenose, in some kind take off the lustre and dignity of the University ... [Is it possible] to ascertain to whom those houses belong, and the value thereof ... [?]'[299] That triggered a number of competing claimants. Christ Church, for one, was anxious to contest the 'unfounded claims set up by Brasenose to Black Hall, Glazing Hall, and Staple Hall, which lie between St. Mary's and the Schools'.[300] But before much progress could be made, events of more immediate import supervened. Principal Radcliffe was thrown back on the affairs of Brasenose.

During the mid-1630s Radcliffe funded several building works designed to accommodate the pre-civil-war boom in undergraduate recruitment. In 1635

---

[295] Hurst Oxford r 7, cited in *VCH Oxon.*, iii. 215 (corrected).

[296] Hurst College: Chapel, 3, cited ibid. 216 (corrected).

[297] Ibid. 217; *Quat. Mon.* III, 16.

[298] Laud, *Works*, iii. 254; *A Breviate of the Life of William Laud, Extracted from his Own Diary* (1644), 28; *Collectanea*, iv. 200.

[299] *Cal. State Papers Domestic* 1629–31, 46–7: 1 Sept. 1629.

[300] Ibid. 57: 12 Sept. 1629.

he personally 'payd for ye Buildinge of ye Cocklofts [and] Battlements' on the south side of the quadrangle 'out of his owne purse'. That is, he constructed a third storey on the hall side to match the range of dormers already added from 1604 onwards to the east, west, and north. The total cost was more than £200.[301] About the same time he made considerable improvements to the Lodgings: 'compass' or oriel windows facing School Street; new 'stayers, closets, studdyes, hangings, furniture'; an heraldic chimneypiece and 'flowring wainscot' in one room on staircase VI (now the Principal's drawing room); and a beamed and patterned ceiling in the room above the gateway (now the Tower Bursary).[302]

But he was determined to go still further. In his will he left money to build 'a Chappell on ye backe of ye hall... which chapell soe erected will make ye south side of a Quadrangle answearable to ye Hall yt. maketh ye north side'. There was also to be 'a [library] buildinge upon Pillars... which will make a walke under it, ye greate want of Brasennose Colledge, and this will make ye East side of a Quadrangle and the Kitchen ye West side'.[303] For this purpose Radcliffe bequeathed the whole of his estate of Piddington Grange in Northamptonshire; its sale value came to £1,850.[304] Roughly speaking, the new library was to occupy the site of old Salissury Hall. The new chapel—dedicated to St Hugh and St Chad: representing the old collegiate dioceses of Lincoln and Lichfield—was to stand on the site of the former Little St Edmund Hall. As he lay dying in the Lodgings—the staircase guarded by Lord Pembroke's musketeers—Radcliffe may perhaps have drawn some comfort from this forty-year-old dream. One day there would be not only a new quadrangle, but a grandiose frontage facing a spacious academic forum (pl. 7).

The new chapel, library, and cloister were not to be completed until eighteen years after Radcliffe's death. The foundations of the chapel—in places 20 ft deep—were begun in June 1656. 'The Little Cloyster began to be digged' in March 1657. The foundation of the library 'began to be layd' in

---

[301] Clennell A 3.20 tipped in, and Hurst College: Buildings 5, 8, 10, 11. The mason was Richard Maude. The carpenter was Chrysostom Parks. Chambers had already been built in 1605–7 over the old chapel and old library (Hurst College: Buildings 2). The visit of James I to Brasenose in 1605 may give a clue to the dating of this work. But no documentation survives to date the dormer ranges, except on the southern side. See also *Quat. Mon.* III, 12, 23 and E. Boardman in *Brazen Nose*, xxxv. 28 *et seq.* 'Dagg' or 'Dog Lane'—the passage from the Old Quad into the later 'Deer Park'—had been created in 1609 (dated spandrel, since removed).

[302] *Quat. Mon.* III, 13. Radcliffe's arms survive on the (Old Parlour) oriel, between what were originally those of Smith and Sutton. Those of the matching oriel on the northern side have been restored away. Inside VI, 4 his arms are still emblazoned alongside those of Smith and Sutton.

[303] Hurst College: Principal 4 (copy of will dated 24 Apr. 1648, cited by Boardman in *Brazen Nose*, xxxv. 30–1); 'Principal Yate's Book', fo. 225; *Quat. Mon.* III, 15 and IV, 23.

[304] Clennell A 3.20, tipped in.

March 1658. Then came the slow process of construction. Not until 1664 did the library receive its books.[305] Not until 1666 would the chapel be consecrated. The date of construction for the balancing screen wall—hiding the kitchen entrance and shown in Loggan's print of 1675 (pl. 7) and Williams's of 1730—is not exactly clear. But by the end of 1666 each of the three main elements of the programme was at last in use. In total, nearly £4,000 had been spent.[306] Of this very considerable sum almost half came from the estate of Samuel Radcliffe. We can therefore forgive two striking armorial conceits. Inside the chapel it is Radcliffe's coat of arms, rather than any religious symbol, that boldly confronts the altar. And outside, on the east front, it is again Radcliffe's escutcheon—not the arms of Brasenose—that greets the eyes of countless tourists as they wander in Radcliffe Square. The arms of Yate are restricted to the interior of the library.

Unlike the first programme of building at Brasenose, this second, seventeenth-century phase is well documented. Bursar Houghton kept meticulous accounts: from 'mending a mattock, 2d.', to 'Mr. John Jackson, overseer of the Building, his wages...20s per week'.[307] Here we can watch the progress of the new chapel from 1656 to 1663, from foundation to glazing. After that we have details of chapel fittings and consecration: purple velvet on altar, pulpit, and cushions; crimson damask and golden fringe; and '2 great brasse branches' or candlesticks. And both before and after these items in Houghton's record, we have notes in the Principal's Fine Book, detailing for example the cutting of timber in Myncherey Wood, Headington, and the felling of trees for scaffolding at Tiptofts in Essex.[308] We know the master joiner: John Wild of London. We know the master carver: a local man, Simon White (22d. per day). He carved the urns of Burford stone—described as 'Bottle creasts'—over each of the chapel buttresses; he received £1 for the 'two Ionick capitals' hung with garlands, on the north doorway of the antechapel; in 1659 he carved 'the frontispiece over the cloyster door [fronting School Street]...with ye King's arms [placed optimistically] over a shield'; and in 1666 he received £52 10s. 0d. for laying the floor of chapel and antechapel

[305] Tables were bought in 1672; extra chains in 1673. Portraits of Joyce Frankland, Lord Mordaunt, and Dean Nowell—variants of those in hall today—hung in the library until displaced by books in 1771. See Wood, *Colleges and Halls: Appendix*, 275; Bodl. MS Top. Oxon. e 286, fos. 110–11 (56ᵛ–57ʳ). They were then transferred to the Tower Bursary, and then to the SCR (Frankland), Lodgings (Mordaunt), and Bodleian (Nowell).
[306] Calculated from A 3.20 by E. W. Allfrey, in *Quat. Mon.* III, 24.
[307] Houghton's 'Book of Accounts of the New Buildings at Brasenose' (Clennell A 3.20, fos. 3 and 7). Selected details quoted by Allfrey, in *Quat. Mon.* III, 14 *et seq.* and by Boardman, in *Brazen Nose*, xxxv, 31–2. Bursar's accounts (1644–1799) and tradesmen's bills (1691–1810) survive.
[308] Organized by Houghton and Petty (Principal's Fine Book: B 1d 36, 7 Mar. 1651 and 9 Apr. 1658). See *Quat. Mon.* III, 16 and 63–4.

with black and white marble sections.[309] Most important of all, we know the name of the master mason or 'overseer' of the whole operation: 'Mr. Jackson surveyor'. Both prefix and suffix are significant. In the slow emerging of the architectural profession, *Mr* Jackson had a particular part to play. It was he who supplied the 'modell' for the elaborate wood and plaster fan vault: for this, 'and his paines taken about it', he received £20 on 5 November 1659. He had already been responsible for building Canterbury Quadrangle at St John's and the Baroque porch of St Mary's. He rests today in the church of St Mary Magdalen, 'an ingenious artist, a loyall subject, an honest man and a good neighbour'.[310] Brasenose has good reason to remember him.

When the site of old St Mary's College—later the site of Frewin Hall—was let out in 1649, Brasenose had reserved the right 'to enter in with workmen and labourers, carts and horses, to pull down the old Chapel, and to carry away the materials to build the new Chapel according to the intentions of the last will and testament of Samuel Radcliffe'. Now St Mary's had been a monastic foundation, a college for Augustinian canons. Erasmus had studied there during his months in Oxford. Like Oseney and Godstow, like Abingdon and Rewley, it eventually succumbed to the Reformation. Its buildings were secularized and its lands were sold. It was the Earl of Huntingdon who, in 1580, made it over to Brasenose.[311] And it was the policy of Brasenose that turned it, effectively, into a quarry. By June 1656, when the foundations of Radcliffe's new chapel had at last been begun, arrangements were already in place to transfer any surviving building materials from New Inn Hall Street to School Street. During March and April 1656 'ye Roofe of ye Old Chapple' was dismantled, piece by piece, and transported in carts to Brasenose. No doubt the labourers' 'bevers'—that is, their daily refreshments—were particularly welcome on this occasion, 'the work being very dangerous'. And as the building began to rise, another set of fragments was brought in: 'Payd Wm. Redhead one days work with his Team, in bringing ye window James [jambs] from ye old Chapel.' Just before Christmas 1657 the bones of the new roof were hauled into place, by means of a 'brass pullye to wind up the great Tymber of the chapple'.[312]

---

[309] Clennell A 3.20; *Quat. Mon.* III, 22, 24.

[310] Epitaph quoted in Wood, *City of Oxford*, iii. 142–3. For the 'modell', see A 3.20, fo. 87.

[311] Hurst: Oxford u 2–3, 21; 'Principal Yate's Book', 126–7. See also J. Blair, in *Harlaxton Symposium* (1999), ed. J. Stratford and C. M. Barron (Donington, 2002), and *Brazen Nose*, xvii, 236–9. Camden called him "a zealous Puritan" (*Complete Peerage* vi, 657).

[312] Clennell A 3.20 quoted in J. Blair, 'Frewin Hall', *Oxoniensia*, 43 (1978), 72 *et seq*. For a definitive explanation of the ceiling vault, its genesis and construction, see ibid. 78 *et seq*. In 1675 'ye old chapell doore' from the former St Mary's College (not, presumably, the old Brasenose chapel on staircase I) was sold off to the University Church for £15 (B 2a. 42: Coxhill's notes, 1675).

1. **Lady Margaret Beaufort, Countess of Richmond and Derby (1443–1509).**

   Posthumous portrait, on canvas, in Common Room; bequeathed to
   Brasenose by a descendant of her dean of chapel.

   Mother of Henry VII; benefactress of education; patron of William Smith,
   Bishop of Lincoln, and of Sir Richard Sutton.

2. **William Smith, Bishop of Lincoln (1460–1514).**
Portrait in stained glass, in Hall, *c.*1635.
Co-Founder of Brasenose.

3. Sir Richard Sutton (*c.*1460–1524).
Portrait in stained glass, in Hall, *c.*1635.
Co-Founder of Brasenose.

4. **The Brazen Nose (12th Century).**
    The brass sanctuary knocker from which, according to tradition, Brasenose
    takes its name. It was recovered from Stamford, Lincolnshire, in 1890, and
    set up over High Table.

5. **A. The Brazen Nose over the college gateway.** Recorded as early as 1534.

B. Caricature Nose (*c.*1635). Stained glass in Hall, north bay window.

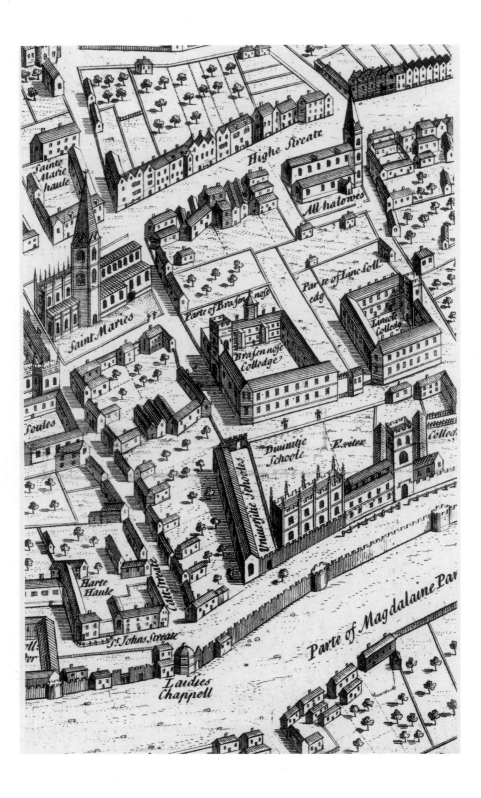

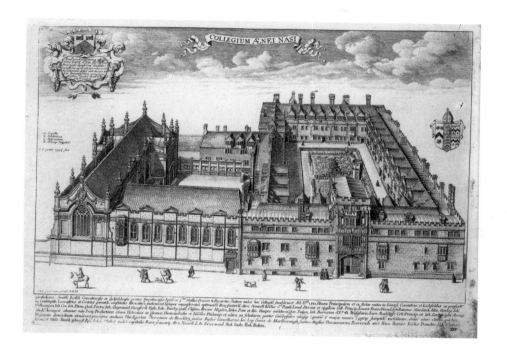

7. **Brasenose College, 1674.**
Engraved by David Loggan for *Oxonia Illustrata* (1675).
Note the formal garden in Old Quad, and cloister in Deer Park

(opposite)

6. **Bird's eye view of Brasenose, 1578.**
From a map of Oxford (1578), drawn by Radulph Agas; re-engraved from a copy by
Whittlesey, 1728.

8. **Pair of chalices and pattens, silver-gilt (1498–9).**
   Hall-marked 1498–9; re-gilded 1676 and 1749.
   Presented to Brasenose by William Smith, Bishop of Lincoln, probably before 1509.
   Rare survivals of the Reformation and Civil War.

9. **Alexander Nowell (1507–1601).**
Master of Westminster School; Dean of St. Paul's; Principal in 1595.
Portrait in Hall, perhaps contemporary, inscribed 'Piscator Hominum'.
Benefactor; angler; 'inventor' of bottled beer. His fishing rods hang above him.
One of the founding-fathers of the Anglican Reformation.

10. **Joyce Frankland (née Trappes; 1531–87).**

Portrait, on canvas, 1586.

Mrs. Frankland was the daughter and heiress of Robert Trappes, twice Prime Warden of the Goldsmiths' Company of London.

Benefactress.

11. **John, 2nd Baron Mordaunt (1508–71).**

Portrait, on canvas, in Hall, by Gilbert Jackson, *c.*1638; after original on panel in the Principal's Lodgings, 1564.

Benefactor.

The crucifix emphasises the Mordaunt family's Catholicism.

12. **Samuel Radcliffe (1580–1648).**
    Principal, 1614–48.
    Portrait, on canvas, in the Principal's Lodgings, 1623.
    Benefactor.
    Died in the Old Lodgings, with Parliamentary soldiers at the door.

13. **Thomas Yate (1603–1681).**

Principal, 1648 and 1660–81.

Contemporary portrait, on canvas, in Hall.

Twice Principal of Brasenose: elected by the Fellows 1648; removed by
Parliamentary Commissioners 1648; restored by Royal Commissioners 1660.

14. **Robert Burton** (1577–1640).
   Portrait, on canvas, in Common Room, by Gilbert Jackson, 1635.
   Author of *The Anatomy of Melancholy* (1621).

15. Sir William Petty, F.R.S. (1623–87).

Portrait by Isaac Fuller.

A 'universal genius'. 'One of the most rational men that I ever heard speak' (Samuel Pepys).

'His emphasis on the division of labour anticipates Adam Smith; his views on taxation anticipate Ricardo; and his macroeconomic outlook often anticipates Keynes' (Peter Sinclair).

16. The Radcliffe Cup (1610).

Silver-gilt, hall-marked 1610.

Presented to Samuel Radcliffe during his Proctorial year 1610, by Lord Chancellor Egerton, later Lord Ellesmere. Bequeathed to Brasenose in 1648 by Principal Radcliffe, for use at the Audit Feast on St. Thomas's Day, 21st December.

It was the survival of all these materials that dictated the form of the new building. Second-hand windows, second-hand roofing: Jackson had to cut his conception according to his cloth. At the same time, no architectural statement in Oxford could afford to ignore the current visual conventions. Two in particular: the survival of Gothic and the importation of Baroque. Hence the style—the perplexing, intriguingly hybrid style—of Brasenose College chapel.

Look at two features in particular: the traceried tableau of the exterior, facing east (pl. 7); and the strange fan vaulting of the interior (pl. 54). As seen from All Souls, the east front of Brasenose chapel is a conundrum. Its framework is Baroque: a pair of Corinthian pilasters, a Vignolan pediment broken and scrolled, and a battery of swags and urns. Its centrepiece, however, is Gothic: a traceried window, amended and adapted from fragments in old St Mary's. The link between these two elements—the germ of the whole conceit—may well lie in the woodcut frontispiece of a book published in Paris some twenty years before: J. Barbet's *Livre d'architecture* (1633).[313] There was, after all, a copy in the Bodleian. Whatever its source, Brasenose now had a chapel with a grand façade. And it faced not inwards towards the college, but outwards: towards an unbuilt square that would one day be named after another patron with a familiar surname, a fashionable physician called John Radcliffe.

The cloister through which the chapel was originally entered is oddly eclectic: narrow, late Gothic windows, stumpy classical pilasters, and a crudely detailed barrel vault (pl. 62). But the interior of the chapel is more intriguing still (pl. 54). Here the early sixteenth-century hammer-beamed roof, imported from old St Mary's, has been ingeniously disguised by a hanging fan vault of wood and plaster. The decision to adopt this prestigious device may have been taken during 1658, while work was temporarily suspended. In 1909 E. W. Allfrey explained the process of design:

The points of the hammer-beams gave [Jackson] the line for his pendents . . . from these the ribs of the vaulting spring . . . The hammer-beams themselves gave him a springing for short, low-pitched tunnel vaults, running north and south, to connect the wall above the window heads with the rest of his vaulting. These are stepped . . . in two levels. If he

---

[313] I owe this suggestion to Sir Howard Colvin. In 1845 the decayed tracery of the east window was replaced by Philip Hardwick; the old masonry was built into the garden wall of Denton House, near Cuddesdon (*Quat. Mon.* III, 32). There are other echoes elsewhere. The chapel of old Tabley Hall, Cheshire—built by Sir Peter Leycester in 1675–8—followed the interior of his own college chapel in several particulars. 'Ephraim Broadhurst of Knutsford, joyner, took his pattern [e.g. for the pulpit] from Brasenose College chapel in Oxford' (MS quoted by C. Hussey in *Country Life*, 66 (1923), 120). The chalice and paten presented to Tabley by Leycester in 1678 bear the same maker's mark (T.C.), as a pair of tripod candlesticks ('branches') at Brasenose (*Brazen Nose*, iii. 283). For Leycester, see *ODNB*.

had run his tunnel vault through at one level, the crown of it would have run out high above the head of the windows, and necessitated a gable over each window. The hammer-beams and the brackets below them are left to show below the new vault, and are ingeniously worked into the new design. All the rest of the old roof is up above, and out of sight. The effect . . . is successful.[314]

Indeed it is. Jackson the 'overseer', Jackson the 'surveyor'—more than a mason, less than an architect—has somehow subsumed archaeology and invention, image and actuality, into a single, soaring cadenza.

The rationale of late Gothic—survival or revival—has been the subject of prolonged debate. This mixture of late Decorated tracery and Perpendicular vaulting; this curious marriage of Renaissance and Gothic: what exactly is it? Mid-Victorian critics regarded it with distaste.[315] Mid-twentieth-century scholars viewed it with caution.[316] More recent judgements tend to be couched in relativistic terms: John Jackson emerges almost as a proto-postmodern eclectic.[317] And lately debate has shifted yet again, to conservationist arguments about polychrome.[318] Whatever the aesthetic verdict, here is an achievement all the more remarkable given the impermanence of its political context. This was a building programme—an Anglican manifesto—which ran right through both civil war and Interregnum. During the actual years of construction, nobody could predict the future of the college. 'God knows', Greenwood remarked at one point, 'how soon we may be dispersed'.[319]

[314] *Quat. Mon.* III, 28. For a cross-section, see R.C.H.M., *Oxford*, 27–8, pl. 77. The roof-space, floored at collar level, can still be entered through an external trap-door.

[315] E. A. Freeman was an exception: he regarded it as 'a daring piece of eclecticism . . . a living, developing, eclectic style' (*History of Architecture* (1849), 439–40). Ruskin was surprisingly generous: he admired the wreaths and swags on the Radcliffe Square front (*Works*, ed. E. T. Cook and A. Wedderburn I (1903), 121 n.: 'The Poetry of Architecture', para. 153).

[316] H. M. Colvin, 'Gothic Survival and Gothick Revival', in *Essays in English Architectural History* (1999), 217–44; A. Oswald in *Country Life*, 77 (1935), 192–7, 216–21.

[317] T. Mowl and B. Earnshaw, *Architecture without Kings* (Manchester, 1995), 198, pl. 105.

[318] When finished in January 1662, the ceiling was simply covered with 'whitening'. The first polychrome scheme—'blazon'd fair from roof to floor'—was devised by J. C. Buckler in 1859; the second by C. E. Kempe in 1895. Kempe's work was compromised in 1951 and 1980: the dark green walls were repainted, first in 'apricot cream' and then in off-white and magnolia (*Brazen Nose*, xvii. 98; xvii, no.1, 8 and no. 2, 115).

[319] *Quat. Mon.* XI, 60. The original seating arrangements are recorded in an almanac of Sir Holland Egerton, Bt. (MPP 10 A1), cited by R. W. Jeffery in *Brazen Nose*, iv. 185. The Principal and Vice-Principal sat where they do now, but the stalls next to each were reserved for the nobility. The adjacent stalls, that is the next three seats facing each other on either side, were for the six senior Fellows. The stalls after the first steps were given to the junior Fellows and MAs; and the last stalls on north and south were taken by 'Scholar Bachelors'. The lower row was divided into three, as now, on either side. The first block contained the gentlemen commoners, the second the commoner bachelors, and the third the junior commoners. In front of these was the 'Knife Board': a simple seat without any frontal praying desk. Here sat the 'Scholars and Bachelors'. In later years, Dean and Junior Dean sat in seats at the east or chancel end of the chapel.

But completed the chapel was, and the library and cloister too. And as the college moved prosperously through the later years of Charles II, improvements and refurbishments must have made the whole place increasingly agreeable. Not entirely, of course. Brasenose plumbing in the later seventeenth century remained obstinately primitive; pestilentially so. The construction of Radcliffe's new quadrangle may actually have made things worse.

To the west of the Chapel lay the College privy, indelicately known as the 'bogg house', with a vault beneath it some forty feet long, ten feet wide and twenty feet deep. This had been emptied every sixteen years or so by digging a hole in the open yard in front of it, removing the contents of the vault and recovering it with earth, all at a cost of about £30 a time. However, 'after this Court or Yard had the new Chappell, the Cloyster & Library built upon it...there was then no way left to emptie it but at a farr greater charg then usually, and without a very great annoyance both to the Colledg: and all the Neighbourhood about it'...

[The] vault under the privy [now became] 'full within a very little of the florre' A system of drains and filters was [therefore] constructed, which could double as a tunnel for access when clearing the vault was necessary; the entrance was apparently in the College wood yard south of the Chapel. One of the side effects of this was to increase the difficulty of clearing the vault; by 1792 it was costing £115 and taking thirty weeks.[320]

Even so, the Fellows must have been understandably proud. They had spent some £4,000 on new buildings without incurring any significant debt. By 1680 college revenue was reckoned at a healthy £600 p.a.[321] There were new cellars south of the tower to accommodate the Principal's kitchen. There was a new chimneypiece and new panelling in what is now the Tower Bursary;[322] and Tudor wainscoting from the hall had been redistributed among several rooms around the first quadrangle.[323] The old chapel and antechapel had already been converted into rooms in 1667. There was at last—from 1682 at least—a Senior Common Room (i.e. the Common Fire

[320] Boardman, in *Brazen Nose*, xxxv. 32, citing Clennell A 3.19 and *Quat. Mon.* III, appendix D, 67–8. The layout of the 'bogg house'—otherwise known as 'the Confables' or 'House of Office'—is shown in W. Williams, *Oxonia Depicta* (1730–3), pl. xxxv.

[321] Bodl. MS Eng. Hist. d1, pp. 108–9. However, this represented only half that of Merton and Corpus; less than half that of All Souls; one-fifth of New College; one-sixth of Magdalen; and only one-tenth of Christ Church.

[322] In 1863, J. C. Buckler thought that the original couplet windows had been made 'triplets at the expense of the blank tracery' (V-P's Reg. 21 Dec. 1863, fo. 190). In fact these triplets—with timber mullions of 1817 by Hakewill (V-P's Reg. Mich. 1817, fo. 99)—must themselves have replaced early 18th-century sashes. Buckler regretted that his restoration work—Taynton instead of Headington stone—stopped short at the interior: he found that a Tudor chimneypiece in the tower had been 'shockingly defaced' in the late 17th century.

[323] *Quat. Mon.* III, 39.

Room, probably II, 3).[324] There were—improbably enough—vines climbing
up the sunny southern side of the new chapel; from 1696 there would even be
a new brew house, fairly close to the kitchen.[325] And from 1700 onwards Ale
Verses would be recited annually in hall, on the occasion of the Shrove
Tuesday feast. The Restoration had clearly given Brasenose new impetus.
From 1663 the very nose on the college gate had begun to shine with
unaccustomed 'guilding'. In that year the old library on staircase IV had
been 'converted into a Chamber and two Studies'. And in 1678 the same
rooms were handsomely repanelled in Flanders oak at a cost of £45, by the
ablest joiner in Oxford, Arthur Frogley.[326]

It was Frogley too—'ffrogley ye Joyner'—who was chiefly responsible for
the transformation of the hall. First, in 1680, came the raising of the floor
level to accommodate a new wine cellar. Then in 1683 came the removal of
the minstrels' gallery and reconstruction of the roof, once again using
materials from old St Mary's. This involved the installation of high-arched
open timbering: cambered collar-beam trusses, with wind-braces between the
purlins. Not until 1751–2 would this grand but rustic roof—smoke blackened
and grimy no doubt—be disguised by a chastely plastered barrel vault.
Finally, it must also have been in 1683–4 that the hall was widened towards
the south with another bay or 'compassed window' at the dais end; at the
same time all the old wainscoting was removed and replaced right up to
cornice level. Brasenose now possessed a dining hall which was considerably
grander, in fact it was virtually new (pl. 69).

Frogley's bill, dated 18 November 1684,[327] for panelling the hall in oak and
making tables and benches, is so resonant with associations that it merits
reprinting in full. Here are the doors, the tables, the very benches, that have
served Brasenose so well for more than three centuries.

---

[324] Merton, Lincoln, and Trinity had introduced Senior Common Rooms in the 1660s.
Staircase II formerly boasted an exterior inscription, long illegible and now removed. Smith's
arms are discernible on the upper floor in Williams, *Oxonia Depicta*, pl. xxxvi.

[325] '1691 To Tom for training and nailing the vines behind the chapel. 1s 7d.' (B 2a. 42:
Coxhill's notes). For the brew house, see Hurst College: Buildings 21, cited by Boardman in
Brazen Nose, xxxv. 37. The jocular term 'Deer Park' dates only from the mid 19th C.

[326] Principal's Fine Book: B1d 36, 1691; R.C.H.M., *Oxford*, 25–6; Wood, *Colleges and Halls*,
371. See also *Quat. Mon.* III, 37–8; VIII, 7; XII, 13; XIII, 52; *Brazen Nose*, iv. 23, citing Bursar's
rolls of account. Thomas Hinde, the Bursar, did not enjoy the new IV, 4 for long: he resigned
in 1670 to become Dean of Limerick. His carved chimneypiece has gone, and the two coats of
arms. For gilding the nose, see Jeffery in *Brazen Nose*, iv. 30, citing Bursar's rolls of account,
11 July 1663.

[327] *Quat. Mon.* III, 66. For the wine cellar, with its three pillars, one marked 1680, see *Brazen
Nose*, iv. 22–3. The details of the new roof are by no means clear. But Madan found that 'the
principal rafters of the chapel and of the western part of the hall are numbered consecutively,
as if they once belonged to a single building' (i.e. old St Mary's College). See A. Clark (ed.), *The
Colleges of Oxford* (1891), 266. The future James II visited the college in May 1683.

	£	s	d
379yds 2ft of Wainscot at 8/6 ye yd	161	3	6
For 2 planks to make uprights to set ye benches on	2	0	0
For boards to line ye top of ye cornish round ye Hall		10	0
For 2 pair of open doors in ye Skreen	4	0	0
For taking down ye old Wainscot & [wall] benches		10	0
For ye upper tables [i.e. table tops]	10	0	0
For four formes [i.e. benches]	2	4	0
For a chair	1	0	0
For a side table with two drawers in it	1	10	0
For another side table		12	0
for a desk	4	0	0
for toners [i.e. polishers] & frames for six tables	28	0	0
for ten formes [i.e. benches]	6	0	0
For a salt box & 3 [notice] boards for [examination] schemes		15	0
	£222	4	6

In the same year, 1684, John Hugeloot 'ye carver' was paid £12 'for carving ye King's Arms' over high table, plus £1 16s 0d. for 'carving ye founders' Arms' above the screens passage. And it was Frogley who set up for posterity those flamboyant symbols of college loyalty—the rampant lion, the priapic unicorn—fixing them firmly with 'stuff and glew'.[328]

But Brasenose had one more storm to navigate before it could settle into the quieter waters of the eighteenth century. There had been no difficulty over loyalty to the restored monarchy. When the King's Commissioners arrived in February 1661 to administer the Oaths of Supremacy and Allegiance, they were welcomed by the Fellowship and entertained with 'Biskets ... and 4 bottle of sack'.[329] Religion, however, was more of a problem. The Restoration settlement had reimposed the Laudian church. By the Act of Uniformity (1662), every Fellow had to accept the 'liturgy of the Church of England as it is now by law established'.[330] The penalty for refusal was deprivation of office; such 'promotions [being] void as if [the incumbent] was naturally dead'. Principal Yate had publicly to subscribe to the Thirty-Nine Articles and Book of Common Prayer. In his case that was easily done. For others it was less straightforward. Thomas Adams, a Fellow since 1652, resigned rather than compromise. He was eventually found a post as chaplain to the Dowager Countess of Clare. Bursar

---

[328] *Brazen Nose*, iv. 23, citing Bursar's Accounts. For specific donations towards refurbishment, 1683–4, see *Quat. Mon.* IV, 53–4.

[329] Bursar's rolls of account, 11 Feb. 1661, cited by Jeffery in *Brazen Nose*, iv. 26. For the activities of the Commissioners, 11 Sept. 1660–24 July 1662, see Bodl. MS Top. Oxon. d 157.

[330] 14 Car. II, c. 4: *Statutes of the Realm*, v. 364–70; Wood, *Colleges and Halls*, 108. College services, however, could still be conducted in Latin.

Houghton—not necessarily for religious reasons—secured himself an equally timely retreat. He moved into Black Hall, just opposite the college gateway, and rented out rooms to selected scholars. He even added a three-storey wing to his new home.[331] When he died there in 1677 he was buried in the very cloister he had recently constructed. Otherwise, the Fellowship raised no objection to the new regime. The rearrangements of 1660 were clearly less acrimonious than those of 1648. Like most other colleges—like the rest of the country in fact—Brasenose had simply had enough of revolutions.

One example of this process—a weary acceptance of the inevitable; rebellion dwindling into royalism—will have to suffice. Richard Norton matriculated in 1631. He began as one of Cromwell's colonels of horse; he fought at the siege of Basing House; he sat in both the Long Parliament and the Cavalier Parliament; and he ended as a prime supporter of the Restoration settlement. First Calvinist, then Presbyterian, then Independent, then royalist, 'idle Dick Norton' relearned his loyalty the hard way. Having resisted the unparliamentary governance of Strafford and Laud; having endured the repression of puritan rule, he settled in the end for a procrustean Anglican establishment, the regime of Clarendon and Sheldon.[332]

From this settlement of 1660–2, however, two groups were rigidly excluded: Roman Catholics and Dissenters. The Prayer Book returned in monopoly form. At college level, altar rails came back and the order for holy communion seven times a year was reimposed.[333] Each college became a miniature stronghold of the established Church; a bastion based on two pillars: the Authorized Bible of 1611 and the Prayer Book of 1662. Only noblemen, and those under 16, were exempt from the oaths. There must have been occasional instances of nominal subscription. Charles Ingleby, of Yorkshire, for example, did not allow his Catholicism to stand in the way of matriculation in 1662.[334] And some do seem to have survived by remaining

---

[331] V-P's Reg. 18 Oct. 1662, fo. 92ᵛ; Clennell B 1d. 36: Principal's Fine Book, 16 June 1666; Wood, *Life and Times*, ii. 388 and *Colleges and Halls*, 378. Thomas Adams justified his position in *The Main Principles of Christian Religion in an 107 Short Articles or Aphorisms* (1675). His brother Richard, once a Fellow, later Rector of St Mildred's, Bread Street, London, was also ejected (A. G. Matthews, *Calamy Revised* (Oxford, 1934), [2].)

[332] *ODNB*; *Hist. Parl.: Commons*, 1660–1690, iii. 160–1.

[333] V-P's Reg. 8 Sept. 1660, f. 88v; Wood, *Life and Times*, i. 313. The arrangement of the chapel is indicated in Williams, *Oxonia Depicta*, pl. xxxv. Morning prayers were at 5 or 6 a.m.; evening prayers at 5 or 5.30, according to season. The seven 'sacrament days' were: 1st Sunday in Lent, Easter Day, Whitsunday, 1st Sunday after Act Sunday, 1st Sunday after Michaelmas, Sunday after All Souls'/Saints' Day, Christmas Day (*Notes and Queries*, ser. 9/3, 123).

[334] H. Aveling, 'The Catholic Recusants of the West Riding of Yorkshire, 1558–1790', *Proceedings of the Leeds Philosophical and Literary Soc.* 10 (1963), 254. However, in 1693 he refused the Oath of Allegiance, having in 1680 been tried and acquitted for complicity in the Gascoigne Plot. When in 1679 a return of papists in the University was compiled, none was reported at Brasenose (OU Arch. WP/a/11/1).

quietly on the fringe. Thomas Martindale, son of a prominent Lancashire nonconformist, received private tuition at Brasenose but did not become a member of the college.[335] On the whole, however, there was no escape. From this constitutional straitjacket came the Oxford crisis of 1688.

Anthony Wood believed that those Oxford Fellows who were reinstated in 1660 scarcely amounted to one-sixth of those previously 'outed; many being now either dead, or married, or had changed their Religion'. That was an exaggeration. In Brasenose the six 'returners' amounted to a third of the Fellowship; and among the Interregnum Fellows only Adams made a stand against the Prayer Book. Other colleges were less lucky. Between 1660 and 1662 eleven heads, thirty-nine Fellows, and three chaplains were removed. To this we must add—thanks to the Act of Uniformity—three more heads, four more Fellows, and half a dozen graduate or undergraduate scholars.[336] For Brasenose, the real losses occurred outside college. The number of ejected clergy—that is, Brasenose graduates removed from their livings under the Act of Uniformity—ran to twenty-three. That was only a third of the number, for example, suffered by Exeter College. Even so, it was significant. Bradshaw and Ince we have already met. They belonged to that cohort of the 1630s—ten of them at least—who cut their teeth in opposition to Chancellor Laud, then found themselves in the 1660s looking for outside employment as nonconformist pastors. Some of this generation emigrated. Others were reduced to charity. 'Praying' Ince is said to have spent his later years keeping sheep. Others were more active—John Miles, for example. He went up in 1636 at the age of 15, then turned exclusion to good advantage. He became a founder of the Baptist movement in south Wales, and ended his days in Massachusetts. The puritan exodus to the New World had in fact been significant since the early 1630s. One early emigrant from Brasenose— he escaped to New England in 1635—was Richard Mather, father of Increase Mather and grandfather of Cotton Mather. His experience sums up the intolerance of the Laudian regime. In 1633 he was suspended by the epis-copal Visitor from his benefice at Toxteth for failing to wear a surplice: 'What...preach fifteen years and never wear a Surpless! It had been better for him that he had gotten Seven Bastards.'[337]

---

[335] R. Parkinson (ed.), *Life of Adam Martindale* (Chetham Soc. 4, 1845), 187–8. From 1666 scholars had also to take the Oxford Oath, consequent on the Five Mile Act imposed by the Oxford Parliament of 1665 (V-P's Reg. 1666, fo. 97ʳ).

[336] Compare Wood, *Annals*, ii. 700 *et seq.* with Matthews, *Calamy Revised*, p. xiii. Several later returned as 'after-conformists' (Beddard, in *HUO* iv. 852).

[337] *ODNB*. The following is a list of Brasenose clergy ejected from their livings in 1660–2: Richard Adams, Peter Aspinwall, Samuel Birch, James Bradshawe, Isaac Clifford, Thomas Crompton, Thomas Crumpton, Richard Ferrand, John Fogg, Samuel Grasty, John Harvey, Joseph Hayhurst, Peter Ince, Gamaliel Marsden, John Mawton, Joshua Richardson, William

So at last in 1660—after turmoil and trouble—the old order returned to Brasenose, and with it practices that were to become only too familiar in the eighteenth century. Consider for a moment—before we examine the crisis of 1688—the regime of Thomas Yate (pl. 13).

The new Principal seems to have been almost the embodiment of the nepotic principle. His first move, in 1661, was to arrange for his younger brother Samuel to be appointed Rector of Middleton Cheney. That was comparatively straightforward. His next move was trickier. Anthony Wood picks up the story. In 1667 'a fellowship... being void, 2 or 3 able and indigent scholars stood for it'. Yate, 'being minded to prefer a kinsman [William Yate], took all occasions to bring him in but could not because he was a dunce and altogeather uncapable. At length certain of the fellowes being absent or out of towne on preaching, [he] called a meeting, and, making a party, elected him. This it seems was soe much resented that Mr. [George] Vernon [formerly of Brasenose, by then chaplain of All Souls] in a sermon at [St] Marie's told the auditory at a distance of it, and Mr. [Ralph] Turnbull of Xt. Ch. more openly there when he said that "men of merit were not preferred, but dunces and squint-eyed fellows".'[338] And that was just the beginning. In 1677 Principal Yate arranged for another of his brothers, Jeremiah, to be elected Clerk of Accounts, that is Steward or 'clericus computi'. In all, no fewer than seven members of the Yate family—the Principal and his wife, the Steward, two nephews: the 'dunce' and his brother a Fellow from 1670, as well as the Principal's wife's widowed sister and daughter—were eventually buried in the cloister.[339] Such nepotism seems to have caused neither surprise nor resentment. Brasenose had suffered too much in the previous generation from the pursuit of conviction and principle. Both sides in the civil war had by now subsumed their old allegiances in pursuit of more immediately profitable goals. In 1675–6, for example, we find the Fellowship happily accommodating ex-Principal Greenwood's nephew Nathaniel alongside two of Principal Yate's nephews, Thomas and William; while at the same time appointing Jeremiah Yate as Clerk of

Thomas, William Turton, William Voyle, Samuel Wickham, John Wilson, Joshua Witton, John Wright (Matthews, *Calamy Revised, passim*; MPP 75 A1). Eight of these came from Lancashire, six from Cheshire. For the Mather family, see R. Middlekauff, *The Mathers* (New York, 1971). The father of the first native-born American poet, Benjamin Thompson, was also a Brasenose man.

[338] Wood, *Life and Times*, ii. 107–8.

[339] A great-nephew of Principal Yate—a third Thomas Yate—held a Fellowship from 1690 to 1699. The Principal's wife was Elizabeth (d. 1688; née Bartlett), widow of Sir Richard Cave, Kt. (who was killed fighting for the King at Naseby, 1645). Her sister Catherine (d. 1681) was widow of Sir Allen Boteler, Kt.; and her daughter Laetitia (d. 1674) was widow of both Sir Francis de Sylva and Sir John Mules, both Portuguese. All three ladies lived and died in the Lodgings (Wood, *Colleges and Halls*, 371, 376, 378).

Accounts, and making another of the ex-Principal's nephews, Moses Green-wood, First Master of Charlbury School.[340] Oxford was now less interested in the drama of high politics than in the loaves and fishes of academic patronage.

But the Fellows of Brasenose, in those palmy days of Charles II, were by no means all 'dunces'. When James Alban Gibbes—one of England's last Latin poets: 'the Horace of his age'—took his D.Med. by diploma in 1673, he cannot have been short of interesting company. Sixsmith we have already encountered. All kissing spent, perhaps; but no doubt his reading lists were still being digested. And there were others also who were effective scholars. In 1676 George Clarke—the future doyen of Oxford Palladians—went up to Brasenose and was assigned to the care of another man we have already met: Ralph Rawson. 'An old Cavalier and an admirable tutor', Rawson had been elected in 1642, extruded in 1648, and reinstated in 1660. But he still retained a zest for teaching. 'He used', Clarke recalled, 'to read to us constantly twice a day, not excepting Sundays'. And he cannot have been wholly unusual. When Rawson retired to a college living at Great Rollright, Clarke managed to secure a conscientious substitute: 'I . . . took Mr. Thomas Millington, a very ingenious fellow of the college, into my chamber, and had his friendship and assistance when I doubted of anything in my studies.'[341] Now Clarke of course was studying the traditional curriculum. 'Modern' subjects were less well catered for. If the later seventeenth century was a golden age for Oxford science, then it has to be admitted that Brasenose had little or no part to play in it.[342] Only in the person of William Petty—so briefly a Lecturer in Natural Philosophy—did the college come near to cutting-edge thinking in applied mathematics and medicine. From 1620 all Oxford students had to attend lectures on geometry in their third to fifth years; and lectures on astronomy in their sixth and seventh. In 1644–5, while he was at Brasenose, Elias Ashmole could make a particular study of natural philosophy, mathematics, astron-omy, and astrology. But teaching provision remained patchy. As with college offices, the various lectureships were handed round from Fellow to Fellow

[340] V-P's Reg. 8 Jan. 1675, fo. 110 and 10 Jan. 1676, fo. 111ᵛ. In all, two of Greenwood's nephews and two of his great-nephews became Fellows of Brasenose. It was another nephew, also a graduate, who became master of Charlbury School.

[341] V-P's Reg. 24 Dec. 1667, fo. 100. Millington was 'found dead in his bed April 8th 1689' (HMC, *Leybourne–Popham MSS*, 260–1). Rawson had been implicated in Sir George Booth's plot (Wood, *Athenae*, ii. 1045). Because of his contentious sermons in St Mary's, he became known as 'the querelous divine' (Wood, *Life and Times*, i. 310). For Gibbes—a Catholic, buried in the Pantheon in Rome—see *ODNB*.

[342] For humanistic studies, see M. Feingold, in *HUO* iv. 211 *et seq.* For sciences see ibid. 359 ff. and N. Tyacke, 'Science and Religion at Oxford before the Civil War', in D. Penning-ton and K. Thomas (eds.), *Puritans and Revolutionaries* (Oxford, 1979), 73–93.

with little concern for specialism. Tenure of Fellowship was in any case seldom prolonged. Brasenose had no Mathematical Lecturer at all until 1700. And the Hebrew Lectureship seems to have become largely honorific: between 1691 and 1697 teaching was farmed out to 'Rabbi Aboudanak'.[343] As in a number of colleges, such extraneous topics often required the purchase of additional tuition.

That did not matter to Clarke. He was a prosperous commoner, the son of a gentleman. He was not short of money. Others were less fortunate. By the end of the seventeenth century, a batteller at Brasenose had to manage on £3 per quarter for living expenses, a commoner on £4. A gentleman (or fellow) commoner on the other hand, could afford to pay out about £5 per quarter on battels, and might on occasion face a bill running to double that amount, not to mention a variety of ancillary costs.[344] At the lower end of the scale William Dean, a servitor who arrived in 1659, found that 72 per cent of his outgoings went on residence, 13 per cent on clothing, and 11 per cent on books. His tutoring was free; his Mordaunt Scholarship, plus payment for serving other students, reduced his costs from a nominal £16 17s. 8d. p.a. to £9 12s. 0d. p.a. A gentleman commoner could spend as much as that on buttons.[345] During this period systematic details of undergraduate expenditure are hard to come by. But records of the first-year expenses for a number of Ralph Eaton's pupils, between 1658 and 1682, do survive. Gentlemen commoners' living costs (£74–£90) could be up to five times those of servitors (£7–£23), and more than twice the expenses of commoners (£32–£50).[346]

And what did they read, for profit or pleasure, these Brasenose men of the later seventeenth century? As a conscientious tutor, Ralph Eaton purchased quite a number of books on his pupils' behalf.[347] Logic is there: Gisbert ab Isendoorn's *Logica Peripatetica*, and Robert Sanderson's *Logicae Artis Compendium*. Philosophy is there too: Daniel Stahl's *Axiomata Philosophica*. And ancient history: Lucius Florus' *De Gestis Romanorum Historiarum*, lib. iv. Theology appears in the shape of Joannes Wollebius, *Compendium Theologiae*

---

[343] Bursar's Account Books, cited by Jeffery in *Brazen Nose*, iv. 28.

[344] A. Bryant, *Postman's Horn* (1936), 45–6, 50. Compare BL Add. MS 46, 955 B, fos.138, 142–3: John Percevale of Christ Church to his uncle, Sir Robert Southwell, 9 Oct. 1678, justifying his expenditure, e.g. 'pocket money' (travel, entertainment, clothing), occasional costs ('Gloves, Candles, Quills, Paper . . . Furniture . . . Bookseller'), as well as 'sett charge[s]' for 'Tutering, Chamber Commons and all ye Colledge servants . . . as Landress Servitor Bedmaker and ye like'.

[345] Porter, in *HUO* iv. 86–7, citing Eaton's 'Pupill Booke', MPP 8 A1, formerly MS 85, fos.82ᵛ–83ᵛ.

[346] *HUO* iv. 87–8, citing 'Pupill Booke', fos. 11ᵛ–101ᵛ.

[347] *Quat. Mon.* XI, 19–20, citing 'Pupill Booke'.

Christianae; and dogmatics in the guise of William Lydford's *Principles of Faith and Good Conscience Digested into a Catechetical Forme*. But there is some lighter reading in the list as well; for example Sir Philip Sidney's *The Countess of Pembroke's Arcadia*. These volumes suggest not just the programme of a professional scholar but the reading of an educated gentleman.

One such gentleman commoner who came up in 1670—one of nine that year—was Richard Myddelton of Chirk Castle, Denbighshire. At matriculation Myddelton was no more than 15 years of age. But he was heir to a baronetcy, a churchman, and a Tory; and one day he would be MP for his county in no fewer than thirteen Parliaments. Thanks to the survival of book-buying inventories, we can begin to build up a picture of his undergraduate reading. There is nothing too disturbing on the list. After all, the works of Hobbes and Milton would be burned in 1683 in the quadrangle of the Old Schools. Most of Myddelton's purchases consisted of standard classical literature and ancient history. In addition, however, he bought biographies and travel books, and volumes of modern history. These would amplify his general education. Here was mental preparation for public life. Camden's *Annales* and *Remaines*, Raleigh's *History of the World*, Milton's *History of Britain*, Walton's *Lives*, Spottiswoode's *Church of Scotland*, Heylin's *Help to English History*, Heath's *Brief Chronicle*, Castlemaine's *War between the English and Dutch*, and Bentivoglio's *Warrs of Flanders*: such was the reading of at least one gentleman commoner, one of England's future legislators.[348]

But the emphasis in teaching was still verbal. The ideal was linguistic and dialectical dexterity. Seating arrangements in the new antechapel reflected this conservative pedagogic process. Here Saturday disputations continued to be held throughout the later seventeenth century. By the side of what is now the organ-loft staircase was the seat of the 'responding bachelor'. The 'opposing bachelor' and bachelor-spectators sat under the west window; and behind them the noblemen and gentlemen commoners. 'Schollars, Battelars and Servitors' sat in the south-east corner. In the centre of the south wall stood the seat of the supervisory Dean.[349]

Of course there was more to Restoration Oxford than disputation. In the general relaxation of manners that followed the collapse of puritan rule, Brasenose was by no means abstinent. Christmas dinners grew more elaborate, with a choice of beef, duck, wigeon, capon, turkey, teal, and wild boar. And the annual celebration of Charles II's return from exile on 29 May—Oak Apple Day—provided an excuse for eating on a heroic scale. The menu for

---

[348] Feingold, in *HUO* iv. 342 n. 360 (corrected), citing Nat. Lib. Wales, Chirk Castle MS 10, 597 and W. Myddelton (ed.), *Chirk Castle Accounts, 1660–1753* (Manchester, 1931). See also *Hist. Parl.: Commons,* 1660–1690, iii. 122–4 and 1690–1715, iv. 998–1000.

[349] Plans in Sir Holland Egerton's almanac (MPP 10 A1).

1693 included: seven jacks (small pike), fourteen perch, a catch of eels, two Westphalia hams, beef, mutton, lamb, veal, two lamb pies, six pigs, fourteen geese, fourteen ducks, thirty chickens, forty-eight pigeons, two hundred spears of sparrowgrass (asparagus), fruit and vegetables galore, oysters, cheese, salmon, and rabbits.[350] And what about wine? Such a feast demanded appropriate contributions from the cellar. One example will suffice. Drinking at the proctorial dinner in college in 1669—following 'a very great and splendid Act' in the new Sheldonian—seems to have been quite gargantuan. According to Anthony Wood, the participants 'drank out in wine at dinner...the sum of £80'.[351] That no doubt was exceptional. But in 1672 one college dinner bill alone included nine quarts of claret (9s. 0d.), nine quarts of canary (19s. 6d.), and a formidable quantity of tobacco and pipes (£1 0s. 7d.).[352] Nor were entertainments of a grosser kind wanting. In June 1683 there was at least one memorable proctorial arrest. The daughter of an Oxford burgher, Samuel Clerk, was apprehended for 'dancing in the Miter Inn with Br[asenose] men in boy's apparell'. Apparently, she was 'seised on next morning in her bed by proctor [Arthur] Charlet'.[353] And on 22 October 1671, at 8 o'clock one moonless night, a baby was actually heard crying among the trees in the front quadrangle (pl. 7). Apparently the child had been abandoned. Vice-Principal Duckworth—whom we last met as master bell-ringer of Steeple Aston—emerged from his rooms and went into the buttery to fetch a candle in order to find it. While he was there, some shadowy 'Bachelor of Arts' carried the child away under his gown.[354] No names; no penalty. But such incidents—like the Revd Mr Duckworth's candle perhaps—throw a suggestive light on Oxford customs in the reign of the Merry Monarch.

Traditionally, Oxford combined ceremony and humour on one particular occasion: the summer celebration known as the Act (the predecessor of Encaenia). Star of the show was the *terrae filius*, a kind of licensed jester to Convocation. Brasenose produced *terrae filii* in 1655 and 1669. On the first occasion the Act was still performed in St Mary's Church. After several years of suppression 'during the time of the calamity', 'it was such a novelty to the Students...that there was great rudeness committed, both by them and by the concourse of people who attended...Whereupon the Vice-Chancellor,

---

[350] E. Boardman in *Brazen Nose*, xl. 111–12, citing Hurst College Dinners 2 and Hurst Bursarial Tradesmen's Bills, 10. Oak Apple Day was not removed from the Book of Common Prayer until 1859, along with the feast of King Charles the Martyr and the commemoration of the Gunpowder Plot.

[351] Wood, *Life and Times*, ii. 165.

[352] Quoted in *Quat. Mon.* XII, 14.

[353] Wood, *Life and Times*, iii. 57.

[354] Ibid. ii. 233.

Dr. Greenwood of Brasenose, a severe and choleric governour, was forced to get several guards of Musquetiers, out of the Parliament garrison then in Oxford, to keep all the doors and avenues and to let nobody in, except those the Vice-Chancellor or his Deputies appointed. There was then great quarrelling between the Scholars and the Soldiers, and thereupon blows and bloody noses followed.'[355] John Glendole of Brasenose—*terrae filius* that year: 'a good Humourist...of a waggish wit'—was so popular that he extended his repertoire to several venues around the town.

A great mimic, [he] acted well in several plays, which the Scholars acted by stealth, either in the stone house behind and southward from Pembroke College, or in Kettle Hall [in Broad Street], or at Holywell Mill, or in the Refectory at Gloucester Hall. Anthony Wood was well aquainted with him and delighted in his company.[356]

When the Sheldonian was at last ready in 1669, one of the *terrae filii* was another Brasenose man, Thomas Hayes. On this occasion, the inauguration of the Theatre called for particular solemnity. John Evelyn—about to receive his doctorate—was therefore shocked by the levity displayed:

The *Terrae filius* (the *Universitie Buffoone*) entertained the auditorie with a tedious, abusive, sarcastical rhapsodie, most unbecoming the gravity of the Universitie...ye Vice-Chancellor and severall heads of houses...were perfectly asham'd of it...[for] 'twas rather licentious lyeing and railing than genuine and noble witt. In my life I was never witnesse of so shamefull entertainment.[357]

No wonder Hayes was 'expelled'. 'No wit', notes Wood curtly; just 'scurrilous'.[358]

From such 'raillying' and 'ribauldry' Oxford would soon have to shake itself free. The Restoration years proved to be a brief moment of excess. The Act was forbidden altogether—temporarily at any rate—in 1687. By then there were more serious things to think about.

The Restoration settlement had re-established the established Church. The terms of that settlement were based on a compact—an identity of interest—between Church and Crown. No provision was made for a monarch whose loyalties lay not with Canterbury but with Rome. James II's attempt to open the machinery of the Anglican state to non-Anglicans—in particular to Roman Catholics—was therefore a recipe for constitutional deadlock. It

---

[355] *Oxoniana*, i. 104–10; *Life of Anthony Wood*, ed. Bliss (1848), 108, 185, 232, 237–8, 245–6.

[356] C. Wordsworth, *Social Life at the English Universities in the 18th Century* (1874), 296–7; Wood, *Annals*, ii, pt. ii, 707. A Cambridge man, Glendole was intruded in 1651; he was buried in St Mary's in 1660.

[357] J. Evelyn, *Diary and Correspondence*, ii (1906), 238–9: 10 June 1669.

[358] Wood, *Life and Times*, ii. 166. Hayes was, unusually, a medical student. The last Act occurred in 1733.

revived the whole question of extra-parliamentary rule. The legions of 1641 rearmed; and once again the battlefield was the University of Oxford.[359]

It was in March 1686 that the Revd Obadiah Walker, Master of University College, lit one of several fuses that precipitated the Glorious Revolution. After some deliberation at Court, Dr Walker 'declared himself a Romish Priest'. This he was able to do—while retaining his Mastership—thanks to the royal dispensing power. He had been dispensed by royal prerogative— that is by order under the Great Seal—from the operation of parliamentary Acts enforcing the Oaths of Allegiance and Supremacy, as well as from the Declaration enjoined by the Act of Uniformity.[360] Others followed his example. Dr John Mill, Principal of St Edmund Hall, recorded this sequence of events in graphic terms:

... old Obadiah is now ... an open Papist and a Priest; and ye Seals are passing [from the King] for a Dispensation to him to say Masse in his College, and to exercise his Religion publickly. His Congregation consists of no less than four, he himself making one of ye number, 2 poor sorry Fellows of his own College [Nathaniel Boyse and Thomas Deane] and a shatterheaded fellow of Brazen-nose College one Bernard. They sing Mattins and Vespers very devoutly (for aught I know) in Their way, but they are become extremely despicable. Ridiculous to that degree, yt. some young Waggs of Ch.Ch. ye other day sent old Job (a poor Naturall, who looks after their College Dishes and Trenchers) with this song, wch. he sung at Walker's door.

> 'O old Obadiah
> Sing Ave Maria
> But so will not I—a
>   for why-a
> I had rather be a Fool than a Knave-a'.[361]

If 'Lillibulero' sang King James out of three kingdoms, perhaps it was old Job's ditty that drove the Pope from four colleges.

---

[359] For the unfolding revolution, see Beddard, in *HUO* iv. 907–54; *A Kingdom without a King* (1988) and *The Revolutions of* 1688 (1991); also J. R. Jones, *The Revolution of* 1688 *in England* (1972).

[360] Following the judgement in *Godden* v. *Hales*, 1686 (W. C. Costin and J. S. Watson, *Law and Working of the Constitution*, i. (1952), 256–8). James II's warrant, dated 3 May 1686, was transcribed—without comment—in V-P's Reg. under July 1686, fos. 132–3. It set aside the Oaths of Allegiance and Supremacy, and the 1662 Act of Uniformity against Dissenters as well as the penal laws, 1581 onwards, against Roman Catholics (Gutch, *Collectanea Curiosa*, i. 287; Evelyn, *Diary*, 5 May 1686).

[361] HMC, *Le Fleming MSS*, 198–200; *The Flemings in Oxford*, ii (OHS lxii), 153–8: 16 May, 19 May, and 3 June, 1686; Wood, *Life and Times*, iii. 196. In 1678 Walker had published an edition of Spelman's *Alfred*, emphasizing that King's status as founder of the University and the Pope's anointed superior of the English Church (Tyacke, in *HUO* iv. 610). He was also the author of *The Life and Death of Our Lord Jesus Christ* (Oxford, 1685).

Who was this 'shatterheaded Fellow of Brazen-nose'? John Augustine Bernard was a grandson of Peter Heylin, Laud's Arminian chaplain and biographer. Soon after graduating from Lincoln he was elected Higden Fellow of Brasenose in June 1681, three years before taking holy orders. Freshly ordained, he fell under the influence of 'old Obadiah'. In the winter of 1685–6, he was converted to Catholicism: he absented himself from college communion on Easter Day 1686. Suddenly he found himself in the front line of religious debate. In March 1687 he was absolved by royal fiat, from the 'pains and penalties' of recusancy; and then, by letters patent from the King, he was elected Lecturer in Moral Philosophy. His inaugural discourse two months later—on the iniquities of Reformation no less—proved to be an occasion of some tension. Wood records that those attending were uncertain whether to approve or disapprove: '5 or 6 hist [hissed] at the conclusion, supposing the rest would follow (but did not).'[362] Now observant Catholics in England and Wales amounted at this point to no more than 1 per cent of the population. But 'popery' was still tainted with treachery; it was linked with the politics of treason; at the very least it was a potent symbol of factional strife. Young Bernard found himself caught up in national events over which he had no control. He became, in effect, a pawn in James II's attempt to fracture Oxford's Anglican monopoly.

By the end of 1687 there was a Catholic Master of University College, a Catholic Dean of Christ Church, and a Catholic President of Magdalen. There were Catholic Fellows at University College, Brasenose, Trinity, Magdalen, and All Souls. Magdalen, in particular—thanks to the King's intervention—looked likely to be transformed into a veritable 'Romish college'. There were Catholic gentlemen commoners at University College and Christ Church. There was a Catholic scholar at Balliol. There were Catholic chapels at University College and Christ Church, serviced by Jesuits and open to public use.[363] There was even a Catholic Sheriff of Oxfordshire. And—crucially—there was still a Catholic King. All that James II needed now was a Catholic Prince of Wales.

On 10 October 1688 the birth of the future Old Pretender was greeted in Oxford with very modified rapture. Bernard—by now nominally a Fellow of Magdalen too—penned a Latin poem of congratulation. It was officially

---

[362] HMC, *Downshire MSS*, i, pt. i, 162: Dr O. Wynne to Sir William Trumbull, 6 May 1686; Wood, *Life and Times*, iii. 171, 177, 182–6, 213–15, 217, 219, 245, 287, 296; Beddard, in *HUO* iv. 916 *et seq.*

[363] Wood, *Life and Times*, iii. 194, 223, 253–4, 276, 285, 298. Some of those who attended mass were soldiers from the regiment of Henry Mordaunt, Earl of Peterborough—a Catholic and ally of James II—quartered nearby. For Magdalen, see L. Brockliss, G. Harriss, and A. Macintyre, *Magdalen College and the Crown* (Oxford, 1988).

dispatched to Whitehall.[364] But 'noe colleges or halls', Anthony Wood observed, 'besides [Magdalen and Christ Church] took any notice of the birth...either by bonfier or ringing of bells—knowing full well that if [the Prince] lives he is to be bred up a papist and so consequently the crowne of England and popish religion will never part'.[365] One month later, Guy Fawkes bonfires were blazing all over Oxford 'in spite to the papists'.[366] That very day, 5 November 1688, the Protestant William of Orange, husband of the King's daughter Mary, landed at Torbay on the coast of Devon. Within weeks James II was in exile over the water, leaving the throne conveniently vacant. Obadiah Walker found himself in the Tower of London. One of the few who volunteered to fight for the King was Walker's protégé and pupil John Augustine Bernard: that 'shatterheaded Fellow of Brazen-nose'.[367]

With Bernard's removal—to Ireland, Cheshire, and ultimately Lincoln-shire—Brasenose was able to resume its wonted ways: serious learning, moderately serious religion, and—from time to time—immoderately serious eating and drinking. With the departure of James II much of the poison had been drained from Oxford politics. The age of ideology was nearly over.

---

[364] *Sterenae Natalitiae Academiae Oxoniensis in Celsissimum Principem* (Oxford, 1688); Wood, *Life and Times*, iii. 272. For Bernard's nomination for Magdalen, see J. R. Bloxam (ed.), *Magdalen College and King James II* (OHS vi), 238, no. 274: 24 Feb. 1688.

[365] Wood, *Life and Times*, iii. 255, 268.

[366] Ibid. 281.

[367] Ibid. 288–91, 296; Beddard, in *HUO* iv. 953. On 4 Dec. Bernard was given permission to absent himself from college (V-P's Reg. 4 Dec. 1688, fo. 137ᵛ). He resigned his Fellowship on 27 Dec. 1688 (V-P's Reg. 27 Dec. 1688, fo. 138), and his Lectureship on 5 Jan. 1689. He followed King James to Ireland; but by Sept. 1689 he was said to be back in Chester, 'very poor and bare', reconciled to the Church of England, and 'maintained with victuals...by the Bishop' ('I do not believe this': Wood, *Life and Times*, iii. 340). 'We are in great pain for honest Dr. Bernard', wrote Dr Arthur Charlett to Sir William Trumbull in 1696; 'fearing that he was taken in the packet boat by the French, it being a month since he embarked from Holland' (HMC, *Downshire MSS*, i, pt. ii, 705: 10 Nov. 1696). Through his godfather, Bishop Gardiner of Lincoln, Bernard was given the livings of Ludford Parva and Kelstern, Lincs., in 1701–2. He maintained a heated correspondence on theological issues with Bishop Wake of Lincoln (Ch. Ch., Oxford, Wake MSS iv, fos. 205–339). Although at different times both sequestrated and excommunicated, he seems to have died as Vicar of Kelstern, some time after 1713 (*ODNB*).

1688–1785

Georgian Brasenose: Tories and Jacobites, Methodists and Freemasons

Between the Glorious Revolution and the accession of George III, Brasenose had only three Principals, two undistinguished and one notorious. John Meare and Francis Yarborough left little impact on the college, and even less on the University. Robert Shippen was a different matter. He is remembered for reasons that are best forgotten. After Yarborough's death in 1770, there were three more, eminently forgettable Principals: William Gwyn, Ralph Cawley, and Thomas Barker. Their brief periods of office mark a pause or intermission prior to the Brasenose renaissance of the 1780s and 1790s. None of these men—except perhaps Shippen—had any real effect on the expanding reputation of the place. None could match the influence of two outstanding benefactors: Sarah, Duchess of Somerset, and William Hulme of Manchester. And none of them played much of a role in recreating the image of the college. Under their rule Brasenose might well have remained little more than a Lancastrian colony, a Jacobite backwater. The crucial factor in the process of change turned out to be not personal but architectural. Brasenose emerged as a major Oxford college thanks to a triumphant accident of topography: the opening of Radcliffe Square and the building of the Radcliffe Camera.

The Revolution of 1688 confirmed Oxford as the citadel of established Anglicanism. James II's infiltration of Magdalen, Christ Church, and University College—to say nothing of his own Catholicism—made acceptance of William and Mary inevitable. Apart from a handful of stalwarts, four Brasenose men among them, Oxford agreed to swallow its legitimist principles and swear allegiance to the new regime.[1] In this the University echoed the English

---

[1] HMC, *Le Fleming MSS*, 252; Bodl. MS Ballard 3, no. 18; C. Wordsworth, *Social Life at the English Universities in the 18th Century* (1874), 604–5. The Brasenose non-jurors were two undergraduates (Robert Bolton and Stephen Bowdler) and two Fellows (Stephen Sagar and William Pincocke). The last of these 'absconded in Lancashire for fear of his creditors ... for near six years', and was 'deprived' in 1692 (HMC, *Finch MSS*, iii. 282–3; Wood, *Life and Times*, iii. 382: 29 Jan. 1692). He had already been suspended from his Fellowship by the Visitor in

Church as a whole. Only about 4 per cent of Anglican clergy became non-jurors after 1688.[2] Nor was the situation changed by the Hanoverian accession of 1714. Broadly speaking, Oxford accepted the Revolution Settlement as a *fait accompli*. Faced with a choice between Church and King, dons plumped unhesitatingly for Church. Henceforward every matriculating Brasenose man over the age of 16 would be required to subscribe to the Thirty-Nine Articles (1562); every graduand had to take the Oaths of Supremacy and Allegiance (1689) as well as the Oath of Abjuration (1701); every Fellow had to reconfirm in like fashion his loyalty to college, University, Church, and Crown[3] And this conformity was enforced. In 1774 the Fellows of Brasenose 'agreed that, for the future, all Under-Graduates and Bachelors should be rusticated for 3 months that absent themselves from the sacrament [at Easter and Whitsun]'.[4] Of course the college was not exactly a pious community. But solemn oaths and religious observance did define the nature of the place: politically, religiously, culturally. Georgian Oxford embodied the Church of England in academic dress. It might also be described as a monument to the politics of exclusion.

But within and between colleges there was considerable variation. Brasenose at this point was small in size and middling in rank. In 1689, for example, the college had only six senior Fellows. By comparison, New College had 13 senior Fellows; Magdalen had 40 Fellows, excluding Demies; and Christ Church had 101 Students. When it came to Convocation, Magdalen had some 47 votes, Brasenose fewer than 20, counting senior and junior

---

1684 for a debt of £166 12*s*. 13/4*d*. incurred in his capacity as Bursar (V-P's Reg. 16 Apr. 1684, fo. 127ᵛ). George Newton, matriculating as a commoner in 1669, was deprived of his preferments at Cheadle and Prestbury in 1690 (*Brasenose Reg*. 221). Thomas Bennett, a Cheshire batteler matriculating 1716, ordained 1720, became master of Tarporley Grammar School, although a non-juror (Bodl. MS Eng. Hist. d. 1, p. 197). Robert Whitehead, a Lancashire batteler matriculating 1694, was ordained as a non-juror by Bishop Nathaniel Spinckes, *c*.1710–20 (ibid. 195).

[2] P. K. Monod, *Jacobitism and the English People, 1688–1788* (Cambridge, 1989), 142. These included some 10 peers and 60 MPs, and perhaps 100 gentry families. The Archbishop of Canterbury, five bishops and some 400 clergy were excluded. Hearne attributed as many as seven suicides among Oxford clergy to remorse at taking these 'abominable Oaths' (*Hearne's Collections*, vii. 296: 11 Nov. 1721). For early exclusion lists see G. Hickes, *Life of John Kettlewell* (1718), appendix vi; J. H. Overton, *The Non-Jurors* (1902), 467–96; and C. E. Mallet, *History of the University of Oxford*, iii (1927), 4 n. 3.

[3] For lists of Brasenose Fellows taking Oaths of Allegiance at Oxford Quarter Sessions, see HMC *Finch MSS*, iii. 282–3: [n.d.; *c*. 7–12 Oct. 1691]. Proctors also retook the Oaths of Supremacy and Allegiance, and received holy communion, on assuming office (W. N. Hargreaves-Mawdsley (ed.), *Woodforde at Oxford, 1759–1776* (OHS NS xxi, 1969), 221: 1 May 1774 and 223: 7 May 1774). Holt, LCJ, gave it as his opinion that the Oath of Allegiance was merely 'an Oath of Legal Obedience' (Bodl. MS Ballard 3: no. 28).

[4] Clennell B 53.3: Cawley Notebook i, fo. 36 and vi, fo. 37: 3 May 1774.

Fellows; though in practical voting power Brasenose probably ranked sixth or seventh among colleges. In terms of politics there was certainly no such thing as collegiate uniformity. Between the 1690s and the 1740s only Pembroke, Exeter, Wadham, and Merton could be labelled consistently Whig. Others ran the gamut from Hanoverian Tory to crypto-Jacobite. Brasenose was tactically Hanoverian but Jacobite by instinct. Between 1701 and 1711, for example—thanks to a bequest from Sir Francis Bridgeman—an annual panegyric continued to be delivered in memory of James II.[5] Socially and religiously, the image of the college was still defined by its pattern of recruitment. Collegiate links with Manchester, for instance, were to prove doubly compromising. Manchester was a stronghold of non-jurors, and in Lancashire as a whole Catholicism remained statistically strong. The roots of collegiate loyalty, therefore, lay outside the political establishment. Socially too, here was a college on the periphery of power. Brasenose men spoke with a northern accent. The corner of Brasenose Lane and Turl Street must have echoed with competing vowels: Welshmen from Jesus, West Country men from Exeter, Lancastrians from Brasenose. Between 1690 and 1719, out of a total entry of 599, no fewer than 315 came to Brasenose from Lancashire and Cheshire. This process of pre-selection applied to gentlemen commoners too: as many as thirty-four during this same period, drawn almost entirely from the gentry families of those two counties. And these local loyalties persisted. During the period 1690–1799, of the 1,846 men who came to Brasenose more than half (950) seem to have hailed from the north, predominantly from Lancashire (491) and Cheshire (393).[6]

As a result of these factors, at least until the 1760s, Brasenose was very far from being a fashionable place. In fact its status at this point has been defined as 'a college of exceptionally depressed social composition'.[7] Over the decade 1690–1700, the record of matriculations lists only 19 gentlemen commoners as against 64 commoners and 122 battelers. Of these batellers—none of whom dined formally in hall: they took their commons from the buttery—by far the greater number, 65 in fact, were categorized as 'plebeian', that is they lacked the armigerous status and/or the financial standing requisite for gentility. And within that category of batteler there were no fewer than 19 who could be labelled *pauper puer*: poor boys working their way through college as servitors or servants. Again, between 1690 and 1719 as many as 340 batellers were admitted as against only 204 commoners. Many of those who

---

[5] Clennell B 53.1*: Cawley Notebook i, fo. 25. By a Decree in Chancery, 1711, this was replaced by an oration on art or science (*Quat. Mon.* IV, 31; *Gent's. Mag.* liii (1783), 628 n.). The tradition survives vestigially as the Bridgeman Prize.

[6] G. V. Bennett, in *HUO* v. 381, 385; V. H. H. Green, ibid. 315.

[7] For the following figures, see Bennett, ibid. 366, 381.

entered as battelers, however, ended as scholars of the college: no fewer than 195 during the period 1690–1719. And many of these in turn became clergymen or schoolmasters. Occasionally they became Fellows too. These trends continued throughout the early Georgian period. In terms of class, therefore, early Georgian Brasenose can be regarded as a kind of primitive escalator of status, at least as regards progress from proletarian to professional rank. Compared with several more prestigious colleges at this time—most notably Christ Church, and to a lesser extent Magdalen and New College—its intake had yet to be significantly gentrified.

The Principal himself was certainly not a gentleman. John Meare was a plebeian scholar from Cheshire who came up as a batteler on the Frankland foundation in 1665 at the age of 16. His career followed a standard clerical pattern: Fellow, Junior Bursar, Rector of Great Rollright, and Rector of Middleton Cheney; then Principal in 1681, and Vice-Chancellor in 1697. Predictably, his relatives benefited too: his son John Meare II became a Fellow in 1704, and Vice-Principal in 1712; his nephew Thomas Meare became a Fellow in 1698 and Rector of Cottingham in 1714. In all, no fewer than eight members of the family were enrolled as Brasenose men in less than forty years. Several of these—as well as the Principal's infant daughter Elizabeth—were buried in chapel or cloister. So was his elder daughter, 'Peggy Meare'. According to Hearne, she was 'supposed to be [secretly] married to Mr. Edward Radclyffe, one of the Fellows'.[8] But none of this family has a memorial; and Meare himself has no portrait. His reign ended miserably. He died insane in 1710, ignored and insulted by the Fellowship.

As Principal and Vice-Chancellor, Meare was an overly acquiescent supporter of the Revolution settlement. He may well have been, in Arthur Charlett's words, 'a very fair, Friendly candid Man'; but his credibility among the majority of Tory heads was constantly undermined by 'Infelicities' of speech and action.[9] In 1688 we find him sycophantically deploring James II's policies. In 1689 he is to be seen again, hastening to take the Oath of Allegiance on the very same day as the Vice-Chancellor.[10] And when in 1697 the moment comes for his own Vice-Chancellorship, he seizes the opportunity—almost too readily—to celebrate William III's triumph at Ryswick.

The day was solemnised with all decency possible [he informed the MP for Oxford University, Sir William Trumbull]. We went to [St Mary's] at nine in the morning, the whole service being read by [myself], set off with very excellent music; after that a

---

[8] *Hearne's Collections*, vi. 223: 5 Sept. 1718. Radclyffe became Vice-Principal, and died in 1723. For the death of Meare's daughter Elizabeth, see V-P's Reg. 15 Sept. 1685, fo. 130.

[9] Bennett, in *HUO* v. 53, citing Bodl. MS Tanner 22, fo.54.

[10] HMC, *7th Report*, 417–18: 23 Nov. 1688, Meare to Lord Preston; Wood, *Life and Times*, iii. 305: 8 July 1689.

very excellent sermon and suitable to the occasion. A bonfire was lighted as we came out at the Church door, with the bells ringing. A little past 12 we went to the [Sheldonian] Theatre, all things having been disposed before by the Curators and Proctors. After music, [I] signified to the Orator to begin. The whole exercise after was performed by handsome young gentlemen of quality, with very great applause, which ended not till near four. The Theatre was very full. There went a vein of loyalty and affection through the whole performance. The evening was concluded with ringing of bells, bonfires and illuminations.[11]

Oxford Tories were less happy. The Warden of All Souls prayed for Meare's transportation to the colonies.[12] And a number of Brasenose Fellows would seem to have agreed with him. That would become plain in 1710 at the next Principalian election. The winner on that occasion would be Robert Shippen, leader of Oxford's crypto-Jacobite faction. Of him we shall hear more, a good deal more.

Meanwhile what of the social composition of the college? By 1710 the Fellowship consisted almost entirely of youthful clerics from Lancashire and Cheshire. Of the eighteen then in post seven were from Cheshire, four from Lancashire, including three Hulme Exhibitioners. They had little social standing. Only two (Leigh Brooke and Edward Radclyffe) were armigerous. Seven were clergymen's sons, eight had been batelers, three ranked as plebeian, and one (a Yorkshireman named George Freeman) had been listed as a *pauper puer* or servitor. And they were all alumni: the college looked after its own. Two generations later little had changed. Take the list for 1770. By then there were twenty Fellows in post, senior and junior, of whom eighteen were alumni: fourteen—including one bateler—ended as scholars (including seven Somerset Scholars) and four remained as commoners. The remaining two came from Queen's and Magdalen. Their average age in 1770 was nearly 29; and ten seem to have lived in college. As regards origins, nine came from Cheshire, seven from Lancashire, two from Herefordshire, and one each from Yorkshire and Buckinghamshire. Six were products of Manchester Grammar School. Their average age at matriculation was just over 17; their age at election to Fellowship averaged out at 23. They held their Fellowships for an average of just under sixteen years. Three died in office; fifteen left for college livings; six of them were Freemasons.[13] All led uneventful lives, except that is for three: John Napleton (pl. 27), William Cleaver, and John Kynaston. Napleton, as we shall see, would make his name as a university reformer.

[11] HMC, *Downshire MSS*, i. 770–1: 3 Dec. 1697, Meare to Trumbull; Trumbull, 'Diary', BL Add. MS 72571.

[12] Bennett, in *H.U.O.* v. 53, citing Longleat, Thynne MS xvii, fo. 251.

[13] Calculations in MPP 80 A3: W. T. Coxhill, 'Ralph Cawley, 1770–1777' (B.Litt., Oxford, 1946), 31.

Cleaver (pl. 24) would be Principal, and a bishop three times over. Kynaston would come to a curious and unfortunate end: he was banished from his Fellowship in 1764 after propagating unproven charges of adultery against a former Fellow, Matthew Maddock.[14]

Gentlemen commoners paid handsomely for their position. From the beginning, their fees were high. When Edward Greene matriculated in 1723, the ceremony alone cost his mother more than £20:[15]

Bought of Mr. Wise, Mercer in Oxford,	£	s	d
a Gent. Com's Gown, Nightgown and Bands	9..	1 2 ..	00
To the Principle for Caution Money	8..	00 ..	00
Entrance into the Butler's Book	0..	10 ..	00
Pd to Mr. Vice Principle	1..	01 ..	00
Pd Matriculation (and Man, 6d)	0..	16 ..	06
Pd Senr. Burser for Admission	0..	13 ..	04

By 1787 a gentleman commoner's caution money had risen to £30; and to £50 if he came from abroad.[16] On the other hand, a gentleman commoner's status permitted graduation after twelve terms rather than sixteen—each year still consisting of four terms—that is, he was able to graduate after three years rather than four.

But as the eighteenth century progressed, gentlemen commoners at Brasenose began to lose some of their special privileges. In 1768 and again in 1791 they lost their exemptions from various academic exercises, as well as their right to keep private servants in college garrets. In 1786 they lost their right to dine at high table, along with their special places in chapel and their right to use the Senior Common Room.[17] Meanwhile, the cost of a gentleman's

---

[14] 'I have always heard', noted George Ormerod years later, 'that the *imputed* guilt to which the decision of the college relates was of a more disgusting description' (R. Churton, *Supplement to... Smyth and Sutton* (Oxford, 1803), lvii, MS Addenda). Kynaston was offered a benefice in America, but retired in the end to Wigan, where he died in 1783. See V-P's Reg. 22 Mar. 1764, fo. 48ʳ and 27 June 1768, fo. 75ʳ; *Register of Manchester School*, i. 27; *Gent's. Mag.* 53 (1783), 627–8 and 55 (1785), 846; J. Nichols, *Literary Anecdotes*, ii (1812), 42 n. 66; *Bodleian Library Record*, 3 (1950–1), 60; W. Hone, *The Every Day Book*, ii (1831), 305. Kynaston had been chaplain to the Cartwrights of Aynho; Maddock chaplain to the Duke of Manchester. Kynaston became an antiquarian contributor to the *Gentleman's Magazine*. See also his letters to D. Prince, Bodl. MS Top. Oxon. b. 42 k: 1782–3. He was criticized for his ministration to Mary Blandy, hanged in Oxford for poisoning her father (*Gent's. Mag.* 22 (1752), 108–16, 188–9 and 53 (1783), 803). Maddock became Rector of Catworth Magna, Hunts., and committed suicide on 22 Jan. 1788.
[15] Greene MSS, quoted in *Brazen Nose*, xi. 23.
[16] V-P's Reg. 18 Mar. 1787, fo. 36. This rule was prompted no doubt by the prospective matriculation in 1788 of Robert Forrest, born in the East Indies, and Bryan Mackey, born in Jamaica.
[17] V-P's Reg. 31 Oct. 1768, fo. 17 and 4 Mar. 1786, fo. 30; *Quat. Mon.* XIII, 43. From 1768 gentlemen commoners had to 'write and show up a Theme weekly with the other undergraduates' (V-P's Reg. 9 Nov. 1768, fo. 8). From 1791 they had to 'do the exercise of Narrare in the Hall personally in their turn with the other undergraduates' (V-P's Reg. 1 Dec. 1791, fo. 47).

time at Oxford had for some time been rising steeply. When Geoffrey Shakerley—born armigerous and himself a future knight—went up to Brasenose in 1638, £60 p.a. had seen him through. When his son Peter went up in 1677—a gentleman commoner, and like his father a future MP for Wigan—that figure had risen to £70. When Peter's half-brother George went up in 1698—a future Jacobite Tory—he found £70 was nowhere near enough. By 1714 such a sum would scarcely suffice for a commoner; and twice as much might be spent by a commoner of gentle status. No doubt some of this was due to inflation. But expectations had clearly changed. By the start of the eighteenth century, George complained, no gentleman could be expected to live 'sneakingly'.[18] And by the end of the century, gentlemen commoners had become—paradoxically—both rather less privileged and very much richer.

Even as early as the 1720s there can have been few sneakers among gentlemen commoners at Brasenose. With their silken gowns and flaxen tie-wigs; with their cocked hats, white stockings, ruffled shirts, and thin Spanish leather shoes, each must have cut a striking figure as they strolled about the Old Quad.[19] Two of them, Edward Greene of Cheshire and Wyndham Napier of Dorset, went up in 1723 and clearly belonged—with their friends Edmund Bolton and Thomas Alford—to a hard-drinking set. On Sunday, 12 December 1725, several of them attended a party in college which seems to have been disorderly indeed. Bolton's letter to Greene, telling the story of that evening, gives us a rare glimpse into early eighteenth-century undergraduate life.

On...Sunday last, a Company of fellow-Collegians were assembled in Napier's room to pass the ev'ning over a bowl of Punch...Every one at first design'd to get drunk soberly, & took their Glasses together very friendly: each drinking his right-hand man's good health over ye left thumb. They had scarce gone round, & each pledg'd every man's health in the room, when Trogee, an old experience'd soldier, whose great soul was much larger than Napier's bowl, grew upon the Heroick strain, & thought it look'd mean to confine himself to the narrow limits of a small Glass. Immediately he raised the bowl to his mouth, &, swearing he'd drink at the fountain's head, swig'd mightily, & defy'd the whole Company to answer him in the like. Now there sat on the opposite side a young Warriour, distinguisht by the name of General, one of great Valour but no Conduct. He, full of indignation and envy, cou'd not bear the defiance, but with a glorious volly of oaths challeng'd him to the drinking Combat. Now glasses clash'd with glasses, & pipes with pipes in terrible

---

[18] Verney MSS (partly printed in F. P. Verney (ed.) *Memoirs of the Verney Family*, ii. 1925), quoted in A. Bryant (ed.), *Postman's Horn* (1936), 44–53. George's mother, Jane Shakerley, was alarmed at her son's extravagance: 'If you do not get some schooling we are undone, and it will be impossible to live easy here [at Gwersyllt, Denbighshire] for three score pounds a year...I do not clear twenty betwixt repairs and taxes.' George's tutor was Thomas Smith.

[19] N. Amhurst, *Terrae-Filius* (1721; 1726), 254 *et seq.*

Confusion, and the punch ran in rapid streams down their throats, as down
a Channel...At last the General...was forc'd to yield himself Vanquish'd by
the Mightier Trogee...[Whereupon] the General plai'd 1,000 mad tricks, threw
down the Jordan in the middle of the floor, wallow'd in it, and at last grew
so troublesome to the Company that they resolv'd to get him to bed. Trogee was
the cheif man in this resolution [but] was so much the worse for drinking that
he was the most unfit man amongst 'em all to do it. He brought him out as far
as the stairs head, where the struggle had like to have had a very tragical end: for
the General unluckily kick'd him from the top of the stairs, & he wou'd inevitably
have broke his scull, had not Alford catch'd him at the bottom. As he was Coming
up again, he was saluted with half a dozen kicks on the face from ye same
Gentleman, & with a great many bruises on the sides. Then they both came into
the room again, where Trogee fell upon him & exerted all his strength to beat
him; but alas! it was all in vain, poor Trogee was so weak with his fall and blows
that he could do nothing. The Company parted them, & having with much adieu
got the General to bed, some hurt, & some unhurt in ye scuffle they went to
bed themselves, and so very prettily concluded the Sunday night. Trogee is gone
down into the Country, & has carry'd with him a terrible black Eye, & Bruis'd face.
Oh Tempora Oh Mores!...[20]

Plus ça change. But gentlemen commoners were always a special case. The
lowly status of Brasenose in the early eighteenth century was sufficiently well
known to feature in at least one popular play, a comedy by Thomas Baker
entitled *An Act at Oxford* (1704). Its leading character is *Chum*, a servitor at
Brasenose. His father was 'a Chimney-sweeper and his Mother a poor
Gingerbread Woman at *Cow-Cross*'. He acts as servant to *Smart*, a London
visitor, and to *Bloom*, a gentleman commoner. His business, he explains, 'is to
wait upon Gentlemen Commoners, to dress 'em, pimp for 'em, clean their
Shoes, and make [i.e. write out] their Exercises; and the difference, Sir,
between Servitors and Gentlemen Commoners, is this, we are Men of Wit
and no Fortune, and they are Men of Fortune and no Wit'. His possessions
are few: 'old shoes which Gentlemen-commoners leave off, two raggs call'd
shirts, a dog's eard *Grammar*, and a piece of an *Ovid de Tristibus*'. But in the
end, all is well: *Chum* manages to impersonate *Smart*, winning for him the
hand of the beautiful Berynthia, the 'Tost o'the University'. For this he is
rewarded with 500 guineas.[21]

Until late in the century, Brasenose apparently retained something of this
same reputation for *gaucherie*. In Hannah Cowley's *Who's the Dupe?* (1779),
Gradus—a provincial pedant—is portrayed as a scholar of Brasenose. His

[20] Greene MSS, quoted in *Brazen Nose*, xi. 23–7 and *Oxford Mag.* 66 (1947–8), 88–92.
[21] T. Baker, *An Act at Oxford* (1704), Act I, scene 1. See also Wordsworth, *English
Universities*, 289–95.

appearance is out of date: 'a grizzle wig curled as stiffly as *Sir Cloudesley Shovel's* in [Westminster] Abbey—a dingy brown coat with vellum button-holes—and cambric enough in his ruffles to make his [grandson's] shirt'. Worse still, he cannot understand the fashionable slang:

Charlotte. Knowledge, as you arrange it, is a downright bore.

Gradus. 'Boar!' What relation can there be between knowledge and a 'hog'!

Charlotte. Lord bless me! How ridiculous. You must have spent your life in learning dead languages, and are ignorant of the living. Why sir, 'bore' is all the 'ton'.

Gradus. 'Ton'! 'ton'! What may that be? It cannot be orthology: I do not recollect its root in the present languages.

Charlotte. Ha, ha, ha! better and better. Why, sir, 'ton' means—'ton' is—Pho! What signifies where the root is? These kinds of words are the short hand of conversation, and convey whole sentences at once. All one likes is 'ton', and all one hates is 'bore'.[22]

Actually, by the date of that play, the image of the college had already begun to change. The days when Brasenose was regarded as hopelessly unsmart were almost over.

After mid-century Brasenose became not only richer but more visibly rich. The Radcliffe Camera was opened with great ceremony in 1749.[23] The college was now incontestably at the centre of Oxford. Recruitment expanded, rental income rose, social status increased. At a time when recruitment to the University in general was static or declining, the average Brasenose intake between the 1740s and the 1780s almost doubled. In 1761 the college books had shown a deficit of £444. By 1781 there was a surplus of £476. In between, in 1771, the surplus stood at something over £200. At this date, college accounts were still presented in Latin, with Roman numerals. Arabic numbers were not introduced until 1773; and Latin survived until 1835. That must have made accurate accounting difficult. But an attempt has been made—by W. T. Coxhill in 1944—to translate these arcane figures into intelligible terms. The table of income and expenditure for 1771 comes out, in money of that day, as follows:[24]

---

[22] H. Cowley, *Who's the Dupe?* (1779), Act I, scene 3, quoted in Wordsworth, *English Universities*, 307, 404, 473.

[23] For this moment of 'Grand Hurly Burly', see letters by Bray and Kennicott, 1749, printed in *Bodleian Quarterly Record*, 1 (1914–16), 165–72. For the text, in Latin and English, of Dr William King's Jacobite sermon, see Gough Oxf. 81 (5) and GA Oxon. 8vo 62 (3).

[24] Coxhill, 'Ralph Cawley', 237, based on Clennell B 53.7: Cawley Notebook vii.

Receipts	£	s	d
Rents	1615	1	6
do. Thornhill	272	7	7
do. Hinksey	30	0	0
Dividends	188	0	0
Room Rents	115	10	0
Admission Fees	8	8	4
Degree Fees	31	0	0
Payments			
Principal & Fellows	792	19	9
Scholars and Exhibitioners	303	2	9
College Entertainments	118	10	9
Agency and Management	86	5	$5\frac{1}{2}$
Maintenance of Establishment	77	19	0
Taxes (College)	24	18	$8\frac{1}{2}$
Quit Rents	25	12	$6\frac{1}{2}$
Brewing Account—loss	4	0	$0\frac{1}{2}$
Donations &c	19	7	0
Repairs—College	302	7	$3\frac{1}{2}$
Benefices, Augmentation of	130	0	0
Trusts, fixed payments	137	10	0

By 1771, then, with a surplus of £200 or so, Brasenose was beginning to advance. There would be deficits again; perhaps more than £500 in 1791 and 1801. But these were temporary difficulties. Benefactions increased. Rentals rose higher. The course of the college was now set fair.

To understand the emergence of Brasenose as a fashionable institution, one has first to grapple with the shifting roles of gentleman commoner, commoner, scholar, batteler, and servitor. The title gentleman commoner carried with it privileges of dress, diet, service, and accommodation. These privileges diminished with each downward step of the social ziggurat. Until 1768—at Brasenose at any rate—the gentleman commoner dined at high table; the commoner and the scholar dined in hall; the batteler fetched his commons from the buttery; and the servitor—almost literally—ate the crumbs from the rich man's table.[25] Commoners took precedence over scholars, at least that was the ruling in 1776.[26] And in hall a system of eight separate tables existed. On the dais, High Mess: one for senior Fellows and noblemen; one for junior Fellows and gentlemen commoners. In the body of the hall: masters, bach-

---

[25] Clennell B 53.14: Cawley Notebook, xiv, inside cover, 6 Jan. 1760. The butler is directed to 'have an eye towards the window where the Bread and Butter stands, for several have been found guilty of putting loaves in their sleeves and not putting on for them' (ibid., fo. 12).

[26] Clennell B 53.6: Cawley Notebook, vi, fo. 19: 2 July 1776.

elors, senior commoners, junior commoners, scholars, and battellers.[27] The servitor of the mid-eighteenth century performed many of the functions of the nineteenth- and early twentieth-century scout. So at the beginning of the eighteenth century there were actually no more than three bedmakers or scouts regularly employed at Brasenose. The other servants were the cook and the cook's assistant, the scullion, the butler and the butler's servant, the common-room man, the hall man and his servant, the barbitonsor, the porter, the gardener, and the bursar's man.[28] These were all remunerated through a complicated system of customary fees and perquisites known as 'styles'. And each gradation was formally expressed in a conventional code of manners. 'All ye Servants', noted the college butler at the beginning of the eighteenth century, 'Cap, i.e. go bare to Mr. Principal, and all Masters of Arts [cap] Fellows, especially in ye Buttery, Kitchen and Quadrangle. All ye House of what rank so ever cap Mr. Principal, and all Bachelors of Art and undergraduates except Gentle Men Commoners [go bareheaded] to Mr. Principal. Bachelors of Arts and undergraduates are not to come into ye Buttery tho' Bachelors are commonly connived at, but always go out if a Senior Fellow comes in. Undergraduates are often scons'd for it.'[29]

Such customs may have faded a little as the century progressed. But not until 1780 did battelers lose their service duties; not until the early 1790s were powdered wigs abandoned at dinner by gentlemen and commoners alike. And not until 1799 did Brasenose servitors cease to wait in hall.[30] Differentiated dress was certainly the rule until the 1770s: noblemen in gold lace, gentlemen in silk and velvet, commoners in bombazine, servitors in stuff. And dressing for dinner, in white waistcoat and stockings, sombre coat, and black pumps, continued throughout the century. Even so, from mid-century onwards, the social balance of the college was changing: battelers and servitors both belonged to dying species; commoners were getting richer, and gentlemen commoners were becoming very rich indeed.

Towards the end of the eighteenth century the payment of servants had reached a state of extraordinary complexity.[31] Wages taken in the form of

[27] Clennell B 53.14: Cawley [Shippary] Notebook, xiv, fo. 3. A plan of *c*.1705 shows six tables arranged about the central hearth, plus two high tables, one for senior, one for junior Fellows (almanac of Sir Holland Egerton, Bt., MPP 10 A1; cited by Jeffery in *Brazen Nose*, iv. 183–6). These gradations were reflected in the silver customarily presented to the college: in 1731 commoners gave pint mugs, scholars half-pint mugs, and battelers quarter-pint mugs. In 1758 three gentlemen commoners (William Lloyd, John Sneyd, and Richard Gorges) presented a fine silver tureen by Paul de Lamerie (H. Clifford, in *Studies in the Decorative Arts*, iii, no. 1 (1995–6), 2–28, and *A Treasured Inheritance* (Oxford, 2004), 31, 91–2).

[28] *Quat. Mon.* XIII, 45 n. 4.

[29] Clennell B 53.14: Cawley [Shippary] Notebook, xiv, fo. 17.

[30] *Quat. Mon.* XIII, 45; *Gent's Mag.* 57 (1787), 1146.

[31] For what follows, see Servants Wages 2, cited in Coxhill, 'Ralph Cawley', 188, 228–9.

'styles' must have been difficult to calculate and were certainly open to abuse. In 1773, for example, the porter was paid as follows:

a. Stipend [paid at Michaelmas]	£ 3.	o.	o.
b. Xtmas Box	o.	13.	4.
c. Stipend for lighting College lamps [paid in November]	1.	10.	o.
d. Attendance at the gate and			
e. for errands &c	101.	8.	1.
	106.	11.	5.

That represented a threefold increase on the porter's perquisites for the year 1753. The point was that perquisites varied according to the wealth and habits of undergraduates. Janitor's fees, for example, that is gate fines, were accumulated as follows:

For knocking in [after 9, and until Morning Prayers]
    2d. before, and 6d. after 11 o'clock
    1s. after 12.
    1s. 6d. after 1.
    2s. after 2.
    2s. 6d. after 3.
    3s. after 4.
    3s. 6d. after 5.
    4s. after 6.
    4s. 6d. after 7
For knocking out
    1d. at any hour.

The cost of staying out late escalated alarmingly hour by hour; and the porter's perquisites for errands were even more precisely graded.

½ penny	for an errand at a short distance
1d.	to Post-office or about that distance
1½ d.	to Water side or about that distance
2d.	for hiring an horse
1d.	for taking an horse home
½ d.	for drawing boots off
1½ d.	for cleaning boots and spurs
1d.	for cleaning shoes and buckles
1d.	for lighting fire and candle
½ d.	for lighting candle
1d.	for lighting chafing dish and filling kettle
½ d.	for filling kettle
½ d.	for carrying bread and butter to a Gentmans room.

In this way the head porter sometimes managed to bring in more cash than the head butler, whose perquisites—£101 1s. 1d. in 1771—were partly

measured out in barrels of ale. Either way, payments such as these, official—
and of course unofficial—survived in modified form until 1864. The gate fine
of 2*d*. for knocking in between 9 and 11 o'clock, imposed by the statutes of
1521, remained in force until 30 September 1932. Meanwhile the presence of
richer undergraduates—richer and gradually more numerous—obviously
had its advantages. As the social status of the college rose, so the value of
perquisites increased.

But Georgian Brasenose remained far from exclusive, at least by comparison with several other colleges. Early eighteenth-century matriculation and
buttery lists survive to show the wide variety of undergraduates. Two college
butlers (John Featly and Edward Shippary), for example, make their appearance, as well as two college cooks (Will Cookco and John Prickett). If we look
at the roll-call for 1712, we find that the twenty-three undergraduates who
arrived that year included two Grosvenors and an Egerton; but they also
included fifteen battelers, ten of them listed as plebeian. One of the commoners that year turned out to be a physician of some promise, Dr Jonathon
Goldsmith. He died aged 38, shortly after his election as Fellow of the Royal
Society. His portrait still graces the SCR.[32]

Things could be very different elsewhere. At New College, composed
largely of Wykehamists, there were no commoners at all until 1854. Instead
there might be up to a dozen gentlemen commoners resident in any one year.
By these terms Brasenose was certainly not smart. Nor as a college was it
particularly riotous. Still, there was the occasional incident. As pro-proctor in
1774—dressed up in bob-wig, cap, and gown—it fell to a Fellow of New
College, the future Parson Woodforde, to patrol the streets of Oxford at
night, looking for miscreants to include in his Proctor's Black Book.

Took a walk [he noted in July that year,] between 11 and 12 this Evening and
returned a little after 12. I met with one Mr. [William] Broome...of Brasenose
College [a commoner from Didsbury, Lancashire] very much in Liquor and who
talked rather saucily to me—but I saw him to his Coll.: and desired his Company to—
Morrow Morning...[When] Mr. Broome waited on me...with an Epistle [that is, a
formal apology]...I set him one of Swift's Sermons to translate into Latin for the
Offence he was guilty of.[33]

Unless he relied on a cooperative chum, Broome's Latin cannot have been all
that rusty: he handed in his translation within twenty-four hours.

Whatever the misdeeds of saucy Mr Broome, Brasenose was not in the same
league as richer colleges at this time when it came to bad behaviour. In 1775
New College was famed for the excesses of its gentlemen commoners. These
'black Guards of New College', so Woodforde reported, were notorious for

---

[32] Presented by Miss Constance Eastwick (V-P's Reg. 17 June 1970, fo. 137).
[33] Hargreaves-Mawdsley (ed.), *Woodforde at Oxford*, 236–7: 5–7 July 1774.

'very great Hollowing'; on one occasion they even pulled down the chimney-piece in their JCR. Brasenose, by comparison, appears rather low key in its manners. And sometimes those manners—by modern standards at least—must have been fairly crude. Take two items at random from the Bursar's accounts:

1754 A dog whip for the porter.
1777 Spitting basons [for] Common Room.[34]

Even so, by the 1760s, Brasenose had begun to expand its numbers and to rise in the social scale. The names of county families begin to appear more frequently in the matriculation lists—in 1758, for example, Hobhouse of Somerset, Sandbach of Cheshire, and Wodhull of Northamptonshire; in 1760 Foley of Herefordshire, Knightley of Northamptonshire, and Rawstorne of Lancashire; in 1769 Gennys of Devon, Lister of Yorkshire, and Sneyd of Staffordshire. And none of these were the sons of Brasenose men. But though the intake was becoming more genteel and more homogenized, there were still exceptions. In 1763, for instance, along with a Dashwood from Oxfordshire and a Noel from Leicestershire, the list of matriculands included one Thomas Clack, whose father owned the Lamb Inn at Wallingford, Berkshire. Apparently Lord Courtenay had fallen in love with Clack's sister. He sent young Thomas to Brasenose, and later presented him with two church livings. Such exceptions however only serve to prove the rule. The general trend towards gentility is clear.

Compare the intake of 1723 (Edward Greene's year) with the intake of 1774 (William Broome's year). In the first year there are only fourteen names to consider. Exactly half are plebeian battelers. Of the remaining seven only two, William Lenthall of Burford and Wyndham Napier—whom we last met drinking heavily with Greene—are listed as gentlemen commoners. Of the final five not one came from a grand gentry background.

Now look at the twenty-seven undergraduates in Broome's year, 1774. There are five gentlemen commoners: Samuel Bagshaw (Irish gentry), Penn Curzon (son of a Viscount), John Fazakerley (a Lancashire Etonian), Charles Drake (Buckinghamshire gentry), and William Assheton (Cheshire gentry). Three of these come from Brasenose families. Then there are six commoners listed as armigerous (John Harries, Benjamin Hobhouse, Edward Meyrick, William Muckleston, Richard Salmon, and Broome himself); and seven more who scrape into the gentry as 'generosus' (Samuel Antrobus, John Collet, William Dickenson, Thomas Gildart, John Longford, Richard Richardson, and Robert Wroe). To these we should perhaps add John Jackson, son of a Brasenose cleric, and Thomas Shepherd, also a clergyman's son but this time

---

[34] B 2a 42: Madan's notes. For New College, see Hargreaves-Mawdsley (ed.), *Woodforde at Oxford*, 309: 28 Nov. 1775.

a product of Eton. That leaves seven: only seven out of twenty-seven who were not—in the technical sense—gentlemen. Having their own way to make, all seven achieved successful careers. Henry Addington, the son of a doctor, has his own niche in history: he ended up as Viscount Sidmouth, BNC's first Prime Minister. Samuel Bethel, son of a cleric, stayed on as Fellow, Vice-Principal, and Junior Bursar. Robert Morres, son of a doctor, became a Fellow and then Prebendary of Salisbury. And four plebeian battelers—Matthew Blow, Joshua Brookes, Samuel Kent, and William Smith: the first two from Manchester Grammar School—followed the safe and customary path of cleric and schoolmaster. It has to be said that apart from Addington and Hobhouse—Hobhouse followed the future Prime Minister into government—only two members of Broome's year, Thomas Gilbert and John Harries, led lives that can remotely be described as dramatic. Gilbert, a Lancashire commoner, became a captain in Tarleton's Legion, a ferocious group of colonial loyalists in the American War of Independence. And Harries, a commoner from Pembrokeshire, ended as captain of the 33rd Foot; he was killed at the battle on the Brandywine in that same unhappy conflict.[35]

To recapitulate: it is not until the third quarter of the eighteenth century that Brasenose begins to become fashionable. Before that, except for a brief florescence of recruitment during Queen Anne's reign, the Georgian college was neither numerous nor smart. On the other hand the Senior Common Room seems early on to have established a reputation for indulgence. This particular Brasenose attribute was apparently common knowledge by the 1720s. According to Nicholas Amhurst's *Terrae-Filius*, Brasenose was known to engross good livings, and to brew ale strong enough to disturb the seasoned head of an Essex squire. In one play—James Miller's *Humours of Oxford* (1730)—a man who wishes to be taken for a Fellow of Brasenose has to use a large pillow for a stomach.[36]

More than enough evidence survives to illustrate the digestive capacity of Brasenose men at mid-century. When three Fellows went on a three-day progress to Great Rollright, they were more than adequately provisioned. With a 'Fricassey of chicken', a 'chine of mutton', and a 'Chalves head'—to say nothing of beer, bread, and 'pudden'—the bill came to £5 13s. 9d. And the general college bill for ale in 1762–3 suggests a very considerable thirst.

---

[35] For Addington and Hobhouse, see *ODNB*. Another Brasenose near contemporary, Thomas Lister, 1st Baron Ribblesdale, also raised a regiment, known as 'Lister's light dragoons', at the time of the American War.

[36] Amhurst, *Terrae-Filius* (1726), cited in Wordsworth, *English Universities*, 305.

1762.	Nov 24–Feb. 7. 1763 to Alderman Jues for Ale	£36	18	9
1763.	Feb. 11–May 11	£34	2	6
	May 19–Aug. 3.............................	£20	1	3
	Aug. 22–Nov. 9............................	£25	17	6.

These are formidable quantities: strong ale at this time was bought by the college at £1 10s. a barrel, and small beer at 7s. 6d. a barrel. Each barrel held 36 gallons.[37]

When it came to food, the quantities consumed were equally impressive. Dinner at Brasenose—the main meal of the day—moved gradually forward during the eighteenth century, from 11 a.m. in 1730, to 1 p.m. in 1753, to 4 p.m. in the 1790s. As dinner became later, so breakfast developed as a sociable meal, in order to balance the day. Supper in turn advanced correspondingly, from six in the evening to nine. In addition, of course, there were the informal meals—most famously sausages and mutton pies—surreptitiously swallowed in hostelries nearby. Still, whatever its official time, formal dinner in hall remained supreme as the social event of the day.

The manciple's order for the gaudy held on 29 May 1762—along with the butler's comments—deserves to be recorded.

23lb. Fresh Fish	...	£1. 4.0	*Jack* [pike] *too large.*
Salmon 36lb. at 10d	...	1. 10.0	
Hams 108lb. at 8d.	...	3. 11.4	*Hams too much.*
Lobster 50lb. at 10d.	...	2. 1. 8	*Lobsters too many.*
Pease	...	5. 0	
32 Chichings at 1/6	...	2. 8. 0	
18 Ducks at 1/6	...	1. 7. 0	
12 Geese	...	1. 16. 0	2 *geese supplied for High Table.*
Mutton 74 lb.	...	1. 4. 8	
Sr Beefe 78 lb.	...	1. 6. 0	*Beef too much by half.*
two tongues and Udders	...	10. 0	
Crawfish	...	10. 0	
Roots	...	6. 0	
Wine [and] Ancovies	...	5. 0	
Currin Jelley	...	2. 6	
Sugar [and] Spice	...	3. 0	
Lemmons and Oringes	...	4. 0	
Gravey Meat	...	5. 0	
Bread flower and eggs	...	3. 6	
Oyl vinegar and must[ard]	...	2. 6	
20lb. Butter	...	13. 4	
Garnish	...	2. 0	

[37] Clennell B 53.14, fo. 17; *Quat. Mon.* XIII, 53; R. W. Jeffery, *The Manors and Advowson of Great Rollright* (Oxford Record Soc., 1927), 184: appendix B.

	£	s	d	
6 dozen. Tarts	...	18. 0	*5 doz. enough.*	
6 dozen cheesecakes	...	12. 0	*5 doz. enough.*	
4 doz. custards	...	8. 0	*3 doz. enough.*	
Sallad and Cucumbers		10. 0	*Cucumbers unnecessary*	

At least the Butler drew the line at cucumbers.[38]
Nine years later, the Gaudy fare was less lavish, but still substantial.[39]

May 29th 1771.

	£	s	d
Two Turbet	2	10	1
24 Chickens	2	8	0
42lb. Bacon	1	11	6
5 Hd. Asparagus		12	6
Tongue, Udder		6	6
Pigg		6	0
Two Marrow puddings	1	10	0
Three Ducks		6	0
30 lb. Salmon	1	5	0
Lobsters		5	0
Two Ducks		4	0
Pudings		15	0
50 lb. Beef		18	3
36 Mutton		13	6
Butter Cheese		4	0
Cucumbers		9	0
Lettice		4	0
Currin Jelly		1	0
Onions H[orse] Radish			8
Lemmins Anchoveys		2	0
Oil Vinagar Mustard		1	6
Gravy Meat		3	6
Wine, Spice		2	6
Bread Eggs flour		1	0
Butter		7	6
Roots		2	6
[Supper at] Night			
Four Qr. Lamb		7	0
Sallad Cucumbers		2	6
Two Lobsters		3	0
Pye		2	6

[38] *Quat. Mon.* XIII, 56.
[39] Hurst Bursarial: Trades Bills 86, cited in Coxhill, 'Ralph Cawley', 124.

Every gaudy, of course, involved traditional formalities. Dinner and supper, with a break between for prayers, occupied more than five hours. Thanks to Principal Cawley's notebooks, we can follow the procedure in 1771–3 exactly.

The Speech was spoken at 2 o'clock. Dinner was served up immediately after. From the Hall the company retired to the Common Room...After the usual general Toasts, viz. Church and King, Queen and Royal Family, Chancellor and the University, all our Colleges and all our absent Members and Incumbents, they proceeded to toast a Gentleman and Lady together, in rotation. The Gentleman on my Right Hand was call'd upon to name a Gent., and the Gentleman on the Right Hand of that Gent., who sat opposite to me, was called upon to name a Lady. Then the 2nd Gentleman on the Right Hand of him, who sat opposite to me, [proposed] a Gentleman, and the 2nd on my Right Hand a Lady. And so on 'till all the Company had toasted. Then they proceeded to Sentimental toasts. [In 1771] I did not return [for supper] in the evening, nor did I wear the scarlet gown...After Grace, the Grace Cup went round. The Person that drinks stands up, and 2 more with him who are the nearest to him: After he has drank, he gives the Cup to one of those that first stood up with him and sits down; then another rises to make up the Triumvirate; and so on. In the yr. 1772 I was absent. But in 1773 present. I continued in the Common Room till near 7 o'clock, and missed Prayers. Coffee etc. came in about 6 o'clock.[40]

'Pan Cakes' on Shrove Tuesday, as well as 'Plumb Cake, Wassall and...verses by the Butler'; 'Snipes', 'Wood Cocks', 'Sweet Breads', 'Nets Tongue', and 'Tanzey Pudding' at the Betty Morley; baked cakes for the Principal each Epiphany; 'a Barrel of Oisters and...Dish of Neats' Tongues...with a Bottle of Sack, Buttery Ale, and Buttered Ale in abundance' at breakfast on the first Monday of Lent term: the diet of mid-Georgian dons can hardly be described as sparse.[41] No wonder the butler notes, circa 1706, 'that Green-Tea Bohea and Coffee & Chocolate are of late years thought fitter Break-Fasts for Philosophers'.[42] And no wonder, perhaps, that in 1788 James Brucker, the common-room man, found so much indulgence all too tempting: he stole 570 bottles of red port from the cellar. Committed to Oxford Castle, and condemned to death, he was eventually 'respited' and sent out to Botany Bay.[43]

---

[40] Clennell B 53.3: Cawley Notebook i, fo. 28.

[41] Ibid., fo. 18; Hurst Bursarial: Trades Bills 86–7, among tradesmen's bills 1691–1810.

[42] Clennell B 53.14: Cawley [Shippary] Notebook xiv, fo. 4. The first Monday breakfast of Lent term was followed at dinner by 'a Breast of Veal' and 'a Chine of Fowls', plus more oysters and neats' tongues, 'and 3 Bottles of wine or more according to ye greatness of ye Company'.

[43] *Jackson's Oxford Jnl.*, 5 June 1788, 9 July 1788, and 8 Apr. 1789.

Even feasts that did not rank as gaudies were to modern eyes gargantuan. On St Thomas's Day, 21 December 1771—the shortest day and the longest meal—the programme ran as follows:[44]

Dinner at 2 o'clock. 15 sat down, viz. 10 Fellows, 1 Gent. Commoner, Mrs. Huddesford [wife of the Keeper of the Ashmolean], Rawlins [Clerk of Accounts], myself and Mrs. Cawley—Prayers were put off till 5 o'clock. None of the company except the Vice Princ. (Mr. Cleaver) attended them, who read Prayers. We drank Tea and Coffee about 6 o'clock, and then sat down to Cards: there were two Tables. We continu'd at them till 9 o'clock, wn we sat down to Supper, a Barrel of oisters, and a plentiful cold Collation. Much more was provided for Supper than necessary [the surplus, of course, went to the servants]. The Company stay'd till ½ hour after 11 o'clock. 2 Bottles of Madeira and 3 of Lisbon were us'd at Dinner; and 1 Bottle of Madeira and 2 of Lisbon at supper and the evening: 5 bottles of Red Port were us'd at Dinner, and 2 at Supper.

Bill of Fare at Dinner

1st Course

Cod's Head and a Qr. Of Hundred of Smelts from London (at Oxon. much cheaper)	£1. 10. 6
To a Piece of Roast Beef Wt. 60lb. 4 oz.	1. 0. 0
To a Mock-Turtle	12. 0
To Cutletts (Mutton)	6
To Tongue	3. 0
To Sallad	1. 0
To Mince-Pies	3. 0
To Couple of Chickens	2. 8

2nd Course

To a Ragout	3. 0
To a Turkey	7. 0
To a Trifle	3. 6
To an Hundred of Asparagus	5. 0
To Apples stew'd	1. 0
To a Couple of Teal	3. 0
To Cheese-Cakes	1. 6
To Stew'd Pears	1. 0
To a Dozn of Larks	1. 3
To Tarts	1. 0
To 5 B. of Red Port, 2 B. of Madeira, 3 B. of Lisbon. In Toto	1. 1. 6
To Apples, Almonds and Raisins & Sweet Meats of various kinds	4. 0
To Bread & Beer & Butter	14. 0
To a bottle of Rum for Serv'ts	3. 0

---

[44] B 53.3: Cawley Notebook i, fo. 14^v–16; L. H. D. Buxton and S. Gibson, *Oxford University Ceremonies* (1935), 32 n.

Eggs and Lemons	5. o
To Coffee, Tea and Cards	6. o

Bill of Fare for Supper, all cold.

To a Couple of Fowls		2. 8
To a fore Qr. of Lamb		15. 8
To 2 small Lobsters		2. 3
To cold Tonge	charg'd before	
To potted Beef	..	
To Brawn	..	
To Tarts	..	
To Cheese-cakes	..	
To Stew'd Pears	..	
To Stew'd Apples	..	
To Blomonge		2. o
To a Barrel of Oisters on Side-Board		4. 6
To 2 B. of Red Port, 1 B. of Madeira and 2 B. of Lisbon		10.6
To Bread & Beer		1. o
To 8 Spermacet Candles at Cards and 4 at Supper		3. o

Note: this was a dinner and supper for no more than fifteen. It probably took place in the new Principal's Lodgings on the High.

So in Georgian Brasenose food was ample, and on occasion it was served with ceremony. What of the educational menu? It is tempting to assume that little teaching actually took place. Tempting, but not entirely true. Brasenose dons may not have matched in idleness Gibbon's notorious 'monks of Magdalen'. On the other hand, there is little evidence of pedagogic zeal. Professorial lectures in Oxford were famously infrequent; college tuition was haphazard. Georgian Fellows acted as moral tutors, but academic tuition can scarcely have been an overriding priority, except for scholars of the college. In effect, a Fellowship was a temporary billet for underemployed clergy; a bolthole for unmarried ordinands, pending the arrival of a benefice.

> ...listless, in the common room,
> They dream of happiness to come;
> And, weary of their learned life,
> Sigh for a living, or a wife.[45]

Thomas Hearne notes two instances of apparent neglect. Thomas Winder came up to Brasenose from Preston in 1726. 'He was a very civil, pretty, comely Gentleman, who wanted to be taken care of by his Tutor and others,

[45] 'K' [of Brasenose?], 1780, in *Poems Chiefly by Gentlemen of Devonshire and Cornwall*, ii (1792), 170.

that were to inspect him. But they were remiss.' Young Winder left for St Edmund Hall and proceeded to holy orders. He would have done better to go home and study Lancashire antiquities. Instead, he was appointed Vicar of Cockerham, and ended up insane.[46] Three years later Theodore Inge, son of a Staffordshire MP and antiquary, went up as a gentleman commoner. His father, Hearne tells us, was 'mighty desirous that his son should study our Antiquities'. Francis Yarborough was assigned as tutor. But the teaching seems to have made little impression. After Inge Sen.'s death, the young man abandoned Anglo-Saxon altogether, 'contrary to his father's design'.[47] Perhaps he simply preferred the duties of High Sheriff. At this distance of time, we cannot be sure. Clearly much depended upon individual motivation. There were no doubt a number of hard-reading men. In 1729 Charles Wesley gave it as his opinion that four hours' work a day was 'wretchedly lazy'.[48] But such judgements are notoriously subjective.

If we turn to the official roster of weekly teaching in Ralph Cawley's Notebook of circa 1770, we find a formidably prescriptive timetable:

Logical Lectures. Mondays, Wednesdays, Fridays in the Morning immediately after Prayers by the Dean & another. *Themes* on Saturdays given to the Dean. *Exercise pro Termino* to Ditto. *Vacation Exercise* to Ditto. *Mathematical Lecture* on Tuesdays at 9 o'clock, Morning. *Greek Lecture* on Thursdays at 9 in the Morning. *Declamations by undergraduates* on Wednesdays & Saturdays in *full Term* immediately after Dinner. Requir'd by the Vice-Princ. on *Wednesdays* & by the Dean *on Saturdays*. *Disputations by Bachelors* on Wednesdays & Fridays in the Ante-Chapel, immediately before Evening Prayer, in full Term. *Disputations by Undergraduates* on Mondays, Wednesdays & Fridays in full Term immediately before Dinner.

Such a timetable was not peculiar to Brasenose. The four-year course of study suggested by an anonymous don in *Advice to a Young Student by a Tutor* (1725) prescribes philosophy every morning and evening, classical literature in the afternoons, divinity on Sundays and church festivals. And the recommended bibliography is no laughing matter: from Cicero to Grotius, from Juvenal to Sophocles, from Newton's *Optics* to Locke's *An Essay Concerning Human Understanding*.

But these were surely counsels of perfection. In actual fact the regime at Brasenose—as elsewhere—must have been a good deal less onerous. In any case study tended to be enlivened by good living. At significant moments academic exercises were sweetened with agreeable ceremony. On New Year's Day, for example, Cawley noted that 'the Scholars bring the Principal each a Latin Epistle or Address . . . and he gives them each ½ a roasted Fowl. But

---

[46] *Hearne's Collections*, xi. 415: 24 Jan. 1734–5; MPP 56 F4/1.
[47] *Hearne's Collections*, x 134: 21 May 1729 and xi. 72: 22 June 1732.
[48] V. H. H. Green, *Young Mr. Wesley* (1961), 149.

in...1772 he gave them also each a Pint of Red Port. There were 6 Scholars: Fowls 5s. od. Wine 5s. In Toto 10s. od.'⁴⁹

Two important letters survive, written to Lloyd Kenyon in 1750, one from John Kenrick and one from George Kenyon. These do suggest a certain regard for the conditions of learning. But at the same time they hint at an element of laxity in practice. Kenrick was a batteler, Kenyon a commoner. Both matriculated in the same year. In October 1750 Kenrick underwent his 'examination for admission'. Having been well drilled at school, this caused him little difficulty.

My tutor first of all tried me in epics and Horace; the next day the Principal [Yarborough] sent for me, and put a Horace in my hand, and then Virgil, and lastly Sophocles, where I read half a dozen lines...[Finally] he gave me a theme to make.

Having negotiated this 'farce', Kenrick then settled down to his first term. He found that although hard reading was not obligatory, the conditions for study were certainly there.

We...are not absolutely obliged to pursue our studies, but...there are so many restraints laid upon us, that [the Fellows] almost put it out of our power to avoid it. For, if we appear out [side college], we are in danger of being taken by the Proctors, or of being branded by names of loungers; besides, we have duties in...college to attend, all [of] which...make our confinement here as great as at school, [though] far [less] disagreeable, for...we can employ some part of the day with a great deal of pleasure in our private chambers, exclusive of all obligation.

As to formal lessons,

First...with our private tutor we are lectured in Plato's Dialogues and logic, whenever he pleases to call upon us; for our public lectures in the hall, we have particular days in the week, which consists of Xenophon's *Memorabilia,* and Horace, by two different lecturers, one of whom is Mr. [Roger] Mather, a very ingenious man...As for our exercises, they are disputations, three times a week, besides a declamation every term.

'Last week', he concludes, 'I [began] to dispute...a work which I do not like much as yet, though I chop logic pretty fast.'

This account seems to have left Kenrick's guardian, the future Lord Kenyon, rather bemused. Surely an Oxford college should be rather less constricting? Kenyon's son George was able to put his father's mind at rest. Oxford, he explained,

---

⁴⁹ Clennell B 53.3: Cawley Notebook i, fos. 17 and 27. See also C. Wordsworth, *Scholae Academicae: Some Account of the Studies at the English Universities in the Eighteenth Century* (Cambridge, 1877).

is indeed a very different place to different persons. The [commoner's] gown a man wears excuses him from many exercises, as a lower [batteler's] gown obliges him to them. Besides this [Kenrick] has got an office that obliges him to attend morning, noon and night, so that he can never be away six hours together. This ... is confinement indeed, and no wonder he ... prefer[s] school to it. However, he will be eased of this in a little time. The only exercises we have to do is to repeat a passage out of a classic; every day at dinner, when it comes to our turns; to dispute in turns; to make a theme once a week and a declamation once a term, and to read the lessons in chapel, when we are a year's standing, in turn. Most of these, you see, come to us one after another, so that we are not often plagued with them, and the rest, if a man will, may very easily be slubbered over.[50]

So there it is, mid-Georgian pedagogy at Brasenose: daily tutorial classes, regular lectures and disputations; weekly themes; termly declamations. The framework of tuition was there, albeit narrowly tied to Greek, Latin, and mathematics. But in practice the system seems to have atrophied into ritual. The emphasis is on verbal facility. But the exercises are mostly formulaic; rote learning and memory work, with small scope for development and little sense of competition. Crucially, there was no notion of verifiable standards: curriculum-based final examinations had yet to emerge. The medieval system of disputation—Opponent versus Respondent in the Examination Schools—had degenerated into a charade performed with proctorial connivance and the use of syllogistical cribs. What was once a serious trial of wits had declined into nothing more than a ceremony.[51]

If there were serious scholars at Brasenose during this period, they tended to come from Manchester Grammar School. In the thirty-five years 1738–73 there were some eighty entrants from Manchester to Brasenose. They arrived at a rate of two or three per year; and they represented perhaps one-sixth of the total intake. On the face of it, that seems a fairly low percentage. But their impact on the college was out of all proportion to their numbers: no less than eighteen became Fellows. Most of them then proceeded to go into the Church fairly quickly. Some later returned to Manchester; some went into college benefices via short-lived college Fellowships. But all of them must have had an identifiably Mancunian stamp: academic learning of metropolitan standard, minus the dubious polish of the metropolis.

The links between Brasenose and Manchester had been amply strengthened in the 1680s by the bounty of Sarah, Dowager Duchess of Somerset (pl. 22).

---

[50] HMC, *Kenyon MSS*, 492: 14 Nov. 1750 and 16 Nov. 1750. Mather is the only member of Brasenose to have been Public Orator; in his time the post was worth £6 13s. 4d. p.a. For a portrait of Mather with his pupil Assheton Curzon, see *Polite Society by Arthur Devis* (Preston, 1983), 104, no. 34.

[51] *Gent's Mag.* l (1780), 119, 277: Observations on the 'Examination system'.

Born about 1630, she was the daughter and co-heiress of Edward Alston, a leading London physician. Her first husband, George Grimston, was a Brasenose lawyer: he died at the age of 23. Her second husband was a Whig MP, the Hon. John Seymour, subsequently fourth Duke of Somerset: he died in 1674. Her third husband was Henry Hare, second Baron Coleraine: he was an antiquary from whom she quickly separated. All three husbands were rich; but her father was richest of all. From each of her marriages, but especially from her father's estate, the future benefactress drew substantial property. Some of this went eventually to St John's College Cambridge. But much was directed towards Brasenose. From 1679 onwards four Somerset Scholars, educated at Manchester—with preference for those born in the counties of Lancashire, Cheshire, or Hereford—were to be elected each year. Their endowment—which stayed with the college until 1894—consisted of tenanted farms within the manor of Iver, Buckinghamshire. Somerset Scholars were provided with rooms and sustenance, as well as caps and gowns; and they had to converse in Latin, with a fine of twopence for each breach of the rule. From 1686 and 1691 onwards, several more scholars each year were privileged to follow the same path, from Manchester, Hereford, and Marlborough schools. Their endowments were the estates of Thornhill and Wootton Rivers, in Wiltshire. At its peak, the Somerset foundation supplied four Somerset (Iver) Scholars and eighteen Somerset (Thornhill) Scholars each year. As her monument in Westminster Abbey proclaims, Sarah's 'never failing generosity to the poor'—among her many other good works—had 'richly endowed for all time' the King's Hall and College of Brasenose.[52]

But all this was surpassed by the legacy of William Hulme. The Hulmes were minor Lancashire gentry, Anglican and royalist, with sizeable land holdings in the Manchester area. As Manchester grew in wealth, so the value of the Hulme property increased. And so, from William Hulme of Kearsley—Manchester Grammar School, Brasenose, and Gray's Inn—came the endowment that has supported generations of Senior Hulme Scholars. In 1691 the income from the Hulme Trust was £80 p.a. Two hundred years later its endowment had multiplied hugely: from the Hulme Surplus Fund came the capital that paid for the late Victorian building programme at Brasenose.

---

[52] Somerset bequests 1679, 1686, 1691 (Hereford Cathedral Archives, 1536); *Property and Income of Oxford and Cambridge* (Cleveland Commission), ii (1874), 607–8; *ODNB*: s.v. Alston, Coleraine; A. A. Mumford, *Manchester Grammar School, 1515–1915* (1919), 111–13; A. D. Briscoe, *A Stuart Benefactress* (Lavenham, 1973), 196–201. Portrait in hall: copy by Thomas Gibson, 1728 (Hurst Bursarial, Tradesman's Bills 35; *Quat. Mon.* IV, 27–8). Coleraine's heir, the 3rd Baron, became Grand Master of Freemasons in 1727, and a member of William Stukeley's Brazen-nose Society at Stamford. For Grinling Gibbons' monument to the Duchess (illus. Dart, *Westminster*, ii. 5; reduced 1876), see J. D. Stewart in *Burlington Mag.*, Mar. 1963.

By the twentieth century the value of the Hulmeian assets ran into millions. Hulme's only child, Banaster Hulme, had died young—the result of a schoolboy tussle at the age of 15—just as he was due to go up to university.[53] From this tragedy came much good. From 1691 onwards dates the trust—deriving from property at Heaton-Norris, Denton, Ashton-under-Lyne, Redditch, Manchester, and Harwood—which has bolstered so many post-graduate careers. It was a highly enlightened endowment—up to 'four Exhibitions, for the poorest sort of Bachelors of Art for the space of four years'—and its origins deserve a moment's pause.

James Grundy of Bolton le Moors [recalled] ... that William Hulme had ... noticed that the county of Lancaster, especially about Manchester, had sent more scholars to the University than any other county or place, but that many who sent their sons were not able to maintain them in the University any longer than to make them Bachelors of Arts, and consequently such young scholars were necessitated to turn preachers before they were qualified for that work ... [Hence his decision to maintain] four such Bachelors of Arts that were Lancashire scholars especially of this part of the county where he lived, and had not wherewith to maintain themselves any longer in the University.[54]

Scholars from Manchester Grammar School—'School Exhibitioners'—had long been subsidized at Brasenose out of school funds. And they would continue in an unbroken line until 1856. But these new Hulme Scholarships were different. They were for graduates proceeding to MA status: 640 of them between 1691 and 1881. It is an impressive record. As the trust increased in value so its benefits were expanded. After a redistribution of assets in 1881, they included undergraduate scholarships for pupils from the newly founded Hulme Grammar Schools in Manchester, Oldham, and Bury. Socially, and even academically, Manchester Grammar School went into a

---

[53] The injury may have triggered some form of meningitis. The evidence for Hulme of Kearsley's own education at MGS is slim. Rather stronger is the Hulme connection with BNC.: Thomas Hulme went up in 1586; John and Samuel Hulme of Redditch in 1625 and 1632; and William Hulme himself in the ominous year 1648. There are brasses to William Hulme (1691) in Manchester Cathedral, and in the hall at Brasenose. Curiously, his name was not added to the list of benefactors in the Long Grace—along with that of Maurice Platnauer—until 1975 (V-P's Reg. 30 Apr., fo. 38).

[54] W. H. Whatton, in S. Hibbert-Ware (ed.), *History of the Foundations in Manchester etc.*, iii (Manchester, 1834); Benefactors Book, 1691; *Quat. Mon.* IV, 30; *ODNB* s.v. Hulme. Up to 1870, £80,000 was spent in the purchase of benefices for former exhibitioners. The stipulation relating to 'scholars of the poorest sort' was not very strictly interpreted: in the decade up to 1700, six out of twelve were sons of clerics, three of 'plebeians', and two of 'generosi'. *Ex inf.* Dr I. D. Fallows. For lists of the various Hulme Acts governing the operation of the Hulme Trust, see *Quat. Mon.* VIII, 28. For a clear exposition, by Sir Noel Hall, see V-P's Reg. 17 June 1972, fo. 139.

period of comparative decline after the 1780s. But the prestige of the Hulme awards continued—and continues—to increase.

Education at Manchester Grammar School was sufficiently liberal in the mid-eighteenth century to produce several Brasenose men of unusual scholastic talents—James Walker, FRS, for example, who returned eventually to practise at Manchester Infirmary. Or Joshua Brookes, the son of a shoemaker, who came up late to Brasenose at the age of 20 but never forsook his roots. As schoolmaster and chaplain—eccentric, uncouth, prodigiously learned—'Jotty Bruks' was one of the best-known Mancunians of his day.[55] The intake of the school at this time—at least until the 1780s—was extraordinarily wide: families like the Stanleys and the Egertons sitting side by side with the sons of cobblers and weavers, dyers, bakers, and fustian cutters. In four successive quinquennia, 1765–85, the sons of the nobility and gentry almost exactly balanced the numbers drawn from manufacturing and mercantile families; with the numbers from both those categories together almost exactly balancing the numbers drawn from shopkeeping and artisan backgrounds.[56] Thereafter the intake begins to narrow towards the centre of the social spectrum: the numbers from gentry and artisan families diminish; the numbers from manufacturing backgrounds increase. The basis of the school curriculum throughout this period was still, of course, the study of Latin and Greek. And that is reflected in the Brasenose intake. One list survives with the names of pupils who delivered the Latin Speech each Christmas. Between 1750 and 1785 at least nine of these star pupils went on to Brasenose. During the 1770s and 1780s Manchester Grammar School produced seven successive Brasenose Vice-Principals. One of them was a curiosity. His name was Samuel Henshall. Now Henshall, it seems, may have been less than sane. J. M. Kemble called him an 'irrecoverable madman'. But he was certainly capable of learned works—*The Saxon and English Languages Reciprocally Illustrative of Each Other* (1798), for example. And when his scholarship was impugned by 'idle blockheads' in the *Gentleman's Magazine,* he stoutly defended his Mancunian training: first and foremost, he took pride in being 'a sound Manchester schoolboy'.[57]

What of non-academic concerns? Mid-Georgian undergraduates took sport rather less seriously than their Victorian successors. Some of their games

---

[55] J. F. Finch (ed.), *Manchester School Register,* i (Chetham Soc. 69, 1866), 109–13; *ODNB.* Brookes is portrayed by Mrs G. Linnaeus Banks (née Isabella Varley) in *The Manchester Man* (1870; 5th edn. 1882), appendix i.

[56] Mumford, *Manchester Grammar School,* 530.

[57] *ODNB*; *Brazen Nose,* xvi, no. 3, 47. The Latin prizewinners were John Darwall, James Wilde, (?) George Hodson, Thomas Breithweite, John Gill, Thomas Sutton, Abraham Ashworth, and (?) John Fenwicke (Mumford, in Chetham Soc., NS. 80, 1921, 12–13). During the same period 124 pupils went on to Oxford (Mumford, *Manchester Grammar School,* 529).

were innocent enough: fives, skittles, boating, or billiards. Others were less innocent: bull baiting at Carfax, cock fighting in Holywell. In 1772 horse racing and cock fighting had to be forbidden by statute, 'forasmuch as the unbridled and deadly love of games for a monied stake has in some measure made inroads upon the University itself, whereby the fame and reputation of the University may be stained from the hearts of young men being set upon horse-racing and cock-fighting'.[58] No doubt some Brasenose men found ways to circumvent these restrictions, as they most surely did the University's attempt in 1785 to restrict the ownership of horses to those of MA status. But then race meetings had always been considered 'fast'; other pastimes were cheaper. At Christ Church John Wesley is known to have played real tennis; at New College Parson Woodforde was an early enthusiast for cricket. And both men occasionally shot and fished. But Brasenose at mid-century was a poorer place than either of those colleges. There were few who could pay to hire horses regularly, and fewer still who could afford to keep their own. At Brasenose early eighteenth-century undergraduates seem to have ridden little and hunted less.

For those unable to afford riding or field sports, open-air recreation seems mostly to have consisted of long walks, and very long walks. When young John Byrom of Manchester visited Oxford in 1731, he spent several days eating plain meals and strolling the Thames Valley and the Cotswolds. Byrom was a gent, and already something of a poet. He was also a Cambridge man; though he had friends at Oxford. His contacts at Brasenose were three fellow Lancastrians: John Clayton—a Hulme Exhibitioner—and two undergraduates, William Parker and Thomas Foxley. One Thursday morning in June Byrom decided to walk from Maidenhead to Oxford, via Henley and Dorchester, 'drinking cider and water only by the way'. With his relative Thomas Houghton as companion, he reached Brasenose at 11 o'clock that night.

We found Mr. Clayton in his room...drank cider, and ate nothing; next morning breakfasted at Mr. Clayton's. Mr. Parker, Mr. Foxley there but did not drink tea because [Clayton] said it made his hand shake. I went into the library of Brasenose between eleven and twelve, met with nothing extraordinary; we are going to dine in Mr. Clayton's room, Houghton is gone to bathe him.

The following morning, Saturday, Byrom set out with Houghton and Clayton and four more Brasenose friends—Robert Thyer, Thomas Alcock, John Smith, and Thomas Maddock—to walk to Woodstock and Blenheim.

[We] set out...at half-past three [a.m.] and came to Woodstock about 5 o'clock, had tea, coffee, bread and butter, 5s 4d. Houghton, Thyer, Alcock, gave me half a guinea

---

[58] *Quat. Mon.* XIII, 46–7. For sports, see G. Midgley, *University Life in 18th Century Oxford* (1996), ch. ix.

apiece, and Smith and Madock 1s. apiece, and we treated Clayton; we walked all to Blenheim, and there Clayton and Smith took leave of us [presumably to take a coach back], and we came on to [Chipping Norton] twenty minutes before 11 o'clock, it being a fine day for walking, being a brisk wind. [Then back by coach to Oxford]. We had a dish of fish and pease [they were, after all, Lancashire men] at Mr. Clayton's; went to the Bodleian library in the afternoon . . . Supped at Clayton's, had a bottle of mead, of which I drank most, and it agreed with me very well, and made me sleep, and I lay till eleven o'clock . . . [Then] we dined with Mr. Foxley . . . and Mr. Parker on fish and pease, and about three [p.m.] went to Queen's College . . . [Next] we saw . . . [Christ Church] library . . . [and] the library of Corpus Christi College; we supped at Mr. Foxley's. Clayton's old bedmaker called me at 3 [a.m.], and I rose up, and the other gentlemen, and we sallied forth; I gave 1s. apiece to two men and a woman at Mr. Foxley's, and 2s. to Mr. Clayton's old woman for her and Mary, and forgot the barber.

Next day they went on to Moreton in Marsh, resting there for tea and cider, 'for we had walked fast'. Then on to Broadway, for a supper of 'bacon and eggs'. And the day after that they pressed on via Pershore ('pudding and fowl' for dinner), in time to eat 'chickens and asparagus' at 1s. apiece at Worcester ('very reasonable'). There, alas, they found that 'the box from Oxford was left at Moreton that had our linen in; I bought a shirt 6s. 6d., stock 7d., pair of thread stockings 3s. 3d., pair of gloves 2s.' Still the day ended well, with a moonlight stroll to the cathedral, and bed at nearly 12 o'clock.

Next day they took a boat to Bridgnorth, dining at Bewdley on the way: 'a very good dinner and beer and ale, all for 5s. 9d., with ale for the waterman, we had boiled fowl and bacon, with fillet of veal roasted, calves' feet, two fine pickled trout, and half a dozen very fresh good cheesecakes, and civil folks.' Next morning Byrom was the only one awake.

I called them up . . . at six o'clock, and rang a bell that was on the staircase, but yet they none of 'em heard it, and I said to them:

> Ye men that came from Brazen Nose
> Into Bridgnorth upon your toes,
> Pray on your beds no longer lie
> If you would see fair Shrewsbury.

When they got back to Manchester, several days later, 'the bells rang upon [their] coming'.[59]

Byrom's weekend interlude that summer term in 1731, with Clayton, Foxley, Thyer, and the rest, tells us something about the lives of one particular group of early Georgian Brasenose men. They are serious minded, sober, and not particularly rich. They are too solemn for the usual undergraduate pastimes of

---

[59] *Literary Remains of John Byrom*, ed. R. Parkinson, i/2 (Chetham Soc. 34, 1855), 314–17: 3–6 June 1731. For Robert Thyer see *Manchester School Register*, i. 39–42.

billiards, skittles, or cards. Their sympathies are high Anglican and Jacobite; and they are mostly Lancashire born and bred. We will meet them again, under less happy circumstances, in 1745. But first we must deal with the man who dominated Brasenose in the first half of the eighteenth century: the Revd Dr Robert Shippen (pl. 17).

Robert Shippen—Principal for thirty-five years, 1710–45—might almost stand as an archetype of unreformed Oxford. He came to Brasenose from Merton; ultimately from Stockport Grammar School in Cheshire. And he achieved a Fellowship by trickery: he was elected Williamson Fellow in 1698 on the basis of a false pedigree.[60] The next step was ordination. Shippen's career in the Church clearly involved no sense of vocation: he was, first and last, a clerical *politique*. His Toryism—many called it Jacobitism—was sufficiently elastic to encompass both support for the high-church views of Dr Sacheverell and acceptance of the Revolution Settlement.[61] His next big promotion came in 1705, as Gresham Professor of Music in London. This was characterized at the time as no more than a 'Piece of Impudence'. He knew little of music; and the post was so obviously a sinecure that it could be handed on eventually to his eldest brother Edward, also a Brasenose man.[62] Then in 1710 came the Principalship. Like his election as FRS in 1706, this can only be ascribed to his connections and to his talent for intrigue. Finally, there was his apotheosis as Vice-Chancellor of Oxford, in 1718–23. This appointment—renewed, most unusually, for five successive years—was essentially a tactical compact. The Chancellor, Lord Arran, was in the same political camp as another of Shippen's brothers—and another Brasenose man—'Honest' Will Shippen, Tory leader in the House of Commons.

These are just the highlights in a career notorious even by the standards of early eighteenth-century Oxford. The evidence is contained in letters and journals of the period. Of course they must be used with caution. The colourful language in Thomas Hearne's diary has sometimes to be taken with a pinch of salt. Shippen was in fact by no means wholly hostile to Hearne: he protected rather than prosecuted that wayward scholar.[63] Hearne, however, continued to nurture a sense of grievance. He relishes every chance to blacken Shippen's name. Even so, in matters of fact we can probably trust

---

[60] Muniments a 1; MPP 56 F4/10: R. W. Jeffery, 'Robert Shippen' (MS, n.d.), 13–16. His grandfather, Anthony Alcocke, had been a Nowell Scholar at Brasenose in 1624, and became Sub-Dean of York.

[61] HMC, *Kenyon MSS*, 447: R. K[enyon] to Mrs Kenyon, 27 Oct. 1711.

[62] Jeffery, 'Shippen', 18; *Hearne's Collections*, iii. 8: 2 June 1710. He defeated 'ye ingenious Mr. Estwick, formerly of Christ-Church, who . . . understand [s] Musick as well as any Man in England'.

[63] *Hearne's Collections*, vi. 395: 14 Oct. 1718 and 398–401: 21 Oct. 1718; HMC, *Portland MSS*, vii. 245: 29 Oct. 1718.

him. And there is testimony elsewhere. Dr William Stratford, Canon of Christ Church, is an equally damning, and rather more circumspect, witness.[64] Politically, Hearne and Stratford were both allies of Shippen. All three hated the Whigs. But politics was not the problem. It was on personal grounds that Shippen was despised. And the weight of evidence is compelling. Shippen of Brasenose was an intriguer, a trickster, a bully, and a womanizer.

It was on 2 June 1710 that Shippen secured the Principalship. At that point there were still only six senior Fellows. They had grown used to a lax regime. John Meare had been Principal since 1681, and as we have seen he achieved the office of Vice-Chancellor in 1697. But he seems never to have been 'noted for Learning or anything else'.[65] Like the bulk of Brasenose Fellows he had compromised with the Whig regime. As Vice-Chancellor, however, he went further. He alienated many by currying favour with London. As the years went by, he grew increasingly incapable; in truth increasingly insane. By 1705 there seemed no hope of recovery.[66] In 1707—the year Shippen became a senior Fellow—Meare's 'great Indisposition' finally presented Shippen and his 'cronies' with an opportunity to take control. First they tried to persuade the Visitor—Dr Wake, Bishop of Lincoln—to remove their ailing Principal altogether. This the Visitor declined to do. He vowed, in fact, to protect 'the poor man' against 'any such hard, however Statutable, Tiger from falling upon Him'.[67] After all, the college seemed safe enough; it was effectively in the hands of a sound Vice-Principal named James Smethurst: 'a good Scholar, an Honest man, and a true and faithful Friend to his College'.[68] But when Smethurst died suddenly on 5 March 1709, the 'Shippen gang' (William Thompson, Thomas Slade, Henry Newcome, and Shippen himself) mounted a *coup d'état*. Without Meare's knowledge or sanction they elected Thompson as Vice-Principal.[69]

---

[64] e.g. his account of Shippen's unpopularity as Vice-Chancellor in his letters to Edward Harley, 2nd Earl of Oxford (HMC, *Portland MSS*, vii. 252–3, 271, 300–1, 318, 335, 354, 360–1). 'So corrupt a man' (ibid. 72).

[65] *Hearne's Collections*, ii. 395: 19 May 1710. For Meare's diary as Vice-Chancellor, 7 Sept.–4 Dec. 1697, see Hurst College Principal, 36–7. See also *Oxford Mag.* 2, 9 Feb. 1911, 169–70 and 188–90.

[66] Bodl. MS Ballard 3, no. 48: Wake to Charlett, 16 Feb. 1709.

[67] Ibid., nos. 38–9: 10 Jan. 1706 and 16 Mar. 1707; V-P's Reg. 23 Dec. 1707, fos. 165ᵛ–166.

[68] *Hearne's Collections*, ii. 127, 173–4, 452–3. Smethurst was buried in chapel on 10 Mar. 1709.

[69] Meare was at this point *hors de combat*: 'per adversam valetudinem impeditus' (Bodl. MS Rawl. D 912, fo. 303ʳ). George Freeman, John Hyde, and Thomas Stanley, who had been outvoted by Shippen's 'gang', protested to the Visitor against this 'pretended election' (V-P's Reg. 16 Mar. 1709, fo. 168). It may have been at this point that they put out an offer of the Principalship to one elderly Brasenose establishmentarian, William Assheton (*ODNB*).

Now Thompson seems to have been quite unsuitable. One of Wake's correspondents—admittedly an anonymous informer—described him as 'a sot and gambler . . . a Blockhead and Illiterate'.[70] Be that as it may, the Visitor expressed his 'astonishment', and immediately denounced the proceeding as 'RASH, PRESUMPTUOUS, and UNWARRENTABLE'; in fact 'NULL and of no Force'.[71] Clearly Dr Wake was not to be browbeaten. But the younger Fellows would have none of him. He was after all a Whig; and Shippen, their preferred nominee, was very much a Tory. Even so, Wake remained obdurate in the face of pressure. He formally declared Thompson's election void. 'If somewhat be not done for this unfortunate College', he wrote 'it will I doubt come to ruine.'[72] The omens of succession, however, were clear. Slade died in October 1709. During 1710 the three senior Fellows who had taken the Visitor's side—George Freeman, John Hyde, and Thomas Stanley—departed to rectories at Steeple Aston, Middleton Cheney, and Didcot. They had few prospects in Brasenose. For on 18 May 1710 Dr Meare had died at last. And within three weeks it was Shippen who was chosen to succeed him.[73]

'The Competitors' in this election, Hearne tells us, 'were Dr. Smith, Principal of Hart Hall and formerly Fellow [of Brasenose] . . . and Mr. Robert Shippen . . . Mr. Shippen carried it by one vote.' Hearne considered Smith 'a Man of Learning and a good Disciplinarian'; though the Visitor noted he was also a heavy drinker. Anyway, it was Shippen who won the day. Hearne did not mince words: 'being a sly, worldly Man and having no small stock of Confidence (without anything of Letters) and being withall but young . . . and having wheedled himself into ye Affections of the greatest Part of the College, who expect to live easy under him, without Prosecution of Studies (according to the modern Custom) [Shippen] carried his Point . . . easily.'[74] And there was another factor too: 1710 was the year of the Sacheverell frenzy. It was a good moment to be an Oxford Tory. Within weeks Smith

[70] Wake to Charlett: Bodl. MS Ballard 3, nos. 48, 76, 93, 95, and 35 no. 117.

[71] V-P's Reg. 22 Mar. 1709, fos. 168ᵛ–169ᵛ; Bodl. MS Ballard 3, no. 51: Wake to Charlett, 19 Apr. 1709. The election seems to have been effected by 'a Fellow [Thompson] going out of Town, to let another into the Seniority to vote for him . . . [in a matter] in which He is expresly forbidden to Vote for Himselfe'. In *Quat. Mon.* XII, 25–6 Lodge cites a MS List of Officers drawn up by John Holmes (Fellow 1770–88). Thompson died 4 Apr. 1713, and was buried in the cloister.

[72] Bodl. MS Ballard 3, no. 51: Wake to Charlett, 19 Apr. 1709.

[73] *Hearne's Collections*, ii. 295: 28 Oct. 1709; V-P's Reg. 22 Oct. 1709, fos. 170ᵛ, 22 Dec. 1709, fo. 171, and 18 May 1710, fo. 172ʳ⁻ᵛ. Hearne claims that Meare was buried in chapel on 20 May 1710, but there is no memorial.

[74] Bodl. MS Ballard 3, no. 48: Wake to Charlett, 16 Feb. 1709; *Hearne's Collections*, iii. 8: 2 June 1710. Smith died a few weeks later, in July 1710, thus vacating the Brasenose benefice of Great Billing (ibid. 25). See Christ Church MS Arch. W. Epist. 16, no. 216 [316].

was dead, and the new Principal was wearing a doctoral gown. And so was
one of his allies in the recent election, Robert Bavand. According to Hearne,
this Bavand was no more than 'a white liver'd, sneaking, mean-spirited and
hypochondriacal Fellow'.[75]

But first things first. Within five months of his election, in time for the
start of Michaelmas term 1710, Shippen had found himself a wife. She was
Frances, widow of Sir Gilbert Clarke. The couple had probably known each
other for some time: she was the sister of Dr Calverley Legh—'Stag' Legh of
Brasenose and All Souls—and like Shippen she came from a Cheshire family.
Two things she shared with her brother: she liked to drink, and she liked to
quarrel. 'This Dr. Leigh', notes Hearne, 'was a terrible hard Drinker (which
shortened his life) and very troublesome [in college], he taking delight to
foment Differences.'[76] The gossips soon had plenty to talk about. Lady
Clarke was perhaps seventeen years Shippen's senior, and she had already
buried three husbands. But the Principal knew what he was doing: she had
'500 libs. per an. Rent-Charge, besides a great Sum of Money'.[77] No doubt
she found the Lodgings somewhat cramped. Within weeks the Shippens had
taken over several adjacent rooms next to the new Library.[78] By the 1720s
they had seven servants. Their social life oscillated between Oxford and
London, and between Newcome's house at Ewelme and their own country
residence, Appleton Manor, Berkshire.[79] When it came to high living, Lady
Clarke—she retained her old title—seems to have matched her fourth
husband blow for blow. 'She was a very proud Woman', noted Hearne at
her death in 1725; 'given much to drinking and gaming, and did no good.'[80]

In one year, 1710, Shippen had thus secured the Principalship and a rich
wife, as well as a non-resident rectory at Great Billing in Northamptonshire.
He had the grace to surrender his chair at Gresham College. But he was still
not satisfied. That same year Brasenose purchased the advowsons of Stepney
and several other churches in East London.[81] Among these was the rectory

---

[75] *Hearne's Collections*, iii. 21: 7 July 1710.

[76] Ibid., ix. 302: 30 Apr. 1727.

[77] Ibid., iii. 72: 25 Oct. 1710.

[78] V-P's Reg. 11 Jan. 1711, fo. 6. By the 1720s they had two maids and a scullion living in,
plus two male servants, a coachman and a groom, living out. These were reduced to one maid,
one manservant, and a groom after Lady Clarke's death (Bursar's Account Books, cited in
Jeffery, 'Shippen').

[79] *Hearne's Collections*, ix. 283: 5 Mar. 1727. For some years Shippen owned a property in
Goodman's Fields, close to a Jacobite 'safe house' and to Dr Welton's non-juring chapel
(R. Sharp, *The Engraved Record of the Jacobite Movement* (1996), no. 659; Monod, *Jacobitism*, 156).

[80] *Hearne's Collections*, x. 53: 3 Oct. 1728; V-P's Reg. 2 Oct. 1728, fo. 65. She may have been
buried in chapel, but there is no memorial.

[81] *An act for confirming . . . the purchase of the advowsons of Stepney and other churches . . .* [9 Anne c. 16,
Private] (1710). Bodl. GA Oxon. c. 223.

of Whitechapel. This prize Shippen selected for himself. But first he had to remove the current incumbent, the Revd Dr Richard Welton. Now Welton was a Jacobite. Shippen was a Hanoverian Jacobite: he was only too willing to compromise in pursuit of office. Welton was less malleable: he was disinclined to swear allegiance to a head of the Church of England who was not only a Lutheran but a German. In September 1715, therefore, Shippen seized his chance. He arranged for Welton to be summoned, at short notice and in his absence, to take the Oaths of Allegiance and Abjuration before two Essex magistrates. As expected, the Rector failed to appear. Whereupon, in March 1716, two Brasenose clerics—George Freeman of Steeple Aston and Thomas Meare Jun. of Cottingham—proceeded to announce themselves patrons with powers of presentation. By September, by 'Institution and Induction under Seal', Shippen was safely in possession. The Bishop of London, John Robinson—the last bishop, incidentally, to hold Cabinet office—decided not to intervene. He was, after all, yet another Brasenose man. Shippen arrived in Whitechapel with a 'Flourish' and a 'Noise of Bells'. Understandably, the parishioners were by no means pleased. 'Really Dr. Shippen', one protested, 'You are...a Principal of Brazen-nose with a Corinthian Forehead [of brass]'; to satisfy 'your Ambition and Covetousness...You have Committed a Theft and a Violence upon Dr. Welton's Prerogative'; in fact you notoriously 'Pursue the Honours and Wealth of the World by...Crooked Ways'.[82]

This attack on Shippen—published anonymously in 1716—was entitled *The Spiritual Intruder Unmask'd*. 'When the Book came out', noted Hearne, 'Shippen was devilishly nettled, and got all [copies] bought up, being not at any time able to bear anything against himself in print.'[83] The Principal's embarrassment was understandable. 'This Shippen', Hearne explained, 'is so illiterate a Man that he understands nothing of Latin. Nor can I learn that he ever yet preached. He is a meer Hocus-Pocus, and very unfit for a Cure of Souls.'[84] Nevertheless Shippen was now in possession of the field, and he rounded off his victory with an unrepentant rejoinder: *The Case of Not Taking Oaths and the Conviction thereupon as of Popish Recusancy* (1717). The same year he joined with other heads in sponsoring an Assize Sermon on the same theme by a sympathetic Fellow of Brasenose, Thomas Dod. Hearne noted waspishly

---

[82] *The Spiritual Intruder Unmask'd in a Letter from the Orthodox in Whitechapel to Dr. Shippen* (1716; price 2*s*.), 18, 19, 27 [Bras. S 19]. Welton had made himself unpopular with the Whig hierarchy in 1713–14 by commissioning an altarpiece which portrayed as Judas the Whig Dean of Peterborough, Dr White Kennett (Sharp, *Jacobite Movement*, no. 714 illus.; G. V. Bennett, *White Kennett, 1660–1728, Bishop of Peterborough* (1957), 127–32).

[83] *Hearne's Collections*, xi. 41: 22 Mar. 1732. At first Hearne suspected the author was a 'Non-Juror...Mr. Lawrence'; then he heard it was Samuel Brewster, formerly of Balliol, a Whig lawyer (ibid., vi. 17: 26 Jan. 1717 and 19: 4 Feb. 1717; vii. 80: 14 Dec. 1719).

[84] Ibid., vi. 15–16: 18 Jan. 1717.

that it was really designed by the Hebdomadal oligarchs to 'ingratiate them-selves' with the Hanoverian regime.[85] In effect it signalled the eclipse of non-juring prospects within the Anglican Church. Welton was reduced to opening a chapel of his own within the same Whitechapel parish. Before long he was both celebrity and martyr.[86] Colley Cibber decided to target him with a comedy entitled *The Non Juror*, and George I made a point of repeatedly attending performances at Drury Lane. The bulk of higher church patronage was now very clearly in Whig hands. Understandably, Welton decided to emigrate. He ended his career as a non-juring Bishop of Christ Church, Philadelphia. Shippen—in Hearne's dismissive phrase—had 'play'd the Knave' again.[87]

In fact Shippen was already playing a deeper, and more serious game. He wanted to be Vice-Chancellor. To this end he had first to establish his Tory credentials. In December 1717 he moved the following motion in Convoca-tion: '[H.M. King George I] is unacquainted with our Language and Con-stitution . . . His British Ministers [should therefore] inform Him that our Government does not stand on the same Foundation with His German Dominions'.[88] The motion was lost. Most heads must have thought it more than a little impertinent. But no doubt Chancellor Arran paid due attention. Within a year Shippen would achieve his greatest ambition. The Vice-Chan-cellor's powers of influence and patronage were soon to be at his disposal.

When it came to patronage Shippen was indefatigable. He interfered with elections at the Ashmolean. He interfered with appointments in the Bodleian Library.[89] He interfered at the Physic Garden.[90] He interfered at Balliol.[91] He interfered at Oriel.[92] He interfered at Univ. In fact at University College the so-called 'Cockman–Denison Case' suggests that once an intrigue had begun in earnest Shippen could become almost deranged.[93]

For seven full years, between 1722 and 1729, the Mastership of University College was in dispute. Originally, there had been three candidates: Thomas Cockman (five votes), William Denison (four votes), and George 'Jolly' Ward

[85] *Hearne's Collections*, 33: 26 Mar. 1717.

[86] Ibid. 107: 14 Nov. 1717; 124: 31 Dec. 1717; 128: 8 Jan. 1718. To pay the costs of the case, Welton 'had his very Bedds seized from his Family, his Daughter was drove to a delirious state by their Cruelty, and [had to be] held down in her Bedd by her Mother and Friends; yet that very Bedd was she forc'd from. His Books which in their Plunder they omitted were sent away *per amicos*' (ibid., vii. 41: anon. letter to Hearne, 23 Aug. 1719).

[87] Ibid., vi. 15–16: 19 Jan. 1717. See also R. W. Jeffery in *Brazen Nose*, v. 41–7; and *ODNB*.

[88] Bodl. MS Ballard 21, fos. 206–7.

[89] *Hearne's Collections*, x. 208: 5 Dec. 1729.

[90] In 1719 he abruptly removed the aged Jacob Bobart from office (ibid., vii. 29).

[91] Ibid., xi. 41: 22 Mar. 1732.

[92] Bodl. MS.Top. Oxon. d. 5: Shippen to Newcome at Ewelme, 6 Feb. 1729.

[93] See Jeffery in *Brazen Nose*, v. 79–90, 136–47.

(one vote). On the face of it, Cockman would seem to be the winner. But Denison disputed the validity of Cockman's majority—the majority after all was not absolute—and thus Shippen saw a chance to intervene. Normally such disputes would be decided by the Visitor. But just as there were two claimants to the Mastership (Cockman and Denison), so there turned out to be two potential Visitors: the Vice-Chancellor, Proctors, and resident Doctors of Divinity (representing the University) and the Crown (representing the putative founder of the college, King Alfred). 'There seems to be a party', noted William Stratford in 1723, 'set to turn . . . poor [Cockman] . . . out of his headship, to which he has as undoubted a right as to any shilling he has in his pocket. If he should have any spirit, this may be an affair that may prove of very fatal consequence to the whole university . . . Here [surely] is sport for Westminster Hall.'[94]

Sport indeed. As the dispute progressed, it descended into farce. One Fellow purloined the college seal and secreted it in the country. Another— the ineffable 'Jolly' Ward—struck out Cockman's name from the Buttery Book, sat in his place in chapel, and removed his chair from the hall. The Jacobite Duke of Beaufort, then an undergraduate at Univ. and a relative of Chancellor Arran, teamed up with Shippen and Ward, to organize 'a great Bonfire and abundance of Ale' for the town mob.[95] Rooms were barricaded. Lawyers were drafted in from London. Shippen not only supported Denison, he threw into the battle the whole weight of his Vice-Cancellarial authority. He seems indeed to have been behind the Chancellor's ultimate appeal to the Attorney General.[96] But in the end Cockman carried heavier guns. He had behind him the Court of King's Bench, sitting in Westminster Hall. There it was eventually decided that in this case Visitatorial powers did indeed reside with the Crown, if only on the hypothesis of the Alfredian legend. Thus Cockman was confirmed, and Shippen discomforted. More to the point, Tory Oxford had been led by its overweening Vice-Chancellor into a losing

[94] HMC, *Portland MSS*, vii. 369–70: 13 Dec. 1723. See also ibid. 346–52, 462–3, 472. For a spirited account of these proceedings, see *Hearne's Collections*, viii. 29–30, 32, 58, 71, 122; x. 322–5; x. 15: 21 May 1728 and 183: 3 Oct. 1729. See also R. Darwall-Smith, 'The Great Mastership Dispute', *University College Record*, 12/3 (1999), 58–85.

[95] *Hearne's Collections*, viii. 25: 18 Dec. 1722. Jolly Ward—'that vicious, lewd Fellow'—was tutor to Henry, 3rd Duke of Beaufort, and his younger brother Charles, the future 4th Duke, who eventually migrated to Brasenose and later became one of the Radcliffe Trustees. On one occasion during the Cockman–Denison affair 'it is said they . . . sate up 'till [2 o'clock] drinking. Ward was so drunk that he vomited four times between Queen's Lane and East Gate' (ibid. 24: 15 Dec. 1722 and 384: 23 June 1725).

[96] HMC, *Portland MSS*, vii. 362: 23 June 1723 and 462: 13 May 1728; *Hearne's Collections*, viii. 89: 18 June 1723. Following an appeal by Cockman's supporters, Shippen's group were summoned to appear by the Attorney General (Sir Robert Raymond) at his chambers in Lincoln's Inn (ibid. 58: 26 Mar. 1723).

(and quite unnecessary) dispute with the Whig establishment in London. 'I am afraid', Stratford concluded in 1728, 'Mr. Cockman owes this success to the general hatred of Dr. Shippen as much as to the goodness of his cause.'[97] Shippen, in effect, had come near to triggering the very event that Oxford Tories always feared: a Crown Visitation of the University.[98]

Even without the Cockman–Denison affair, Shippen's reputation as Vice-Chancellor was low. This is demonstrated by the fiasco of the Sheldonian curatorship in March 1723. The curatorship was a merely honorific office; but it was an honour Shippen coveted. For some time he had dreamed of succeeding Sir Christopher Wren. Having packed the nominating committee—in this case the Delegates of Accounts—his hopes were high when news came at last of the aged architect's demise. 'But', Stratford tells us, 'there appeared a strange aversion in the whole university to the Vice-Chancellor.' When it came to Convocation's ratifying vote, Shippen was trounced by the President of Magdalen, a man on whom he had previously relied. 'Never', Stratford concludes, 'was there a public mark of detestation so remarkable . . . The Masters cried aloud in the Convocation House that . . . they should have no more of [Shippen] . . . If [Chancellor Arran] continues to countenance this man and his cronies he will find a great majority here in revolt.' All true, all true. Next year there was a new Vice-Chancellor.[99]

The opposition to Shippen was not political. His unpopularity, over a period of many years, was essentially personal. When in 1721 he swept the Whig satirists from the coffee houses of Oxford, his action was widely approved.[100] But he seems to have had a compulsive appetite for intrigue. After the Whitechapel affair, he was for ever 'the Spiritual Intruder'. Thanks to the Cockman–Denison saga he was nicknamed 'Fergusson the Tricker' or 'Fergusson the Plotter', after Robert Fergusson the Jacobite double agent whom Dryden immortalized as 'Judas' in *Absolom and Achitophel*.[101] In pursuit

---

[97] HMC, *Portland MSS*, vii. 463: 23 May 1728; Bodl. MS Top. Oxon. d. 5, fos. 2–11.

[98] Some of Shippen's opponents suspected that Denison's supporters—'the most . . . notorious Jacobites in the whole University'—were trying in fact to lure the Crown into repeating the mistakes of James II by invading the rights of the University (BL Add. MS 35584, fo. 310: [May 1728].) In the end the heads of houses—with the Vice-Chancellor abstaining—voted to discontinue proceedings, in effect admitting defeat (BL Add. MS 36137, fo. 63: Bishop of Llandaff to Bishop of London, 20 May 1728). Cockman was finally installed as Master by order of seven Crown Commissioners in May 1729 (*Hearne's Collections*, x. 129: 11 May 1729).

[99] HMC, *Portland MSS*, vii. 335: 5 Oct. 1722 and 347–8: 2 Mar. 1722/3.

[100] It was Amhurst's *Terrae-Filius* which was suppressed. See *Terrae-Filius*, ed. W. E. Rivers (Newark, 2004), 15, 420 n.

[101] *Hearne's Collections*, v. 189: 27 Mar. 1716; x. 406–7: 18 Apr. 1731; and xi. 18–19: 19 Jan. 1732. Fergusson was an adherent of Monmouth, involved in the Rye House Plot. He joined William of Orange but went over to the Jacobites. He then betrayed the Jacobites in Lovat's Plot, but was sent to Newgate in 1704 on a charge of treason. He died in poverty 1714. See W. Beamont (ed.), *Jacobite Trials* (1694); (Chetham Soc. 28, 1853), pp. lxxix–lxxxiii; and *ODNB*.

of office he was certainly greedy. He accumulated benefices at Great Billing, Whitechapel, and Amersham. And he took as much as he could from college and University. The Principalship itself was worth no more than perhaps £100 p.a.[102] But it carried generous allowances. Best of all, there were fees—or fines as they were called—payable on the renewal of leases. As Vice-Chancellor, Shippen could also look forward to sizeable fees for the renewal of licences. On the death of Mrs Tomlins of the Three Tuns, for example, the renewal of its licence brought £500 into Shippen's pocket.[103]

The Principal of Brasenose was certainly not averse to high living. His 'boon Companion' in college was Henry Newcome, another Cheshire man, elected Fellow in 1700. Within weeks of becoming Principal, Shippen had arranged for Newcome to become Rector of Didcot, and soon afterwards—thanks to Harcourt and Arran—for the same 'very infamous' man to be master of the Free School at Ewelme. Both Shippen and Newcome were Jacobites at heart, and many a toast would seem to have been raised in the privacy of the master's dwelling. Nor, apparently, were other pleasures absent. The master's house seemed destined to become—according to Stratford—positively notorious. 'Instead of a school', he told Harley, '[it] will be a bawdy-house.'[104]

Perhaps Shippen's closest ally in college was his nephew Robert Leybourne. It was in 1711 that Leybourne arrived at Brasenose from Christ Church. He became Frankland Fellow in 1715 and chaplain to Chancellor Arran; then Proctor in 1723, Lecturer at Whitechapel in the same year, Grammar Lecturer at Brasenose—after 'a great struggle'—in 1723, and eventually Junior Bursar in 1727.[105] When he then became Rector of Stepney and of Limehouse in 1729 he had of course to resign his Fellowship.[106] But he continued to enjoy a comfortable career, and it was Shippen who made the whole thing possible. Leybourne had a reputation as 'a boon blade': he seems, for instance, to have broken the heart of John Wesley's sister.[107] He was very much Shippen's *bon ami*. Uncle and nephew worked in tandem for many years, even though Leybourne quarrelled with 'Honest' Will Shippen

[102] That was the salary fixed in 1749 (V-P's Reg.16 June 1749, fo. 151; *Quat. Mon.* XIII, 60).
[103] *Hearne's Collections*, vii. 7: 12 May 1719.
[104] Ibid., v. 43: 11 Apr. 1715; HMC, *Portland MSS*, vii. 181–2: 23 Feb. 1714. In 1731 Hearne noted that Newcome had 'never taught so much as one boy since he hath had the School' (*Hearne's Collections*, xi. 15: 11 Jan. 1732). Newcome had spent his wife's fortune of £1,500; even so 'they proved a very loving couple' (ibid., xi. 42–3: 28 Mar. 1732).
[105] Ibid., viii. 10: 29 Oct. 1722; 69: 24 Apr. 1723; 99–100: 20 July 1723. The Brasenose Lectureship was worth £25 p.a.
[106] Resigned 5 Dec. 1730 (V-P's Reg. 1730, fo. 73).
[107] 'When I loved L[eybourne] he loved not me, though he was rogue enough to persuade me he did…For near half a year I never slept half a night' (Emily to John Wesley, 7 Feb. 1733, quoted in Green, *Young Wesley*, 108 n. 2).

and still more with that politician's wife.[108] Eventually, in 1736, Leybourne received his culminating reward: he was installed as Principal of St Alban Hall.

One particular story of Shippen's appetite for intrigue is irresistible. In April 1731 John Andrews, Fellow of Magdalen and Senior Proctor, was chosen Keeper of the Ashmolean. Shippen was not well pleased. 'The University in general', noted Hearne, 'seems glad that Andrews is in.' Not 'on account of his skill', for he is 'no scholar and understands nothing in the least of Natural History, Mathematicks and Antiquities'; 'but because Dr. Shippen...is hereby baffled, [for Shippen] had a design that the Election should be deferred 'till next Term, and then (there being to be a Proctor of his own House) [i.e. Brasenose] he intended to have got either him, or some one of his...own kidney, Keeper'.[109] By January 1732, however, Shippen seems to have changed his mind. He decided that the post would make an ideal sinecure for one particular head of house. He persuaded Andrews to call on George Huddesford, President of Trinity, and 'surrender the keys to him'. Andrews was then given £50 compensation, and the Vice-Chancellor was prevailed upon not to intervene. 'This', noted Hearne, 'is an astonishing affair that the University rings of.' Not least because Huddesford was not an ally of Shippen's at all, but an opponent, a Whig. At this point Hearne reveals the reason: 'Dr Shippen...is a strange lover of Women, [and] he used, and does still use, to go often to Hudsford's wife, a very pretty Woman, and 'tis on that account partly that he was so zealous for Hudsford.'[110]

Such things, apparently, were not unknown in Brasenose. 'Dr. Shippen', Hearne noted the following spring, 'is a most lecherous man'; 'some years since [he] debauched a very pretty Woman, one Mrs. Churchill, the wife and afterwards the widow of one Churchill, a bookbinder in Oxford, one of the prettiest Women in England. He poxed her, of which she died in a sad Condition. The thing is so notorious that 'tis frequently talked of to this day.'[111]

Not surprisingly, Shippen's manoeuvring sometimes rebounded against his chosen candidate. In 1716 and 1718 John Featly, who succeeded Edward

[108] Margaret Shippen—heiress to Sir Richard Stote—seems to have had little to recommend her but her fortune of £70,000. Leybourne—who was himself no paragon—called her a 'stinking, greedy, Ugly, Ill-natured, Covetous, Beggarly, proud Barrowful of Tripes' (Bodl. MS Top. Oxon. c. 107, p. 163: R. Leybourne to R. Shippen, 27 July 1732). She ended her days living at Richmond while her husband remained in Norfolk St., London.

[109] *Hearne's Collections*, x. 406–7: 18 Apr. 1731.

[110] Ibid., xi. 31: 22 Jan. 1732. Shippen's patronage stretched beyond the grave: George Huddesford held the Keepership from 1730 to 1755; his son William inherited the post, holding it from 1755 to 1772.

[111] Ibid., xi. 41: 22 Mar. 1732. See also Bodl. MS, Hearne's Diaries, 95, fo. 61: 15 Dec. 1722. She was said to be a college tenant in High Street.

Shippary as head butler at Brasenose, competed twice for ceremonial office, first as Inferior Beadle of Arts, then as Yeoman Beadle of Law. Featly, Hearne tells us, 'a very honest, modest Man', had once been a poor scholar, but 'now...wears no Gown and never intends it more'. Shippen 'made all the Interest he could...he [even] came from London and brought several Votes with him'. But in vain: the majority of Congregation opposed Shippen on personal grounds. Indeed they 'were resolved to thwart him'.[112] And so in the end they did.

Now these were all University matters. But even in Brasenose itself Shippen's writ did not run smoothly. In January 1718 he again came up from London, this time to prevent William Wright being elected Fellow. Inevitably, Shippen had a candidate of his own. But the Principal's choice was defeated, so Hearne assures us, by 'Mr. Leigh and ye honest part of ye College...[So Shippen] is gone back to London displeased.'[113] Similarly, in March 1720, the Principal—by then Vice-Chancellor—proceeded to expel a servitor called Thomas Ball; nominally for 'Heterodoxy', actually because he hoped to install 'a creature of his own'. Ball's tutors, however, appealed to the Visitor, Dr Gibson—a Whig, and no friend of Shippen—and within weeks the offender had been reinstated. In vain, now wearing his Vice-Chancellor's robes, Shippen next attempted to expel Mr Ball from the University altogether. That would indeed have been 'very improper'. Again Shippen had to admit defeat.[114]

Any eighteenth-century Principal—still more so any eighteenth-century Vice-Chancellor—was an obvious and accepted fount of patronage. 'All the Servants', noted the Brasenose butler circa 1706, 'are put in by Mr. Principal's Sole Power & the Goldsmith ye Plummr the Iron-monger the Glazier ye Brazier ye Chandler the Smith & ye Butcher are put in by him allso.'[115] In Georgian Oxford patronage filtered down from the highest to the lowest. It was the glue that held the whole system together; and unless we come to terms with this process we can never understand the mechanics of the University in its unreformed state. For example, when a new head cook was appointed at Brasenose early in Shippen's reign, Hearne reports that the job went to 'a North Countrey (I think, a Cumberland) Man', called Simpson; he 'got his Place by the Interest of My Lady Clark'. When Simpson died in

---

[112] *Hearne's Collections*, v. 189: 27 Mar. 1716; vi. 177: 17 May 1718. Featly 'died of a Dropsy, after a long time's confinement...He had the palsy in the head for many years to a strange degree. He has left a widow, but no child. He was once a Gownsman, a Servitore of the College [matric. pleb. 1705]. He was hardly 50 years old. He was an understanding, modest man and honest' (ibid., xi. 110: 17 Sept. 1732).

[113] Ibid., vi. 131: 20 Jan. 1717/18.

[114] Ibid., vii. 131: 25 May 1720; HMC, *Portland MSS*, vii. 276: 31 May 1720.

[115] Clennell B 53.14: Cawley [Shippary] Notebook xiv, fo. 16.

March 1721, this office—being a piece of property—was passed on to his son, 'a Boy of about three Years old'. Alas, 'the Bells went' for him too, within days of the death of his father.[116] Patronage was indeed universal; but occasionally it had its tragic side.

Can nothing then be said for Shippen? He inherited from his father William Shippen Sen. a collection of manuscripts relating to English monasteries. These had probably been accumulated from anti-popish motives. Still, the son seems to have adopted his father's antiquarian interests, and eventually he left a tenth-century copy of Terence to the College.[117] Again, Shippen supported genuine scholars: he encouraged Browne Willis in his antiquarian researches, and he showed some interest in Anthony Wood's *History*. He had an interest in current French literature.[118] He even seems to have shown belated generosity to Dr Welton of Whitechapel.[119] In 1724— the very year Welton left for America—Richard Welton Jun. appeared at Brasenose, at the age of 16. Two years after that he was awarded a Mordaunt Scholarship.

So maybe there was another side to Shippen after all. He certainly had the wit to appoint an apparently blameless curate to look after Whitechapel. This was Charles Huxley, Fellow, 'a sober man [who] dyed with drinking tea'.[120] But Shippen cannot be said to have raised either the moral or the academic standard of Brasenose. Take the case of the election of George Hammond as Fellow in 1720. This event might almost be said to set the tone for the whole period. Hammond was elected on production of a false birth certificate; 'pretending that Gosworth was really in Prestbury'. Not that it mattered much. He was, notes Hearne, 'a very obscure Man, and of no Merit that I can hear of'.[121] That comment has the ring of truth. In terms of collegiate history, Shippen's tenure shows Brasenose at its least illustrious. Nor did he add anything to the glory of the Vice-Chancellor's office. He seems, for example, to have been a poor public speaker: at his readmission in 1720 'his Speech was sad wretched stuff'.[122] In the end it is hard to avoid a negative verdict.

---

[116] *Hearne's Collections*, vii. 223: 12 Mar. 1721 and 338: 14 Mar. 1722.

[117] Once in the possession of Cardinal Bembo; now Bodl. Lib. William Shippen Sen. had been active at the time of the Popish Plot in conspiring with Israel Tonge, Fellow of Univ., 'to have Mr. [Obadiah] Walker turned out [of Univ.] for being a Papist, [so that] one of them might succeed [to the Mastership]; base ingratitude and false' (*Hearne's Collections*, x. 348: 6 Nov. 1730; 436: 14 July 1731; Wood, *Life and Times*, ii. 422: 30 Oct. 1678).

[118] *Hearne's Collections*, vii. 166: 8 Sept. 1720; 182: 24 Oct. 1720; 272–3: 28 Aug. 1721; M. Feingold, in *HUO* iv. 275.

[119] *Hearne's Collections*, vi. 21: 13 Feb. 1716/17.

[120] Ibid., xi. 148: 17 Jan. 1733.

[121] Ibid., vii. 93: 27 Jan. 1720; V-P's Reg. 25 Jan. 1720, f. 41 He had previously been headmaster of Macclesfield School.

[122] HMC, *Portland MSS*, vii. 243; *Hearne's Collections*, vii. 175: 7 Oct. 1720.

Shippen's morals and intrigues confirm only too well the reputation of early eighteenth-century Oxford. Politics in the University took precedence over scholarship, and over religion too.

Ultimately, Shippen's greatest—some would say his only—contribution to Brasenose was the decision to purchase eight crucial sites: one next to the chapel, seven more facing outwards towards the High Street. When he became Principal in 1710, the college owned no freehold property in the High. During his term of office seven High Street frontages were acquired in 1715, 1724, 1727, and 1736.[123] The future expansion of Brasenose was thus secured. For that the college should be grateful. No doubt the Fellows who elected him were grateful too for the handsome panelling of their new Common Room, completed as soon as Shippen became Principal.[124] Perhaps they were also enthusiastic for one extraordinary flourish of philistinism: the insertion of more than twenty sash windows inside and outside the Old Quad; fifteen facing inwards, half a dozen facing out. Here only too obviously Shippen left his mark.[125]

During Shippen's Principalship the college made a series of grandiose attempts to inflate its architectural presence. At the start of his tenure Brasenose was still essentially the college created in the sixteenth and seventeenth centuries. It still retained, for example, its formal garden in the Old Quad. This dated back, in origin, to the early sixteenth century, and was the last significant example of its kind in Oxford. Doubtless it suffered minor changes over the years. The double-noosed knot pattern shown in Loggan's engraving of 1675 (pl. 7), is said to have had a grisly origin: it was apparently invented by the Duke of Buckingham as a device for hanging two men simultaneously. Whatever the truth of that story, by the early eighteenth century these box parterres had become shaded by trees—probably lime and

---

[123] MPP 56 F/10: Jeffery, 'Shippen', 67 n. 1; *Quat. Mon.* VI, 42–3. Seven properties were bought in 1736 from All Souls, New College, and Christ Church, following the Radcliffe Library Act (7 Geo. I, c. 13), whose passage Shippen and Clarke had done much to assist.

[124] For the development of the Common Room, see *Quat. Mon.* III, 37; IV, 58–9. In 1707 it was transferred from II, 3 where it had been since at least 1682 (*Quat. Mon.* XIII, 10). Its panelling dates from 1708–11. It was refurbished in 1783 when the arms of Smith, Sutton and Nowell seem to have been transferred from the hall. T. G. Jackson's jib staircase dates from 1898 (B 1076). His smoking room was added in 1899 (B 272–80), and extended to designs by Sir Guy Dawber in 1936. Those who originally contributed to the Common Room's adornment—'...ut elegantius exornaretur nova Camera Communis...'—were at that time commemorated with coats of arms: T. Willis, F. Powlet, N. Wrighte, J. Dod, G. Shakerley, P. Starkie, H. Egerton (*Quat. Mon.* IV, 58). The dining chairs formed part of the 'refurnishing' of 1834 (V-P's Reg. 13 Mar. 1834, fo. 203: £100).

[125] For the appearance of Old Quad in 1732, with its full array of sash windows, see W. Williams, *Oxonia Depicta* (1730–3), pl. xxxvi; for another view, in 1805, see J. Skelton, *Oxonia Antiqua Restaurata*, ii (Oxford, 1823), 105 (from J. M. W. Turner's *Almanack* drawing).

yew—planted around their periphery. It was these that Shippen decided to
banish as part of a general scheme of improvement. And so, early in 1727, we
find Shippen as Principal and Leybourne as Bursar spending a good deal of
time—and a good deal of college money—in London.[126] Almost certainly
they were plotting architectural schemes and arranging for the purchase of a
striking statue, a centrepiece for a very different quadrangle that would
symbolize the burgeoning status of the college. No doubt the decision for
this ornament was Shippen's. But the idea must have come from a rather more
sympathetic person, one of Ralph Rawson's old pupils: Dr George Clarke.

Like Shippen Clarke was a Hanoverian Tory. He had once been an ally of
the second Duke of Ormonde, Chancellor over the water.[127] Then he aligned
with Arran and Shippen on the Tory-Jacobite wing of politics. He had a long
parliamentary career, from 1685 onwards, almost continuously as MP for the
University. When he stood in the election of 1722, Shippen made sure that he
received twenty-one out of twenty-three possible Brasenose votes.[128] But on
that occasion it was not enough to return him at the head of the poll. It seems
he was insufficiently Tory. All Oxford knew that he had long since made his
peace with the Whigs. Hearne dismissed him as 'a pitiful, proud Sneaker and
an Enemy to true Loyalty'.[129] But such aspersions have done his memory no
harm. Today Clarke is honoured as one of the stars of Oxford's architectural
history.

Dr Clarke had gone up to Brasenose in 1675.[130] By 1680 he was a Fellow of
All Souls. In Parliament and Whitehall, under James II, William and Mary,
and Queen Anne, he was the acceptable face of Oxford at the centre of
political power. After 1714, however, he concentrated his energies in the
University, overseeing a series of major architectural projects: the Clarendon

---

[126] Bursar's Account Book 1727, cited in Jeffery, 'Shippen'. For the old garden, see
D. Loggan, *Oxonia Illustrata* (1675) and R. Plot, *The Natural History of Oxfordshire* (Oxford,
1677), 260.

[127] *Hearne's Collections*, vii. 318: 18 Jan. 1722.

[128] *A True Copy of the Poll for Members of Parliament for the University of Oxford Digested into an
Alphabetical Order* (Oxford, 1722). Hearne disputed this: 'This most silly Paper ... drawn up and
published by the most egregious Coxcomb and Rascal, Joseph Bowles, Head Keeper of the
Bodlejan Library ... is called a *true Copy*, whereas 'tis a most false one.' It was contradicted by
another *Account of the Late Election of the University of Oxford for Members of Parliament*. See *Hearne's
Collections*, vii. 349, 394; HMC, *Portland MSS*, vii. 318; and *Hist. Parl.: Commons, 1715–54*, i (1970),
305–6, 554–5. It is worth noting that as late as the early 1740s between a quarter and a half of
Tory MPs were openly sympathetic to the Jacobite cause (I. R. Christie, in *Historical Jnl.* 30
(1987), 930).

[129] *Hearne's Collections*, vii. 341–2: 22 Mar. 1722. By 1728, for example, Clarke was close to
the Whig Duchess of Marlborough (ibid., x. 53: 2 Sept. 1728).

[130] In 1677 he was the first commoner to wear a square cap in Oxford (Clarke, 'Autobiography', in HMC xlix, *Leybourne–Popham MSS*, (1899), 259–61).

Building, Christ Church Library, Queen's College, University College, All Souls, and Worcester. Clarke was a virtuoso, an amateur architect of more than amateur skill. After the death of Dean Aldrich in 1710 he became the acknowledged master of Oxford building.[131] He has some claim to be regarded as a founder of English Palladianism. What could be more natural, towards the end of his life, than to involve himself with the fabric of his own college?

It was almost certainly Clarke who introduced Nicholas Hawksmoor to the University, and thus to Principal Shippen. From the partnership of these three men stemmed a series of hyper-ambitious projects, which might have transformed Brasenose into the grandest classical college in Oxford. In all Hawksmoor produced at least five designs. The first, dating from 1712–13, formed part of a prodigious scheme for the replanning of the entire city centre. This envisaged a rebuilt Brasenose facing a rebuilt All Souls across what would eventually become Radcliffe Square. The University would thus have acquired a new academic forum, with Brasenose at its very heart.[132] Hawksmoor's second scheme, dating from 1719–20, has come down to us in the shape of two particularly dramatic perspectives.[133] In these engravings Brasenose boasts a mighty, six-columned Corinthian portico on the High Street, leading into a spacious new quadrangle bordered by continuous arcades. Behind it, the Old Quad has been recast in classical dress. And in the centre, between the two quadrangles, stands a new chapel—apsed and pillared—fronted with an engaged colonnade of no less than eight

---

[131] See H. M. Colvin, *Biographical Dictionary of British Architects 1600–1840* (1995), 250–1. Shippen never received the royal chaplaincy that he hoped Clarke would secure him (Bodl. MS Top. Oxon. c. 107, fo. 95: R. Leybourne to Shippen, 17 June 1727). But on Clarke's death in 1736, Shippen became executor of his will. Thus it was via Shippen that many of the Clarke papers—including part of Inigo Jones's collection—became the property of Worcester College (J. Nichols (ed.), *Illustrations of the Literary History of the 18th Century* (1817–58), viii. 291). Other papers descended via Leybourne to the Revd D. Taylor. In 1725 Clarke presented two silver decanters, together worth £40, to the Brasenose commoners' table (*Hearne's Collections*, ix. 39: 10 Oct. 1725; *Quat. Mon.* V, pl. viii).

[132] Clennell B 15.1 (S), reprod. in *Quat. Mon.* III, pl. xvi and R. White (ed.), *Nicholas Hawksmoor and the Replanning of Oxford* (1997), no. 90. See also Bodl. MS Top. Oxon. a. 26 (R), redrawn in H. M. Colvin, *Unbuilt Oxford* (1983), pl. 74. There is some evidence that the idea of Radcliffe Square can be attributed in the first place to Clarke (Hawksmoor to Clarke, All Souls MSS, cited in V. Hart, *Nicholas Hawksmoor* (2002), 278 n. 7).

[133] Williams, *Oxonia Depicta*, p. xxxvii, dedicated to the Cartwright family, reprod. in *Quat. Mon.* III, pl. xviii and Colvin, *Unbuilt Oxford*, pl. 156. Plans of this scheme survive as Clennell B 15.1 (e.g. Williams, pl. xxxv) and as Worcester Coll. MSS no. 65 (H. M. Colvin, *Architectural Drawings... Worcester Coll. Oxford* (1964), pls. 87–8). The *Almanack* of 1723, by G. Virtue, appears in Skelton, *Oxonia Antiqua Restaurata*, i. 26. See also H. M. Petter, *The Oxford Almanacks* (Oxford, 1974).

Corinthian columns. The general layout of this plan—twin courtyards, central chapel, atrium or 'peristylium': what Hawksmoor called 'the Antique disposition'—has been traced back to Palladio's reconstruction of a Roman house as described by Vitruvius; and further back still, via the Escurial in Spain, to the layout of Solomon's Temple as recorded by Ezekiel.[134] Such things are hard to prove. But Hawksmoor was certainly intrigued by architectural antiquities. In any case, here was a plan which might have given Brasenose a dominant place in the architectural history of Oxford. It would certainly have combined some much-needed accommodation with a striking profile and silhouette. The new quadrangle was designed to incorporate eight or ten staircases; and its roofline was to be varied by no fewer than four monumental cupolas. In the version engraved for the *Oxford Almanack* of 1723 (pl. 18), the whole composition is placed in an allegorical setting. The new building itself becomes a backdrop to a procession of college benefactors. The achievements of Sutton and Smith are promulgated by Apollo, master of the muses, and their names are recorded in the book of time.

Baroque indeed. But nothing was built. As some compensation, the college decided to renew the sundial on the sunny south side of the Old Quad's northern wall.[135] That was in 1719. In 1727 this was followed by the installation of the statue that Clarke had secured in London. Here was a gesture designed to astonish Oxford. It took the form of a lead version, by John van Nost the Younger, of Giambologna's famous *Samson and the Philistine* (1560–2) (pl. 19).

Last Week [complained Hearne] they cut down the fine pleasant Garden in Brasenose College Quadrangle, which was not only a great Ornament to it, and was agreeable to the Quadrangles of our old Monasteries, but was a delightful and pleasant Shade in Summer Time, and made the rooms in hot Seasons much cooler than otherwise they would have been. This is done ... purely to turn it into a Grass Plot, and to erect some silly Statue there ... [This] fine Garden ... [was] the only one of that kind remaining in Oxford [It had been there] ... from the very Foundation of the College ... This [vandalism] is an argument of the decay of Letters, which love Retirement and sweet shady Places. Dr. Robert Shippen ... was the chief occasion thereof.[136]

Some economy was clearly involved. The resulting 'grass-plott' had merely to be mown at a cost of £2 p.a.; while 'the Fellows' garden and that near the

---

[134] Hart, *Hawksmoor*, 203–4.

[135] Thomas Wildgoss received 7 guineas for 'painting and Guilding the Diall with ye ... blew'; Thomas Cookson 7s. 6d. 'for drawing the Lines of the Dial'; George Cooke 15s. 'for a Noman [i.e. gnomon] to Sun Dial' (Hurst Bursarial: Trades Bills, 27). In 1962, at the entrance to the hall, 'a correction table' was set up by Alexander Thom, 'to enable Greenwich Time to be calculated at all periods of the year' (V-P's Reg. 17 Oct. 1962, fo. 1).

[136] *Hearne's Collections*, ix. 361: 25 Oct. 1727 and 405: 2 Mar. 1728. See also E. S. Rohde, *Oxford's College Gardens* (1932); M. Batey, *Historic Gardens of Oxford and Cambridge* (1989), 51.

Chapel'—planted with herbs and flowers for the table—cost as much as 3 guineas p.a. to maintain.[137] But economy was not a priority.

The 'fine tho. Shocking Statue' which formed the centrepiece of Clarke's scheme has always been known at Brasenose as 'Cain and Abel'.

> How the knave jowls it to the ground, as if it were
> Cain's jaw-bone, that did the *first murder*!

'Kain and Abel' is indeed the description in the bill made out to Clarke by van Nost:

August ye 23	1728		
For a Statue Kain and Abel	£30.	0.	0.
For a Box	1.	4.	0.
For a carte to Queen hith	4.	0.	
For Worfidg & Crane	1.	6.	
	31.	9.	6.

The name of bargman is Larans for Oxon
put on ye barge on Thursday afternoon
  Recd. Sep. ye 6 1728
  ye full cont of this Bill and demands
    Jno. Nost.[138]

Giambologna's statue, in its original marble form, had come to England in 1623. It had been presented by Philip IV of Spain to the future Charles I, at that time Prince of Wales. He in turn gave it to his ill-starred favourite, the first Duke of Buckingham. After Buckingham's assassination in 1628, the statue remained in London, in the garden of York House or Buckingham House, until the reign of George III. It then came into the hands of the King's Surveyor General, Thomas Worsley of Hovingham Hall, Yorkshire; and from the Worsley collection it eventually found its way to the Victoria and Albert Museum in 1953. Meanwhile versions in lead had been produced in London, and distributed via the sculpting dynasties of van Nost and Cheere. Brasenose had one of the earliest. At least eight survive today: at Chatsworth in Derbyshire, at Drayton, Boughton, and Harrowden in Northamptonshire, at St Paul's Walden Bury in Hertfordshire, at Southill in Bedfordshire, at Seaton Delaval in Northumberland, and in the gardens of the Palace of Queluz near Lisbon. During the nineteenth century the Brasenose version came to symbolize the college's sporting prowess. It seemed a

---

[137] In 1772 the head porter acted as College Hortulanus, supervising the gardener Richard Hayward and his two boys. Herbs included rocket, thyme, marjoram, rue, balm, and sage. Table flowers included carnations, pinks, sweet peas, narcissus, lupins, and lilies of the valley (Clennell B 53. 3: Cawley Notebook i, fo. 24 and Hurst Bursarial: Trades Bills 86). The 'grass plott' and newly staked fence in Old Quad is visible in Williams, *Oxonia Depicta*, pl. xxxvi.

[138] Hurst Bursarial: Trades Bills, Buildings 35; Shakespeare, *Hamlet* V, i.

very icon of muscularity. In the eighteenth century it had proved rather less iconic. Still—unlike those sash windows—it was a not ignoble symbol of Shippen's ignoble reign.[139]

Nothing else ever came of all Hawksmoor's ambitious plans. In 1734—as part of the Radcliffe Square programme—at least three more variant schemes had been produced. These accepted the fact that college access to the High was likely to remain restricted. Instead of a mighty portico, therefore, Hawksmoor now suggested a comparatively modest entrance, set between existing houses and broadening out into a Corinthian atrium, or colonnaded court, in the centre of the college. The chapel was to remain, balanced by a new hall and vaulted kitchen. A 'direct vista' was thus opened up, bisecting the college, from the new High Street entrance right through to the Old Quad, aligned on the figure of *Cain and Abel*. The Principal's Lodgings were to be extended along the site of the old hall, with a new parlour and columned library; and a new Senior Common Room—also columned, perhaps domed—was to be inserted more or less on the site of the later Eckersley Room.[140] There was much to be said for these plans. Brasenose would have gained a new hall, kitchen, and buttery; the Principal would have acquired ceremonial access plus a splendid suite of rooms; the Fellows would have been given a very desirable Common Room; and the college would at least have secured its entrance from the High. There was even to be a coach yard and stables on one side of the 'direct vista', and a hidden set of privies—Hawksmoor called them 'the publick Necessaire'—on the other side. At the same time, yet another scheme—the fifth in the series—suggested an apsed hall, two bell turrets, and a curved colonnade with space for both a Fellows' and a Principal's garden. But again nothing came of this. Hawksmoor died in 1736; and by then there were other, more pressing, operations close at hand. The time was at last approaching when Brasenose would command a view across the noblest panorama in Oxford: 'Ratcliffe's piazza'.

Shippen's last years must have been dominated by this prospect: the construction of the Radcliffe Camera, looming larger and larger day by day, over the windows of the Principal's Lodgings (frontispiece). Since 1715 the Radcliffe Trustees—all Tory allies of Dr Shippen—had been accumulating land, item by item. A private Act of Parliament had to be drawn up in 1720–1. Oriel, Magdalen, and University Colleges were all involved; and Brasenose supplied a final piece in the jigsaw puzzle: the 'Principal's Stable and Garden

---

[139] J. Pointer, *Oxoniensis Academia* (1749), 70; *Notes and Queries*, ser. 4/3, 83; 6/4, 517; 8/6, 285, 437, 497; M. Baker, 'Giambologna's Samson and a Philistine and its Later Copies', *Antologia di belle arti*, NS 23–4 (1984), 62–71.

[140] Plans survive: Clennell B 15.1, reprod. *Quat Mon.* III, pl. xix; Worcester Coll., nos. 67–8: 27 Apr. and 5 May 1734, reprod. Colvin, *Unbuilt Oxford*, 89, pls. 157–8 and Colvin, *Architectural Drawings... Worcester Coll.*, pls. 89–90.

etc.', to the north of St Mary's Church, were sold on Lady Day 1737.[141] That spring James Gibbs produced his ultimate design: a sublime rotunda that would change for ever the skyline of Oxford. Its plan tells us something about the circumstances of its conception. Its arcades are aligned not on All Souls, not on the Bodleian, not even directly on the University Church; but directly onto Brasenose. By March 1743 the dome had at last been completed. But the celebrations did not pass without drama. Even as the scaffolding was being removed, two workmen 'had their brains beat out, and died on the spot'. One of them must have been a servant at Brasenose. Responsibility for distributing the £20 that went to his widow and children fell to a man not otherwise known for charity, Dr Robert Shippen.[142]

When Shippen eventually died at the age of 70, a martyr to the stone, on 24 November 1745,[143] there can have been few mourners. 'Truculent, dishonest, interfering...sensual'—the words are those of R. W. Jeffery[144]—he was a Principal of whom Brasenose can scarcely be proud. His idealized bust in the antechapel—sculpted by Taylor of the Taylorian and paid for by the incorrigible Leybourne—suggests a character of rather more nobility (pl. 17).[145]

Even as Shippen lay dying, the Jacobite drama in which Brasenose had long played a peripheral role was drawing to a tragic conclusion. Brasenose of course was a Tory college. But it was more than that: it was Tory for a good reason. Its collegiate constituency was fundamentally anti-Whig. That, as Shippen put it in 1711, was 'the present humour' of the place.[146] No wonder a Whig like John Russell escaped in 1715 to a Fellowship at Merton. Brasenose was no place for a Russell.[147] When, in the same year, there were riots against a group of young Whigs who styled themselves the

---

[141] Clennell B 53.6: Cawley Notebook vi, fo. 167; Clennell B 1d. 37: Fine Book, p. 76. Cawley built a new coach-house in Holywell, on land leased from Merton (*Quat. Mon.* IV, 37).

[142] S. G. Gillam, *Building Accounts of the Radcliffe Camera* (OHS, NS xiii, 1958), p. xvii.

[143] V-P's Reg. 24 Nov. 1745, fo. 128. For his medical history, see *A View of the Present Evidence for and against Mrs Stephens' Medicine as a Solvent for the Stones* (1739), case lv.

[144] In *Brazen Nose*, v. 192–3. The memorial's fulsome inscription was composed by Shippen's old ally Dr Frewin. Compare N. Amhurst, *Oculus Britanniae* (1724).

[145] The monument was originally placed lower on the wall, at eye level. Marble steps were removed in 1860 (V.-P.'s Reg. 19 June 1860, f. 42). The sculptor was the future Sir Robert Taylor, architect and founder of the Taylorian Institution (Bodl. MS Top. Oxon. c. 33; Designs for Monuments, Taylorian Library). He is said to have relied much upon assistant carvers (*Gent's. Mag.* 58 (1788), 930).

[146] HMC, *Kenyon MSS*, 447: 27 Oct. 1711, R. K[enyon] to Mrs Kenyon, regarding acceptance of [Robert Entwistle]. The Principal's brother, 'Honest Will' Shippen, was MP for Newton, Lancs.

[147] W. R. Ward, *Georgian Oxford* (Oxford, 1958), 80, 99–100, 103. Russell was especially critical of compulsory subscription to the Thirty-Nine Articles at matriculation. Hence Shippen's hostility (Bodl. MS Ballard 21: Shippen to A. Charlett, 3 Feb. 1720/1).

Constitution Club, Brasenose naturally took the side of the rioters. 'As part of [the Jacobite mob] were passing by Oriel', notes Stratford, 'a gun was fired out of an upper chamber in that College, and wounded a Brasenose man... The person who fired it was one Ingram [brother to Lord Irwin]...Much work was made in the town for glaziers.'[148] No wonder Hanoverian troops patrolled the streets of Oxford for two years, in 1715–17. But when Brasenose Tories rioted, they rioted as individuals. There was no corporate disobedience. On the night of the Old Pretender's birthday, 10 June 1715, it was a Fellow of Brasenose, Thomas Dod, who—in his proctorial capacity—made sure the rioting was strictly limited.[149] Oxford might well be 'the Jacobite capital of England';[150] but its loyalties were seldom consistently expressed.

Brasenose did, however, contain quite a few Jacobites; a sufficient number to attract the attentions of a blackmailer.

Yesterday [noted Hearne, on 23 September 1721] a Man was whipp'd at the Cart's Tail from Cairfax to East Gate...He was a perfect Stranger...[who] came into Brazen-Nose Coll. Common Room, and into some Chambers of the same Coll., uninvited and against all People's Wills, took up the Glass, and propos'd and drank the Health of King James, the Duke of Ormond, etc., on purpose to trepan [entrap] Gentlemen; upon which, complaint being made to the Vice-Chancellor, he was apprehended, and committed to the Castle [at Oxford], and being try'd at this Assizes, he was sentenc'd to be whipt, and 'tis found that he is a Rogue that goes about to ensnare Men.[151]

The blackmailer on this occasion may actually have been rather well informed. That very summer a Brasenose non-juror named Thomas Carte was in fact travelling England at the behest of Bishop Atterbury, making secret preparations for a Jacobite invasion.[152] Carte was a serious scholar who graduated from Brasenose in 1702 before transferring to Cambridge. 'I have a very great Honour and Respect for him', wrote Hearne in 1714, 'particularly for his late excellent Vindication of the blessed St. and Martyr King Ch. 1st.'[153]

---

[148] HMC, *Portland MSS*, vii. 222/3 (misdated 1717). See also *Hearne's Collections*, v. 62–3: 29 May 1715; HMC, *Various Collections*, viii. 99 (misdated 1717); P. Rae, *History of the Rebellion...against H.M. King George I* (2nd edn. 1746), 140; N. Amhurst, *Terrae-Filius* (1726 edn.), 120 *et seq.* (misdated 1714).

[149] *Hearne's Collections*, v. 65: 10 June 1715 ('White Rose Day').

[150] J. R. Green in *Oxford Chronicle*, 17 Sept. 1859; repr. in *Studies in Oxford History* (OHS xli), 122. See also J. Oates, 'The Rise and Fall of Jacobitism in Oxford', *Oxoniensia*, 68 (2003), 89–111.

[151] *Hearne's Collections*, vii. 261: 23 July 1721.

[152] G. V. Bennett, *The Tory Crisis in Church and State, 1688–1730: The Career of Francis Atterbury, Bishop of Rochester* (Oxford, 1975), 236–7, 254. For more on the Atterbury plot see HMC, *Portland MSS*, vii. 326: 5 June 1722 and 332: 22 Aug. 1722.

[153] *Hearne's Collections*, iv. 433–4: 30 Nov. 1714.

17. **Robert Shippen (1675–1745).**
   Principal, 1710–45; Vice-Chancellor, 1718–22.
   Memorial bust in the antechapel, sculpted by Sir Robert Taylor.
   'Truculent, dishonest, interfering, sensual'.

18. **Nicholas Hawksmoor: Baroque design for reconstructing Brasenose (1719–20).**
From the *Oxford Almanack* of 1723.
The benefactions of Smith and Sutton are promulgated by Apollo, master of the
Muses, and their names are recorded in the book of time.

19. **'Samson and the Philistine' (known as 'Cain and Abel').**

A lead version by John van Nost the Younger from the marble original (1560–62) by Giambologna; installed 1728; sold for scrap 1881, following a Bump Supper riot.

Its destruction was 'an utterly inexcusable act of vandalism' (*Encyclopaedia Britannica*, 1881).

A

B

20. A. **[Sir] John Soane: Gothic design for enlarging Old Quad (1804).**
The 17th century silhouette of Old Quad would have been destroyed.

B. **Philip Hardwick: Gothic design for a new High Street front (1810).**
A speculative scheme.

A

B

21. A. [Sir] John Soane: Roman design for a new High Street front (1807).
     More than a hint of Parisian Neo Classicism.

     B. [Sir] John Soane: Grecian design for a new High Street front (1807).
     An avant garde Greek Revival project, anticipating elements in Soane's Bank
     of England, London.

22. **Sarah Alston, Duchess of Somerset** (*c.*1642–92).
Portrait in Hall; copy by Thomas Gibson, 1728.
Daughter of a rich physician; thrice widowed; major benefactress.
Buried in Westminster Abbey, beneath a monument by Grinling Gibbons.

23. Old Quad in 1861.

Photograph taken after the oriel window of the Old Parlour had been inserted (1860),
but before the sash windows of Staircase VII (1720s) had been replaced with mullions
(1863). It also shows the Tower Bursary after its triple wooden mullions (1816) had replaced
sash windows (1720s: see Frontispiece); but before they were in turn replaced by double
stone mullions (1863).

A VIEW from BRAZEN NOSE COLLEGE, OXFORD.

24. William Cleaver (1742–1815).

Principal, 1785–1809. Successively Bishop of Chester, Bangor and St. Asaph.
'A View from Brazen Nose College': caricature by Robert Dighton (1808).
'A splendid pluralist, armed with diocesan thunder and lightning' (De Quincy).

25. **Frodsham Hodson (1771–1822).**
Principal, 1809–22; Vice-Chancellor, 1818; Regius Professor of Divinity, 1820.
Portrait, formerly in Hall, by Thomas Phillips (1822).
'The most important man in Oxford'.

Brazen Nose, Oxford.

26. Henry Halliwell (1765–1835).
    'Dr. Toe': caricature by Thomas Rowlandson (*c.*1802).
    Bursar Halliwell was immortalised by Reginald Heber in *The Whippiad* (*c.*1802).

27. John Napleton (?1738 –1817).

Vice-Principal 1769–70; Senior Bursar 1771–2, 1773–4, 1775–6.

A 'martinet' who enjoyed 'anecdote and told a story well'. He was the first to propose a coherent reform of Oxford's examination system.

Portrait by Arthur William Devis (1817), showing Napleton as Prebendary of Hereford with the plan of St. Katherine's Hospital, Ledbury.

28. **Francis Yarborough** (1696–1770).

Principal, 1745–70.

Benefactor: he bequeathed his library to the college and paid for several improvements in Hall.

Portrait, formerly in Hall, by Tilly Kettle (1763).

29. **The Library, in 1935.**
    Begun 1657, completed 1664: John Jackson, 'overseer' and 'surveyor'.
    The columns and coved plaster ceiling were inserted by James Wyatt in 1779–82.
    The windows overlooking the Deer Park – blocked in 1779 – were not re-opened until 1954.

30. **Reginald Heber (1783–1826).**
Bishop of Calcutta, 1823–26.
Portrait by Thomas Phillips, 1823.
Tennyson thought 'Holy, Holy, Holy' was 'the finest hymn in the English language'.

31. Henry Hart Milman (1791–1868).
Professor of Poetry, 1821–31; Dean of St. Paul's 1849–68.
'A kind of Christian Gibbon'.

32. The Antechapel and Organ Screen, in 1935.

The Antechapel was used, historically, for teaching and disputation, as well as for college memorials. C. S. Lewis's legendary wardrobe – the cupboard entrance to the kingdom of Narnia – is partly visible to the right of the organ-loft staircase.

But Carte used his researches as cover for less innocent operations. By the summer of 1722, there was a price of £1,000 on his head. The *London Gazette* put out an alert:

[Wanted] of a middle stature, a raw-boned man, goes a little stooping, a sallow complexion, with a full grey or blue eye, his eyelids fair, inclining to red, and commonly wears a light-coloured peruke.[154]

Carte managed to escape to France, and lived to conspire another day, notably in 1745. But he was too talkative to make a good plotter. And his importance in the long run was merely historiographical. His *History of England* (4 vols., 1747–55) was based on significant documentary material, much of which found its way eventually to the Bodleian Library.[155]

The extent of Shippen's own Jacobitism is difficult now to determine. As brother to 'Honest' Will Shippen, he must have been privy to that murky area of parliamentary politics in which Tory principle shaded into Jacobite sympathy. As a tactical ally of Arran, Atterbury, and Harcourt his instincts certainly lay with the highest of high-church Anglicans. His London house in Goodman's Fields was close to a Jacobite sanctuary as well as to a non-juring chapel. And he must surely have known of Thomas Carte. But Shippen was an academic politician, not a conspirator. He shunned all contact with treasonable practice. He was a Hanoverian Tory. In that respect he echoed the mood of Oxford high tables. Most Fellows were content to prevaricate. They drank equivocal toasts, and kept their powder dry. There was some support for the Old Pretender in 1715; little or none for Prince Charlie in 1745. Shippen judged the climate well. In the jargon of the day he may well have been 'Jackish'; but he was Jacobite in sentiment alone.

The same could not be said for Brasenose in general. Its hinterland, after all, was Lancashire and Cheshire. When the Ale Verses were performed in 1709, the college drank toasts to 'our true *English* King', not to some putative Hanoverian claimant. Brasenose men might occasionally appear as time-servers; but more often than not they were loyal to some half-forgotten Stuart dream. For every Richard Blacow—a Mancunian loyalist who ended up Canon of Windsor—there was always a Thomas Patten: a Lancastrian who dabbled in Hutchinsonian heresy.[156] And for every royal chaplain— Thomas Bradshaigh to George I, Charles Jenner to George II—there were sad, shadowy figures like Henry Hall, tutor to gentlemen commoners, 'a

---

[154] Quoted in *ODNB*. He was able to return to England on the accession of George II.

[155] Bodl. MSS 10447–10724. His Tory *History* was the first book placed in the Radcliffe Camera (Bodl. MS Ballard 2, fo. 185). He also wrote a *Life of James, Duke of Ormonde* (1736).

[156] Ward, *Georgian Oxford*, 170–1, 205–6, 283. In 1747 Blacow reported several Balliol men for shouting 'God Bless King James'; they were prosecuted for treason in the Court of King's Bench, and Blacow was rewarded with a canonry at Windsor (*Gent's. Mag.* 25 (1755), 168).

conscientious Nonjuror [who] never attended the College Prayers', and
ended his days in exile in Madrid, as chaplain to the Duke of Ormonde.
There was no consistent college line. Brasenose might well be expected to
nurture elements of opposition. Nicholas Fazakerley, for instance, MP for
Preston—Horace Walpole's 'tiresome Jacobite lawyer'—was a Liverpudlian
Tory, though never a Westminster Jacobite.[157] But Oxford opponents of
Whiggery are seldom easy to categorize. Jacobites, non-jurors, high Anglicans, Tories—even, as we shall see, some of the earliest Methodists—
they add up to no more than a shifting coalition of discontent. Not all of
them would have recognized each other as allies. And from a Brasenose
point of view it turned out to be not Principal Shippen nor any of his Fellows,
but two rogue Methodists from Manchester Grammar who proved to be the
college's most committed Jacobites.

It was in November 1729 that John and Charles Wesley, of Lincoln and
Christ Church, began those private prayer meetings in college rooms from
which the worldwide Methodist Movement sprang.[158] By 1730 their little
group of 'enthusiasts' had been given a nickname: the Holy Club. They had
other names too: the Godly Club, the Bible-Moths, the Bible-Bigots, the
Supererogation Men, the Sacramentarians. Among their number was Clayton
of Brasenose, whom we last encountered on a walk to Woodstock. The son
of a bookseller, John Clayton had come up to Oxford from Manchester
Grammar School in 1725 at the age of 15. He joined the Holy Club in April
1732.[159] So he was certainly not the first Methodist. But he may have been the
first to call himself one. Certainly Clayton's is the first recorded, self-con-
scious use—in September 1732—of that 'honourable appellation'.[160] Now
the 'method' employed—at this point by no more than a handful of devout
young men—involved Bible study (in Greek), prayer, fasting, good works,
communion, and confession. There is no hint yet of separation from the
established Church. These 'enthusiasts' set out simply to galvanize the
formalism of Oxford religion; to tip the balance of Anglican thinking away
from reason and back again to faith. In August 1732, as Tutor and Hulme
Exhibitioner, Clayton could report to Wesley that he brought with him to the

[157] *ODNB*. For Hall, see *Hearne's Collections*, xi. 7: 14 Dec. 1731 and 17: 15 Jan. 1732.
[158] *Journal of John Wesley*, ed. N. Curnock, i (1909), 87 ff.; L. Tyerman, *The Oxford Methodists* (1873), 157–62.
[159] J. Wesley, *Works*, i (n.d.), 13: 18 Oct. 1732; *Works*, xviii (Nashville, 1988), 131–2, Journal, preface.
[160] In a letter of 6 Sept. 1732 to John Wesley (*Journal*, viii (1916), 281). The inventor of the term in this context may have been a Christ Church man (T. Jackson, *Life of the Rev. Charles Wesley*, i (1841), 15–19). It had previously been used in 17th-century theology (L. Tyerman, *John Wesley*, (1870), i. 67; J. Wesley, *Works*, vii (Nashville, 1983), 402).

group a 'little flock'—two or three at least—of his own pupils. 'God be praised', he wrote, they are 'true to their principles and I hope to themselves too.' Principled they certainly had to be, for Clayton followed a strenuous regime. 'I thank God', he writes primly, 'I have fully conquered my affection for a morning nap, and rise constantly by five o'clock.'[161]

It should be emphasized at this point that these young Methodists were still firmly within the high-church camp. But they were also notoriously outside the mainstream of Anglican sympathy. One of those closest to John Wesley as an undergraduate, for example, had been the Revd Jonathon Colley, formerly of Brasenose latterly of Christ Church, whom even Hearne regarded as 'crazed': 'an apocalyptic Man . . . much given to Books upon the Revelation.'[162] Even so, in one respect members of the Holy Club had a significant reputation. They surprised Oxford by their social conscience: their care for prisoners in the city jails; their interest in the paupers who populated the local workhouses. In August 1732, for instance, we find Clayton sending Wesley fairly detailed accounts of his efforts to teach such people to read and understand the Bible.[163] Here was a new spirit in the University. But Clayton himself did not stay long. In May 1733 he went back to Manchester, to Trinity Chapel, Salford. There he became increasingly high church—indeed dangerously so. He fell in with non-jurors, notably a local Jacobite, the Revd Dr Thomas Deacon. And on 29 November 1745 he was found, on his knees, blessing the Young Pretender in the streets of Salford.[164] Among those present that fateful day was another Brasenose man, the Revd Thomas Coppock, chaplain to the Jacobite Regiment of Manchester. Clayton was suspended for three years by the Bishop of Chester.[165] Coppock's fate was rather more severe: he was butchered at Harrowby gallows on the outskirts of Carlisle.

The story of the Manchester Jacobites, encouraged in their folly by these two Brasenose priests, is curious and tragic. The rebellion of 1715—at least as regards England—had depended heavily on the support of Catholic squires in Lancashire. They surrendered ignominiously at Preston.[166] In

---

[161] J. Wesley, *Works*, xxv (Oxford, 1980), 331–4: 1 Aug. 1732. An attack on the affected austerities of 'these Methodists' in *Fogg's Weekly Jnl.* 9 Dec. 1732, was answered by [William Law?], *The Oxford Methodists* (1733; 2nd. edn. 1738).

[162] *Hearne's Collections*, ix. 197: 28 Sept. 1726; xi. 189: 24 Apr. 1733.

[163] Tyerman, *John Wesley*, i. 83–4; quoted in part in *Quat. Mon.* XIII, 20–1: 1 Aug. 1732.

[164] *ODNB*. Deacon had been involved in the 1715 Rebellion. He moved from London to Manchester in 1726, and was much influenced by William Law. Deacon, Byrom, Clayton, and Thyer met regularly at Chetham's Library in the 1730s.

[165] Tyerman, *Oxford Methodists*, 49. His residence was in Greengate, Salford; the Methodist chapel in Gravel Lane later stood on the site of his garden.

[166] Details in BL Add. MS 33954, fo. 30; *5th Report, Deputy Keeper Public Records* (1844), 152–67; *Lancs. Memorials of the Rebellion, 1715* (Chetham Soc., NS 5, 1845); G. Blackwood, 'Lancashire Catholics, Protestants and Jacobites during the 1715 Rebellion', *Recusant History*, 22 (1994–5), 41–59.

1745 the numbers were smaller, but the basis of support was more varied. Manchester—that is the so-called Manchester Regiment—supplied the largest constituency of Englishmen in the rebel army.[167] Some of the officers were certainly Catholic, and minor gentry too. But many were manufacturers and warehousemen; most were high-church or non-juring Anglicans; and quite a few had come under the influence of Clayton himself. The fact that their chaplain, 'Parson' Coppock, was also a Brasenose graduate is more than just coincidence. Manchester Grammar School contained Jacobite sympathizers until the end of the eighteenth century.[168] The collegiate church of Manchester—in effect Manchester's cathedral chapter—remained a Jacobite haven until 1754 at least.[169]

In an attempt to root out these priestly rebels, a new Warden, Samuel Peploe, had been put in place in 1717. Now Peploe was a staunch Whig. 'Peeploe, Peeploe', remarked George I prophetically, 'he shall Peep High'.[170] When Peploe also became Bishop of Chester in 1726—and thus Visitor and Warden simultaneously—tension rose very high indeed. 'The gentlemen of that diocese', it was remarked in 1725, 'are all Jacobites.' And the collegiate church became a focus for the Jacobite sentiments of the whole area. Of the ten collegiate fellows elected under George II, no less than seven were Brasenose clerics: Richard Assheton, Thomas Cattell, Thomas Wroe, Thomas Moss, Thomas Foxley, John Crouchley, and John Clayton. They were Jackish to a man.[171] And Peploe—'Pope Hildebrand-Firebrand' as Deacon called him—was determined to expose them. 'I see some', he warned the Duke of Newcastle early in 1746, 'who like the pay of a Coll. very well, but seem afraid of facing an enemy.'[172] Three Brasenose men in particular were now within his sights: Thomas Cattell, John Clayton, and William Shrigley, at that time incumbent of Newton Chapel. Cattell and Clayton had attended the Pretender's levee; Shrigley read prayers for the Highland chiefs on St

[167] P. K. Monod, *Jacobitism and the English People,* 1688–1788 (Cambridge, 1989), 331. To these must be added supporters among the Welsh gentry (P. D. G. Thomas, 'Jacobitism in Wales', *Welsh Hist. Rev.* 1 (1960–3), 179–300).

[168] Henry Brooke, headmaster 1730–49, was a Whig; but Charles Lawson, headmaster 1764–1807, was still considered a Jacobite in 1801 (Mumford, *Manchester Grammar School,* 168–9, 192, 233). For Lawson's epitaph, composed by Frodsham Hodson, see ibid. 241.

[169] That is, until the foundation of St John's Church, Deansgate (ibid. 161). The collegiate church received cathedral status in 1847.

[170] Ibid. 133. Peploe succeeded a moderate Whig, 'Silver Tongued' Richard Wroe.

[171] HMC, *Portland MSS,* vii. 419: 29 Jan. 1726.

[172] *Literary Remains of John Byrom,* ed. R. Parkinson, i/1 (Chetham Soc. 32, 1854), 233: Deacon to Byrom, 6 Dec. 1762; B. Stott, 'The Informations Laid against Certain Townsmen of Manchester in 1746', *Trans. Lancs. and Cheshire Antiquarian Soc.* 42 (1925), 27: Peploe to Newcastle, 29 Jan. 1746.

Andrew's Day. All were 'determined men against the Govt.'[173] One of the collegiate chaplains, the Revd Richard Assheton—Brasenose, like several generations of his family—had some years before that refused to pray for a Hanoverian king, and narrowly escaped exclusion.[174] The case against Cattell and Shrigley, however, was at this stage slim. That was not the situation with Clayton. He was a much more public figure. Clad in gown and cassock, with a white band in his hat, he had greeted the Young Chevalier with reverence. 'God Bless Your Royal Highness Prince Charles', he shouted; 'and the Croud ... cryed out, Long live Parson Clayton.'[175] Such things could not go unnoticed. But Clayton seems to have had influential connections. As chaplain to the High Sheriff of Lancashire—Sir Darcy Lever, one of his local pupils and yet another Brasenose man—he had managed to become a chaplain of the collegiate church in 1740; in 1746 he was to survive his reckless show of sympathy with the rebels; and in 1760 he was rewarded at last with a collegiate fellowship. Things were more difficult for Coppock.

Coppock was the son of a tailor, who had gone up from Manchester Grammar School to Brasenose in 1739. There he seems to have gravitated towards the Methodist group, and perhaps became one of their itinerant preachers after graduation. At that point he began to fish in troubled waters. Thanks to a forged testimony he managed to secure a curacy at Snave in Kent, a parish in the Romney Marsh area known at that time for smugglers and Jacobites. When his forgery was exposed, he joined the rebel army in November 1745 as chaplain and quartermaster to the Manchester Regiment.[176]

When the Young Pretender arrived in Manchester, the chaplains and fellows of Manchester collegiate church rejoiced. In the marketplace, at the Bull's Head Tavern, Coppock sat drinking with Jacobite officers. Among their company was Oswald Mosely. Now Mosely's father was the Lord of the Manor of Manchester, Sir Oswald Mosely, Bt., yet another Brasenose man.[177]

---

[173] Stott, 'The Informations', 28: Peploe to Newcastle, 8 Mar. 1746; *Literary Remains of John Byrom*, ed. R. Parkinson, ii/2 (Chetham Soc. 44, 1857), 449: 14 July 1748.

[174] His son, Richard Assheton jun., also of Brasenose, later succeeded Samuel Peploe sen. and jun. as Warden in 1782. He in turn was succeeded by another Brasenose man, Thomas Blackburne, in 1800. See F. R. Raines (ed.), *Wardens of the Collegiate Church* (Chetham Soc., NS 6, 1885), 157–78; H. A. Hudson, 'Wardens of the College of Manchester', *Trans. Lancs. and Cheshire Antiquarian Soc.* 33 (1915), 190; S. Hibbert-Ware (ed.), *History of the Foundations in Manchester of Christ's College, Chetham's Hospital, and the Free Grammar School*, ii (Manchester, 1830), 72–5. For Bishop Peploe, see also HMC, *Portland MSS*, vii. 474–7.

[175] Stott, 'The Informations', 31, 37.

[176] B. Stott, 'Parson Coppock', *Trans. Lancs. and Cheshire Antiquarian Soc.* 40 (1923), 45–75.

[177] PRO KB.33/4/1, cited in Monod, *Jacobitism*, 335. The Young Pretender spent some time at Mosely's seat, Ancoats Hall, prior to the rebellion. See J. Wheeler, *Manchester: Its Political, Social and Commercial History* (Manchester, 1836). Sir Oswald had been the focus of 'talk of an opposition' in the Oxford elections held on George II's accession (HMC, *Portland MSS*, vii. 450: 29 July 1727).

And at the same time, in a nearby house in Market Street later known as the 'Palace Inn', Clayton—acting as 'a sort of Royal Chaplain'—said formal grace for the Young Chevalier.[178] 'Liberty and Property'; 'Church and King': the regimental banners in the street proclaimed messages long familiar in Brasenose. But now the toasts were in deadly earnest. Earnestness did not save them. Within weeks the rebellion was over. Three of 'Bishop' Deacon's sons—all Salford pupils of John Clayton—died as a result of the affray. One was executed on Kennington Common, and his skull was brought back to Manchester on a pike. Eight of their fellow officers were also hanged at Kennington; their bodies dismembered as a warning to rebels.[179] Coppock himself—the only English clergyman in the rebel army—was condemned for high treason. Despite several appeals, he was hanged and quartered at Carlisle. He met his fate with a defiant speech:

I should rejoice without Measure could this single Head of mine be fix'd on all Cathedral and Parish Churches in Christendom, to satisfy the whole Christian World of the honesty of my Intensions, and Integrity of my Principles, and could it be engraven on my Tombstone, 'underneath are enterred the ashes of that only English Protestant Clergyman whose Honour, Zeal, Courage and Loyalty were conspicuous in his royal Majesty's cause'.[180]

Coppock's head was fixed on a pole and placed on the English Gate at the entrance to the city.

Clayton was certainly luckier. He was indicted for treason at Lancaster as 'a person evilly disposed and of an Impious Iniquitous ffactious Seditious Turbulant and Rebellious Mind and Disposition'. But his connections seem to have been stronger than the evidence against him. The indictment was withdrawn, and Parson Clayton lived on to preach once more.[181] After three years' suspension he boldly fashioned his first sermon—delivered in Peploe's presence—as an address on the following theme: 'I became dumb, and opened not my mouth, for Thou didst it.'[182] By that time Peploe himself seems to have mellowed. Bowing to local pressure, he had surrendered the collegiate Wardenship—admittedly in favour of his own son—as early as

[178] Tyerman, *Oxford Methodists*, 49.

[179] Ibid. 46; Mumford, *Manchester Grammar School*, 162. One son died in custody; one after transportation. For details of the '45 in Lancashire and Cheshire, see [J. Byrom, T. Deacon, et al.] *Manchester Vindicated* (Chester, 1749); *5th Report, Deputy Keeper Public Records* (1844), 171–93; Hibbert-Ware, *History of the Foundations in Manchester* 97–125 and F. J. McLynn, *The Jacobite Army in England,* 1745 (Edinburgh, 1983).

[180] 'Last Speech and Dying Words', partly printed in *Brazen Nose*, iii. 284–5. For a variant speech (18 Oct. 1746), see BL Add. MS 33954, fo. 75. See also Stott, 'The Informations', 25–52.

[181] Stott, 'The Information', 37–42.

[182] Tyerman, *Oxford Methodists*, 49.

1738. In the meantime Clayton had managed to make his peace with the establishment.[183] As Wesley moved away from hierarchy—'the world [is] my parish'—so Clayton became more orthodox.[184] When the Wesleys returned to Manchester to preach, Clayton thought it politic to ignore them.[185] By then he was, after all, collegiate chaplain and headmaster of Salford Grammar School. And it is as a local schoolmaster that Clayton is now remembered. Refounded in 1735, and at first known as St Cyprian's—after the patron saint of non-jurors—Salford School came dangerously close to being a nursery of Jacobitism. Even after the fiasco of '45, the sons of local Tories continued to imbibe high-church principles there, at least until Clayton's death in 1773. We leave him, a figure of local celebrity, wandering the back streets of Manchester with 'a great sweeping nosegay' in a vain attempt to keep out the smells of the city.[186]

Back at Brasenose, Clayton's early associates had long since dispersed. One of his Methodist pupils had been William Nowell, a Lancastrian of founder's kin. He came up at the age of 16; later became a Hulme Exhibitioner; and later still removed to Oriel. Another was Thomas Patten, whom we have already met; a Mancunian and Hutchinsonian. He too came up at 16, but later moved to Corpus.[187] Another was Robert Thyer: like Clayton, as we have seen, he returned to Manchester and there became Chetham's librarian.[188] A fourth Brasenose Methodist was Matthew Salmon. He was an exact contemporary of Patten, though from Cheshire rather than Lancashire. He must have been a paragon of the new religion. John Wesley described him as 'in person, in natural temper, and in piety, one of the loveliest young men

---

[183] See a caricature of Clayton as Janus, labelled 'the art of trimming' (ibid. 50).

[184] J. Wesley to (?) Clayton (*Works*, xxv. 616: 28 Mar. 1739?).

[185] After 1738 Charles Wesley described Clayton as 'my *former* friend' (C. Wesley, *Journal*, ed. T. Jackson, ii (1849), 134). However in 1752 he still thought Clayton read the prayers on Good Friday more 'distinctly, solemnly, and gracefully... [than] any man I... ever heard' (*Works*, xx (Nashville, 1991), 413: Journal, 27 Mar. 1752). In Dec. 1738 George Whitefield had been especially impressed 'by dear Clayton's judicious Christian conversation', and by his services at Trinity Chapel: 'Blessed be God for my coming to Manchester' (*Literary Remains of John Byrom*, ed. R. Parkinson, ii/1 (Chetham Soc. 40, 1856), 218: 2 Dec. 1738). Even so, by Feb. 1739 it was reported that Clayton had 'left the society of Methodists upon seeing their oddities' (ibid. 238: 19 Feb. 1739).

[186] Byrom, *Literary Remains*, 55 n. and *Trans. Lancs. and Cheshire Antiquarian Soc.* 23, 185. Portraits of Clayton in F. R. Raines, *Fellows of the Collegiate Church*, ed. F. Renaud (Chetham Soc. NS. 23, 1891), frontispiece; and 'Breaking-up Day at Dr. Clayton's School in Salford' (*c.* 1738–40), illus. in *Polite Society by Arthur Devis* (Preston, 1983), 42–3, no. 9. Tory dinners in Clayton's memory continued long after his death.

[187] *ODNB*. He was highly regarded by Dr Johnson (*Boswell's Life of Johnson*, ed. G. Birkbeck Hill, iv (Oxford, 1887), 162).

[188] Portrait by Romney, Egerton coll., reprod. in *Butter's Poetical Remains*, ed. R. Thyer (1827 edn.).

I have ever known'.[189] Indeed in 1735 he would gladly have followed the
Wesley brothers to Georgia, in their attempt to proselytize the New World.
His own relatives, however, prevented it.[190]

The number of these early Methodists in Oxford, inside or outside the
University, was never large. Perhaps fifteen in 1735; never as many as thirty.
But Brasenose supplied several of the founders. And the years 1729–35
remained vividly present in John Wesley's spiritual memory. In those years
the seed was sown. 'I often cry out', he wrote in 1772, 'Let me be again an
Oxford Methodist!'[191]

In Oxford generally Methodism made little headway. It was progressively
frozen out by the University establishment. By the time John Wesley experienced his great 'conversion' in 1738, there were few known Methodists in
residence. By the time he resigned his Fellowship at Lincoln in 1751, there
were fewer still. When Charles Wesley went back to Oxford in July 1737, he
must have been agreeably surprised to encounter one of the early Holy Club
members, strolling down the Long Walk in Christ Church Meadows. The
young man's name was Matthew Robinson; originally an undergraduate at
Lincoln, later a Fellow of Brasenose. By that date Robinson was already
ordained; but he had abandoned all his old 'enthusiasm'. His former mentor
could do no more than remonstrate. 'Remember', he told his ex-protégé, 'you
will be of my mind when you come to die.'[192] Ironically, two of the very
books almost certainly studied by Robinson at the Holy Club were written by
a man with Brasenose affiliation: Jeremy Taylor's *Holy Living* and *Holy Dying*
(1650–1). Wesley—like Bishop Warburton—always regarded Taylor as 'a
man of the sublimest piety, and one of the greatest geniuses upon earth'.[193]

In Oxford terms at least, Jacobites and Methodists faded away together.
But before we consign them to the limbo of lost causes—Methodism, of
course, had a future elsewhere—it is time to consider a curious outgrowth of
the Jacobite phenomenon, the origins of Freemasonry at Oxford.

With a warrant from the fifth Duke of Beaufort, Grand Master and Jacobite,
'The Lodge of Alfred in the University of Oxford' was established at
Brasenose in 1769. This was the University's first Masonic Lodge. Its origin-
ators were a group of six Brasenose Masons, four of them Fellows: Hercules

---

[189] J. Wesley, *Works*, xxiii (Nashville, 1995), 123: Journal, 6 Apr. 1779.

[190] Soon afterwards he abandoned Methodism altogether. See *ODNB*; Tyerman, *Oxford
Methodists*, 65; Green, *Young Wesley*, 177 n. 1. He became Vicar of Godmanchester, 1782–97,
and wrote *The Foreigner's Companion through the Universities of Oxford and Cambridge* (1748).

[191] J. Wesley, *Letters*, ed. J. Telford, vi (1931), 6: 15 Dec. 1772.

[192] *The Journal of the Rev. Charles Wesley*, i (1849), 73. Robinson resigned his Fellowship in
1739; he became Master of Boston Grammar School.

[193] J. Wesley, *Works*, iii (Nashville, 1986), 425; Tyerman, *John Wesley*, i. 35.

Durham, a gentleman commoner from Scotland; the Revd Dr Robert Markham, Junior Bursar; the Revd James Wood, Fellow; the Revd John Napleton, Vice-Principal and future reformer; the Revd Giles Haddon, Senior Bursar; and John Willis commoner, the son of George III's doctor. This was the group that James Woodforde of New College—the future Parson Woodforde—joined in 1774. 'It is a very honourable and charitable Institution', he wrote; 'much more than I could conceive it was. Am very glad being a Member of it.' His entrance fee was £3 5s. 0d.; his quarterly subscription 13s. 0d. Monthly meetings, which had begun at the King's Head in Cornmarket, were by this time normally held at the New Inn, sometimes with postprandial singing at the Mitre. Woodforde's dining companions—apart from Wood and Napleton—included several other Brasenose *literati*: Bennett Dorset, Charles Francis, and Ralph Cawley.[194] Membership was curiously mixed, town and gown together, with an occasional oddity like Paniattotti Ballanchi, the University fencing master. But the life of this body was short. In about 1782 it ceased to exist as a college institution. It vanished completely in 1790, only to re-emerge in 1814 in the form of a non-University Lodge.[195]

But that was not the end of it. The Alfred Lodge left behind it one conspicuous memento. In the very year of its foundation, 1769, there appeared in hall—in place of honour over high table—a massive portrait of King Alfred, eponymous patron of the Lodge, and mythical founder of 'the King's Hall'. The donor was J.H. Smith Barry, a Jackish landowner from Cheshire and Co. Cork. The money came from the estate of another Brasenose man, a Jacobite Irish magnate who died in 1751: James Smith Barry, later fifth Earl of Barrymore. And the date of presentation marked the birth of his grandson, the future seventh Earl, a notorious roué known as 'Hellgate'.[196] Now the fourth Earl of Barrymore had been a committed

---

[194] Hargreaves-Mawdsley (ed.), *Woodforde at Oxford*, 217–18, 222, 231, 239, 257, 273, 280, 291, 323: 1774–6. Other Brasenose members were James Barton, Thomas Calley, Allan Eccles, Thomas Evanson, Gervas Ker, William Muckleston, Thomas Roberts, Richard Salmon, James Strode, James Stronge, and James Woodcock. Durham—son of James Durham of Kirkaldy, Fife—was elected first Master, aged 25, prior to his matriculation. See membership list in E. L. Hawkins, 'Two Old Oxford Lodges', *Trans. Quatuor Coronati Lodge*, 22 (1909), 139 *et seq*. In 1772 a silver Lodge medal was struck; there is an example in the Ashmolean. See also *Trans. Quatuor Coronati Lodge*, 43. 238; *Masonic Mag.* 7. 437; D. Knoop, *University Masonic Lodges* (1945); E. L. Hawkins, *Freemasonry in Oxfordshire* (Oxford, 1882), 3–10.

[195] United Grand Lodge MSS and Apollo Lodge MSS; *Brazen Nose*, iii. 212–13. For Paniattotti, see *Jackson's Oxford Jnl.*, 16 Mar. 1793.

[196] The painting cost £25 (*Quat. Mon.* IV, 37 and VII, 23). The 7th Earl of Barrymore seems to have been 'a great rogue', but 'exceedingly good company' (*Prince of Wales Correspondence*, ii. 736: Duke of York to Prince of Wales, 19 Mar. 1793; *Gent's Mag.* (1793), i. 284). He built a

Jacobite and non-juror.[197] As MP for Wigan he represented a constituency sympathetic to the Pretenders. In 1744 he had been active in promoting the possibility of a French invasion. In 1747, just before his death, he narrowly escaped prosecution. But with the collapse of the '45, and with the accession of an identifiably English monarch in 1760, Jacobite sentiment retreated into dining clubs and drinking parties, secret associations for the maintenance of myth.[198] Among these not the least were the Masonic Lodges that multiplied in increasing numbers around 1760.[199] It takes only a small leap of imagination to see Oxford's Alfred Lodge as part of this same process. Oxford's mythical originator—the equally mythical founder of Brasenose—emerges as a substitute focus for the loyalties of Old England, an escape from the humiliation of Hanoverian rule. At Brasenose the painting of King Alfred remained in place until 1903. In that year the icon was demoted; relegated to a position at the opposite end of the hall, prior to exile in 1926 on the Old Lodge staircase and eventual destruction in 1952.[200]

So at this point a touch of speculation is legitimate. The rise of organized Freemasonry in Britain has been traced in part to the waning of Jacobitism during the middle years of the eighteenth century. One secretive sect gave

celebrated private theatre at Barrymore House, Wargrave, Berks. (S. Rosenfield, *Temples of Thespis* (1978), ch. vii). One lame brother was known as 'Cripplegate'; another, criminally inclined, was known as 'Newgate'; their foul-mouthed sister was known as 'Billingsgate'. The family owned considerable estates at Belmont, Cheshire, and Fota Island, Co. Cork. For their eccentricities see J. R. Robinson, *The Last Earls of Barrymore*, 1769–1824 (1894); *Notes and Queries*, 5th ser. 10, 68, 110, 376, 476 and 11, 276; also *ODNB*.

[197] E. E. Cruickshanks, *Political Untouchables: The Tories and the '45* (1979), pl. 4; R. R. Sedgwick (ed.), *Hist. Parl.: Commons, 1715–54*, i (1970), 440–2.

[198] During the 1750s, toasts in Oxford were still being drunk in Jacobite glasses: 'The Society being met and the cut Glasses representing the figure of the Young Chevalier drest in Plaid being brought in...' (quoted from an Oxford newspaper of 1753, in *The Field* (Nov. 2005), 39: Drambuie Collection). In the 1760s, however, Catholic loyalty to the Stuarts evaporated. In 1766 the Vatican ordered that George III be prayed for at mass (Monod, *Jacobitism*, 329). In 1774 the University elected Lord North as Chancellor: he was thus Prime Minister to a Hanoverian King whose portrait could now hang even in St John's.

[199] J. P. Jenkins, 'Jacobites and Freemasons in 18th century Wales', *Welsh Hist. Rev.* 9 (1979), 391–406.

[200] The decision was taken by E. G. Collieu. Its removal from hall coincided closely with a similar decision by University College. 'King Alfred to be removed. Bishop Smith to be put in his place. Sir Richard Sutton to be placed where Bishop Smith now is. Dean Nowell to go in Sir R. Sutton's place. Lord Mordaunt to replace Dean Nowell. Robert Burton to replace Lord Mordaunt. The portrait of Samuel Radcliffe on the north wall to replace Burton; balancing the portrait of Radcliffe, on the other side of the Duchess of Somerset' (V-P's Reg. 21 Jan. 1903). The portrait of Alfred has been attributed to Edward Penny; it was inscribed 'Ichnographia Aulae Regiae'. See R. L. Poole, *Catalogue of Oxford Portraits*, ii (OHS lxxxi), 243; *Hearne's Collections*, iv. 313–14: 24 Feb. 1714; and *Brazen Nose*, iii. 213.

impetus to another.[201] In Brasenose, the foundation of the Alfred Lodge followed soon after the final collapse of Jacobite hopes in 1759–60. Certainly that is intriguing. But what is doubly intriguing is the fact that the subsequent demise of the Alfred Lodge—for some years symbolized by a portrait commemorating the birth of 'Hellgate' Barrymore—coincided almost exactly with the birth of Oxford's oldest dining club, a club designed to perpetuate a diabolically secret toast: the Phoenix Common Room. Two of its early members, in 1813 and 1816, turn out to be illegitimate sons of the donor of the Alfredian portrait. Perhaps there are clues here to an abiding Brasenose mystery. Did Jacobitism go underground as Freemasonry and emerge as a convivial society dressed up in ritualized form? Could it be that the Phoenix actually rose not from the ashes of some forgotten Hell Fire Club but from the embers of Alfred Lodge? These are deep waters. The first members of the Phoenix are not known to have been Freemasons. But their sympathies may well have been Jacobite. Their founder, Joseph Alderson, was connected to a family notorious for its Jacobitism and crypto-Catholicism: the Westbys of Mowbreck Hall, Lancashire. But firm evidence is hard to come by. The name Phoenix has always been presumed to presuppose an earlier society. But the title could just as well refer to the name of a very Brasenose watering hole: the Phoenix Inn, 'a victualling house' conveniently close to All Saints Church in the High. So much is speculation. In any case details of further Masonic doings at Brasenose—to say nothing of the Phoenix itself—must wait for a later chapter. But at this point it is worth remembering that college traditions—toasting an unmentionable absent friend for instance—may sometimes turn out to contain vestiges of fact.[202]

One thing at any rate is clear. These early Brasenose Freemasons could never be described as Oxford Methodists. They were careerists not pietists; and they were college men through and through. Two of them eventually became Principal: Ralph Cawley and William Cleaver. Cawley we already know. Cleaver is a bigger figure, and he deserves at least half a chapter to himself.

---

[201] Monod, *Jacobitism*, 300–7. For example, in the 1760s J. P. Pryse of Gogerddan—a Jacobite from Oriel, a satellite of the Tory Duke of Beaufort, and a close friend of the radical John Wilkes—was both a Mason and a member of a local 'Lunatick Club', that is a Welsh offshoot of the Medmenham Hell Fire Club (Jenkins, *Welsh Hist. Rev.* 9 (1979), 399).

[202] There is at least one known parallel: the leading Jacobite society in Wales—the Cycle of the White Rose—survived as a social club for the gentry of Denbighshire until 1869 (Thomas, *Welsh Hist. Rev.* 1 (1960–3), 299). As late as 1923, Evelyn Waugh joined a White Rose club at Oxford (Waugh, *A Little Learning* (1964), 183). For the Phoenix Inn see Wood, *City of Oxford*, i, 80, 480, 524. Alderson was born circa 1762, son of Joseph Alderson sen. of King's Lynn, Norfolk. For links with the Westby family see J. Burke, *Landed Gentry* (1837 edn.), i. 598 n. and J. M. Robinson, *Country Houses of the North West* (1988), 222, 229.

Cawley's regime is memorable now only for the notebooks he left behind. Without them the record of Brasenose during most of the eighteenth century would certainly be a great deal thinner. But Cawley's immediate predecessor, William Gwyn, has his own part in this story too. For Gwyn was not a Freemason, but he was very much a Manchester product. His father was Rector of Prescot, and a Fellow of King's College Cambridge. For a career such as his, all the omens were good. But his tenure turned out to be brief: the briefest of any Brasenose Principal. After less than one hundred days in office, he was found dead in the lanes of Brighton, at the age of 35.

This gentleman arrived at Brighthelmstone on Friday morning [17 Aug. 1770], and ordered a dinner to be ready by two o'clock: in the interim he went to take a walk, but not returning, enquiries and diligent search were made for him by his servant and others, but to no purpose; the next day (Saturday) the search was renewed, to as little effect; when it was generally supposed that he was drowned: on Sunday [19 August] however, the body was discovered by the edge of a pathway, west of the town, *a little above the church*, lying with the face downwards, *among standing barley*. There were several guineas, a pocket-book, etc. found about him; the body was brought to the New Ship, and examined by [Brighton's] principal physician Dr. Awsiter, who gave it as his opinion, that he fell in a fit, and was suffocated for want of timely assistance.[203]

Otherwise we know little of Gwyn. Curiously, we know not a great deal more about his own immediate predecessor—one of the longest serving of all Brasenose Principals—the Revd Dr Francis Yarborough. But with Yarborough one thing is certain: this phase in college history—Brasenose as a Lancastrian Jacobite Tory backwater—comes finally and irrevocably to its end.

Yarborough came from Yorkshire gentry stock. His father was a Serjeant-at-Law. He graduated at University College in 1716, and became Higdon Fellow of Brasenose three years later. During the long years of Shippen's rule, he stayed on as a bachelor and cleric, acting as Junior and Senior Bursar before moving in 1739 to the enviable rectory of Aynho. Summoned back as Principal in 1745, he passed no fewer than twenty-five years in collegiate calm before dying at Bath in 1770. Even the omniscient *Gentleman's Magazine* omits all mention of his death. Once his portrait by Tilly Kettle (pl. 28) hung magisterially in hall. Today he looks out quizzically across a less prestigious kingdom: he has been exiled to staircase XI.[204]

---

[203] *London Chronicle*, 21 Aug. 1770 and Cole coll., BL Add. MS 5847, p. 450, quoted in *Gent's Mag.* N.S. 8 (1837), 489–90. His library was sold by Fletcher of Oxford (a Brasenose man) in 1771 (Nichols, *Literary Anecdotes*, iii. 677). He was buried at St Nicholas, Brighton.

[204] *Jackson's Oxford Jnl.*, 24 Apr. 1770; Burke, *Landed Gentry* (7th edn. 1886; 15th edn. 1937): Yarborough of Campsmount; *Quat. Mon.* XIII, pl. i; V-P's Reg. Mich. 1817, fos. 106 [portrait], 116.

Yarborough wrote nothing. But he possessed a fine collection of scientific, philosophical, and deistic books. Its inheritance by the college in 1772 prompted the reordering of Radcliffe's library and the insertion of an elegant coved ceiling, designed by James Wyatt in 1779–82 (pl. 29). In effect, the library became a book-lined open space—suitable for lectures or receptions—lit only by windows on its Radcliffe Square side. The ceiling was originally uncoloured; the columns were of siena-tinted scagliola. The removal of the seventeenth century shelving meant that the older books were at last unchained—almost the last major library in England to be freed in this way—even though undergraduate access was still severely restricted.[205] By this date Yarborough had already presided over several improvements in hall (pl. 69). In 1748 a handsome new chimneypiece was installed.[206] In 1751 replacement glazing was inserted; and in the same year a new ceiling. Barrel vaulted and stuccoed, this elegant covering enveloped but did not replace the hall's original sixteenth-century beams; and in 1774 its appearance was enhanced by the addition of two splendidly gilded chandeliers. In 1752 a new steel grate, hearth-back, and fire irons were installed. In 1753 a new cupola was fixed upon the belfry. In 1763 both hall and screens passage were paved throughout with black and white marble. And in 1775 reglazing of the windows on the southern side was begun, resplendent with the arms of founders and benefactors.[207]

Quite a number of these improvements were paid for by Yarborough. And his example was followed by several richer collegians.[208] With Yarborough at the helm Brasenose prospered materially. As the college rose in wealth and standing after the middle years of the century, the need for improvements—in particular for new accommodation—became obvious. But in 1770—that

[205] *Quat. Mon.* III, 34 and XIII, 7. The glazing had been renewed in 1751 (*Quat. Mon.* IV, 34). Wyatt's drawings (Clennell B 15.1: July 1779) show an open layout, with blocked windows facing the Deer Park. These blocked windows attracted damp, and had to be renewed by Philip Hardwick in 1845 (*Quat. Mon.* III, 32). They were not opened until 1954 (*Brazen Nose*, x. 99). Yarborough's books were valued at £350 (Coxhill, 'Cawley', 56; *VCH Oxon.*, iii. 213). The chains in Magdalen library were not removed until 1799 (B. H. Streeter, *The Chained Library* (1931), p. xiv).

[206] Paid for by Assheton Curzon, later 1st Viscount Curzon (Benefactors Book, 1748; *Quat. Mon.* IV, 34).

[207] Benefactors Book, 1775, gift of Richard Beaumont. Arms by Eginton, 1821: Clifton, Mordaunt, and Frankland; Williamson, Chichester, and Higden; Elton, Somerset, and Darbie. For ceiling, chimneypiece, flooring, furniture, etc., see *Quat. Mon.* III, 40, 42–3 and IV, 34–6, 38. Around this time it was Yarborough who paid for plastering the gate lodge and library staircase. The hall chandeliers (presented by Richard Brooke) were replaced with gaslights in 1839. The cupola was removed c.1948 and replaced in 2010 (V.-P.'s Reg. 30 July 1948, f. 127; 15 Dec. 1948, f. 134).

[208] IV, 3 was refurbished in 1748, by Assheton Curzon; IV, 4 in 1753, by Sir Peter Leicester, Bt. (Benefactors Book, 1748, 1753; *Quat. Mon.* IV, 34 and 35).

complicated year of three Principals—it cannot have been exactly clear how this could be achieved. Brasenose took its decision stage by stage. In February the college bought in the leases of two houses in the High Street, purchased originally from Christ Church in 1736. In April both premises were fitted up as 'Gentlemen's lodgings'. Only then, after Gwyn's election, was it decided to convert them into 'a Lodge for the Principal'.[209] Gwyn himself never lived to see this change. But nearly £2,000 was spent on improvements to the fabric.[210] At the same time the Old Lodge was divided up between Bursar and Fellows. 'At Mich's, 1771', Cawley was at last able to report, 'the Principal left the old Lodge, & went to the new one.'[211] And there, in a plain stone-fronted house facing onto the High Street, one shop away from St Mary's Church, the Principals of Brasenose would reside until 1886 (pl. 53B).

Ralph Cawley, whose notebooks we have had good reason to quote, was not a gentleman and not very much of a scholar. His father had been master of Wigan Grammar School. He matriculated as a plebeian batteler in 1738, became a Fellow in 1744, and would never have emerged from his rectory at Stepney had it not been for the sudden death of Principal Gwyn. But he was a loyal Brasenose man. He left a useful collection of books to his successors;[212] he placed a memorial to Bishop Smith in Lincoln Cathedral in 1775; and he donated painted glass for the east (later west) window of the college chapel in 1776.[213] Almost his only claim to fame is the fact that in 1783 his wife Ann— by that date his widow—acted as private tutor to the young Jane Austen.[214]

[209] Clennell B 53.6: Cawley Notebook vi, fo. 18; Hurst Bursarial: Trades Bill 82; Clennell B1 d 37: Principal's Fine Book, 1705–1804.

[210] *Quat. Mon.* III, 40–3, 57–8, pl. xxvii. For kitchen plans, see Clennell B 15.1. For decorative details (e.g. 'Common Parlour', 'Best Parlour', 'Large Dining Room', 'Little Dining Room'), see Hurst Bursarial: Trades Bills 82, 83, 87; for the site, see *Brazen Nose*, iii. 107.

[211] Clennell B 53.1: Cawley Notebook vii, fo. 15. From 1772, Cleaver moved from II, 3 and 5 into Old Lodge, 5, 6, and 7 (Room Book, 1764–74).

[212] Listed in Coxhill, 'Cawley', 248–56: mostly classics and theology. These were moved from the Tower to the Principal's Lodgings by Principal Gilbert in 1823.

[213] The memorial to Smith at Lincoln—a marble tablet with Latin inscription near the west door—cost £35; the east window in Brasenose chapel cost £240 (*Jackson's Oxford Jnl.* 25 Jan. 1777; *Quat. Mon.* IV, 38; R. Churton, *The Lives of William Smyth, Bishop of Lincoln, and Sir Richard Sutton, Knight, Founders of Brozen Nose College* (1800), 358–60).

[214] 'Stiff-mannered' Mrs Cawley took her pupil on sightseeing tours: 'They dragged me through so many dismal chapels, dusty libraries, and greasy halls, that it gave me the vapours for two days afterwards' (Jane Austen, quoted—perhaps apocryphally—in P. Honan, *Jane Austen* (1987), 31). Mrs Cawley died in London in 1787 at her brother-in-law's house in Norfolk St., Strand (*Jackson's Oxford Jnl.* 8 Nov. 1787). Despite treating himself with digitalis, Cawley died of a heart condition, aged 56, in 1777; he was buried in the antechapel (E. Boardman, in *Brazen Nose*, xxxviii. 60).

As the college prospered so its comfort improved; and with these improvements the spirit of Brasenose moved further and further away from its homespun northern roots. Brasenose had never been as numerously Methodist as, for example, Lincoln or even Christ Church. Principal Shippen was scarcely likely to be a sympathizer. Nor, a little later, was Cawley's successor Principal Barker. In 1778 we find Robert Wroe—yet another Brasenose Mancunian of methodistical instincts—applying to Barker for authority to proceed to ordination. He received short shrift. Apparently Wroe had attended Methodist meetings not only in Oxford but in Macclesfield too. Worse still, he had 'repeatedly denied the necessity of episcopal ordination'. Methodism was becoming bolder. In fact the whole Wesleyan phenomenon was fast outgrowing its Anglican origins. The break came in 1784 when Wesley finally threw off episcopal control. 'It does not appear to me possible', Barker informed the Bishop of Lincoln in 1778, 'that the College should sign any [graduating] testimonial of Mr. Roe's.'[215] By that date Wesley was no longer a Fellow of Lincoln. But his last sermon at St Mary's in 1774 can surely not have been forgotten:

We were last Friday [noted William Blackstone] entertained at St. Mary's by a curious Sermon from Wesley the Methodist. Among other equally modest Particulars, he informed us, 1st That there was not one Christian among all the Heads of Houses, 2ndly that Pride, Gluttony, Avarice, Luxury, Sensuality, and Drunkenness were the general Characteristicks of all Fellows of Colleges, who were useless to a proverbial Uselessness. Lastly, that the younger Part of the University were a Generation of Triflers, all of them perjured, and not one of them of any Religion at all.[216]

No wonder young Wroe never received that testimonial. The spirit of Methodism was never integral to Brasenose, and it was worlds away from the Oxford of Parson Woodforde.

James Woodforde of New College—at this point senior Fellow and proproctor—supped three times at Brasenose in 1774–6. On the first occasion (17 November 1774) he was invited by a fellow Freemason, James Wood. There were three other guests from Exeter, and one from Oriel.

We had for Supper a Hare rosted, Veal-Collops & one Woodcock. We all eat very hearty. Port Wine & Punch to drink after Supper. We played at Whist [in the SCR] both before and after Supper. I won at Whist this evening 5s. od. We did not break up till very near 12 o'clock.[217]

---

[215] Visitor uncatalogued (Tower MSS), 18 Dec. 1778. For Wroe's brief career, see J. S. Reynolds, *The Evangelicals at Oxford* (Oxford, 1975), 51–2. Wesley himself had been ordained by Bishop Potter, who was sympathetic to Methodism: 'These gentlemen are irregular; but they have done good; and I pray God to bless them' (Tyerman, *John Wesley*, i. 43).

[216] Charterhouse Archives: Blackstone to S. Richmond, 28 Aug. 1744, quoted by Green, in *HUO* v (1986), 455. The sermon's text is given verbatim in Tyerman, *John Wesley*, i. 450–2.

[217] Hargreaves-Maudsley (ed.), *Woodforde at Oxford*, 259: 17 Nov. 1758.

On the second occasion (28 Feb. 1775) Wood again was his host.

It being Shrove Tuesday we had Lambs Wool to drink, a Composition of Ale, Sugar etc. Lobsters, Pancakes etc. to eat at Supper, and the Butler there gives a Plumb-Cake with a Copy of Verses of his own making upon it. There were present Napleton, Wood...cum multis aliis [from other colleges]. We played at Cards till after 12 at night. At Whist I lost 6s. od.[218]

On the third occasion (26 January 1776) Woodforde went to Brasenose in his 'Visitatorial capacity', as senior Fellow of New College. 'Did nothing at all', he notes contentedly, 'only received for my trouble as usual os. 8d. [i.e. 4 groats].' But then comes the timetable, and—more importantly—the menu.

...bitter cold all the day...Between 8 and 9 this morning...to [Bursar] Napleton's rooms, went with him immediately to their Chapel to Prayers, sat next to the Principal's Seat—After Prayers I went into their Bursary and breakfasted with Napleton, Cle[a]ver, [Houstonne] Radcliffe & a Stranger. We had Chocolate, Coffee and Tea...Their Bursary is very handsome, the room immediately over the Gate-way...[Then back to New College, losing on the way 'one of my gold Buttons out of the Sleeve of my Shirt...']. Was invited also to Dinner...at 3, and dined and spent the Afternoon in the same Room with Napleton...Cle[a]ver, Radcliffe, Bower the Stranger mentioned above, Dr. Wall and Lucas of [New] College.—We had a very elegant Dinner. First Course Cod & Oyster Sauce, Rost Beef, Tongue & boiled Chicken, Peas Soup & Roots—The second Course, a boiled Turkey by Mistake of the Manciple which should have been rosted, a brace of Partridges rosted, 4 Snipes & some Larkes rosted, also, an Orange Pudding, Syllabubs & Jellies. Madeira and Port Wines to drink and a dish of Fruit. Dr. Wall, myself and Lucas came away about 7. Great Quantity of very fine Plate made use of there...[219]

Present that day in 1776, breakfasting and dining in the Tower Bursary, were two men who would one day transform Brasenose and go some way towards transforming the University: William Cleaver (pl. 24) and John Napleton (pl. 27). Cleaver would make Brasenose socially glittering and scholastically formidable. Napleton would set in motion a movement for academic reform that would radiate through Oxford. The University of Parson Woodforde— with its claret and roast partridge, its codfish and oyster sauce; with its sclerotic syllabus and its archaic examination system—was at last coming peacefully to an end.

218 Hargreaves-Maudsley (ed.), *Woodforde at Oxford*, 275: 28 Feb. 1775.
219 Ibid. 323: 26 Jan. 1776.

3
1785–1822

'The First College in Oxford': Cleaver, Hodson, and the Hebers

Modern Oxford begins towards the end of the eighteenth century. Or rather the steps by which the University acquired its insignia of modernity can be traced back to 1773. That was the year in which the Revd John Napleton—whom we last encountered dining with Parson Woodforde—published *Considerations on the Public Exercises for the First and Second Degrees in the University of Oxford*. Napleton (pl. 27) was a product of Manchester Grammar School. He had gone up to Brasenose in 1755, and he held a Fellowship for seventeen years before moving on to a diocesan career in Hereford. A sound logician and conscientious tutor, a 'martinet' who enjoyed 'anecdote and told a story well',[1] he was in effect the first to propose a coherent reform of Oxford's formulaic system of examinations.

Of course he was not alone. The unreformed examination system was described by John Scott—the future Lord Eldon, who took his BA in 1770—as, quite simply, 'a farce'. Vicesimus Knox, author of *Liberal Education* (1781), was equally damning. 'The poor young man to be examined in the sciences', he complained, 'often knows no more of them than his bed-maker, and the Masters who examine [him] are sometimes equally unacquainted with such mysteries. But *schemes*, as they are called, or little books containing 40 or 50 questions in each science, are handed down from age to age, from one to another. The Candidate to be examined employs three or four days in learning these by heart, and the Examiners, having done the same before him when they were examined, know what questions to ask, and so all goes on smoothly.'[2]

---

[1] R. Polwhele, *Traditions and Recollections* (1826), i. 107 and ii. 182. See also *Gent's Mag.* 1817, pt. ii, 630. Thanks to the Foley family, he became Rector of Stoke Edith and Master of St Katherine's Hospital, Ledbury (Hereford Cathedral Archives 6434). Napleton's proposals are summarized in *Quat. Mon.* XIII, 25–6. In 1771 he was also in advance of his time in setting up an annuity fund for families of deceased Fellows. This investment (in 3% consols) was forgotten by the college after 1782, and rediscovered in 1821 by Cocks Biddulph's Bank (V-P's Reg. May 1823, fo. 220).

[2] *The Works of Dr. Vicesimus Knox*, i (1824), 377–80; originally no. 77, of *Essays, Moral and Literary*, i (1782), 332–6.

Oxford, he concluded—and this was the year of the French Revolution—was sunk in 'monkery, popery, slavery and Gothicism'.[3] Unless the University could be reformed voluntarily, it was clearly vulnerable to less palatable forms of change. By the 1790s quite a number of dons were toying with examination reform as a defence against the spread of revolutionary ideas: Ralph Churton—BNC's first historian—for one. From the pulpit of St Mary's, he denounced 'the want of subordination, the impatience of discipline', endemic in French universities. If 'there is the remotest Tendency to similar passions' in Oxford, he added, 'we should crush the growing evil in the bud'.[4]

Churton we shall meet again. But in discussions of academic change, Napleton comes first; and anyway he was more specific. What he wanted to do was to revitalize traditional disputations by turning them into vehicles of public interrogation. By aiming to test a specific body of knowledge, he foreshadowed a modern system of examination in which the viva would linger on as no more than a token of pre-nineteenth-century practice. Change came slowly. But from Napleton's initiative—and from the example of Oriel and Christ Church—emerged eventually the New Examination Statute (1800); the first Examination Lists (1802); and the first systems of classification (1807–9). At the same time a system of Responsions was established, that is a preliminary examination in classics, logic, and geometry; and Literae Humaniores was separated in Final Honours from maths and physics, thus making possible the celebrated 'double First'. Henceforward Oxford's BA examinations—at least for the happy few who aspired to Honours—would be competitive, public, and graded; based on a specified syllabus in classics, mathematics, and divinity.

All these changes were internal reforms, sponsored by the University itself. They did not affect the structure of University administration, still less the autonomy of colleges. That would come later, with the reforms imposed from outside by the parliamentary Commissions of 1850–2 and 1872–7. Meanwhile, Oxford took its own medicine, and emerged refreshed by the experience of change. There was even an improvement in the industry and sobriety of undergraduates.[5] Two men who played a part, albeit obliquely, in this therapeutic process were successive Principals of Brasenose: William Cleaver (pl. 24) and Frodsham Hodson(pl. 25).

Cleaver arrived at Brasenose from Magdalen in 1762; he moved on from Fellow to Vice-Principal and thence to Senior Bursar, before becoming

---

[3] V. Knox, *A Letter to the Rt. Hon. Lord North* (1789), quoted by V. H. H. Green in *H.U.O.* v. 620. For 18th-century examination conventions—'huddling', 'stringing', 'doing quodlibets', etc.—see C. Wordsworth, *Scholae Academicae* (Cambridge, 1877), 214–15, 228–34.

[4] Quoted by Green, in *HUO* v. 622. For other ideas of reform, see S. Rothblatt, in L. Stone (ed.), *The University in Society*, i (1975), 280 *et seq.*

[5] M. G. Brock, in *HUO* vi, pt. i, 26.

Principal in 1785. The contrast with his predecessor, Thomas Barker, could hardly have been greater. Barker came from a modest background. He was a brother of the college butler. And this particular butler lived out his retirement in Catte Street, just a stroll away from the Principal's lodgings.[6] Now Barker was not entirely negligible. He gave money which paid for the refurbishment of the library. But he was not the man to elevate the standing of the college, or to exploit its transformed location overlooking Radcliffe Square. Cleaver belonged to rather a different world. His family had been minor gentry since the sixteenth century. His father was master of a fashionable private school; his brother became Archbishop of Dublin; and his patron throughout was a magnate of immense influence: George Nugent-Temple-Grenville, lord of Stowe and first Marquess of Buckingham.

From the outset Cleaver courted the rich and powerful. He had no wish to be head of 'a college of paupers'.[7] He had style, and he had presence. First as Principal, then as Bishop, he was not content with the customary doctor's robes. He wore lawn sleeves to meetings of the Hebdomadal Board; he even wore them at home in the Lodgings. In Dighton's celebrated caricature (pl. 24), he sports the 'big wig' of a Bishop—'bushy, cauliflower'd, round'—as well as 'gloves of bright Bishop's purple'. All this accentuated his bearing: he was 'a tall man, with good features and stately gait'. 'He looked', as the Brasenose porter used to say, 'quite the Bishop'. And 'the effect... was not a little increased by a habit of walking with both his hands upon his chest'.[8] Quite so. But Cleaver was not simply a bishop: he was a bishop three times over. In 1768, 'after a close neck-and-neck contest',[9] he just failed to become Bodley's librarian. So he looked for preferment elsewhere. He became tutor to the Buckingham family. That was a very astute

[6] G. V. Cox, *Recollections of Oxford* (1868), 162. Dr Henry Richards, Rector of Exeter and Vice-Chancellor in 1806, married the daughter of the college cook. Another head of house, 'not far from Exeter', did the same; though, unlike Mrs Richards, she was 'a very lady-like person, and her brother was a Fellow of Pembroke' (ibid. 190). Jeremiah Yate, brother of Principal Yate, had been Steward of Brasenose; he was buried in the cloisters in 1681. Principal Barker was buried in Manchester.

[7] For an account of his Principalship, see [A. Heber (ed.)], *Life of Reginald Heber*, i (1830). For Cleaver's pedigree, going back to the 16th century, see Bodl. GA Oxon. 4 to 599. Several of his relatives are buried at Old, Northants.

[8] Cox, *Recollections*, 159. R. Dighton's print—'A View from Brazen Nose College, Oxford'— appeared in the series 'Oxford Caricatures'. Cleaver's wife, from an Irish Catholic family— Ashton of Downham—was reputed to be 'more than half crazy'; at BNC she was known for 'her absurd questions and remarks' (Cox, *Recollections*, 161: MS additions by George Hornby). Cleaver himself 'was inclined to a kind of claustromania', and locked 'his [college] gates every night at eight o'clock' (*Notes and Queries*, 178 (1940), 204).

[9] Cox, *Recollections*, 210 n. The votes were tied, and the prize went by seniority (*Gent's Mag.* 85, (1815), pt. i, 563).

move, both for himself and for the college. The Marquess's eldest son, Earl Temple—later MP for Buckinghamshire and eventually both Marquess and Duke—became a Brasenose undergraduate. So did his younger brother, Lord George Grenville. Their uncle, William Wyndham, first Baron Grenville, became Chancellor of the University. Cleaver's courting of the Buckingham–Grenville clan brought Brasenose influence and endowment. And it brought Cleaver himself three bishoprics in succession—Chester, Bangor, and St Asaph—each of which he held simultaneously with the Principalship of Brasenose. No wonder De Quincey described him as 'a splendid pluralist, armed with diocesan thunder and lightning'.[10]

Cleaver knew how to use his power to good effect. For all his pluralism, he was admitted to be 'a wise, temperate and successful reformer'; he was even mildly interested in the education of women.[11] In fact Cleaver was a Principal who presided over something of a golden age. During his reign, the college enjoyed 'an unexampled increase in its members, its revenue and its fame'.[12] In terms of numbers, the annual undergraduate recruitment during Cleaver's regime went up from nine in 1785 to twenty-seven in 1809; and that at a time when University recruitment as a whole was static or declining. Partly this was due to the availability of bursaries. Perhaps 10 per cent of undergraduates—sixty-nine between 1770 and 1795—were in receipt of Hulmeian awards.[13] But there was another factor at work. The change in terms of social class was even more striking than the simple increase in numbers. Of the nine freshmen in 1785, only one could call himself a gentleman in the armigerous sense; of the twenty-seven freshmen in 1809, perhaps twenty could lay claim to that distinction. Brasenose had come up in the world. And occasionally Cleaver's gentlemen commoners turned out to be gentlemen

[10] T. De Quincey, *Confessions of an English Opium Eater* (1862 edn.), 122–8. Both the 1st and 2nd Marquesses of Buckingham supplemented the Somerset foundation, and nominated candidates for 'Grenville' scholarships. In 1815 the 2nd Marquess presented the college with a portrait of his father to hang in hall 'by the side of his most illustrious kinswoman, Sarah, Duchess of Somerset' (V-P's Reg. 11 Nov. 1813, fo. 152 and 24 Nov. 1815, fo. 37). The painting, by John Jackson, was exhibited at the Royal Academy in 1814, removed from BNC to Wotton, Bucks., in 1890 (B4 b10, ii, 14 Feb. 1890), and in 1947 transferred to Christ Church.

[11] *Gent's Mag.* 85 (1815), pt. i, 563–4 and pt. ii, 213. In old age he chose to educate a young girl in part of the Bishop's Palace at St Asaph (letter from Revd R. Stephens, in *Brazen Nose*, iii. 216). The see of St. Asaph was worth £6000 p.a. (*ODNB*).

[12] V-P's Reg. 31 Oct. 1809, fo. 23. On the presentation of a 'silver Terrein' by Rundell and Bridge, 'in memoriam beneficiorum acceptorum' (ibid. 15 Feb. 1810, fo. 33 and 31 Mar. 1810, fo. 59). He resigned unexpectedly, via a Birmingham notary, on his way back to St Asaph (Heber MSS, Hodnet: Richard Heber to Reginald Heber Sen, 10 June 1809).

[13] *Ex inf.* Dr I. D. Fallows, citing Hulme Trustees MSS.

scholars too—Andrew Crosse, for example, who came up from Somerset in 1802. He eventually emerged as a distinguished electro-crystallographer.[14]

In terms of income, the college had now entered upon a period of notable prosperity. On 24 December 1794, Joseph Farington, RA—brother of the Revd Robert Farington, Fellow, Vice-Principal, and Bursar—noted in his diary:

On Monday last the Principal (Bishop of Chester) and Fellows of Brazen-nose-college unanimously agreed to raise the livings belonging to that College...in London...to [a minimum of] £350 a year, and...in the Country to £300 a year. The deficiency to be made up from the Domus accumulation arising from the estates belonging to the College. A Senior Fellowship of Brazen-nose is worth on average about £200 a year. A Junior Fellowship not above £140 a year. Brazen-nose-College is the best endowed College in the University of Oxford.[15]

That was an exaggeration. But college income did double between 1790 and 1810—from £4,700 to £9,200 p.a.—a rate of growth faster than that of any other college. Hamlett Harrison, who managed BNC's landed property during Cleaver's time, clearly achieved impressive results.[16] Brasenose was no longer among the lesser colleges of Oxford. In revenue, in numbers, in class, Cleaver had lifted BNC into an altogether higher league. Cleaver's Brasenose was not only the college of the Grenvilles. It was the college of Fortescues and Egertons, of Drakes and Moseleys, of Hebers and Cholmondeleys. It was the college of Richard Rainshaw Rothwell I, a gentleman capitalist worth £50,000 p.a. It was the college of the young Tatton Sykes, a figure who comes down to us as a veritable Sir Roger de Coverley: farmer, horse breeder, doyen of the hunting field, and crack-shot marksman; the grandest sporting man in Yorkshire.[17] Brasenose had become almost a rival to Christ Church, without abandoning its roots in Lancashire and Cheshire. And not the least of Cleaver's contributions was the recruitment of one

---

[14] Crosse had been trained in a hard school at The Fort, Bristol, under the Revd Mr Seyer, where he was caned three times a day for seven years (Boase, i. 772). Cleaver took care to arrange for young Lord George Grenville to be tutored by learned men: George Glover and Henry Halliwell, both of Manchester Grammar School and BNC (J. F. Smith (ed.), ii *Manchester School Register*, (Chetham Soc. 73 1838), 196, 247).

[15] *Diary of Joseph Farington*, i (1978), 280: 24 Dec. 1794.

[16] In 1805 he was presented with 'a silver waiter (value fifty guineas)...as an acknowledgement of his skill and attention to the landed property of the Society' (*Brasenose Reg.*, 384). In 1810 BNC's income (£9,200) was however considerably less than that of Christ Church and New College (*HUO* v. 300: table 10.6).

[17] At Brasenose Rothwell 'was celebrated for the manner in which he read the Liturgy' (*Brasenose Reg.* 396). Later Rector of Sefton, Lancs. For Sykes, see obit, *The Times*, 23 Mar. 1863, p. 6; 'Thormanby' [W. Wilmott Dixon], *Famous Racing Men* (1882), 82–8 and *Kings of the Turf* (1898), 164–76; 'The Druid' [H. Hall Dixon], *Saddle and Sirloin* (1878), 221–53 and *Scott and Sebright* (1878), 9–14, 131–42, 325; also *ODNB*.

particular northerner, the star of Manchester Grammar School: a Liverpudlian named Frodsham Hodson (pl. 25).

The name of Frodsham Hodson—there were family links with Frodsham in Cheshire—is stamped indelibly on early nineteenth-century Brasenose. G. V. Cox, grandest of Esquire Bedells, watched him closely over many years. 'Hodson', he recalled in 1868, 'was in many respects a superior person. He had long been known as a first-rate College Tutor and Public Examiner [in 1808 he even examined the future Prime Minister, Robert Peel. He had] the rare advantage of a good figure, handsome countenance, and a winning address. He was a devoted supporter of the Grenville and Buckingham party... [and in return] the family exerted their interest for [his] promotion;... [As] Vice-Chancellor... his courteous manner gained him "golden opinions".'[18] Lord Liverpool thought him 'the most important' man in Oxford.[19] Hodson certainly took the role of educator seriously. In his early twenties he won the Chancellor's English Essay Prize with a treatise on *The Influence of Education and Government on National Character* (1792; 1836). Thereafter education and government were never separated in his mind; and his capacity for working in both spheres was formidable. 'In 99 cases out of 100', he told Reginald Heber, 'I answer my letters by return.'[20] On the other hand, he did have a private side. Cox paints an attractive picture of the great man *en famille*, clad in Vice-Cancellarial robes but surrounded by a troop of infant daughters: 'It was a pleasing sight to see them clinging to him as he left home for Convocation, when he would gently shake them off, with "Away, ye dear little Incumbrances!"'[21]

As Vice-Chancellor, Frodsham Hodson gave Oxford a national profile; and as Principal of Brasenose, he asserted the right of the college to stand at the summit of University affairs. In 1808 the exiled Louis XVIII had visited BNC.[22] The French royal family had, in effect, been offered asylum by the first Marquess of Buckingham. Their visit to Brasenose received little publicity: in wartime even the Bourbons preferred understatement. But things were

---

[18] Cox, *Recollections*, 193. He acted as Public Examiner in 1802, 1803, 1806, and 1808–10.

[19] *Letters of George IV*, ed. A. Aspinall, ii (Cambridge, 1938), 492, Earl of Liverpool to George IV:19 Jan. 1822. When a few months after his death the archbishopric of Dublin became vacant, Lord Liverpool was at a loss: 'The man whom I destined for this post is dead' (*Manchester School Reg.* ii. 127).

[20] Heber MSS, Hodnet: Hodson to Reginald Heber, 7 Mar. 1817.

[21] Cox, *Recollections*, 194 n. Apparently, on several occasions he took his wife to Prescot in Lancashire hoping that she would give birth to a son who might—as a local scholar—succeed him in a Brasenose Fellowship (ibid. 195 n.). In the event, his only son, Grenville Heber Frodsham Hodson, went up to BNC in 1839.

[22] A 'cold collation' was prepared in hall on 11 Jan. 1808. Stained glass by Eginton of Birmingham commemorating this visit—with the arms of Cleaver and Hodson, Sutton and Smith—was placed in the south dais window in 1821 (V-P's Reg. 26 Apr. 1821, fo. 170ᵛ); this was replaced by T. G. Jackson 'architectus' and James Powell 'vitrarius' in 1889 (*Brazen Nose*, vi. 327).

different in 1814. That summer the allied sovereigns—the Prince Regent, the Emperor of Russia, and the King of Prussia—visited Oxford in great state. They dined in the Radcliffe Camera with undergraduates gawping from the balconies. They posed and paraded in Brasenose: library and hall were transformed for the occasion into 'drawing rooms for the company to assemble in before dinner'.[23] Of course Christ Church hogged much of the limelight. But the food was prepared by the Brasenose kitchen. Under Hodson the college clearly took every opportunity to turn its special location to advantage. To crown it all, in 1815 BNC went head of the river for the first time, in the first recorded inter-college race.

Frodsham Hodson lived up to his ambitions. In fact, he lived like a prince of the Church. At high table even the toasted cheese was served in a silver dish made by the incomparable Paul Storr. And when he travelled, the Principal of Brasenose progressed *en prince*. Mark Pattison records the definitive story:

After one Long Vacation Hodson drove the last stage into Oxford with [a team of four] post-horses. The reason he gave for this piece of ostentation, was that 'it should not be said that the first tutor of the first College of the first University in the world entered it with a pair'.[24]

Only one thing was missing: a grand entrance from the High Street. Since the abandonment of Hawksmoor's dream (pl. 18), hopes of a new quadrangle had been quiescent. But they had not been forgotten. In particular, the Hulme Trustees had been pressing since 1795 for new buildings to house their exhibitioners. Local builders were consulted. And then, in 1800, Cleaver aimed higher. He approached the King's Surveyor General, James Wyatt. That was not such an outlandish idea. Wyatt had already worked at Brasenose; and now he was recommended by the Earl of Wilton, for whom he had recently designed one of Lancashire's grandest houses, Heaton Hall, near Manchester. Alas, Wyatt lived up to his reputation: he proved 'extremely negligent'. Another big name was therefore suggested: John Nash.[25] Once

---

[23] V-P's Reg. 12 June 1814, fos. 172–3. For details of the ceremonies, see *Gent's Mag.* 84 (1814), i. 616. Food was passed from hand to hand—from Brasenose to the Camera—by a troop of dismounted cavalry. Afterwards the soldiers feasted on the remnants (U. Aylmer (ed.), *Oxford Food* (Oxford, 1995), 66–9).

[24] M. Pattison, *Memoirs* (1885), 3. Pattison's father went up to BNC in 1805. His friends were John Le Mesurier, John Blackburne, John Ford, William Wheatley, and Thomas Farrer: neither the smart set nor the reading set. 'His favourite book was Aristophanes. One night he was caught by Hodson on the back of Cain and Abel. On being asked what he was doing there, he replied: Ἀεροβατῶ καὶ περιφονῶ τὸν ἥλιον. "Oh!, cried Hodson, "it's only Aristophanic Pattison" (ibid. 6–7). Socrates' words—'I walk on air and contemplate the sun'—eventually became the motto of the OU Air Squadron (*ex inf.* Revd R. Smail).

[25] For Wyatt and Nash, see minutes of Hulme Trustees: 12 Nov. 1800. *Ex inf.* Dr I. D. Fallows.

again, no designs were forthcoming. In any case, by this time Cleaver was more interested in creating a second quadrangle ample enough to incorporate a new set of Principal's Lodgings. That meant replacing the college kitchen as well. So Brasenose tried a new tack. In 1804 Cleaver requested a fresh set of plans from the man who was currently the most favoured architect at Stowe: John Soane.

From Soane's office in Lincoln's Inn Fields—over a period of four years, 1804–8—came no fewer than three schemes: Roman, Greek, and Gothic. The Gothic proposal (pl. 20A) was unexciting: a sequence of dull extensions to the Old Quad.[26] All the dormer windows were to go; extra rooms were to be secured by inserting corridors along the top storey; and the whole thing was to be disguised by a predictable array of battlements. Each set of chambers would have been spacious; bedroom, study, and sitting room. But the singular charm of the quadrangle, its variety and silhouette, would have been destroyed. Happily, nothing came of this. The Roman scheme (pl. 21A) was much grander.[27] It proposed a formidable Corinthian portico on the High, flanked—in one variant at least—by domed terminal pavilions. This design had a French flavour; in fact it was positively Parisian. But the third scheme, the Greek Revival design (pl. 21B), was stylistically even more advanced.[28] For this Soane postulated a giant Doric colonnade, running along the High Street front, with terminal columns set in pairs: a battery of fourteen Doric columns in all. Inside, there were to be vestibules and corridors; contrived vistas and multiplied spaces; the sort of thing Soane later achieved on a much larger scale at the Bank of England in London. Had it been built, this would have been extraordinarily doctrinaire for its date. But it was all a pipe dream.[29] Soane estimated his Grecian design at £56,400; and his Roman scheme at £58,700. Both sums were well beyond college resources. Instead, in 1807, additional room space was created by turning the cloister beneath the library into a series of four sets for Hulmeian Scholars.[30] All three grand designs had been essentially hypothetical. Full control of the High Street site had yet to be secured. And Cleaver was already looking elsewhere. He resigned in 1809.

[26] Soane Museum, drawer 33, set 4 (1804–8); B 15.1, reprod. in *Quat. Mon.* III, pls. xx–xxi (unsigned; 25 Apr. 1804).

[27] B 15.1: 4 July 1807, reprod. in *Quat. Mon.* III, pl. xxiv.

[28] B 15.1: 4 July 1807; reprod. in *Quat. Mon.* III, pl. xxiii; redrawn by G. Richardson, reprod. in J. Mordaunt Crook, *The Greek Revival: Neo-Classical Attitudes in British Architecture, 1760–1870* (1972), pl. 165: Victoria and Albert Museum.

[29] For estimates see D 356. See also *Lords Jnls.* 29 Mar. 1827; *Apollo* (2004), 23; H. Colvin, *Unbuilt Oxford* (1983), 153 citing Bodl. GA Oxon. a. 249, p. 28.

[30] Hurst College Buildings 27. Converted for use as Hulme Common Room in 1972, until transfer to III, 3 in 2008. Burials had continued until 1754.

It was at this moment that yet another architect—Philip Hardwick—
decided to try his luck. He submitted designs for a new quadrangle fronting
the High Street, with only the plainest of Gothic trim (pl. 20B).[31] Fortunately,
once again nothing came of it. Instead the college settled for two buildings of
a distinctly impermanent kind, both situated in the Fellows' Garden, at right
angles to the antechapel. One was called New Buildings.[32] The other was
called Garden Buildings or Garden Court.[33] New Buildings seems to have
been an enlargement of earlier work dating back to 1740; it survived until
1887. Garden Court was built afresh in 1810; it survived until 1883.[34] Placed
opposite each other, with balancing screen walls of flimsily Gothic style, they
did make a naive attempt at symmetry. But their life expectancy must always
have been short. The problem was that as long as they were there, nothing
serious could be built. Soane therefore resigned himself to the inevitable.
In 1814 he belatedly submitted bills for £207 11s. 0d. for the designs he had
produced in 1804, 1806, and 1807.[35]

Curiously, the only relic of this whole episode—apart from three simple
doors by Soane in the library cloister (pl. 63)—is a caricature of 1811 by
Thomas Rowlandson: 'Bacon Faced Fellows of Brasen Nose Broke Loose'
(pl. IV).[36] A crowd of rubicund dons, bewigged and gowned, tumble out of
chapel on their way to dinner. Their surroundings are fanciful; but the college
is identified by several brazen noses, to say nothing of the allusion to Friar
Bacon. As the Fellows proceed through the entrance lodge, they seem to
celebrate their order of release. BNC has at last broken loose from its
cramped, unworthy site. That at least is one interpretation. It makes sense
of a note which appeared in the *Gentleman's Magazine* that very year:

Oxford, already one of the most beautiful cities in the Empire, is about to experience
some very considerable improvements. A great number of indifferent houses
belonging to [Christ Church] . . . and Brasenose Colleges, are on the early expiration
of the present leases, to be pulled down, and the streets are to be widened etc . . . [37]

[31] B 15.1: 26 June 1810, reprod. in *Quat. Mon.* III, pl. xxv.

[32] Later known as Old Staircase X, later still (1883–7) as Old Staircase IX; near the southern
corner of the antechapel and the northern boundary of the Principal's Lodgings; demolished
1887 (illus. *Quat. Mon.* III, pl. xxviii and *Brazen Nose*, xxi. 44).

[33] Later known as Old Staircase IX; near the northern corner of the antechapel and the
south-west corner of the kitchen; demolished 1883 (illus. *Quat. Mon.* III, pl. xxix).

[34] V-P's Reg. 15 Feb. 1810, fo. 34. Hodson set up a Building Fund (e.g. Fees on graduation
'pro instaurationibus'), and £1,500 of 3% reduced stock was sold to cover the cost of 'New
Buildings' (V-P's Reg. 1 Nov. 1809, fos. 26–7 and 9 Nov. 1810, fo. 68).

[35] V-P's Reg. 21 Oct. 1814, fo. 178.

[36] M. D. George, *Political and Personal Satires*, ix: 1811–19 (British Museum, 1949), 57: 26 Feb.
1811. The college later purchased a variant preliminary drawing (reversed) by Rowlandson entitled
'Brazen Nose Chapel Broke Loose' (Sotheby's, up to £625: V-P's Reg. 17 June 1970, fo. 141).

[37] *Gent's. Mag.* 81 (1811), i. 178.

That was over-optimistic. It would be another century or more before the Fellows of Brasenose finally broke out.

During Hodson's reign there were to be no more building projects, except for Gothic windows in the Tower Bursary.[38] There were other things to do. In 1809—the first year of the new Principalship—a regime of 'terminal Collections' was set up to supplement 'the established system of private lectures'.[39] These traditional lectures had been occasionally effective; Robert Farington's Greek discourses were apparently 'excellent'. But they lacked teeth. Hence the sanction of a regular report. At the same time, recognizing that the University's new method of examining and classifying had made the custom of disputation irrelevant, Hodson instituted a practice of regular formalized declamation.[40] Every Wednesday during full term, scholars and exhibitioners read out their essays in the antechapel; a special literary lecture was delivered every Saturday morning; an annual audit of library books was arranged for the first time; and because of 'the great increase in the number of undergraduates', a Sub-Dean was appointed to assist the Dean in his supervision of their 'weekly exercises'. All this in addition to the customary catechetical classes, and the 'Declamations of the Bachelors and the exercises for Degrees', which continued to fill the antechapel on special occasions.[41] Finally and crucially, in 1816 the college declared its intention to award Fellowships primarily on the basis of the new system of classified examinations. Those examinations now included, of course, obligatory papers in

[38] D 353 and B 15.1: 'new windows…at each end of the Bursary, after a design by Mr. [Henry] Hakewill', Dec. 1816 (V-P's Reg. Mich. 1817, fo. 99). These were executed in wood; they had to be remodelled in stone by J. C. Buckler (George Wyatt of Oxford, builder) in 1861–3 (V-P's Reg. 21 Dec. 1863, fo. 190). About 1816 the three oriel windows facing Radcliffe Square were also replaced (compare engraved views by R. Ackermann, 1813, and N. Wittock, 1829). The oriel windows facing into the Old Quad from IV, 4 and the Old Parlour date from Buckler's intervention (1861–3) (pls. 23, 47B). In 1817–19 the Wyatt family were the builders who fitted up the room over the Tower Bursary as 'an Archive room' (D 353; V-P's Reg. 20 May 1819, fo. 132 and 1821, fo. 182).

[39] V-P's Reg. 31 Oct. 1809, fo. 24; Collections Books, 1811 onwards. Each undergraduate had to 'give an account of the nature and extent of his Studies during the term', before the Principal, Vice-Principal, Senior Fellow, Tutor, and Dean. From 1815 such interviews were registered in the Collections Book 'as a memorial of the diligence and proficiency of each undergraduate' (ibid., 28 Oct. 1815, fo. 35).

[40] For Farington's lectures see Revd T. Whalley, in *Diary of Joseph Farington*, vii. 2613: 14 Sept. 1805. For reforms see V-P's Reg. 1809, fos. 24, 35. Mark Pattison summed up the reform of the examination system (1800, 1807, etc.) as a change from medieval to modern, 'from disputation (dialectical) to composition (rhetorical). Instead of being trained to argue, men were trained to write with ease' (OU Commn., *PP* (1852), xxii, Evidence, 46).

[41] V-P's Reg. 31 Oct. 1809, fo. 24; 21 Dec. 1810, fo. 72; 22 Apr. 1815, fo. 16. The Library visitation was fixed for 24 June, to coincide with the commemoration of Dr Grimbaldson, benefactor of the library. The library was insured for £1,000 (ibid., 11 Mar. 1809, fo. 10).

mathematics and natural philosophy, i.e. science. Not one of the five Fellows, it was noted, elected immediately prior to that date had mastered even 'the Elements of Euclid'.[42]

Such good intentions were only slowly fulfilled. Almost immediately in fact, in 1819, Hodson suffered a rare reversal. Three years before, a third-class graduate named James Smith of Chester had sent in an application for a Fellowship backed by two pedigrees. One showed him to be twelfth cousin four times removed of the daughters and co-heiresses of Sir John Port II; the other showed him to be the Port co-heiresses' fifth cousin eleven times removed. Hodson protested vehemently. Surely such relationships were impossibly distant; valid only in the past. Alas, precedent proved too strong. 'I hasten . . . to express my astonishment', announced Windsor Herald—with all the authority of the College of Arms—'that a Christian teacher should pretend to assert that consanguinity can ever wear out or extinguish so long as the posterity of Adam continues to exist.' The Visitor was duly abashed. Smith was elected, and Hodson discomforted.[43] Not for another generation would elections to Fellowships at BNC be regularized by the reforms of the 1850s.

Even so Regency Oxford prepared the way for change, and the contribution of Brasenose was by no means negligible. Academic results certainly began to improve. In thirty-two years, 1801–33, BNC won twelve University prizes, six for English verse, six for Latin: only Christ Church won more. In 1807 the college won the Craven Scholarship as well as the Chancellor's Essay Prize. And in 1809 occurred a triumph which is still hard to believe. In the Lit. Hum. list that Easter, every single First came from BNC. Classical studies were of course still compulsory for all undergraduates in the University. But that year there were only three Firsts: Edward Cardwell, Robert Garden, and Samuel Hall. And they were all Brasenose men. Cardwell in particular had a formidable career ahead of him. He became secretary to three successive Chancellors: Grenville, Wellington, and Derby. Some said he was the most powerful man in Oxford. The class list did not lie. Admittedly, Hodson was one of the examiners that year; but he was only one of four. And that record tally was not really so unusual. In the years 1808–10, BNC took seven out of thirty-seven Firsts; in Michaelmas 1810, two out of six; in

---

[42] Ibid., 22 Feb. 1816, fo. 51. Whatever the truth of that claim, there was certainly no election to the Lectureship in Natural Philosophy between 1803 and 1812. For a First as one criterion of election, see ibid., 6 Feb. 1817, fo. 88. In 1818 a Junior Mathematical Lecturer was appointed; maths and natural philosophy were established as part of the future examinations for Fellowships; and tutors were made responsible for the preparation of pupils in Euclid for Responsions. In 1833 mathematical lectures were made compulsory for freshmen (V-P's Reg. 19 Dec 1818, fo. 121 and 24 Jan. 1833, fo. 174).

[43] Ibid., 1819, fo. 136 and 1843, fo. 27; G. D. Squibb, *Founder's Kin* (Oxford, 1972), 68–9.

Michaelmas 1814, two out of eight; in Michaelmas 1815, two out of five; in Michaelmas 1817, two out of seven; and in Michaelmas 1819, two out of five. After that there was a falling off, although at Easter 1837 the college revived somewhat with three Firsts out of seven. Perhaps the most dazzling of these results was the First awarded to William Gregson in 1810. The examiners thought it the best they had ever seen. He lived to be the barrister who drafted the Great Reform Bill.

Gregson's year was also the year of Henry Hart Milman's arrival at Brasenose. Ensconced on staircase III, in a veritable 'chaos of literature', he found the teaching at Brasenose rather less impressive than that at Eton. 'Of our three tutors', he wrote, 'one can lecture and never does, another cannot and always does, the third neither can nor does.'[44] Fortunately, he was quite happy working on his own. Milman (pl. 31) is now a forgotten mind. But in his day he was a giant. At Brasenose he notched up not only the expected First, but the University prizes for English and Latin verse as well as the English and Latin Essay Prizes.[45]

> His lines on Apollo
> Beat all the rest hollow,
> And gain'd him the Newdigate Prize.

It was the start of a career which would take him from a Brasenose Fellowship and the Professorship of Poetry—via multiple volumes on the history of Jewry and Christianity—to the deanery of St Paul's. His verse today suffers from excessive Latinity: his professorial lectures were actually delivered in Latin. But as an Anglican critic of uncritical Catholicity—'a kind of Christian Gibbon'—he was, in his time, a potent liberal force.[46] When it came to recruitment, Cleaver and Hodson had plainly hit upon a winning formula: scholars to work and gentlemen to pay.

In early nineteenth-century Oxford only three colleges managed to combine a fashionable clientele with high academic standing: Brasenose, Christ Church, and Oriel. All three had waiting lists; elsewhere there were places to spare. In 1800 Brasenose was described as 'superabundantly full';[47] by 1810— as we have seen—the college was erecting new buildings in the Fellows' Garden. The intake in Hodson's time was particularly buoyant, rising steadily

---

[44] Quoted in A. Milman, *Henry Hart Milman* (1900), 22.

[45] Because of the 'unexampled honour' Milman brought to the college, he was presented with the *Graeciae Orationes* and a 'splendidly bound' set of Clarendon's *History of the Great Rebellion* (V-P's Reg. 10 June 1813, fo. 143 and 7 June 1816, fo. 73).

[46] For Lecky's tribute, see Milman, *Milman*, 311–12. For more recent assessments see C. H. E. Smyth, *Dean Milman* (1949), 7, 20–1; G. M. Young, *Daylight and Champagne* (1937), 110–11; D. Forbes, *The Liberal Anglican Idea of History* (1952); and *ODNB*.

[47] [Heber], *Life of Reginald Heber*, 1. 22–3.

from thirty to forty a year, at a time when University recruitment—though generally increasing—remained noticeably volatile.

So how did they live, these Brasenose men of the Regency? Richard Baker came up in October 1801, at the age of 17, and immediately wrote off to his cousins, describing his first impressions of college life. His family was not particularly rich, and he found the accommodation more than adequate.

My rooms [Old Lodge 6]... are much more comfortable than I expected—my sitting room is as large as your little parlour and to appearance much more comfortable—a bureau, 5 chairs, and a table in it. My drawing room (for so I please to call it) is smaller, but neater, a glass door out of my sitting room to it with two chairs and two tables. My bedroom is a little larger than [my] sitting room with a very comfortable bed, bureau etc., altogether as if it were our three parlours at Highfields, but a door to each out of my S.R. I have been this morning with some of the Tutors to buy myself a set of tea-things, Candlesticks, silver tea-spoons, sheets, towels etc.... Figure to yourself a venerable elderly man and myself with our caps and gowns choosing and buying the best China...We all dine together in the Common Hall with servants to wait, and you order what you like. Supper at 9. Prayers 7 morning, 5 evening.

What is particularly valuable about this correspondence is young Baker's description of the new system of examinations, instituted after the reforms of 1800.

Our examinations for degrees have always hitherto been laughed at as a trifling and a mere matter of form, but now they have assumed a very serious aspect...[For] the end Examination... there is now a large room [in Old Schools] fitted up for the purpose which will contain, I should imagine 300 persons; there are benches for the Vice-Chancellor, Proctors, Drs., Heads of Colleges and Halls etc., who are all required to attend at this most solemn occasion, and about 200 auditors. There are perhaps six examined at a time and this occupies from 9 in the morning till 3 in the afternoon; so that whoever thinks of taking a degree [at least with Honours] must fag...[48]

Well yes: Baker must have decided that he could never face such an ordeal. Six hours a day, he thought, was quite enough time for study. He went down in 1804 without an Honours degree, entered the army, and died three years later in St Helena.

Reginald Heber (pl. 30)—being a gentleman as well as a scholar—was rather more critical of living conditions. As a younger son, destined for the Church, he was not a gentleman commoner; and that meant sharing the commoners' table. 'The dinners we get here', he told Richard Thornton in 1801, 'at least for the commoners (for the gentlemen commoners have a table to themselves, and fare very well) are the most beastly things that ever graced

[48] R. D. Baker, 14 Oct. 1801, quoted in *Quat. Mon.* XIII, 63–4.

the table of a poor house or house of correction.' On the other hand, Cleaver had already spotted him as a future star. 'I am to have a private tutor [Revd T. S. Smyth]', he told Thornton in 1800, 'to keep me out of drinking parties'; the Principal has 'cautioned me strongly against too numerous an acquaintance'. So while the gentlemen commoners dined handsomely, young Heber had to read out his verses in hall. But scholars were almost a protected species. 'No man is obliged to drink more than he pleases', he reported, and there are none of the 'tricks on freshmen which ... were normal forty or fifty years ago'. Compared to some less ruly colleges, teaching was in fact well organized. 'In the economy of time', Heber explained, we 'are perfect Cartesians; we admit of no vacuum'.[49] The secret was that Brasenose now served two distinct clienteles. Cleaver and Hodson had created a fashionable college within a framework of respectable scholarship.

Some of the Fellows—Hornby for instance—were gentlemen. Others— Tench in particular—were rough diamonds. But nearly all were men of learning. When George Eliot, in *Middlemarch*, wished to conjure up the fate that awaited Casaubon at the hands of reviewers, she had only to hint at Dr Carp—or was it Tench?—'and the leading minds of Brasenose'. John Tench in fact was a mathematician; very fierce, and definitely 'an odd fish'. Between 1788 and 1812, as Fellow, Bursar, and Vice-Principal, he remained notoriously farouche. He is remembered as 'wearing a vulgar-looking, powdered one-curled wig, speaking with a strong Lancashire dialect, and reading [in chapel] with a voice of thunder'. Hodson shuddered at his 'nasty fustian breeches and filthy worsted stockings'. Hornby recalled that 'one could hear him reading in chapel as far off as the archway into the quad'; in fact, as Cox put it, 'his enunciation of the oaths and exhortations on Degree Days was an awful infliction on the drum of one's ear'.[50] No doubt there was some relief in 1811 when he moved on to the living of Great Rollright. Under the unreformed system, only a few senior Fellows were permanent fixtures; junior Fellows were birds of passage, on their way to a comfortable perch. Those who intended to stay had to work their way to the top of the college hierarchy. Frodsham Hodson (pl. 25) was the classic example.

Hodson's career was a remarkable tale of upward mobility. He set out to capture every one of Oxford's commanding heights. First in 1787 came a scholarship from MGS to BNC—his father, a clergyman, had been there thirty years before—followed by a Fellowship in 1794, promotion to Senior

---

[49] [Heber], *Life of Reginald Heber*, i. 20, 22, 24, 26, 27.

[50] Cox, *Recollections*, 203 (Hornby MS); *Quat. Mon.* XIII, 30. He died, as Rector of Great Rollright, in 1848, aged 82 (V-P's Reg. 23 Jan. 1848, fo. 77). One likely model for Dr Casaubon is R. W. Mackay who came up to BNC from Winchester in 1821. He was a comparative mythologist, and George Eliot's first article in the *Westminster* was a review of his *Progress of the Intellect as Exemplified in the Religious Development of the Greeks and Hebrews* (1850). See *ODNB*.

Bursar in 1803, and election as Principal in 1809. Then came the bigger prizes: the Vice-Chancellorship in 1818 and the Regius Professorship of Divinity in 1820, with its attendant canonry of Christ Church.[51] At this point Hodson was on the brink of holding four posts simultaneously: Principalship, Professorship, Vice-Chancellorship, and canonry. He had the good grace not to appropriate the canonry—there was no love lost between Brasenose and Christ Church—and he stepped down from the office of Vice-Chancellor. Still, it was an impressive tally; and as Kingmaker he went even further. Two prizes remained: the University's parliamentary seat and the University's Chancellorship. For the parliamentary seat Hodson needed a politically minded Brasenose squire with the reputation of a scholar. He found one in Richard Heber. For the Chancellorship he needed a nobleman with the highest political connections and long-standing college loyalties. He found just the man in the shape of Lord Grenville. Now Grenville was a former Prime Minister, as well as uncle to Cleaver's favourite pupils. He was also a bibliophile and man of letters. In 1809 he was duly elected Chancellor. Henceforward Brasenose would have influence at the very summit of University politics. In 1809–10, all three Grenvilles—Baron, Marquess, and Earl—received the honour of DCL in the Sheldonian. Brasenose was now a power on the Hebdomadal Board. Such influence, however, had its price. In 1811 Hodson found himself attacked in the *Anti-Jacobin Review*. The college reacted swiftly. The editor was forced into public apology, and the publishers were charged with libel in the Court of King's Bench.[52] With the Grenvilles on his side, Hodson seemed invincible. And in 1821, it was Heber's turn to benefit. At the second attempt, he at last won a seat in the Commons. Hodson's upward career had stretched over more than a quarter of a century, and it was a story of almost continuous triumph. But at the last minute he was denied his final honour. He died in 1822, aged

---

[51] He claimed that the numbers (310) wishing to attend his inaugural were too many for the lecture room at Christ Church; he therefore chose to deliver it in the chapel and antechapel at BNC (V-P's Reg., 16 May 1821, fo. 172). In truth, Christ Church was most unhappy at Hodson's appointment (BL Add. MS3828646, fo. 352, 38369, fos. 313–14, 40342, fo. 194, and 40344, fo. 61). See also Richard, 2nd. Duke of Buckingham, *Memoirs of the Court of George IV* (1859), i. 52.

[52] The offending passage seems to have been removed in bound versions. 'We acknowledge the receipt of an "extraordinary letter", accompanied by an extraordinary present, and by an extraordinary request. The letter, however, shall be kept [secret] as desired; the present [as settlement] shall be given to some object of charity; and the request [for removal] shall be complied with' (*Anti-Jacobin Rev.* 39 (1811), 112). The Revd W. Agutter published a retraction in the *Sun*, *Courier*, *Morning Post*, *Morning Chronicle*, and *Observer*, and in the Oxford, Cambridge, Manchester, Liverpool, and Chester papers. Messrs Cradock and Joy, publishers, were prosecuted in the Court of King's Bench (V-P's Reg., 16 May, 17 May, and 26 June 1811, fos. 85–6, 90–1).

only 51—brought down by 'high living and neglect of exercise'—[53] just as a bishopric was within his grasp. Earl Temple—by now both a Marquess and a Duke—marched in the Principalian funeral procession. And so did Richard Heber, MP.

The Hebers were very much a Brasenose dynasty. In fact they were collateral descendents of Dean Nowell.[54] Between 1673 and 1802, no fewer than seven of them were admitted to BNC. Fourth in line was the Revd Reginald Heber of Chelsea, a clerical squire with lands in Yorkshire, Shropshire, and Cheshire. He produced three sons—Richard, Reginald Jun., and Thomas—all of whom he sent to Brasenose. Thomas followed his father into a Fellowship, then became Rector on the family estate of Marton in Yorkshire. He remained a bachelor, devoted to genealogy, heraldry, and church brasses. Reginald jun. might well have done the same: he followed his father into another family rectory, this time at Hodnet in Shropshire. But he was destined for far greater things. He became Bishop of Calcutta and one of the leading hymnologists of the age. As for Richard—'Heber the Magnificent' as Sir Walter Scott christened him[55]—he emerged as England's greatest book collector, but a man destroyed by public rejection and private doubt. His career, in fact, is almost a moral fable. Heber was a bibliophile who succumbed to bibliomania.

Now the Hebers were well-established gentry. But their wealth had multiplied dramatically thanks to the construction of the Leeds–Liverpool Canal between 1774 and 1816. When Richard Heber went up to BNC in 1790, aged no more than 16, Ralph Churton was the obvious choice as tutor. After all he had been born in the Heber parish of Malpas in Cheshire. The future book collector was given his uncle's old rooms (VI, 3), a set later occupied by his half-brother the future Bishop. Ever afterwards they would be known as 'Heber's rooms'. They 'are very pleasant', noted Reginald Heber Sen., 'having

---

[53] Cox, *Recollections*, 194 n. Gilbert gives a more graphic description: his bowels were afflicted with 'some secret mischief which medicine could not reach'; after twelve days' illness, 'the animal functions ceased, and the spirit was loosened from its clay' (V-P's Reg. 18 Jan. 1822, fos. 184 and 187). Hodson was thought to be a 'hypochondriac', but his suspicions of his own imminent mortality proved well founded ([Heber], *Life of Reginald Heber*, ii. 51: 22 Jan. 1822 to C. W. Williams Wynn). There is a monument to Hodson by Bacon—costing £150—in the antechapel, with a Latin inscription by E. Cardwell. The funeral was limited to family and college: the Dean of Christ Church was refused admission. A year later a portrait by Phillips was placed in hall, 'on the south wall near the oriel window'; a copy was made for St Mary's Hall (V-P's Reg. 30 Dec. 1823, fo. 1 and 10 Oct. 1824, fo. 12).

[54] Pedigree in R. Churton, *The Life of Alexander Nowell* (Oxford, 1809), 390.

[55] W. Scott, to G. Ellis, quoted in J. G. Lockhart, *Memoirs of Walter Scott*, i (1900), 429; Scott, *Marmion*, introd. Canto vi.

a window to Radclyffe's Area and another to Exeter Gardens, with a convenient study, the only inconvenience is the smallness of the bed-space'.[56]

Richard Heber's first friends in college were not particularly grand. John Stonard, Hugh Cholmondeley, and Thomas Smyth all became clerics; Henry Hobhouse became a civil service lawyer, and ended up editing the state papers of Henry VIII. But before long he moved into a more glamorous world. His allies now included Sydney Smith, founder of the *Edinburgh Review*, and two rising literary stars: Robert Southey and Walter Scott. Nearly all this group—certainly all the Hebers—were staunch anti-Gallicans: they rallied to the Pittite cause against the threat of Jacobin France. And from their letters we can reconstruct the atmosphere at Brasenose during the long struggle against Napoleon. Most unusually, we have sufficient evidence to plot the political and social attitudes of senior and junior members alike. When in 1792 subscriptions were collected for French refugee clergy, for example, 'Brasenose distinguished itself, the College voted £30, the Principal gave £20, and the contributions of individuals amounted to £50 more. Stonard was particularly active.'[57] Stonard in fact was almost a caricature patriot: a clerical hearty, xenophobic, fond of feasting, and rather too fond of port. 'Glad the famous Robespierre is gone at last', he wrote to Heber in 1794; 'gone to Hell as sure as he is born: and Barrère and all the tribe of them. I only wish that all the French Convention were gone with 'em. Aye, and the French Nation too. Hope we shall drive the Ragamuffins back . . . I do on my conscience believe that Divine Wrath is manifesting itself against the sinful nations of Europe.'[58]

Unlike the future Bishop Heber—and unlike most of his friends at BNC—Richard Heber never seriously wished, and never really needed, to go into the Church. His friend Hugh Cholmondeley had less choice. So Cholmondeley's attitude to clerical, and academic, life is rather more typical of this Brasenose generation. He is worth a moment's pause. In 1796 he secured a Williamson Port Fellowship by ingeniously tracing his ancestry back to a sixteenth-century knight, Sir Thomas Gresley; thus establishing that he was the sixth cousin five times removed of the granddaughter of Sir John Port II. Ordination followed fairly quickly. 'After much consideration,' he told Richard Heber in 1798, 'I have almost resolved to take Orders next Trinity Sunday. It is an object to me to get settled upon some

---

[56] R. H. Cholmondeley (ed.), *The Heber Letters* (1950), 61. Sitting room and bedroom were together rearranged as the Principal's study in 1956.

[57] Ibid. 162: John Richardson to Richard Heber, 18 Nov. 1792.

[58] Ibid. 165–6: Stonard to Richard Heber, 17 Aug. 1794 and 26 Feb. 1795. He hated the international moneyed interest: 'I wish you would turn Baring, Ricardo and Rothschild and the whole gang of Jew speculators and moneylenders and loanraisers out of Parliament. I hate to see their names in the newspapers, a set of vagrant Countryless Raggamuffins' (ibid. 302–3: 31 Dec. 1822).

Curacy or other, for this wandering kind of life will not do for me . . . I am not particularly anxious to go into the Church, but as it must be my profession the sooner I take it up the better . . .'[59] By 1799, as both priest and Fellow, he was immersed in college affairs, disciplinary as well as scholastic. In May that year, for example, he wrote to Heber describing a theft in college.

A few days after you left us I had my bureau broken open and 29 guineas of Common Room money stolen. Charles the hall boy is now in [Oxford] Castle for it and will be convicted next Assizes. The money except one guinea I recovered very luckily. There were others concerned whom I took infinite pains to bring the charge home to, but the Vice-Chancellor is very stupid and cautious.[60]

Six years later, still a Brasenose Fellow, Cholmondeley was presented with the deanery of Chester. 'My friends', he noted, 'have been wonderfully zealous'. Indeed they had; and the methods they employed—the nuts and bolts of patronage—merit at least a little scrutiny. Here we can see, in almost comic detail, just how the system operated. The previous Dean of Chester was scarcely in his coffin before Cholmondeley's brother Thomas, MP for Cheshire, had been tipped off by his brother-in-law, the Revd Thomas Parker. The news came to Parker on a Friday. He 'instantly sent off an Express [letter] . . . which on Saturday afternoon found [the MP] just returned from a capital run at Belvoir [Castle]. He instantly set out in a hack-chaise for [London] where about 12 o'clock on Sunday he arrived [to find Prime Minister Pitt out of town, taking the waters. So] about 2 o'clock [the same day] he started again for Bath.' There he found that the Grosvenor family were already pulling strings for a rival candidate. But 'I spoke to [Mr Pitt] like a man and a relation', Thomas Cholmondeley reported proudly; he was after all the Prime Minister's second cousin. Meanwhile, Lord Chatham had already written to Pitt in Cholmondeley's favour, the letter timed to coincide exactly with the death of the Dean. Within days, Pitt himself was dead. The Cholmondeleys had got there just in time. Heber's old friend succeeded to the deanery, with only hours to spare. Within weeks he was giving a dinner party in Brasenose Common Room for 'all the Resident fellows, Masters etc.' 'I shall give them', he told Heber, 'as good a dinner as can be got and the best wines I have.' The system was now working smoothly, and its machinery did not stop there. The deanery was worth £400–500 p.a. But within two years Cholmondeley was intriguing again, for a particularly desirable rectory, at Tarporley in Cheshire. 'As we know by experience of College Elections', he reminded Heber, 'nothing can be reckoned upon till it's finally fixed.' But by this time Cholmondeley was well practised in the arts of patronage. In April

[59] R. H. Cholmondeley (ed.), *The Heber Letters* 170–1: 15 May 1798. For his ancestry and Fellowship, see Squibb, *Founder's Kin*, 107–9, 174.
[60] Cholmondeley (ed.), *Heber Letters*, 172: 26 May 1799.

1808, he achieved his ambition. The Chester Chapter duly elected their own Dean to the comfortable living of Tarporley.[61]

Cholmondeley it seems had to watch the pounds, if not the pennies. Richard Heber was under no such obligation. As an undergraduate he spent freely, especially on wine, books, and music lessons. His rooms overflowed with books. 'I must say', his father wrote in 1792, 'Richard is very inconsiderate and very unreasonable in contracting debt after debt for me to pay.'[62] But at least he had serious interests. He was already developing an appetite for politics. In 1795 he had to fight so hard to hear the Commons debate on Wilberforce's motion for peace with France that he lost both his shoes and had half his tailcoat torn off.[63]

These were interesting times. England was at war, and Brasenose was in ferment.

Everything at Oxford [Heber reported in 1797] wears a most martial appearance. The haunts of the Muses are molested by the din of arms and nothing but words of command and volleys are to be heard from morning to night. A corps of five hundred men and upward has been raised and embodied for the defence of the University, composed indiscriminately from all ages and ranks ... The Oxford [Volunteer] Regiment ... are indefatigable in attending to their drill twice a day, having regular sergeants to instruct them. Their uniforms are determined upon but not arrived yet.[64]

When they did arrive—and were inspected on Port Meadow by the Duke of York—those uniforms must have cut quite a dash: blue coats faced with white, black bearskins, duck pantaloons, and short black gaiters.[65]

Young Heber was certainly a loyal Pittite. In May 1802 we find him celebrating the Prime Minister's birthday at Merchant Taylors' Hall; singing along to Canning's chorus: 'The Pilot who weathered the storm'.[66] In the summer of 1803 he raised a company of volunteers at Hodnet.[67] He even managed to practise drilling, under the eye of a sergeant of the Guards, in his sister's 'little garden' in London.[68] As heir to the Marton estates in Yorkshire, he also became a colonel of the Craven Legion. That meant it was young Reginald who had to look after operations in Shropshire while Richard was

---

[61] Ibid. 158–9, 169–72, 198, 208–9, 213, 219; *Diary of Joseph Farington*, vii (1982), 2275: 20 Apr. 1806. Cholmondeley also secured the post of Regius Concionator (i.e. Preacher) at Whitehall. He was buried in the antechapel. The monument is by Chantrey; its Latin inscription by Reginald Heber (Heber MSS, Hodnet: F. Hodson to Reginald Heber, 7 Nov. 1816).

[62] Cholmondeley (ed.), *Heber Letters*, 68–9: 26 Feb. 1792.

[63] Ibid. 91: 3 June 1795.

[64] Ibid. 105: 28 Nov. 1797.

[65] Cox, *Recollections*, 33–4.

[66] Cholmondeley (ed.), *Heber Letters*, 136–7: 31 May 1802.

[67] Ibid. 143: 8 Aug. 1803.

[68] Ibid. 144: 18 Aug. 1803.

away in Yorkshire. But military discipline did have its compensations. In October 1804 the future Bishop explained that mess life in the Volunteers was in some ways an improvement on BNC.

> You have compared your mess [at Craven] to the B.N.C. [Phoenix] club, I think ours [at Hodnet] resembles the Brasenose Hall as the set [i.e. company] is excessively good or infamously bad according to one's good or bad fortune in getting a seat. There are two favourable circumstances which destroy the resemblance, one that the [mess] dinners are excellent, the other that the [local] raffs are all sober [i.e. unlike those at BNC] and leave as soon as they have finished their pint...[69]

Wartime meals at Brasenose were scarcely Lucullan. In 1812 pastries were dropped from the menu because of 'the high price of corn' and the 'apprehension of scarcity'; in 1817 'the difficulties of the time' meant that there could be no more 'wheaten bread'.[70] The cost of living rose, with consequent pressure on the level of wages. Bedmakers had to be paid more. In 1812 their pay went up by 2*s*. 6*d*. to 13*s*. per quarter for every commoner, and by 5*s*. to £1 per quarter for every gentleman commoner. In return, they had to 'wash their respective staircases and brush them, three times a week, at least'; to report any broken windows; and, 'whenever a porter is not [available], to give immediate attention to their masters'.[71] Even in wartime, apparently, the proprieties had to be preserved. And, war or no war, all servants continued to troop into the antechapel once a week for Sunday evening prayers.[72]

But the wartime college—first the Revolutionary, then the Napoleonic War—must have seemed distinctly unacademic. Not many Brasenose men were regular soldiers. Edmund Jodrell and Charles Sibthorp, for example, served in the Peninsula; John Thoyts was taken prisoner at Waterloo; Samuel Briscall served as chaplain to Wellington in both Spain and France. And quite a few followed the gentry route into local magistracy and yeomanry: William Hulton, for example—Constable of Lancaster Castle—who on 16 August 1819 gave the fateful order which precipitated the Peterloo Massacre.[73] But there was no strong military tradition in college. When it came to home security, however, there was a good deal of enthusiasm. In 1794 the college contributed £105 towards the cost of local defence; in 1798 the servants alone collected £16 15*s*. 6*d*.[74] And in the latter year, when Hugh Cholmondeley went back to college—this time with ordination in mind—he found the whole place operating like a military school.

---

[69] Cholmondeley (ed.), *Heber Letters*, 154: Oct. 1804.

[70] V-P's Reg. 1 May 1812, fo. 108 and 6 Feb. 1817, fo. 89.

[71] Ibid. 17 Dec. 1812, fos. 122–3.

[72] Ibid. 31 Oct. 1809, fo. 22.

[73] As magistrate responsible for the Cheshire Yeomanry (*Brasenose Reg.* 414).

[74] V-P's Reg. 11 Apr. 1794; *Brazen Nose*, vii. 2.

There are here nothing but soldiers now. They get up and are at Prayers at six. Immediately afterwards go to Exercise till ½ past eight. They begin again at ¼ before two and continue it till ½ past three and dine at four and Chapel at six. This all the Fellows except Parsons, Farington and Halliwell join in ... I do not think they will be able, nor will it be quite fair, to keep the men to their duty during the Long Vacation. They say they must have 120 gentlemen (and they have got above 500 names set down by the different Colleges and given to the Vice- Chancellor) to be in Oxford during the Vacation. This will be a bore to many.[75]

Yet study still went on, and we do know something of the syllabus and the methods of tuition. In August 1793 we find Churton making sure that Richard Heber did not neglect his vacation reading:

If you have not carefully read Herodotus, Thucydides, and Xenophon's Hellenica, you cannot in the present period of your academic studies, do better than read them and in the order mentioned. You will of course take with you the collateral aids of geography and chronology. As to the later subject, Hebricus's tables are useful and that at the end of Bentham's Orationes Funèbres etc. [i.e. Funeral Eulogies in Greek]. It is also very expedient to make short abstracts of the history for yourself especially in reading Herodotus whose work is in a degree a miscellaneous or general history, and this justly celebrated Father of History is a very pleasing and honest writer who gives you his authorities fairly, whether they rest on his own knowledge or were told him by Egyptian priests or others.[76]

By 1800 Heber was himself giving advice to the Revd Thomas Smyth, then preparing for a Prize Fellowship examination at Oriel. 'I tremble at the thought of the examination', Smyth told Heber; 'though I have certainly read more than I could possibly have expected and in compliance with your advice, have frequently composed in my leisure hours. Before [sitting the examination], I shall have read all Aeschylus except the Chorus's three times over, all Sophocles as often, and five or six plays in Euripides, the greater part of Demosthenes, all Juvenal, the 1st book of Thucydides and all the speeches three times over ... [So] if I have any luck I may pass ... '[77] Well, pass he did; young Smyth was duly elected. During the previous summer vacation, he had found himself largely alone, while the business of college life dwindled all around him. 'I have been fagging very hard for Oriel', he reported to Heber, 'and have just finished the Persae of Aeschylus. College is thinning very fast. [As for the Fellows], Harper is very busy arranging the Library, Halliwell is inventing methods to make men attend prayers more regularly, Boswell [jun., later Heber's colleague in the Roxburghe Club] is haranguing

[75] Cholmondeley (ed.), *Heber Letters*, 171–2: Cholmondeley to Richard Heber, 20 May 1798.

[76] Ibid. 164: 1 Aug. 1793. For Churton's orotund letter of advice to Richard Heber, prior to a journey to Rome, see ibid. 185–6: 29 Dec. 1802. In 1805 he was presented with the archdeaconry of St David's, a post worth £50 p.a. (ibid. 198: 31 July 1805).

[77] Ibid. 173–4: 15 Mar. 1800.

against College discipline, Palmer and Popham [are engaged] in bathing and fishing, and your humble servant is poring over Greek and writing Prose Latin.'[78]

Reginald Heber Sen. had made sure that 'dear Richard', as he invariably called him, was well trained in classics and mathematics. He sent him to a curiously exclusive school in Essex, run by Dr Samuel Glasse, FRS. The boy's immediate contemporaries included five future earls and two sons of a marquess.[79] In 1804 the future book collector inherited over 6,000 acres, divided between Yorkshire and Shropshire.[80] But by then he had already been infected with bibliomania. As early as 1789, his father had warned him that even then he had too many books: 'ten times more than were ever read or even looked into. Of multiplying books, my dear Richard, there is neither end nor use. The Cacoethes of collecting books draws men into ruinous extravagancies. It is an itch which grows by indulgence and should be nipt in the bud.'[81] That advice, of course, was ignored.

Before bibliomania took total control, Heber did have hopes of a political career; and the saga of his election for Oxford University tells us a good deal about BNC during the Regency period. It was in November 1806 that Heber first stood for one of the two University seats in Parliament. Churton recommended him to Pitt as an ideal candidate. Despite the support of Brasenose; despite the particular support of Frodsham Hodson, he ended bottom of the poll. He received only 275 votes, against 651 for Sir William Scott and 404 for Charles Abbot. Now Abbot was already Speaker of the House of Commons—later he became Baron Colchester—and he could rely on Treasury support. But Heber's allies at Brasenose were by no means dismayed by the result. 'Your minority', wrote Hodson, is 'glorious'. 'The glorious 275', added Churton, 'would have carried almost every election, however hardly contested, in any time till the present, when Royal Dukes and Dukes not Royal, Committees of the Treasury, East India Company and that great body of Christ Church overpowered us.'[82] Heber's old friend Stonard

---

[78] Cholmondeley (ed.), *Heber Letters*, 173: 3 July 1799.

[79] Ibid. 18–20. He may have had education of another kind from the proprietor's son, Dr G. H. Glasse, who published extensively but ran through a fortune and eventually hanged himself in a London hostelry (*ODNB*).

[80] The Yorkshire estates, centred on West Marton Hall—and later on Airmyn Hall, Howden—had been acquired by the Hebers in the 16th century; in the 18th century they inherited the Hodnet estate in Shropshire (J. Burke, *Landed Gentry* (7th edn. 1886): Heber of Hodnet). For the impact of the canal, planned by James Brindley, see G. Murray, *Yorkshire* (1882), 424. By 1873 the Shropshire land (2,791 acres) was worth £5,576 p.a.; the Yorkshire land (3,899 acres) was worth £7,406 p.a. (*Return of Owners of Land*, 1873).

[81] Cholmondeley (ed.), *Heber Letters*, 52: 15 Apr. 1789.

[82] Ibid. 213–14: 6 Nov. 1806, 7 Nov. 1806. See also *Hist. Parl.: Commons, 1790–1820*, ii (1986), 329.

had no vote, otherwise he would have protested formally at the tactics of the Duke of Marlborough and the Dean of Christ Church. 'The numbers [that] were lost by the villainy of the Dean', Stonard complained, 'is prodigious ... [and] if Abbot is not expelled, the University is turned into a dirty rotten Minister's borough. I hate to think of the little nasty stinking Imp [i.e. Abbot], a mere ... lickspittle of the Duke of [Marlborough], the refuse of the offscourings of Woodstock.'[83]

Three years later the election of Lord Grenville as Chancellor of the University revealed that Brasenose opinion was far from united. Thanks to Frodsham Hodson the college officially supported the Pitt–Grenville connection; indeed Hodson spent several frantic weeks canvassing absent Brasenose men by post. In Gillray's famous cartoon (pl. I) it is Hodson's hot air that floats the triumphant Grenville high up above the ranks of dons, massing below in Radcliffe Square. Once victory was in the bag, Hodson went about 'radiant and triumphant'. But not all the Fellows endorsed Grenville's politics. This election 'has staggered and confounded all hopes and prospects', Churton reported to Heber; still 'our duty, thank God is the same as ever, to adorn and defend the University, the Church and State by honourable and prudent Christian conduct'.[84] Heber was not so sure. In London he was beginning to be known as 'an illuminé'; he was rumoured to have helped in the new Chancellor's campaign; and he even sympathized with Grenville's inclination to emancipate Irish Catholics. But to Churton the

---

[83] Cholmondeley (ed.), *Heber Letters*, 215: letters of 17 Nov. and 6 Dec. 1806, conflated. Abbot had been MP for Woodstock, 1802–6. George Spencer, a Christ Church man and Treasury Lord, later 5th Duke of Marlborough, was particularly active in this election. Heber repaid his supporters in college by presenting the Common Room with a set of curtains to go with the newly laid carpet (ibid. 213: 16 Mar. 1806).

[84] Ibid. 229: 22 Dec. 1809, Archdeacon Churton to Richard Heber; Cox, *Recollections*, 62 (Hornby MS). In fact Grenville won by only 13 votes out of 1,037. As a 'slight testimony of gratitude', Grenville presented the college with a marble bust of himself by Nollekens; a pedestal was later presented by the Marquess of Buckingham (V-P's Reg. 9 Apr. 1811, fo. 83 and 20 Dec. 1812, fo. 103). There is another version in the Royal Collection. Cox remembered Grenville as 'the proudest-looking man I ever saw'; in Hornby's words, he actually looked 'like a marble bust' (Cox, *Recollections*, 190: Hornby MS). For Hodson's enthusiastic canvassing, see *Law Mag.* 44, quoted in H. Twiss, *Life of Lord Chancellor Eldon*, ii (1844), 110 n. A flysheet protest against the dangers of Catholic Emancipation—addressed to 'John Bull Jnr. [i.e. Richard Heber], B.N.C., B.A., F.A.S., J.P. etc.'—appeared c.1810 (exhib. Stampex, Royal Horticultural Hall, London, Oct. 2005). For Gillray's cartoon of Grenville's Installation, see George, *Political and Personal Satires*, viii, no. 11570, pp. 942–4. Compare nos. 11384 and 11534. For James Sadler's balloon ascent, see *The Times*, 9 July 1810. One pirate version satirized such Broad-Bottom liberalism as a product of 'Broad Bum College, Oxford' (pl. I). Three 'delegates' were nominated by BNC to deliver congratulatory addresses: 'a nobleman, a man of property, and a clever man—the latter is [Charles Henry] Johnson, the John the Baptist [prize poem] man' (quoted in Milman, *Milman*, 20).

prospect of Whiggish reform was frightening. 'There is I fear, everything to dread', he told Heber; 'this disastrous election [in the teeth of opposition from twenty Heads of Houses and three quarters of the University] may very probably be the beginning of mischief... [Soon] there may be no University, no Church and no State in this envied land. Do not fancy my fears Utopian: Heaven grant they may be so!'[85]

What terrified Churton was the prospect of Catholic Emancipation, and with it the disintegration of the Anglican Settlement and the Protestant Constitution. 'I have not seen or heard of a single argument in support of [Grenville's position] except that one gentleman of Brasenose used the term "union" or "uniting", that is uniting light and darkness, one subject to King George alone and one subject to the pope and the pope to Bonaparte... [Grenville's] principles as to the Roman Catholics and breaking down the ancient barriers of the Constitution, if they prevail, cannot but be the ruin of the country... [Our situation] is strange and unprecedented... Three Heads [of Houses] just elected espouse the candidate whom all the seniores and discretiores steadily oppose! The Princess of Wales and the Royal Dukes canvas for the avowed opponent of the wishes and principles of the King their Father! The Chancellor of Cambridge a Socinian! The Chancellor of Oxford the advocate of the pope's vassals! So is the purest Church on earth protected!!'[86]

By 1813 Churton had become thoroughly alarmed. When an article appeared in the *Anti-Jacobin* advocating rights for Irish Catholics, he warned Heber it was enough to make any man tremble who had 'either religion, life, liberty or property to lose'.[87] When in 1814 Heber was again thinking of standing for the University, his old tutor determined to put him to the test. 'That most woeful election of Lord Grenville', warned Churton, 'created an almost universal hostility to our dear Brazenose and caste a suspicion on almost all his partizans and supporters. I greatly fear that any candidate from Brazenose, known to have been friendly with Lord Grenville, will not be very

[85] Cholmondeley (ed.), *Heber Letters*, 229: 22 Dec. 1809.

[86] Ibid. 230. George III complained that 'Cambridge had a Unitarian Chancellor [the Duke of Grafton], and Oxford a [pro-]Popish one [Grenville]'. Quoted in Twiss, *Eldon*, ii. 110. His Catholic sympathies are satirized in Gillray's 'The Brazen Image, set up at Oxford' (George, *Political and Personal Satires*, viii, no. 11534, p. 916: 1810); and 'The Introduction of the Pope to the Convocation at Oxford, the Cardinal Broad-Bottom' (ibid., no. 11384, p. 850: 1809). Grenville hoped to abolish slavery, liberalize trade, and emancipate Irish Catholics; Churton would have been horrified to know that most of the bishops voted for him (*Diary of Joseph Farington*, x (1982), 3588: 16 Dec. 1809). He was a noted bibliophile: his library at Dropmore, Bucks., was celebrated; and he was a major landowner: his marriage to Anne Pitt brought him the considerable estate of Boconnoc in Cornwall. See also E. P. Williams, *Poets and Statesmen* (1856), s.v. Grenville.

[87] Cholmondeley (ed.), *Heber Letters*, 253: 12 Jan. 1813.

favourably received by the University; [and] unless it is clearly understood that he does not coincide with his Lordship as to Roman Catholic Emancipation...he will have no chance whatsoever.' This 'matter of the Roman Catholics', he added, 'is truly momentous'. Apart from 'the incurable hostility of that idolatrous Church to Protestants...[they] rob the King...of half his Prerogative...[for] our invaluable Constitution [is] the source under Providence of all our strength and property...[and] if we surrender it, as we should do if we transferred half of the Imperial Prerogative of the Crown to the Pope or to any foreign power, [then] tyranny, slavery, anarchy and confusion would ensue'. What Churton wanted was an MP who was 'an independent country gentleman...a man of talent and literature...[like] dear Sir R. Newdigate, Sir W. Dolben, Mr. [Francis] Page and Lord Cornbury'.[88] They may not have been 'men of shining abilities or of great learning'. But they were figures 'of good family and independent fortune'; not one of them was a mere politician, the sort who would willingly 'barter the honour and interests of his seat for promotion'.[89]

To all this, Heber seems to have returned an answer answerless. Churton was apparently persuaded that his pupil remained 'the same true and steady Church and King man [he] always hoped and believed [him] to be'. As evidence, Heber had been able to point to the Yorkshire election of 1807, when the local Whigs 'engaged all the horses for two stages round York', and Heber walked 'twenty miles' to 'vote for Mr. Lascelles'.[90] A nice enough story; it may even have been true. But there were Tories and Tories. Heber belonged to the liberal, Canningite wing, supporters of pragmatic reform and incremental emancipation. Heber's tactic, as regards Brasenose—and still more as regards the University—was somehow to keep the Ultra Tories on board while at the same time refusing to compromise his liberal instincts. All this he managed to do. In a letter to the Vice-Chancellor, he vowed to 'protect...[the University's] rights, privileges and interests...[and] to perpetuate our Constitution in Church and State, cemented as it is with the blood of Patriots and Martyrs'. Oxford's curriculum, he solemnly declared— 'Ancient Literature, the Evidences of Christianity and the Volume of Holy Scriptures'—was the key to 'our National character' and 'our present and future happiness'.[91] In 1821 his diplomacy was at last rewarded. The by-election of that year saw him scrape home by thirteen votes out of 1,131. His opponent was Sir John Nicholl of St John's, a man with a record of strong

---

[88] For all these, see *Hist. Parl.: Commons* 1754–90 (1964).
[89] Cholmondeley (ed.), *Heber Letters*, 263–4: 25 Mar. 1814.
[90] Ibid. 265–6: 5 Apr. 1814. In vain: Lascelles lost.
[91] Ibid. 288–9: 24 Aug. 1821. Reginald Heber seems also to have believed that his brother was an opponent of Catholic Emancipation ([Heber], *Life of Reginald Heber*, ii. 48).

opposition to Catholic Emancipation and parliamentary reform. Heber's prevarication had paid off.[92]

But there would have been no victory without the support of Frodsham Hodson. Now Hodson was a staunch Pittite, but a Pittite Tory with the instincts of a Whig. He believed Mr Pitt to be 'the ablest Minister in Europe'; and he regarded Pitt's resignation in 1801 on the issue of Catholic Emancipation as a 'cause for national mourning', evidence indeed of the King's 'insanity'. 'My spirits', he told Heber on that occasion, 'were never so low!... His loss is irreparable.'[93] No doubt this depression was ameliorated by the fact that Pitt's temporary successor, Henry Addington—a stout opponent of reform—was at least a Brasenose man. But thereafter Hodson steered his college firmly in the direction of Pitt's progressive Toryism, and in 1821 it was Richard Heber who turned out to be the principal beneficiary. Despite increasing sickness, it was Hodson who masterminded Heber's election. The electoral contest was spread out over three days; and every Oxford MA had a vote. On the night before the poll opened, one hundred supporters dined together in Brasenose hall. Heber's old friends Stonard and Boswell were there; and so of course was the choleric Churton. Heber knew he could rely on his old tutor for at least a 'silent' vote. But what about the others? On the first day the poll was practically even; Nicholl may even have been in the lead. Doubts in Brasenose began to spread. But that very night the Principal revealed his 'secret' plan. He had 'directed that the household troops should be kept in reserve till the [second] day ... [Then] the following words on a slip of paper [should be] produced in the handwriting of General Hodson, "Let forty B.N.C. men go up and vote".' The plan 'was obeyed with military precision'. That day 383 votes were cast for Heber, 270 for Nicholl. 'The countenances', of our opponents, noted James Boswell, 'became strictly academical "colore sub fusca"...' On the last day, Heber romped home by 612 to 519.[94] The names of all those Brasenose men who supported Heber—159 of them—were inscribed in triumph in the Vice-Principal's Register; and 'gratuities [were] paid to the College servants for their extraordinary services' in preparing accommodation and distributing refreshments. The Seniority voted to place a portrait of Heber in hall.[95] That night

---

[92] Lord Colchester, *Diary and Correspondence*, ii (1861), 234. Hodson was similarly equivocal: in 1813 his High Street windows were 'completely demolished' by local 'patriots' (*Brazen Nose*, xiv. 76–7).

[93] Cholmondeley (ed.), *Heber Letters*, 176–7: 2 Feb. 1801 and 21 Mar. 1801.

[94] Bodl. MS Top. Oxon. c. 32: 'Mr. Heber's Cheque'; Cholmondeley (ed.), *Heber Letters*, 290–2: 29 Aug. 1821, James Boswell to Richard Heber. A different distribution of votes over the three days is suggested in V-P's Reg., 24 Sept. 1821, fo. 175ʳ.

[95] V-P's Reg. 24 Sept. 1821, fos. 174–6: £5 to the porter, plus £5 for his two assistants; 3 gns. to each of four bed-makers; 3gns. to 'Blake, the Common Room man ... and the person who assisted him'; £5 to the shoeblack.

'we had a grand symposium at [BNC]', Boswell reported, and 'Hodson, I thought imprudently, attended but seemed a new man. He made one or two speeches which were admirable.' But old John Dean—last of the Latin speakers in Congregation: a don with 'the activity of a parched pea and the loquacity of a popinjay'—'proposed the health of Churton...and the old gentleman babbled o' green fields'. Still, eccentricity was forgiven in the general euphoria. 'It was a glorious struggle and a triumphant victory', noted one participant; 'Waterloo was a joke to it...Poor Jemmy Boswell was only intelligible till the cloth was removed.'[96] Another supporter observed that it was just as well the undergraduates were on vacation: 'the uproarious proceedings in Brasenose' would certainly have 'scandalised...the junior part of the University'.[97]

That presupposed a rather rosy view of undergraduate attitudes. The Brasenose of Frodsham Hodson was in fact notoriously 'fast'. In October 1811 we find a scholarship boy from Chester—on his way to holy orders—writing home to his father after a two-day coach journey to Oxford in the rain:

I shall endeavour as much as possible to govern myself by [the advice of my tutor, Mr Hodgkinson]...I trust also that through Divine Grace I shall be kept unspotted from the contagion of vice and immorality that too much prevails in this place.[98]

Young Mr Janion had good reason to be apprehensive. He was in a minority in a college of swells. No Oxford undergraduate of this period was smarter than Lord George Grenville: see him dressed up in Dighton's caricature, 'A View from B.N.C. Gateway'. No man in the University had access to more cash than Ralph Franco, heir to the name and fortune of Sir Manasseh Lopes: he would soon inherit £800,000. And none could possibly be wilder than 'Squire' Osbaldeston (pl. 55), a roaring boy from Eton who hunted thrice weekly in term time. It was at BNC that Osbaldeston began his career in the field by buying a pack of dwarf foxhounds from the Earl of Jersey. Later he moved on to the Monson, the Atherstone, the Quorn, and the Pytchley, before becoming MP for East Retford as well as High Sheriff and Deputy Lieutenant of Yorkshire. His manners were alarming. Once, when dining in hall after a hard day's hunting, he noticed that two undergraduates

[96] Cholmondeley (ed.), *Heber Letters*, 292: 24 Sept. 1821, Sir Archibald MacDonald to Richard Heber.

[97] Ibid. 292: 24 Sept. 1821, Sir John B. Bosanquet to Richard Heber. Afterwards the victor's health was even 'drunk with cordiality in the Common Room of St. John's'. See Heber MSS, Hodnet: Reginald Heber to M. Stow, 3 Oct. [1821].

[98] Richard Janion to Joseph Janion: 17 Oct. 1811 (typescript tipped into MPP 56 F4/1). Prostitution in Oxford and Cambridge remained sufficiently serious to justify the appointment of special constables, see *PP* (1825), iii. 639–40.

were wearing powdered wigs. Incensed at their ultra Toryism — liberals at that date wore their own hair—he emptied a gravy boat over their heads. That was too much for Frodsham Hodson. He denounced Osbaldeston for behaviour more appropriate to 'a drayman or coal heaver in a low coffee-shop'.[99] The victims on this occasion turn out to have been a pair of Lancashire Harrovians, Thomas and William Farrer—'the Dumb Twins'—members of a family later known as solicitors to the Crown. On another occasion, Osbaldeston rode 200 miles in ten hours for a bet, changing horses every four miles. As a marksman, he was legendary. His shooting career began with ramrods and ended with breech-loaders. One day he bagged forty partridge in forty shots. And on another occasion, at Lynford in East Anglia, he clocked up ninety-eight pheasant with one hundred shots. Two pricked birds were recovered shortly afterwards, making his score an astonishing 100 per cent.[100]

And how much did it all cost? When Archer Clive went up to BNC from Harrow in 1817—one of his school friends was the future Principal Harington (pl. 35)—his father gave him an allowance of £300 p.a. At the end of three years he found he was £200 in debt. He did not live luxuriously: 'Some riding and hunting but moderately for I had no horse of my own and I could not afford to hunt often. Some boating in the season, which I liked much.' On the other hand, his closest associates—Henry Buckley (later Fellow of Merton), Henry Perceval (son of the Prime Minister), Frederick Shaw (son of a Dublin banker), and Charles Beckford (later Fellow of All Souls)—were all members of the Phoenix. We shall encounter their revels again, when we come to deal with that club. Meanwhile it is enough to note that by any reasonable measure of comparison, every one of these young men was extremely well off. When Looker the under butler retired in 1825 at the age of 75, after forty-four years' service, he received a pension of only £10 p.a.[101] It cost nearly a third of that sum each year to polish a gentleman commoner's Wellington boots.[102] Still, Clive's set was not particularly fast; their pleasures were not excessive; and of the five friends four ended up in holy orders. Clive himself was not averse to staying up in the Easter vacation in order to

---

[99] *Squire Osbaldeston: His Autobiography*, ed. E. D. Cuming (1926), 21; *Brazen Nose*, iv. 104–5 (corrected). He seems to have been egged on by Lord George Grenville. The Brasenose barber from 1774 to 1816—when the office was abolished—was Arthur Routledge, Tonsor, of St Mary's Parish (*Oxford*, 8/2, Summer 1943).

[100] For these and comparable feats, see Sir Hugh Gladstone, *Record Bags and Shooting Records* (1922); also 'Thormanby' [W. Wilmott Dixon], *Kings of the Hunting Field* (1899). Gambling was Osbaldeston's undoing: he lost *c.* £200,000 on horses, and was forced to sell his estates in 1848. (*ODNB*).

[101] V-P's Reg. 17 Nov. 1825, fo. 40.

[102] Ibid. 31 May 1819, fo. 133. The shoeblack's quarterly rate was raised in that year from 4*s.* 6*d.* to 6*s.* for commoners, and from 5 to 7*s.* for gentlemen commoners.

continue studying. Looking back in 1850—the year he became a Prebendary of Hereford—he regretted only one thing: 'the want [of] interest in learning beyond what was necessary for the purposes of a degree, which our tutors ought to have...encouraged, but did not. Mine [his tutor was the future Principal Gilbert] certainly not. I believe Cardwell [a Fellow, and future Camden Professor] did more, but [even] he only a very little. They were all deficient in anything beyond their actual work—very little English and no foreign learning at all. No science or encouragement to attain it, so that beyond books necessary for my 2nd class viz.: Herodotus, Thucydides, Aeschylus, Euripides, Livy, Horace, Virgil—Aristotle's Ethics—Logic and a very small smattering of divinity, I learnt nothing at Oxford, and most of my contemporaries did much less than me.'[103]

It is a familiar story. Once the examination system had taken hold—even in rudimentary form—its minimum requirements came to be treated as a maximum. Undergraduates increasingly found their greatest stimulus outside the digestion of prescribed texts. The vacuity of catetechizical classes—that is, group teaching of set books—re-emphasized the social value of under-graduate clubs. From this period, therefore, we can date at least three college and inter-college associations which still survive: the Phoenix, The Club, and the Apollo Lodge. It is time to examine their origins in detail.

The Phoenix—technically the Phoenix Common Room—traces its foundation to 1786, or perhaps to 1782. Whether, as we have seen, its origins can be traced further back to some manifestation of the Medmenham Hell Fire Club has long been a subject for speculation. Sir Francis Dashwood—patron of 'the monks of Medmenham'—had died just before, in 1781. He had been a warm favourite of Oxford Jacobites: he even received an honorary doctorate at the opening of the Radcliffe Camera in 1749. And Joseph Alderson, founder of the Phoenix, may perhaps have been connected with him in some way. But that is speculation. The Phoenix might just as easily have emerged—via the Alfred Lodge—from the mysterious world of post-Jacobite clubs and lodges examined in Chapter 2. Or again its name may simply represent an echo of the Phoenix Inn. There is no clear evidence either way. What is beyond dispute is that the Phoenix remains the oldest dining club in Oxford. Its records are unique, and its story is integral to the history of Brasenose.[104] From the start, membership was limited to

---

[103] Clive MSS, Whitfield (*ex inf.* Edward Clive). The Revd Archer Clive, of Whitfield House, Herefordshire, was a kinsman of Clive of India, and a noted breeder and exhibitor of stock. For serious scholars there was no lack of available reading, e.g. *List of* [more than 400] *Books Recommended to the Students in Divinity on Mr. Hulme's Foundation in Brasen Nose College, Oxford* (Oxford, 1815).

[104] F. Madan, *Century of the Phoenix Common Room, 1786–1886* (1888) and *Quat. Mon.* XIV. ii, 93–135. The PCR's motto—'Uno avulso non deficit alter' (*Aeneid* vi. 215)—suggests, like the

a maximum of twelve. That meant only a handful of elections each year. Hence its reputation for exclusivity. The 'Phoenix Society or Junior Common Room of Brasenose' first appears under that name in 1782, thanks to the initiative of 'Joseph Alderson and his friends', Robert Hesketh, James Pemberton, and George Powell. They were followed by two more founder members, R. W. Blencowe and F. H. Rodd. The Phoenix Common Room proper dates from 1786, that is from the admission of George Terry, Robert Crowther, Robert Symonds, William Heron, William Bagshaw, and Charles Mainwaring.

Note: these names are not particularly grand. Alderson himself would end his days as an undistinguished clergyman: Rector of Oxwick, one of the dimmest parishes in Norfolk. In these early lists there is not a single gentleman commoner. What we find instead are a set of upward achievers appropriate to the age of Cleaver and Hodson. Five of the first thirteen members were elected to Oxford Fellowships; seven more elections to Fellowships followed before the end of the century. Frodsham Hodson (pl. 25) himself became a member in 1787 and Reginald Heber (pl. 30) in 1801. One founder member, John Latham, became President of the Royal College of Physicians. No fewer than nine Fellows of All Souls were drawn from the ranks of the Phoenix between 1801 and 1822. Mixed in with these aspirant academics were the sporting gentry more usually associated with BNC: Luttrell and Bouverie, Fane and Vane, Marriott, Isham, and Poulett. But gradually the balance began to shift. The social element came to dominate the academic. Within a generation the Phoenix had developed from a convenient system of dining in rotation—there was still of course no JCR—into a focus of social ambition. In the process, it took on many of the accoutrements of status: rules, constitution, uniform, codes of practice. In 1822, for example, Richard Harington (pl. 35)—a future Principal—is reproved for being improperly dressed: on one occasion 'white Turkish trousers and flowered black waistcoat'; on another a pair of 'striped worsted stockings'. By 1823, members had begun to wear the uniform which still survives: white tie and waistcoat, and tail coats—first claret, then brown—with facings of creamy silk. And of course they dined well. In 1800, there were already 175 dozen of madeira in the PCR cellar, priced at 72*s.* a dozen.

Such indulgence aroused hostility. By 1821 the exclusivity of the Phoenix was beginning to create 'violent opposition throughout the College'. Nor did its behaviour always match the increasing decorum of a less boisterous age. In 1810 two members—George Camplin and John Spicer—were gated for a

Phoenix symbol itself, continuity through co-optation. For Sir Francis Dashwood, 1st Bt., see *ODNB.* Henry Dashwood, later 3rd Bt. and MP for Woodstock, matriculated at Brasenose in 1763. Alderson, aged 25, migrated to Trinity College, Cambridge, before becoming Rector of Oxwick, Norfolk, in 1810 (*Admissions to Trin. Coll. Camb.* iii (1911), 305; *Gent's Mag.* 80 (1810), pt. i, 276). A portrait of Thomas Reynolds, the PCR servant, then aged 56, was drawn by Delamotte and engraved by Cheeseman in 1801 (*Quat. Mon.* VII, 31).

term for 'misconduct', and condemned to transcribe several books of Aristotle.[105] In 1832 nearly half the active members—Thomas Shafto, Mervyn Archdale, and John Conolly—were sent down for misbehaviour; and in 1840–2, as we shall see, the PCR faced a major crisis, a crisis all the more serious for being self-inflicted. Nevertheless, the Phoenix survived. Not for the last time, it proved to be a bird not easily put down.

The Phoenix also survived two scandals for which it probably had no responsibility at all. In January 1828 a third-year man, Houstonne Radcliffe, was sent down for feeding strong liquor to a woman of the town. Her name was Ann Prees (alias Crotchley), and she was 24 years of age. One evening the previous December she had apparently knocked at an undergraduate's ground-floor rooms. Radcliffe seems to have been one of a party there; he rewarded her with a teapot-full of brandy. This she proceeded to drink from between the bars of a low-lying window. Having staggered as far as Blue Boar Lane, she was found several hours later 'in a dying state'. She had been the victim of a particularly brutal assault. Two watchmen carried her home in a wheelbarrow, or so *The Times* reported, 'weltering in her blood'. Within twenty-four hours she was dead. Over Christmas the murder was a national sensation. Both the University and the City offered £100 reward. But the crime was never solved, even though the corpse was medically examined before burial, then disinterred and examined again. Radcliffe himself died less than two years later. And six years after this unsavoury episode, on 3 April 1834, another scandal occurred. On this occasion a second-year man, E. L. Trafford, dropped dead at a dinner party in his college rooms (III, 3), it was thought through alcoholic excess. He was the son of a Cheshire landowner, Trafford Trafford of Outhrington, and unlike Ann Crotchley he was accorded a solemn burial in St Mary's churchyard. Neither event did much to improve BNC's reputation as a place of learning. But neither Radcliffe nor Trafford was ever a member of the Phoenix; and only imagination can link them with the existence of any sort of diabolical society. Evidence, moreover, to connect either event to the so-called Hell Fire rooms (VI, 1), is slim. If Radcliffe was there he must have been a guest. So much for legend.[106]

---

[105] V-P's Reg. 28 Mar. 1810, fo. 57.

[106] The Room Books confirm the fact that Radcliffe's rooms in 1827–8 were Garden Court 9 (later Old Staircase IX; demolished 1883); and that in 1834 Trafford's were Old Quad III, 3 overlooking Brasenose Lane. A local man, a picture-framer named John Williams, was acquitted of Crotchley's 'shocking and mysterious murder'. See *Jackson's Oxford Journal*, 15 Dec. 1827, 22 Dec. 1827, and 19 Jan. 1828; *The Times*, 14 Dec. 1827, 3–4, 21 Dec. 1827, 2, 22 Dec. 1827, 2, 24 Dec. 1827, 3, 26 Dec. 1827, 3, 28 Dec. 1827, 3, 31 Dec. 1827, 2, 3 Jan. 1828, 4. The V-P's Reg. gives few details about either occurrence: see 31 Jan. 1828, fo. 101, 3 Mar. 1834, fo. 201, and 6 Mar. 1834, fos. 202–3. College legend has confused the date and place of both events (e.g. W. Maskell, *Odds and Ends* (1872), 108–12; F. G. Lee, *Glimpses of the Supernatural*, ii. (1872), 207).

What then of the Apollo and The Club? It was on 24 May 1818 that five Oxford Freemasons met in the rooms of Lambert Blackwell Larking (Old Lodge 4), and founded the Apollo Lodge. Larking was an Etonian, with a lengthy clerical and antiquarian career ahead of him. Bearing a warrant from the Duke of Sussex, Grand Master of the Order, the Lodge held its first meeting in the Star Hotel, in Cornmarket, on 19 February 1819. From the start, strict rules of secrecy meant that membership was sometimes curiously diverse. In the first year initiates included two waiters from the Star and three titled members of Christ Church. But on the whole, recruits were chosen from the nobility and gentry. It comes as no surprise to see that Lord Augustus Fitz-Clarence of Brasenose—son of the Duke of Clarence and Mrs Jordan, and a future chaplain to Queen Victoria—was admitted in 1826. Between 1825 and 1844, initiates included 'five Marquises, two Earls, four Viscounts and thirteen Lords'. Apollo had become Oxford's 'premier social club'.[107] And in 1826–7 and 1832 the Lodge Master was a Brasenose man: a future Principal, Richard Harington (pl. 35). Numbers expanded fast. Between 1820 and 1825 there were seventy-five new members, BNC supplying more than any other college. From 1825 to 1844 the average annual intake was fourteen; from 1853 to 1865, no fewer than forty-three. The number of recruits from Brasenose dropped at this point, though seven were elected in one exceptional year, 1864. But whatever the numbers, exclusivity was maintained. At Brasenose, for example, among the freshmen of 1858, all five initiates were members of the Phoenix.

The Brethren of Apollo Lodge quickly formed part of a supra-collegiate network of patronage and philanthropy. They long retained their original uniform: knee-breeches and tails, white tie, silk stockings, and pumps. The fact of membership was no secret: it was seen as a token of status. In the University, Freemasons played a prominent and visible role. At college level membership became, at the very least, a useful guarantee of loyalty. At social events—notably the Masonic Ball and Masonic Fête in Eights Week—membership was publicly displayed. And within the Lodge itself ceremonies became increasingly elaborate. By 1832 the Brethren had their own house in Alfred Street. In 1864 they moved to improved quarters in Frewin Court; in 1926 to larger premises in the High Street, before transferring to 333 Banbury Road in 1961.

---

[107] D. Wright in *Isis*, 24 Oct. 1923, 15–16 and 7 Nov. 1923, 11–12; H. A. Pickard, F. P. Morrell, and E. L. Hawkins, *By-Laws of the Apollo University Lodge . . . List of Members etc.* (privately printed, Oxford, 1881; spiked proofs in Bodl. GA Oxon. 16mo. 197 (1), coll. A. E. Cowley); [W. C. Costin], 'Apollo University Lodge, 1819–1969' (typescript, Bodl. 24791 e. 331). Fifty-eight members of Apollo Lodge were killed in the First World War (*Masonic Roll of Honour* 1914–1918 (1921), 14–15). By 1988 there were no fewer than sixteen Lodges in Oxford (C. Hibbert, *Encyclopaedia of Oxford* (1988), 146). See Apollo records, Bodl. MS. Eng. c. 7363–78, d. 3732–7.

By comparison The Club was a small-scale operation. THE Club, as it came to be known, was a University dining society limited to ten or twelve senior members. It was established in 1790—originally to propagate liberal principles—and five of its founder members were Brasenose men: George Harper, James Pemberton, J. H. Hindley, Mark Sykes, and Samuel Bethell. Thereafter BNC's involvement is less noticeable, though scholars like Edward Cardwell and J. J. Lowe continued to be elected. And with the arrival of Falconer Madan, The Club amply revived its original Brasenose spirit. Since Madan's time, circumstances have changed, and qualifications for entry have varied. But in its low-key way The Club remains unique in the social politics of Oxford.[108] Appropriately, Madan became its historian. He was well aware of its complicated antecedents. First through the Alfred Lodge (1769), then through the Phoenix (1782), then through The Club (1790), and then through the Apollo (1819), Brasenose played a conspicuous part in socializing the upper echelons of the University.

Richard Heber had joined The Club about 1796, shortly before he joined the Phoenix. These were comparatively small steps in his social progression. In the year of his election as MP he would become High Sheriff of Shropshire. By 1824 he was one of the founder members of the Athenaeum.[109] He was already a pillar of the Roxburghe Club. He was rich, he was learned, he was charming, he was popular. Byron revered him. The Revd T. F. Dibdin thought him quite brilliant: 'He would moot Greek metres with my friend Mr. [Henry] Drury, and fight over derivatives and etymons with Roger Wilbraham ... His memory was only exceeded by that of Porson.' He could quote at length from both classical and late Latin poets—Lucan, Claudian, Silius Italicus—as well as from late medieval Latin authors like Politian, Sannazarius, and Vida.[110] He was notoriously short-sighted, but handsome, with dark eyes and a high domed forehead. There was even talk of his marrying a rich lady book collector, Mary Richardson Currer of Eshton

---

[108] 'About 1862 or 1863 a second society, calling itself The Club, was founded at Oxford ... The effect of the title on the older club is that when it is desirable to distinguish between them it is now proper to accentuate the word "The" in the title of the older of the two' (F. Madan, *Records of The Club at Oxford, 1790–1917* (privately printed, Oxford, 1917), 12). Members of this second club (limited to 21; refounded *c.*1890; no longer extant) included Reynolds, Heberden, Lodge, Watson, and Buchan, all of BNC. For lists see Bodl. GA Oxon. 4 to 599.

[109] 'Mr. Heber has lately been ... in great force, full of frolick; and very intent on the formation of a New Club which is to be called the Atheneum, and to contain as many eminent persons in letters, science, or rank, as can be comprised in a thousand names' (Heber MSS, Hodnet: J. J. Blunt to Reginald Heber, 14 Dec. 1824).

[110] T. F. Dibdin, *Reminiscences of a Literary Life*, i (1836), 431–2. He united 'all the activity of De Witt and Lomenie, with the retentiveness of Magliabecchi and the learning of Le Long'.

Hall, Yorkshire. Alas, he was probably less interested in the lady than in her library of 15,000–20,000 volumes.[111]

By the end of his life Heber had at least eight libraries. He bought books compulsively, almost without limit. Dibdin said he had a 'book appetite' of 'cormorant-capacity'. One hostile critic described him as 'a bibliomaniac in the most unpleasant sense of the word—no confirmed drunkard, no incurable opium-eater has less self-control'. He would buy whole libraries at a time. As a minimum he claimed to need three copies of every book: one for reading, one for show, and one for lending. No doubt there was also an element of self-aggrandizement, the thrill of defeating competitors.[112] But, unlike Dibdin, Heber was a serious scholar. He was fluent in Greek and Latin, Italian and French, Spanish and Portuguese. He began the first catalogue of his collection at the age of 8. At 9 he was producing metrical versions of Ovid, Virgil, and Horace. At the age of 10 he was already a noted book buyer. As a schoolboy he began an edition of Persius. As an undergraduate he began editions of Silius Italicus and Claudian. All these appeared in limited form during the early 1790s; but significantly, none was ever quite finished. And having gone to considerable lengths to get himself a seat in Parliament, he apparently never spoke a word. Somehow, the accumulation of books became an end in itself, a substitute for action. It was not that he overspent: he did build himself a new library at Hodnet; and he did take out two mortgages on his estates, though they were not irreversibly crippling.[113] What was more serious was the effect of all this book collecting on his sense of purpose.

Nobody knows how many books he owned. Dibdin suggested 127,500; Allibone calculated 146,827, excluding pamphlets.[114] Some said there were 200,000. They were rumoured to have cost him £100,000 in money of that day. His country house library held 12,000; there were two houses in London, one in York Street, off Great James Street, Westminster—which he seems to have used as a warehouse—and another, Pimlico Lodge, known locally as

[111] T. F. Dibdin, *Reminiscences of a Literary Life*, ii (1836), 949–57 and idem, *Bibliographical Tour*, ii (1838), 181–90. Her library was sold for *c.* £6,000 in 1862 (*ODNB*).

[112] T. F. Dibdin, *Bibliomania* (revised edn., 1842), 93; J. Ferriar, *The Bibliomania, an Epistle* [to Richard Heber Esq.] (1809); *Gent's Mag.*, NS i (1834), 105–9. In fact Heber's generosity made his library 'a feature in the literary geography of Europe' (J. H. Burton, *The Book Hunter* (1862; 1885), 100).

[113] Mortgages were taken out on land at Marton in Yorkshire and at Wicklewood in Norfolk. At Hodnet Hall—then half-timbered—the library was doubled in space. Churton was delighted with the setting of the house; Heber dismissively called it 'an old ragamuffin mansion' (Cholmondeley (ed.), *Heber Letters*, 220: 15 July 1808 and 237: 25 Dec, 1810). Hodnet was rebuilt in 1870 to designs by A. Salvin.

[114] S. A. Allibone, *Critical Dictionary of English Literature and British and American Authors*, i (Philadelphia, 1859), 816; Dibdin, *Reminiscences*, i. 442–3 n.

'The Hermitage'; and yet another house in the High Street at Oxford, stacked with books from cellar to attic. Abroad, he had one library in Ghent, another in Antwerp, another in Brussels, and an especially large one in Paris, not far from the Quai Voltaire; and there were yet further depositories in Nuremberg, in Louvain, in Leyden, and in The Hague. His Paris house alone—a huge mansion, nicknamed the 'Grand Hotel Bibliomanesque'—held 30,000 books.[115] What Dibdin called Heber's 'ungovernable passion' sometimes drove him to extreme lengths: he would 'put himself into the mail coach, and travel three, four or five hundred miles' by road, rather than 'entrust his commission to a letter'.[116]

Not surprisingly, Heber spent a good deal of time on the Continent, bidding at auction and instructing agents. But there were rumoured to be other reasons. As MP for Oxford University Heber had always been a Tory, but a Tory with liberal instincts. That made him the target of Ultra Tory Anglicans. Ugly stories began to circulate. And by the end of 1822—little more than a year after taking his seat—Heber was looking for a way out. In January 1823 he thought he had found it. The previous month, his half-brother Reginald had been offered a bishopric abroad: he was to be the second Bishop of Calcutta, in effect Primate of all India. Richard offered himself as Reginald's replacement in the family rectory of Hodnet.[117] Now Heber had never seriously considered the Church. But the Hodnet benefice was worth £2,000 p.a., a not insignificant sum.[118] And, as he explained to his sister, he was so 'unpopular' in Oxford that he was in 'fear of being turned out'. His friends counselled otherwise, and his sister laughed him out of the idea: taking orders 'would be a fatal step in every point of view'.[119] But his debts were mounting, and the rumours were starting to multiply.

In May 1826, *John Bull*, carried the following titbit of gossip: 'Mr. Heber, the late Member for Oxford University, will not return to this country for some time . . . [His] complaint, for which he is recommended to travel, is said to have been produced by an over addiction to Hartshorn.'[120]

Now 'Hartshorn' (a kind of smelling salts) was fairly obvious code for Charles Hartshorne, a Cambridge undergraduate whose potential Heber had spotted while he was still a schoolboy. In June 1824, young Hartshorne had been admitted—without right of membership—to the private revels of the

[115] Dibdin, *Bibliomania*, 93–4. Mostly from the Boulard Library which Heber bought *en bloc*.

[116] *Gent's Mag.*, NS 1 (1834), 109.

[117] Heber MSS, Hodnet: Richard Heber to Reginald Heber, 16 Jan. 1823. 'Most private . . . strictest secrecy'.

[118] *The Times*, 2 Jan. 1827, 3.

[119] Heber MSS, Hodnet: Mary Cholmondeley to Reginald Heber, 20 Nov. [1823]. 'I never believed it for a moment.'

[120] *John Bull*, 7 May 1826, 150, and 14 May 1826, 158.

Roxburghe Club. 'At about half past ten', recorded one member, 'when our mirth seemed near its highest noon, after a . . . speech from [Mr Dibdin] . . . seconded by Mr. Heber . . . there was admitted to the honour of a sitting that truly bibliomaniacal spirit Mr. Charles Hartshorne.'[121] This was unprecedented. Dibdin and most of the others stayed till one o'clock; Heber and Hartshorne lingered on, drinking red wine and curaçao till four in the morning. Stories of such behaviour—and whispers of unnatural vice— quickly found their way back to Oxford. Maybe the rumours were false, a mere calumny on a bookish bachelor. Almost certainly, they were exaggerated. But Heber refused to issue a denial. 'Always a shy, proud man', noted one Oxford diarist, 'he could not face [his accusers], and resigned.'[122] To cover his tracks, he told his sister that he simply found the House of Commons 'a fag and a bore'.[123] In truth, he had delayed so long in issuing a denial that he was left with little alternative but resignation; unless of course he was prepared to sue. But as yet no actionable article had appeared. In September 1825, several months before the publication of the notice in *John Bull*, Heber seems to have made up his mind: he explained to the Vice-Chancellor that he hoped 'to save the University all unnecessary trouble and ferment'.[124] Early in January 1826 he told his family he was going;[125] and later that month he notified his friends at Brasenose that he was applying for the Chiltern Hundreds. His letter was addressed from Brussels.[126] In effect he had fled the country, leaving the Athenaeum as a forwarding address for correspondence with the unhappy Hartshorne. The rumours became more sinister. But *John Bull*, which had criticized Heber for his silence over the Catholic question, now affected to regret his going, calling him 'a munificent patron of literature, and one of the best read men in Europe'.[127] Within weeks, however, came the much-quoted canard about 'Hartshorn'.

[121] Joseph Haslewood, quoted in A. Hunt, 'A Study in Bibliomania: C. H. Hartshorne and Richard Heber', *Book Collector*, 42 (1993), 39.

[122] Cox, *Recollections*, 109.

[123] Cholmondeley (ed.), *Heber Letters*, 330–1: 15 Sept. 1825. 'I should pass my time more agreeably among my neighbours, my books, and my trees at Hodnet, than amidst the bad air, and bad blood of St. Stephen's Chapel [Westminster]' (Heber MSS, Hodnet: Richard Heber to Reginald Heber, 16 Jan. 1823). 'My opinion is, he was tired of expecting [i.e. waiting for the seat] before he had it, and [Frodsham] Hodson being gone, and most of his early friends, the Place is irksome to him' (Heber MSS, Hodnet: Mary Cholmondeley to Reginald Heber, 7 Feb. 1826).

[124] Hunt, 'Hartshorne and Heber', 185.

[125] Heber MSS, Hodnet: Richard Heber to Reginald Heber, 17 Jan. 1826.

[126] V-P's Reg. 21 Jan. 1826, fo. 49. 'A beautiful letter . . . Heber's farewell, I call it'; reprinted in the *St James's Chronicle* (Heber MSS, Hodnet: Mary Cholmondeley to Reginald Heber, 7 Feb. 1826 and 2 Mar. 1826).

[127] Heber MSS, Hodnet: Mary Cholmondeley to Reginald Heber [2 Mar. 1826]. Criticism of Heber's silence on the Catholic question was echoed from the opposite side by Copleston of Oriel (ibid: E. Copleston to Reginald Heber, 16 May 1825).

Heber's friends were horrified. 'Dreadful surmises', wrote Crabb Robinson in his diary; 'Broke?... No, worse than that... Shocking whispers!'[128] Sir Walter Scott was appalled:

'This horrible business... [has] really haunted me like a nightmare... Here is learning, wit, gaiety of temper, high station in society and complete reception everywhere, all at once debased and lost by... degrading bestiality... What a world we live in! ... We are come back to the days of Juvenal.[129]

Now Heber could afford to respond by doing nothing, and that suited his procrastinating temperament. He simply stayed abroad for five years until ill health brought him back to England in 1831. But Hartshorne still had his career to make. He brought an action for criminal libel against *John Bull*, and he won. Heber's friends rallied round: they held three dinners at the Athenaeum in Hartshorne's support. But he won no damages because it was a criminal trial. And what of his career? He had been relying on Heber to secure him a post in the King's Library at the British Museum. No hope of that now. So in 1827, as soon as the case in the King's Bench was settled, he found himself a snug parish in Shropshire, embraced holy orders, and married an heiress.[130] The Revd Mr Hartshorne then proceeded to produce fourteen children. Nearly thirty years later, in 1864, he was at last elected to the Roxburghe Club, just a few months before his death.

Heber's ending was less happy. When he returned to London in 1831, he was coolly received in clubland. At Brasenose he was discreetly forgotten. His portrait—which was to have signalled forever his triumph of 1821— seems to have hung in hall only briefly. Sick and reclusive, ordering books to the very moment of his death, Heber the Magnificent died alone in Pimlico in 1833, in the very room in which he had been born; excluded from society, like Beckford before him.[131] He is remembered as 'the archetype of the bibliomaniac, a man whose passion for books was a manifestation of a deeper abnormality'.[132]

Heber's personal property—some £200,000 excluding land—went to his sister Mary Cholmondeley. But what about his books? In a series of sales, spread over three years, 1834–7, the Bibliotheca Heberiana was 'slaughtered': dumped

---

[128] Quoted by Hunt, 'Hartshorne and Heber', 187: 16 Apr. 1826.

[129] Scott, *Letters*, ed. H. J. C. Grierson, x (1936), 68: 30 June 1826, 73: 10 July 1826; and 101: 8 Sept. 1826; *Journal*, ed. W. E. K. Anderson (Oxford, 1972), 162, 170.

[130] Hunt, 'Hartshorne and Heber', 197.

[131] *ODNB*. The dealers did not forsake him: his last visitor, the night before he died, was the bookseller Thomas Rodd of Great Newport Street.

[132] Hunt, 'Hartshorne and Heber', 208.

on the market, at bargain prices.[133] Many of Heber's purchases had been made when the market was high. In the years after Waterloo, the economy faltered and prices fell. By the mid-1830s—in Dibdin's graphic phrase—a sort of 'torpor and satiety' settled over the book market. In 216 days of sales, some 150,000 volumes fetched only £65,000.[134]

It was a curious anticlimax to a Brasenose career which had once promised so well. Meanwhile, what of his half-brother Reginald (pl. 30), whom we last encountered drilling troops with the Volunteers?

Reginald Heber's undergraduate years had been dazzling. In 1800 he won the prize for the 'Carmen Saeculare', a Latin poem on the commencement of the new century; in 1803 the Newdigate Prize for English verse with an epic poem on 'Palestine'. In 1805 he gained the award for the best English essay, with a disquisition on 'The Sense of Honour'. In the same year he was elected a Fellow of All Souls. Young Heber was the toast of Oxford. Walter Scott came to breakfast just before the completion of 'Palestine', and pointed out one slight omission: the building of Solomon's Temple had been a phenomenon remarkable for its silence. Heber left the table, perched for a moment on the window seat overlooking Radcliffe Square, then jotted down some memorable lines:

> No hammer fell, no ponderous axes rung,
> Like some tall palm the mystic fabric sprung.
> Majestic silence![135]

A few days later, to rapturous applause, he declaimed the poem in the Sheldonian Theatre, then returned alone to his rooms. His mother found him on his knees in prayer. Then came an unconventional Grand Tour: Scandinavia, Russia, the Crimea, Austria, Hungary, and Germany. And then

---

[133] e.g. items bought by William Henry Miller (d. 1848), founder of the Britwell Library (*The Times*, 9 Apr. 1927). He bought *The Pylgremage of the Soule* (1483), printed at Westminster by William Caxton, previously in the Spencer Library, for only 18 gns. (pt. iv, lot 2686).

[134] The first seven sales alone—nearly 40,000 lots; say 80,000 volumes—fetched over £34,000 (Dibdin, *Reminiscences*, i. 366 n.). The final total for the nine sales in England (166 days) was £47,265 2s. od. (*Gent's Mag.*, NS 5 (1836), 413). Two sales in Paris (Silvestre, 15 Mar. etc. and 7 Oct. etc. 1836: 2058 and 1267 lots), and one in Ghent (Ch. Citerene, 26 Oct. 1835 etc.: 1792 and 292 lots) brought the grand total to c. £65,000. By comparison, Mr Hibbert's library fetched £21,700; Sir M. M. Sykes', £18,700; Mr Dent's £15,000; and the Duke of Marlborough's £14,482 (Dibdin, *Reminiscences*, i. 461 n.).

[135] [Heber], *Life of Reginald Heber*, i. 29–33. The printed edition gives a different reading. 'No one who heard Reginald Heber recite "Palestine" in that magnificent theatre, will ever forget [it; for] . . . this was not the mere display of the skill and ingenuity of a clever youth . . . here was a poet indeed' (Sir Charles Grey, in *Blackwood's Mag.* 22 (1827), 619). Others claimed evidence of plagiarism (G. Murray, *The Oxford Ars Poetica: or How to Write a Newdigate*, 1853). The building of Solomon's temple is described in 1 Kings 6–7.

back he went to the village of Hodnet for sixteen years as a parish priest. Despite this retreat, his literary fame continued to grow. By 1817 Frodsham Hodson was thinking of putting him up for the Wardenship of All Souls.[136] Destiny, however, would take him further afield. In 1823 came the bishopric of Calcutta.[137]

At Calcutta—in effect, as Primate of India, Australia, and Southern Africa— Heber laboured heroically. For some years he had been interested in missionary work, of an understated, interdenominational kind. Now he set about pursuing his ecumenical ambitions over a diocese the size of three continents. 'Never', he believed, 'was any people entrusted with such power of doing good as England now is!' Such ambitions proved abortive. He died at Trichinopoly after scarcely three years in office, and today even his poems are unread. But who has not sung 'From Greenland's icy mountains...'? There are worse fates than to be remembered for just a handful of anthems. Tennyson thought 'Holy, Holy, Holy' was 'the finest hymn in the English language'.

At the very least, Bishop Heber had a nice ear for parody. One anecdote is too good to leave out. In June 1802, Bursar Halliwell was disturbed in his rooms in Old Quad by the repeated cracking of a whip. The miscreant turned out to be a recent graduate—and member of the Phoenix—named Bernard Port. Halliwell was an unpopular figure, a disciplinarian known from his awkward posture as 'Dr Toe'(pl. 26). Unwisely, he tried to wrestle the whip from the hands of the younger man and ended up flat on his back: a parody of the struggle between Cain and Abel. Heber immortalized both combatants in a mock-heroic poem entitled *The Whippiad*. First of all he sets out the scene:

> Where whiten'd Cain the curse of Heaven defies,
> And leaden slumber seals his brother's eyes,
> Where o'er the porch in brazen splendour glows
> The vast projection of the mystic nose,
> Triumph erewhile of Bacon's fabled arts,
> Now well hung symbol of the student's parts...

Then comes the denouement. Halliwell calls in vain for help:

> Scouts, porters, shoe-blacks, whatsoe'er your trade,
> All, all attend, your master's fist to aid!'
> They heard his voice and trembling at the sound
> The half-breeched legions swarmed like moths around...
> [But] while for servile aid the Doctor calls,
> By Port subverted, prone to earth he sprawls.

---

[136] Heber MSS, Hodnet: Richard Heber to Reginald Heber, 17 June 1817.

[137] The offer came via his friend C. W. Williams Wynn, President of the Board of Control for India. For an assessment of his work, see *The Times*, 31 Aug. 1826, 3, via the *Bombay Courier*, 22 Apr. 1826; also D. Hughes, *Bishop Sahib: A Life of Reginald Heber* (1986).

'This is not the first time', notes Heber, 'the Doctor has been overcome by port.'[138]

When it came to humour, the future Bishop did not have it all his own way. His close contemporary—he went up in 1801—was Thomas Dunbar, later Keeper of the Ashmolean, the wittiest man in Oxford. Tuckwell tells the best story.

One of the Heads of Houses had four daughters—Mary, a 'don'; Lucy, a bluestocking; Susan, a simpleton; Fanny, a sweet unaffected girl. Asked by Lucy the meaning of the word alliteration, with scarcely a pause he replied:

> Minerva-like, majestic Mary moves;
> Law, Latin, Logic, learned Lucy loves;
> Serenely silent, Susan's smiles surprise;
> From fops, from flatterers, fairest Fanny flies.[139]

Reginald Heber's later years at Brasenose saw the first glimmerings of what he christened 'a general change of manners'. This was a phenomenon by no means limited to BNC. The excesses of Regency England were about to give way to the soberer world of the young Victoria. Heber sensed this when he returned to Oxford in 1818, and found the University 'a curious gerometer' of custom.

In Oxford, notwithstanding [an] outward monotony, there are certain changes which [one]...cannot fail to discover...[Even] Christ Church [is no longer] an absolute monarchy...My old college is less altered in this respect; but the tutors there, as elsewhere in the university, are [a very]...different race from the former stock... The old boys never stirred from home; these pass their whole vacations on the continent, are geologists, system-mongers, and I know not what...Of the young men...the general story is, that they were never so diligent and orderly as at present, all which is put down to...the [new] system of examination. There is really, I think, much less lounging than formerly, which is produced, of course, by the greater

---

[138] *Blackwood's Mag.* 54 (1843), 100–8; *Quat. Mon.* XII, 30–1. When Arabella Hornsby, daughter of the Savilian Professor of Astronomy, spurned Dr Toe for a mere footman, Heber produced the following squib: ''Twixt footman John and Doctor Toe | A rivalship befell | Which of the two should be the Beau | To bear away the Belle! | The footman won the lady's heart | And who can blame her? No man | The whole prevailed against the part | Twas Foot-man versus Toe-man.' Halliwell spent years working on the Oxford edition of Strabo's *Geography* (2 vols., 1807); it was derided by [R. Payne Knight] as a 'ponderous monument of operose ignorance' (*Edinbugh Rev.* 14 (1809), 441). He ended his days as a High Tory, anti-Catholic Rector in the Brasenose living of Clayton, Sussex (£800 p.a.). At his death his cellar included 'one hundred dozens' of 'fine old port wine', variously labelled 'rich flavoured', 'full flavoured', 'curious', and 'excellent' (*Manchester School Reg.* ii. 247–50; *ODNB*).

[139] W. Tuckwell, *Reminiscences of Oxford* (1901 edn.), 14. Dunbar was the son of a baronet, and author of *The Brase Nose Garlande* [?1811]. He was 'Poet Laureate' to 'the Brazen Nose Chesse Club', founded 1810, 'the first chess club that ever existed at Oxford' (*British Chess Mag.* (Oct. 1932), 43, quoted in *Brazen Nose*, v. 241). For anecdotes see obit tipped into MPP 56 F4/1.

frequency and regularity of lectures; but hunting seems practised to a degree considerably beyond our times . . . [even] if Bacchus is somewhat less honoured.[140]

The status of scholars was beginning to change too. After 1799 servitors no longer waited in hall. But when Mark Pattison's father went up to Brasenose in 1805, 'the "scholars" were still not regarded as gentlemen. They did not associate with the commoners but lived among themselves, or with the bible clerks. They were nicknamed "charity boys" . . . twenty-five years [later] this had quite changed. The scholar's gown, from being the badge of an inferior order, had become a coveted distinction.'[141] And attendance in chapel was being tightened up too. Bedmakers were given lighter duties on Sundays, so that they might attend divine service.[142] And in 1818 it was 'resolved that the Porter be directed to lock the Chapel door at the commencement of the Psalms both at morning and evening prayers'. As a concession, 'commencement' was then altered to 'conclusion'.[143]

Such developments suggest that by the 1820s the roistering days of BNC—the days of Sykes and Osbaldeston—were nearly over. Nearly, but not quite. In 1824 Cruikshank still thought the activities of Brasenose men a suitable subject for satire: smuggling girls into college in a laundry basket for example.[144] Evenings in Regency BNC can seldom have been silent. One night in May 1822, looking down from his garret rooms (IV, 5) in Old Quad, a second-year man named W. G. Meredith was astonished by the amount of noise.

I am in rather a bad way this morning [he wrote to his friend Benjamin Disraeli] as my slumbers were totally spoiled last night by . . . tumultuous shouting and sing-ing . . . [The] the noise in our quad . . . usually takes place at about 11 or 12 o'clock. After liberally imbibing the liquors which are of every description from champagne to gin and water, they institute what is called a Vauxhall, and promenade up and down the grass plot smoking, and drinking malt, till a very late hour. . . . Some mornings ago at half past one, a man was perched on the shoulders of the statue in the middle of the College, drinking the health of the Vice-Principal, which was seconded by loud acclamation.[145]

Brasenose would keep its boisterous reputation for some time yet. Even so, the world of R. H. Barham—he of the *Ingoldsby Legends*—had indeed

---

[140] [Heber], *Life of Reginald Heber*, i. 498–9.

[141] Pattison, *Memoirs*, 26–7, 72; Gallia Collis [W. T. Coxhill], *Aeneinasensiana* (1941; 1946), 20.

[142] V-P's Reg. 10 Mar. 1820, fo. 168.

[143] Ibid. 26 Nov. 1818, fo. 120. Later the chapel door was left open, but the Bible Clerk's 'Imposter' made a list of all who were 'tardy' in attendance (ibid. 18 Dec. 1827, fo. 97).

[144] R. Cruikshank, 'Capping a Proctor, or Oxford Bull-dogs, detecting Brazen Smugglers' (published 1 Mar. 1824 by Sherwood, Jones, & Co.).

[145] W. G. Meredith to B. Disraeli, 13 May 1822, Bodl. Dep. Hughendon 12/1, fo. 6, partly quoted in *Brazen Nose*, xiii. 113.

begun to fade. Barham came up in 1807, in possession of 'a perilous abundance of funds'. As a gentleman commoner, already a man of infinite jest—in Buchan's phrase, 'an acrobat of style'—he worked little and gambled hard, specializing in 'unlimited loo'. On one occasion Principal Hodson summoned him to explain his continued absence from morning chapel. Barham was unabashed.

'The fact is, sir, you are *too late* for me'.
'Too late!'
'Yes, sir—*too late*. I cannot sit up till seven o'clock in the morning: I am a man of regular habits; and unless I get to bed by four or five at the latest, I am really fit for nothing next day'.[146]

That happy state of decadence did not last. Towards the end of his time at BNC, Barham experienced a shock that may well have tipped him in the direction of holy orders.

Brasenose had for some time been known as an 'expensive' college. In Barham's year more than two-thirds of the intake could be classified as gentry. And several of his close contemporaries were very rich indeed. The wealth of the Grenvilles was legendary; William Vane was heir to the millionaire dukedom of Cleveland; Richard Glyn belonged to a dynasty of bankers; Ralph Franco would soon inherit a vast estate in Devon and a colossal fortune based on slaves and sugar. BNC that year was no place for poor men. But of those who went up in 1807, there was one undergraduate who was certainly not rich: a friend of Barham's named Robert Andrews. A scholar from Rugby, the son of 'a gentleman of respectable standing, but straitened means', Andrews unwisely tried to keep up with the fast set. 'He launched into the gaieties of college life'; he fell into debt; and in April 1810, close to suicide, he was forced to write for help to his father, at that time an indigent clergyman in Lancashire. Back came a letter containing the promise of emergency funds, but it arrived several hours too late. The frantic parent—fearing the worst—had tipped the mail guard a guinea to deliver the envelope by hand. When the wretched messenger did arrive, already 'reeling drunk', he found a coroner's inquest in progress, 'over the body of [the twenty year old undergraduate] whose head was shattered to atoms by a pistol-ball'.[147]

Andrews was buried in the antechapel. His memorial bears no reference to the circumstances of his death, and the college records are silent. Golden ages are not all gold.

---

[146] R. H. D. Barham, *Life and Letters of R. H. Barham*, i (1870), 20. His facility in rhyme made 'Byron and Browning look like bunglers' (*The Times*, 25 Sept. 1930). A jolly bohemian and high-church Tory, he was equally opposed to popery and Dissent. See Buchan, in *Quat. Mon.* XIV. ii, 11–13; *ODNB*.

[147] *Life and Letters of Barham*, 26–8.

4
1822–1853

Religion and Reform: The Brasenose
of Gilbert and Harington

'23 Nov. 1835: Resolved that the College accounts be henceforward kept in English, and that the Bursar be desired to prepare his scheme for the ensuing audit in that language.'[1] Too much should never be read into a single fragment of evidence. But between the 1820s and the 1850s the institutions of England underwent a reordering of their very foundations. The practice of central and local government, the principles of administration and representation, the status of Church and law, even the governance of ancient universities—all these were subject to change. And that Governing Body resolution, refashioning the budget of a single college, tells us a good deal about this spirit of reform. Latin was to be no longer the language of accountancy. Even in Oxford, utility had made its mark.

There were seven men present on that occasion, seven senior Fellows: the Seniority of Brasenose. They were, of course, all clerics; and all were in the process of climbing the clerical ladder via the route of collegiate patronage. All were Oxford classicists, except Joseph Walker, who was a mathematician from Cambridge. And all were respectable scholars: only James Smith, by now a popular Vice-Principal, had failed to achieve a First in Schools. Thomas Ormerod and the two Churtons, Thomas and Whitaker, belonged to loyal Brasenose families: the Churtons produced four BNC men, the Ormerods eight. But whereas the Churtons came from clerical stock, Ormerod was a gentleman commoner.[2] He proceeded from MGS to BNC, and so via the Phoenix and the Inner Temple to a comfortable Norfolk living. Thomas Bazely was Ormerod's exact contemporary at Brasenose, and like him he published variously on ecclesiastical politics.

[1] V-P's Reg. 21 Nov. 1835, fo. 16. College accounts have been printed and published since 1882; the Bursar has issued an annual report since 1885 (B272–80).

[2] At Sedbury Park, Glos., Ormerod built up a considerable library, sold at Sotheby's in 1875 for £2,200 (Boase, ii. 1257–8). For Walker, see ibid., vi. 760.

But none of this group ever became a public figure, except that is for the Principal: Ashurst Turner Gilbert (pl. 34). And Gilbert's career deserves a moment's pause.

The election of Gilbert as Principal in 1822 had been unexpected. He was not yet 36; and of the seven electors (including himself), four were senior to him. But at least he looked the part. He had a 'fine tall figure and handsome face, white hair and dark eyes'.[3] He was not by origin a gentleman. His father was a captain in the Royal Marines. A succession of scholarships had taken him from MGS to BNC, where a First in Greats—in the same year as Robert Peel—had secured him a Fellowship in 1809. But he only found himself a Fellow thanks to an accident of consanguinity: he successfully claimed kinship to both Joyce Frankland and Bishop Smith. With remarkable candour he openly admitted that he had never been by nature a teacher: he 'had very early conceived a dislike to the labour of . . . education'. It was just that he had 'no other means of obtaining bread'. Anyway, thanks to his providential election as Principal, he had now risen beyond the level of mere tutorials, happily exchanging—in his own words—'drudgery' for 'responsibility'.[4] Within months he had married, and settled down to bringing up a family of eleven children in the Principal's Lodgings. By 1836 he was Vice-Chancellor of the University. By 1842 he was Bishop of Chichester.

That final leap came as a surprise to many.[5] But it can hardly have been unexpected in Brasenose. Peel's Conservatives were in power and Gilbert had been piling up support on the Tory side for quite a while. His campaign really took off with the Hampden Case. When in 1836 Lord Melbourne appointed Dr R. D. Hampden as Regius Professor of Divinity, Oxford's high-church Tories rose up in protest. Hampden had been a brilliant tutor at Oriel and an enterprising Principal of St Mary Hall. He had even scored a double First without the aid of a private coach. But in theological terms he was a liberal evangelical. He regarded the Tractarians—that is, the high-church supporters of *Tracts for the Times* (1834–41)—as Romish obscurantists. In 1833 he had been a contentious Bampton Lecturer; and the ground of contention was only too familiar: he placed the evidence of Scripture above the authority of the Church.[6] Having bravely delivered his inaugural—facing down Tractarians in the Divinity School itself—he

---

[3] *The Times*, 22 Feb. 1870, 10.

[4] A. T. Gilbert to Revd R. Dawson, 3 Feb. 1822, quoted in *Brazen Nose*, v. 248–50. For Gilbert's pedigree see Muniments B 5 and G. D. Squibb, *Founders' Kin* (Oxford, 1972), 28–9.

[5] G. V. Cox, *Recollections of Oxford* (1868), 306.

[6] R. D. Hampden, *The Scholastic Philosophy Considered in Relation to Christian Theology* (1833); *ODNB*.

became the focus of bitter debate.[7] Among those most heavily involved was the Principal of Brasenose.

As Principal, Pro-Vice-Chancellor and Vice-Chancellor in turn, Gilbert had no doubt at all where he should stand. Neither right nor left; neither Tractarian nor evangelical; he rallied BNC to the cause of Church and state. On 22 March 1836, 400 non-resident MAs crowded the Sheldonian, calling down judgement on the aberrant Hampden. Tempers were running high. A vote of censure was announced: 'Placet or Non-placet'. With 'a tremendous shout of Placet', the motion was carried, and then vetoed by the Proctors. At this, there was a huge commotion, and 'a general cry rose up—"to Brasenose Hall"...' Many of the protesters clutched in their hands Dr Arnold's slashing attack on Oxford's Tractarian 'Malignants', published that very day in the *Edinburgh Review*.[8] A mass petition was prepared, and Gilbert vowed to prevent a single Brasenose man attending Hampden's 'rationalistic' lectures[9]. But Hampden held on, thanks to Whig support, despite a second censure in Congregation. Eventually, in 1847, Lord John Russell made him Bishop of Hereford. But by then the atmosphere in Oxford had changed. Newman had gone over to Rome in 1845. The Tractarian fever had passed its peak. And Brasenose had a rather different Principal, a man more concerned with threats to the University than with disruption in the Church of England.

Unlike Gilbert, Principal Harington (pl. 35) was very much a gentleman, the son of a baronet in fact. He had been to Harrow and then to Christ Church: he even married a daughter of the Dean. By the time of his election as Principal, he had already been Master of the Apollo Lodge, not once but three times over. One thing he did share with Gilbert: a serious interest in ecclesiology. He was President of the Oxford Architectural Society, and broadly speaking his instincts were high church. But he tried hard to keep extreme opinions out of college life. In 1845 the Dean of Manchester—a Trustee of the Hulme foundation—decided to block the award of an exhibition to one Theophilus Jones, an undergraduate of Tractarian sympathies. Harington accused the Dean of turning a charitable fund into 'a hot-bed of

---

[7] Some forty-five books and pamphlets appeared on the subject, e.g. by Pusey, Newman, and Keble. Oxford became 'a kind of image of...Florence...in the days of Savonarola' (R. W. Church, *The Oxford Movement* (1891; 1922), 161).

[8] [T. Arnold], *Edinburgh Rev.* 63, 225–39. For the whole episode, see *Letters of Rev. J. B. Mozley* (1885), 54–5; *Letters of Frederic Lord Blachford*, ed. G. E. Mandarin (1896), 28–30; W. R. Ward, *Victorian Oxford* (1965), 101.

[9] Cox, *Recollections*, 264, 280; Ward, *Victorian Oxford*, 360 n. 100. Gilbert refused to sign testimonials for those who had attended. As Vice-Chancellor, in 1839, Gilbert was less contentiously involved in the award of honorary degrees to Grand Duke Alexander of Russia (later Alexander II) and Prince (later King) William of the Netherlands. A seating plan for the grand banquet held on that occasion in Brasenose hall survives (*Brazen Nose*, iii. 213–14).

acrimonious and implacable controversy'. Such a proceeding, he thundered, was 'unparalleled...since the declaration required of the Jansenists in France, by Pope Alexander VII, at the instigation of the Jesuits'. All to no avail: the Dean of Manchester got his way. Harington, it seems, was less disposed to litigation than Dr Gilbert would prove to be.[10] In any case, the style of these two Principals was fundamentally different. At Phoenix dinners Harington was something of a dandy; on the river he was quite a swell. In 1830 Mark Pattison noticed that as a tutor he did little for BNC's academic standing.

Brasenose had the reputation of being rowdy and drinking; and though the tutors, Hall, Churton, and Richard Harington, were first class men, yet the tuition was not esteemed good. Hall was getting old and weary of it; Tommy Churton I afterwards came to know as a 'stick'; and Harington was a fine Gentleman, who sailed his own pinnace on the river, and dined out too much.[11]

He was also, as Principal, too conscious of his own dignity. Seventy years after the event, one Brasenose freshman still remembered him with 'hate and loathing'. 'Handshaking'—that is leave-taking at the end of each year—had apparently been reduced by Harington to the level of an icy ritual.

Principal Harington made all the young men pass through the scullery in the [eighteenth-century Lodgings] in the back quad and touch his outstretched finger as he stood at the corner of his rug [in the drawing room, just before the undergraduates] passed through the street door into the High Street. [In] so doing he insulted God much more than the young men, showing that that was his idea of fulfilling to them his idea of doing his duty to them at the most critical epoch of their life.[12]

[10] *Correspondence between the Hon. and Very Rev. the Dean of Manchester and the Principal of Brasenose College, Oxford* (Oxford, 1846), 12, 35. Harington studied ecclesiology in the context of architectural history (*The Ecclesiologist*, 12, NS 9 (1851), 289). He was closely involved in Buckler's restoration of St Mary's.

[11] M. Pattison, *Memoirs* (1885), 23. Hall retreated to Middleton Cheney in 1831. Harington had been elected Fellow in 1822 and Mathematical Lecturer in 1823 (VP's Reg. 16 Mar. 1822, fo. 198 and 29 May 1823, fo. 225). Madan noted that his portrait, taken after death and before burial, used to hang in Cradock's dining room. 'Mrs. C. was frightened and put it in the servants' hall; sold with Dr. C's things, and Newman (Common Room man) saw it in a sale and bought it for a few shillings. We agreed to give him 5 gns.' (B4 b10, tipped in).

[12] W. D. V. Duncombe to [R.W. Jeffery], 16 Dec. 1922, tipped into MPP 56 F 4/1. Harington was buried in the antechapel in 1853 along with his first wife and daughter. A south window in his memory, by Wailes of Newcastle, was installed in 1860 (V.-P.'s Reg. 21 Dec. 1860, f. 49v; *Oxford Guide* [1862], 142). A new east window, made by Hardman to Street's design, had been installed in his memory in 1853; it was replaced by Kempe in 1894–6, the old glass being given to Sir Richard Harington, 11th Bt., of Whitbourne Court, Herefordshire

Other undergraduates used language which was rather less high-flown. 'If the Principal was made a Bishop', announced G. R. Winter in 1850, 'I would take the keys of the college, throw them down the bog and bog upon them.'[13]

In the year of Harington's election—1842—Brasenose ranked high among the colleges of Oxford. Only Christ Church was significantly bigger. Apart from the Principal, there were 20 Fellows, resident and non-resident; 121 undergraduates or endowed graduates—that is, 26 scholars, 95 commoners—plus 61 BAs and 177 MAs still 'on the books'. By 1851 the grand total was 408.[14] Numerically at least, BNC was more than three times the size of Merton, more than five times the size of New College, and more than nine times the size of Magdalen. No wonder Harington felt he had nothing to fear from the threat of a Royal Commission. The total college revenue—difficult to calculate exactly—increased during the 1840s and 1850s to as much as £15,000 p.a. by the end of the 1860s. Of this, at least in 1842, £1,725 went to the Principal, £3,640 to the Fellows, and £750 to the scholars. Most of the income was the product of property and endowment, but some £750 came from tuition fees and perhaps £600 from the rent of rooms.[15] The disparities built into such a structure were obvious. As Principal, for example, Harington

(V.-P.'s Reg. 13 Dec. 1853, fos. 158–9; 21 Dec. 1860, fo. 50; 18 Mar. 1896, fo. 86; 6 May 1896, fo. 88). One window on the south side, by Wailes, memorializes Revd J. W. Barlow, Fellow (d. 1859); another, also by Wailes, commemorates J. P. Harris, a hero of the siege of Lucknow (d. 1864).

[13] 'The [E. V.] Amery Gallery' [i.e. sketches by G. R. Winter, c.1850, ex colls. J. W. Cobb and F. Madan], Bodl. MS Top. Oxon. d. 335, fo. 77 ult. Several of Winter's contemporaries appear, as E. Waller, staggering home by moonlight on the arm of 'Brother Bossum', the porter; J. A. Dawkins, 'after a night's debauch'; and J. H. Milne, with ladies of the town: 'having totally reformed, [he] tries his strength of mind, as an opportunity occurs, and finds his determination as firm as a Rock' (ibid. fo. 76). Waller became High Sheriff of Gloucestershire; Milne became a chaplain at Dinan and Avranche; Dawkins became Rector of Farmington, Glos., and Daylesford, Worcs. Winter himself rowed in the BNC Eight (1846–8) and became Rector of East Bradenham, Norfolk. He published *The Oxford Doughnut* and *Recollections of Eton and Oxford*.

[14] OU Commn. (*PP* (1852), xxii), Report, 227. The figures in *OU Calendar* (1842), used here for undergraduates and endowed graduates—whether actually in residence or not—differ from those tabulated in J. Heywood, *The Recommendations of the O.U. Commissioners* (1853), opp. p. 1, and those prepared by H. L. Jones, for V. A. Hüber, *English Universities*, ed. F. W. Newman, ii, pt. 2 (1843), 576. Heywood's table—originally in *Quarterly Jnl. of the Statistical Society of London*, 5 (1842), 243–9—claimed to represent numbers actually in residence in May 1842, and is used in *HUO*. vi, pt. i, 159.

[15] BNC's annual income between 1858 and 1867 was tabulated in decennial form at the behest of the Commissioners (Clennell, B2 b 12: 25 Sept. 1869). It was the Colleges Estates Acts of 1858 and 1860 which made possible a general improvement in college incomes prior to the decline of agricultural revenues in the 1870s.

received nearly half as much as all twenty Fellows put together; though it has to be said that he was a poor man compared with the Dean of Christ Church and the Provost of Oriel. More striking still was the comparative wealth of this one college and the poverty of the University as a whole. During the 1850s and 1860s BNC's income continued to rise: 'dividends from money in the funds', for example, increased from £167 to £412 p.a. between 1858 and 1867. But the ordinary annual income of the University itself was reckoned in 1850 at no more than £7,500; plus a separate parliamentary grant of £1,042 for the payment of several professors. That was rather less than the annual revenue received by the University from the printing of Bibles and Prayer Books; and a mere fraction of the £150,000 received each year by the colleges from their own accumulated endowments.[16] The colleges were rich and the University was poor. The Royal Commission of 1850 was, in effect, the first of a whole series of attempts to swing the balance of power the other way, from college to University; from a congeries of private corporations to a cohesive institution of national standing. This process of shifting the balance—recovering the territory ceded by the University to the colleges as long ago as the sixteenth century—would continue throughout the nineteenth and twentieth centuries.[17] And the issue of relative power—University versus college, centre versus periphery, science versus arts—has remained since then in a state of continuous tension.

In the earlier nineteenth century the focus of that tension—as so often since—was the examination system. Colleges taught; the University examined. When the University reformed the system, the colleges had to live with the consequences. Chief of these was the fact that, for the majority of undergraduates, the new process was too severe. In 1830, in order to reduce the numbers who left without any degree at all, a Fourth class was established and Honours degrees were separated from Pass (or Ordinary) degrees. Honours continued to be demanding. The number of successful Finalists in 1845–8, for example, averaged only 287 out of 387, and the number obtaining a First in classics only 10 out of 90.[18] A 'double First', in classics

---

[16] Heywood, p. xix; OU. Commn. (*PP* (1852), xxii), Report, 125–7, 151.

[17] 'The Colleges absorbed the University; so that practically, they shut up its Schools and silenced its Professors' (OU Commn., *PP* (1852), xxii, Report, Application of College Revenues, p. iv). 'Laud sealed the victory of the [colleges] by forcing all the Undergraduates within their walls: but Laud only systematized what was already done. The Fellows had become... the practical rulers and teachers of the University... the College Foundations have become Institutions of the University; and in common justice their new position subjects them to principles of interference not contemplated at the outset' (Revd F. Temple, in OU Commn., *PP* (1852), xxii, Evidence, 131). 'Is it not almost absurd to attribute to the wishes of a fallible man, living in the 13th or 14th century, a power of binding in perpetuity a corporate body endowed with an artificial existence by the law alone?' (Sir E. Head, ibid. 158).

[18] Ibid., Report, 61 quoting figures returned to the House of Commons, 5 Jan. 1850 (ibid., appendix K, 69–70).

GREAT GUNS OF OXFORD.   B.N.C.

33. **Edward Tindal Turner (1822–1911).**

Fellow, 1845 onwards; Senior Bursar, 1866–70; Vice-Principal, 1870–81; Registrar of the University, 1870–97.

Shrimpton's 'Great Guns of Oxford', no. lxi (suppressed by Turner).

To the parents of an undergraduate who died in his first term: 'It may be of some consolation to you to know that the young man would in any case have had to go down owing to his failure to pass Responsions'.

THE CHICHESTER EXTINGUISHER.

Bishop of Chichester. "GO! GO! YOU INSOLENT, REBELLIOUS BOY. WHAT WITH YOUR NONSENSE AND INCENSE AND CANDLES YOU'LL BE SETTING THE CHURCH ON FIRE."

Master P-ch-s. "JUST WHAT I'D LIKE TO DO. THERE!"

34. Ashurst Turner Gilbert (1786–1870).
Principal, 1832–42; Vice-Chancellor, 1836–40; Bishop of Chichester, 1842–70.
'The Chichester Extinguisher': Bishop Gilbert punishing Revd. John Purchas for ritualistic practices in Brighton.
Punch 25 Oct. 1868.

35. **Richard Harington** (1800–53).

Principal, 1842–53.

'A fine Gentleman, who sailed his own pinnace on the river, and dined out too much' (Mark Pattison).
An arch-opponent of reform.

36. **Edward Hartopp Cradock [formerly Grove] (1810–86).**
Principal, 1853–86.
'The Chief': 'Everybody can do something better than anybody else'.
It was Dr. Cradock who first established B.N.C.'s sporting reputation.

37. **Walter Pater in 1872, as an 'aesthetic young man'.**
Fellow, 1858–94.
'Faint, pale, embarrassed, exquisite Pater! He is the mask
without the face' (Henry James).

38. **The Fellows, in 1861.**

STANDING: Revd. J.W. Knott. Revd. T.H.R. Shand (Junior Bursar). Revd. J.A. Ormerod (Senior Bursar). Revd. F. Menzies (Vice-Principal). Revd. S. H. Reynolds.

SITTING: Mr. C. J. Wood (Tutor). Revd. R.S. Wilson. Revd. W. Yates (Tutor and Junior Dean). Revd. A. Watson (Tutor and Librarian).

These Fellows were all elected under the old statutes, before the reforms of the 1850s.

(opposite)

39. A. **'Brasenose Ale', 1886.**

Caricature of 'Toby' Watson, newly elected Principal. Published by A. T. Shrimpton, Oxford.

B. **Walter Pater: in Oxford and in London.**

Drawings by C. J. Holmes: Oxford 1887; London 1890–91.

A

B

40. John Bossum (d. 1861).
   Head Porter, photographed 14 April 1860.
   A mountainous figure, weighing 22 stone: 'Cerberus at the gate'.

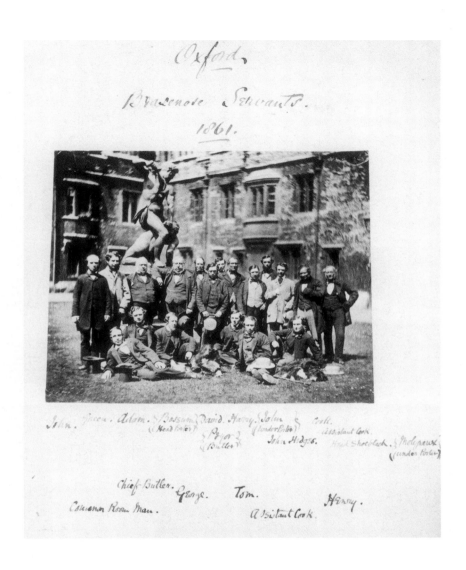

41. Brasenose Servants, 1861.

STANDING: *Back row:* John Hinton. Thomas Green. Adam Owen. John Bossum (Head Porter). David East. *Middle row:* John Prior (Butler). Henry Charlwood (Pater's scout). John Hawkins (Under Porter). John Hedges. *Front row:* Thomas Wells (Manciple / Cook). Assistant Cook. Head Shoeblack. John Molyneux (Under Porter / Messenger).

SITTING: Common Room Man. Chief Butler. George. Tom. Assistant Cook. Harry.

43. **The Prince of Wales, while in residence at Frewin Hall, 1859–60.**

   The future King Edward VII (standing), with (left to right) the Prince's Governor, Major-General Robert Bruce; the Prince's Law and History Tutor, Herbert Fisher; and Rear Admiral Sir Henry Keppel.

(opposite)

42. **Undergraduate Lodgings, *c*.1862.**

   A. Above Standen's outfitters in Catte Street (later part of Hertford College). A. C. Plowden, founder of the Vampires, wears a turned-down bowler hat. Hartwell Grissell is immediately on his right. C.E. Harris, Secretary of the Phoenix, is on the far left in the same window. E. W. Knollys appears on the left of the right hand window.

   B. Interior. Centre: H. Grissell. E. W. Knollys, A. C. Plowden and G. J. Barry.

**44. Walter Bradford Woodgate [11st. 4lb., left] and
Weldon Champneys [11st. 0lb., right], at Henley.**

Champions in the Silver Goblets, Henley, 1861 and 1862.

'Guts' Woodgate's terrier Jenny is wearing B.N.C. colours.

'The everlasting Woodgate [8 years in the 1st Eight] was again to the fore
and concluded this brilliant regatta [of 1862] with another brilliant victory'.

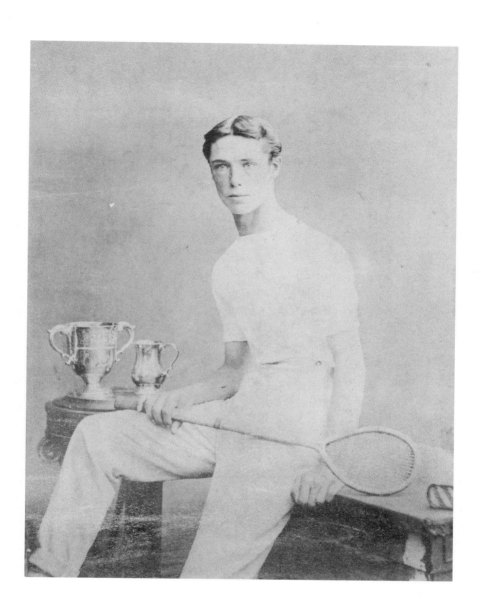

45. **C. J. Ottaway** (1850–78).
  With Blues for cricket, tennis, rackets, football and athletics – as well as a First in Classical
  Mods – he was 'the greatest athletic hero known at Oxford till C.B. Fry'.

46. The Brasenose Coach, *c.*1863.

Undergraduates setting out from Radcliffe Square.

Note the entrance lodge and tower, freshly restored by J. C. Buckler.

(opposite)

47. A. The Octagon, 1867.

Photographed outside II, 1.

BACK ROW: <u>A.G.H. James</u>. <u>B. de M. Egerton</u>. <u>C.W. Everard</u>. <u>A. Nash</u>. <u>M. Prower</u>.
FRONT ROW: <u>F. W. Percival</u>. L. B. Vawdrey [President]. <u>P.R. Gorringe</u>.

Underlined names: Founder Members.

Prower, top right, was the last undergraduate to be mortally injured – 'inter tumultum plebis' – during a Town v. Gown riot.

B. Old Quad, *c.*1891.

Note the decayed stonework, progressively replaced during the 20th century; and the battlements over the hall bay window, removed in 1958.

A

B

48. The Phoenix, Chapel steps, 1861.

STANDING: *J. Dunn (Radley). A. Henry (Radley). F. Brandt [guest] (Cheltenham). *P. H. Lee (Rugby). H. Grissell [guest] (Harrow). *W. H. Erskine [11th Earl of Mar and Kellie](Radley). * P. Arden (Harrow).

SITTING: *J. H. Gumbleton (Harrow). R. B. Leach [guest] (Marlborough). W. I. Allgood ( ). *J. B. Orme (Radley). F. G. Farquhar (Harrow).

* = member of Apollo Lodge.

and mathematics, was of course rarer still. By comparison, the Pass degree did little more than formalize a system of preparation from classical cribs: 'four plays of Euripides, four or five books of Herodotus ... six Books of Livy ... half of Horace, four Books of Euclid or ... Aldrich's Compendium of Logic to the end of the Reduction of Syllogisms'.[19] And even this bibliography was too much for many Pass men. During the later 1830s, reported one examiner, 'the proportion of [Pass] candidates who were rejected, was usually about 30%; the proportion who withdrew voluntarily was about the same; so that of about 160 candidates for the ordinary [Pass] examination [in any one year], 60 would disappear altogether, 90 would obtain ordinary [Pass] certificates, and about 10 would be placed by the Examiners in the fourth class of honours'.[20] In this way college lectures—that is, classes designed, at BNC as elsewhere, for Pass and class men simultaneously—became increasingly formulaic. Professorial lectures were a different matter; but they belonged to the University sector, and many of their subjects—law, medicine, modern history, etc.—lay outside the Schools curriculum. Before the reforms of the 1850s, the compulsory syllabus consisted solely of the rudiments of Christian religion (the Gospels, the Articles, Paley's *Evidences*); Literae Humaniores (Greek, Latin, ancient history, and philosophy); and the elements of mathematics and physics. In most colleges, these were all taught by two or three tutors, chosen not with regard to their expertise but simply according to seniority. The result, as Pattison discovered even at Oriel, was an empty ritual, tedious for teachers and taught. The examination reforms which had begun so hopefully in 1800 had yet to be translated into an adequate system of instruction. For Honours men that meant private coaching.[21] For Pass men, it supplied a perfect alibi. And that suited BNC: the college consisted largely of Pass men.

Edward Caswall—who arrived at Brasenose in 1832, and lived to write hymns still sung across the globe—deftly parodied at least twenty types of undergraduate:

He that goeth to the Ascot races. He that loungeth in Quad. He that readeth many books. He that readeth few books. He that readeth no books. He that readeth novels ... He that sporteth many new whips. He that knoweth many pretty girls. He that knoweth one pretty girl. He that hateth Greek. He that being poor sporteth champagne. He that hath gone a second time to a dog fight. He that is a radical albeit

---

[19] Ibid. 63: Requirements for a Common Degree.

[20] T. Twiss, ibid., Evidence, 294.

[21] 'The real business of education has passed from the hands of the College Lecturers to those of the Private Tutors ... Thus a vast body of "cram" is perpetuated from one generation to another' (G. O. Morgan, ibid., Evidence, 196).

his father was a Tory, for such a one thinketh himself clever. He that weareth white kid gloves when shooting. He that breaketh lamps in the street. He that learneth more than two instruments of music. He that eateth too much pudding. He that hath a lock of hair in his desk. He that thinketh he will be plucked. He that thinketh he will not be plucked.[22]

Perhaps it was just as well that the butler was forbidden to serve beer before one o'clock.[23]

Not that Brasenose held any sort of monopoly in idleness. Christ Church at this time spawned several clubs whose high spirits led to their suppression: the Isis and the Quintain, for example. And BNC could hardly match the Bullingdon. Still, under Harington, it was scarcely a sober place; and like Christ Church it was subject to the usual temptations of rich young men: 'houses of ill fame, tandem-driving, intoxication, horse-racing, steeple-chases etc.'[24] For undergraduates who were less well off, there were always the minor distractions of college life. In 1845, by 'way of relieving the tedium of the Lent term . . . a fancy-dress ball [was held at BNC]'; male guests attended dressed as ladies; and 'the best mimic among the undergraduates . . . appeared in lawn sleeves, and made a speech at supper in the exact imitation of the tone and manner of . . . Dr. Gilbert'.[25]

Brasenose at this time was certainly 'not a reading College'.[26] During the 1840s its tally of Firsts fell sharply.[27] But in the University as a whole—apart from Balliol—a similar, and growing, imbalance of scholars to non-scholars can also be detected. By 1850, even for those undergraduates who did read, the list of authors studied for Lit. Hum. had shrunk from more than twenty in the 1820s to little more than a dozen. In philosophy, Aristotle's *Ethics*, *Rhetoric*, or *Politics*, plus two or three Dialogues of Plato, Butler's *Analogy* or his *Sermons*; in ancient history, Herodotus, Thucydides, the first or second Decade of Livy, the *Annals* or the *Histories* of Tacitus; in poetry, Aeschylus, Sophocles, Aristophanes, Virgil, Horace, and Juvenal: that was the sum of the

---

[22] 'Scriblerus Redivivus' [E. Caswall], *A New Art, Teaching how to be Plucked, a Treatise after the Fashion of Aristotle* (1837). Caswall became a Catholic in 1846, and followed Newman into the Birmingham Oratory after his wife's death in 1848. Obit, *The Guardian*, 9 Jan. 1878; *ODNB*.

[23] VP's Reg. 2 Mar. 1833, fo. 176.

[24] Revd W. E. Jelf, OU Commn. (*PP* (1852), xxii), Evidence, 182–3. During Ascot week dinner in hall was compulsory: names were monitored by the Impostor (V-P's Reg. 22 May 1841, fo. 164).

[25] W. K. R. Bedford, 'The O.D.A.', in L. M. Quiller Couch (ed.), *Reminiscences of Oxford* (OHS xxii, 1892), 377–8; *Morning Post*, 31 Jan. 1845 ('Fancy Dress and Polka Ball').

[26] B. O. Jones in *Brazen Nose*, iii. 255. In the 1840s and 1850s the ratio of scholars to commoners varied between one in three and one in four (tabulated in J. E. Thorold Rogers, *Education in Oxford* (1861), 174). More important, the majority of commoners were Pass men.

[27] Tables for 1838–48 in Sir W. Hamilton, *Discussions on Philosophy and Literature* (1866 edn.), 744–5; tables for 1840–59 in Rogers, *Education in Oxford*, 172.

reading of even the most diligent scholar; though this was supplemented by the growing study of complementary commentaries and histories, for example those of Niebuhr and Grote[28] Diligent scholars, of course, represented only a minority of undergraduates, and even those seemed then to be dwindling. Between 1839 and 1848 an average of only 92 candidates from all colleges achieved classical Honours, as against an average of 115 for the years 1831–8. As for Honours in mathematics and physics, the numbers by mid-century were very small: only 20, for example, in 1846. Some colleges provided no mathematical instruction whatsoever. Brasenose was unusual in starting to take the subject seriously: there were seven Firsts in maths during the 1840s, more than any other college.[29] But there must still have been a good deal of time wasting. After 1850, therefore, the system was tightened up. Responsions—known since their introduction in 1808 as 'Little Go': they included simple mathematics as well as one Greek and one Latin author—were brought forward from the $6^{th}/9^{th}$ term to the $3^{rd}/7^{th}$ term; a new Intermediate Examination—compulsory classical Mods.—was instituted; and Final Examinations or 'Great Go' were revised to include a syllabus for both Pass and Honours degrees, the Honours section linking compulsory Lit. Hum. papers with alternative programmes in mathematics, natural science, and law and modern history. That was certainly a heavy burden, and it had to be eased in 1865 and 1871 by making optional the taking of a second Final School, first for Honours men and then for Pass candidates. But one key change, which would transform the undergraduate intake, had yet to be accepted: a matriculation examination, taken prior to admission. Some colleges had informally adopted such a system by 1850; others—and these included BNC—erected no such hurdle, least of all for gentlemen commoners.[30] And the question of broadening, or reviving, the range of subjects studied had scarcely begun to be tackled.

---

[28] OU Commn. (*PP* (1852), xxii), Report, 62–3: Requirements for Honours and Uncertainty in Examinations. It was Dr Sheppard who added Aristotle's *Ethics* to the list in 1806; and it was Dr Hampden who introduced Butler. Bacon's *Novum Organon* first appeared in 1852. For the post-1850 syllabus, see ibid. 64–8: Statute of 1850, and M. Burrows, *Pass and Class* (1861), 10–15.

[29] Revd W. W. Stodart, in OU Commn. *(PP* (1852), xxii), Evidence, 231; Select Committee on ... Oxford and Cambridge, *PP* (1867), xiii, appendix 4.

[30] OU Commn. (*PP* (1852), xxii), Report, 68–70: Proposal to establish a Matriculation Examination. 'The university continues to shrink...[from] a public entrance examination...[for] fear of excluding the scions of noble families' (*Eclectic Rev.* 5th ser. 4 (1852), 229). By 1867 Responsions were 'verging towards a matriculation examination' (Revd H. G. Liddell, Select Committee, *PP* (1867), xiii. 262). But change was still resisted: 'This obvious remedy...[has] since the days of [Richard] Whately [of Oriel]...been constantly recommended by unanswerable arguments, and constantly defeated' (Goldwin Smith, in *Macmillan's Mag.* 35 (1877), 289).

Extraordinary, really: post-medieval Oxford, prior to 1850, taught little or nothing in the way of law, or medicine, modern languages, or even theology. There was some mathematics, a little physics, a very little chemistry, and of course a touch of divinity. But the bulk of college teaching scarcely spread beyond a conventional range of Greek and Latin texts, plus a smattering of ancient history, logic, and philosophy. And this in the university of Locke and Butler.[31] As for higher degrees, these had atrophied over the years into little more than relics of the medieval Faculty system. Oxford education in the 1840s may have been liberal, but it was also very limited. A whole spectrum of subjects—what Halford Vaughan neatly termed 'delightful gymnastics of the mind'—[32] had been effectively excluded from the University curriculum. The emancipation of the sciences—that is their examination in a separate School, independent of the classical curriculum—arrived only in 1849; law and modern history followed with their own School in 1850, though their separation had to wait until 1872. Meanwhile, the Brasenose of Gilbert and Harington—unchanged and unrepentant—awaited its deliverance at the hands of the reformers. Academically speaking, during the 1830s and 1840s, BNC was marking time. Gilbert was preoccupied with the distractions of religion; Harington with resistance to the whole notion of reform.

In 1837 Gilbert had been anti-Hampden, but certainly not pro-Tractarian. He was an old-fashioned High and Dry churchman, never a ritualist. Broad-church liberals and popish fellow-travellers were to him equally abhorrent. But it was Tractarian thinking which seemed to pose the most immediate threat. In March 1841, therefore, he joined the Hebdomadal Board in censuring Newman's *Tract XC*.[33] And in November that same year he took

[31] For example, 'the Chair of Moral Philosophy was virtually suppressed from 1673 to 1829, by the custom of giving it to the Senior Proctor, himself being one of the Electors' (OU Commn. (*PP* (1852), xxii), Report, 102, 105). Similarly, 'the Physical Sciences' were, before 1849, largely 'ignored in our Academical system' (Prof. C. Daubeny, ibid., Evidence, 268); the University seemed 'dead to the value of [Natural Science] as a gymnasium of the mind' (N. S. Maskelyne, ibid., Evidence, 286).

[32] Prof. H. H. Vaughan, ibid., Evidence, 86. He prophesied that there would be little progress 'in physical, historical and mathematical instruction' until the examination system had been 'emancipated . . . from classical and theological studies'. He also called for new chairs in aesthetics, moral philosophy, English history, European history, etc. (ibid. 87–8).

[33] Newman set out to demonstrate that the Thirty-Nine Articles were compatible with traditional Catholic teaching. In effect he was claiming, in Hurrell Froude's words: 'We are Catholics without the Popery, and Church of England men without the Protestantism' (*Remains of the Late Richard Hurrell Froude*, i (1838), 404: 25 Feb. 1835). This prompted a public protest by Thomas Churton of BNC—an evangelical disapproved of by Gilbert—and three other senior tutors. See R. W. Greaves, 'Golightly and Newman, 1824–45', *Jnl. Eccles. Hist.* 9 (1958), 209 *et seq.*

the lead in opposing Isaac Williams as a candidate for the Professorship of Poetry. Now Williams was indeed a poet; but he was also a Puseyite. So Gilbert nominated James Garbett, a Brasenose Tory with evangelical leanings. For his part, Garbett knew little of poetry.[34] But he shared with Gilbert an almost obsessive suspicion of Rome. Like Gilbert he was also a strong opponent of Whiggish schemes for university reconstruction. Garbett's election, therefore, became a symbolic defeat for both ritualism and reform. Within months Prime Minister Peel made Gilbert the ninety-second Bishop of Chichester, and Gilbert presented Garbett with a prebendal stall in that same delectable see.[35]

As Vice-Chancellor in 1836–40, it had fallen to Gilbert to lead the Oxford colleges in their resistance to the Whig programme of investigation and reform. Having pocketed his reward from the Tories, he settled down in Sussex to a new career as hammer of the ritualists. He fought the Revd John Purchas over incense; he fought the Revd A. D. Wagner over crucifixes; he fought the Revd J. M. Neale over confession. Each case became a *cause célèbre*.[36] Meanwhile, the Tractarians whom he had left behind in Oxford— outmanoeuvred and restless—blamed Gilbert's previous instrument of obstruction, the Erastian Hebdomadal Board. 'Ensconced in cod-fish and oyster-sauce', noted J. D. Dalgairns in 1844; 'impenetrable in their leather arm-chairs', the heads of houses had apparently 'turned out all the learning and earnestness' of the English Church; 'alas for Oxford! Rome, Rome, Rome, will be the only shelter for weary feet'.[37] And so in 1845 it proved, at least for quite a few. Safely installed at Chichester, Garbett remained loyal to his old Principal, publishing pamphlets in the Bishop's defence. Gilbert gratefully promoted him to an archdeaconry. And when in 1870 the time

---

[34] His only publication in this field was *De Rei Poeticae Idea* (1843). See Boase, i. 1120. Some of Williams's verses—'Keble and water'—appeared as *Lyra Apostolica* (1836). See *ODNB*.

[35] A. T. Gilbert, *Letter to Dr. Pusey about the Professorship of Poetry* (1841); Ward, *Victorian Oxford*, 114; *Letters of Rev. J. B. Mozley* (1885), 123, 126–7. Williams withdrew after an informal canvass showing him trailing Garbett by 623 votes to 921. Brasenose, New College, and St John's voted Garbett 'to a man'. The Fellows of BNC put up £80 to cover the 'peculiar circumstances' of the contest (V-P's Reg. 1835–43, fo. 175).

[36] A. T. Gilbert, *Proceedings . . . against . . . the Warden of Sackville College* (1853); *Pictorial Crucifixes: A Letter to the Rev. A. D. Wagner* (1852). See also A. O. J. Cockshut, *Anglican Attitudes: A Study of Victorian Religious Controversies* (1958); J. Bentley, *Ritualism and Politics in Victorian Britain* (Oxford, 1978); and *ODNB*. For a caricature of Gilbert punishing Purchas—'The Chichester Extinguisher'— see *Punch*, 25 Oct. 1868, 173 (pl. 34). His portrait at BNC by T. Phillips was exhibited at the RA in 1835.

[37] J. D. Dalgairns to J. M. Gresley: 10 Dec. 1844, quoted in Ward, *Victorian Oxford*, 116. For the flavour of contemporary debate, 1843–5, see [H. Rogers], 'Puseyism, or the Oxford Tractarian School', *Edinburgh Rev.* 77 (1843), 501–62 and 'Recent Developments of Puseyism', ibid. 80 (1844), 309–75; also [N. W. Senior], 'Oxford and Mr. Ward', ibid. 81 (1845), 385–98.

came for the Bishop's funeral eulogy, a Brasenose man was once again conveniently to hand. Gilbert's old colleague Whittaker Churton was by that date—to nobody's surprise—a Prebendary of Chichester.[38]

As Principal and Vice-Chancellor, Gilbert's disciplinary regime had been strict. In 1838 he warned the House of Lords Committee on the Great Western Railway Bill that this new form of transport might pose a novel threat to Oxford morals: the fleshpots of London were now too easily enjoyed.[39] But his control of undergraduates was not obtrusive. Over-frequent roll-calls, he believed, would represent 'a Mode of Discipline unsuited to the Age and Station and the manly Character of the young Men themselves; we cannot institute Military Discipline in the University; it must be one combining Restraint and Freedom'.[40] In matters of religion, however, Gilbert was clearly less tolerant; he certainly did nothing to soothe the religious turmoil of early Victorian Oxford. When in 1842 he bade farewell to BNC—accepting a presentation of silver in the library—he left behind him a college not entirely compatible with his own ecclesiastical image.

Look at the intake of 1837, and then—after a pause—at the intake of 1840. In 1837 there were thirty-five freshmen. Only seven came from major schools. Nine were from Lancashire or Cheshire, including four from MGS. Seven were the sons of clergymen, and no less than twenty became clerics themselves. Of these quite a number might be counted high church. Two actually went over to Rome: John Walker in the same year as Newman, 1845; Charles Garside as a result of the Gorham Judgement in 1850.[41] It was not a year for hearties: only three took up rowing seriously, and only one went into the army. And it was not a good year for gentry. Scarcely half a dozen came from landed families. There was only one gentleman commoner and he came to an unhappy end. His name was John Woodhouse.

---

[38] Obit, *The Guardian*, 23 Feb, 1870. See also J. F. Smith (ed.), *Manchester School Register*, ii (*Chetham Soc.* 73, 1868), 221–4; *The Times*, 22 Feb. 1870, 10 (obit) and 26 Feb. 1870, 5 (funeral). The bishopric of Chichester was worth £4,200 p.a., and included the patronage of forty livings. Gilbert materially assisted his blind daughter Elizabeth in her educational and philanthropic work for the blind (*O.D.N.B.; Brazen Nose*, v. 250). He was buried at West Hampnett, Sussex, where there is a memorial window by Clayton and Bell (1867).

[39] *PP* (1837–8), House of Lords, xx. 728, 756. Gambling was a particular temptation: 'there is no Vice which [is] more destructive' (ibid. 728).

[40] Ibid. 767. As Principal, Gilbert managed to prevent three 'improvident marriages' between rich BNC men and 'Female Characters . . . of the very lowest Description in Oxford' (ibid. 738). Gilbert's apprehensions with regard to railway travel were confirmed in the next generation by E. B. Pusey and T. V. Bayne (Select Committee, *PP* (1867), xiii. 378–407).

[41] He had been a curate at Margaret Street Chapel, then became chaplain to the last Catholic Earl of Shrewsbury. He wrote *The Impiety of Bartering Faith for Opinion* (1850) and *The Sacrifice of the Eucharist, and Other Doctrines of the Catholic Church Explained and Vindicated* (1875).

It was on 1 November 1840—a Sunday night, the eve of All Souls, at a meeting of the Phoenix—that Woodhouse raised his glass to the Devil, and dropped down dead at the dinner table. That is the legend, and there may be a measure of truth in it. The Vice-Principal at the time, the Revd Thomas Churton, returning down Brasenose Lane to his own rooms in VI, 4, claimed to see the ghost of the blasphemer being dragged through the bars of a window by a shadowy, diabolical figure. He raced round to the Lodge and hammered on the door. The porter gravely announced the death of Mr Woodhouse. Now the date is certainly correct. So is the fact of the dinner, and the identity of Woodhouse's rooms (III, 5). On the other hand, Woodhouse himself was not yet a member of the Phoenix, and his rooms—unlike those of Trafford in 1834—did not overlook Brasenose Lane. Did the fatal meeting therefore take place in a neighbouring room, the already ill-omened III, 3? On balance, that seems likely. Whatever the precise circumstances— such legends grow in the telling—the dinner party was hurriedly dissolved. Several Phoenix men resigned, including the college's leading oarsman, J. J. T. Somers Cocks. Pressure was brought to bear on the club by an angry SCR. Sunday meetings were abolished;[42] so too were toasts to His Satanic Majesty: a deplorable 'remnant of heathenism'.[43] As a peace offering, the remaining members presented the college with a boating prize known as 'the Phoenix Sculls', with silver medals to be competed for annually.[44] It would be going too far to point to this episode as a turning point in the history of BNC: in with Victorian morality, out with the riotous days of the Regency. But the college was indeed evolving, and the death of Woodhouse did have an effect. There would be no more gentlemen commoners. That epoch had ended. Somers Cocks—who eventually became a Roman Catholic—might legitim- ately be seen as a typal figure of the new Brasenose, in all its Christian muscularity.[45]

The strongest voices on the religious side among the intake of 1837 came from two evangelicals—Edward Garbett and T. G. Hatchard—and from one

[42] Phoenix Minutes, 3 Feb.1842 (SL.11 A 1/1/10).

[43] Ibid., 6 Nov. 1844; *Quat. Mon.* XIV. ii. 110. Garbled versions of this story—confused with the scandals of 1828 and 1834—are to be found in W. Maskell, *Odds and Ends* (1872), 108–12 and F. G. Lee, *Glimpses of the Supernatural*, ii (1872), 207. The next occupant of III, 3 was a stout Protestant, the Revd G. T. Driffield, author of *Popery Productive of Infidelity.*

[44] *Quat. Mon.* XIV. ii, 131: 1845.

[45] The Revd and Hon. J. J. T. Somers Cocks, scion of the Whig family of Somers, became Rector of Sheviocke, Cornwall; then seceded to Rome in 1856. He stroked the BNC Eight when it was head of the river in 1840, as well as the losing Oxford Eights of 1840 and 1841. The title of gentleman commoner was revived in 1908 as part of the quatercentenary celebrations.

man whose religious position defies definition: F. W. Robertson. Garbett was the younger brother of James Garbett, Gilbert's nominee as Professor of Poetry. As editor of *The Record* and the *Christian Advocate*, he broadcast evangelical opinions to a committed audience over a period of many years. The tone of his writings is best suggested by one of his early titles: *An Aggressive Protestantism the Best Safeguard against Romish Encroachment* (1851).[46] Like his elder brother, he became Bampton Lecturer at Oxford; like him too he had no sympathy at all with the Tractarians. Thomas Hatchard, on the other hand, son of the publisher and a homiletic author in his own right, adopted a rather more moderate position. Accordingly he rose steadily in the Church: he married a daughter of the Bishop of Jerusalem, and ended up Bishop of Mauritius.[47] In their different ways, Garbett and Hatchard both became men of influence; but neither achieved the celebrity of F. W. Robertson.

Pulpit oratory is an ephemeral art. Robertson is scarcely remembered now, outside ecclesiastical circles. But in his heyday—six tempestuous years as 'Robertson of Brighton', between 1847 and 1853—he was regarded as a phenomenon, the most charismatic preacher of the age. His religious views were idiosyncratic: neither high nor low, nor yet exactly broad; neither fundamentalist nor ritualistic, but with a distinct bias towards the 'theological left'. His mental development—from evangelical dogma to a kind of liberal 'inclusiveness'—chimed in well with the uncertainties of his generation.[48] Among his most significant writings was *An Analysis of Tennyson's In Memoriam* (1862). But in the end his influence depended not on his thinking but on his speaking. In an age of pulpit power, he was the preacher's preacher. And it is worth pondering for a moment just how he did it. 'The word extempore', he explained, 'does not exactly describe the way I preach. I first make copious notes; then draw out a form; afterwards write copiously, sometimes twice or thrice, the thoughts, to disentangle them, into a connected whole; then make a syllabus; and, lastly, a skeleton, which I take into the pulpit.'[49] Whatever the method, the result was volcanic. Dean Stanley called him 'the greatest preacher of the century'; Dickens said he was one of the greatest masters of elocution he had ever heard.[50]

As an undergraduate of older years—he came to Brasenose from Edinburgh—Robertson felt able to resist Newman. 'A man who crouches before

---

[46] Obits *The Record*, 14 and 21 Oct. 1887; *ODNB*.

[47] Obits *The Guardian*, 30 Mar. 1837, 367 and 6 Apr. 1870, 399; *ODNB*.

[48] S. A. Brooke, *Life and Letters of F. W. Robertson*, ii (1866), 150, liii [1852].

[49] Some of the notes for his sermons survive (ibid. ii, Appendix iii).

[50] Mozley, *Letters* (1885), 335: 1 Dec. 1873; *ODNB*. His only rivals were Thomas Chalmers of Scotland and Henry Melvill of St Paul's; and perhaps the great Unitarian preachers, W. E. Channing and James Martineau.

a crucifix', he explained, 'or trembles before the sacrament, and does not bow his whole heart in adoration of the good, the holy, the true, is not religious but superstitious...It is all cowardice.'[51] As a young ordinand in Cheltenham, however, he rejected with equal vehemence the dogmatism of the evangelicals: 'They tell lies in the name of God.'[52] Language like that left him vulnerable to both sides of the debate; he became a kind of 'theological Ishmael'.[53] In some ways he occupied a central position, placing himself vaguely within the spectrum of broad-church opinion. He certainly preferred Jowett and Stanley to Keble and Pusey. But he never took up the challenge of German higher criticism; and he preferred the thinking of Andrewes and Hooker to that of any contemporary.[54] All this made him difficult to accommodate. Samuel Wilberforce—'I give my clergy a large circle to work in'—assigned him to the poor parish of St Ebbe's. That suited Robertson's sense of mission: 'I am not, and never shall be, at ease with the upper classes.'[55] But at St Ebbe's the undergraduates attended too: they 'hung breathlessly on every word he uttered'; they loved [that] 'tremulous, clear-ringing, musical voice'.[56] Trinity Chapel Brighton, however, offered Robertson something still more precious: the prospect of independence.[57] In Brighton his audience expanded hugely and his sermons became electrifying:

motionlessly erect in the pulpit [recalled Stopford Brooke] hands loosely lying by his sides or grasping his gown; his pale, thin face, and tall, emaciated form, seeming, as he spoke, to be glowing as alabaster glows when lit up by an inward fire. And, indeed, brain and heart were on fire. He was being self-consumed...he would go on uninterruptedly for hours...[58]

Not all his congregation were enthusiastic. Some mistook his radicalism for socialism. True, the Chartists, and the revolutionaries of 1848, did ignite his imagination; but his instincts were essentially High Tory. He was a

---

[51] Brooke, *Robertson*, ii. 275: 28 Sept. [1846], to his wife.

[52] Ibid., i (1866), 108 [1843]. Robertson was bitterly attacked in *The Record* (ibid., ii (1866), 17–18, 76).

[53] Ibid., i (1866), 110: 1843; ii (1866), 149, liii. He thought the eucharist was more than commemoration, but less than transmutation (ibid., i (1866), 161–3: 3 Jan. 1849 and ii (1866), 162–4). He thought baptism confirmatory rather than miraculous. See ibid., i (1866), 126; 162–3: Jan. 1849; 334: 9 Mar. [1850]; ii (1866), 66–70 xxix [1851].

[54] For a summary of the broad-church position, see [Frederick Harrison], 'Neo-Christianity', [a review of] *Essays and Reviews* (1860) in *Westminster Rev.* 74, NS 18 (1860), 293–332.

[55] Brooke, *Robertson*, i. 125 and 128–9: 3 May 1847; ii (1866), 285–6: 11 Nov. [1846].

[56] Ibid., i (1866), 129; ii (1866), 317: A. J. Ross.

[57] Built in 1817 by Thomas Read Kemp as a Dissenting chapel; bought for the Church of England in 1825 by the Revd Robert Anderson; its central feature was a pulpit 'resembling a huge vase standing on an Ionic fluted column' (H. Henson, *Robertson of Brighton* (1915), 106–8).

[58] Brooke, *Robertson*, i. 190–3.

romantic paternalist with a smouldering social conscience. 'My tastes are with the aristocrat', he explained, 'my principles with the mob.'[59] He preferred Carlyle and Ruskin to Fourier or Louis Blanc.[60] But religion in his scheme of things was potentially a powerful social force. 'Christianity', he believed, 'must come in to balance and modify political economy'.[61] Ultimately he regarded the 'fossils' of religious dogma as simply symbolic truths; symbols which reinforced the 'sublime feeling of a Presence', the 'realities' of 'moral goodness and moral beauty'. Those were his yardsticks, not the 'Bibliolatry' of the evangelicals or 'the infallibility of Romanism'.[62] 'My God is not a philosopher's god', he concluded; 'not a first cause, nor a machinist . . . [He is] the Lord of Right and Love.'[63] By comparison, he concluded, 'Romanism is not finality, but only uncouth stammerings of truth.'[64]

Robertson lived out his life in mental turmoil. His vitality—the 'lightning' of his intellect—was extraordinary. In Lady Byron's glorious phrase, 'his very calm was a hurricane'.[65] He belonged to no party; he founded no school; and his reputation—except in America—lasted little longer than the memory of his voice. In the end he died of 'brain fever', at the age of 37; and the Brighton shopkeepers cried in the street.[66]

[59] Brooke, *Robertson*, i (1866), 126, xli: 1852. He favoured Catholic Emancipation, and thought that 'retribution' would overtake Irish landlords (ibid., 140, l: 1852; ii (1866), 140–2, l).

[60] Ibid., i (1866), 97 [1843]; i (1866), 270–1 [1850]; ii (1866), 24–6 [1851], and 50 [June 1851].

[61] Ibid., ii (1866), 8: July 1851. 'To get a dish of green peas, or young potatoes, on a West-End table, how much toil and unknown deprivation must be gone through by human beings!' (ibid., ii (1866), 53: June 1851). On the other hand, he foresaw the danger of over-mighty trade unions: 'they will be [the] bloated aristocracies of the year 2000' (*ibid.* 55, xxiii [1851]).

[62] Ibid., i (1866), 120, xv: 1846 and 181, xxviii [?1850]; ii (1866), 92, 149, liii: 1852. 'He is liberal in his opinions; and though he is alarmed by the Puseyites, he seems to dislike the Evangelicals much more. I like him much' (H. Crabb Robinson, *Diary, Reminiscences and Correspondence*, iii (1869), 281: 23 Oct. 1846).

[63] Brooke, *Robertson*, i. 343–41, lxxx: Sept. 1850; ii (1866), 42: 21 May 1851. 'There may be a First Cause . . . but . . . I only believe in him as I believe in electricity [or] gravitation. . . . Truth is felt, not reasoned out.'

[64] Ibid., ii (1866), 55–8, xxiv: 1 July 1851, to a Roman Catholic friend, 'Mrs. . . . '. 'Mariolatry and purgatory are material and gross statements of spiritual facts'; 'fossils' rather than 'lies' (ibid., i (1866), 178: Oct. 1849 and ii (1866), 40, 161: 17 May 1851).

[65] Ibid., ii (1866), 324, 330, quoted by A. J. Ross.

[66] Ibid., ii (1866), 242–7; F. Arnold, *Robertson of Brighton* (1886), 249, 250, 254, 273, 287. He was buried in Brighton Cemetery. A memorial window by Wailes of Newcastle was placed on the north side of Brasenose Chapel in 1861–2 (V-P's Reg. 11 June 1861, fos. 61, 73; 11 April 1862, f. 73v), 'and the sun shines now through the letters of his name upon the spot where he dedicated his youth to God' (Brooke, *Robertson*, ii. 256–7). Subscribers included Tennyson and Ruskin. A bust (1853) by W. Pepper sen. was presented to Brighton Pavilion, with versions for the Bodleian Gallery and BNC. Another version was presented to the college in 1914 (V-P's Reg. 2 Dec. 1914, fo. 57); it was damaged and replaced by a replica in 1937 (V-P's Reg. 10 Feb. 1937, fo. 209). By 1866 fourteen editions of the first volume of Robertson's *Sermons* had been

But then Robertson was not a typical Brasenose man. He enjoyed moments of college life: entertaining in Eights Week in his quarters (I, 5) next to the SCR; pacing Old Quad with Tommy Churton, locked in theological debate. But he had no wish for 'an Oxford fellow's selfish, dronish life'. In fact he condemned Oxford for its 'deadly torpor... the curse of God will fall on it'.[67] What he sensed, no doubt, was the presence of too much religion and too little faith.

There was certainly plenty of formal religion at Brasenose in the 1840s. And sometimes it was deeply felt: Frederick and John Marshall were sent down in 1843 for demonstrating in the Sheldonian against the award of an honorary doctorate to a Unitarian.[68] But on the whole the formularies of religion were diluted by the social and sporting interests of undergraduates and dons. These are the attitudes that we have to examine—robust, low-temperature Anglicanism—if we are ever to understand early Victorian Brasenose.

Take the intake of 1840. There were thirty-one freshmen that year, plus two who migrated from elsewhere. Very few came from top public schools: one from Eton, three from Harrow, four from Rugby. The majority hailed from less fashionable places: one each, for example, from Tonbridge and Haileybury; one each from Wakefield, Newark, and Oswestry; and of course three more from MGS. Socially speaking, the freshmen of 1840 were scarcely smart. Apart from Samuel Reynolds Hole and Alexander Penrose Forbes—both of whom deserve separate treatment—only four can be classified as gentry: G. H. Egerton (younger son of a baronet), Llewellyn Irby (younger son of a baron), Charles Isham (heir to a baronetcy), and John Tyrwitt Drake (of Shardeloes in Buckinghamshire; master of point-to-point). There was a sprinkling of commercial money: Richard Barton, for example, scion of a wine-shipping family from Liverpool. But the Brasenose cohort of 1840 was by no means plutocratic. Geographically, its catchment area followed college tradition: thirteen of the thirty-one were born in Lancashire or Cheshire. And, again traditionally, all but seven out of thirty-three came up as commoners. They had not been chosen for their learning. Only two took Firsts: J. E. Cook, a future barrister and E. T. Turner (pl. 33), a future Fellow, of whom more

published, twelve of the second, twelve of the third, and three of the fourth (ibid., ii (1866), 255). For later selections, see *F. W. Robertson's Sermons*, ed. E. Rhys, 3 vols. (1906); *Lectures, Addresses, etc. of F. W. Robertson*, ed. S.A. Brooke (1876); C. B. Robertson and I. Maclaren (eds.), *Sermons Preached at Brighton* (1898); C. Smyth, *The Art of Preaching* (1940); *The Preaching of F. W. Robertson*, ed. G. E. Doan (Philadelphia, 1964).

[67] Brooke, *Robertson*, i. 33–4, 47, 128: 1839, 1840, 1847. Robertson resented the inadequate care he received from Thomas Bazely, but Thomas and Whitaker Churton guided him helpfully towards ordination (ibid. 35, 37: 1840).

[68] For this event, see V. H. H. Green, *Religion at Oxford and Cambridge* (1964), 273–4.

later. What marked out these men of 1840 was their straightforward acceptance of the established Church. Only six out of thirty-three were themselves the sons of clergy; but no fewer than twenty-one—nearly two-thirds of the intake—went into holy orders. By contrast, only three went into law, and only one into the army. Of course, clerical ambitions did not necessarily guarantee good behaviour. In November 1843, Holland Lomas, J. H. Sykes, Arthur Evans, and Edward Pickering were discovered 'playing at cards'—a euphemism for gambling—one Sunday evening. Apparently they carried on well into Monday morning. Lomas was sent down—after all they were using his rooms (III, 3 again)—the others were simply rusticated.[69] But all four proceeded to go into the Church. Pickering became a chaplain in South Africa. Lomas even published an essay entitled *The Unfruitful Vineyard*. For most of this generation of Brasenose men the Church of England remained central to their view of a career. Some, like J. C. Bagshaw, became missionaries in the colonies. Others, and they were the majority, followed high church routes to preferment. Hole became Dean of Rochester; Samuel Plant and G. H. Egerton became Prebendaries of Lichfield; J. T. Pigot a Prebendary of Exeter. Rather more famously, Forbes became Bishop of Brechin; a very high churchman in a land of Presbyterians, in effect the Scottish Pusey.

But before we come to Bishop Forbes, first of all a word about Dean Hole. Samuel Reynolds Hole came from a family of Nottinghamshire gentry with business interests in Manchester and the West Indies. He went up to BNC in March 1840, intending to read for a First in preparation for the Church. On arrival, his rooms (IV, 6) struck him first of all as a refuge: 'small but snug... the bedroom a mere slice of masonry, just holding the inmate and his appurtenances; but of all dormitories [it was] the most delightful.' His possessions seemed more than enough: 'item, one joint-stock servant... 6 dessert and 6 tea spoons, real silver, hall marked and engraved with family crest, three dozen of port and ditto sherry, an armchair which might have been made for Falstaff, and a series of richly coloured prints.'[70] Here was 'stillness and peace'; here too, however, was temptation.

In October 1840, the future Dean encountered John Tyrwritt Drake. This 'siren' of Old Quad—'black velvet cap and scarlet coat, a bird's-eye blue tie, buff kerseymere waistcoat, buckskin breeches and pale top [boots]'—proceeded to introduce him to the hunting field.[71] From now on it would be the Bicester and the Heythrop rather than the Bodleian and the Radcliffe Camera. Together Hole and Drake were recruited to the Phoenix; together

---

[69] V-P's Reg. 11 Nov. 1843, fo. 11.
[70] *The Memories of Dean Hole* (1892), 322.
[71] *The Letters of Samuel Reynolds Hole*, ed. G. A. B. Dewar (1907), 6.

they discovered the delights of point-to-point;[72] together they defied the wrath of the Vice-Principal.

> How jollily, how joyously we live at B.N.C.!
> Our reading is all moonshine—the wind is not more free.[73]

Hole was not a rowing man. Hunting and boating were in practice incompatible. But it was during his time that Brasenose first staked out its status as a seriously sporting college. Football was not yet in vogue; rugby was scarcely formalized; golf had yet to come south; athletics had yet to be regularized; lawn tennis had yet to be invented. That left cricket in the summer and boating in the winter. The Varsity cricket match against Cambridge dates from 1827: the patron saint of rugby, BNC's William Webb Ellis, was actually in the team. The Oxford–Cambridge Boat Race dates from 1829.[74] But at college level, organized teams emerged more slowly. There was a BNC cricket team from at least 1835—only Brasenose and Christ Church had their own grounds—though there was little competition from other colleges until the 1850s. In rowing, however, inter-college rivalry was already fierce. Brasenose had staked its claim to boating supremacy as early as 1815, when it defeated Jesus for headship of the river. 'The Childe of Hale' went head again in 1822, 1826, and 1827. After that, as far as we know from sketchy records, there was something of a falling back. But in 1840–1 the college led the river again with no fewer than five men in the Varsity Eight: R. G. Walls, E. Royds, G. Meynell, J. J. T. Somers Cocks, and W. B. Garnett as steerer. The college colours had yet to be formalized. Blue and gold in 1839, red and gold in 1845, blue and yellow in 1857: it was not until 1858 that the Brasenose crew appeared definitively in sable and gold.[75] But whatever the colours, the spirit was already there. In 1846 Brasenose was one of the first colleges to boast a barge, taken over from the University Boat Club. In 1847 there were three BNC men in the Oxford boat; in 1851 and 1852 three more.[76] In the 1850s, and again in the 1860s, the college went head of the river in four successive years.

---

[72] 'At Brasenose we invented "The Grind" . . . [that is] a small company of undergraduates, meeting, after lectures and luncheon, at a rendezvous outside of Oxford, mounted on the ordinary hack, selecting some building or plantation two or three miles away, and racing towards it as our winning post' (Hole, *Memories*, 347).

[73] [Hole], Ale Verse, 1841. Another example of light verse is Hole's *Hints to Freshmen* (1847).

[74] S. E. Green, in *Oxford Today* (Michaelmas 2002), 66. Ellis became Rector of Menton, in the south of France, and was buried there in 1872, just a few weeks before the first Varsity rugger match. At BNC—living in I, 8 in 1828—he held an Ogle Scholarship (£1 per quarter) and a Somerset Iver Scholarship (5s. 9d. per quarter).

[75] *The Times*, July 1939, p. 18; [W. T. Coxhill], *Aeneinasensiana* (1941), 32.

[76] Details in *Brazen Nose*, iii., 244. Godfrey Meynell, who rowed four times for BNC and twice for Oxford, was the original 'Billy Blades' of *Verdant Green*.

This growth of collegiate action echoes a wider general enthusiasm. Georgian field sports had been individualist pursuits; now they were giving way increasingly to the corporate games of the Victorians. 'How they loved the river, and the boat', Hole remembered fifty years later; 'those grand, genial, brave-hearted, strong armed men! Again I see those eager faces... as they listen for the signal... and the eight oars dip and rise as one... "Bravo Brasenose!"'[77] Perhaps he was thinking of Edward Royds, a Cheshire cleric who rowed three times for Oxford and five times for BNC. In 1843 he joined the sporting immortals as one of the seven oarsmen—yes, seven—who defeated a full Cambridge Eight in the Grand Challenge Cup at Henley. When the Oxford stroke fell down in a dead faint just before the start, Cambridge refused to allow a substitute; some said because of the large sums of money already wagered on the result. Oxford stepped up gallantly, 'with seven working hands only... the bow oar being absent. Loud shouts of applause greeted this behaviour, and the Oxonians acknowledg[ed] it with a bow.' Hole was there to record the scene.

I shall never forget the roar of 'Bravo Oxford!' which reached us as the boats came into view, nor the amazement, which could not believe what it saw—the boats close together, and our own gradually drawing ahead, until the race was over, and, by half a boat's length, Oxford beat Cambridge with seven oars! Had they been the Seven before Thebes or the Seven Champions of Christendom, or the Seven Bishops, who stepped out of their boat at the Tower [of London], they could not have been cheered more heartily... some regarded [the result] as supernatural...[78]

Such excitement was not conducive to steady work. In 1843—the year he was initiated into the Apollo Lodge—Hole was rusticated for two terms 'for visiting, in company with an out-college man, the rooms of several undergraduates, and destroying their property'.[79] That out-college felon was presumably Drake: he went down the same year without taking a degree, and ended up—still hunting—at a rectory in Northamptonshire. Hole sailed on to a Pass degree. But in 1845 he seems to have turned over a new leaf. He joined the Ecclesiological Society, and embarked on a clerical career as a moderate high churchman. Once there, he managed to develop his skills as an occasional writer, while remaining essentially a sporting squarson. At Caunton in Nottinghamshire he was both priest and proprietor, a well-known hunting man and a famous gardener. He grew 400 varieties of roses on his estate; at Rochester, there were 135 varieties in his

[77] Hole, *Memories*, 348.
[78] Ibid. 348–50; *Quat. Mon.* XIV. i, 15; W. Tuckwell, *Reminiscences of Oxford* (1901 edn.), 113–14.
[79] V-P's Reg. 17 Feb. 1843, fo. 201.

deanery garden.[80] But he never lost his youthful appetite for words. Stainer set his hymns to music. John Leech introduced him to the table at *Punch*. Thackeray put him up for the Garrick and invited him to contribute to the *Cornhill Magazine*. As first President of the National Rose Society, he became an international figure. Tennyson christened him 'the Rose King'. In politics he was a staunch Conservative with Gladstonian sympathies. And as a popular preacher—fluent, plain spoken, down to earth; playing whist for small stakes, drinking in moderation—he retained a sizeable following, in England and in America too. His commanding presence— 6 ft 4 in, with a rasping voice—made him a powerful speaker at St Paul's; his enthusiasm for good company made him Grand Chaplain of Freemasons.[81] He even went back to Oxford, as Select Preacher in 1885– 6—forty-two years after rustication—in time to preside over the centenary dinner of the Phoenix.[82]

Hole's religious position was representative of his Brasenose generation. By 1840 undergraduates had begun to find the etiolated Anglicanism of chapel services dispiriting and drab. At that time, for example, there was no cross in BNC chapel, let alone a crucifix. All his life Dean Hole remained a loyal supporter of the established Church. When a memorial statue to Cardinal Newman was proposed in Broad Street, he denounced the idea as preposterous: 'the representation of a deserter...in a barrack-yard of the Church Militant'. But he was also a lifelong advocate of the 'reunion of Christendom on Catholic principles'; and he could well understand the hunger of his contemporaries for a more sympathetic expression of the Anglican tradition. 'I never heard a note of music in our college chapel', he recalled; 'the University sermons (I do not remember that any were preached in college) failed to impress the undergraduate mind, except when Newman, or Pusey, or Claughton [of Trinity] preached...It was a time in which ugliness and dirt were regarded as bulwarks of the Protestant faith, and beauty and order were "marks of the beast". Doctrine was bigotry, reverence was idolatry, and zeal was superstition.' In other words, cut off from both Catholic aesthetics and evangelical fervour, pre-Oxford Movement

---

[80] He wrote *A Book About Roses* (1869), which went through at least nineteen editions. His favourite roses were Gloire de Dijon (the old glory rose), La France, Mrs John Laing, and Marie van Houtte (*Country Life*, 14 Oct. 2004, 98–9: photo of Hole at Caunton Manor, 1899). Besides Caunton Manor, the Holes owned Guiana Island, Antigua.

[81] He joined the Apollo Lodge in 1842.

[82] *ODNB;* obits *The Times*, 29 Aug. 1904, p. 8 and *The Guardian*, 31 Aug. 1904, pp. 148–9; *Gardener's Chronicle*, 3 Sept. 1904 (portraits); *Vanity Fair*, 1895 (cartoon); W. P. Frith, *John Leech*, ii (1891), 80–8. Dean Hole believed that Rochester was the only place to order decanal gaiters: 'there is only one man in England who can make gaiters—all the others are alligators' (F. Pigou, *Phases of my Life* (1898), 355–6).

Anglicanism—and scholarship too—seemed in danger of shrivelling into monotony. Not that the Fellows themselves were necessarily to blame. Heads of houses—Gilbert in the 1830s, Harington in the 1840s—were respected dignitaries, but 'figure-heads rather than pilots ... sitting in serene expectation of bishoprics and deaneries'. College tutors—in the 1850s Thomas Chaffers would stand as a warning—were often men whose scholarly sympathies had apparently atrophied into pedantry. 'Learned ... just ... patient and kind', Hole admitted, they were often 'men of high moral integrity', even if they showed too much 'appreciation of their good old common-room port'. It was just that their roles had become habitual. They preached little and they published less. Their tenure was either too brief (a preliminary to marriage and a rectory), or too prolonged (a refuge in celibate old age). Their attitude to teaching and pastoral care was at best idiosyncratic, at worst negligent. 'No advice was offered', Hole remembered, 'no sympathy shown'. An undergraduate in search of moral counsel might well be met with incomprehension. 'If he meant confession and that sort of thing', one was curtly informed, 'he had better go to some popish priest'.[83]

Such was the mentality—wary of 'enthusiasm', suspicious of the very notion of sacramentality—that Hole's exact contemporary, Alexander Penrose Forbes, set out to change. Forbes of Brechin is now hardly a name to conjure with, but in his day he was a doughty polemicist and pastor. At Brasenose he was an unusual undergraduate. When he arrived in 1840 at the age of 22—descendant of an ancient Scottish house—he had behind him a varied education at Edinburgh Academy, at Glasgow University, and at Haileybury College. He had developed a talent for oriental languages, and he had already sampled a career as an administrator in India. Had it not been for several bouts of fever, he might well have stayed on in Madras. Instead he went back to university, and there encountered the Oxford Movement at full blast. Now it is worth emphasizing that the chronological span of this phase was

---

[83] Hole, *Memories*, 164–5, 316, 329–33. For a view by R. W. Buss, of 1842, showing a voluntary Sunday afternoon service at BNC, see V. A. Hüber and F. W. Newman, *The English Universities* (1843). This shows two candles on the altar; but the eagle lectern of 1731 still dominates, immediately in front of the altar rail; there is no inlaid marble cross, merely 'a large glory' on the reredos of 1733, regilded in 1819 (*Quat. Mon.* III, 29–30, pls. viii–ix and IV, pl. iv). The cross—minus the crucifix added in 1980—arrived only with Buckler's redecoration of 1860 (V-P's Reg. 1860, fos. 34, 37, 42, 44, 46, 49, 69). It was later hidden by a painting. The lectern was lowered c. 1860. The two chandeliers were replaced by gas lamps in 1865, and exiled to Coleshill church, near Amersham. They returned in 1887 (V-P's Reg. 20 June 1865, fo. 123 and 14 Dec. 1886, fo. 165). Weldon Champneys, Whittaker Churton, and (eventually) John Knott were evangelical influences. Hole set out his own position—Anglican but Catholic—in *The Catholicity of the English Church* (1878) and *Ritualism* (1883).

brief: 1833 Keble's Assize Sermon; 1841 Newman's *Tract XC*; 1845 the condemnation of 'Ideal' Ward by Convocation, and then Newman's departure for Rome. After that, the pendulum swung back the other way, towards liberalism and reform. Still, the impact of those twelve years on Oxford was seismic. Even Brasenose did not escape.

On [Newman's] afternoon sermons at St. Mary's, [Forbes recalled] men hung in rapt attention. Young men from the manor-houses and parsonages of the country, from the streets and squares of the city... came term by term under the charm of Oxford, and, in many cases, to Oxford owed their immortal souls... [Some] assembled in each other's rooms to sing the Canonical Hours in Latin during the season of Lent... [there was even] abstinence from hall on fasting-days,... conscientious attendance at Chapel,... evening sittings of the Mendicity Society... regular frequentation of the early Communion at St. Mary's... conscientious study... plenteous alms-deeds.[84]

Over to Rome went four prominent Brasenose men of an earlier generation: Edward Caswall, hymnologist, whom we have already met; William Leigh, church builder and patron;[85] Edward Badeley, Tractarian lawyer and enemy of the Privy Council;[86] and Samuel Grimshaw, ecclesiologist and landowner.[87] Over too went two of Forbes's closest contemporaries: Charles Garside, once curate of Margaret Street Chapel;[88] and R. K. Sconce, the grandson of Vicesimus Knox.[89] All six might be counted victims of 'Newmania'. But not Forbes. His career is worth at least a parenthesis.

As an MA and gentleman commoner, Forbes dined at high table, and customarily took his place with the Fellows in Common Room. Pusey became his closest friend; Gladstone his most influential patron; he was even trusted by Newman to seek out rare books on the Continent.[90] In those days, Hole found Forbes 'a delightful companion. No man could have [had] more solemn convictions, or a more reverential spirit; but the sunlit, silvery

[84] *Remains of the Late Rev. Arthur West Haddon*, ed. A. P. Forbes (1876), pp. xi–xii. For the impact of Newman's sermons, see R. W. Church, *The Oxford Movement* (1891; 1922), 139–45. One near contemporary at BNC, the Revd H. B. Bulteel, bitterly attacked Newman from an Irvingite perspective, in *The Oxford Argo* (1845). But many thought Bulteel 'deranged'; others even doubted his authorship of the *Argo*, suggesting R. Burdon. See Bodl. MS Top. Oxon. e. 165; also *ODNB* and Mozley, *Letters* (1885), 25: Feb. 1832.

[85] Converted 1844; endowed Adelaide Cathedral; began building Woodchester Park, and a monastery at Northfield, Glos.

[86] Converted 1850; supported Philpotts of Exeter in the Gorham case. See *Gent's Mag.*, NS 5 (1868), 688; *Letters of Mr. J. R. Hope-Scott*, ed. R. Ormsby (1884) and *ODNB*.

[87] Of Ernwood, Buxton, Derbys.; a neighbour of A. J. B. Beresford Hope.

[88] Converted 1850, following the Gorham Judgement. See *ODNB*.

[89] Converted 1848; to Australia as Rector of St Andrew, Sydney.

[90] *Letters and Diaries of J. H. Newman*, viii (Oxford, 1999), 301: 17 Oct. 1841 and 457: 9 Feb. 1842.

waves of his humour danced and gleamed above the depths.'[91] Others were
equally impressed. Matthew Arnold remarked on his 'experience of the
world'.[92] Dean Plumptre remembered him—with his 'dark hair and eyes,
his swarthy olive complexion'—like some Italian Jesuit transplanted into
Oxford: 'supple, subtle, courteous . . . with an underlying thoroughness and
earnestness of character'.[93] After winning the Boden Scholarship for Sanskrit
in 1841, Forbes was clearly marked out for promotion. By 1845 he was curate
of St Thomas's, Oxford;[94] by 1847 he was Vicar of St Saviour's, Leeds, a
powerhouse of northern ecclesiology. And when in 1848 the bishopric of
Brechin fell vacant Gladstone had no doubts: 'how about young Forbes?'[95]

Once established in the Scottish episcopate, 'young Forbes'—he was
scarcely 30 at consecration—wasted no time in stating his theological position. But it was only ten years later that matters came to a head. The
inheritance of the Scottish Episcopal Church was primarily a non-juring
high-church tradition. To this Forbes added his own experience of the
leading Oxford Tractarians. That involved, in Newman's phrase, the acceptance of dogma as 'mystery'; the notion of 'doctrine lying hid in language'.[96]
North of the border ideas like that—words as an engine of supernatural
truth—were inevitably suspect. On 5 August 1857 Forbes's Primary Charge
to the Diocesan Synod took the form of a manifesto on the eucharistic
presence. The burden of his argument lay in the presumption of Christ's
presence in the eucharist, a presence not 'symbolic' but 'objective'; not
'virtual' but 'real'.[97] The Scottish College of Bishops reacted angrily: they
suspected more than a whiff of popery. And there was opposition in England
too. In a sense, Forbes was replaying in Scotland—with encouragement from
Pusey and Keble—the earlier campaigns of the Tractarians. In doing so, as
Forbes himself admitted to Gladstone, he had allowed himself to be drawn
into a 'terrible mess'.[98] Despite written support from Keble, Forbes was
reprimanded in Synod by the majority of his episcopal colleagues. After a

[91] Hole, *Memories*, 163.

[92] Quoted in D. J. Mackey, *Bishop Forbes: A Memoir* (1888), p. xxix.

[93] Ibid.

[94] This included responsibility for the Boatmen's Floating Chapel, a barge on the canal
which served as a school on weekdays, and a chapel for boatmen and their families on Sundays
(T. Squires (ed.), *In West Oxford* (1928), 18–19).

[95] Mackey, *Forbes*, 59; R. Strong, *Alexander Forbes of Brechin: The First Tractarian Bishop* (Oxford,
1995), 48, 51.

[96] Quoted in A. Hardelin, *The Tractarian Understanding of the Eucharist* (1965), n. 31.

[97] In 1860 Forbes reiterated his belief in the 'real though not local, Objective Presence', that
is the 'real supernatural Presence of the Body and Blood of Christ, yea of Christ Himself,
my Lord and my God, in that Holy Sacrament' (quoted, Mackey, *Forbes*, 113 n. and Strong,
Forbes, 143).

[98] Quoted in Strong, *Forbes*, 115.

celebrated trial—with Keble himself attending—in February and March 1860, Forbes was formally subjected to a 'Declaration of Censure and Admonition'.[99] At least it was not an outright condemnation. On behalf of English high churchmen, A. J. B. Beresford Hope bade him take heart and be of good cheer: '10,000 congratulations. Benedictus! soft words butter no parsnips, ergo, censures break no bones.'[100] But after that trial Forbes found it difficult to regain his theological momentum. He would never be the leader of an Oxford Movement in Scotland.

Such dramas had little effect on Forbes's pastoral work. Church building, school building, hospital building; the foundation of sisterhoods; the establishment of libraries and lodging houses; visiting the sick, visiting the imprisoned: he exhausted himself in work for the poor and needy. 'When the cholera raged in Dundee [in 1853], he was to be seen among the afflicted ones, with his cholera mixture in one hand and his Prayer-book in the other.'[101] In the depths of that industrialized city—a Babylon of jute mills and tenements—Forbes was operating at the cutting edge of mid-Victorian capitalism. 'Upon what a fearful structure of practical atheism is the commercial success of this country founded! The creation of a God-forgetting, God-despising class seems the condition of our social advancement…'[102] Hence his need to proselytize and preach: Forbes was a Tory paternalist with the eye of a prophet. And yet there was still time for scholarship. 'After a day of district visiting in the slums…his great refreshment was a Canto of Dante.'[103]

Forbes's status as a theologian—he was closely involved with Dollinger and the Old Catholics—made him a figure of European standing.[104] He did not engage with the imperatives of evolutionary thinking. The knowledge of God as revealed in Scripture, he believed, could not be 'improved upon' like some steam engine or telegraph system.[105] So much for 'the Roman Catholic…theory of development'.[106] But that did not rule out a wider ecumenical approach. Hence his commitment to the Association for the Promotion

---

[99] Mackey, *Forbes*, 114; Strong, *Forbes*, 153.

[100] Quoted in Strong, *Forbes*, 153: 16 Mar. 1860.

[101] Dean Nicolson, quoted Mackey, *Forbes*, 91.

[102] Quoted in Strong, *Forbes*, 95.

[103] Quoted ibid. 69.

[104] Forbes's correspondence with Old Catholic Leaders such as Dr Ignaz von Dollinger of Munich, Bishop Hefelé, Archbishop Georges Darboy, and Cardinal J.-B. Pitra is preserved among the Brechin Diocese Papers, Dundee University Library.

[105] Quoted in Strong, *Forbes*, 96.

[106] Quoted ibid. 104–5, with reference to Newman's *Essay on the Development of Doctrine* (1845).

of the Unity of Christendom.[107] 'The present condition of Anglicanism', he warned Gladstone in 1867, 'is not only essentially provisional, but universally perilous. The days of establishments are past, and the two issues are Rationalism or Catholicity.'[108] The collective enemy now was the new liberalism—the 'advancing and all devouring Rationalism of the 19th century'.[109]

When Forbes died in 1875 aged only 58, worn out by years of controversy, thousands followed his coffin. One of his opponents in the trial of 1860 acted as pall bearer at his funeral.[110] The aged Pusey—with whom Forbes had often lodged at Christ Church—was heart-broken: 'When I think of him, my head gets dizzy; and when I speak of him I choke.'[111] From the pulpit of All Saints, Margaret Street, he was hailed as 'the Athanasius of modern times'.[112] Since then his reputation has faded. But his scholarship in matters theological—patristic, medieval, and modern—still ranks high.[113] His time may come again.

Not so those who opposed the Royal Commission of 1850. It is time to consider this episode more closely. After it, Brasenose would never be the same. Ever since the dramas of 1845—the persecution of Newman, the degradation of 'Ideal' Ward—Oxford Liberals had been determined on reform. Their chance came with Lord John Russell's Commission of Inquiry in May 1850. The Commissioners set about their work by first defining the collegiate ideal, and then drawing attention to its current deficiencies.

Colleges...may be defined as Charitable Foundations for the support of poor Scholars, with perpetual succession, devoting themselves to study and prayer,

---

[107] It received its *coup de grâce* with the Vatican's rejections of Anglican orders in 1896. See C. Butler, *The Life and Times of Bishop Ullathorne* (1926), i. 334–68; E. Norman, *The English Catholic Church in the 19th century* (Oxford, 1985), 215; M. D. Chapman, 'The Fantasy of Reunion: The Rise and Fall of the A.P.U.C.', *Jnl. Ecclesiastical Hist.* 58/1 (2007), 49–74. On the Anglican side, the APUC's founding father was the Revd F. G. Lee of Lambeth; on the Roman Catholic side, Ambrose Phillipps de Lisle of Leicestershire. In France its leading spirits were the Abbé Guettée, Cardinal J.-B. Pitra, and Archbishop Georges Darboy.

[108] Gladstone Papers, BL Add. MS, 44154, fo. 305: 15 Aug. 1867.

[109] Quoted in Strong, *Forbes*, 222.

[110] Ibid. 217. 'The event will be memorable in the annals of Dundee' (*The Times*, 16 Oct. 1875, p. 10).

[111] Quoted in Mackey, *Forbes*, 215.

[112] Commemorative sermon, quoted ibid. 208.

[113] For a bibliography of Forbes's writings, see Strong, *Forbes*, 261–3. These include *A Plea for Sisterhoods* [1849]; *The Sanctity of Christian Art* (Edinburgh, 1862); *The Church of England and...Papal Infallibility* (Oxford, 1871); *A Short Explanation of the Nicene Creed* (Oxford, 1852; enlarged 1866); *An Explanation of the Thirty-Nine Articles*, 2 vols. (Oxford, 1867–8); and *The Notes of Unity and Sanctity in Reference to Modern Scepticism* (1864). He translated the Scottish communion office into Greek (1865), and edited *Kalendars of Scottish Saints* (Edinburgh, 1872). His sermons were collected in four volumes (1857, 1860, 1862, 1870). Much of his correspondence is preserved in Pusey House, Oxford.

administering their own affairs, under the presidency of a Head within, and the control of a Visitor without, according to Statutes which were to be neither altered nor modified, and which were sanctioned by solemn oaths.[114]

In practice, Oxford fell short of that ideal in almost every respect. Undergraduate numbers had fallen catastrophically since the seventeenth century. By the end of the 1840s, there were only half as many residents as there had been in 1612;[115] and they were mostly young men of independent means. In a number of colleges, provision for the poor had wholly vanished. 'Oxford', announced the *Edinburgh Review*, 'has become simply a great public school.'[116] Non-residence was rife among the Fellows, and religious observance was frequently tokenistic. Tuition had in effect been privatized, through delegation to independent coaches. Professorial seminars on Germanic lines were still a very long way off. Only 22 out of 542 Fellowships were open: 12 at Oriel, 10 at Balliol. All the rest were hedged about with restrictions dating back centuries: that is, restrictions relating to locality or birth, patronage or education. There were even insufficient First-class graduates to fill the 35 or so closed Fellowships which fell vacant every year: the annual average number of Firsts was only 13.[117]

Nothing [complained the Revd Frederick Temple] could possibly be further from the founders' intentions than the present system. They meant the fellows to be resident. A large proportion hardly ever come near the place. They meant the fellows to live a strict and severe life. The comfortable common-rooms and £200 a year do not represent that. They meant the fellows to be bona fide students. Nothing could be more absurd than to call the present body such... In fact, it could hardly be possible to imagine a greater contrast than that between the ideal present to the Founders' minds of a poor hard-working student of theology, copying manuscripts, disputing in the Schools, living a life of monastic severity, and the fellow as he at present exists, with his comfortable rooms, liberty to roam over the world, and £200 a year with nothing to do for it... In short, a literal interpretation of the Founders' wills has become a mere superstition... [Reform] is not an interference with private property, for the property is not private; it is not the betrayal of a trust, for the trust was essentially conditional; it is not a departure from the intentions of the founders... [namely] the advancement of learning and religion... [Finally] it is demanded by common justice, for the colleges are now injuring the University, under whose shelter they were meant to live.[118]

---

[114] OU Commn. (*PP* (1852), xxii), Report, 136, 143–6.

[115] Calculations by C. P. Eden, quoted in Ward, *Victorian Oxford*, 140.

[116] *Edinburgh Rev.* 96 (1852), 242.

[117] Ward, *Victorian Oxford*, 162.

[118] 'If no other change were made than to throw all the fellowships open and secure that the elections were honest, all other reforms would follow spontaneously' (Revd F. Temple, in OU Commn. (*PP* (1852), xxii), Evidence, 129).

It was time—in Brodrick's trenchant phrase—to assert 'the interests of the living against the posthumous control of the dead'.[119]

At Brasenose the dead hands of past benefactors had by no means been eliminated. Over the course of three centuries nearly 100 Fellows had been elected on the basis of kinship: 34 Port, 24 Williamson, 19 Elton, 21 Frankland. Such elections were not invariably unworthy. Many of those appointed turned out to be reputable scholars. Since the days of Frodsham Hodson indeed, the college had done its best to appoint on merit. But without some form of competition, even the most scrupulous election could be said to lack validity. Over the years applications for closed Fellowships had been based on arguments of consanguinity or affinity that even then seemed quite fantastic. H. W. Maddock acquired a Williamson Port Fellowship in 1827 by tracing his pedigree back twenty generations to Stephen de Longspee, Justicion of Ireland in 1260, descendants of whom had married, three centuries later, each of the three daughters and co-heiresses of Sir John Port II. Nor was that the most extraordinary claim. In 1846 J. W. Barlow secured a Fellowship on the same foundation on grounds of his cousinage with Ferdinando Hastings, sixth Earl of Huntingdon, a great-great-grandson of one of the co-heirs of Sir John Port II, by virtue of their common descent from the first Baron Stanley (1406–59), whose great-great-great-great-great-granddaughter was Ferdinando's mother.[120] Well, Barlow was the last to hold such a Fellowship. At his death in 1859 he was commemorated by a stained glass window in chapel.

The argument for some form of redistribution—transferring college endowments to University lectureships and chairs—was in general hard to refute. The argument for opening Fellowships to competition by merit—regardless of local or sectarian affiliation—was in practice unanswerable. Likewise the closed links between particular schools and particular colleges: in the long run they would have to go too. The case for an equitable expansion of undergraduate numbers, based on a wider system of competitive scholarships, was an idea whose time was certainly overdue; similarly, the argument for a radical broadening of the syllabus. And as for streamlining administration—rationalizing representation and expanding the executive functions of Congregation at the expense of both Hebdomadal Board and Convocation—that was a cry which would resonate endlessly down the years. But these things take time. The Royal Commission was appointed in 1850, and reported in 1852. Then came the response, the Report and Evidence of the

---

[119] G. C. Brodrick, *What are Liberal Principles?* (1877).
[120] G. D. Squibb, *Founder's Kin* (Oxford, 1972), 107, 109, 111; E. G. C[ollieu], in *Brazen Nose*, xvi/1. 49–53.

Hebdomadal Board. Parliamentary legislation followed in 1854; implementation by parliamentary Executive Commissioners was not completed until 1858.[121] The process was slow; but the momentum was unstoppable. Oxford emerged, after eight years of dispute, irreversibly changed. By the end of the 1850s, Fellowships had been largely opened to laymen, even if they were still supposed to be celibate; undergraduate numbers had begun to expand; syllabus reform had been given fresh impetus; and Dissenters had been admitted as undergraduates, even if they had to wait until 1871 for full equality at degree level. And the symbols had changed too. The annual University sermon commemorating King Charles's Martyrdom was allowed to lapse. So was the annual Brasenose service commemorating Charles II's return. Congregation was now actually debating in English rather than Latin.[122] 'Everything cannot go exactly as we wish', remarked Max Müller with satisfaction; 'but the avalanche rolls in the right direction.'[123]

Under Principal Harington (pl. 35), Brasenose did its best to ignore the Royal Commission altogether. The Common Room was by no means wholly Tory: John Ormerod might well have been elected Regius Professor of History on the death of Dr Arnold, had he not been too well known as a Whig.[124] But the Principal could rely on the support of several Fellows. James Garbett, for one: he dismissed the establishment of the Commission as an echo of Stuart autocracy; 'a despotic stretch of antiquated prerogative'.[125] As for the Governing Body as a whole, when approached by the Commission, it drafted a negative reply which comes down to us as magisterial even in summary form:

The [old] Statutes have worked very well and there is [already] a workable method existing for changing or improving them. If a College is delinquent in monetary

[121] The opening of Brasenose Fellowships was smoothly settled by Jan. 1856; under the new arrangement, Fellows had to take holy orders within ten years of their MA (Goldwin Smith to Gladstone, BL Add. MS 44303, fos. 93: 1 Feb. 1856 and 117: 19 June 1867). See also MSS of the OU Commn., PRO HO 73/37–40.

[122] 'It is a strange solecism to conduct the business of the nineteenth in the language of the first [century] . . . If our statutes are intended to be understood and obeyed, they ought to be written in the vernacular language, and not in a style of barbarous Latin, which would puzzle Cicero as much as it does the moderns' (H. E. Strickland in OU Commn. (*PP* (1852), xxii), Evidence, 99).

[123] *Life and Letters of . . . Max Müller*, ed. Mrs Müller (1902), i. 173–4. 'Young Oxford is all with you. Every year more men obtain the reward of their industry through your legislation. But old Oxford takes a long time in dying' (Goldwin Smith to Gladstone, BL Add. MS 44303, fo. 140: 19 June 1859).

[124] Peel Papers, BL Add. MS 40510, fos. 239, 243; and J.P. Wynter to Duke of Wellington, 20 July 1842, in BL Add. MS 40459, fo. 257.

[125] Cox, *Recollections*, 356, 388. For a spirited defence of the status quo, see *Quarterly Rev.* 61 (1838), 203–38.

matters, the Courts of Common Law are open. The proposal invades rights, destroys the visitatorial jurisdiction, introduces new Statutes, prejudices the independence of the College and is detrimental to the general interests of Learning, Virtue and Religion.[126]

On the Hebdomadal Board, Harington was among the leaders in securing counsel's opinion against the Commission's constitutional legality. BNC recruited four weighty lawyers from Lincoln's Inn, and weighty too was their opinion. But they in turn were trumped by three Law Officers of the Crown.[127] 'Grounds of public policy' upstaged once and for all the 'legal hocus-pocus' of reversionary privilege.[128] In Convocation, however, Harington continued to argue against cooperation with the Commission.[129] Memories of James II and the siege of Magdalen; appeals to the statutory rights of independent corporations; cries of the 'Church in Danger': Harington could count on a substantial body of support, particularly among the other heads of houses. But with the Whigs in power in London, and the Liberals ascendant in Oxford, the movement for reform began to appear irresistible. BNC was left with one last card to play. The college refused even to give evidence to the Commission. Its position was by no means indefensible. Legal opinion was divided; and Brasenose—by comparison with Magdalen, Merton, New College, or even Queen's—could be presented as almost a paragon of progress. Not that its recent record was blameless. In 1838 J. A. Ormerod had been elected to a Fellowship on very vague grounds of consanguinity: probably some putative kinship with Principal Meare.[130] But in general the Fellows seem to have been anxious to put their house in order. As early as 1827 the college had petitioned the Hulme Trustees to open up their

---

[126] Petition [*c.*1851], summary: Press mark 42.25.

[127] OU Commn. (*PP* (1852), xxii), appendix B, 27–38. An appeal by both Brasenose and the University to the Queen in Council was equally fruitless. BNC's petition contains a prophetic note: 'If the authority of this Commission is admitted, the College may be exposed, at all future times, in the fluctuation of Political parties, to attacks and influences very injurious to its peace, and to the steady performance of its duties' (MR 5 L7/41). Lord Robert Cecil was similarly perceptive: reform of Oxford by Parliament would eventually turn Oxford and Cambridge into 'pensioners of the State' (*Hansard*, cxxxii, cols. 711–14: 7 Apr. 1854).

[128] C. Neate, in OU Commn. (*PP* (1852), xxii), Evidence, 239. This had been Sir William Hamilton's argument in 1834: 'A University is a trust confided by the State to certain hands for the common interest of the nation; ... [but] a University may, and ought, by the State to be from time to time corrected, reformed, or recast' (*Discussions of Philosophy* (1852), 538).

[129] Bodl. MS Top. Oxon. c. 286, fos. 3–12. In 1850 it was Harington who moved the resolution that Jeune of Pembroke, a leading reformer, be excluded from the Board's discussions; not surprisingly, a state of 'feud' existed between Mrs Harington and Mrs Jeune (J. H. C. Leach, *Sparks of Reform* (Oxford, 1994), 35). But Harington and most of the BNC Fellows had confidence in Gladstone's management of change through his position as MP for Oxford University (BL Add. MS 44372, fos. 77, 88 and 44373, fo. 313: 1852–3).

[130] Squibb, *Founder's Kin*, 76.

endowments to full-scale competition; and ever since Frodsham Hodson, First-class men had been consistently recruited to Fellowships and Tutor-ships.[131] Only Christ Church could point to greater numbers. Only Oriel and Balliol could claim higher academic distinction. On the eve of reform, BNC was prosperous, populous, and proud.

But by 1850 that was no longer enough. Brasenose was still in some ways a very 'close' college. Like New College and St John's, it had links with particular schools—Manchester, Marlborough, Hereford—which smacked too much of monopoly. Its richest source of income, the Hulme Trust, was vulnerable to charges of exclusivity. Like Queen's, however, Brasenose cherished its territorial loyalties, in particular to Lancashire and Cheshire. These had once been a source of strength; in the railway age they seemed anachronistic.[132] In any case, by the end of the 1840s, the nature of Oxford discourse had shifted: from theology to economics; from religion to re-form.[133] Harington was caught in that transition. And, at a crucial moment, fate took a decisive hand. When the Commissioners' Report—'the Great Blue Book'—appeared at last in May 1852, it became compulsory reading, not least for the Chancellor of the University. On 14 September the aged Duke of Wellington took it to his bedroom 'with a pencil in it'. 'I shall never get through it', he was heard to mutter; 'but I must work on.'[134] Next day he

---

[131] 'The College of Brazen Nose takes, next to Christ Church, the largest share in the education of Oxford youth, and in proportion to the number of members on its foundation, a larger [share] than even Christ Church itself. It does this under the further disadvantage, that all its Fellowships are restricted to certain Parishes, Counties, or Kindred. Fortunate it is for the College that the accidental claim to locality or birth is so frequently combined with the highest literary distinction. But it is not in the nature of things that this should always be the case' (VP's Reg. 2 Mar. 1827, fo. 75). In 1850, out of fourteen Fellow-Tutors, all but two had Oxford Firsts; the only Cambridge man, J. Walker, had been eighth wrangler in 1830 (Gladstone Papers: BL Add. MS 44566, fo. 297). For notices advertising vacancies of a Port Fellowship (1846) and a Foundation Fellowship (1849), see ibid., fos. 299–300. See also Ward, *Victorian Oxford*, 161.

[132] Even though, in practice, Lancashire and Cheshire represented a populous catchment area ('Correspondence respecting...Improvement in the Universities and Colleges of Oxford and Cambridge' (*PP* (1854), l, 246–7).

[133] 'Controversy had worn itself out; the *ferrea via*, or railroad...attracted even the clergy more than the *via media*. Instead of High Church, Low Church or Broad Church, they talked of high embankments, the broad gauge, and low dividends: Brunel and Stephenson were in men's mouths instead of Dr. Pusey and Mr. Golightly; Mr. Hudson [the Railway King, whose son was entered for Christ Church] was in the ascendant instead of Dr. Faussett, and speculative theology gave way to speculations in railroad shares' (Cox, *Recollections*, 338).

[134] Ibid. 386. The Report was welcomed by *The Times* (22 May 1852, 6 and 28 Aug. 1852, 8); endorsed by *The Guardian* (1852, 45, 345, 681); and opposed (by J. B. Mozley) in the *Quarterly Rev.* (93 (1853), 152–238). Wellington was not wholly immobile: 'There is in Oxford not a Gentleman who dislikes innovation and change as much as I do. But I live in the World' (Wellington to Gilbert: 5 Nov. 1837, quoted in E. Longford, *Wellington*, ii (1972), 345).

was found dead in an armchair, and with his departure went the last obstacle to reform. Three months later Harington too was dead—the last Principal to be buried in chapel—and Brasenose turned its back on the politics of obstruction. BNC entered a new era with a new Visitor —the Bishop of Lincoln had also died in 1853—as well as a new Principal, a Principal committed to change.[135]

BNC's opposition had been based on concern for collegiate autonomy.[136] But in the end the college had little difficulty in swallowing the Commission's specific ordinances. In effect, the result of the Commission had been an acceptable compromise. The Oxford University Act of 1854 simply enabled each college to alter its statutes under the direction of a Board of Executive Commissioners. The colleges retained most of their independence vis-à-vis the University. Heads of houses kept much of their Hebdomadal power. Fellows escaped—thanks to a newly formed Tutors' Association—the full impact of professorial rule. It was an arrangement that BNC was very willing to endorse. By the end of 1853, as one Brasenose Fellow informed Gladstone, even 'anti-Reformers [had now come round to the] feeling that Reform must come'.[137]

Opening their governance to all Fellows, junior as well as senior; exposing Fellowships to open competition, free of limitation as to locality or birth;[138]

---

[135] G. F. Bowen told Gladstone that 'nothing but [these] successive deaths...had prevented us from maturing our plans [for reform] at an earlier period...The [new] Principal... will be supported by the whole body of the Fellows in removing all local restrictions, in throwing open to general competition all our Fellowships and Scholarships, and in carrying out all the other views embodied in Lord Palmerston's letter to the Chancellor, except that of making Fellowships terminable' (BL Add. MS 44377, fos. 96–7: 24 Jan. 1854). Cradock assured Palmerston that Brasenose wished to see 'the advantages of University education extended to a greater number of students, especially to those of limited pecuniary means' ('Correspondence respecting...Improvement' (*PP* (1854), l), 246: 8 Feb. 1854). In 1854 he provided £100 out of the emoluments of his own office for the maintenance of two open scholarships (V-P's Reg. 18 May 1854, fo. 169).

[136] 'The Principal and Fellows of this College...do not conceive themselves at liberty to publish information concerning their Corporate Revenues, or other internal affairs of their Society, at the instance of parties with the object of whose inquiries they are unacquainted, and for whose authority to inquire they can find no warrant, either in the Statutes of their Founders or in the Charter of their Incorporation' (Revd R. Harington to Revd A. P. Stanley: 2 Dec. 1850 in OU Commn. (*PP* (1852), xxii), Evidence, 335). The replies of Magdalen and Trinity were equally abrupt (ibid. 334 and 340).

[137] G. F. Bowen to Gladstone: 27 Dec. 1853 (BL Add. MS 44376, fos. 238–40). For the context of this grudging acceptance of reform, see the Hebdomadal Board's reply to the Commission: *Report and Evidence Upon the Recommendations of H.M.'s Commissioners for Inquiring into the State of the University of Oxford* (Oxford, 1853). For the Tutors' Association, see *Papers Published by the Tutors' Association* (Oxford, 1853–4), and A. J. Engel, *From Clergyman to Don* (Oxford, 1983), 43–9.

[138] V-P's Reg. 11 May 1856, fo. 192.

capping, even equalizing, the stipends of senior and junior Fellows;[139] abolishing seven tied scholarships and suppressing four Fellowships, while applying their endowments (£1,190 p.a.) to the funding of twelve open scholarships;[140] rearranging the Somerset and Hulme foundations; removing a variety of obsolete rules and titles;[141] even installing in their Common Room the Camden Professor of Ancient History:[142] all these changes could be tolerated by BNC once the legitimacy of the Royal Commission had been accepted. Much more drastic were the recommendations of the Commission as regards the University as a whole. The remodelling of its administration; the expansion of its mandate into the field of collegiate registration; the multiplication of professorships and lectureships; the reconstitution of the 'departments of Physical Science'; the redistribution of Fellowship endowments, upwards to professors, downwards to scholars;[143] the creation of new Fellowships in new subjects;[144] to say nothing of a veritable bonfire of supposedly irrefragable oaths—here indeed was a programme for radical change.

[139] 'In Brasenose College the duty or the power of sealing leases belongs to a seniority of six, and all fines or foregifts are divided between those who are intrusted with it. The practice [resulting in 'a too great inequality... between the Senior and Junior Fellows; a few Fellowships being worth upwards of £500 a year.'] ... is at variance both with the letter and the spirit of the Statutes, and is injurious to the best interests of the Society' (OU Commn. (*PP* (1852), xxii), Report, 170: Limitation in the Value of Fellowships). Fourteen Brasenose Fellows formally accepted a commutation of fines in 1857–8 (MR 5 L7/20; V.-P.'s Reg. 21 Dec. 1857, fo. 3). The Principal had already commuted his double share of fines (c. £714 p.a.) to £600 p.a. (V-P's Reg. 18 May 1854, fo. 169; Ordinance III, 3, 1857).

[140] V-P's Reg. 24 May 1856, fo. 194ᵛ (Fellowships). Frankland, Claymond, Ogle, Binks (Stoddard), Henley, Church, and Yate Scholarships were all abolished in 1857.

[141] e.g. the need to appoint 'a Lecturer to train Students in Sophistry, Declamations, Recitations, and Doubts' (OU Commn. (*PP* (1852), xxii), Report, 228: Brasenose). For negotiations 1856–7 between Brasenose and the Commissioners, see MR 5 L7/35–45. For the new Ordinances, see *London Gazette*, supplement 2 July 1857, pp. 2296–301 and *Ordinances Framed by the University Commissioners... in Relation to Brasenose College* (Oxford, 1862).

[142] J. A. Ormerod privately protested. 'Objectionable: Exeter and Lincoln are not saddled' (MR 5 L7/35–45). But he still believed that, with judicious reform, BNC could 'stand... among the very first [colleges] in the University' (BL Add. MS 44377, fo. 106: Ormerod to Bowen, 20 Jan. 1854). BNC agreed to a subvention for both the Camden Professor and the Reader in Ancient History, from the funds of a fifth suppressed Fellowship. Since 1889 the Camden Professor has been, ex officio, a Fellow of Brasenose.

[143] 'What the State and the Church require... is not poor men, but good and able men, whether poor or rich' (OU Commn. (*PP* (1852), xxii), Report, 174: Application of College Revenues, iii).

[144] 'At present [Fellowships] are practically devoted to the Literae Humaniores... Mathematics in Oxford are a bad investment for intellectual, physical and pecuniary capital... This consideration is one of vast importance' (Prof. H. Vaughan, in OU Commn. (*PP* (1852), xxii), Evidence, 90).

But three major planks in the reform platform were still by no means in place: first the expansion of undergraduate numbers via a system of cheaper, non-collegiate residence;[145] second, the abolition of celibacy requirements;[146] and third, the final abrogation of religious tests.[147] All three would have to wait until the changes set in train by the Commissions of 1871 and 1877. Oxford would retain its status as a fortress of celibate Anglicanism for a little while longer. And any significant expansion of numbers would take longer still. When a select committee of the House of Commons returned to the subject in 1867 it found that the pace of change had slowed to a standstill. One history examiner complained that 'the tone of the place' was still 'aristocratic', 'luxurious', even 'apolaustic'; sport had become 'a positive nuisance'; the standard of Pass degrees was utterly 'miserable'; and 'ability...all over the country' was 'quenched and stunted

---

[145] Eventually resolved by the establishment of a Delegacy for Unattached (later Non-Collegiate) Students, living in licensed lodgings.

[146] Restrictions on marriage had two advantages: the maintenance of residential college life, and a faster turnover of Fellowships, which prevented 'the choking of Foundations, through the too long retention of Fellowships' (Revd R. Scott, ibid., Evidence, 113). 'After a lengthened discussion and much variety of opinion' (e.g. V-P.'s Reg. 20 June 1870, fos. 183, 185; 21 Dec. 1870, fo. 190; and 17 Mar. 1871, fo. 194), the Governing Body of BNC 'failed to arrive at a decision as to the best solution [to the question of marriage]; but no member maintained that the obligation to celibacy should be enforced in every case and under all circumstances' (Selborne Commn. (*PP* (1881), lvi), pt. ii, 109). Albert Watson proposed that for Official Fellows, permission to marry should be considered 'an exceptional privilege, and not...a general right' (ibid. 129). In the end, the Fellows accepted from the Commission new statutes, drawn up in 1878, and approved by the Queen in Council in 1882. These provided for two Fellows in holy orders, one being responsible for chapel services; and four Fellows resident in college, 'of whom three at least shall be unmarried, and one shall be the Vice-Principal'. The marriage of Fellows was permitted, subject to a two-thirds majority vote in a secret ballot of the Governing Body; the Principal retaining two votes. Ormerod thought this 'most invidious' (M R 5 R10: MSS relating to 1st and 2nd Commissions; Statutes made...by the University of Oxford Commissioners...in pursuance of the...Act, 1877 (*PP* (1882), li), 334).

[147] Subscription to the Thirty-Nine Articles (of 1562) remained a condition of matriculation until 1803, and of graduation until 1854; the bar to MA status—and thus to Fellowships—was removed in 1871. Before the University Tests Act of 1871 (35 and 36 Vict. c. 26), a Fellow might be deprived for 'contumaciously ceasing to conform to the Church of England and Ireland' (Ordinances III, 33, 1857: L. Campbell, *On the Nationalisation of Old English Universities* (1901), 171). For oaths and declarations prior to that date, see ibid. 172–5. The 1857 Ordinances (III, 34) made declarations an alternative to oaths. In 1870—despite a petition from 136 old members, including 25 former Fellows—Brasenose resisted pressure to oppose the removal of religious tests for Fellowships (V-P's Reg. 18 Mar. 1870, fo. 177). By 1850 attendance in chapel—once daily, twice on Sundays—had, in many colleges, become 'practically optional' (J. Heywood, *The Recommendations of the O.U. Commission* (1853), 463). By the 1860s, at BNC and elsewhere, such attendance—a service of only fifteen minutes—had become in effect a register of residence (Ward, *Victorian Oxford*, 314). Compulsory chapel at Brasenose survived in vestigial form—as an alternative roll-call: 'holy rollers'—until 1932 (*Brazen Nose* v. 310).

by want of opportunity'.[148] Not surprisingly there were calls for another inquest, another reform. But the next Royal Commission—the Cleveland Commission of 1871–3—limited itself to financial matters, and then made recommendations which turned out to be over-optimistic. The enactments of its successor, the Selborne Commission of 1877–82, had to be geared to a collegiate economy which was already shifting into reverse.[149] Between the 1880s and the 1890s a decline in agricultural rents meant that proposals for wider science provision were mostly delayed; and proposals for any form of large-scale extra-collegiate recruitment were put on indefinite hold.[150] It was not until the First World War that the University began to make significant inroads on collegiate autonomy. That involved the agency of governmental finance. Public funding, in turn, brought with it the imperatives of public policy. And so, in the mid-twentieth century, Oxford at last opened its doors—as the 1850 Commissioners had hoped—to 'the most able and promising of the youth' of a different and wider world.[151]

Oxford, and Brasenose too, was at a turning point. And at this stage it is worth reminding ourselves of the bigger picture. In 1850 not more than 5,000 or 6,000 schoolchildren in the whole of England were receiving an education that fitted them for university.[152] The fees and living costs of the average Oxford undergraduate ran out at £200 to £300 p.a.[153] Oxford education was still a very expensive luxury. Jowett's dream of expansion in the direction of 'the lower and middling classes'[154] would have to wait until after the First

---

[148] C. S. Roundell, Fellow of Merton, 2 July 1867, to Select Committee on...Oxford and Cambridge (*PP* (1867), xiii), 208, 211, 214, 220. The progress of science was especially disappointing: 'Oxford really does not touch the general education of the country at all; it is simply a university for the wealthier classes...and it would be a very good thing indeed if you could induce the middle classes to come and get the benefit of a University education' (Sir B. Brodie, Bt., Waynflete Professor of Chemistry, 2 July 1867, ibid. 196).

[149] For evidence to the Selborne Commission regarding science provision, professorial teaching, research, etc., see *PP* (1881), lvi. Under the Oxford and Cambridge Act of 1877, Brasenose eventually received its amended statutes from the University Commissioners in 1881 (*PP* (1882), li. 330–46).

[150] For a detailed discussion of collegiate finance, see J. P. D. Dunbabin, in *Econ. Hist. Rev.* 2nd ser. 28 (1975), 631 *et seq.*; A. Engel, ibid., 31 (1978), 836–45, and Dunbabin, ibid. 446–9.

[151] OU Commn. (*PP* (1852), xxii), Report, 18: Numbers. 'We have no wish to encourage "poor scholars" to come to the University merely because they are poor...What is needed is encouragement to merit and industry; so that every promising youth, however poor, shall be able to command assistance to support him in the University' (ibid. 40: University Extension).

[152] Revd B. Jowett, ibid., Evidence, 32.

[153] Revd F. Temple, ibid. 126; Revd W. C. Lake, ibid. 169. 'An Oxford education costs a thousand pounds. It might be done for a hundred' (J. E. Thorold Rogers, *Education in Oxford* (1861), 203–4).

[154] Revd B. Jowett, in PP (1852), xxii, Evidence, 33: 'a matter of duty and justice'. See also *ODNB*. Goldwin Smith—assistant to A. P. Stanley, the Commission's secretary—published

World War. In 1868 he told a Commons Committee that the only hope for Oxford was to 'draw . . . [its] students from a much larger area . . . At present consider what a small portion of society it is that you draw from . . . [no more than] the upper hundred thousand at most.' One fragment of dialogue on that occasion still reverberates down the years.

Beresford Hope: How far down in the social stratum do you think it would be
                              advantageous to go for the supply of University men?
Benjamin Jowett: I can put no limit to it at all.[155]

That particular conundrum—the expanding mirage of higher education— would return with multiplied force at the end of the twentieth century. Meanwhile, BNC faced the second half of the nineteenth century with some confidence. Its governance had been reconstituted; but its ethos and personnel remained fundamentally unchanged. How did this new generation of Brasenose men match up to its predecessors?

There would be nobody to match Forbes—still less Robertson—among the undergraduates of the immediate post-reform era. But by modern standards, the men of the 1850s were still religious, if not exactly devout. Look for a moment at the intake of 1854. There were only twenty-one freshmen that year. In round figures, a quarter came from Lancashire; half went into the Church; and only two could possibly be described as landed gentry. The two gentlemen were H. L. Puxley, an Anglo-Welsh Etonian, and Thomas Grass-yard Edmondson, squire of Gresgarth Hall, near Lancaster. Both belonged to the Phoenix; but they must have been almost the only candidates that year. The circle of J. E. Binney—a future curate at All Saints, Margaret Street, and domestic chaplain to the Duke of Buccleuch—was much more typical. A lifelong bachelor, and convivial high churchman, Binney's friends included J. M. Austen, J. H. Rawdon, and C. J. Astbury: serious men all of them; a little solemn, and all from northern schools. They used to breakfast together each Sunday. Other friends from adjacent years included Principal Harington's nephew John Oakley, a future 'red' Dean of Manchester. Oakley was a jovial pianist, with rooms which were dangerously accessible on the ground floor. He 'achieved the distinction of being simultaneously plucked for Greats and elected President of the Union. Most of his friends were extreme ritualists of

pointed comments on its unfinished business in *The Reorganization of the University of Oxford* (1868).

[155] Revd B. Jowett, 16 July 1867, to Select Committee (*PP* (1867), xiii), 337, 339. 'At present not a tenth or a twentieth part of the ability of the country comes to the University . . . the great difficulty in [rectifying this] is the present state of the Grammar schools' (quoted in G. Faber, *Jowett* (1957), 347).

other colleges.'[156] Then there was G. H. Mullins, for thirty-five years a master at Uppingham; A. B. Shepherd, later a distinguished physician; Brooke Lambert, who would spend much of his clerical career ministering in Whitechapel; and one exact contemporary who cut a rather more colourful figure than any of these: Cormell Price, the first open scholar at BNC.

'Crom' Price is forgotten now; but he has his own niche in history. He was once the boon companion of William Morris and Edward Burne Jones; he could claim to be one of the godfathers of the Pre-Raphaelite Movement; and he was the mentor of Rudyard Kipling. Price's garret rooms (VI, 6) were next door to those of William Berkly, a future Fellow of Trinity. Price remembered him as 'one of the most winning characters and one of the deepest thinkers I ever met with'.[157] In effect Price, Berkly, and another freshman, F. L. Latham, formed a 'set': artistic rather then sporty, bourgeois rather than gentry. Price was happy there: he stayed in the same rooms for four years, 1854–8. But he had other friends, and they were at other colleges.

Price came from Birmingham, and his closest allies were two more Birmingham boys, Edward Burne-Jones of Exeter and C. J. Faulkner of Pembroke. But it was William Morris, also of Exeter College, who emerged as this group's leading light.[158] Price might play a hard game of fives, or enjoy gymnastics at Maclaren's in Oriel Street; but most of his time was spent talking late into the night, either at Exeter with Burne-Jones and Morris, or at Pembroke with Faulkner, William Fulford, and R.W. Dixon, or else in his own rooms overlooking Radcliffe Square. Here Price would declaim Shakespeare, and Morris would recite Malory or Chaucer. Here the 'Brotherhood' would gather 'to settle once for all how people should think'.[159] Medievalism was their credo. But only Burne-Jones was especially high church; the Pembroke set were evangelical. Yet whatever their churchmanship, they shared in particular Morris' rejection of capitalist ethics. 'Topsy [Morris] has got the real grit in him', noted Price; 'but we shall all go to Heaven.'[160] Morris must often have stumped up the stairs of staircase VI, tiptoeing past the shuttered oak of the Revd E. T. Turner. But the climb was worth making: Price could be relied on to serve punch and tobacco.

---

[156] Cormell Price, in *Brazen Nose*, i. 192. In fact he was sent down for non-attendance at chapel: the services must have been insufficiently high (*ODNB*). For Binney's obit, see *Brazen Nose*, i. 373–4.

[157] *Brazen Nose*, i. 192.

[158] Other Birmingham products were William Fulford, R. W. Dixon, and Edwin Hatch of Pembroke, and H. J. Macdonald of Corpus (*Brazen Nose*, i. 189–90).

[159] Burne-Jones, quoted in J. W. Mackail, *Life of William Morris*, i (1899), 33.

[160] Quoted, ibid. 91. Price also sat to Morris 'for a clay head which he was modelling; it was never finished, because whenever Morris grew impatient he flew at it and smashed it up' (ibid. 129).

And what did they talk about? It was thanks in part to Price that this brilliant knot of enthusiasts managed to couch their Pre-Raphaelite dreams in the language of social reform. Most of their conversations must have been the staple fare of undergraduates. As Burne Jones put it in a letter to Price, they talked of 'Eclectics, Syncretics, Rationalists, Pantheists, Atheists, and all names that are named in this age of "isms" . . .'[161] But Price was there too, to bring these musings down to earth. Morris and Burne Jones had come up to Oxford intent on a career in the Church. As the religious ferment of Oxford in the early 1840s began to wane, the next generation started to look to other forms of expression: to art and poetry, and thus to politics and economics.

Things were at their worst [Price recalled] in the forties and fifties. There was no protection for the mill-hand or miner—no amusements but prize-fighting, dog-fighting, cock-fighting and drinking. When a little boy I saw many prize-fights, bestial scenes: at one a combatant was killed. The country was going to hell apace. At [King Edward's School] Birmingham, a considerable section of the upper boys were quite awake to the crying evils of the period; social reform was a common topic of conversation. We were nearly all day boys, and we could not make short cuts to school without passing through slums of shocking squalor and misery, and often coming across incredible scenes of debauchery and brutality. I remember one Saturday night walking five miles from Birmingham into the Black Country, and in the last three miles I counted more than thirty lying dead drunk on the ground, nearly half of them women.[162]

Thanks to Cormell Price—a born schoolmaster, even before he graduated—Oxford's eager young Pre-Raphaelites came to see the evils of their time as in some way symbolized by the decadence of conventional art. Their Brotherhood became a 'Crusade and Holy Warfare against the age'.[163] The Christian socialism of Maurice and Kingsley, the feudal socialism of Carlyle, the aesthetic socialism of Ruskin, and the revolutionary socialism of Marx and Engels—all these emerged as part of this new generation's stock of conversation, but spiced of course with a dash of youthful nonsense. Only Morris translated their early dreams into the realities of adult politics. But much of the romance of Pre-Raphaelitism stemmed in good measure from the evils of the Hungry Forties.

In 1856, with help from a few Cambridge friends, Price's group decided to put their ideas into print by launching a monthly journal called the *Oxford and Cambridge Magazine*.[164] Morris supplied the financial backing; but he looked to

[161] Quoted in G.B.J., *Memorials of Edward Burne Jones*, i (1904), 82–3: 1853.
[162] Quoted in Mackail, *Morris*, i. 64.
[163] Burne Jones, quoted ibid. 63: 1853. A 'godly crusade against falsehood, doubt and wretched fashion, against hypocrisy and mammon, and lack of earnestness' (*Oxford and Cambridge Mag.* 7, 1856).
[164] For full details see *Wellesley Index*, ii (1972), 723–31.

Price for the prospectus and programme.[165] It was through this magazine that Rossetti's 'Blessed Damozel' began to reach a wider public. Some of the articles—for example Price on industrial working conditions—were concerned with social politics. But most of them, notably Morris's poems, were tales of myth and legend and romance revived: 'a dream remembered in a dream.'[166]

Morris and Burne-Jones left Oxford for London in the autumn of 1856. But Price stayed on at BNC. In the winter of 1857–8 Burne-Jones and Morris came back with Rossetti, to paint the murals of the Oxford Union. Those were years when Brasenose was a dominant force in the Union: there were three BNC Presidents in three successive years, 1855, 1856, 1857.[167] And when it came to murals, Price could at least help out as a model. '18 Oct. 1857', runs Price's diary: 'Stood for Top[sy] for two hours in a dalmatic.'[168] As the painting progressed hilariously, awash with tempera and soda water— 'Oh tempora, Oh Morris!'—the chief participants would find their way back of an evening to Price's rooms in Brasenose. Morris, Burne-Jones, Rossetti, and Swinburne too: they turned VI, 6 into 'a veritable nest of poets'. There they devoured Chaucer and Malory, glorying in the romance of *Morte d'Arthur*. There they feasted on Ruskin, with Morris in particular chanting aloud those 'weltering oceans of eloquence'.[169]

It cannot have been entirely coincidence that 1859—Price's last year—was also the year in which J. C. Buckler at last advised the Fellowship to repave the chapel with Minton tiles, to illuminate its walls with painted canvas, and to redecorate its ceiling in shades of blue, gold, and vermilion with stars of gold in inset panels (pl. 54).[170] Within four years not only the chapel but the entrance tower—decayed and neglected, inside and out—had been restored by Buckler with scholarly precision (pl. 46). Crisp Taynton masonry replaced

---

[165] 6 Nov. 1855. 'After Hall, to Faulkner's where I helped Top [prepare] a letter to the publishers'; 22 Nov. 1855. 'Ground out a prospectus with Top. In the evening to Pembroke and go on with the prospectus, Fulford joining in and doing lion's share' (Price's diary, quoted in Mackail, *Morris*, i. 87–8).

[166] Ibid. 134.

[167] D. C. Lathbury, John Oakley, and T. R. Halcomb. For photographs of the murals in the old Union debating hall, later library, see H. A. Morrah, *The Oxford Union 1823–1923* (1923).

[168] Quoted in Mackail, *Morris*, i. 126.

[169] *Brazen Nose*, i. 190; Mackail, *Morris*, i. 47.

[170] V.-P.'s Reg. 4 June 1860, f. 37; 19 June 1860, f. 42. 'To my taste, Buckler is satisfied in his sanguine expectations that the whole effect will be beautiful. I do not like to say much about it, as it is a question of taste only. But I may mention that the decoration of the Easternmost Bay is extremely Brilliant, a great deal too much so to be carried on to the succeeding Bays ... [The] stars are cast in lead, gilt and fixed on, so as to look in relief.... The beading will be *gold upon red* in the one bay, and red upon white *or stone colour* in the other Bays. The Blue tint for the ground is very charming' (Frederick Menzies to Cradock, B 503: 16 Aug. 1860).

the crumbling Headington stone. BNC was enjoying a belated medieval revival.[171] Georgian Oxford had begun to seem far away. Studying Tennyson on 'hot dreamy afternoons'; playing whist into the small hours; 'pouring basons of water' from upstairs windows over roistering crowds on May Day evening; lingering in the cloisters of New College, or loitering in Merton Street: 'a vision of grey-roofed houses and...the sound of many bells'; singing plain chant in Holywell Music Room; eating 'innumerable cherries'; or just laughing 'a great deal'—it was all 'such fun, by Jove'. And despite all the nonsense, it was the dreaming of this one particular Brasenose group that gave shape and substance to the thinking of the early Pre-Raphaelite Movement.[172]

Brasenose in the 1850s was comparatively staid, at least by comparison with the days of Frodsham Hodson. As Burne Jones remarked to Price in 1854, 'the Brasenose of old times [must have been] very fast indeed'.[173] In Price's day, things were quieter. 'Breakfasts' and 'wines' were the chief medium of entertainment: small groups in private rooms; larger parties, up to fifty strong, in lecture room VII. With the Phoenix going through a thin patch—'kept going by a solitary individual'—Price was happy to belong to 'a small coterie called the "Owls"'; their 'raison d'etre was chat and dessert after Hall', with 'devilled' oranges prominent on the menu. Members included Anthony Adams Reilly, 'a charming Irishman of serene temperament, rich at that time', later a distinguished Alpinist. Then there was J. W. Mollet, 'a man of tempestuous character, an excellent companion, everyone's friend but his own'; fluent in French and German, later secretary to a bank, a man who spent much of his later life in Java. By contrast, another member of this group was L. O. Pike, a future keeper at the Public Record Office. Pike was among the sternest of palaeographers, and his *Yearbooks of Edward III* (Rolls Series, 1885–1908) raise pedantry to a form of art. Then there was W. W. Waddington, 'a jovial Yorkshireman', who studied sheep rearing with Mollet in Switzerland, before becoming a master at Hartley College, Southampton. Another 'Owl' was C. J. Stone. He and Price used to holiday together in Broadway Tower—a spectacular Cotswold folly—with William Morris as a frequent guest. Alas, Stone died young in 1886, 'dejected through total loss of his patrimony in a law-suit and lack of appreciation of his [only] two books': *Cradle-land of Arts and Creeds* (1880) and *Christianity before Christ* (1885).[174]

---

[171] Builder: George Wyatt of Oxford. See Hurst, College Buildings, 24. Also V-P's Reg. 12 June 1862, fo. 75; 26 June 1862, fo. 76; 30 June 1862, fo. 79; 4 Dec. 1862, fo. 82; 20 Oct. 1863, fo. 96; 21 Dec. 1863, fo. 190; 13 June 1864, fo. 110; 19 June 1865, fo. 121.

[172] *Quat. Mon.* III, 32; G.B.J., *Memorials*, i. 77, 181; Mackail, *Morris*, i. 29.

[173] Quoted in G.B.J., *Memorials*, i. 98.

[174] Cornell Price, in *Brazen Nose*, i. 190–2.

After the 'Owls', and a short spell studying medicine, Cormell Price went out to Russia as tutor to the Orloff Davidoff family. Then in 1874 he set up a school of his own for the sons of naval and military personnel. The United Services College, as it came to be called—Price was headmaster there for twenty years—was bracingly positioned at Westward Ho!, a holiday resort on the north Devon coast. That choice of location was a cunning move: Charles Kingsley's novel of the same name (1855) had made the place familiar to many prospective parents. Rudyard Kipling was sent there in 1878, and his portrait of the headmaster—'the Proosian Bates'—in *Stalky and Co.* (1899) came near to making Price immortal.[175] One of the assistant masters was another Brasenose figure, W. C. Crofts: the greatest oarsman who never rowed for Oxford.[176]

Finally, two more members of Price's generation deserve separate mention. In May 1856 Francis Latham and Henry Wace entered for the same scholarship examination, sitting next to each other in hall. Both would take Firsts—Latham in classics, Wace in maths—and both would remain loyal college men for nearly three-quarters of a century. Latham went on to be a barrister at the Inner Temple, and Advocate General in Bombay.[177] Wace became Professor of Ecclesiastical History and Principal of King's College London; as well as chaplain to the Queen and eventually Dean of Canterbury. Delane employed him regularly as a *Times* leader writer: he wrote, for example, a tribute on the death of Dickens. Whatever he did, he did with all his might. He was a doughty fighter, a 'Reformation man', a veritable Protestant champion.[178] His qualities—'robustness and humanity...hatred of foppery and dishonesty'—were qualities 'of the Brasenose kind'.[179] His son, H. C.—'Daddy'—Wace, became chaplain at BNC, and eventually Bursar, and kept up the spirit of his father's no-nonsense low churchmanship well into the 1920s.[180]

What Latham found when he arrived at Brasenose was not, in academic terms, exactly impressive. 'Our system of tuition was chaotic,' he recalled; and 'I was excused all College teaching when I was found to be working

---

[175] R. Kipling, *Stalky and Co.* (2001 edn.), 134. 'Kind and generous...somewhat inscrutable, with [a] half-quizzical smile...heroic of purpose, sincere in friendship...and not without a touch of greatness' (E. H. Blakeny, in *The Times*, 16 May 1910, 10), Price published at least two teaching aids: *German Declension* (1886) and *Practical French Gender Card* (1887). The school merged with Haileybury in 1962.

[176] Crofts appears as 'King' in *Stalky and Co.* Twice winner of the Diamond Sculls, he was drowned off Sark in 1912. Photo in L. C. Dunsterville, *Stalky's Reminiscences* (1927).

[177] He wrote on *The Law of Window Lights* (1867) and *The Odes of Horace* (1910).

[178] Obit, *The Times*, 10 Jan. 1924. His writings include *The Foundation of Faith* (1879), *First Principles of the Reformation* (1883), and *Christianity and Agnosticism* (1895). He edited *A Dictionary of Christian Biography* (1877–87) and *The Primary Works of Luther* (1896).

[179] Obit by R. W. J.[effery], *Brazen Nose*, iii. 325–8.

[180] See p. 316, 344 below.

seriously for Honours ... [In fact that was] the best thing that could have been done for me.'[181] A story like that is not quite as odd as it might seem. Classes were geared to Pass men; and Fellows regularly had to operate outside the range of their expertise. Tutorials were a little more efficient. Latham and his friend Berkly were, as a pair, apparently well groomed for Greats. But good teaching seems to have been a matter of luck. Not that other colleges were much better; hence the widespread recourse to private coaches. One kindly Brasenose Fellow at this time actually paid a poor scholar's coaching fees, knowing full well that he was not up to doing the teaching himself.[182] Not surprisingly Latham and Berkly jumped at the chance of attending Jowett's professorial lectures at Balliol. But in the end perhaps it scarcely mattered. This generation—like most undergraduate generations—effectively educated each other. Cormell Price taught them about the Pre-Raphaelites; Brooke Lambert brought a touch of Christian socialism. There were some 'hard-reading men', like Austen, Morshead, and Mullins from Marlborough. And Lancashire and Cheshire still supplied a handful of serious scholars—James Rawdon and Albert Weigall, for instance—spurred on by Hulmeian Exhibitions. But Oxford in the 1850s had yet to assimilate the beneficial results of reform. Between 1855 and 1863 for example, there were no Fellowship elections of any kind at Brasenose: Latham, Wace, and Berkly had to look outside college for advancement. James Marshall was the first Fellow to be elected under the new system, in 1864. The dividends of change came slowly.

They were never to be reaped by Principal Harington (pl. 35). In effect Harington's early death in 1853 let Brasenose off a rather awkward hook. As head of house, he carried too much conservative baggage ever to be easy under the reformed regime. Once he had gone—and once their Visitor had gone too—the Fellows could openly change tack. They could absorb reform under the leadership of a new Principal. Astutely, they chose a liberal-minded cleric with administrative talent; a progressive who believed that 'College Reform is the royal road to University Reform';[183] a broad churchman who was actually married to a relative of the arch-reformer Lord John Russell.[184] Friends reported that he was 'a scholar and a gentleman, thoroughly

---

[181] *Brazen Nose*, i. 159.

[182] Ibid. 160. The Fellow in question was Albert Watson: his Mods teaching seems to have been hopeless; his ancient history teaching for Greats, however, was apparently excellent.

[183] 'I see my way clearly as to what is right in College improvement [but on] University Reform ... my opinion is far from matured' (BL Add. MS 44377, fo. 101: Cradock to Bowen, 19 Jan. 1854).

[184] The label 'broad church'—as opposed to high or low—seems to have been coined by A. H. Clough before 1850 (*OED*); it was given definitive currency by A. P. Stanley in *Edinburgh Rev.*, July (1850), 266 and by W. J. Conybeare, ibid. 98 (1853), 330.

well-disposed towards University progress and improvement'; he had only 'average talent and acquirement'; but he had efficiently managed the finances of Worcester Cathedral; he was 'a sensible and impressive preacher'; at the very least he was 'a good specimen of a producible man'.[185] His name was Edward Hartopp Cradock (pl. 36). We shall hear from him again.

Meanwhile one last look at BNC in the days before reform. Arthur Evans, uncle to a greater Brasenose man, the archaeologist Sir Arthur Evans, matriculated in 1840. He lodged in 'back buildings'—or New Building, as it was known—'next door to the shoe- boot- and knife cleaning establishment'. His rooms were also not far from a rather less welcome facility: 'the salutiferous exhalations of a certain capacious necessary', in other words the college privy. Otherwise there was no plumbing at all. Each morning the scout delivered a pitcher of cold water, which frequently froze during winter. Living conditions—this is true of course for Oxford as a whole—were both grand and primitive. And teaching, to say nothing of pastoral care, could best be described as vestigial. Evans's description of undergraduate life in 1841 is telling.

There are three tutors whose lectures, at least some of them, I am obliged to attend to the amount of 12–16 a week; first Churton or Tommy, then Chaffers, and next Walker or Joey. Tommy is a very good-natured sort of fellow who means all very well, but has a habit of lending all freshmen 'little Books' to read, which he says 'won't take five minutes', the little books usually being octavo's of about a hundred or two pages. He gives besides small parties of a Sunday Evening on the 'tea and prayers for tea' principle, when you get nothing to eat except, if you have good luck, a small fragment of dry toast, and afterwards have to sit and listen for two mortal hours to a prosy and drawling discussion respecting the derivatives and significations of some words or other in the Greek Test[ament] ... Chaffers is a very different sort of fellow, [he] would not much care if all his pupils went to the Devil, if they only got up their lectures pretty well. He's the sort of fellow that fancies himself a kind of Sphinx of private life, and tries to come the facetiously satirical over one in lectures, but it generally won't do. Walker [a mathematician] is the kind of fellow that always has a glass in his eye, and wears a subrufous wig, and always calls one Mister... Besides these three is Whittaker Churton who I have nothing to do with. He is ... too good for this world a great deal and speaks as if he were in a mortal funk of having his head cut off if he is heard above two yards off'.[186]

Evans's comments on the Revd Thomas Chaffers add flesh to an otherwise shadowy Brasenose 'character'. Chaffers arrived at BNC in 1831, as a

---

[185] BL Add. MS 44376, fos. 238, 240: Bowen to Gladstone, 27 Dec. 1853 ('Our choice seems to be universally approved in Oxford'). Also Knowsley Papers 93/3: E. Cardwell to Lord Derby, 15 Mar. 1858, cited in Ward, *Victorian Oxford*, 378 n. 69.

[186] *Brazen Nose*, vi. 219: 28 Feb. 1841. For living conditions, compare F. W. Robertson's experience in 1837–40 (Brooke, *Robertson*, i. 39: May 1838).

Hulme Exhibitioner from Manchester Grammar School. With a First in Greats, a Founders' Fellowship, and a college living in Stepney, 'Chiffie' moved smoothly up the *cursus honorum*: Tutor, Junior Bursar, Vice-Principal, and Proctor. His eccentricities became legendary: his lectures involved a kind of theatrical fidgeting. He was popularly thought to be the last surviving member of the Hell Fire Club. That seems unlikely on a number of counts. But his attitude to religion was certainly whimsical. One undergraduate decided to tease him by pretending to have doubts about the Trinity. He called on Chaffers in IV, 4 to discuss the problem. 'Wait a minute', murmured Chaffers, diving into his library and returning with a huge folio. 'Here, Mr. . . . , is the first volume of the works of St. Athanasius; and, when you have finished it, I shall be happy to lend you the other two.'[187]

Whatever his shortcomings, Chaffers was a learned man, and not incapable of wit. A certain J. B. Litler was apparently an idle student: 'Mr. Litler, I see you have no idea of grammatical construction. You are ignorant of the very elements of grammar. Why, sir . . . your very name is ungrammatical.'[188] We know his appearance.[189] We know the arrangement of his rooms.[190] We know, alas, his habits. The regime of pre-reform Oxford—too much time and too little accountability—proved in the end to be his undoing. He was 'a brilliant man', recalled one pupil, 'ruined by the old celibate Common Room life'.[191] W. B. Woodgate gives the best account of his decline.

He was a quaint character with nez retroussé . . . a great scholar; brusque, but kindly-hearted under a rough exterior; nobody's enemy but his own; he 'lifted his elbow' too much; and when, Whit Tuesday, 1859, he roared from his window to the College porter for more soda water, there culminated a scandal which led to his resignation of [the Vice-Principalian] office . . . [On one occasion] he had dined in Exeter (well); for safety's sake Tommy Shepherd, chaplain of Exeter, undertook to see him safe home, just before midnight. Down Brasenose Lane they came; Chaffers, three sheets to the wind, could not port his helm to fetch BNC. lodge gate, and sailed across to [the] railings of [the] Radcliffe [Camera], to which he held taut. Shepherd tugged at his gown tail. 'Let go, Chaffy; come on to the college before it strikes twelve; consider the undergraduates; they may be looking at you!'

[187] *Brazen Nose*, i. 159.

[188] A. C. Plowden, *Grain or Chaff? The Autobiography of a Police Magistrate* (1903), 62. For other anecdotes, see *Brazen Nose*, i. 200–1, 236–8, and iii. 256.

[189] Drawn by Revd G. R. Winter in 'Science in the Divinity School' (pub. Ryman, 1850).

[190] Drawn by J. B. Pyne, *c.*1858, prior to the insertion of the oriel window, *c.*1861.

[191] See F. L. Latham, in *Brazen Nose*, i. 159. He was by no means opposed to sensible reform, and welcomed Cradock as 'an able and judicious adviser' (BL Add. MS 44377, fos. 103–5: Chaffers to Bowen, 18 Jan. 1854). For Chaffers's death see V-P's Reg. 4 June 1860, fo. 38.

Chaffers: 'Ye——fool, Tommy, can't you see the quad's going round? Wait till the lodge comes by, and we'll go in.'[192]

Within a few months he was dead, at the early age of 48. And with the passing of Chaffers—a don who could laugh at his own learning—went half the spirit of Brasenose before reform.

---

[192] W. B. Woodgate, *Reminiscences of an Old Sportsman* (1909), 107. Shepherd preferred 'the Brasenose tap' to dining at Exeter; so he was made an hon. member of the BNC Common Room (ibid. 165). So, apparently, did another friend of Chaffers, 'Tommy Short' of Trinity (*Brazen Nose*, iii. 255).

5
1853–1886

The Age of Athletic Prizemen:
Walter Pater and 'the Chief'

'I wish they wouldn't call me a hedonist', Walter Pater remarked to Edmund
Gosse in 1876; 'it produces such a bad effect on the minds of people who
don't know Greek.'[1] By that date Pater (pl. 37) had been a Fellow of
Brasenose for twelve years, an aesthete outnumbered by athletes. Born the
son of an East End doctor, orphaned before he left King's School, Canterbury, he emerged from Queen's College in 1862 without resources—and
without a First—but with a glowing recommendation from Benjamin Jowett.
'I think', Jowett announced, 'you have a mind that will come to great
eminence.'[2] From the outset, a career in the Church was blocked: when he
applied for ordination he was denounced by a school friend as a sceptic.[3] But
in 1864 he competed for a non-clerical fellowship by examination at BNC;
and the Fellows elected him unanimously.[4]

Perhaps without realizing their luck, the Fellows of Brasenose had acquired one of the most remarkable stylists in the history of the English
language. Here was a writer who would begin by exploring the origins of
Renaissance painting, and end by revolutionizing our understanding of
artistic perception. That meant, first of all, disentangling Ruskin's confusion
of art and morality, ethics and aesthetics. Then it involved abandoning the
conventions of pictorial analysis, by translating narrative images into sequen-
tial impressions. And finally it meant dissolving the whole apparatus of
pictorial tradition into a series of ocular sensations. Pater would inspire
Wilde and Proust; he would anticipate Berenson and Fry. He would lay the

---

[1] E. Gosse, 'Walter Pater', in *Critical Kit-Kats* (1896), 258.

[2] Ibid. 249.

[3] In December 1862 J. R. McQueen protested to the Bishop of London (T. Wright, *The Life
of Walter Pater*, i (1907), 207).

[4] 'Per maximam partem suffragantium' (V-P's Reg. 5 Feb. 1864, fo. 104). He defeated
eleven other candidates. In 1865 his Fellowship was confirmed after the usual one year's
probation (ibid., 5 Feb. 1865, fo. 117).

foundation—though that is too pedestrian a metaphor—for a modern theory of abstract art. All this in an allusive, evocative style; mannered no doubt, precious even, but never trivial, never dull. His famous description of the *Mona Lisa*, for example, would one day be chopped up into short lines by W. B. Yeats and printed as the first poem in the *Oxford Book of Modern Verse* (1939). But in 1864 all that lay in the future. He had been recruited by BNC as a classicist, a college tutor; and that would be his primary duty for upwards of thirty years.

The Common Room that Pater joined comprised just fourteen Fellows, with only a handful of resident dons. Miraculously, one photograph survives from the year 1861 (pl. 38), showing the bulk of the Fellowship in all its bewhiskered glory. The Principal is not there. Nor is Edward Turner, absent no doubt on University business. J. W. Knott will soon be off to India, C. J. Wood to Jersey. R. S. Wilson will be almost the last election under the old statutes, and in any case he will soon be gone. As for J. A. Ormerod, he will soon be dead. Otherwise, these are the men—plus a couple of later elections—who will elect unanimously the brilliant young aesthete from Queen's. Not all of them attend every meeting of the governing body. There will be just eight names on Pater's endorsement as Actual Fellow in 1865. All but one of these—J. D. Davenport, like Pater a non-clerical Fellow—will be ordained Anglicans, elected under the old statutes. Frederick Menzies, T. H. R. Shand, and William Yates will all end up in college livings.[5] They are clergymen first, and scholars second. Edward Turner (pl. 33) and Albert Watson (pl. 50) will both have long-running Brasenose careers: Turner—martinet and bibliophile—as Vice-Principal and University Registrar; Watson—'dear, shy, shrinking, genial, learned Albert Watson'—as Senior Bursar and eventually Principal.[6] Both are college men first and clergymen second. As for the rest, J. J. Hornby and E. H. Cradock are clerics

---

[5] Davenport became a Chancery lawyer. For Yates see Boase, vi. 973. For Shand, a Scots mathematician, see obit, *Daily Telegraph*, 20 Feb. 1914.

[6] T. H. Ward, 'Reminiscences', in *Quat. Mon.* XIV. ii, 76. Undergraduates once tried to block the entrance to Turner's rooms (VI, 4) with snow; he escaped via the Tower Bursary and watched their operations with amusement (F. Weatherley, *Piano and Gown* (1926), 63). 'He was a don very much of the old type. He wore an eyeglass [pl. 33], which emphasised somewhat his "you be dammed" expression of countenance . . . [He once] wrote to the parents of a Brasenose undergraduate who died in the middle of his first term . . . It may be of some consolation to you to know that the young man would in any case have had to go down at the end of the present term owing to his failure to pass Responsions' (G. B. Grundy, *Fifty Five Years at Oxford* (1945), 79). He tutored in divinity, that is the Gospels and Acts of the Apostles, in Greek. Late in life he married the daughter of Rector Lightfoot of Exeter. A Tory bibliophile, he was also a member of the Roxburghe Club. For Shrimpton's caricature, see Madan coll., II, 325. For Bussell's obit of Turner, see *Brazen Nose*, i. 167–8, illus.

as well; but first and foremost they are gentry. Hornby, the son of an admiral, had rowed bow for Oxford in 1851 and will go on to be headmaster and provost of Eton, and chaplain to the Queen. As for Cradock, he will become one of the longest-serving Principals in the history of Brasenose.

Unlike most of his colleagues Edward Hartopp Cradock (pl. 36) was not a bachelor. In fact his whole career stemmed from a network of conjugal patronage. In 1844—on moving to parish work—he had married well, choosing the Hon. Harriet Lister, one of Queen Victoria's Maids of Honour. Besides her connections—her relatives were Russells and Ribblesdales—she was a novelist and artist in her own right.[7] In 1849, as if to consolidate his progress, the future Principal proceeded to change his name, from Grove to Cradock, on inheriting property from Sir Edmund Cradock Hartopp, first Baronet, a maternal uncle who had himself changed his name from Bunney.[8] Now the Groves of Shenstone Park, Staffordshire, were certainly gentry; so were the Cradocks of Knighton, Leicestershire. But the future Principal, as the son of a second wife, had been forced to make his own way. He rose through marriage and the Church. As a cleric, as a don, Cradock was a pre-Tractarian Anglican of mildly Liberal persuasion.[9] He welcomed University reform, but passively rather than actively. He was not particularly interested in scholarship: his only publications were a sermon at a Three Choirs Festival and an obituary poem on Wordsworth.[10] A degree in classics at Balliol, a rural parish in Herefordshire, a canonry at Worcester, a series of college posts: his early career was in no way remarkable. Except in one respect. What marked him out was his engagement with a new social phenomenon, the emerging dynamic of organized games. From the date of his election, Principal Cradock exploited the potential of competitive sport. In effect, he enlisted the enthusiasms of a whole generation in pursuit of collegiate cohesion. More

[7] Boase, iii. 130 (3rd Baron Ribblesdale, horse breeder and gambler). The 4th Baron, a celebrated Master of the Royal Buck Hounds, was famously portrayed by Sargent. Mrs Cradock was the author of a number of novels, notably *Anne Grey* (1834); also *Views in Elf Land, Designed and Executed by Mrs. Weird*, ed. [really written] by Mrs Cradock (1878). She kept a garden in Holywell, a cottage at West Malvern, and a retreat above Grasmere. For the Cradocks playing croquet, *c.*1869, see Shrimpton caricature, Madan coll., I, 4.

[8] Boase, i. 1747; E. Walford, *County Families* (1860), 293 and (1878), 238.

[9] In early years he belonged to the 'progressive' camp of Francis Jeune, J. M. Wilson, Goldwin Smith, and Halford Vaughan. A high point of this phase was his defeat of F. C. Plumptre of Univ. in the elections of 1857 for a seat on the new Hebdomadal Council. As Vice-Chancellor, it had been Plumptre who in 1852 protested on behalf of the old Hebdomadal Board against the proposed Commission. When weighing up his vote for Sir W. Heathcote in January 1854, Cradock wondered: 'surely he is or was, (nobody is) a Protectionist and not exactly a liberal according to my idea...' (BL Add. MS 44377, fo. 102). See also W. R. Ward, *Victorian Oxford* (1965), 189, 216.

[10] *A Sermon Preached in the Cathedral of Worcester, at the Triennial Meeting of the Three Choirs* (1851); *The Stone Steps* (an elegy on William Wordsworth), (Oxford, 1860).

than anyone, it was Cradock—universally known as the Chief—Principal for thirty-three years, from 1853 to 1886, who created the muscular image of BNC. Curiously, though in many ways his antithesis, Pater seems to have found him a congenial colleague. Both were Liberals; and they did have Wordsworth in common.

Cradock had been elected to a Fellowship in 1833, under the pre-reform dispensation; and for twenty years after his arrival, Fellows continued to be chosen according to the unreformed statutes. It was a system that placed a high premium—too high in many cases—on the integrity of an individual Fellow.

Occasionally the right choice was made. Samuel Harvey Reynolds— almost the last Brasenose Fellow to be elected under the old system—arrived from Exeter College in 1855, with the Newdigate Prize as well as Firsts in Mods and Greats. After taking his MA, he began reading for the bar at Lincoln's Inn; but he had an accident to his eye, and decided—curiously— that he could be a scholar with defective eyesight but not a barrister. So he went back to Oxford and took holy orders. There he became an effective tutor and a common-sense counterpoint to Walter Pater, bridging the gap between pre- and post-reform Fellows. His range was certainly impressive. He edited twelve books of the *Iliad* (1870); he was an essayist and minor poet, and a speculative historian. He was a progressive Liberal in University politics: he even wore a red shirt. And he could write. George Saintsbury noted 'the freshness, the vigour, and above all the geniality (in the foreign as well as the English sense) of his mind'.[11] In fact Reynolds was enough of a critic to be considered for the chair of Poetry in succession to Matthew Arnold.[12] When he married in 1871, Brasenose presented him with what was then a valuable living in an obscure, quiet place, East Ham. When he arrived the population there was under 2,000; when he left it was 45,000. He needed a sense of humour, and a generous spirit—in fact, a Christian spirit—and he had both. It must have required more than ordinary dedication to keep going, at the same time producing scholarly editions of Selden's *Table Talk*, and Bacon's *Essays*; plus about 2,000 articles for *The Times* over a period of twenty years. When he retired in 1893, he settled in Abingdon—'to be near enough to the Bodleian for study, and not near enough to Oxford for society'. His *Times* obituary noted his Swiftian tolerance, 'sturdy common-sense...hatred of cant...and...abiding sanity of judgement, not unworthy of [Dr] Johnson himself'.[13] Wit, raconteur, stylist, and scholar; Reynolds was rowing for the

[11] BNC Members 31b: letter from Revd J. Darlington, 1 Mar. 1909; George Saintsbury, in S. H. Reynolds, *Studies upon Many Subjects* (1898). L. A. Tollmache (ed.), *Rev. S. H. Reynolds* (1922). Reynolds wrote *The Reciprocal Action of the Physical and Moral Constitution of Countries upon each Other* (1856), and *The System of Modern History* (1865).

[12] T. D. Raikes (ed.), *Sicut Columbae: Fifty Years of St. Peter's College, Radley* (1897), 19.

[13] Memoir, *Essex Review*, 6 (1897), 69–71; *The Times*, 10 Feb. 1897, p. 10.

first Eight about the time he was examining young Lord Rosebery in Greats. He even took reading groups to the Island of Sark, rejoicing in sea, and sunshine, and fresh air.

> This huge-framed, gold spectacled philosopher...swimming or ashore...reminded us of some old sea-god, at one with Nature. In the evening the sea-god played whist; in the morning...he would discourse with gusto on the virtues of [Bacon's] *Novum Organum*, on the greatness of Professor J. M.Wilson [of Corpus], on the irrefragibility of Comte's Positive Politics, and on the invading absurdities...of the Oxford Hegelians.[14]

Few Fellows made the transition from pre- to post-reform Oxford as well as Reynolds. But in the last resort, they could always retire and take refuge in a rectory. Such transfers could of course result in unsuitable appointments. In 1848, for example, Joseph Brooks exchanged his Senior Bursarship for a college benefice at Great Rollright. His first move was a grandiose reconstruction of Ralph Rawson's old rectory. 'Give me air', he told the builders; 'give me space!' Within three years he was hopelessly in debt. 'Forgive us our debts', he announced from the pulpit; 'as we forgive our debtors.' With that, he turned his back on the bewildered congregation and fled abroad, to Bavaria.[15] But then Brooks was a Phoenix man. Such behaviour was scarcely an option for Brasenose servants. They were, perforce, a hardy and tenacious breed. Their appointments were frequently lifelong and occasionally even hereditary. University reform had little effect on their daily existence.

When Pater arrived in 1864, the head porter who greeted him was John Hawkins. In 1861 he had succeeded the legendary John Bossum. Both men appear in a remarkable photograph taken that very year—the year of Bossum's death—showing the servants of Brasenose assembled (pl. 41).[16] This image is worth a moment's study.

Near the centre of this photograph, leaning heavily on Cain and Abel, stands Bossum himself, a mountainous figure weighing twenty-two stone (pl. 40). Normally, he sits at his window in the Lodge, with a tankard of Brasenose ale before him, a veritable Cerberus at the gate. Bossum is a loyal Freemason; he has a powerful singing voice; and he is famous for his rendition of 'New Mown Hay'. How much does he earn? A head porter's wages about this time stood at £120 p.a. plus £3 from the Senior Bursar, and one shilling for every matriculation.[17] But formal payments were only the

---

[14] T. H. Ward, 'Reminiscences', in *Quat.Mon.* XIV. ii, 77. Wilson, Professor of Moral Philosophy and President of Corpus, was a noted Liberal, instrumental in the abolition of religious tests and in furthering the 1st and 2nd parliamentary Commissions (*ODNB*).

[15] R. W. Jeffery, *The Manor and Advowson of Great Rollright* (Oxford Record Soc., 1927), 163, 166.

[16] MPP 42 A1 (Shepherd Album).

[17] For official wages, see V-P's Reg. 15 June 1858, fo. 10; 24 Apr. 1863, fo. 90; 7 Feb. 1869, fo. 167; 5 Feb. 1870, fo. 175; 15 Feb. 1872, fo. 210; 30 Apr. 1872, fo. 212; 18 Nov. 1873, fo. 228.

beginning of a servant's pay. On Bossum's right we see three scouts: portly Adam Owen, obliging Thomas Green, and shy John Hinton. On Bossum's left, in central place of honour, stands John Prior the butler, hero of many a Shrovetide Ale. His salary is £250 per annum, half as much as a junior Fellow, even allowing for a Fellow's supplementary earnings. He is clearly a man to reckon with. He will live to serve the college for fifty-two years.[18] Behind Prior stand two more scouts, David East and Harry Charlwood. It is Charlwood—'a good looking man of middle height'; later known for his 'dark whiskers and fresh complexion'—who will soon be chosen as Pater's scout. Twenty years after that he will die in a lunatic asylum.[19] The retirement of David East will be rather more content. He will rise to be head scout; the owner of 'a large section of Long Wall Street—provision for his old age—out of the earnings of his trade'. Such wealth is not as surprising as it might seem: the head porter at Trinity reputedly left £15,000–20,000. College service was almost a model of an informal, black economy. Senior servants received regular retainers from the tradesmen of the town in return for guaranteed custom; junior scouts could count on perquisites in the form of tips and unused provisions. This was the world immortalized in one classic Oxford comedy, *The Adventures of Mr. Verdant Green* (1853).[20] In front of Charlwood, and a little to his left, stands John Hawkins the first under porter. Within a few months he will succeed Bossum, doubling his wages in the process. In front of Hawkins, and to his left, we see John Hedges, one of a dynasty of servants living close by, in a property off the High Street known as

In 1852 Bossum was living at 1 Longwall Street. When Bossum's successor, John Hawkins, died in 1866, the responsibilities of the head porter were rearranged, at wages of £75 p.a. (ibid., 3 Feb, 1866, fo. 132). The head porter of Trinity reputedly made his fortune through a charge of one halfpenny on every letter delivered to the Lodge (*Oxford Undergraduate's Jnl.*, 10 Nov. 1866, p. 86).

[18] *Brazen Nose*, iv. 8. In 1852 he was living at 28 Holywell Street. Adam Owen once knocked the Mayor of Henley downstairs when he mistook him for a gatecrasher at an undergraduate review. See W. K. R. Bedford, 'The O.D.A.', in L. M. Quiller-Couch (ed.), *Reminiscences of Oxford* (OHS xxii, 1892).

[19] Wright, *Pater*, i. 216. Prior to his death, Charlwood was also Phoenix Common Room man. He was succeeded as Pater's scout by Frank Walker, a fourth-generation scout, 'a spruce, obliging man' (ibid., ii. 49), who came to BNC as a messenger in 1873, was a bedmaker from 1881 to 1915, and died in 1934 aged 78 (*Brazen Nose*, v. 346). To Walker Pater left the minor contents of his rooms (MPP 134 C1).

[20] By 'Cuthbert Bede, B.A.' [Edward Bradley]. By 1873 over 100,000 copies had been sold; by 1890, 130,000 (*ODNB*). Bradley was the inventor of the double acrostic, and thus the grandfather of the crossword puzzle. T. Green remained in charge of the SCR until 1888 when he was succeeded by E. Newman (*Brazen Nose*, iv. 51–2). For servants' perquisites, see also W. B. Woodgate, *Reminiscences of an old Sportsman* (1909), 116, 119, 120–1. Pater's underscout, W. H. Tombs, came to BNC in 1884 at the age of 13, and survived until 1968. Each morning he brought in a pitcher of cold water for Pater's hip-bath (*Brazen Nose*, xiii. 255 and xiv. 207).

Amsterdam. To Hedges's left, behind and in front, stand the manciple or cook, Thomas Wells, and the cook's assistant; left again we see the head shoeblack (£130 p.a. in 1870)—a busy person, no doubt, in an age of shiny boots—and the second under porter and messenger, John Molyneux (£40 p.a.). At the very front, with their tall hats and their boaters, their canes and their pet dogs—reclining in mock-patrician manner—we see six more assorted figures. From left to right: first the common-room man and the chief butler (a rather more professional person with an especially shiny top hat); then two more scouts, George and Tom; and finally another assistant cook and another scout named Henry.

Nineteen men in all. Their clothes are graded according to rank, from frock jacket to symbolic top hat and waistcoat; each, in different degree, formal but dishevelled. Each man knows his place in the hierarchy of service. And this hierarchy is replicated in the college as a whole. The servants admire the sportsmen, cheering them on at Henley; the sportsmen respect the Fellows; and all revere the Chief.

That photograph was taken in 1861. What of the finances by which this service economy was sustained? In 1871 the college produced a breakdown of its income and expenditure in the form of a tabulated return to the second Royal Commission.[21] Here, in snapshot form, we catch a glimpse of the college's mid-Victorian economy. From external sources—lands, house property, stocks, shares, and trusts—Brasenose received an income of just over £9,600; from internal sources—room rents, fees, tuition charges, etc.— just over £6,700; making a total of a little more than £16,000. Against this, expenditure was running at rather more than £13,600: the Principal drew £1,439 8s. 9d.; the twelve Fellows £2,925 19s. 4d.; and the servants £1,476 16s. 11d.; with £1,387 16s. 0d. going on scholarships, exhibitions, library, etc. In other words, during that year the college managed to show a healthy balance. In addition, of course, there were as many as twenty-two benefices; financially less than rewarding, but components all of them in the network of collegiate patronage. What might appear to be the college's greatest asset— over 4,600 acres of land—produced in fact only a low return, being mostly let out not at 'rack rents' but on 'beneficial leases'. By the mid-1870s, college income was beginning to dip.[22] It was only in the 1880s and 1890s that the income from urban rents began to show an appreciably higher return. This shift in the balance of income was important. But BNC suffered less than many colleges from the general decline in agricultural rents that set in during

---

[21] Cleveland Commn. (1874) (*PP* (1873), xxxvii), pt. i, summary: 91–5; pt. ii, details: 579–613.

[22] Return to the Selborne Commission, supplementing returns to the Cleveland Commission, 29 Oct. 1877 (*PP* (1881), lvi, pt. ii, 55–7).

the final quarter of the century.[23] Even the onset of collegiate taxation for University purposes—a by-product of the Selborne Commission—caused little more than a ripple on the balance sheet.

So the successes of BNC under Cradock's regime rested on a sound financial basis. Christ Church, Magdalen, and New College were richer; so now were St John's, Merton, Oriel, and Queen's. But in terms of income Brasenose would overtake several of these by the end of the century. By modern standards, the Common Room was still small. In 1878, for example, there were ten Fellows plus a Reader in Ancient History. One Fellow—E. T. Turner—elected before 1854, received £366 p.a. with allowances; the remaining nine received £200 p.a. in 1872–6 and £230 in 1877, plus allowances; the Reader similarly received £200. Seven had tenure for life, one for 'so long as he serves the college'; the tenure of four was linked to holy orders; the tenure of eight was tied to stipulations regarding marriage and property.[24] Various college lectureships—Hebrew, maths, classics, law, history, and divinity—provided the Fellows with supplementary earnings; and the duties and perquisites of the chaplain were shared between those in holy orders.

These salaries and modes of tenure were not noticeably different from those of other colleges. All over Oxford, the formula is much the same. But it is possible to sense a collegiate identity here, independent of the statistical evidence. The undergraduates attracted to the college in the mid-Victorian period were identifiably Brasenose men: civil and plain spoken; loyal to a fault; social but not too smart, churchy but not pious, athletic but not irredeemably philistine. It was also a college capable of generating intense loyalty: 'Good Old BNC'. In the jargon of the day, these men had 'pluck'. And—socially speaking—Brasenose held one additional trump card. In 1859–60 the Prince of Wales was in Oxford. He was an undergraduate at Christ Church; but he resided in a BNC property: Frewin Hall (pl. 43).

So what held the college together? First there was a code of mutually acceptable behaviour, based on a set of shared assumptions. Second, it has to be repeated, Brasenose was still part of the educational armoury of the Church of England. Religious tests and compulsory chapel; dons mostly unmarried and in holy orders; plus a sizeable majority of undergraduates from clerical backgrounds: only gradually, through the reforms of the 1850s and the 1870s, was the Church establishment's grip on Oxford education eventually loosened. Third, of course, there was Cradock's obsession with organized games. And

---

[23] Merton, Magdalen, Brasenose, and St John's experienced an aggregate rise in net external income, between 1883 and 1903, of between 17 and 18% (A. Engel, in *Econ. Hist. Rev.* 2nd ser. 31 (1978), 442). For a discussion of these matters, see also J. P. D. Dunbabin, in *Econ. Hist. Rev.* 2nd ser. 28 (1975), 631 ff. and 31 (1978), 446–9.

[24] *PP* (1881), lvi, pt. ii, 88–90.

fourthly there was the tug of institutional pride: once again 'Good Old BNC'. College allegiance transcended generations, transcended class. It was this pervasive sense of loyalty that underwrote the premium placed upon sporting achievement by mid-Victorian Brasenose men.

To all this Pater raised no objection. He had aesthetic reasons for admiring sportsmen, and he was not averse to the status that accrued to even the most junior of Fellowships. But first and foremost the college made it possible for him to write. Brasenose might boast of its sporting prowess, but it was also a place where scholarship could still be taken seriously. The easy tempo of college life fostered Pater's development as an essayist. Within ten years of his election, he had opened up new pathways into the *mentalité* of the Renaissance; within twenty he had recreated the spiritual milieu of early Roman Christianity; and within thirty he had even managed to reconstitute the aesthetic premisses of Platonic thinking.

Cradock's overriding principle was that 'every member of the college should do something for its credit... When any of his lads gained what he considered a solid distinction, whether of body or brain, he used to ask the performer to dine, and proudly introduce the young man to his guests.'[25] In 1861, for example, W. B. Woodgate (pl. 44)—champion in sculls and pairs—found himself dining with W. L. Stonhouse, winner of the Chancellor's Prize for Latin verse. Mrs Cradock—'Bunny' to her friends—was adept at bringing together disparate interests and age groups. Her drawing room was a veritable 'oasis in [a] wilderness of celibates'. Jowett even managed a little mild flirtation with a daughter of the Dean of Bristol. Goldwin Smith was enchanted. 'Mrs. Cradock', he recalled, 'was very bright, full of anecdote and fun... [She supplied] genuine Afternoon Tea, a meeting of a few people for real enjoyment, with talk, music and reading aloud; far different from the social battue of people crowded into a house in which there is hardly room for them to stand, and talking against a hubbub, into which Afternoon Tea has grown.'[26] There was hymn singing on Sunday evenings, and amateur *fêtes champêtres* in Bunny's rose garden in summer.[27] Cradock himself enjoyed a wide range of company. But he always put Brasenose first. He 'could not forgive a man who was no good to the college. And if he happened to come across such a failure he would speak his mind with refreshing frankness.'[28] Physical idleness was especially reprehensible. On one occasion, 'pronouncing sentence on an unruly member of the College, [the Chief] told him he must go down as he was "no good to the

[25] Woodgate, *Reminiscences*, 126–7.

[26] G. Smith, *Reminiscences* (New York, 1911), 280.

[27] E. Abbott and L. Campbell, *Life and Letters of Benjamin Jowett*, i (1897), 267; G. Faber, *Jowett* (1957), 301–4.

[28] A. C. Plowden, *Grain or Chaff? The Autobiography of a Police Magistrate* (1903), 61–2. 'Everybody', Cradock used to say, 'can do something better than anybody else' (*Brazen Nose*, i. 19).

College, physically, mentally or morally". The order of preference was characteristic.'[29]

Many of the incidents relating to Cradock's regime are recorded in Woodgate's *Reminiscences of an Old Sportsman* (1909). Walter Bradford Woodgate (pl. 57) is remembered today as the founder of Vincent's; the finest oarsman of his generation.[30] His eccentricity was unstudied, in costume, manner, and speech. In winter he wore a low-crowned 'John Bull' hat; in summer—at least in his early days—a white top hat of excessive height. Throughout a long life as a barrister, he maintained his early reputation for anecdote and salty language. He arrived at Brasenose from Radley in 1859, went straight into the first Eight, and stayed there for eight seasons, the last three as a graduate. Prompted no doubt by S. H. Reynolds's connection with the school, there were five Radleians that year out of an overall intake of thirty. Of these five, 'Guts' Woodgate was the only scholar. He was able enough as an undergraduate to earn pocket money by writing sermons for idle incumbents. But scholarship scarcely figured on his agenda. Good manners certainly did. 'B.N.C. was a comparatively quiet college in those days', he recalled; 'we did not fall foul of our dons as in other colleges.' At Merton, for example, in 1865, Mob Quad was nearly destroyed in a Guy Fawkes riot; and in 1879, at Wadham, the college was reduced to employing a private detective to investigate disorder.[31] At Univ., tutors and pupils led a veritable 'cat and dog' existence; 'screwing up' the oaks of unpopular dons was commonplace; and in Trinity term, 1880, the same college endured the ignominy of mass rustication.[32] At Brasenose, by contrast, there was mutual forbearance. The sportsmen acted on the principle that 'every don [was] a gentleman until he proved himself to the contrary'. As a freshman Woodgate was sufficiently confident in this assumption to invite Vice-Principal Menzies to

[29] F. Weatherley, *Piano and Gown* (1926), 44. For Cradock in sporting mode, see Shrimpton caricature, Madan coll., II, 277.

[30] *ODNB*; obits, *The Times*, 2 Nov. 1920 and *The Field*, 6, 13 Nov. 1920. 'He was in the Oxford winning crews of 1862 and 1863, and won the university pairs three times and the sculls twice; at Henley he won the Grand Challenge cup in 1865, the Steward's cup in 1862, the Diamond sculls in 1864 and the Goblets in 1861, 1862, 1863, 1866 and 1868. He also held the Wingfield sculls in 1862, 1864 and 1867' (*ODNB*). Two of his books, *Oars and Sculls* (1875) and *Boating* (1888), remain classics. As 'Wat Brandwood', he wrote *O.V.H., or How Mr. Blake became an M.F.H.*, and its sequel *Ensemble*.

[31] Woodgate, *Reminiscences*, 106; J. Covert, *A Victorian Marriage: Mandell and Louise Creighton* (2000), 40; *Oxford and Cambridge Undergraduate's Jnl.* 29 May and 5 June 1879, 434, 449.

[32] Woodgate, *Reminiscences*, 123–4; *Oxford and Cambridge Undergraduate's Jnl.* 13 and 20 May 1880, 410, 426–7, 431–2; *Oxford Chronicle*, 15 and 22 May 1880; *Oxford Mail*, 21 Aug. 1935. The cricket match between Univ. and BNC in 1880 had to be cancelled. Part of the trouble at Univ. stemmed from an attempt to eliminate the keeping of pet dogs (W. E. Sherwood, *Oxford Yesterday* (Oxford, 1927), 31). These were permitted at BNC by this time, although they had been banned in 1851 (V-P's Reg. 13 Feb. 1851, fo. 121). Woodgate's black and tan fox terrier, Jenny, wore Brasenose colours at Henley (Woodgate, *Reminiscences*, 112, 115).

lunch. And when Stonehewer Illingworth—immortal name!—became drunk and disorderly at a bump supper in 1865, Menzies was quite unperturbed. 'Shake hands Mr. Illingworth', he announced next morning; 'We don't go head of the river every day.' A year later Illingworth repaid the courtesy: he helped Menzies settle into his new rectory at Great Shefford.[33]

Sometimes the mores of an aggressively male college in the mid-nineteenth century are difficult to translate into modern terms. BNC was famous at this time for its amateur theatricals. These included a good deal of amiable cross-dressing. William Allgood and Gordon Haigh, for example, had been the stars of 1858, in a performance of *Still Waters Run Deep*. This seems to have been the earliest instance of college theatricals in Oxford. Before that, there were occasional inter-college performances, with imported actresses, located outside proctorial jurisdiction: *The Travestie of Macbeth* for example, put on by the Oxford Dramatic Amateurs at Henley in 1847.[34] In 1859 it was Woodgate's turn. That January he was already in training for Torpids, eating raw steaks, and running in the Parks before morning chapel. 'I was', however, 'very effeminate in appearance', he recalled. In fact he was nicknamed the Apollo of Brasenose. 'This at once helped me into the best set (Phoenix) ... to play ... Lady Barbara in *The Little Savage.*' After the performance, there was 'a supper on the usual College lines of those days; pretty substantial—oysters, dressed crab, grilled bones, poached eggs etc ... after a 6pm. dinner in hall. Then an adjournment to other rooms where stood four steaming punchbowls—whisky, rum, gin and brandy. Every one had taken wine with me (twice over) at the heavy section of the meal, first as a lady, secondly as a freshman. My head swam before I reached the punch room. I was still in my petticoats (velvet dress and lace) ... My ... memory is a blank till the next morning, when I woke with awful "hot coppers". I tumbled up to chapel, my rouge of the play still thick on my cheeks (simple cold bath had not removed it). As I came out of chapel, I ... found myself famous ... I had an instant levee in the cloisters; "Lady Barbara!" ... "What a painted Jezabel!" ... At least half-a-dozen off-hand invitations to breakfast: but I had to feed with the Torpid ... I nearly died at the smell of fragrant mutton chops; but ... I was fairly fit for afternoon rowing ... I received not even reproof from a tutor ... [Apparently, the night before] I had been carried out to the open air, and laid on a mat on chilly quadrangle turf to recover, and then carted off to bed.'[35]

---

[33] Woodgate, *Reminiscences*, 106, 125; F. Menzies, *Some Village Sermons*, intro L. G. Smith (1903).

[34] G. R. Winter, artist and oarsman, appeared as MacDuff wearing his Oxford Eight boater, 'his helmet having been mislaid'. A sketch of the finale was made by G. A. Sala for 'Sugary' Thompson, the Oxford print seller (Bedford, in Quiller-Couch (ed.), *Reminiscences*, 381).

[35] Woodgate, *Reminiscences*, 102–4. Another 'capital actor' was D. L. Landale, who starred in 1863 in *A Wonderful Woman*, in Holywell Music Room. He was soon afterwards lost in the bush

The freshmen of Woodgate's year, 1859, came mostly from clerical families. The great majority were Pass men; their interests were overwhelmingly
sporting. Only eight out of thirty took Honours degrees. There were two Ivy
League Americans: Frank Dean and Henry Taylor. Of these Taylor in
particular set Oxford conventions at defiance. He hunted in pink, smoked
cigars in the street, and was caricatured in *Punch*: addressing a Proctor as 'old
hoss' and offering him a fiver.[36] But the intake as a whole was by no means
plutocratic. At least eleven of the thirty were sons of clergymen; and thirteen
became clergymen themselves. One was a Wykehamist: A. M. Lipscomb.
Two were Harrovians: Hartwell Grissell and J. H. Gumbleton. Otherwise
they mostly came from schools of lesser rank. Apart from the five Radleians,
for instance, St Paul's, Rossall, and King's Canterbury all supplied two each.
It was not a year that was academically distinguished. In fact there were only
two first-rate scholars: Francis Chancellor, a mathematician from Oundle;
and W. H. Maber, a classicist from Marlborough. Both died in their twenties.
On the other hand, two figures from that year did live long enough to enjoy
lives of agreeably peripheral learning. Hartwell de la Garde Grissell (pl. 51)—
in Woodgate's words, 'a non athlete, but... popular'—inherited part of a
building fortune from Thomas Grissell of Norbury Park; after appointment
as chamberlain to the Pope, in time for the Vatican Council of 1869–70, he
eventually bequeathed a collection of papal coins to the Ashmolean.[37]
Wladyslaw Somerville Lach-Szyrma, the son of a famous Polish exile, held
a series of Cornish livings—as well as chaplaincies at Spa, Marienbad, and
Aix-La-Chapelle—and is chiefly remembered as a West Country topographer.[38] But these men were exceptions. The cohort of 1859 was un-
ashamedly muscular. That summer the first Eight—in the first of
Woodgate's eight years—made no fewer than five bumps, a feat not equalled
by the college until 1922.[39] 'I had the luck', Woodgate recalled, 'never to be
bumped in Eights; and only once in Torpids, with a broken oar... The only
bump which befell B.N.C. during my career... was in 1861, by Trinity, and

near Mt. Bischoff, Tasmania (ibid. 121). Undergraduate theatricals in which women took
men's parts were banned by the University in 1871, and were not permitted again until 1883
when performances were restricted to Shakespeare, the female roles being played by lady
amateurs (M. G. Brock, in *HUO* vii. 35).

[36] Woodgate, *Reminiscences*, 134–5; *Punch*, 36 (1859), 151. Taylor had already been rusticated
from Harvard.

[37] Woodgate, *Reminiscences*, 174. At Oxford he was friendly with Oscar Wilde and David
Hunter Blair, the future Benedictine Abbot and Baronet (*Letters of Oscar Wilde*, ed. M. Holland
and R. Hart-Davis (2000), 61).

[38] He also published poems and novels.

[39] Photo of crew sent with letter to R. W. Jeffery by Revd J. B. Orme, 7 June 1922 (MPP 56
F 4/1).

I was out of the boat that day—crippled. Our Coxswain—"Sally" Parkin (so called from playing the slavey "Sally" in *Whitebait at Greenwich*) had made a swipe at my face at dinner, forgetting that "she" was holding a knife. I just parried it, to save my nose, and got it in the fleshy outside of my right hand. It had to be sewed up: I remember that when the blood spurted, our tall no. 5, "Long" Coxe—now Rector of Stoke Bruerne, Northamptonshire—gave a grunt and turned over, falling like a log on the floor. (Blood upsets some stomachs after a full meal) . . .'[40]

No wonder Walter Pater thought the hearties of BNC were 'like playful young tigers [recently] fed'.[41] To Pater we will return; but first a few more exploits of Brasenose sportsmen. Some were certainly wild. 'Jack' Morley—a cousin of the Liberal statesman—seems to have been a veritable caricature. 'Comical to look at, as broad as he was long; enormous calves and arms. As a freshman [1859] he used to amuse himself by bending all the pokers in front quad rooms into hoops, round his bull neck.'[42] After dinner one evening in London, he bet Woodgate a sovereign that he could not walk that night from Mayfair to Oxford. Starting out in his dinner suit at 9 p.m., Woodgate reached Henley at 6, in time for light refreshment. By 11 he was strolling home across Magdalen Bridge. 'My waistcoat and trousers', he recalled, 'were badly spotted with the perspiration that had dropped all night from my face. My kid, elastic-sided evening boots (the fashion of that day) had split . . . and I had torn my pocket-handkerchief into strips to bind them up. After I had tubbed and breakfasted . . . for wanton bravado, I [then] went down to the river, got my sculling boat, and sculled to Nuneham . . . and back. I slept well that night . . . [but missed] chapel on Good Friday morning.' Woodgate clearly had formidable stamina: he once went three rounds with Tom Sayers; he even swam in the Channel with Captain Webb.[43]

And then there was 'Springy' Colmore. T. M. Colmore was a Rugbeian who could run like the wind. Of course he won the 100 yards sprint for Oxford against Cambridge in 1866. But what was extraordinary was his speed over the middle distance of the race. 'From about the thirtieth to the eightieth yard, [he] was simply marvellous: to an onlooker he seemed to be in air all the

---

[40] Woodgate, *Reminiscences*, 179.

[41] Gosse, *Critical Kit-Kats*, 270. Once 'two exuberant sportsmen upset a large can of paraffin [in the rooms above him] . . . Slowly the contents trickled between the ancient floorboards, and finally dripped steadily onto Pater's head as he lay sleeping' (C. J. Holmes, *Self and Partners* (1936), 103).

[42] Woodgate, *Reminiscences*, 108.

[43] Ibid. 155–6, 170–1, 448. Woodgate always denied that rowing was harmful to health: 'My own experience of rowing is that heart and lungs never suffer, with a man in real training . . . [In 1871] I was passed by an Insurance Office as A 1 . . . [though] I believe I have rowed more than any other amateur or professional' (Woodgate, in J. E. Morgan (ed.), *University Oars . . . a Critical Enquiry into the After-Health of the Men who Rowed in the Oxford and Cambridge Boat-Race* (1873), 255).

time: his feet—to the eye—off the ground all the way, like an artist's sketch of a galloping horse.'[44] That simile was too good to miss. Bets were taken: could Colmore out-race a galloping horse, running 90 yards while the horse did 100? 'Bobby' O'Neill—son of the Revd Baron O'Neill—supplied the requisite steed; the astonished horse did manage to win, and by two lengths, but only after ferocious application of the whip.

One or two of Woodgate's contemporaries were slightly less boisterous. Samuel Waddington and A. C. Plowden arrived at Brasenose in 1862, aged only 17. Both were Pass men; both were early members of Vincent's; Plowden was also in the Phoenix, and in 1865 he founded the Vampires. But both eventually settled into useful careers, in civil service and the law. Waddington turned out to be not a bad poet, and Plowden ended up as a liberal and witty magistrate. Both left thoughtful memoirs, and through these we have a rather different measure of the tempo of mid-Victorian BNC.

First Waddington, tucked away for three years high up in the attic of staircase VI, his latticed window shaded by the chestnuts of Exeter garden. Waddington was on the progressive side—Jowett rather than Pusey; Kingsley rather than Newman—and his moderate churchmanship eventually faded into rationalism.

We used to go and bathe in the river at 7am returning to college in time for morning chapel at 8. The hours between breakfast and lunch were fully occupied in attending college 'lectures', and the afternoon was usually spent on the river, or in long walks in the country, or in reading at the Union [Brasenose library was still at that time reserved for dons]. It was therefore only for an hour before dining in hall, and afterwards in the evening, that we were ever much alone… [Besides, we] were also most diligent in attending breakfast-parties, luncheon-parties, and 'wines' after dinner. The hours passed smoothly and merrily; and… owing to exercise—rowing, walking and swimming—excellent food, Brasenose ale which was at that time celebrated for its strength-giving properties, and port wine, we hourly and daily increased in bodily vigour, and after three years' residence left the university certainly stronger and, we will hope, wiser men.[45]

Reading books—and Waddington read a good deal, mostly English poetry and French philosophy—was obviously reserved for the vacation.

The memoirs of 'Baby' Plowden (pl. 42) are less rose-tinted. 'No-one was more popular in his day', recalled Woodgate; 'he made quite a pretty girl, as a lady of the harem in *Barefaced Imposters*… in 1863.'[46] But years later, when he came to write his recollections, he did not mince words. The age of top hats and Dundreary whiskers, of dog-carts and rat-hunts, had been too often also an age

---

[44] Woodgate, *Reminiscences*, 222.

[45] S. Waddington, *Chapters of my Life* (1909), 30–1, 45–6. He published several books of sonnets, a study of A. H. Clough (1883), and *Some Views Respecting a Future Life* (1917).

[46] Woodgate, *Reminiscences*, 180.

of idleness: gambling and excessive drinking were common. 'There was a very large margin of leisure', Plowden remembered, 'at the disposal of an idle undergraduate, and if there was abundant leisure there was certainly also abundant temptation... The wonder is that one didn't come to grief altogether.' There were no restrictions except 'morning chapel, occasional lectures, and... being within the college walls by midnight... In the summer term everybody was in the playing fields till 9 o'clock, and the college was practically deserted.' No wonder the temptation to smash windows or climb lamp-posts sometimes proved irresistible. In any case, subsequent punishment was light. 'Many an evening during...'gating [the Senior Bursar, T. H. R. Shand] would lighten up my captivity by inviting me to dine in his rooms [VII, 2] , 'and very pleasant little dinners they were'. In effect, dons and undergraduates seem to have agreed between themselves to keep up a polite conspiracy of convenience. Four very basic Pass degree papers, spread over a minimum of three years, each taken up to three times if necessary, with extra terms thrown in for the asking: 'the waste of time', Plowden concludes, was 'ridiculous'.[47]

Academic study was not completely ignored. And this fact has to be emphasized, since BNC's sporting triumphs are all too easily remembered. Between Reynolds's election in 1855 and Pater's resignation of his Tutorship in 1883 Brasenose scored forty-eight Firsts in classical Mods and eleven in Greats. To put this in a wider perspective: in 1865 BNC's three Firsts in Mods represented a quarter of the University total; in 1871 a score of three more accounted for approximately one-fifth; and a total of four in 1875 represented exactly one-seventh. And of the eleven men taking Firsts in Greats, six later achieved Oxford Fellowships. This was way behind Balliol and Corpus; but it was eminently respectable. At least one New College man—Lionel Johnson—was wistfully envious: 'Oh, to be reading Greats at B.N.C.!'[48] Other subjects were not quite as strong, but they were by no means weak. During the same period of twenty-eight years there were eighteen Firsts in mathematics Mods—a much smaller University list, of course—and ten in the maths and physics Schools. Only Balliol and Queen's were consistently stronger. There were just two Firsts in the brand new School of Modern History. But in 1874

[47] Plowden, *Grain or Chaff?*, 49–50, 52–3, 58, 61. 'A [Pass] degree may be attained... by the work of about an hour or two daily. The vast majority of Pass men do not read so much' (J. E. Thorold Rogers, *Education in Oxford* (1861), 150). 'The mere Pass can never be considered justifiable for any man of commonly good abilities, commonly good health, and commonly good education' (M. Burrows, *Pass and Class* (1861), 23). For contemporary attitudes to study, see also Sherwood, *Oxford Yesterday, passim*.

[48] [L. Johnson] reviewing *Plato and Platonism* in *Westminster Gazette* (1893); reprinted in T. Whittemore (ed.), *Post Liminium* (1911). For a poem by Johnson on Pater, and an obituary of Johnson, see *The Academy*, 11 Oct. 1902, 397–8.

one was a name to remember: Arthur J. Evans, later of Knossos and the Ashmolean.[49] Even so, it was the athletes who set the pace. That is the paradox of mid-Victorian Brasenose. There were a number of effective tutors: Turner, Reynolds, and Marshall; even Shand and Yates. Several Fellows were outstanding in their field. G. Baldwin Brown, for example, a Fellow in 1874–7, became a pioneer in the study of Saxon art. Each year a handful of under-graduate scholars maintained respectable academic standards. But the athletes created the image of the place. It was their achievements that were popularly recognized, especially in the 1860s and 1870s. One other factor in the make-up of the college is worth remembering too. Every resident member still attended chapel once a day and twice on Sundays. In the 1860s the number of undergraduates who went into holy orders remained—to modern eyes—surprisingly high; higher indeed than the numbers reached in the days of the Oxford Movement. The generation of the 1830s, as often as not, ended up high church. The Revd Bryan King of St George's in the East, London, became particularly notorious. By the 1860s, however, undergraduate atti-tudes had cooled. Quite a number belonged to the evangelical wing. Henry Bazely, 'the Oxford Evangelist', is one example. John Knott, who gave up a Tractarian plum posting at St Saviour's, Leeds, to travel out to India as a missionary in 1869, had been another. But high or low, during the 1860s and 1870s well over 50 per cent of Brasenose men went into the Church.[50]

All this ties in closely with Cradock's policy of recruitment. His attitudes were liberal. He regarded the college as a 'free trade' zone in matters of faith. During his reign, religious friction diminished, and the number of matricu-lations increased steadily. As agricultural rents began to fall in the 1870s—and as stock market returns began to waver—the need to increase college revenue through additional recruitment became quite clear. In the University as a whole, matriculations increased significantly; but at BNC the intake rose dramatically, tripling between 1860 and 1875. By the latter date numbers were almost back to their level in the palmy days of Frodsham Hodson. That meant, in particular, recruits from the top public schools: during the early 1870s their numbers rose to more than 73 per cent of the annual intake.[51] The

[49] 'The "first" which I . . . wrung for him out of the obdurate Stubbs' (J. R. Green to E. A. Freeman: *Letters of J. R. Green*, ed. L. Stephen (1901), 422). In 1878 Evans married Freeman's daughter Margaret (d. 1893).

[50] By comparison, in 1854–63, 63.3% of Oxford graduates took holy orders; in 1882–91 only 38.8% (figures calculated by M. Curthoys). For chapel attendance, see V-P's Reg. 21 Dec. 1857, fo. 4. For BNC evangelicals, see J. S. Reynolds, *The Evangelicals at Oxford 1735–1871* (Oxford, 1975). Like Bazely, most came under the influence of Revd A. M. W. Christopher at St Aldate's (E. L. Hicks, *Henry Bazely*, 1886). For W. Whitaker on tutors in his time, see *Brazen Nose*, iii. 256.

[51] A. J. Jenkinson, 'The Schools, University Honours, and Professions of Brasenose Men in the 19th Century', in *Quat. Mon.* XIV. ii, 37.

numbers from Manchester Grammar School correspondingly dwindled—
halving in fact between the 1840s and the 1870s—partly because of the
declining value of Somerset Scholarships. On the other hand, numbers of
sportsmen—Champneys, Coxe, and Pocklington (pls. 56, 57) for example—
were subsidized by Hulme Exhibitions. That hardly chimed in with William
Hulme's original concern for poor scholars. But it certainly bolstered BNC's
muscular intake. Not surprisingly, we see a drastic decline during this period
in the number of men reading for Honours. The four years 1871–5 marked
the high (or low) point in this process: 142 commoners to 32 scholars. This
did not go unnoticed in the wider world. On 19 October 1878 an amusing
advertisement appeared in the *Whitehall Review*:

Wanted, every October, for four £80 scholarships a few really good men for the
University Eight and Eleven. Papers will be set in Lillywhite's *Cricketing Annual* and
Woodgate's *Notes on Rowing*... They must produce certificates of biceps, breadth of
chest, and size of calves...

Of course Brasenose was not unique in its enthusiams. In 1867 one Fellow of
Merton told a Commons Committee that the current 'idolatry of athleticism'
was 'one of the greatest mischiefs of the day'.[52] It was just that, when it came
to organized games, Cradock knew how to pick a winner. And he had no
objection to boisterous behaviour.

High jinks occasionally spilled over into something more sinister. In April
1869 BNC recruited a rather unusual freshman. His name was Llewellyn Jones,
son of Ernest Jones, Chartist.[53] Now Jones Sen. had been a gentleman
Chartist—a godson of the Duke of Cumberland—but a Chartist none the
less, and a physical-force man to boot. He called for revolution, the bloodier
the better. With the collapse of the Chartist Movement, he ended his days in
penury; and it was only with the help of sympathetic friends that his son was
able to go as a scholarship boy, via Manchester Grammar School, to Brasenose.
He arrived at a comparatively mature age: 21. And he found himself, the son of
a notorious rebel, surrounded—in Matthew Arnold's phrase—by barbarians.

I was at a College where learning played a very subordinate part to sports; Eton,
Harrow, and the other great public schools sent contingents of lusty athletes of the
aristocracy and upper middle class to spend three years in pursuit of pleasure,
qualified only by a thin veneer of learning sufficient to satisfy the requests of
an indulgent authority. There were indeed hard-working students, scholars from
provincial grammar schools... They moiled and toiled by day and by night to obtain

---

[52] C. S. Roundell, 2 July 1867 to Select Committee... on Oxford and Cambridge (*PP*
(1867), xiii), 214. He was himself a cricket blue.

[53] Obit, *The Times*, 27, 29 Jan. 1869 and 27, 31 Mar. 1869. See also J. Saville (ed.), *Ernest Jones:
Chartist* (1952).

a degree with honours, and . . . entered on the battle for life physically and mentally enfeebled.[54]

That is a little wide of the mark. Eton and Harrow have never dominated the intake at BNC. And in reality there was scarcely an aristocrat among the thirty-one freshmen that year; fifteen were the sons of clergymen; and seven were actually scholars. The bulk of the cohort, however, were indeed of public school origin, with a fair sprinkling of gentry. Strictly speaking, young Jones was gentry too; but his father's career had placed him well beyond the pale.

One night in March 1870 there was a debate in college on the issue of Irish nationalism. Jones spoke out in support of the Fenians.

The hot-heads of this sanctuary of Tories could not brook this outrage; and a night or two after, after returning to my rooms, I found my bedding lying soaked in water at the bottom of three flights of stairs and my room [old X, 8] wrecked. The young barbarians had wreaked their vengeance, and for a time the placid life of the college was disturbed by a feud between those who favoured my aggressors and those who sympathised with their victim.[55]

At that time there were several Anglo-Irish hearties at BNC, on whom suspicion might well have fallen. James Stronge, then in his second year, perhaps: a future major in the Inniskillings, High Sheriff of Tyrone and Armagh, and secretary to the Ulster Defence Union;[56] or the Hon. Bernard Fitzpatrick, heir to the barony of Castletown, then in his third year: a headstrong tearaway who fought a duel with the future Duke of Wellington, and kept a 15 ft python in his rooms in college [II, 2].[57] But no: the perpetrator turned out to be a young Rugbeian, born in Russia, named Samuel Keate Gwyer. Not only had he committed 'this outrage'; he also refused to apologize. A special meeting of the Governing Body was called. Cradock, Shand, Turner, Watson, Pater, Wordsworth, and Ward were all present. Gwyer was rusticated for the rest of the year.[58] In fact he never reappeared at all. Young Jones went on to the Inner Temple and became Mr Justice Atherley-Jones, KC, JP; for nearly thirty years Liberal MP for Durham North West.[59]

Much more violent than this event were the Town v. Gown riots which still disfigured public occasions. On the Prince of Wales's birthday in 1860—he was at that time resident in Frewin—there was a firework display in

---

[54] L. A. Atherley-Jones, *Looking Back* (privately printed 1925; presented to BNC library by E. G. Collieu), 17.

[55] Ibid. 18.

[56] 5th Bt., of Tynan Abbey, Co. Armagh (destroyed by the IRA, 1981).

[57] Obit, *Daily Express*, 1 Dec. 1925. See also Castletown's autobiography, *Ego* (1924).

[58] V-P's Reg. Mar. 1870, fo. 177.

[59] Obit, *The Times*, 17 June, 1929, 19. He published, anonymously, a number of novels including *The Fall of Lord Paddockslea*.

Merton Meadow. Two BNC men, John Brown and Francis Farquhar, were cornered by 'town roughs'—30 to 2—and 'cut up badly...by some iron implement. The leader of this massacre', Woodgate recalled, 'was...a notorious lickspittle rough known as Oxford George'.[60] In 1867, the usual 5 November troubles were particularly wild. Mervyn Prower (pl. 47A), then in his second year, was seriously injured by a butcher's knife—as his memorial in chapel explains—'inter tumultum plebis'. A fortnight later he was dead.[61] In 1869 Brasenose was besieged by Guy Fawkes rioters with flaming torches; and in 1876, one BNC freshman—E. R. Turton, then lodging in the Turl—was reduced to driving back a posse of townsmen with a well-aimed riding whip. Such battles were fortunately rare. But Brasenose hearties might well have been better advised to restrict their activities to college premises: clambering over battlements at midnight,[62] or spattering Cain and Abel with red paint.[63] By modern standards, mid-Victorian Oxford was certainly a boisterous place. The solemnities of Encaenia, for example, were sometimes noisier than Last Night at the Proms.

The social life of Brasenose in the early 1860s is unusually well documented. We have the memoirs; we have the photographs, in college and out; we know the smartest lodgings: at 59 the High and over Standen's outfitters in Catte Street (pls. 42A and B).[64] We know where the evangelicals met for evening prayer meetings: in A. C. Downer's rooms on old staircase X, Back Quad.[65] We have the menus of private suppers: oysters, lobsters, mulled ale. We know all the Masonic affiliations: one-third of Woodgate's year were members

[60] Woodgate, *Reminiscences*, 154–5.

[61] He was injured on 9 Nov. 1867. He then apparently contracted typhoid fever, and died in college on 28 Nov. 1867 (V-P's Reg. 28 Nov. 1867, fo. 152^v; *Oxford Undergraduate's Jnl.* 5 Dec. 1867, 218). For 5 Nov. 1869 and 1876, see *Brazen Nose*, iv. 197.

[62] Entwistle and Pauncefote caused 'considerable damage by displacing tiles etc.', and were rusticated. If they had not confessed, they would have been treated more harshly (V-P's Reg. 9 Mar. 1869, fo. 167). Two years later W. B. Hornby was involved in a similar escapade above staircases V and VI.

[63] As in *c*.1874: 'It was a dark night, and no murder was ever planned more secretly. There was not a soul about the Quad, but next morning the perpetrator was sent for by the Vice-Principal, Revd. E. T. Turner (who we believed wore glasses [pl. 33] to prevent him seeing too much).' The sinner was C. Coltman Rogers, 'a keen musician and most delightful man', later MP for Radnorshire and author of *Conifers and their Characteristics* (1920) (Canon Egerton Leigh, in *Brazen Nose*, iv. 453; and C. C. Eley, ibid, ix. 393).

[64] Photos survive (MPP 41 A2) of these 'digs', showing *inter alia* C. E. Harris, C. Grissell, G. J. Barry, A. C. Plowden, and E. W. Knollys (pls. 42A and B). See also Plowden, *Grain or Chaff?*, 58.

[65] Cradock accepted 'free trade' in college religion. Evangelical prayer meetings began in Eights Week 1867. Downer later published *Mountaineering Ballads* (n.d.), and ended as chaplain at Biarritz (A. C. Downer, *A Century of Evangelical Religion in Oxford* (1938), 44).

of Apollo Lodge, that is exactly ten out of thirty.[66] We know who drank the best port: C. E. Harris, secretary of the Phoenix (pl. 42A).[67] We even have nearly thirty names of one particular group of undergraduates, burned into the windowsills of one particular room. The room in question is II, 3: a panelled study on the first floor, with a tiny bedroom; both rooms looking out over Old Quad towards Radcliffe Square. For two years, 1862–4, this was the private empire of J. C. Daubuz, a Harrovian banker with an estate at Killiow in Cornwall. He played no games and he took no degree; but he was clearly a college man through and through. When he went down in 1864 he made a present of silver to the college; and the year before that, he commissioned a record of the appearance of his study: a watercolour by J. B. Pyne. That image still hangs in II, 3; and in the mid-twentieth century generations of historians must have idly noticed it during tutorials with Eric Collieu. What few seem to have spotted is the fact that thirty of these windowsill inscriptions date from exactly the same period: the two years of Daubuz's occupancy. Here then is an identifiable 'set': a group of undergraduates breakfasting and lunching together—whist and 'vingt-et-un' were popular games—and recording their participation with a red-hot poker.

What do we find? Daubuz himself, of course, is there; and 'Baby' Plowden and Weldon Champneys; and 'Bobby' Shepherd and Duncan Pocklington (pl. 56); as well as R. T. Whittington, P. A. Latham, and A. J. Richards—all names to conjure with in Brasenose rowing. Here too is W. E. Heap, a prodigious runner; and E. L. Fellowes, a more than prodigious fast bowler. And of course there are the names of those who seem to have done nothing in particular. But this is by no means the smartest set. There are hardly any names from the Phoenix. The range of backgrounds is fairly uniform; understandably so, given the homogeneous intake of the period. There is scarcely a scholar in the list. All much as one might expect. But one common denominator comes rather as a surprise. Over half this group—18 out of 30—have directly clerical affiliations. That is, they are either the sons of clergymen, or they are future clergymen themselves; or both. Mid-Victorian Brasenose was certainly muscular, but it was above all muscularly Christian.[68]

---

[66] Woodgate never progressed beyond Master Mason; he was instituted at the Apollo Lodge with his friend W. H. Erskine—later Earl of Mar and Kellie, of Alloa House, Clackmannan and Kellie Castle, Fife—who eventually became Deputy Grand Master (Scotland). Bossum the porter was a regular guest at the Apollo Lodge, as was Spiers, proprietor of a 'fancy goods emporium in the High' (Woodgate, *Reminiscences*, 120, 166, 198).

[67] Later C. E. Harris-St John. 'I fear he pays for it now—with gout, at West Court, Finchampstead' (ibid. 180).

[68] Several of this group appear in one photograph (MPP 203 A1; reproduced in *Brazen Nose*, i. 274 with key ibid., i. 304). The term 'muscular Christian' seems first to have been used by T. C. Sandars in the *Saturday Rev.* (1857), vis-à-vis Charles Kingsley. Once, when BNC and

Woodgate himself is missing from this list. But then he was not in the Phoenix either. In 1861 half the Phoenix men were his fellow Radleians (pl. 48); but there seems to have been no room for Woodgate: he was always a wayward spirit. More to the point, his horizons were University-wide, not college based. Hence his enthusiasm for Apollo Lodge: he was the Apollo of Apollo. Hence too his greatest social achievement, the foundation of Vincent's in 1863. This was to be a club much broader than mere collegiate societies; but at the same time more exclusive than the University Union or the OUBC. In fact it began with just forty of Woodgate's 'special friends'. Its inaugural meeting was held in BNC, but not in Woodgate's own rooms (V, 4); by that time he was living out.[69] Instead he chose the headquarters of a close friend, the 'crack sprinter' W. E. Heap (III, 3, now HCR);[70] Thereafter, the club was attached to no particular college. Its name was taken from that of Vincent, the University printer, whose High Street rooms were at first rented by Woodgate for £100 p.a. (pl. 52A).[71] Naturally, Brasenose supplied a nucleus, eleven founder members in fact: W. H. Dunn, L. Garnett, A. W. Grant, C. E. Harris, R. B. Leach, W. E. Heap, S. E. Illingworth, P. A. Latham, S. Phillips, A. C. Plowden, and of course Woodgate himself.[72] Four Radleians, three Etonians; hunting, rowing, cricket, sprinting—from the start this was a club for sportsmen and gentlemen. And for Freemasons too: six of the eleven Brasenose founders were Apollo men, including of course Woodgate himself. It was not a club exclusively for blues: as late as the 1890s, they supplied less than half the membership. But it was a club that was by definition exclusive. Over the years, its definition of eligibility has of course altered a good deal. Oxford evolves; but Vincent's flourishes still.

So too, for another century at least, did both the Vampires and the Octagon. Vincent's 1863; the Vampires 1865; the Octagon 1866: mid-Victorian Brasenose was prolific in the founding of clubs. With breakfast, lunch, and tea all taken in private rooms—and still no JCR—there was inevitably a tendency to fragment. This process was not peculiar to one

---

Ch. Ch. men were accused of reading questionable French novels and defacing Bibles, John Cartwright rose to their defence: 'Brasenose and Christ Church men may be fast, but they are not sacrilegious' (*Oxford Undergraduate's Jnl.* 20 Nov. 1873, 83).

[69] At Cattel's lodgings, later part of Univ., on the corner of High St. and Logic Lane (Woodgate, *Reminiscences*, 112). For a view of Woodgate's college rooms in Dec. 1861, see his *Reminiscences*, 180. Present: Illingworth, Champneys, Erskine, Garnett, Heap, Leach, Phillips, Allgood, and a Radley friend not in fact at BNC, Col. Sir H. Oldham.

[70] Ibid. 187.

[71] By 1909 the club had moved four times. Its first servant was John Brown, the second his son 'young' John Brown (ibid. 186, 191).

[72] Ibid. 186–7, 189, 191. One black ball in eight excluded. 'The fun was great and the dinners vile' (H. A. N. Smith, in *Brazen Nose*, iii. 112).

college. Christ Church, for instance, boasted a number of clubs at this time, notably Loder's and Rouser's. The Gridiron, an intercollegiate coterie, was founded in 1884. Regular breakfasting and lunching in college halls began only with the foundation of Keble in 1868. The formation of clubs was thus part of the natural evolution of Oxford life. It was a process facilitated by the traditional staircase plan: a tradition, again, first broken by the Spartan corridors of Keble. When 'Baby' Plowden founded the Vampires, he was thus following a well-worn path. He designed it as a cricket club that did not take cricket too seriously. Sunday lunch was a major consideration.[73] Similarly, the Octagon. This was a dining club founded as a junior Phoenix; fine dining, but with rather less flummery. With octagonal plates and an octagonal minute book—to say nothing eventually of velvet smoking jackets—the Octagon might be thought to have outsmarted its senior rival. In a group photograph of 1867 (pl. 47A) they pose elegantly enough against a crumbling wall festooned with clematis.[74] But appearances are deceptive. What one would never guess—given the club's later reputation—is that no fewer than six of the eight founder members were prospective clergymen. Perhaps the Octagon began as a clerical counter to the notorious secularity of the Phoenix. Anyway, two of these three clubs—Vincent's and the Octagon—survive to this day.

Other institutions of mid-Victorian Oxford have proved to be less durable—'Show Sunday' and 'The Procession of Boats', for example.

'Show Sunday'... took place on the Sunday in Commemoration Week. After the Cathedral Service [at Christ Church] it was the custom for all Oxford, in cap and gown, to go into the Broad Walk and to promenade slowly up and down in two opposite streams. It was the great chance to show our friends, who had come up for the festivities of the ensuing week, all the celebrities of Oxford, since in a walk of only about a mile we met each of them four times over... The next night, Monday, was the Procession of Boats... The Head of the River, in a light racing boat, was moored opposite to the Varsity Barge [decked out, like all the barges, with flags]; and all the others in gig boats in their order on the river, followed by all the Torpids, rowed up from the Long Bridges and saluted the head boat in line, ship's fashion, by tossing their oars. They then went on through Folly Bridge, turned in the Pool, and passed down again to the Long Bridges. Thus we had about forty crews, all wearing their college hats and blazers [and in the case of BNC at least, broad scarves], and with banners bearing their college arms floating behind the coxwain's seat, passing

---

[73] One handwritten menu for 9 June 1906 survives: a substantial cold collation of salmon mayonnaise; cold roast beef, veal and ham pie, pressed beef or lamb; and macedoine of fruit, gooseberry tart or sponge cakes in custard (Ingram MSS).

[74] SL 11 B8/2. Loder's club had been founded as the Christ Church Society in 1814. The Octagon may have originated in a coterie known in 1862 as The Tome, which in turn grew out of the Torpid of 1861 (*Brazen Nose*, i. 73–5). The original eight members were Brooke Egerton, Charles Everard, Peter Gorringe, Alfred James, Richard Milne, Alexander Nash, Francis Percival, and Harvey Taverner (pl. 47A).

up and down in a double stream, like the people in the Broad Walk the evening
before, whilst the college barges [BNC had a splendid new barge from 1882
onwards] all flew their boating flags and the band played on the Varsity Barge.

Finally, after each of these functions, came the ritual ceremony of the
Nuneham picnic.

Men took their friends, their lady friends especially, down [the river] in all sorts of
boats... the ordinary pleasure boat for a small party [or] the larger 'company boats',
which were mostly the large racing eights of the 1820s and 1830s... towed by a horse
[or, for still] larger parties... one of the house-boats which required a couple of horses
to tow it.[75]

To round off the festivities came the Masonic Garden Party or 'Musical Fête'
in St John's, New College, or Worcester, and the Masonic Ball at the Corn
Exchange. The years 1863–5, when BNC held successive Lodge Masterships,
were particularly memorable. Photographs show Brasenose men well to the
fore, their Masonic garb vying for notice with the more elaborate dresses of
female guests. There was nothing secret about these Oxford Freemasons. In
fact Apollo Lodge remained fashionable and influential throughout this
period: Oscar Wilde was initiated in 1875, Cecil Rhodes in 1877.[76]

    Show Sunday lasted until the end of the 1870s; the Procession of Boats
until 1893. Throughout this period BNC figured prominently. The college
rowed head of the river on thirty consecutive nights in 1852–5; and in two of
those years, 1852 and 1853, held the headship simultaneously in both Eights
and Torpids. Among the stars of that generation—in their blue and yellow
striped jerseys and their boaters of ribboned straw—were J. J. Hornby,
William Houghton, Kenrick Prescot, Richard Greenall, and J. E. Codrington:
four of these were Lancastrians, and all five took holy orders. In 1852 in
particular, Greenall hit a 'terrific pace', stroking—with the shorter oars of
those days—an amazing 52 to the minute. Then came the glory years, 1860–7:
Henry Fleming Baxter had gone down, but 'Guts' Woodgate and Weldon
Champneys amply replaced him; not to mention 'Bobby' Shepherd, Fred
Crowder, and Duncan Pocklington: seven blues in as many years (pls. 47, 57).
W. C. Crofts, another star of this generation, twice won the Diamond Sculls
at Henley, in 1867 and 1869, after taking a First in classical Mods; but he

---

[75] Sherwood, *Oxford Yesterday*, 48–49. See also idem, *Oxford Rowing* (1900), 98–100. For the
first BNC barge (1846–82), see C. Sheriff, *The Oxford College Barges* (2003), 55, photo 1876. The
barge of 1882 (pl. 76) was replaced in 1926 (pl. 77), and replaced again by a boathouse in 1959
(illus., *Brazen Nose*, xii). The barge of 1926 is now moored at Henley.

[76] For Wilde's Masonic regalia, see *Letters of Oscar Wilde* (2000), 62 n. 1. For garden party
programmes (1857–1903), see Bodl. GA Oxon 8vo 1120. In 1884 no fewer than 1,597 people
attended the fête in Worcester College gardens (Apollo Lodge MSS: Minutes, 18 June 1884).
The Ball of 1883 was held in the new Examination Schools; none was held after 1914.

never achieved a blue: he was too 'opinioné', and in any case there was too much competition.[77]

The typical training schedule of those days makes alarming reading now. 'Breakfast of chops and steaks, bread and butter, and tea [after a mile run before chapel]. Lunch, a half-pint of beer and bread and butter, or a sandwich and a glass of sherry... For dinner [after a mile rowing] four days a week beef or mutton, and on the others fowls, fish for Sunday, and once or twice a light pudding... [and] always... one pint of beer every day. After dinner two glasses of port... [and] occasionally... an extra glass. For supper a basin of gruel or a cup of chocolate, and to bed at 10.30 sharp.'[78] These were clearly men with energy to burn. In 1862 George Morrison presented the OUBC with a new Head of the River Cup; Brasenose won it seven times before the end of the century. In 1866 the college was once again head in both Eights and Torpids. And ten years after that, coincident with the introduction of sliding seats in 1873—outriggers had been in use since 1846—Brasenose entered a period of remarkable success. For six consecutive years, 1874–9—including the famous dead-heat of 1877—the Oxford boat was stroked by BNC. Some said that the 1878 crew was the fastest ever.[79] The heroes of that time were J. P. Way, T. C. Edwards-Moss, and H. P. Marriott. All three stroked the Oxford Eight; six times between them in as many years. 'Cottie' Edwards-Moss, in particular— 'the paragon no. 7 of his day'—was a great favourite of the Chief. After all, he did win the Diamond Sculls two years running, in 1877 and 1878. It was even said that Cradock 'deferred to [him] upon sundry matters of college [business]'.[80] Only the great Sam Butler had equal influence in the Principal's Lodge. And that brings us to the Chief's final sporting obsession: cricket.

In Woodgate's year BNC had two men in the Oxford Eleven. One was the poker-bender himself, Jack Morley: he died in his twenties in Australia. The other was Francis Brandt, a bewhiskered fast bowler who captained the University in 1861 and ended as a judge of the High Court in Madras.[81]

---

[77] Woodgate, *Reminiscences*, 319, 369. The Oxford–Cambridge Boat Race became an annual event from 1856, keel-less boats being introduced in 1857.

[78] W. E. Sherwood, *Oxford Rowing* (Oxford, 1900), 60–1: Oxford Boat 1861. By 1913 this regime had been lightened. Breakfast: fresh fish, eggs, toast, tea; lunch: cold beef or chicken and tomatoes; dinner: beef, mutton, etc., and one glass of port; supper: milk or barley water (A. C. M. Croome (ed.), *Fifty Years of Sport*, i (1913), 194).

[79] Woodgate, *Reminiscences*, 371; Croome (ed.), *Fifty Years of Sport*, i. 208. For memories of BNC's head of the river crew in 1866 see *Brazen Nose*, i. 70–3. For illustrations of the 1877 race against Cambridge, and portraits of crew, see *Illustrated London News*, 24 Mar. 1877; for a photo of the 1878 Oxford crew see *Fifty Years of Sport*, i. 213.

[80] Woodgate, *Reminiscences*, 128. Edwards-Moss presented the OUBC Torpids Challenge Cup in 1878.

[81] Obit, *The Times*, 20 June 1925 and *Brazen Nose*, iv. 113–41; photo in W. K. R. Bedford, *Annals of the Free Foresters* (1895).

Then came R. D. Walker (pl. 55). A cricket blue five years running—and for
four years a blue in rackets as well—Walker was one of seven brothers, all
bachelors, a veritable tribe of athletes. The Walkers were major London
brewers: one of them was the only millionaire to play cricket for England.[82]
And 'Russy' Walker was perhaps the greatest all-round games player of the
whole family. His eye was extraordinary: when batting, he didn't even wear
gloves or pads. In fact his *Times* obituary suggested that he was 'probably the
best all-round player of games that ever lived'. Cricket, billiards, rackets,
tennis, croquet, chess, fishing: Walker excelled in every field. He even taught
the future King Edward VII how to play cards. Somehow he managed to find
time for a Second in classical Mods, and became a barrister at Lincoln's Inn.[83]
In the years 1859–65, Morley, Brandt, and Walker made BNC a notable
cricketing college. And there were greater things to come. In 1868–70—in
the shape of E. L. Fellowes and Bernard Pauncefote—Brasenose captained
the Oxford team three years running. Fellowes, a truly muscular Anglican,
was 'a veritable demon bowler'; in 1866—still bowling round-arm—he
skittled out Cambridge, taking six wickets in the first innings and seven in
the second—five of them clean bowled.[84] Two years later three Harrovians—William Evetts, Ernest Mathews, and J. H. Gibbon—joined BNC's
list of cricketing blues. Evetts in particular was 'a frightful punisher of loose
bowling': on the day after the Varsity Match of 1868 he hit 50 against Surrey
off only 12 balls. In 1870 there were six Brasenose men in the Oxford Eleven;
in 1871 no fewer than eight; in 1872 eight again. It is almost a relief to notice
that in 1873 there were only five.[85]

The cricketers of this generation were cast in heroic mould. C. J. Ottaway
(pl. 45) 'was perhaps the greatest athletic hero known at Oxford till C. B. Fry'.
Between 1870 and 1873 he won multiple blues for cricket, rackets, tennis,
athletics, and football—as well as a First in classical Mods. 'No one who saw
him will forget his firm-set mouth, and keen eyes and black hair ... [With]
cricket over for the day [he] would shut himself up in his rooms and grind
away at Moderations work; but alas! he was burning the candle at both ends,

---

[82] Vyell Walker (obit, *The Times*, 23 Mar. 1906; *ODNB*).

[83] W. A. Bettesworth, *The Walkers of Southgate* (1900). Obit, *The Times*, 31 Mar. 1922, 6; *Brazen
Nose*, iii. 190–2. He lived at Southgate House, Arno's Grove, Middlesex, and North Villa,
Regent's Park. His portrait (pl. 55) was hung in the Long Room at Lord's. See 'Veterans of the
University Match', *The Times*, 6 July 1920, p. 7.

[84] *The Times*, 20 June 1866, 6 and 24 July 1896, 8 (obit). His match analysis was 13 for 88.
Fellowes lived at Tackley Park, Oxon., and was Managing Director of a Lighterage company.
He was also President of the Bullingdon.

[85] See F. Madan, 'Notes on Brasenose Cricket', in *Quat. Mon.* XIV. ii, 83 and C. Eccles
Williams, 'The Golden Age of Brasenose', in *Brazen Nose*, iv. 171–82. In 1871 a BNC Sixteen
beat an All England Eleven by eleven wickets; in 1872 a BNC Fourteen beat an All England
Eleven by five wickets; and in 1873 a BNC Sixteen beat the North of England by 131 runs.

MARIVS
THE·EPI
-CVREAN·

49. Walter Pater (1839–94).
'Marius the Epicurean'.
Cartoon by 'J.C.R. Spider' [John Hearn].
'Our greatest artist in prose' (Oscar Wilde).

50. **Albert Watson** (1828–1904).
   Principal, 1886–89.
   'Dear, shy, shrinking, genial, learned Toby Watson'.

51. Hartwell de la Garde Grissell (1839–1907).
Friend of Oscar Wilde; Chamberlain to the Pope.
'A non-athlete, but popular'.

52. **A. Vincent's Club Room, 23 The High, *c*.1892.**
    Vincent's was founded at B.N.C., in III, 3, by 'Guts' Woodgate in 1863.

   B. St. Mary's Chambers, *c*.1892.
    Private rooms 1885 onwards.

53. **A Brasenose: Radcliffe Square front, *c*.1887.**

The funeral hatchment over the gate is that of Principal Cradock, died 1886.

The railings round the Radcliffe Camera were removed in 1936, and replaced in simpler form in 1990.

B. The old High Street frontage in 1887, prior to reconstruction.

This shows, half-right, the second Principal's Lodgings of 1770; they were replaced by Jackson's New Lodgings in 1887.

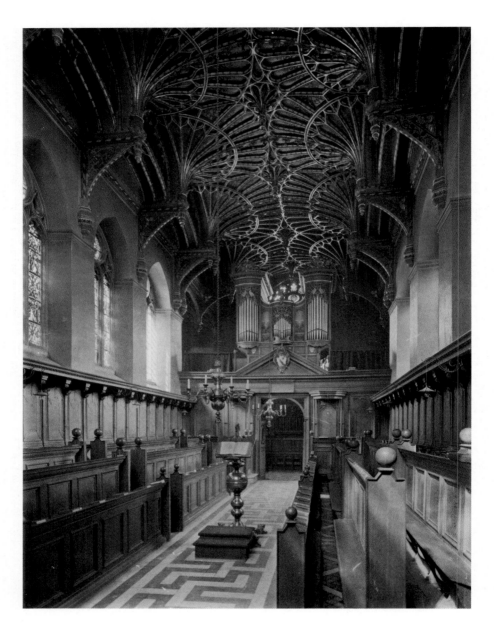

54. The Chapel, in 1935.

Begun 1656; consecrated 1666: John Jackson, 'overseer' and 'surveyor'.

A stylistic hybrid, Gothic and Baroque. The ceiling vault is an exercise in *trompe l'oeil*. Jackson imported a 16th century hammer-beamed roof from St. Mary's College, New Inn Hall Street; then disguised it with a hanging fan-vault of wood and plaster. Originally covered with 'whitening', this ceiling was decorated by J. C. Buckler in 1859–60, and redecorated by C. E. Kempe in 1895. The eagle lectern dates from 1731.

55. Nine Brasenose Cricketers, 19th–20th Centuries.
C. J. Ottaway (1870), W. H. Haddow (1870), V.P.F.A. Royle (1875)
I.A.R. Peebles (1930), M.C. Cowdrey (1952), C.K. Francis (1870)
R. D. Walker (1861), G. Osbaldeston (1808), A.C. Smith (1958).

56. The Torpid, Hilary Term 1861.

STANDING: D. Pocklington (10st.7lb.). S. R. Coxe (10st.12lb.). F. G. Blackburne (9st. 8lb.). R. B. Leach (9st.8lb.). F. J. Huyshe (8st. 11lb.). W. T. Burges (10st. 0lb.).

SITTING: R. Shepherd (11st. 2lb.). W. C. Harris (10st. 6½ lb.). R. T. Whittington (10st. 13lb.). Head of the River: 'Brasenose started at a glorious pace'.

57. The Eight, Trinity Term, 1862.

Photographed outside staircase I.

STANDING: D. L. Landale (11st. 3lb., no. 3). W. C. Harris (10st. 9lb., Bow).
R. T. Whittington (11st. 9lb., no.4). W. T. Burges (10st. 2lb., no.2).
C. I. Parkin (8st. 2lb., Cox).

SITTING: R. Shepherd (11st. 0lb., no. 6). W. B. Woodgate (11st. 4lb., Stroke).
Weldon Champneys (11st.0lb., no.7). R. Burton Leach (9st.8lb.,no.5).

Not a good year: B.N.C. went down from 3rd to 7th, lacking that 'dash which has
hitherto been the distinguishing mark of the Brasenose crew'.

58. The Vampires, 1882.

STANDING: A. O. M. Mackenzie, G. E. Moke, P. Y. Gowlland, A. W. Arkle, G.R. Askwith, A. G. G. Asher, D.H. Barry.

SITTING: H. S. Barton, H. E. Phillips, D. Haig, R. A. Baillie, W. M. Pike, J. L. Puxley, P. F. Du Croz, J. I. Blencowe, G. F. Farnham, T. Hitchcock.

The future Earl Haig is sitting – posed in profile – third from left.

59. The Vampires, 1886.

A.R. Appach, H. L. Popham, A.S. Blair, H.H.E. Nelson-Ward, F. Routledge, A.Pearson, G. E. Rhodes, E. F. Macpherson, J. Methuen, E. Alderson.

J. Tracey, J. H. Ware, W. J. Barry, H.T. Arnall-Thompson, E.H.F. Small, A.E.R. Bedford, J.A. Dun, H.R. Parker, W.W. Rashleigh, J.D. Boswell.

'The aborigines of Brasenose' (Logan Pearsall Smith).

Rashleigh and Boswell – sitting, front row, right – were noted hell-raisers.

60. Dr. Frederick William Bussell (1862–1944).

Drawn by W. Rothenstein in 1894.

'I must confess myself a prig, a pedant and in some ways a poltroon'.

Pater believed he had 'a real touch of genius'.

61. Walter Pater, in 1894.

Drawn by W. Rothenstein.

This image was suppressed by Pater: 'Bussell, do I look like a Barbary ape?'

62. Entrace from Cloister to Chapel, 1935.
Burials in the Cloister continued until 1754.

63. The Cloister from the Chapel, 1935.
Converted into rooms by Sir John Soane in 1807.

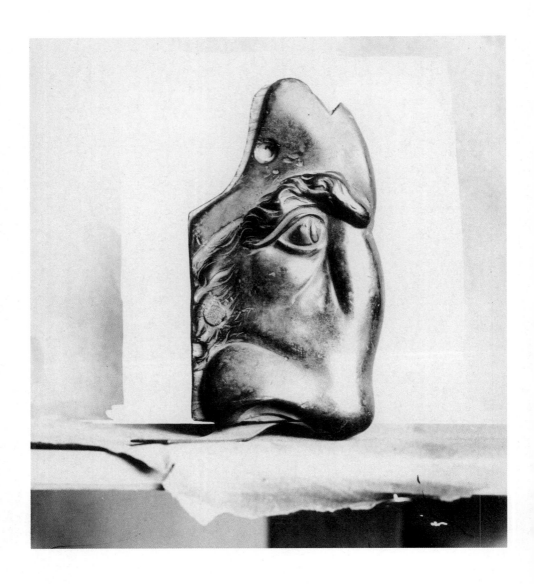

64. The Childe of Hale's Nose (*c.*1850).
   In the early years of Eights Week, this emblem was fixed to the bow of the College Eight.

and died prematurely on 2 April 1878.'[86] Sam Butler was more of a specialist, a fast bowler who in one match became immortal. Playing at Lords on a shooting pitch in 1871—overarm bowling now, since 1869—he took 15 Cambridge wickets for 95 runs: all ten wickets—clean bowled—in the first innings, and five in the second, clean bowling in all no fewer than twelve. This was 'the greatest bowling feat in the whole history of University cricket', recalled R. H. Lyttleton; 'he bowled a terrific pace', and on the first day in particular he was 'unplayable'.[87] He certainly had a mighty arm: he could stand in the Old Quad and throw a rackets ball over the gate tower on to the lantern of the Radcliffe Camera.[88] As a bowler, C. K. Francis (pl. 55) was not far behind Butler; as a bat Pauncefote came close to Ottaway.[89] And as a batsman, bowler, and fielder V. P. F. A. Royle was as good as any. 'Johnny' Royle (pl. 55)—ambidextrous and fast as lightning—was in fact 'one of the most famous cover points that cricket has ever produced'.[90] All these were blues in the 1870s, along with W. H. Hadow (pl. 55), two more Marriotts (C. and G. S.), William Townshend, F. W. Isherwood, William Law, A. H. Heath, and C. A. Wallroth. Of this group, four—Ottaway, Hadow, Butler, and Francis—all played together for the Gentlemen v. Players at Lords. In total, Brasenose notched up thirteen cricket blues in a decade. The schools from which this group of thirteen emerged were of course narrowly based: three each from Harrow and Rugby, two each from Eton, Winchester, and Rossall, and one from Clifton. And the professions that they later followed were equally predictable, mostly law and the Church. But one, A. H. Heath, took up politics on the basis of a fortune in coal and iron. And another—the intrepid Isherwood—went 'boring for Petroleum in the Carpathians'. Together, these men—in their side whiskers and blazers—were the flower of

[86] Madan, 'Brasenose Cricket', 84; *Evening News*, 17 Dec. 1931, quoted in *Brazen Nose*, v. 211–12. Interestingly, in 1874 Pater borrowed two authors for him from BNC library: Hobbes and Locke (B. A. Inman, *Walter Pater's Reading* (1981), 263).

[87] Hon. R. H. Lyttleton, in *Cricket* (Badminton Library, 1920 edn.), 236. 'Butler bowled like a man inspired' (Croome (ed.), *Fifty Years of Sport*, i. 101). His 'yorkers' were legendary: in 1871, against Cambridge, he sent Yardley's middle stump sailing beyond long stop (*Brazen Nose*, iv. 177).

[88] Woodgate, *Reminiscences*, 128.

[89] In the summer of 1869, playing at Lord's for Rugby v. Marlborough, Francis (pl. 55) took 17 wickets, including all 10 in the second innings, of which 9 were clean bowled. In 'Cobden's Match' v. Cambridge in 1870—in which Oxford lost by two runs thanks to a last-minute hat-trick by F. C. Cobden—he took 12 for 161. In February 1872 he also played in the first Varsity rugby match against Cambridge: twenty a side, before the abolition of hacking and mauling; Oxford won by one goal to nil. On 3 June 1867 Pauncefote scored 211 not out v. Corpus; following this with 100 v. Rugby School three days later. Obit, *Brazen Nose*, iv. 115–16.

[90] Obit, *The Times*, 22 May 1929, 10. He was playing for Lancashire before he arrived at BNC, and he went to Australia with Lord Harris's England team of 1878–9. His portrait was hung in the Long Room at Lord's.

Cradock's heyday. In 1880–2, when BNC could boast not a single cricket blue, it was the first time such a calamity had hit the college since 1860.

By 1876–7 the Chief had been in the Principal's Lodge for a quarter of a century. He had made the name of Brasenose synonymous with sport. That year BNC was of course head of the river; Edwards-Moss was the winner of the Diamond Sculls; and Marshall ('Mini') Brooks managed to clear 21 ft 8.5 in in the Varsity long jump, and an astonishing 6 ft 2.5 in in the high jump.[91] Walter Pater rejoiced: 'It is so beautiful to see young men leaping over bars like panthers.'[92]

Even as a young man (pl. 37), a Fellow at 25, Pater had seemed inscrutable. His dress might be striking—ties of apple green, gloves of palest yellow—but there was distance in his smile, a 'weary courtesy' in his greeting. His approach was oblique, cautious rather than camp. Mostly he walked alone, treading 'delicately'; furtively even, with 'evasive eyes and ... surreptitious manner'; his face the colour of old ivory; pondering a phrase, 'like one listening to his own thoughts, occupied with mystical visions of the unseen'.[93] His rooms—Old Lodge 4 and 5 (now 2 and 3), to the left of the library stairs—were a study in understatement. Ebony-tinted doors, stamped with antique iron; primrose-painted panelling, greenish-white in later years; a bowl of dried rose petals; a Persian carpet; tapestry over the chimney; books bound up in palest vellum; blue chintz curtains; lilies of the valley; classical statuettes; a scatter of Greek coins; a table draped in bluish baize; engravings after Michelangelo, Correggio, Ingres: such a contrast to 'the oaken respectability and heaviness of all other dons' rooms at that day'. On one side, at right angles to the fireplace, stood the focus of the room: an oriel window. Here Pater would lounge on cushions, smoking dreamily,[94] while the sun played

[91] He was the second son of the 1st Baron Crawshaw. Photo: *Quat. Mon.* XIV. ii, 90. Brooks's famous high jump—performed at Lillie Bridge Ground, London—stood as a world record until 1887. 'He stalked straight up and from the grass take-off cat-jumped and, amidst thunderous applause, walked back under the lath' (quoted in R. McWhirter and A. Noble, *O.U. R. F. C.* (1969), appendix. 'He was a tall man who ran nearly straight at the bar, and cleared it by sheer spring. If he could have been taught the gymnastic tricks, which nobody then knew, he might have done nearer seven feet than six' (Croome (ed.), *Fifty Years of Sport*, i. 19). As a full-back, he also played rugby for Oxford v. Cambridge in 1873, and for England v. Scotland in 1874 (ibid., ii. 22).

[92] Quoted in J. Buchan, 'Nine Brasenose Worthies', in *Quat. Mon.* XIV. ii, 24. This was before the introduction of the 'Western Roll'.

[93] A. C. Benson, *Walter Pater* (1906), 178, 180; Edward Monson, in *Oxford Mag.* 7 Nov.1906; George Moore, in *Pall Mall Mag.*, Aug. 1904, quoted in Wright, *Pater*, ii. 95; Waddington, *Chapters of my Life*, 35.

[94] L. Jopling, *Twenty Years of my Life, 1867–87* (1925), 273; Pater seems to have given up smoking in later life (*Brazen Nose*, xiii. 256). He was particularly fond of blue, especially 'the colour of the sea' off the north Devon coast ('F.' in *The Speaker*, 26 Aug. 1899, 208).

late upon All Souls; the Camera on his left, St Mary's on his right, half Oxford in his hand. On the opposite side of the room, across a narrow passage filled with cupboards, stood 'a low, ancient, stone-framed, gothic doorway [leading] into a tiny slip of a bedroom, only a few feet wide'. At one end, a small window, looking out over the Old Quad; at the other a projection like a step—the roof in fact of a staircase below—on which rested a simple truckle bed. Nothing else, just a chest of drawers and a cold-water basin. Here Pater slept late, breakfasting later still, feasting on dictionaries, and making notes on tiny slips of paper. This is not the boudoir of an aesthete; it is almost an anchorite's cell.[95]

When Thomas Hardy first met him in 1866, he sensed something of the enigma. Pater seemed almost to tiptoe through life, like 'one carrying weighty ideas without spilling them'.[96] Sometimes he comes down to us as whimsically precious: 'The undergraduate is a child of nature . . . like a wild rose in a country lane'; 'Pansies are like the eyes of angels, given to mankind so that [we] should not weep.'[97] But beneath the affectation—particularly towards the end of his life—lurked uncertainties and doubts. The apparatus of religion fascinated him. With his London friend Richard Jackson,[98] he spent hours trawling the parishes of the East End for services of higher and higher ritual. But the meaning of these ceremonies eluded him. As an undergraduate his preference had been for ritual as theatre: 'It doesn't matter in the least what is said, as long as it is said beautifully.'[99] And in early middle age he was still able to separate performance and purpose: 'The Church of

[95] For Pater's rooms, see Room Book, 1818–67: B 4d 4; Benson, *Pater*, 17–19; Wright, *Pater*, i. 215–16 and ii. 27, 117, with photo opp. p. 226. Pater moved into OL 5 in 1865, and added OL 4 in 1888. See also B. Richards, 'Walter Pater at Oxford', in G. McGrath (ed.), *The Pater Society* (Brasenose, 1986), 1–14. G. H. Wakeling occupied OL 5 from 1895, before moving to VI, 4, XI, 4, and XII, 3. 'It is now tenanted by another . . . but surely as long as English literature lasts it will be "Pater's rooms" . . .' ('F.' in *The Speaker*, 26 Aug. 1899, 208).

[96] T. Hardy, *The Life and Work of Thomas Hardy*, ed. M. Millgate (Athens, Ga., 1985), 187.

[97] Wright, *Pater*, ii. 61, 119. In 1889 he offered personally to return Arthur Symons's copy of Shakespeare's *Sonnets*, 'lest it should get bruised by transit through the post' (*Letters of Walter Pater*, ed. L. Evans (1970), 96: *c.*18 June 1889).

[98] R. C. Jackson—the 'Revd. Brother à Becket'—was a rich collector and ritualist, and an enthusiast for the work of Carlyle and J. M. Neale (*The Times*, 25 July 1923, 15 and 30 July 1923, 8). Pater spent a good deal of time at his house, Bowyer Park, 185 Camberwell Grove (interior photos, Wright, *Pater*, ii. 20–1, 179–80, 184). He was the author of *His Presence: Spiritual Hymns and Poems* (1886) and *In the Wake of Spring: Love Songs and Lyrics* (1898). He bequeathed at least one Rubens to the National Gallery (Sir Charles Holmes in *The Times*, 31 July 1923, 7). For a dismissive account, see R. Ironside, in *Cornhill Mag.* 962 (May 1944).

[99] Wright, *Pater*, i. 201–2 and ii. 26–34. In those days he attended St Thomas's Oxford, enjoying the ritualistic services conducted there by Revd Thomas Chamberlain, founder of *The Ecclesiastic* (1846–68). He later admired Liddon's sermons at St Mary's.

England is nothing to me apart from its ornate services.'[100] Gradually, however, he settled on a ritualized theistic viewpoint, accepting the formularies of the Church without necessarily accepting its metaphysic. He even ended as an advocate of compulsory chapel. 'Theology', he wrote in 1866, is 'a great house, scored all over with hieroglyphics by perished hands'.[101] Ultimately, its mysteries proved impenetrable. Yet his very last essay was on Pascal, the laureate of doubt denied.

Pater's conception of religious belief seems to have broadened over the years. Beginning with Platonic idealism—'a sort of sensuous love of the unseen'—he moved towards the type of 'generous eclecticism'—Christian ethics, pagan aesthetics—that he eventually admired in Dante. Such a relativistic approach, he came to think, might well represent 'the mental attitude of the modern world'; an acceptable religion 'for the modern mind'.[102] 'The beliefs, and the function in the world of the historic church', he explained to Mrs Humphry Ward in 1885, 'form just one of those obscure but all-important possibilities, which the human mind is powerless effectively to dismiss from itself; and might wisely accept, in the first place, as a workable hypothesis'.[103] Her comment on that occasion was not favourable: this

---

[100] Wright, *Pater*, ii. 38. 'He delighted in high altars banked with flowers—the arum, the narcissus, the jonquil—innumerable candles forming a pyramid of points of fire, priests in transplendent copes stiff with gold, incense rising in swelling clouds, bell-ringing, genuflections. But what it was all for did not trouble him' (ibid., ii. 28–31). Pater's favourite services in London at this time were those of St Austin's Priory, Walworth (Fr. G. Nugèe), St Alban's Holborn (Revd A. H. Mackonochie), St Thomas's, Regent Street (Revd A. Bathe), and St Paul's Walworth (Revd J. Gowing). At St Austin's, the black and white marble flooring had been imported from All Souls College, Oxford; at St Paul's, Walworth, there were said to be six curates worth £3,000 p.a. each (ibid., ii. 26–7, 30, 34). Pater thought St Philip's, New Road, Stepney (1888–92), by Arthur Cawston (1857–94) the 'nearest to perfection' in architectural terms ('F.' in *The Speaker*, 26 Aug. 1899, 208).
[101] Pater, 'Coleridge's Writings', *Westminster Rev.* 29 (1866), 129; reprinted in part in *Appreciations* (1889).
[102] Pater's introduction to Shadwell's translation of Dante (1892), quoted in Wright, *Pater*, ii. 166. See also *Times Lit. Supp.* 3 Feb. 1927, 1–2 and Pater to Vernon Lee [Violet Paget], July 1883, quoted in Benson, *Pater*, 89–90. Pater's alter ego, Marius, is portrayed as 'an Imaginary Portrait of a peculiar type of mind in the time of Marcus Aurelius': an Epicurean of the Cyrenaic school who discovers the incompleteness of the Stoic system, and eventually moves from theism towards Christianity, via the aesthetics of ritual. Pascal's position seemed to Pater 'no mere calm supersession of a state of doubt by a state of faith; the doubts never die, they are only just kept down in a perpetual agonia' (Pater, 'Pascal', in *Contemporary Rev.*, Dec. 1894, reprinted in *Miscellaneous Studies*, ed. C. L. Shadwell (1895), 79).
[103] Pater, *Letters*, ed. Evans, 64: 23 Dec. 1885; also Mrs H. Ward, *A Writer's Recollections* (1918), 210. In later years, 'the Bible, the Prayer Book, and the Breviary [translated by John, 3rd Marquess of Bute]' were his 'chief reading' (Wright, *Pater*, ii. 125, 201). At the time of his death, he had all ten volumes of Jeremy Taylor's *Works* out of BNC library (Inman, *Pater's Reading*, 331, 333). Brasenose chapel, meanwhile, continued on its Laudian way with 'several

'acquiescence in the religious order', she decided, was Pater's 'principal intellectual weakness'.[104] In her eyes—and she was the most perceptive of Pater's Christian critics—he had simply abandoned the pursuit of transcendence; taking refuge instead in the therapy of words.

Since his death, Pater has been claimed by both sides: for belief and for unbelief. Like Marius himself—Pater's fictional self-projection, Marius the Epicurean (pl. 49)—he achieved in death the ultimate ambiguity, 'dying ambiguously, half…a Christian'.[105] But his final position in matters of faith, for those who care to look, had been suggested in a review of Mrs Ward's best-selling novel *Robert Elsmere*.

In an age of negation…Robert Elsmere was a type of a large class of minds which cannot be sure that the sacred story is true…But there is also a large class of minds which cannot be sure that it is false…They will think those who are quite sure it is false unphilosophical through lack of doubt…[And] that bare concession of possibility… opens wide the door to hope and love…such persons are…the nucleus of a Church.[106]

Hence the inscription on Pater's gravestone: 'In te domine speravi.'[107]

In public however, he kept up a façade of inscrutability (pl. 49). Behind the shutters, beneath the surface patter, we can still catch glimpses of suppressed

peculiar little ceremonies: the candles are lit at celebrations. The Junior Fellows bring in the elements [of the eucharist] with solemnity from the ante-chapel. When the procession leaves the altar, the dignitaries who carry the alms and the [altar] vessels bow at the lectern to the altar, and to the Principal as they pass his stall. The Vice-Principal bows to the altar on leaving his stall, and [to] the Principal as he passes out' (Benson, *Pater*, 85).

[104] Ward reviewing *Marius the Epicurean*, in *Macmillan's Mag.* 53 (1885), 132–9. She satirized Pater's position as follows: 'pray, weep, dream with the majority while you think with the elect.' Or as Flaubert put it, 'live like a bourgeois and think like a demi-god' (Wright, *Pater*, i. 261).

[105] Arthur Symons, in *Time* (Aug. 1887), 157–62. One of Pater's oldest friends, Ingram Bywater, noted: 'I always thought there was a chance of his ending his days as a Catholic' (W. W. Jackson, *Ingram Bywater: The Memoir of an Oxford Scholar* (Oxford, 1917), 79). He certainly thought 'Newman's features'—as in the Christ Church portrait—'were those of the ideal priest' ('F.' in *The Speaker*, 20 Aug. 1899, 208). A. C. Benson, however, thought him 'a deep though unwilling sceptic', who believed 'that religion in its purest form is not a solution of the world's mystery, but a working theory of morals' (*Walter Pater* (1906), 172–4). George Saintsbury thought him 'most profoundly, sincerely, reverently interested' in religion (*The Bookman* (Aug. 1906), 165–70). To T. H. Warren he seemed 'a kind of quietist' (Benson, *Pater*, 175). For Bussell on Pater's later religious attitudes—'a devout Christian'—see *Oxford Mag.* 13 (17 Oct. 1894), 7–8 and memorial address 14 Oct. 1894, with additions (Bras. B. 132/5).

[106] [Pater] reviewing *Robert Elsmere* in *The Guardian*, 28 Mar. 1888; reprinted in Pater, *Essays from The Guardian* (1896), 72–4. Pater appears in the novel as 'Edward Langham'; 'Robert Elsmere' himself is J. R. Green; 'Mr. Grey' is T. H. Green.

[107] In Holywell Cemetery, Oxford; not far from larger memorials to Churton, Cradock, Watson, Lodge, Turner, and Heberden. Until the 1960s, these memorials were maintained with the help of subventions from Brasenose (V-P's Reg. 13 Oct. 1937, fo. 225; 31 Mar. 1943, fo. 40; 19 June 1963, fo. 26; 13 Nov. 1963, fo. 26).

passions. 'Wouldn't one give much', noted 'Michael Field' mischievously, 'to surprise the Bacchant in Walter Pater!'[108] So much was apparent artifice. Even the moustache was a disguise: 'Bussell, do I look like a Barbary Ape?...I would give ten years of my life to be handsome' (pl. 61).[109] 'Faint, pale, embarrassed, exquisite Pater!'—the words are those of Henry James—'he is the mask without the face'.[110]

A tutor always remembers his earliest students, and three of Pater's first pupils were well worth remembering: C. L. Shadwell, Gerard Manley Hopkins, and Humphry Ward. Of these only Ward was a Brasenose man. He arrived in Pater's first year, 1864. Shadwell and Hopkins were private pupils sent to him in 1864–6 from Christ Church and Balliol respectively. As Pater's celebrity grew, his audience diversified. Oscar Wilde, for example, an undergraduate at Magdalen, attended the master's lectures in 1876–7.[111] In 1888 Bernard Berenson was less lucky: Pater found an excuse to turn him away.[112] But Shadwell—'the handsomest man in the university'—remained a lifelong friend. Together he and Pater visited Ravenna, Florence, and Pisa in 1865; and years later, as Provost of Oriel, it was Shadwell who edited Pater's *Miscellaneous Studies* (1895).[113] Hopkins—that 'star of Balliol'—arrived at Brasenose in April 1866, for extra coaching in Greats. Jowett shrewdly guessed that a touch of Pater would do his own pupil no harm at all; it might even keep him out of Liddon's high-church orbit. 'Coaching with W. H. Pater this term', noted Hopkins on 2 May 1866. 'Walked with him on Monday last, April 30. Fine evening bitterly cold' 'Bleak-faced Neology in cap and gown.' 'No cap and gown but very bleak.' And again, on 31 May: 'A little rain and at evening and night hard rain—Pater talking two hours against Xianity.'[114] With Humphry Ward there were few such differences. Young Ward—destined to vicarious celebrity as consort of Mrs Humphry Ward—took a First in Greats in 1868, and followed Pater into the Brasenose Common Room as a Fellow by examination in 1869.[115] There he lectured

[108] *Works and Days from the Journal of Michael Field* [Katherine Bradley and Edith Cooper], ed. T. and D. C. Sturge Moore (1933), 121.

[109] Wright, *Pater*, i. 192; W. Rothenstein, *Men and Memories*, i (1931), 155. The style of Pater's moustache, in middle age, was known as a 'mudguard'.

[110] *Selected Letters of Henry James to Edmund Gosse, 1882–1915*, ed. R. S. Moore (Baton Rouge, La., 1988), 120.

[111] L. Ellmann, *Oscar Wilde* (1987), 46, 57. 'Pater gives me great praise, so I am vainer than usual' (*Letters of Oscar Wilde* (2000), 60: Wilde to R. Harding, Aug. 1877).

[112] Pater, *Letters*, 172.

[113] Obit, *The Times*, 14 Feb. 1919; Wright, *Pater*, i. 218.

[114] Hopkins, *Journals and Papers*, ed. H. House and G. Storey (1959), 133, 138; D. Donoghue, *Walter Pater* (New York, 1995), 32–3. The label 'Neologist' had been applied to sceptical and liberal Anglicans since the 1830s (*OED*).

[115] He was one of seventeen candidates (V-P's Reg. 1869, fo. 166). J. R. Green was his father's curate at St Barnabas, King's Square, London.

variously on Chaucer, Virgil, ancient Greece, and the Italian Renaissance, as well as coaching Pass men in mathematics.[116] Throughout his sixteen years at BNC, Ward could rely on Cradock. Both took a Liberal viewpoint. But it was to Pater—another Liberal—that he was naturally drawn. As an undergraduate Ward had joined Pater for vacation reading in Sidmouth.[117] Later on, in Ward's rooms (III, 4), overlooking Brasenose Lane—hung round with Japanese prints and engravings after Raphael—the two young Fellows would meet after dinner, declaiming poetry into the early hours. Swinburne was present on at least one occasion. And from 'an upper window . . . thrown open to the summer night', there came the 'music of verse which first outsang and then silenced the nightingales [in Exeter garden], protracting its harmonies until it disconcerted the lark himself at sunrise'.[118]

Humphry Ward belonged to the first generation of dons who were able to marry without necessarily forfeiting their Fellowships. His own marriage turned out to be a veritable literary merger. It was in 1872 that he married Mary Arnold. She was already Dr Arnold's granddaughter and Matthew Arnold's niece; eventually she would become Aldous Huxley's aunt and G. M. Trevelyan's mother-in-law: a veritable epitome of the Victorian intellectual aristocracy. In due course Humphry left Brasenose for *The Times*;[119] and Mary began a career in authorship that, for a while, made her the best-paid woman in England. But before that, in the decade 1872–82, this impressive couple represented a distinctively new breed, the academic families of north Oxford.

Nobody [she recalled] under the rank of a Head of a College, except a very few privileged Professors, possessed as much as a thousand a year. The average income of the new race of married tutors, was not much more than half that sum. Yet we all gave dinner parties and furnished our houses with Morris papers, old chests and cabinets, and blue pots. The dinner parties were simple and short . . . Most of us were very anxious to be up-to-date, and in the fashion, whether in aesthetics, in house-keeping, or education. But our fashion was not that of Belgravia or Mayfair, which indeed we scorned! It was the fashion of the movement which sprang from Morris and Burne-Jones. Liberty stuffs very plain in line, but elaborately 'smocked', were greatly in vogue, and evening dresses, 'cut square', or with 'Watteau pleats', were generally worn, and often in conscious protest against the London 'low dress' which

---

[116] V-P's Reg., Mar. 1877, fo. 177; J. Sutherland, *Mrs. Humphry Ward* (Oxford, 1990), 45. When Hopkins was attached to St Aloysius, Oxford, in 1878–9 Pater seems to have been a frequent visitor (D. A. Downes, *Victorian Portraits: Hopkins and Pater* (New York, 1965), 22–7, 30–3, 44–7).

[117] Benson, *Pater*, 26. In the long vacation, 1867.

[118] Gosse, 'Walter Pater', 254. Later known as the White Room, presumably because the panelling was so painted by Ward in 1870. After 1881 it was used for a while as a lecture room.

[119] On marrying in 1872 he resigned his Fellowship, but remained a Tutor. For some years he was responsible for articles of art criticism in *The Times*. He wrote little independently, e.g. *A History of the Athenaeum, 1824–1925* (1926).

Oxford—young married Oxford—thought both ugly and 'fast'. And when we had donned our Liberty gowns we went out to dinner, the husband walking, the wife in a bath chair, drawn by an ancient member of an ancient and close fraternity—the 'chairmen' of old Oxford... Everybody was equal, nobody was rich, and the intellectual average was naturally high... My friends and I were all on fire for women's education... [120].

Mrs Humphry Ward, Mrs Mandell Creighton, Mrs Max Müller, Mrs J. R. Green, Mrs T. H. Green: from this north Oxford generation emerged the founding spirits of Somerville and Lady Margaret Hall.

Life in Bradmore Road—Pater and his sister Clara at one end of the street, Mr and Mrs Humphry Ward at the other—was certainly economical. Over four years, 1869–72, Ward averaged a total income of just over £500 p.a. as Fellow, Lecturer, Tutor, and Junior Dean—but only by taking on extra pupils inside and outside the University. After marrying—and thus losing his Fellowship—he managed to accumulate sufficient teaching in 1877 to make his Tutorship worth £529 4s. 0d. In the same year Pater received £537 17s. 6d. as Tutor, £119 16s. 8d. as Dean, and £230 as Fellow. That of course excludes the value of accommodation and service. But after resigning his Tutorship, Pater's college income was much reduced. As Fellow, Lecturer, and Senior Dean he received less than £300 p.a.[121] Hence the incentive to write reviews. Principal Cradock, by comparison, received in all not far short of £1,500 p.a. Not surprisingly, north Oxford people like the Paters and the Wards followed a regime that was consciously self-contained. Even their cats were related. Pater rented no. 2 Bradmore Road from 1869 to 1886. He seems, increasingly, to have found college life too public. Later on, in 1886–93, he rented a London house, 12 Earl's Terrace, to escape—at least in vacations—the constriction of Oxford living.[122] But in the end, it was to Oxford that he returned, to die in 1894 at 64 St Giles's. And during the whole of this time, he retained his Brasenose rooms. It was in Oxford that he felt most completely at home.

The drawing room [at 2 Bradmore Rd.] [Mrs Ward remembered] which runs the whole breadth of the house from the road to the garden behind was 'Paterian' in every line and ornament. There was a Morris paper; spindle-legged tables and chairs;

[120] Ward, *Writer's Recollections*, 119–20, 152. See also Covert, *Victorian Marriage*, 84.

[121] Humphry Ward's account book survives (MPP 44 A1). For Pater's income, and Cradock's, see Senior Bursar's Dividend Books, 1867–93 (Clennell B 2a 58–60) and Junior Bursar's Dividend Books, 1855–83 (Clennell B 2a 55–6). A summary statement for 1877 is included in BNC's return to the Selborne Commission (*PP* (1881), lvi, pt. ii, 97).

[122] 'Oxford pains me, slays me! It is impossible there to escape the ruts of convention. Everything follows the most ridiculous precedents and the stupidest of rules. The whole place is cobwebbed over. Oh, it's so delightful to be in Walworth—to be a man for an afternoon, after being an automaton for a month. Oh, I can breathe in Walworth!' (Pater, paraphrased by Jackson, in Wright, *Pater*, ii. 41).

a sparing allowance of blue plates and pots, bought, I think, in Holland, where Oxford residents in my day were always foraging...framed embroidery of the most delicate design and colour...engravings...from Botticelli or Luini, or Mantegna; a few mirrors, and a very few flowers, chosen and arranged with a simple yet conscious art. I see that room always with the sun in it, touching the polished surfaces of wood and brass and china, and bringing out its pure colour.

Her own house, no. 5 (later 17), was much the same, but plainer: it lacked Pater's amber-coloured curtains.

I see, in memory [our] small...room as it was on a winter evening, between nine and midnight, my husband in one corner, preparing his college lectures, or writing a 'Saturday'[Review] 'middle'; my books and I in another; the reading-lamp, always to me a symbol of peace and 'recollection'; the Oxford quiet outside.

And yet, beyond this retreat, lay another world, a world of mental turmoil.

It was not so tranquil as it looked. For beating round us all the time were the spiritual winds of an agitated day. The Oxford of thought was not quiet...Darwinism was penetrating everywhere; Pusey was preaching against its effects on belief; Balliol stood for an unfettered history and [biblical] criticism, Christ Church for authority and creeds.[123]

The BNC of Dr Cradock might not seem quite the place to look for intellectual ferment. But even Brasenose could not escape. In 1873–7 Pater found himself right at the centre of debate.

It was in 1868, in an anonymous notice in the *Westminster Review*, that Pater first set out his credo.

One characteristic of the pagan spirit...[is] the desire of beauty quickened by the sense of death....Not the fruit of experience [therefore] but experience itself is the end [of our existence]. A counted number of pulses only is given to us of a variegated, dramatic life. How may we see in them all that is to be seen in them by the finest senses?...To burn always with this hard gem-like flame, to maintain this ecstasy, is success in life...While all melts under our feet, we may well catch at any...stirring of the senses...Not to discriminate every moment some passionate attitude...[some] brilliance...is on this short day of frost and sun, to sleep before evening...We are all under sentence of death...Some spend this interval in listlessness, some in high passions, the wisest...in art and song.[124]

---

[123] Ward, *Writer's Recollections*, 123–4, 165. The Wards lived there from 1872 to 1881; they bought the house on mortgage for £2,000, and sold it to Henry Nettleship of Balliol for £2,500 (Sutherland, *Mrs. Humphry Ward*, 56, 80). As 'Two Fellows', Mr and Mrs Ward wrote 'A Morning in the Bodleian', in *Dark Blue* (Feb. 1872). Mrs Ward's late novel *Lady Connie* (1916) recalls the Oxford of her girlhood.

[124] [Pater], 'Poems by William Morris', *Westminster Rev.* (Oct. 1868), 302–12. Pater's inclusion of 'song' is interesting: he seems to have had no ear for music (H. Holiday, *Reminiscences of my Life* (1914), 164–5).

The substance of this prose-poem formed the basis of the 'Conclusion' to Pater's *Studies in the History of the Renaissance* (1873). And it was this 'Conclusion' which brought down on him the anathemas of the establishment. Sidney Colvin dismissed it as an invitation to 'general indulgence'.[125] George Eliot called it 'quite poisonous'.[126] Mrs Oliphant thought its 'elegant materialism' was fundamentally decadent: 'rococo from beginning to end'.[127] In April 1875, from the pulpit of Christ Church Cathedral, the Bishop of Oxford denounced Pater as an agent in 'the progress of unbelief'.[128] In effect, Pater faced a double accusation: he was a danger not only to the minds, but to the morals of the young. Here was a tutor who hymned the beauties of adolescent males; who scorned the existence of eternal verities; who openly relished pagan appetites; and who apparently turned *carpe diem* into a programme of physical and mental indulgence. Threatened with ostracism and even prosecution, Pater took fright. He deleted the 'Conclusion' from the second edition of his *Renaissance*—now subtitled *Studies in Art and Poetry* (1877)—on the grounds that it might 'mislead . . . young men'. He only readmitted it to the third edition (1888) after he had published an 'anti-epicurean' exposition of his beliefs in the form of a long fictional study—'the new Cyrenaicism'—set in early Christian Rome and entitled *Marius the Epicurean* (1885). Such contrition was scarcely enough. Wilde revered his master to the end: he christened Pater's *Renaissance* 'the holy writ of beauty'. But even Pater's sympathizers thought him suspect. 'There is a kind of Death clinging to [him]', wrote J. A. Symonds, 'which makes his music (but heavens! how sweet it is!) a little faint and sickly. His view of life gives me the creeps.'[129]

One member of the Brasenose Common Room who found Pater's apparent hedonism too much to swallow was the Revd John Wordsworth. A grand-nephew of the poet, and a future Bishop of Salisbury, Wordsworth was committed to maintaining the clerical character of the college against 'the restless current of modern life'. In particular, he believed that the education of potential clergymen was best secured by electing 'conscientious . . . religious men' as Fellows, not 'brilliant literary or scientific proficients'. In this he was opposed, passively by Pater, actively by Ward. It fell to Ward to speak for the non-clerical Fellowship. 'Clerical Fellows', he told the Selborne Commission, 'are intellectually not quite the equals of lay fellows'; 'the connection between clerical fellowship and research is [just] . . . a dream of the research party'; and finally—here one senses the tension in the air—'universities belong to the

---

[125] *Pall Mall Gazette*, 1 Mar. 1873, 11–12.

[126] *The George Eliot Letters*, ed. G. S. Haight (1954–6), vi. 455: 5 Nov. 1873, to John Blackwood.

[127] *Blackwood's Mag.* 114 (1873), 604–9.

[128] J. F. Mackarness, *A Charge Delivered to the Diocese of Oxford* (1875).

[129] J. A. Symonds, *Letters*, ed. H. M. Schueller and R. L. Peters (1967–9), ii. 273: 20 Feb. 1873 to H. G. Dakyns. See also ibid., iii. 41–2.

nation and not to the church establishment'.[130] Pater would never have spoken so freely. But when his views on life—if not on universities—were at last openly published, Wordsworth felt it his duty to protest. On 17 March 1873, the following letter was delivered to Pater's rooms:

You will, I think, hardly be surprised at my writing to you... No one can admire more than I do the beauty of style and the felicity of thought by which [your work] is distinguished, but... no one can be more grieved than I am at [your] conclusions... [Your] philosophy is an assertion, that no fixed principles either of religion or morality can be regarded as certain, that the only thing worth living for is momentary enjoyment... and that probably or certainly the soul dissolves at death into elements which are destined never to reunite... The difference of opinion... between us must, I fear, become public and avowed, and it may be my duty to oppose you... Would you object to give up... your share in the Divinity Examination in Collections?'[131]

Pater's reply does not survive. But a year later, when it was the turn of Brasenose to nominate a University Proctor, he found himself passed over in favour of a former pupil and junior Fellow, none other than Wordsworth himself.[132]

By that date Pater had become embroiled in something much worse. In February 1874, an undergraduate named William Money Hardinge—unfortunately known as 'the Balliol bugger'—was sent down for 'unnatural behaviour'. 'I can't', announced Jowett, 'allow this sort of thing to go on.' Now Jowett, of course, was Pater's former tutor; he already considered him a 'demoralizing moralizer'; and when he discovered that Pater had written compromising letters to Hardinge, he summoned his old pupil to Balliol for what A. C. Benson later described as a 'dreadful interview'. Pater emerged 'old, crushed, despairing'.[133] After a judicious interval, Hardinge was allowed

---

[130] Selborne Commn. (*PP* (1881), lvi), pt. ii, 146–50, 161–3, 171–3. In all, four Fellows of BNC—Wordsworth, Watson, Whittuck, and Ward—addressed memoranda to the Commission, each with opposing opinions.

[131] Pater, *Letters*, ed. L. Evans, 12–14: 17 Mar. 1873; reprinted with commentary, from E. W. Watson, *Life of Bishop John Wordsworth* (1915), 89–91. After the Act of 1871, acceptance of the Thirty-Nine Articles was no longer obligatory for the taking of University degrees, except for divinity. Wordsworth was elected Fellow in 1867 and acted as college chaplain. See *Brazen Nose*, i. 193–5: illus., and *ODNB*.

[132] The office was worth £300–350 p.a. (Wright, *Pater*, i. 256).

[133] W. Sharp, 'Some Personal Reminiscences of Walter Pater', *Atlantic Monthly*, 74 (1894), 811; A. C. Benson, 'Diary', reprinted in R. M. Seiler, *Walter Pater... A Life Remembered* (Calgary, 1987), 253–61. For the whole episode, see B. A. Inman, 'Estrangement and Connection: Pater, Jowett and Hardinge', in L. Brake and I. Small (eds.), *Pater in the 1990s* (Greenboro, NC, 1991), 1–20; and L. Brake, 'Judas and the Widow', *Prose Studies*, 4 (1981), reprinted in P. Dodd (ed.), *Walter Pater: An Imaginative Sense of Fact* (1981), 39–54. Jowett acted judiciously: he noted that Hardinge's 'conversation and writing were indecent, his acquaintance bad, his work = o × 2.... yet I don't want to ruin the man for life' (Inman, 'Estrangement', 6). Hardinge 'had tried to turn Pater's head [but] Jowett... blamed Pater more than the undergraduate. But it is all so long ago...' (A. Raffalovich to Forest Reid, *c*.1920: PP 1 A 2/7).

to return. Years later he became a successful poet. He even walked, with Viscount Milner, in Jowett's funeral procession. But for Pater there was no easy settlement. He retreated deeper into his shell; operating thereafter behind a carapace of studied ambiguity. He had no appetite for the martyrdom of Reading Jail.

There was however one alibi open to him. Pater's hedonism was concerned with the appreciation of art rather than the conduct of life; it treated art not—in Ruskinian terms—as a moral paradigm, but simply in terms of sensations and impressions; as a key to 'the splendour of our experience' as well as a reminder of what he called the 'awful brevity' of our existence. Here was 'a creed [suitable] only for moral and intellectual aristocrats', a maxim for 'rare souls'.[134] At its best—in his writing on Botticelli or Giorgione, for example—Pater's art criticism sets out to explain the very nature of art: through its origins in the psyche of the artist and its impact on the eye of the spectator.[135] His approach to art was psychologically based, but undidactically so. It was not designed for translation into generalized, demotic terms. Appropriately, some of his most original writings—his essay on Antoine Watteau, for example—take the form of 'Imaginary Portraits': a literary device designed to illuminate the links between art and temperament while avoiding the complications of actuality. Ultimately, Pater was not concerned with conventional art history. Identification, attribution, evaluation: none of these was his main concern. His quarry was the origin of art itself, that is the psychic roots of the creative process. In the end he came to see paintings almost as sign manuals of the soul; but a soul as transient and ephemeral as any of its forms of physical expression.

After the mid-1880s Pater led two distinct lives. 'At Oxford', recalled one pupil, 'his hair was left to grow rather long, his moustaches to droop, his walk was a paddle, and the general effect that of a foreign musician or possibly an organist.' But in London he was a different man. 'There he tripped along in a smart top-hat and black jacket, with a stiff clipped moustache, neatly rolled umbrella and dog-skin gloves. But for the dreamy fixity of his gray eyes he might have been a retired Major in the Rifle Brigade' (pl. 39B).[136] In the metropolis he became quite a feature of the literary scene, at home with exotics like Vernon Lee and Frank Harris; lecturing at the London Institution; or dining out on Sundays at Snow's Restaurant off Piccadilly. On at least

---

[134] Buchan, 'Nine Brasenose Worthies', 27. See also a sermon by Revd J. B. Mayor of Cambridge in *Oxford and Cambridge Undergraduate's Jnl.* 19 Feb. 1880, 249.

[135] R. Wollheim, 'Walter Pater as a Critic of the Arts', in *On Art and the Mind* (1973), 155–76; summarized in J. Turner (ed.), *The Dictionary of Art* (1996), s.v. 'Pater'. See also K. Clark (introd), Pater, *The Renaissance* (Fontana edn., 1961).

[136] C. J. Holmes, *Self and Partners* (1936), 102.

one occasion he feasted *à quatre* with Frank Harris, Matthew Arnold, and Oscar Wilde. Inevitably, they talked about style.[137]

But that was Pater in middle age. It is the young Pater who has come down to us so memorably in the pages of Mallock's *New Republic* (1877).

'I rather look upon life', announced Mr. Rose, 'as a chamber, which we decorate... tinting the walls... with symphonies of subdued colour, and filling it... with flowers, and with strange scents, and with instruments of music... We have learned the weariness of creeds... for us the grave has no secrets... the aim of life is life; and what does successful life consist in? Simply... in the consciousness of exquisite living'. No more 'the warrings of endless doubts'; simply now 'a profounder and more exquisite pleasure in the colour of a crocus, the pulsations of a chord of music or a picture of Sandro Boticelli's'... 'What a very odd man Mr. Rose is', said Lady Ambrose.... 'He always seems to talk of everybody as if they had no clothes on'.[138]

No wonder Pater never became Slade Professor, still less Professor of Poetry.

In Brasenose, however, Pater's position was secure. He was able to lunch in college with louche characters like Harry Melvill and Oscar Wilde, Simeon Solomon and Oscar Browning. To the hearties he became something of a mascot. In the 1860s and 1870s he was nicknamed 'Blue Peter',[139] or 'Sage Green' (echoes of *Verdant Green*), because of his fondness for pastel-coloured neckties. Sometimes he was simply known as 'Judas' (he sat as such for Simeon Solomon).[140] Suspicion certainly lingered. In 1880 C. E. Hutchinson, who had arrived at Brasenose in 1873—the very year of the Balliol scandal—published an anonymous pamphlet entitled *Boy Worship*.

Men of all tastes become boy-worshipers. It is not only Sayge Greene who goes into ecstasies over a boy's face and figure (he may, it is true, express himself more eloquently than some of his more robust brethren), but the devotees of the cricket and football fields have ere now furnished many an ardent follower. The Upper River, as well as a certain College Chapel, has its little band of habitués.[141]

Slender evidence, of course, this curious pamphlet; and it would be foolish to equate homosocial with homosexual behaviour. If mid-Victorian BNC suffered from one particular vice it was likely to be misogyny rather than

---

[137] F. Harris, *Contemporary Portraits*, ii (1919), 212.

[138] W. H. Mallock, *The New Republic* ii (1877), 139. Pater appears as 'Mr. Rose'; Ruskin as 'Mr. Herbert'; and Matthew Arnold as 'Mr. Luke'. For Mallock's critique of liberalism and socialism, see *ODNB*.

[139] Revd J. Darlington (1869) in a letter of 1 Mar. 1909 (Members 31 b).

[140] One of the pictures in Pater's room at BNC (G. G. Monck, quoted in Wright, *Pater*, ii. 118–19).

[141] Quoted in Inman, 'Estrangement', 14.

pederasty. Woodgate for instance once fled from a train compartment rather than travel alone with a lady: he would 'sooner have a mad dog rather than a single woman in the carriage'.[142]

So when the *Oxford Undergraduate's Journal* drew a distinction between Pater and the Aesthetes—between men of sensibility and that 'unwholesome gang of sensualists'—it was probably speaking for the bulk of late Victorian Oxford.[143] Now one of the editors of that particular magazine was in fact a Brasenose man and a pupil of Pater, named F. E. Weatherley. Fred Weatherley was one of the best-known Brasenose men of his generation. He was the author of drawing room ballads without number: 'Danny Boy' and 'Roses of Picardy' will be for ever his memorials. And with his arrival we are back on safer territory; back in the world of tutorials and Torpids, bump suppers and Commems.

It was in spring 1867 that Weatherley first came to BNC from Hereford Cathedral School. He was a scholarship boy, a doctor's son from Somerset. Leaving his luggage at the old Clarendon Hotel in Cornmarket, he picked his way down Brasenose Lane, and emerged—scarcely believing his eyes— amidst the drama of Radcliffe Square. Four Herefordians had recently preceded him: C. C. Prichard, James Mapleton, George Yeld—a Newdigate prizewinner—and Fleming Baxter, already a rowing legend.

It was in Prichard's rooms [VI, 3] that I had my first Oxford lunch. Has any meal afterwards ever seemed so good? I remember the cyder cup in the silver tankard, and the green leaves of the chestnuts that waved and tapped at the windows as they had waved and tapped when Heber...occupied the room, and wrote his famous New-digate, 'Palestine'. To steer a college boat, and to write a Newdigate—those were my first ambitions. The first I achieved, the second never, though I had three shots at it...[That October] I found myself at Baxter's college, Brasenose, head of the river in Eights and Torpids, and with nine men [eight actually] in the Varsity Eleven... I who had never had a study to myself—now found myself with sitting room and bedroom of my own [old X, 7; then III, 6]. My own furniture, my own pictures, and my own piano...my scout, my bedmaker, his wife of course; my linen, my plate ...To be able to order my breakfast, my lunch, in my rooms, alone or with friends. It seemed all so strange...[144]

And then there was Cradock. The Principal turned out to be 'a dear old fellow, far more interested when I was able to tell him that I was steering the Torpid than that I had finished reading the *Odyssey* in the vacation'. But most of the tutors seemed 'remote'; and as for chapel services, 'how lifeless'. Pater was

---

[142] Woodgate, *Reminiscences*, 444.
[143] F. Weatherley, *Piano and Gown* (1926), 75. *Boy Worship* was reviewed and condemned in this journal on 22 and 29 Apr., and 6 May 1880, 351–2, 365, 372, 387–9. The pamphlet was withdrawn from sale, and its stock destroyed after personal intervention from the Vice-Chancellor.
[144] Weatherley, *Piano and Gown*, 41–2.

another matter; he was 'a rare piece of good fortune. I had seen all the other Fellows before I saw him—Shand, "Toby" Watson, "Jacky" Wordsworth... "Sam" Reynolds. They were rough, kind, genial men, untidily clad, of the type of one's masters at school. But Pater was beautifully dressed, he was a dandy with a dash of the eccentric, spoke with a gentle voice, was as polite as a woman, [and] arranged lectures and subjects with a quiet deferential air... At lectures he was too shy to make a good teacher. Rather than hurt a pupil's feelings, he would let even a howler go uncorrected... [But his was] the happiest teaching that I ever got in Oxford... It became my custom to arrive at lectures five or ten minutes too early so that I might listen to him talking about pictures... [Ah,] those few snatched moments of talk with Pater...[145]

Weatherley found cricket and riding too expensive; but, given his diminutive size, coxing suited him well. And that gave him access to the inner circle. In 1868 BNC bent the rules by entering what was in effect the first coxswainless four in the Stewards' Cup at Henley: Champneys and Woodgate of course (steering by pedal and wire), Rumsey and Crofts—with Weatherley sitting in as dummy and throwing himself into the river at the start of the race. It was a good wheeze: BNC won by 100 yards. But victory was quickly followed by disqualification.[146] 'Dear distracting Oxford': lectures in the morning, boating in the afternoon, piano in the evening. There were musical recitals in college with Champneys, Muir-Mackenzie, and H. E. Burgess; fiery debates with Atherley-Jones; and later on the earliest performances put on by OUDS. No wonder Weatherley fell behind in his work, and took to employing private coaches. We even know their names: Godby of New College; little Frank Paravicini of Christ Church, for Virgil; 'Bob' Williams of Merton—'the Stugger'—for Logic. In the end Weatherley took an acceptable degree, joined the Apollo Lodge, and ended up as a private tutor himself; still writing verses, still tinkling his piano, and eventually reading for the bar. In later life, a well-known KC on the western circuit, he wrote something like 3,000 songs. 'No practising barrister', noted his obituarist, 'has ever... produced so much innocent pleasure.'[147]

So how can we define the nature of BNC at this stage in its evolution? Looked at over the Victorian period as a whole, Brasenose—there is no denying it—enjoyed its reputation as a sporting college. Between 1839 and 1891, for example, the first Eight went head of the river on no fewer than 110

---

[145] Ibid. 44–7.

[146] Ibid. 66, 69. For details see *Quat. Mon.* XIV. i, 60–2. Weatherley was a non-swimmer.

[147] Weatherley, *Piano and Gown*, 73, 75, 78, 137; *The Times*, 9 Sept. 1929, p. 7; *ODNB*. Private coaches customarily earned £10 a term, for three hours' teaching per week (M. Burrows, *Pass and Class* (1861), 62). Among Weatherley's pupils were the cricketers E. F. S. Tylecote and K. J. Key, H. G. and G. Marriott, as well as Marshall Brooks the high jumper (Weatherley, *Piano and Gown*, 151). 'The Londonderry Air' was played at Weatherley's funeral in Bath Abbey. He published anonymously *Oxford Days: or How Ross got his Degree* (1879).

nights, nearly twice the number scored by its nearest rival. Now oarsmen, of necessity, are team players not individualists. The spirit of BNC—middling gentry, middle-stump Anglican—was understated and cohesive; seldom flashy, never exhibitionist. Writing in 1891, Falconer Madan—Fellow for three decades—chose his words carefully: 'pertinacity, perseverance, power of endurance, doggedness, patriotism, solidarity... [They] do what they are doing with all their might.'[148] The slang of the period had a single word for it: 'pluck'.

The spirit of a college can also be stated negatively as well as positively. In 1877–8, Brasenose was defined in exactly that way: it proved to be incompatible with its immediate neighbour, Lincoln. In October 1877, worried by his college's declining income, the President of Lincoln, Mark Pattison, paid a personal visit to Cradock. After explaining the situation, he laid his cards on the table: 'Can you take us in?' That winter proposals were drawn up for a united college, to be called 'Brasenose-Lincoln', with new statutes to guarantee joint elections. On 22 March 1878 a 'plenary convention' was held in Brasenose Common Room. It was then that divisions began to emerge. Both Bursars voiced support: there might be economies of scale. One future Principal, Heberden no less, was in favour: the range of teaching provision would increase; besides Lincoln men were 'quiet and good'. Madan was not averse to the proposal: at least a century would be added to the antiquity of the college. Whittuck too was supportive: there might be less emphasis on sport. But two teaching Fellows, Pater and Edmundson, were alarmed: greater numbers would surely mean a greater burden of tuition. The undergraduates of both colleges staged a joint debate. They rejected the proposal, except as regards teaching. At this point Hugh Platt of Lincoln produced a fighting pamphlet: *A Plea for the Preservation of Lincoln College* (Oxford, 1878).[149] That guaranteed deadlock. In November 1878 a majority of BNC Fellows supported integration, but not the two-thirds majority required for change. And among the Fellows of Lincoln there was no prospect of a majority. The nub of the problem had been exposed. In Platt's words, Brasenose was 'eminent as a college for Pass men'; Lincoln was 'a resort for men of simple tastes and habits who came to Oxford for the purposes of study'. So there it was: reading men or sportsmen. There could be no easy rapport between

[148] F. Madan, 'Brasenose College', in A. Clark (ed.), *The Colleges of Oxford* (1891), 265.
[149] For the whole episode, see V. H. H. Green, *Oxford Common Room: A Study of Lincoln College and Mark Pattison* (1957), 298–301. Platt's arguments against over-large administrative units were prescient: 'To my mind, the increasing waste of time and ability on administrative work is one of the worst features which Oxford now presents. So many people who might be studying are disputing about what and how to study. "Research" is so often lost sight of, while discussing the machinery of research. The real purposes of the University are forgotten, and fussiness mistaken for intellectual activity.' For MS notes of preliminary BNC votes, see MR 5R 10/8 and B4 b9 (Madan's notebooks).

Pattison's view of a research community, and a college created in the image of Cradock.

That does not mean there could be no changes at all. In March 1878 Vice-Principal Turner—scarcely a revolutionary figure—'put up the first notice in *English* about reassembling after the Vacation'.[150] But the Chief himself saw no pressing need for change. During his lifetime he weathered three Royal Commissions as well as a Commons select committee. Over the years he recruited Fellows of proven ability. A. W. Rucker, FRS, mathematician and physicist; I. S. Leadam, economist and historian; Thomas Case, an Aristotelian and Baconian philosopher with a talent for music and cricket: all these were briefly Fellows, and leaders in their chosen fields. John Wordsworth was a formidable ecclesiastic, Falconer Madan a great librarian, G. Baldwin Brown a pioneer art historian, Richard Lodge one of the architects of the Oxford History School. And two Fellows, at least, were touched with genius. Walter Pater was the most brilliant stylist of the age; and Alfred Barratt—briefly a Fellow from 1868 onwards—was a prodigy beyond compare: he had no less than five Firsts to his name.[151] Between the First Commission and the Second—technically between 1855 and 1881—all Brasenose Fellows were in effect Prize Fellows, elected by examination. The result was a vintage crop of appointments. Of course examination in itself did not guarantee excellence: Stocker, notoriously, never fulfilled his promise. But the process of college elections was now competitive and transparent. Such was the spirit of reform. And by 1881 the secretary to the Oxford University Commission was actually a Brasenose Fellow: the prodigious Barratt himself.

The college by this time was in better financial health than most of its competitors, thanks to the bounty of the Hulme foundation. And the ethos of its Common Room was Liberal. When Thomas Baring offered to put up £30,000 for the establishment of Fellowships limited to Anglicans only, Brasenose declined the offer.[152] But in terms of image, BNC had emerged as a sporting icon. 'Day after day in summer term [Cradock] might be seen in the early afternoon, looking on at a college match at Cowley Marsh [BNC did not reduce grandpont until 1894], and as the sun declined he would make his way to the tow-path, and wait to see the college eight.' One morning, Woodgate remembered, he saw the Chief 'escorting some ladies round Christ Church meadow... [clad in] full dress robes [as for] the Sheldonian Theatre... I observed the DD. robe, and an arm from it, waving a signal to me to

---

[150] F. Madan, 'Private Book', 19 Mar. 1878.

[151] A Balliol Rugbeian, Alfred Barratt took Firsts in classical and maths Mods (1864), a First in Greats (1865), and Firsts in Final Schools in maths and in law and history (1866). Brasenose elected him to a Fellowship by examination in 1868, but he died in 1881 as secretary to the OU Commission. He wrote *Physical Ethics* (1869) and *Physical Metempiric* (1883). See *ODNB*.

[152] The money went to Hertford College (W. R. Ward, *Victorian Oxford* (1965), 283).

come within hail...' The Chief had a triumphant announcement to make: 'I have just matriculated the stroke of the Eton eight.'[153]

Back in college, Pater pondered the mystery of words.

When he had something new to express [Frank Harris recalled] he used to say the idea over and over again to himself, and then write it fairly on a little slip of paper. He would carry with him for a walk perhaps half a dozen of these slips loose in his pocket. When he found himself in a different mood, by the riverside in Oxford, or under the trees of Kensington Gardens, he would take out a slip, repeat the sentence to himself again, correct the English now here, now there, and finally end by finding a new form altogether for the thought. When he came home he would write this new sentence down and carry it about with him for days till he was certain he could not improve on it. Jeweller's work, or rather the work of some great lapidary, fashioning the stone to the idea in his mind, facet by facet with a loving solicitude, and inexhaustible patience.[154]

Too calculated, no doubt; too much midnight oil. But Oscar Wilde probably got it right: Pater may not have been 'among the greatest prose writers of our literature'; but he was surely 'our greatest artist in prose'.[155]

Let's leave him, counting phrases, in his rooms off the library stairs. In a fictional memoir, written towards the end of his life, he looks out across Radcliffe Square, then back again across Old Quad, conjuring up the ghosts of his predecessors; occupants 'it might be, of his own quaint rooms...just below the roof...[And with their ghosts, he senses their memories too; memories] of what he [still could] see from his windows in the old black front eastwards, with its inestimable patina of ancient smoke and weather and natural decay (when you look close the very stone is a composite of minute dead bodies)....On summer nights the scent of the hay, the wild-flowers, comes across the narrow fringe of town to right and left; seems to come from beyond the Oxford meadows...He looks down upon the green square with the slim, quaint, black, young figures that cross it on the way to chapel on yellow Sunday mornings or upwards to the dome, the spire; can watch them closely in freakish moonlight, or flickering softly by an occasional bonfire in the quadrangle behind him...In truth the memory of Oxford made almost everything he saw after it seem vulgar...'[156]

---

[153] Woodgate, *Reminiscences*, 127–8. The man in question, J. W. McClintock Bunbury, had initially failed the test for matric; but the Boat Club protested to the Chief. 'God bless my soul', replied Cradock; 'Is that so? I will see at once whether anything can be done.' He promptly telegraphed the candidate at Eton: 'What is the perfect of τύπτω?' That was a difficult question; it still requires close scrutiny of Liddell and Scott. But back at once came the correct reply: πέπληγα. So in 1871–2 it was McClintock Bunbury who stroked first the Brasenose and then the Varsity Eight (*Brazen Nose*, iv. 173).

[154] F. Harris, *Contemporary Portraits*, ii (1919), 209–10.

[155] Wilde, reviewing 'Imaginary Portraits', in *Pall Mall Gazette*, 11 June 1887, 2–3.

[156] Pater, 'Emerald Uthwart', *New Review*, June–July 1892; reprinted privately (Canterbury, 1905), 30–1. The topography is vague: there are hints of Queen's College as well.

Pater's masterwork, *Marius the Epicurean*, was published in 1885. It seems unlikely that it was read by Edward Hartopp Cradock. He had only a few months to live. By the mid-1880s the Chief was fading slowly, a laggard from an age before reform. A few weeks before his death, he received a familiar guest.

I had gone to see Trial Eights at Goring [Woodgate recalls] and reached Oxford more or less muddy, in shooting kit. I rang the Chief's bell . . . The butler shook his head. 'He is very ill, sir; I am afraid we are going to lose him, . . . The Chief was in a dressing-gown; looking white and wasted; the hand of Death was already close on him.

Old BNC men had been sending him game and messages of goodwill. Woodgate had one last request: he had heard of a brilliant oarsman from Eton named Holland, just the sort for Brasenose; but he 'had been pluck-ed . . . for Matriculation . . . a college disaster'; what could be done about it? 'The Chief moaned. "It was not my fault, Woodgate; . . . I have been much too ill to attend to any examinations . . . [But] don't let him go to any other college . . . send him up again next January; . . . he is sure to do much better this time; they always do . . . promise me this!" ' And we parted; I never again saw the dear old soul alive.' Cradock died in January 1886. That summer, Claude Holland was rowing for Brasenose; the summer after that for Oxford; and the summer after that he was President of OUBC: a quadruple blue, destined for the captaincy of Leander, and a career in the wine trade. 'How the Chief would have revelled in this.'[157]

---

[157] Woodgate, *Reminiscences*, 129. A window in memory of Cradock, probably by James Powell, was placed on the south side of the ante chapel (V.-P.'s Reg. 21 Jan. 1887, f. 167). The north window opposite, by Whittington, was dedicated to the oarsman Duncan Pocklington in 1871 and renewed in 1894 with an adjacent window to T. C. Edwards-Moss, by Clayton and Bell (Heberden Jnl. MS, 1894; V-P's Reg. 21 Dec. 1870, fo. 188; 6 June 1894). The west window (1775–6, by J. Pearson from cartoons by J. H. Mortimer; transferred from the east end in 1855), was repaired and reset by Kempe in 1894–6 (V-P's Reg. 7 Mar. 1894, fo. 65; 6 May 1894, f. 88; 18 Mar. 1896, f. 86). For engravings of Mortimer's four Evangelists, see BL Add. MS 34873, fos. 2–6. The college repurchased Mortimer's drawing of St Luke in 1971 for £400 (V-P's Reg. 20 Jan. 1971, fo. 37).

6

1886–1918

Officers and Gentlemen: The Days of Haig and Buchan

As Frodsham Hodson lay dying in 1822, he made each Fellow promise never 'to renew the leases of any of the Houses in the High Street'.[1] By that date it had taken the college more than a century to gain control of its southern boundary. The efforts of several generations of Bursars had in fact been directed above all to this one end: the accumulation of a viable site for building.[2] Between the late seventeenth century and the early nineteenth century there had been only two major additions to the stock of undergraduate accommodation: New Building and Garden Court.[3] Neither of these had been remotely worthy of the college. On one occasion, Cradock referred to them as built in the 'lath-and-plastrian' style.[4] But by the mid-Victorian period, after so many aborted schemes, Brasenose was at last ready to break out. The leases on the High Street had finally fallen in. And this time there was no problem about money. Unlike most Oxford colleges, BNC's income in the late 1870s was rising rather than falling. By 1880 the college was eager to build; and its chosen architect was the most fashionable practitioner in Oxford, Thomas Graham Jackson.[5]

By 1880, Jackson had established himself as architect to the Liberals of Oxford. He could almost be described as the darling of the progressives. His Oxford practice had been launched with the new Examination Schools (1876–83); it continued with an impressive series of college extensions: Corpus, Lincoln, and Somerville, Wadham, Trinity, and Hertford. But Brasenose was earlier than any of these. Thanks probably to Humphry Ward, the college engineered his appointment, and thus secured a rising star. Now Jackson's style was distinctive: an eclectic compound of Elizabethan and

---

[1] V-P's Reg. 8 Feb. 1822, fo. 195.   [2] See *Quat. Mon.* III, 3: plan.   [3] See p. 167.

[4] To the OU Architectural and Historical Society, Nov. 1873.

[5] J. Mordaunt Crook, 'T. G. Jackson and the Cult of Eclecticism', in H. Searing (ed.), *In Search of Modern Architecture* (New York, 1982); *ODNB*; W. Whyte, *Oxford Jackson: Architecture, Education, Status, and Style 1835–1924* (Oxford, 2006).

Jacobean, flexible, secular, and picturesque. It was sometimes called 'Advanced Jacobean'.[6] Whatever it was, it represented a calculated escape from the rigidities of collegiate Gothic. And it was a style based on considerable learning. Jackson was a gentleman scholar as well as a gentleman architect.[7] He had no trouble fitting in with the ethos of the Brasenose Common Room. He was already a Fellow of Wadham; he would soon be a Royal Academician; and he would end his days a full-blown baronet.

The 'Anglo-Jackson' style—a phrase borrowed by John Betjeman from Maurice Bowra—was exactly right for Brasenose. In the sixteenth century its buildings had been Gothic Survival; in the seventeenth century a mixture of Gothic Revival and Renaissance. Now they were to be all three simultaneously: Survival, Revival, and Renaissance. No wonder contemporary critics talked of 'progressive eclecticism'.

The first stage of Jackson's scheme was constructed in two phases: new staircases X and XI in 1881–3;[8] new staircase IX in 1886–7.[9] In effect, these made up the west and north sides of a new quadrangle (pl. 71). There were twenty-two undergraduate sets, one commodious set for a resident Fellow, two spacious lecture rooms, and one surprising novelty: an undergraduate reading room, soon to become the college's first JCR (pl. 68). The undergraduate quarters had separate sitting rooms and bedrooms; there were scouts' pantries on each landing. But there would be no internal plumbing for another three-quarters of a century. Until 1910 hip-baths and chamber pots were the order of the day. After that date, until the 1950s, undergraduates continued to use outside facilities, situated along the Lincoln boundary wall. From 1862 onwards these bathrooms—all open access; no doors—had been linked to the first quad by means of a corridor under staircase I. They were accessible, but not exactly convenient. Still, whatever their lack of luxury, Jackson's new buildings were built to last. The interior walling was of friable Headington stone; but the facings were of Gibraltar rag, with Clipsham dressings for string courses, sills, and mullions, plus hard Doulting stone for the rest of the surface work. This was Brasenose, after all: each staircase was designed to withstand heavy treatment. The landings were of flagstones from Castlehill near Thurso. The stairs themselves were composed of massive slabs from the Isle of Portland. Even so, during the next half-

[6] H. E. D. Blakiston, *Trinity College Oxford* (Oxford, 1898), 238.

[7] His writings include: *Modern Gothic Architecture* (1873); *Architecture: A Profession or an Art* (with R. N. Shaw, 1892); *Byzantine and Romanesque Architecture*, 2 vols. (Cambridge, 1913; 2nd edn. 1920); *Gothic Architecture in France, England and Italy*, 2 vols. (Cambridge, 1915); and *The Renaissance of Roman Architecture*, 3 vols. (Cambridge, 1921–3).

[8] B 13.2 (plans and drawings); RA 1882 no. 1136; *The Builder*, 43 (1882) (ii), 535 and 45 (1883), (ii), 570; *Oxford and Cambridge Undergraduate's Jnl.* 19 Oct. 1882, 16–17.

[9] B 13.2 (plans and drawings); *The Builder*, 53 (1887) (ii), 296.

century, their treads would be beaten into semi-sculptural shapes by the pounding of booted feet.

New Quad made good use of Jackson's distinctive vocabulary: Cotswold vernacular with touches of late Gothic and Renaissance. The rhythm of bay and balustrade, chimneystack and gable, has absorbed the traditions of collegiate planning; these traditions have then in turn been synthesized in pursuit of the Picturesque. The result is original, yet laden with associations. The new reading room for example, facing south to catch the sun, conjures up echoes of the 'Tribunal' or Court House at Glastonbury. Perhaps this antiquarian touch was regarded as some compensation for the loss of the old brew house, which had been in use since 1826. Certainly, the heritage aspect of the programme was not ignored. For example, the jumble of cottages around Amsterdam Passage was now swept away; but the college's oldest building, the fifteenth-century kitchen, was consciously and carefully preserved. In this, Jackson dared to contradict the judgement of Walter Pater. It was Pater's view that a new kitchen should be built to the west of the buttery, leaving room for a spacious new quadrangle, unencumbered by the old service buildings. That would certainly have given the chapel greater prominence. But it would also have destroyed the college's picturesque variety. 'The present kitchen', Jackson explained to Cradock, is 'in the most convenient place for the Hall and... When stripped of its ugly outbuildings... [will be] a very picturesque mass of building... [besides it will be] good economy to save it and the sets of rooms [staircase VIII] above it.'[10]

Jackson's view found favour with the Fellowship. Picturesque it was to be. When W. N. Stocker first climbed the steps of staircase XI in October 1883—and looked out over library and chapel towards St Mary's and the Camera—he took possession of a view that was quintessentially Oxford. No wonder he stayed there for the best part of half a century.[11]

With Cradock's death in 1886, the moment for a breakthrough to the High Street had finally arrived. The decision was taken to rebuild the Principal's Lodgings, as part of a brand new entrance frontage. Cradock's successor— shy Albert Watson—seems to have had no intention of staying long in office.

---

[10] College buildings: Jackson to Cradock, 29 Nov. 1880; B4 b10, ii. fs. 201–2: 26 June 1880. Staircase VIII dates mostly from the later 18th century (College Buildings 25 and 29). The 1862 corridor below staircase I did not affect the 16th-century old chapel staircase. It was only in 1936 that Guy Dawber transferred the lower sections of these stairs to the south end of the corridor, at the same time creating the Eckersley Room. Not until the 1960s was the upstairs smoking room extended to the north, thus removing the 17th-century 'corkscrew' staircase which previously gave access to the attic floor. The kitchen's elaborate brick chimneystack—reproducing those of 1509—dates from 1912 (B 272–80). In that year New Quad was finally paved and bordered; it was rearranged and regrassed in 1937 and 1998.

[11] He was elected by examination in 1877, and retired to BNC in 1901.

The future in that respect clearly lay with Heberden. But it was under Watson's nominal leadership that Brasenose at last produced an architectural statement worthy of its ambitions. The new Lodgings would be large. In one respect at least they would be too large: Bunny's rose garden was doomed.

Jackson's High Street programme was constructed in two phases, 1887–90 and 1909–11. First came the Lodgings, the new entrance tower, and staircase XIII; then came Broadgates, Amsterdam, and staircase XII (pl. 71). This time there was a new attention to amenity: there were actually bathrooms on the ground floor. But the main emphasis was still on style. Jackson's design had to look two ways: inward towards the quiet world of the college; outward on to the bustle of the High. The inner front he made appropriately collegiate; it simply followed the pattern of what had already been built. It was the outer front which presented him with problems. How could he create a powerful collegiate image without destroying the random balance of the High Street? It had been Pater's view that the jumble of old shops should stay. But that would have reduced, and reduced drastically, the number of new rooms in the scheme. Besides, Brasenose had not waited all those years merely to create a new quadrangle invisible from the outside world. The Common Room looked to Jackson to supply a prestigious presence. And Jackson looked to the college to give him the chance of creating an architectural statement. But how could he satisfy the Fellows while protecting 'the famous "High"'? After all, as he took care to explain, this was the very 'glory of Oxford'.[12] The commission was certainly a challenge. But it was also—as he informed the Bursar—'a labour of love'.[13]

Brasenose had waited the greater part of two centuries for this opportunity. A symbolic entrance there had to be. That meant at least a gateway. But in Oxford there could be no gateway without a tower. And a conventional tower posed difficulties: it would present too bold a rectangle, too harsh a cube, when placed sequentially between the spire of St Mary's and the steeple of All Saints. Again, a third vertical feature could assume the form of neither steeple nor spire without at least some sense of visual redundancy. So Jackson hit upon a daring compromise: a steeple with an open crown; a multi-buttressed pinnacle—gravity defying, diaphanous—soaring high above the squarest of square towers; the tower itself, pierced at its base with a vaulted ceremonial porch.[14] One final touch: this grand vertical feature was to be set back from the line of the High Street, placed behind an open screen,

---

[12] T. G. Jackson, 'The High Street of Oxford, and Brasenose College', *Mag. of Art*, 8 (1889), 332–40; College Buildings: Jackson to Cradock, 29 Nov. 1880.

[13] B 502: T. G. Jackson to A. J. Butler: 8 Feb. 1890.

[14] B 502: T. G. Jackson to A. J. Butler: 18 Jan. and 26 Feb. 1887.

and entered via a miniature forecourt. In this way Jackson hoped to fly beyond the visual platitude of three tall towers in a row.

It was ingenious; it was bold. The architect's design perspective (pl. 70) was one of the talking points of the 1887 Royal Academy Exhibition.[15] But would it ever be accepted? Some thought this new street frontage too ecclesiastical. 'The style', noted *The Builder* sourly, 'is a hard type of Late Gothic, which we love not.'[16] More to the point, could Brasenose afford it? Bursar Butler, for one, must have had his doubts. Within a year, Jackson produced a modified design; rather less obtrusive, and considerably less expensive (pl. 71).[17] The entrance tower was now reduced in scale. It no longer made any attempt to compete with its High Street neighbours. In its new form the design concentrated its impact on the ornament of the street façade.[18] By replacing that 'hard type' of fourteenth-century tracery with softer, secular Gothic forms—rippling outwards from bay to bay—Jackson remoulded his façade to suit the broken rhythms of the High.[19] From a town-planning point of view, the city was just possibly the loser. A more histrionic silhouette—with echoes of Newcastle and Aberdeen—would certainly have multiplied the drama of Oxford's skyline.[20] But Brasenose must surely have breathed a sigh of relief. William Morris was quite right to warn Butler against such a looming 'mistake'.[21] For the inhabitants of the New Quad, the result might have been nightmare rather than dream.[22]

And what was the eventual cost? Apart from the Examination Schools, this proved to be Jackson's most profitable Oxford project. Staircases IX–XI, and the repairs to the old kitchen area, cost more than £16,000. The High Street frontage—which came in at £1,000 over budget—cost nearly £20,000.[23] Taken together with the cost of sundry works of restoration—notably the reconstruction of Frewin Hall in 1887–94,[24] and the refurbishment of

[15] RA 1887, no. 1689; *The Builder*, 52 (1887), 832; *Quat. Mon.* III, pl. xxx. For debate and eventual rejection, see *Oxford Jnl.* 15 Oct. 1887, p. 5.

[16] *The Builder*, 52 (1887), 827.

[17] RA 1888, nos. 1804, 1815, 1839; *Building News*, 11 May 1888, 666. Houses in St Mary's Entry (occupied by Madan and Wordsworth) were refurbished by T. G. Jackson and H. W. Moore (V.-P.'s Reg. 25–7 May 1887, f. 177 and 16 June 1889, f. 180) (pl. 52B).

[18] The masonry carving was by Farmer and Brindley of 63 Westminster Bridge Rd., London (ills. *Academy Architecture*, 2 (1890), no. 1794, 21; *Quat. Mon.* III, pls. xxxii–xxxiii).

[19] The oriel windows on the High were specifically requested by the Governing Body (V-P's Reg. 11 Mar. 1889, fo. 172).

[20] Drawing by A. E. Perkins, *Quat. Mon.* III, pl. xxxi.

[21] S.B. uncatalogued (New Buildings 1881–1911), 8 Mar. 1887; reprinted *Brazen Nose*, xxii. 33.

[22] J. H. Middleton, Slade Professor at Cambridge, was adamantly opposed: 'the tower with its lantern-crown would be a serious discord in [a] site [which is] architecturally one of the most important in the world' (B 502).

[23] B 13.2 (working drawings); D 819 (Building Accounts, 1881–1911).

[24] *Oxford Architectural and Historical Soc. Proceedings*, NS 6 (1894), 38–47.

chapel and antechapel in 1890–2 and 1894–6[25]—the total expenditure at BNC on building under Jackson's direction cannot have been less than £45,000. Begun under Cradock, continued under Watson, completed under Heberden, New Quad was ultimately the responsibility of two men: the architect Graham Jackson, and the Bursar Alfred Butler. Jackson was the artist; but nothing would have been done without the Bursar. Butler was the presiding genius. Appropriately, New Quad's western wall is marked today with a plaque in Butler's memory.

When the future Earl Haig (pl. 58) arrived at Brasenose in October 1880, all this work had scarcely been begun. He was allocated inferior quarters, in New Building: they were already scheduled for demolition as part of Jackson's grand design. He lost no time in moving to IV, 2. Not only was the Old Quad more comfortable; it was of course the centre of college life. Haig had every intention of enjoying himself.

At his first meeting with the Principal, the future field marshal received one piece of advice. 'Ride, sir, ride', barked Cradock; 'I like to see Brasenose gentlemen in top boots.'[26] Haig required little prompting. Years later, he admitted that during tutorials with Walter Pater he wore hunting kit beneath his trousers, ready for a quick start with the Bicester. Pater responded in kind. Sensing that this man's mind was not on Homer, he set him instead to study Thackeray and Dickens.[27] While still at Clifton, Haig had already decided on a military career. Riding and playing polo—he scored three times against Cambridge—was exactly what he intended to do. Dining in hall that first night, sitting opposite the portrait of Frodsham Hodson, he revealed to the man placed next to him just what he expected from BNC. Oxford was to be a stepping stone to Sandhurst.

Haig's Oxford career can now be fairly well documented. Through it we can conjure up the college life of at least one of Cradock's 'Brasenose

[25] Interior decoration 1894–6 (painting and stained glass by Kempe; stained glass by Clayton and Bell) and 1901 (stained glass and painted decoration by Kempe). See V-P's Reg. 19 June 1891, fo. 79 (Kempe's report), 6 June 1894, fo. 68 (Clayton and Bell's antechapel north window), 5 Dec. 1894, fo. 73 (Kempe's report), 18 Mar. 1896, fo. 86 (Kempe's east window), 19 June 1901 fo. 184 (wall colouring and geometrical marble flooring by Kempe and Mills). Also B4 b10, Madan's notebooks, 6 Dec. 1893 and 6 June 1894. Heberden gave £500 in 1902 for 'the renewal of the marble panelling' of the reredos (*Quat. Mon.* IV, 41). From this period, presumably, dates also the rearrangement of the early 18th-century altar rails (original layout shown in W. Williams, *Oxonia Depicta* (Oxford, 1732–3), pl. xxxv). For the organ case (pl. 32), see A. Freeman, *English Organ Cases* (1921), 120; this was largely paid for by Heberden (benefaction of £1,240 in 1892: *Quat. Mon.* IV, 41). See also V-P's Reg. 23 Oct. 1891, fo. 30 and 3 Dec. 1919, fo. 159. Rebuilt by P. Collins (1972–3); renewed by R. Bower (2001).

[26] Lord Askwith, 'Haig at Oxford', *Oxford Mag.* 23 Feb. 1928, 243–4.

[27] *Brazen Nose*, iv (1928), 368.

gentlemen'. Haig's father, a whisky trader worth £10,000 a year—old family, new money—had died in 1878.[28] His mother died a few months later in 1879. When he arrived at BNC, an orphan at the age of 19, young Haig turned a hard face to the world. Sport must have been a useful shield. 'Cricket', his mother had told him, will 'make you strong and manly', not a 'weakly Cad'.[29] She had nothing against 'Scholarship'; she thought it a useful 'antidote to the vulgarity and narrowness of mind which active commercial pursuits are apt to engender'. But a real university had rather more to offer. 'My idea', she explained, is that 'an Oxford or Cambridge man is of a higher stamp, than those who are not... [after all] you... mix with men in college, who, in the course of a few years will be the great men of the day, statesmen, lawyers, etc. and the training makes a gentleman'.[30] Future statesmen were thin on the ground at Brasenose in Haig's time. But there was a good sprinkling of lawyers—the undergraduate he confided in that first night was the future Lord Askwith—and there were certainly plenty of gentlemen.

Hunting in the Bicester country; polo in Port Meadow; claret at the Octagon; port at the Phoenix; lunching with the Vampires; dining with the Bullingdon; pulling strings at Vincent's on the other side of the High—Haig floated smoothly into the smarter sporting set. Of his sixteen closest friends at BNC, seven were Etonians, three were Harrovians, and not one was a scholar. A few came from abroad: Robert Baillie from Australia, George Moke and Tommy Hitchcock from America (pl. 58).[31] A few, like Haig himself, represented commercial money: H. S. Barton, claret shipper; Douglas and Willie Barry, copper merchants. But they all fitted easily into the category of gentry. In Haig's rooms on staircase IV—ground floor, right-hand side—they spoke in the same language. Few bothered to take a degree, fewer still aspired to Honours. They went to Brasenose to enjoy themselves and to take on by osmosis just a tincture of civility.

> Up! and defend the cause so dear –
> Imperium, Beaconsfield, and beer.[32]

---

[28] G. J. De Groot, *Douglas Haig, 1861–1928* (1988), 9.

[29] Ibid. 16.

[30] Ibid. 13, 14.

[31] Hitchcock belonged simultaneously to five of the world's top clubs: the Knickerbocker in New York, the Somerset in Boston, the Metropolitan in Washington, the St James's in London, and the Travellers in Paris.

[32] C. B. L[ucas], Ale Verse (1880). It was for his activities on behalf of the Conservative interest in the Oxford city by-election of 1880 that Thomas Wells, the Brasenose manciple—a man of some influence in local politics—was found guilty of corruption ('Report [on] Corrupt Practices in the City of Oxford' (*PP* (1881), xliv), 17–18). For Haig's social life, see D. Cooper, *Haig*, i (1935), 31; [Dorothy] Countess Haig, *The Man I Knew* (1936), 21. For the diary of one of Haig's friends, W. J. Barry—a crack-shot country-house guest—see E. Walton, in *The Field*, Jan. 2002, 40–3.

In all this, Haig was fairly typical of his class and generation. Even so, there was an element of calculation about his pleasures. And an element of vanity. He kept early hours; he stayed fit; he studied sufficiently hard to sail through the examinations for a Pass degree in French, political economy, and ancient history. He took care to join the Freemasons.[33] Above all, he never lost sight of his career. Once, on a trip abroad, when friends enticed him to the roulette wheel, he coolly declined: '[I don't want] to play at Soldiering, I'm going in it as a profession, and I am going to do well.'[34] There seem to have been no lady friends. 'Women', he once remarked, 'are at the bottom of all quarrels.'[35] Besides, they held a man back. He did not marry until the age of 44, and then he chose one of the Queen's ladies in waiting. 'If I went into the Church', he used to say, 'I'd be a bishop.'[36]

There was nothing episcopal about Brasenose in the 1880s. In fact, on at least one occasion, on 9 March 1881, the Old Quad was the scene of an extraordinary riot. That afternoon the college Torpid had gone head of the river, catching Keble after a hectic race. The Chief gave permission for a bump supper; a circle of bonfires was ignited; and the figures of Cain and Abel were shadowed in smoke and flame. As it happened, a visiting tutor was watching from a first-floor window.

Warmed, but by no means overcome, by the potent Brasenose ale and perhaps nobler stimulants, the young braves...streamed forth to dance the tribal dance round Cain and Abel...In the flickering light of bonfires thoughtfully arranged by the edge of the grass could be seen the figures of some two hundred young men bounding and leaping high round the images and passing from lurid light into deep shadow alternately; and the leaping was accompanied by terrifying yells and the most fantastic music ever devised by savages standing on the verge of culture; for every one of the participants had equipped himself with his flat-bottomed bath—part of an undergraduate's outfit before college bathrooms were built: this he held in his left hand and his sitting-room poker in his right, and by banging it on the centre of his bath he produced sounds which, multiplied by two hundred others chiming in, might well surpass the same number of bull-roarers in volume and terror. When the tone of the bath was injured by the poker going through the bottom as frequently happened, the dancer threw it away and was immediately supplied with a new one by one of the scouts who stood around in an admiring group away from the inner circle. Till midnight, the full moon, the solemn dome of the Radcliffe, and Cain and Abel looked down on the scene...

[33] Haig passed all his examinations for BA, but 'was never fully qualified by residence' (*Brazen Nose*, iv. 380–83). He was initiated in Elgin's Lodge at Leven on 7 Dec. 1881, but did not become a Master Mason until 2 Feb. 1924 (*ex inf.* J. Daniel and G. Bourne-Taylor).

[34] De Groot, *Haig*, 27.

[35] P. Warner, *Field Marshall Earl Haig* (1991), 28. He was handsome, but had a cast in one eye.

[36] De Groot, *Haig*, 27.

But this long orgy of dance and music was only preliminary to the great final act, the desecration of Cain and Abel. About midnight the tribal leaders produced large pots of variegated and indelible paint, and embellished the statues all over with such astonishing savage designs that in the morning light they were no longer Cain and Abel but monstrous and unspeakable parodies of humanity... [Clearly] the centre of a young man's quadrangle is not a safe place for any monument of art.[37]

Haig must certainly have been present on this occasion. Years later he fondly recalled just such a bonfire, 'as far from the Principal's house as possible'.[38] Three members of the winning crew—Askwith, Puxley, and Barton—were particular friends of his (pl. 58). And this was the only bump supper during his time at BNC. By coincidence, he was absent next term; but on grounds of illness, and not as a result of disciplinary action. In fact no action was taken by the Governing Body against any undergraduate, even though some at least seem to have been as naked as Cain and Abel themselves; and some were actually carted off, insensible, in wheelbarrows.[39] The glory of a bump supper meant that undergraduates were exempt from disciplinary sanction. Instead it was Cain and Abel who were sent down. That summer, the celebrated statue—supposedly 'very dilapidated'[40]—was quietly removed, and sold for scrap to a local blacksmith.

Next Shrove Tuesday there was a ritual protest:

> Yes, where is Cain and Abel, the glory of the quad?
> And Echo, somewhat strangely, seems to answer 'Ichabod'
> ...'twas [just] a gift to Brasenose to be kept for evermore –
> Small wonder that old Dr Clarke turned in his grave and swore!
> The very Nose above our gate turned up in sheer disgust
> At the shameless perpetrators of such a breach of trust.
> Oh ye, whose mighty fiat brought this paltry thing to pass,
> May the ghost of the donor haunt you with the jawbone of an ass![41]

[37] L. R. Farnell, *An Oxonian Looks Back* (1934), 134–5.

[38] *Brazen Nose*, iv. 370.

[39] W. T. S. Stallybrass in *Brazen Nose*, ix. 325. Other forms of rowdyism were treated more harshly: seven undergraduates were gated for between one and three weeks 'in consequence of disturbances in college on the evenings of the 18th and 19th [Feb.]' (V-P's Reg. 22 Feb. 1876, fo. 22); and five were fined and gated for lighting bonfires in 1885–6 (ibid. 28 Nov. 1885 and 10 Nov. 1886). The dons were certainly tolerant. On 30 June 1880, noted Madan, at 1.30 a.m. 'Radley was pushed on a chair down the stairs in [old staircase] no. 9, and was thought to be dying; but it seems that he only got some bruises. Whittuck sat up with him for two hours that night' (B4 b10, ii, f. 186).

[40] V-P's Reg. 15 June 1881, fo. 75. In 1878 Buckler was consulted about repairs: £40 for 'putting on a wooden limb' (B4 b9, i, fos. 64–6, 77). In 1880 the Phoenix paid 2 guineas 'compensation... for damage' (B1 a29: 25 Nov. 1880).

[41] A. W. A[rkle], Ale Verse, 1882.

The *Encyclopaedia Britannica* (9th edn., 1881) was damning: Brasenose had perpetrated 'an utterly inexcusable act of vandalism'. Pater was appalled, but apparently unable to prevent it.[42] He rejoiced in the custom of bonfires: their flickering shadows illuminated the spire of St Mary's 'so beautifully'. He must often have relished the sheer machismo of Giambologna's statue. But naked sportsmen dancing round a naked statue: it would have been unwise for him to take a stand.

Undergraduate memories are short. Stories of this episode, however, must still have been current when John Buchan arrived at BNC in 1895 (pl. 66). The intervening years had seen little change in the ethos of the college. In 1882 BNC fielded its first regular soccer team, thanks to the initiative of two north-country freshmen from footballing schools: Henry Dobinson (Repton) and William Jacques (Shrewsbury). Rugby, of course, had been well established for some time: there were five Brasenose men in the first Oxford team to play Cambridge, in 1872. And in 1874, the first Oxford soccer team against Cambridge was led by the great Ottaway himself. But after that Brasenose footballers played little part in the development of soccer at University level. However the Brasenose rugger teams of the later 1870s could boast at least one England player: A. H. Heath; and in the 1880s a series of powerful blues recruited from Loretto—Mackenzie, Asher, and Berry; Blair, Blyth, and Boswell—made BNC a force to reckon with in the world of rugby football. But the college was still defined by its rowing and its cricket. So much is clear from the memories of G. B. Grundy. The year 1888 was the year of Grundy's arrival, and his memoirs underline the persistent muscularity of late Victorian BNC.

Cradock had admitted sportsmen eagerly; the pace of recruitment scarcely slowed down under his successor, the shy and retiring Watson. 'Toby' Watson was a bachelor classicist with a weak heart and a gentle smile. He had long given up teaching; he seemed almost to have given up speaking. 'To meet Mr. Watson in the street', recalled Falconer Madan, 'you would think that his one desire was to get past you in safety and, if possible, silence.'[43] In University politics he had once been a noted Liberal. But his was an interim Principalship: he was not the man to change the complexion of the college.

[42] T. Wright, *A Life of Walter Pater*, ii (1907), 52, 99; E. Gosse, in *Critical Kit-Kats* (1896), 268–9; J. H. M[iddleton], in *Encyclopaedia Britannica* (1881), s.v. 'Sculpture'.

[43] *Oxford Mag.* 30 Nov. 1904. See also C. B. H[eberden], *Address in Memory of Rev. Albert Watson* (Oxford, 1904). He died within twenty-four hours of his greatest friend and Liberal ally Thomas Fowler of Corpus (Newspaper Gleanings, 21 Nov. 1904, 40). His *Select Letters of Cicero* (1870) was for long a standard work; his knowledge was hidden by shyness; and his headship of a hard-drinking college must always have seemed anomalous (Shrimpton caricature, Madan coll., III, 524, 557 and VI, 1098; pl 39A. Memorial by Eric Gill).

By 1890 there were no fewer than four rowing cups in place of honour in the newly established JCR: for Eights as well as Torpids, plus the Henley Visitors' and Steward's Cups and the BNC–Trinity Challenge Cup. For three years in a row, 1889–91, the BNC Eight stayed head of the river. And for nine years—1886–94: fifty-three consecutive nights—the Torpid remained head as well, a quite extraordinary feat. It took a severe frost in 1895 (when rowing was cancelled), and an accident in 1896 (when bow broke a strap at the start), to interrupt this heroic sequence. That year, stroke wore a black armband in the customary group photograph of the crew. Over the best part of a century BNC's record had been remarkable: head of the river 18 times in 84 years (117 nights); in Torpids 22 times in 62 years (141 nights). No other college could match those figures.

But a counter-revolution was already in train. The man who would ultimately be responsible for this was Charles Buller Heberden (pl. 67), a Devonian classicist who arrived as Fellow—via Harrow and Balliol—in 1872, and became Vice-Principal in 1883, then Principal in 1889.[44] Heberden did not despise competitive sport, far from it; but he regarded it as more than an end in itself. It was part of a much bigger educational game, a wider socializing process: the construction of civility. His chief ally in this operation was the future Sir Richard Lodge.

Heberden was progressive; Lodge was very progressive. He came from a Midlands commercial background, conscientious and Liberal: his elder brother was Sir Oliver Lodge, physicist and psychical researcher; his sister was Eleanor Lodge, later Vice-Principal of Lady Margaret Hall. Lodge's undergraduate career had been dazzling: the Brackenbury Scholarship at Balliol, the Stanhope and Lothian Prizes, and in 1878 election to a Fellowship by examination at BNC within a year of his expected First in history. He stayed at Brasenose sixteen years, becoming Junior Bursar and Vice-Principal before moving to professorial chairs first at Glasgow, then at Edinburgh. He enjoyed the bonhomie of sportsmen: in particular the dozen blues sent up from Loretto during his time at BNC. But his belief in the educative power of history was compelling. He can claim to be one of the founders of the Oxford History School.[45]

---

[44] Heberden produced editions of Euripides' *Medea* (1886) and *Hecuba* (1901); but his greatest contributions were administrative, as Vice-Principal, Principal, and Vice-Chancellor. He spent years editing the *Brasenose Register, 1509–1909*, 2 vols. (Oxford, 1909).

[45] In the written competition for a Brasenose Fellowship—12 candidates—he defeated the formidable T. F. Tout (B4 b9, i: Madan notebook). At Glasgow he defeated H. A. L. Fisher, having himself been defeated at Edinburgh by G. W. Prothero; eventually he became Prothero's successor. His Oxford Ford Lectures appeared as *Great Britain and Prussia in the 18th Century* (1922); but his most widely read textbook was probably *English Political History, 1660–1702* (1909).

'Dickie' Lodge looked 'very tall and gaunt and fierce', recalled Gertrude Bell; 'but [was] not really fierce at all... [in fact he was] very nice and friendly'.[46] His Sunday breakfasts and tea parties, organized by his popular young wife, were hugely popular with undergraduates. One older Fellow remarked that 'sometimes when Lodge looks at me, I have an uneasy feeling that he wants to kick me'. But any hostility was invariably dissolved by Lodge's 'irresistible smile'.[47] In fact 'Dickie' became the darling of the History Faculty: he had to transfer his lectures from BNC to Balliol because the undergraduate audience was so large.[48] In college matters he and Heberden were dominant: in the 1880s and early 1890s, recalled Sir Francis Wylie, 'Brasenose moved round Heberden and Lodge.'[49] Their aim was to raise the intellectual tone of the place. They managed, at last, to persuade Principal Cradock to accept the imposition of a prior matriculation requirement for all candidates: tutors were tired of coaching Pass men for Responsions. The Chief, however, remained unconcerned. As Principal he took no part in teaching; but he did preside over Collections. Once, while invigilating, he glanced over the shoulders of one group of candidate athletes: 'Gentlemen, I should not if I were you translate "an old man" by antiquus vir, but by senex. The tutors will like it better.'[50]

It is worth reminding ourselves, at this point, just what was required—or not required—of a mid-Victorian Pass man. In 1867 the Dean of Christ Church defined the requisite range of study as follows: 'a not very great acquaintance with classics, a very insufficient acquaintance with mathematics, and none [at all] with physical science'. The maths in fact amounted to no more than 'the first two books of Euclid and a certain quantity of arithmetic'; and even this might be replaced by elementary logic if preferred.[51] A Pass man reading law and history could get away with Blackstone's *Real Property* and Lingard's

---

[46] M. Lodge, *Sir Richard Lodge* (1946), 30, 57–8. Gertrude Bell herself took a First in history in 1888, the first woman to do so. The Lodges lived first at 23 Norham Road, then at Brasenose House in All Saints Entry off the High, and finally at 37 St Margaret's Road, which they built in 1887. As Vice-Principal he briefly occupied IV, 4 in college, before its temporary conversion in 1891 into the Fellows' smoking room (V-P's Reg. 8 Oct. 1891, fo. 29).

[47] *ODNB.*

[48] Lodge, *Sir Richard Lodge*, 51, 57. He was also the founder of the *Oxford Magazine*, and acted as treasurer of the BNC Boat Club, 1881–92, during a period of great success. From 1888 the college sports clubs amalgamated for the purpose of collecting subscriptions; from 1892 this was regularized by an amalgamated committee. See cash book 1887 onwards (SL8 A 2/1/1) and minute book 1893 onwards (SL8 A1/1).

[49] [Sir] Francis Wylie, in *Brazen Nose*, vi. 185.

[50] G. B. Grundy, *Fifty-Five Years at Oxford* (1945), 51. These changes were largely due to the Senior Tutor, C. H. Sampson.

[51] Revd H. G. Liddell, 8 July 1867, to Select Committee on ... Oxford and Cambridge (*PP* (1867), xiii), 263.

History of England. His Honours counterpart was a little busier: for history he had to read Lingard, Hallam, Gibbon, Milman, Clarendon, and Ranke; for law it was Blackstone, Wheaton, and Justinian. And both class and Pass men might extend their programme of work—or leisure—over a period as long as four to six years.[52] Much of the time might in fact be spent—or misspent—in passing Responsions. From 1865 onwards, when the Honorary Fourth for Pass men was abolished, there was no inducement for a Pass man to distinguish himself. As Montagu Burrows put it, 'the pass [had been] knocked down to the very lowest limit, in order to let men through'.[53]

With the demise of Cradock, the number of Pass men noticeably declined. In Haig's year (1880) there had been as many as 29 out of 36; in Grundy's year (1888) there were only 18 from exactly the same number. Even so, that figure remained well above the University average. In 1881 only one-third of Oxford degree candidates were Pass men; in 1900 only one-quarter. The number at BNC remained well above those levels.

Brasenose was still defined by its sportsmen. It was they who shaped the image of the college. In the forty years preceding the First World War, Brasenose won the inter-college billiards competition more frequently than any other college. No wonder Vice-Principal Heberden found it hard to impose order. In particular, one future rugby international, J. D. Boswell (pl. 59)—a Scottish Pass man with a taste for riot—proved too much for him. Boswell's partner in crime was William Rashleigh (pl. 59), an all-round sportsman with an eye for mischief. Multiple cricket and rugby blues, a strenuous double Third, a little gentle schoolmastering, and then a spell of clerical life, ending up with minor canonries at Gloucester and Canterbury—Rashleigh's career might seem almost a parody of Brasenose muscularity. He was certainly not unusual. And yet there were conventions of behaviour that made serious academic work still possible. Reading men were not despised; and the Fellows were treated with amused respect. There was 'an unwritten rule', noted Grundy, 'that you must not rag the dons. It was apparently considered an unsporting thing to do, like shooting tame hens or sitting ducks.'[54] Grundy himself lived to become a distinguished ancient historian in his own right. But during the later 1880s he drew his friends chiefly from the Phoenix: 'Fred' Barker and 'Monkey' Tilney, Etonians both and future Masters of Hounds; 'Tommy' Persse, son of a Galway distiller and nephew of Mrs Brassey of Heythrop; and 'Polly' Parkin of Ravenscragg, Ullswater, whose neighbouring kinsman—Parkin of Sharrow Bay—enjoyed the finest

---

[52] Revd H. G. Liddell, 274, 322.   [53] Ibid. 417.

[54] Grundy, *Fifty-Five Years*, 50. Boswell played for Oxford in 1885–7, and for Scotland—winning fifteen caps—in 1889–94. Rashleigh was an impressive full-back for Oxford (1887–8), and the best batsman in the university (as a freshman he scored 107 v. Cambridge in 1886). See obits, *The Times*, 15 Feb. 1937, 7 and 16 Feb. 1937, 6.

view in England on an inheritance of £30,000 per annum.[55] There was certainly a fair amount of trading money among Grundy's BNC contemporaries. James Young, a Wykehamist brewer from Wandsworth; Ernest Johnson, another Wykehamist, but this time a wire maker from Manchester; and Alexander Leith, a Harrovian coal merchant with a fortune in Newcastle iron and steel: all Brasenose men, and all new money. But on the whole, the late Victorian college remained bourgeois rather than plutocratic; County rather than City; provincial rather than metropolitan.

C. J. Holmes—a future Slade Professor, successively Director of the National Portrait Gallery and of the National Gallery—was only a year senior to Grundy. But although he was an Etonian—his uncle was Royal Librarian—he seems to have moved in rather different circles. His best friends were two talented Wykehamists, Harold Child and Reginald Cripps, plus a scholar from Manchester Grammar School named Basil Cornish. His choice of club was different too, neither the Phoenix nor the Octagon; instead he chose the Ingoldsby, an essay club founded in 1879 (pl. 66). His idols were a theologian, W. B. Selbie, and a philosophizing psychologist—E. B. Titchener—known for his intellect as 'God Almighty'. Holmes's allies among the dons were the chaplain, Arthur Chandler—a future Bishop of Bloemfontein—and A. J. Butler, Heberden's financial linchpin, 'the friendly but awe-inspiring Bursar'. The existence of this more sober set helps to put into perspective the otherwise muscle-bound reputation of the college. Brasenose, Holmes explains, 'numbered only about one hundred and twenty, and [at that time] owed its repute to five or six famous rowing men [H. R. Parker, L. Frere, G. E. Rhodes, J. H. Ware, C. W. Kent, and W. F. C. Holland], to a great [rugby] footballer [the incorrigible Boswell], and to the Captain of the Oxford [cricket] XI [the irrepressible Rashleigh]. Behind them came a dozen stout secondary performers, ... reinforced ... by some sixty vigorous, lively young Philistines. The more active scholars kept in touch with this central group.' This mixing of opposites had certain advantages: the scholars became less precious and the sportsmen not so barbarous. Altogether, Holmes concludes—and this might stand as a general comment on the college over a much longer period—it was 'a company tolerant of the genial duffer, [but] merciless to the prig. Brasenose has never been famous for imparting the Oxford voice and manner.'[56] Despite the reputation of Walter Pater, it was a plain-spoken place.

[55] Grundy, *Fifty-Five Years*, 57. Lt. Col. W. H. Parkin became land agent to the Earl of Lonsdale and Deputy Lieutenant of Westmoreland.

[56] C. J. Holmes, *Self and Partners* (1936), 104–5, 109–10. It fell to Butler to arrange the reorganization of college accounts required by the 1877 Commission. Titchener—the son a railway clerk—became Professor of Psychology at Cornell (£750 p.a. in 1905). 'I suppose', he told Heberden, 'that to you at Oxford, Oxford itself seems a wide enough world...To me it doesn't' (Titchener file: 8 Apr. 1905). For Kent's achievements as an oarsman, see *Brazen Nose*, xi. 100–1. For Titchener's 'iconic' status in American psychological literature, see *ODNB*.

And the Common Room, by modern standards, was still very small. In 1885 there were still only twelve Fellows; only seven were involved in teaching; and only three were married. But of the Fellows elected since 1863, all but two had been chosen by competitive examination, and those two—elected in 1883 and 1885—had at least been selected after public advertisement.[57] Apart from this group of 'prize' Fellows, there was a Reader in Ancient History (W. W. Capes) who gave fifty-two lectures a year to audiences of about twenty, and a Camden Professor of Ancient History (George Rawlinson: a prolific writer), who offered thirty-six lectures a year to which—at least in 1885—not a single person came.[58]

For the undergraduates, it must sometimes have seemed like paradise. By any account, it was an agreeable retreat for those who were lucky enough to be there. There was time to think; time to talk; time to stroll still undeveloped fields.

It is impossible [Holmes remembered] to forget the Rubens-like sunsets over the autumnal fields by Water-Eaton, the glories of a June morning on the track down to Bablockhythe, and the great panoramas from sundry high places: from Beckley, from the lonely Boar's Hill, from the then unpolluted Cumnor Hurst. And there was a great walk to Blenheim and Woodstock, made memorable by a midday meal of excellent roast mutton, apple-tart, cheese and ... cider ... at a nameless little inn at Bladon.

'Good old B.N.C.', Holmes concluded, 'had a character of its own ... As Balliol enlisted clever heads, so B.N.C. enlisted stout legs and arms ... Yet a certain standard was maintained.' When a famous Etonian oarsman was rejected towards the end of the 1880s, there was no beating about the bush: 'he couldn't spell; he could hardly even write his own name; we had to draw the line somewhere.'[59]

After Lodge's departure in 1894, Heberden relied principally on the Revd Frederick Bussell (pl. 60) in his campaign to civilize the philistines. Bussell had taken three Firsts at Magdalen—Mods, Greats, and theology—before his election as Fellow of Brasenose in 1886. Thereafter he became Pater's closest friend, and Heberden's staunchest ally. In all he was Vice-Principal for seventeen years (1896–1913), a record surpassed only—in later times—by Stallybrass and Platnauer. Aesthete, polymath, and pluralist, he chalked up

---

[57] 'Return relating to ... Oxford and Cambridge' (*PP* (1886), li), 575. In 1867 Wordsworth was elected from eleven candidates; in 1868 Barratt and Case from twenty; in 1872 Heberden and Leadam from thirty.

[58] Ibid. 541.

[59] Holmes, *Self and Partners*, 100–1, 107–8. This may have been the legendary candidate who 'spelled Jesus with a small g'.

donative benefices in twenty counties; he even joked of his rustication for simony.[60] Bussell rejoiced in his own eccentricity. Once, he was discovered at a race-meeting by an elderly north Oxford lady. 'Mr. Bussell, I thought you were a clergyman.' 'I am, madam', he replied; 'just a little, just a little.' On another occasion, he decided to recuperate from vaccination in a Bath chair: a junior porter wheeled him through the Parks, while undergraduates trailed behind him, reading their essays aloud. In politics he was the most romantic of Tories: he conducted an annual requiem at Pusey House for the soul of Thomas Strafford. Pater was amazed at his versatility, his ability to read early Christian theology and later pagan philosophy 'as other people read the newspapers'. He even wrote a Latin poem in two books, on Merovingian land tenure. Two of his pupils, Holmes and Goodyear, have left us a composite portrait:

his eyeglass and dandified air, his smart riding-breeches and equally smart repartees; his phenomenal knowledge of philosophy and political history, of silver Latin and of stocks and shares; his precocious Doctorate in music and his singing of [negro]-songs in an amazing falsetto treble [all these make Bussell unique]...He talks incomprehensibly on all subjects by their own nature incomprehensible—from the early history of the Papacy down to the Primrose League. He has read innumerable books and begun to write even more...[And] after his death his posthumous works, comprising notes for volumes dealing in all the habitual topics of his conversation, will be issued by *The Times* as a supplement to the *Encyclopaedia Britannica*...[In short], he sees all things, but chaotically.[61]

Bussell's talents were certainly unusual. No doubt he was too eclectic ever to be a profound scholar. But in Pater's words he had 'a real touch of genius'. With Sabine Baring-Gould he collected folk songs among the cottages of Dartmoor, travelling from village to village 'in a coach of his own design, raised so high that from it he could peer over the hedges, and equipped so well that in it he could write at a table, consult books, and obtain refreshment by opening what we would now term a cocktail cabinet'. Back at Brasenose, he entered blithely into undergraduate theatricals, composing incidental

---

[60] He was suspended as Fellow, but not as Vice-Principal, for 14 days (VP's Reg. 12/26 May, 1899, fos. 119–21).

[61] Holmes, *Self and Partners*, 100–1; *Frederick Goodyear: Letters and Remains*, ed. F. W. Leith Ross (1920), 149–54. See also Pater, *Letters of Walter Pater*, ed. L. Evans (1970), 144, 151 n. 3; *Westminster Gazette*, 13 Jan. 1921. Bussell's favourite text for sermons was 'Fear God and honour the King' (*Brazen Nose*, viii. 141 and ix. 100–2, 176, 198). His Disraelian views are summed up in *A New Government for the British Empire* (1912). His most important works were *The School of Plato* (1896); *Marcus Aurelius and the Later Stoicism* (1903); *The Roman Empire: Essays on...Constitutional History*, 2 vols. (1910); and *Religious Thought and Heresy in the Middle Ages* (1918). For Bussell as dandy, see Shrimpton caricature, Madan coll., VI, 1124 and *Brazen Nose*, ix. 259. For Bussell as a collector of folk music—e.g. his encounter with an old Devon woman named Sally Slatterly—see S. Baring-Gould, H. Fleetwood Sheppard, and F. W. Bussell, *Songs of the West* (1889; ed. C. J. Sharp, 1905); also *Daily Telegraph*, 31 Aug. 1981 and C. Lycett Green, *Betjeman: Coming Home* (1997), 164. In *Who's Who* he gave his recreations as 'none'.

music for performances of Shakespeare and Aristophanes, and leading dancing at Commems with a private version of the Lancers. Shrimpton's cartoon shows him as an 1890s dandy, in blue trousers, yellow gloves and spats, a brown bowler, and a monocle. Hand-coloured photographs record his presence at fancy dress parties, surrounded by sportsmen garbed as women (pls. II and III). One, H.D. Murphy of Australia, became a cross-dressing secret service agent. With Pater Bussell used to give luncheon parties, for 'tongue-tied, simple, good-looking youths of the sporting fraternity'. There he would be uncharacteristically quiet: he 'denied himself speech in the companionship of . . . Pater, the Silent'.[62] He was much involved with the Apollo Lodge—he was especially fond of silk stockings—and in 1900 became its Master. But he was 'best remembered [for] his dashing singing of Dinah Doe in [a] high alto voice to his own piano accompaniment'.[63] Eventually he amazed his colleagues, and perhaps even himself, by marrying. The year was 1905. His bride was a well-born Gaiety Girl. And since he had no intention of retiring until his pension was due, nor of surrendering his rooms, the newly-weds seem to have led semi-detached lives. Eventually Bussell did retire, in 1917, to the college living of Northolt, Middlesex. He ended his days in Worthing, Sussex, taking tea with impoverished gentry; defying in old age the rationing of World War II.[64]

Unlike his four predecessors as Vice-Principal—Bebb, Chandler, Heberden, and Whittuck—Bussell knew how to control the bloodies by a combination of firmness and good humour. It was not an easy task.

> Send to Brasenose for Professors
> Of the mystic art of ragging . . .

---

[62] Cornelia Sorabje, in *The Times*, 6 Mar. 1944, p. 6; W. Rothenstein, *Men and Memories*, i (1931), 139. Pater left Bussell his cap and gown, surplice, and two hoods (MPP 134 C1).

[63] MPP 51 (2) and (42); obit, *The Times*, 1 Mar. 1944, 7. He retired on a college pension of £500 p.a. in 1917 at the age of 55 (V-P's Reg. 29 Nov. 1917, fo. 111), and eventually made over all his property to Brasenose in return for a life annuity payable to himself and his wife Mary, daughter of Sir Robert Dibdin (V-P's Reg. 4 Dec. 1937, fo. 231; 9 Feb. 1938, fo. 235; 18 May 1938, fo. 239; 21 Oct. 1943, fo. 44). She wrote *Mr. Wentworth's Daughter* (1889) and *Starting Life* (1890).

[64] V-P's Reg. 3 Oct. 1925, fo. 14. 'W [i.e. Mrs Bussell] and I "divide et impera" she all the ho.work, washing, fowls, baking and brewing—with a distinct flair for growing delicious vegets and a po' of masking the tedium of the weekly joint. We actually sell our eggs and are expecting a visit fr. the Black Marketeers! I do a quite respectable parlour-maid and page-boy, to lay and clear all tables—with the same etalage of silver and crockery as in our palmiest days. Also to open house (in the dark) on . . . winter mornings. We manage to extract various bottles from our merchants—even of gin and whisky; we cannot get rum lower than £1. 1s. a bottle. Whereas my slave-owning gr'sires in Jamaica had more than eno' for nothing . . . We have all the Curates (one by one) to Te and are very liés with an Hon. and Rev. whose remote ancestor was a Scottish "Duke", the family is now a Marquisate' (Bussell to Stallybrass, 1942, quoted in *Brazen Nose*, vii. 233–4).

> Burn the ghastly
> Work of Liddell and of Scott;
> Burn the Lecture-tables; lastly
> Chuck the Dean upon the lot!

When BNC went head in Eights and Torpids, in 1891, the bonfires were particularly alarming

> ...And with each fresh crash the cry rose higher,
> Good Old B.N.C.[65]

On one occasion Vice-Principal Chandler—a future bishop—actually ended up on a bonfire, before being rescued by a posse of scouts. Bussell was more resilient. One day he would fine an undergraduate heavily; next day invite him to dinner. His 'great principle', Stallybrass recalled, 'was that disorder must be corporate. Any private bonfire, any private drunkenness, must be rigidly suppressed.' And it was all done with the lightest of touches. He had a rare talent for self-deprecation. His unfinished memoirs begin: 'I must confess myself a *prig*, a *pedant* and in some ways a *poltroon*.'[66] But as Vice-Principal he was shrewd enough to identify and deflect all serious trouble before it got out of hand. Under his eccentric regime Brasenose actually began to change. Academic work was strengthened. Dickie Lodge and his successor, G. H. Wakeling—of whom more later—overhauled the teaching of history. And in law, the college was already establishing the basis of what would soon be its strongest subject. In ten years, 1894–1904, BNC notched up ten history Firsts. In 1899–1901, the college fielded five candidates for All Souls; and in 1905–6, three more—one of whom, J. L. Brierly, actually pulled off the coveted prize. However the image of the college in the eyes of the world remained very much the same: 'manly, upright, sportsmanlike'. During the 1890s more than 30 per cent of Brasenose men rowed in Eights or Torpids. At the end of the century, despite all Heberden's efforts, there were still more blues than Firsts.[67]

Buchan's prizewinning career did something to rectify this imbalance. But in the long run his novels and writings contributed to BNC's enduring image

[65] *The Undergraduate*, i (1888), 48; Shrimpton caricature, Madan coll., VII, 1151; *Isis*, 29 Oct. 1892; Boat Club records SL8 B10/1. For Madan's notes on indiscipline, see B4 b10, ii, fo. 176: 20 Nov. 1879 ('college notices on fire'; 'Menzies' bed-clothes on [Cain and Abel]', and B4 b11, iii: 7 Nov. 1892 ('the College *has* a bad reputation'). For Stallybrass's stories of the riotous 1890s, see *Brazen Nose*, ix. 350–5.

[66] Bussell MSS, MPP 51 (42).

[67] For discussion of BNC's image—'vigorous, practical...patriotic...[no] loafers'—see [R. L. H. Gough], *Spectator*, 25 Mar. 1899, 414 and R. Baillie, ibid. 15 Apr. 1899, 520. In 1901–10 there were twenty-three Firsts in Final Honour Schools at BNC. Besides Buchan, the other Brasenose candidates for All Souls in 1899–1901 and 1905–6 were G. F. Carter, F. Bradshaw, B. K. Long, and J. D. Quirk (*ex inf.* J. S. G. Simmons).

as a training ground of muscular patriotism. During the 1890s, nearly a quarter of Brasenose graduates went into some form of imperial service or foreign business. The college's sporting ethos—cohesive yet competitive, meritocratic yet egalitarian—led Haig to look back on his years at BNC as 'splendid training'. Appropriately, it fell to Buchan to chronicle the Field Marshal's career in a twenty-four-volume—1,200,000-word—*History of the War*, published even as the struggle ground on, in 1915–19.[68] Fate drew them curiously together. Both men took strength from their Calvinist roots; and both accepted without question the burden of Britain's imperial role. Buchan was first and foremost a romantic, with a romantic's belief in the individual: 'there is in all men, even the basest, some kinship with the divine.'[69] Haig's faith, by contrast, had an almost Cromwellian sense of destiny: 'Every step in my plan has been taken with the Divine help ... We are fighting, for the good of humanity ... [for freedom] from German tyranny ... for Christ and the freedom of mankind.'[70] As early as 1909, at a quatercentenary dinner in London, Haig had warned the college that one day soon it 'might have to fight for [its very] existence'.[71] That day turned out to be not far off. Brasenose 'pluck' was to be cruelly tested on the battlefields of Flanders.

Buchan's own Oxford career is now the stuff of legend. He came up in 1895, a poor boy from a Gorbals manse, and went down in 1899 as President of the Union and a member of Vincent's, with a First in Greats as well as the Bridgeman, Stanhope, and Newdigate prizes. Only All Souls eluded him.[72] Thereafter it was almost continuous success: Member of Parliament, best-selling novelist, biographer, critic, and peer of the realm; he lived to send his sons to Eton, and to exchange confidences—as Governor General of Canada—with the President of the United States. He had achieved all the accoutrements of worldly power; even if the reality somehow eluded him. But it was Oxford, and Brasenose in particular, which retained a particular grip on his affection. His first view of the place had fixed him for life. 'Bitter winter

---

[68] Revised in four volumes as *The History of the Great War* (Boston, 1921–2) and twice abridged in one volume, ed. A. Alington (1936), and V. Neuburg (Moffat, 1991).

[69] Quoted in J. P. Parry, 'From the Thirty-Nine Articles to the Thirty-Nine Steps: Reflections on the Thought of John Buchan', in *Public and Private Doctrine: Essays...Presented to Maurice Cowling* (Cambridge, 1993), 212.

[70] Quoted by N. Cave, 'Haig and Religion', in B. Bond and N. Cave (eds.), *Haig: A Reappraisal Seventy Years on* (1999), 243: 1915–16.

[71] *Brazen Nose*, i. 17. By 1912, the college was already preparing, 'in case of war', to hand over beds and bedding to 'the Military Authorities for Hospital Purposes' (V-P's Reg. 4 Dec. 1912, fo. 19). In the event, blankets were sent to the Mayor of Oxford (V-P's Reg. 3 Oct. 1914, fo. 52).

[72] In 1899 he was beaten by D. O. Malcolm, in 1900 by A. H. D. Steel-Maitland. Malcolm later composed the Latin inscription on Buchan's memorial in the churchyard at Elsfield, Oxfordshire.

weather…blazing fires…and coffee such as I had never known in Scotland…I felt as if I had slipped through some chink in the veil of the past and become a medieval student. Most vividly I recollect walking in the late afternoon in Merton St. and Holywell [after sitting the scholarship exam] and looking at snow-laden gables which had scarcely altered since the Middle Ages. In that hour Oxford claimed me, and her bonds have never been loosed.'[73]

He began with several advantages. At Glasgow University he had studied classics with Gilbert Murray and history with Richard Lodge. It was Lodge who directed him to Brasenose. Unusually, he was already a published author. He had even reviewed Pater's posthumous *Greek Studies*. Most of all, he had a talent which transcended class. He could never be an athlete. But he had the stamina of a mountain goat. At BNC he clearly had the dons on his side: Principal Heberden, musical and kind, with his falsetto voice and scholar's stoop; Bursar Butler, tutor to the Khedive of Egypt; Herbert Fox—of whom more later—a golfing classicist with a handicap of six; Falconer Madan, antiquarian and bibliographer; and of course the Revd F. W. Bussell, that disciplinarian of beguiling charm (pl. 67). These men trusted young Buchan to write a popular history of the college. He produced it in eighteen months flat—working through the night in Heber's rooms on staircase VI—and he published it while still an undergraduate. But 'the aborigines of Brasenose'—the phrase is Logan Pearsall Smith's[74]—took rather more persuading. One Sunday night in November 1898, Bussell was dining out at Keble. The hearties seized their chance, and protested in hall against Heberden's attempt to raise the academic standing of the place. Now the fact of the matter was that Heberden had only recently presided over the purchase and construction of a new cricket ground and pavilion at Grandpont (1894–6). BNC now had the best-placed playing fields in Oxford, right next to the Eights and Torpids finish stone. But the Boat Club had lost the privileged position it held under Cradock. In six years the first Eight had slumped from head to ninth, its lowest position for generations. There were now almost as many Firsts as blues. A drunken scuffle occurred in Deer Park, and Buchan denounced the hooligans like an Old Testament prophet: 'paper-faced babies puking all over the chapel steps'. J.B. himself had a strong head and a stronger heart. He was certainly no puritan, and the bloodies came round in the end. Once, when a serious accident was narrowly averted—a Roman

---

[73] J. Buchan, *Memory Hold-The-Door* (1940), 47 (American title, *Pilgrim's Way*). During the examination Buchan lodged in VIII, 1; during his first year in I, 7; his friend Benjamin ('Taffy') Boulter was in I, 8, just above Prince Synd Ulee Meerza, son of the Nawab of Bengal (B. C. Boulter, *Brazen Nose*, ix. 62–3). For Buchan's 'Tory imagination', see A. Lownie, *John Buchan: The Presbyterian Cavalier* (1995).

[74] Buchan, *Memory*, 47.

candle in the trousers of a Balliol man—the cry went out for Buchan: 'he's the only sober man in B.N.C!'[75]

When Buchan first arrived at Brasenose he could scarcely afford to dine in hall. His undergraduate contemporaries were still very much as they had been in Haig's time. Of the thirty-four freshmen who went up that year, as many as twenty were reading for a Pass degree; and the majority came from leading public schools. Still, only a few of these were really rich. There was new money (iron) in the shape of Lionel Crawshay; old money (banking) with George Biddulph Eaton; and very old money (land) with Robert Ralston-Patrick: he followed no fewer than five hunts, and inherited estates in Scotland which had been in the family since 1663. But on the other hand, more than half of Buchan's immediate contemporaries were destined for conventional careers in the professions: law, teaching, the Church, or the civil service. One or two did well in business: W. J. Thomson in shipping;[76] G. H. Piercy on the Stock Exchange. But there are few high flyers in the list. When it came to pot-hunting, Buchan had no competitors at BNC. Just ahead of him in seniority were scions of plutocratic families like Lloyd and Stewart (iron and steel), Barbour (linen), and Rushton (textile machinery).[77] There was even a budding theatre critic in the shape of Philip Comyns-Carr. And just junior to him were two future authors of some note, Philip Pryce Page and Rolfe Scott James, as well as a notable ironfounder from Falkirk named Douglas Miller.[78] But on the whole, Brasenose men of the early 1890s were rather more obscure: they came from lesser county stock, and they went into solid professional careers.

The cost of three or four years at Brasenose had not changed greatly since the Regency. When C. J. Ingram went up in 1897–8 he had an allowance of £250 p.a.: 'I reckoned after deducting £150 for college fees and battels, I had £100 to play with.' He bought a four-year-old black mare for £25 at Tattersall's in Knightsbridge; found a stable in Oxford for 24s. 6d. per week; and rode to hounds with the Bicester, the South Oxfordshire, and the Old Berks.[79] Men like Ingram read law *faute de mieux*: he later found it useful in South Africa. But his heart was really in the countryside; and that must have been true for most of his contemporaries. Men for example like Frank Bradley Birt—later

---

[75] *Brazen Nose*, vii. 40; Buchan, *Memory*, 50; J. Adam Smith, *John Buchan* (1965), 57. In 1896 Buchan founded a book club, known as the Crocodile Club: its mascot was a stuffed crocodile; its members read and discussed current books of interest (Minutes, B1 a 47).

[76] Glasgow Steam Shipping Company; and Donaldson South American Line.

[77] Rushton of Dobson and Barlow, Bolton; Stewart of Stewart and Lloyds, Coatbridge; Barbour of Belfast; Lloyd of Lloyd and Lloyd, Warwickshire.

[78] James Miller and Son, Glasgow; Abbots Foundry Co., Falkirk. For Scott-James, a noted authority on modernist writing, see *ODNB*.

[79] Ingram MSS: MPP 234 AI.

Frank Bradley Bradley Birt—of Birtsmorton Court, Oxfordshire. Armed with a Second in history in 1896, he went out to India as an Assistant Magistrate in Bengal, worked effectively there, and wrote at length on the customs of that province. In Buchan's own words, a man like Bradley Birt—we might call him 'the average Brasenose man' of the late Victorian period—was essentially English, 'very close to English soil; and from [men like] him I learned some of the secret of the English character'.[80]

Heberden himself was a Liberal—a friend, for example, to women's colleges—a sensitive classicist and talented musician, urbane, civilized, and generous. He was the first layman to be elected Principal in the history of Brasenose. But he deferred to nobody in his commitment to the established Church. It was he who introduced organ music into services in chapel, playing first on a harmonium, then on a small instrument in the antechapel, and finally on a full-scale organ above the seventeenth-century screen—all paid for by himself (pl. 32).[81] It was Heberden—on Lodge's recommendation—who gave Buchan his Junior Hulme, and then Senior Hulme, Scholarship. Buchan in turn took Heberden's part in the troubles of Michaelmas term 1898.

Now the records of the Governing Body ignore this episode altogether. The Fellows—if we trust the written record—appear to have been more exercised by the introduction into college of a new telephone system.[82] But the University as a whole was highly intrigued. Brasenose seemed to be gaining an unenviable reputation, and the *Oxford Magazine* waxed very facetious:

The condition of St. Francis College is giving rise to the greatest anxiety . . . an athletic conspiracy is imminent . . . and several of the College authorities are marked out for destruction . . . a large number of undergraduates have collected in the front quad and are shouting for the Dean . . . Speaking from his window, he said. . . . 'it will ever be my aim to preserve the glorious traditions which have placed this College in the forefront of civilization. With the athletic element we must stand or fall' . . . The President's windows have [now] been broken and the Dean is being burnt in effigy . . . [thus upholding] in all their sanctity those glorious principles of liberty which have made the College a model for the imitation of the whole civilized world.[83]

---

[80] W. Buchan, *John Buchan* (1982), 88.

[81] *Brazen Nose*, iii. 151; *Morning Post*, 31 May 1921. The organ and its casing cost £1,240 (*Quat. Mon.* IV, 41). He left money for an organ scholar in his will. 'Hebbie' was widely revered: H. G. Hanbury remembered his 'simplicity, sweetness and kindness . . . He was . . . the most perfect human being I have ever known' (*Brazen Nose*, xv. 43). Curiously, he was also a keen mountaineer.

[82] V-P's Reg. 15 Mar. 1899, fo. 117. By contrast a Harrovian, G. B. Eaton, had been rusticated 'for breaking the windows of a Fellow' (ibid. 6 June 1897, fo. 101).

[83] *Oxford Mag.* 30 Nov. 1898, 113. See also ibid. 7 Dec. 1898, 129: 'the pros and cons for retaining the Dons were fully and freely debated: some were for lynching them all, and some for simply having them fined and gated . . . [Eventually] the Head . . . was hurled from his . . . much too luxurious lodgings, [and] the Bursar . . . was compelled to eat his own accounts, raw, not "cooked" in the usual manner.'

In fact, Bussell had already defused the crisis. Instead of establishing a disciplinary committee, he set up a good-humoured debate. Under his benevolent eye, the Sutton Society discussed and then rejected a motion 'That the craze for athletics at the present time is an excessive and misdirected enthusiasm'.[84] The speakers were cleverly chosen. W. M. Bouch, an oarsman with a First in Mods, opposed the motion; G. C. Williams, a scholar who would soon score a First in Greats, supported it. And both sides would seem to have retired with honour satisfied.

All this commotion did Buchan's political career no harm at all. That very month he was elected President of the Union by an overwhelming majority.[85] But when, within a few months, the reviews of his new college history began to come in, he received short shrift. The *Oxford Magazine* noted that he had mixed up Duns Scotus with John Scotus Erigena; that the eighteenth-century college had been revealed as not only 'undistinguished' but even 'unpleasantly so'; and that it was 'just as well' that this exiguous chronicle had stopped short of the current disturbances. *The Spectator* was even more caustic; it noted simply that BNC had long boasted the lowest of academic reputations.[86]

This was by no means fair to Heberden. During his Principalship, the college had clearly begun to move—albeit reluctantly—out of the gymnasium and into the academy. There were still plenty of hearties:

> We get up at 7.30 [wrote one American oarsman to his mother in 1906, then] trot out in flannels for a walk of about a mile or so and a short sprint, then back for a cold bath and an enormous Togger breakfast at 8.30—five course always, oatmeal porridge, fish, some meat, chops, steak or chicken as it happens—eggs and toast and marmalade...We have a very light lunch at one, row from two till about 4.00 or 4.30, we have a very light tea...and another enormous meat-dinner in Hall at 7.30...Then we have fruit and so on after it and get to bed at 10.30.[87]

But the tempo of the place was not quite the same. The Senior Common Room, in particular, was rather different. In 1902 two Brasenose Fellows—Henry Pelham and Arthur Evans; respectively Camden Professor and Keeper of the Ashmolean—were elected founder Fellows of the British Academy; Gerard Baldwin Brown followed them in 1924. Two Brasenose physicists—A. W. Reinold and A. W. Rücker—had already climbed the ladder from the Clarendon Laboratory to the Royal Society, during the mid 1880s.[88]

---

[84] The debate itself took place on 30 Oct. 1898 (Sutton Soc. minutes, SL 13 B1/1).

[85] *Oxford Mag.*, 30 Nov. 1898, 117.

[86] Ibid. 1 Mar. 1899, 245; *Spectator*, 18 Mar. 1899, 387.

[87] F. Blanchard, *Frank Aydelotte* (Middletown, Conn., 1970), 77: 11 Feb. 1906.

[88] Rücker began his career with Firsts in maths and natural science at BNC, and a Fellowship by examination in mathematics, and ended as Sir Arthur Rücker, first Principal of London University. He worked with A. W. Reinold on thin liquid films, but was best known for his research in terrestrial magnetism. See *ODNB*.

These were all harbingers of change. However BNC had never been a scientific college. The earlier achievements of Sir William Grove, FRS, in the field of electro-chemistry—and of Sir John Lawes, FRS, in agricultural science—were wholly individual, the work in fact of heroic amateurs.[89] They were scarcely typical members of the college. Throughout the Victorian period the numbers reading natural sciences at Brasenose remained small. Still, during Heberden's time there tended to be a maths or science First in nearly every year. By the turn of the century, Cradock's world had actually begun to fade. And Buchan's career was itself an index of a much wider transformation.

Within two years of leaving Oxford, Buchan had been called to the bar; within three he was Lord Milner's private secretary in South Africa; within eight he had married a Grosvenor, with a Wyndham as best man and a reception in Park Lane at the home of a diamond billionaire. J. M. Barrie's dictum is hard to resist: there is nothing quite so impressive as the sight of a Scotsman on the make. And yet Buchan's style was so easy, so genuine, that he made few enemies and many friends. In 1906 he had joined a publishing firm run by his old Vincent's ally Tommy Nelson. In 1915 he published *The Thirty Nine Steps*; in 1916 *Greenmantle*. And in 1917—already stricken with a duodenal ulcer—he took on a new role as Director of Information, in effect as Lloyd George's wartime Minister of Foreign Propaganda. As such he had direct access to Sir Douglas Haig's GHQ in France.

Now Haig, of course, Buchan already knew.

Once in South Africa I carried despatches to him, and, oversleeping myself, was decanted at Colesberg platform on a bitter winter morning indecently clad in pyjamas and a British-warm. He received my apologies with the remark that Brasenose had never been a dressy college![90]

Curious to us, this meeting on an African railway station: the general and the novelist. Haig with his Lowland lilt, an accent more noticeable as he grew older; and Buchan, speaking—in Arnold Bennett's words—in 'the accent of Kensington tempered...by a shadow of a shade of Scotch'.[91] Years later, as the war in France progressed and casualty lists became horrific, both men must have realized that the resources of civilization were running very close to bankruptcy. Soldier and journalist, participant and observer, both men

[89] Besides a career at the bar—he defended 'Poisoner Palmer' in 1853—Grove was a prominent member of both the Royal Society and the Royal Institution. He became a High Court Judge; but is best remembered for his *Correlation of Physical Forces* (1846 etc.) and for his discovery of the fuel cell (*ODNB*). Sir John Lawes, 1st Bt., founded the Lawes Agricultural Trust on his own estate at Rothampstead in Hertfordshire. Its experiments over many years had a major impact on the development of agricultural chemistry (*ODNB*).
[90] Buchan, *Memory*, 184.
[91] J. Adam Smith, *John Buchan and his World* (1979), 25.

belonged to a generation sleepwalking to disaster. Deadlocked in battle—deadlocked diplomatically, strategically, technologically, ideologically—neither Haig nor Buchan can have seen any alternative to this appalling impasse. One thing, however, was clear. They were witnessing, at close range, the destruction of an order rooted in the rituals of a calmer, kinder world; the world of Lodge and Heberden, of Bussell and Fox, of Pater and the Chief.

Since 1918 Haig's historical standing has oscillated wildly. Praised and vilified in turn—the 'architect of victory', 'the butcher of the Somme'—he has been used, often enough, as a stalking-horse by historians in search of a reputation. These things even out over generations. Two verdicts at least deserve to be repeated here. Both underline the bond that existed right to the end between the commander in chief and his men. William Orpen, a war artist who witnessed at first hand the horrors of the Somme, noted in 1921:

Haig was a strong man, a true Northerner, well inside himself—no pose. It seemed it would be impossible to upset him, impossible to make him show any strong feeling, and yet one felt he understood, knew all, and felt for his men, and that he truly loved them . . . One felt he knew, and would never allow them to suffer and die except for final victory.[92]

Then there is Viscount Trenchard, writing thirty years later, in 1952. Haig was

a great man and a great soldier . . . He had no glib tongue or the gift of words, but his spirit and morale were of the highest . . . [Even] after the terrific battles of the Somme and Passchendaele, and the great offensive of April 1918, all ranks trusted Haig. Their faith in him was unshaken . . . I feel one day in years to come—it may be fifty or even a hundred years—history will relate what the world owes to Haig.[93]

With uncanny predictability, half a century after that judgement, the pendulum has swung back in Haig's direction. Brasenose lauded him consistently: there were celebratory dinners in 1919 and 1927. And this enthusiasm lasted at least until the 1960s. In 1967, however, a tablet bearing his name—a memorial commemorating all Brasenose men who served under his command in the First World War—was summarily removed from the gate lodge. The victor of 1918—and the founder of the British Legion—deserved better than that. For in the final analysis, Haig was the army's ultimate professional; even if, at that terrible moment, professionalism may not have been enough.[94]

---

[92] W. Orpen, *An Onlooker in 1917–1919* (1921; rev. edn. 1924), 27.

[93] Quoted in J. Davidson, *Haig, Master of the Field* (1953), pp. vii, x.

[94] A number of myths regarding Haig's conduct of the war are dispelled in B. Bond (ed.), *Haig: A Reappraisal* (1999) and *The Unquiet Western Front* (2002). See also J. Terraine, *Douglas Haig: The Educated Soldier* (1963) and *To Win a War, 1918: The Year of Victory* (1978); G. Sheffield, *Forgotten Victory: The First World War—Myths and Realities* (2001), and *Haig: War Diaries and Letters*, ed. G. Sheffield and J. Bourne (2005). Haig's campaigns were 'neither futile nor

In those tranquil years leading up to the Great War the Brasenose Common Room was both conservative and progressive. Its achievements were by no means negligible. Its Fellows had reasserted academic values in a college prone to philistinism; and, thanks to a timely reordering of the Hulme foundation, they presided over one of the most successful building programmes in Victorian Oxford. Unusually in an age of declining agricultural rents, Brasenose prospered significantly. Net external income rose from £7,400 in 1871 to £10,300 in 1903; gross income was estimated to rise from £13,000 to £20,000 between 1879 and 1916.[95] This increase in wealth, however, did not disrupt the nature of the Common Room. The Fellows remained a cohesive group: they entertained each other to Sunday breakfast in strict rotation, and three of them—Butler, Madan, and Bebb—all lived within gossiping distance of Banbury Road. Several were committed Liberals: Fox, Heberden, Jenkinson; several—notably Pelham and Evans—were scholars of national standing. The religious tempo was by no means high church. Heberden, Madan, and Wace inclined to the evangelical side. If anything it was a Common Room that was becoming increasingly secular: by 1900 there were only four clerical Fellows out of a total of fourteen.[96] But it was a Common Room with a collective purpose. The college was becoming much more of an academic community. Thanks to its expanding income— mostly urban rentals and investments—Brasenose led the way with several important innovations. From 1877 three out of ten Fellowships were assigned to non-classicists; from 1899 Fellows were entitled to regular sabbatical leave; and from 1903 the college establishment included for the first time the coveted title of Research Fellow.[97] From 1887 there was actually a Junior Common Room (pl. 68). From 1897 the library was no longer reserved for dons.[98] And from 1904 the college could rely on a new accession

pointless, but indefinitive—for good technical reasons' (R. Smith, *The Utility of Force* (2005, 112)). The memorial tablet was to 'be stored until its future location was decided' (V-P's Reg. 26 Apr. 1967, fo. 41).

[95] Gross decennial estimates tabulated in MR 5R 10/1; net external income in Return A. 18, p. 584 (*PP* (1873), xxxvii), pt. ii and *Jnl. Royal Statistical Soc.* 64 (1904), table i, 588. For a list of Brasenose estates, with historical notes, see A. J. Butler, 'The College Estates and . . . Advowsons', *Quat. Mon.* VI, 1–64. For comparisons with other colleges, see A. J. Engel, *From Clergyman to Don* (Oxford, 1983), 204–5.

[96] At this date the Oriel SCR was still entirely clerical; St John's and Queen's predominantly so. See tabulated lists in L. Campbell, *The Nationalisation of the Old English Universities* (1901), 217.

[97] Engel, *From Clergyman to Don*, 218, 260, 265, 276, citing *PP* (1882), li; (1899), lxxvi; (1904), lxxiv–lxxv. In effect, replacing Prize Fellowships, which had frequently been non-resident.

[98] The JCR was in IX, 3 (later the Shackleton Room). Until 1897 the library was reserved for Fellows' use (V-P's Reg. 6 June 1897, fo. 101). After 1879—thanks to Madan, librarian from 1877 at £24 p.a.—access had been permitted for undergraduates, though limited to two

of strength: the recruitment of several Rhodes Scholars each year, from America, Canada, Australia, or Germany. From 1901 admission to the college itself became rather more competitive. Responsions no longer represented a sufficient qualification. There was now an entrance examination. This change of policy, advocated for many years by Fox, went a long way towards guaranteeing renaissance. Of course there was a price to pay. In 1900 the first Eight went down from fourth to tenth; in 1906 the Torpid went down from second to tenth. But the Fellows cannot really have been too unhappy. They no longer presided over a gymnasium.

See them now, posing for the camera, one still June morning in 1907 (pl. 67). They cluster round the entrance to the hall, conscious of their dignity as the college approaches its quatercentenary. There are just eleven of them, artfully grouped according to seniority and friendship. There in the centre, is Principal Heberden—a Brasenose man for half a century; the college's first Vice-Chancellor since 1840—serene and watchful, with just a hint of irony. Bursar Butler is on his left, grave, omniscient, proudly holding the college keys. The irrepressible Bussell sits on Heberden's right—waxed mustachios à la Dali—cradling his Vice-Principal's Register. On Butler's left is Sampson— 'good old Sammy'—looking whimsical; but this shy mathematician is not quite as simple as he looks: he has married a rich wife, and one day he too will be Principal. And on the other side of the photo, just a little apart, Stocker is sitting, deep in thought—or perhaps just sitting—his boots ready waxed for walking. He has given up physics, but he will live to be the last of the life Fellows. Next to him, stout ally on many peregrinations, stands Falconer Madan, less formidable than he seems, despite his clipped beard and formal suit; in sixty-four years he will never miss a term's residence. He is Bodley's learned chatterbox. And next to him, upright and at ease, is H. C. Wace—'Daddy' Wace—one of nature's Pass men, chaplain to the hearties; he will never quite recover from gas poisoning in the Great War. The last subgroup is a little different. In the centre of the back row stand R. W. Leage and A. J. Jenkinson, lawyer and philosopher side by side. Leage—BNC's first law Fellow—is thin-lipped and tense; clear signs of impending mental breakdown: he will never recover from a public argument with A. V. Dicey in 1909. 'Jenkie' Jenkinson looks out into the middle

hours per week (Wednesday and Thursday, 1.30–2.30), 'the Librarian being present during that time' (Madan, 'Private Book', 25 Apr. 1879; V-P's Reg. 25 Apr. 1879, fo. 54). Prior to that date, the room had sometimes been used for undergraduate classes (Madan, 'Private Book', 20 and 23 Mar. 1878). The library had also occasionally served non-academic purposes. In 1867 permission was given for 'a dancing party' to be held there (V-P's Reg. 1 June 1867, fo. 147). Until the installing of bookcases at right angles in 1890 (B4 b10, ii), the space was occasionally used by Fellows for badminton (rackets illus. *Brazen Nose*, xxv. 2, 12). It is perhaps worth noting that undergraduates were not welcome in the Bodleian until 1856.

distance, eyes distracted: he will fall to his death, dramatically, not far from the Devil's Kitchen on Snowdon.[99] Finally, two men of rather more worldly mien: Wakeling and Fox. G. H. Wakeling, a bicycling historian with twinkly eyes, dressed in a fashionable double-breasted suit; and Herbert Fox, tall, debonair, a classicist with a flower in his buttonhole, and a smile just quivering about his lips: one man whose sanity—at least until the onset of war—is not in doubt.

The SCR's *esprit de corps* permeated the college as a whole. In 1904, for example, there were recruits from America (four Rhodes Scholars), Canada, South Africa, Germany, Denmark, Ireland, and Scotland. Their ages at matriculation ranged from 18 to 25. And yet they must have been an instantly cohesive group. At the Freshman's Wine that year, held at the Clarendon Hotel on 24 October, all thirty undergraduates attended. Within days of matriculation, their committee of four had organized a nine-course dinner— hors d'oeuvres, soup, turbot, chicken, lamb, partridge, pudding, sardines, and dessert—washed down with sherry, claret, and hock. Ten of them put on a full programme of music: piano, mandolin, flute, and singing. No doubt there were speeches too. And at the end, all but one of those attending was sufficiently sober to sign the menu.[100]

Now for a last glimpse of this sheltered world, before the coming horror of war. John Middleton Murry—soon to be vicariously famous as the husband of Katherine Mansfield—arrived at BNC in 1908. 'Various people had spoken to me ominously of Brasenose', he recalled. 'It was a college full of "bloods", with a reputation of making the life of its freshmen a little hell on earth.'[101] Murry had good reason to be alarmed. Only five years before, W. H. Elliott— the son of a butcher, educated at Horsham Grammar School—had been so terrorized by the hearties on his first night in college that he spent the whole of his three-year theology course in lodgings.[102] Would Murry fare any better? As he arrived at the college gate, as he entered beneath the brazen nose, he surely

[99] For a moving obituary of Jenkinson by Stallybrass, see *Oxford Mag.* 17 May 1928, 525–6. Jenkinson's family continued to live in Stamford House (built 1895) until *c.*1950. Leage's quarrel with Dicey related to the rotation of examiners in Greats (Bras. Folio Misc. iv, pp. 12–13). For Madan's family, see F. Madan, *The Madan Family* (privately distributed; Oxford, 1933).

[100] Ingram MSS: MPP 61 BI/I. It was apparently the custom for second-year men to pay the bill.

[101] J. Middleton Murry, *Between Two Worlds* (New York, 1936), 84–8. Virginia Woolf thought Murry 'vile'; but she read his autobiography: '[even] carrion has its fascination, like eating high game' (*Letters*, ed. N. Nicolson, v (1979), no. 3048, to Lady Ottoline Morrell [17 July 1935], 418). T. S. Eliot thought him 'very clever', but 'dishonest through and through' (*Diary of Virginia Woolf*, ed. A. O. Bell (1978; 1988 edn), 124–5: 7 June 1921).

[102] *HUO* vii. 547 n. 8. Elliott became a Canon of St Paul's in 1928. See his autobiography, *Undiscovered Ends* (1951).

felt a little nervous. There he was, a scholarship boy from Peckham, full of book learning and apprehension. Even his luggage looked miserably 'unbloodlike'. But the lodge porter proved surprisingly friendly, and his attic rooms over Radcliffe Square opened out on a view in a million. 'I was enchanted', he recalled; 'the enormous lump of coal that blazed upon the fire and roared wastefully up the chimney, welcomed me into a kingdom of more generous living than I had known.' That first night after dinner—a good dinner too—a second-year scholar named Frederick Goodyear, with tousled hair and gown awry, invited him to join the Pater Society: 'I liked him at sight.' 'This isn't a bad place', announced Goodyear, 'not half as bad as they make out. In fact, it's really better than those intellectual forcing houses [Balliol and New College].' And the second-year men who came round later, drinking his beer and criticizing his cigarettes, were really not so bad either. They even called out 'goodnight' to him in cheery voices as they tumbled back downstairs. Perhaps, thought Murry primly, 'I fortified them a little on the intellectual side'. So that first day went well, and next morning he met Fox: a tutor 'in a thousand. Generous, sympathetic, happy-go-lucky, a fine scholar, a fine cricketer—he let in upon me the breath of a larger air. I admired him without reserve.'

H. F. Fox must have had a remarkable presence. He was a free-thinking Liberal—Asquith rather than Lloyd George—with the instincts of a polymath and a genius for friendship. In manner, he was grand as a bishop; in conversation, blunt as a Quaker. He was certainly not a specialist, and he boasted no First of any kind. But he was a born tutor. With Fox and his wife, Murry lunched on Boar's Hill, and read through classical texts at Snape near the Suffolk coast. Even a dose of second-year blues—Oxford seemed 'unreal' after a visit to Paris—could never quite break the spell. Fox nursed this temperamental pupil through every crisis to a First in Mods—there were four of them at BNC that year—and eventually found him a job on the *Westminster Gazette*. Murry never forgot those halcyon terms, days when the world of the mind first opened up for him at Brasenose. Of course it was far from plain sailing. Leaving home, and all the stifling limitations of home, can be a process full of pain. 'The severance from one's family', Murry wrote years later, 'is not a simple thing.' But with Fox all things seemed possible. 'Fox, in some inexplicable way', he remembered, 'was Oxford to me. I felt grateful to Brasenose itself, even, primarily because it gave escape and freedom to Fox, to do in his own way his incomparable work of education . . . and I did not let him down.'[103]

---

[103] Murry, *Between Two Worlds*, 84–8, 91–2, 111. Murry's Junior Hulme Scholarship was worth £100 per annum. See also Murry, *The Evolution of an Intellectual* (1920); obit, *The Times*, 14 Mar. 1957, 15 and 18 Mar. 1957, 10; also *ODNB*. Fox had been a notable classics master at Bath College, and he played cricket occasionally for Somerset between 1882 and 1891. 'Not a great scholar', noted Madan, 'but a perfervid character, with great powers of teaching' (B4 b10,

Murry was free of some of the distractions enjoyed by his better-off contemporaries: Tom Leach and Arthur Ingram, the Egleston brothers, 'Stoney' Wix, and 'Monty' Ravenhill. They could rely on social networks that were independent of college life. Dancing at the Masonic Ball; punting at the end of term with strawberries and a gramophone; tennis parties in the country; weekend motoring; 'ripping two-steps' with the Grid—Murry had no easy access to any of these. But perhaps he attended the Quatercentenary Ball on 21 June 1909. Herr Stanislas Wurm's White Viennese Band were the top attraction, beating out a two-step to the tune of 'Teddy Bear's Picnic'; not to mention a catchy Lancers number by Lionel Monkton entitled 'Our Miss Gibbs'.[104] On that occasion, Bursar Butler and 'Daddy' Wace were on the Committee; but so was a rather more glamorous figure, Denys Finch-Hatton—big-game hunter, pioneer photographer, and future hero of *Out of Africa*—a younger son of the thirteenth Earl of Winchelsea.[105]

Murry scarcely belonged to that world. The centre of his existence at BNC was the Pater Society, founded by Goodyear with Bussell's blessing in 1907. There the talk was of Fauvism and Post-Impressionism, of falsity and truth. One photograph survives, from 1911, showing these Brasenose aesthetes in their brief Edwardian pomp.[106] They were more than poseurs. F. R. Radice won gold and silver medals at Bisley—the coveted King's Prize—as well as a First in history. H. R. Bray, a Rhodes Scholar from Canada, became a successful QC; Philip Landon became Law Fellow and Bursar of Trinity, a celebrated Oxford clubman; and at least three more of them achieved professorships. A. F. Willmer might well have been a Fellow of All Souls.

ii: 24 Jan. 1890). 'To find the secret of Fox's hold on youth one must go to the foundations of it . . . sympathy with youth and perennial delight in it, which kept the man himself a boy to the end . . . His patience . . . was inexhaustible' (obits, *The Times*, 22, 26 Jan. 1926). Through his mother, he was a kinsman of Herbert Bradley, the philosopher. For some years Fox set Latin and Greek verse competitions for the *Westminster Gazette,* see P. Waller, *Writers, Readers and Reputations: Literary Life in Britain, 1870–1918* (2006), 101. For striking obituaries by Stallybrass of Fox and Jenkinson, see *Brazen Nose*, iv. 155–65 and 344–54.

[104] Diary of May Ingram (née Williams), June–July 1908; Quatercentenary Ball programme, 1909 (Ingram MSS: MPP 61 B4/I).

[105] Obit, *The Times*, 15 May 1930, reprinted *Brazen Nose*, v. 160–2. See Baroness K. C. Blixen-Finecke [Karen Blixen, née Dinesen], *Out of Africa* (1937 etc.; film version, 1985, with Robert Redford as Denys Finch-Hatton) and *ODNB*, s.v. 'Blixen'. After one year, Finch-Hatton moved from staircase IX to 117 the High, where the roulette wheel rolled late into the night (S. Wheeler, *Too Close to the Sun* (2006), 38, 41).

[106] SL 7 C 5/7. From 1909 its meetings are chronicled in the *Brazen Nose*. Bussell entertained the Society to a 'Paternal' Dinner on 16 June 1910, with 'Potage à la Marius', 'soles Platoni-ciennes' and 'Sardines à la Renaissance' (*Brazen Nose*, i. 135). On another occasion he planned an iced pudding with hot chocolate sauce; at the appropriate moment he exclaimed, in mock surprise: 'Ah! an oxymoron' (ibid., ix. 176). For minutes 1911–72, see SL14 C1/1–12.

That very year Goodyear and Murry—with Fox's support—set up their own magazine, published to coincide with graduation. Its title was *Rhythm*, and old-style aestheticism was the target of its abuse. It clearly had an impact at BNC. Bussell was seen wandering the front quad repeating over and over again the concluding line of a prose-poem by Francis Carco which had been printed in the very first number: 'Absolument nu! Absolument nu!'[107]

Such enthusiasms would last only a little longer. Eight members of the Pater Society did not return from the war, and they included Goodyear and Willmer, the cleverest of their generation (pl. 74).[108] Willmer's bearing in battle was heroic. At Ypres, with blood pouring from a face wound, his leadership was inspirational: 'Willmer was magnificent.'[109] As for Goodyear, his death is made more memorable by the letters that survive as records of his impressions of the war. As an undergraduate, Goodyear had sometimes been irritated by his more stolid contemporaries; but his loyalty to the college was never in doubt. 'You should not insult the memory of B.N.C.', he wrote from France in 1915; 'there were a good many men who read all sorts of things—[though] we read in (for Oxford) a rather Philistine spirit, as of men making themselves acquainted with some of the less important appendages of life. Possibly we instinctively forescented the war.'[110] If nothing else Brasenose had given him some sense of style. Writing to his mother in May 1917—between amputations at a primitive dressing station—the founder of the Pater Society found time to comment on the sounds of spring: 'I did just hear a nightingale afar off . . . [but sadly] no cuckoo at all.' Even battle had its code: 'It seems to me to be rather bad taste to commit suicide when on active service.'[111]

Brasenose suffered badly in the Great War. Losses were not concentrated in any one particular action; casualties were scattered over more than a dozen regiments. Six hundred and sixty-one members of the college served in the forces and of those 114 never returned. The numbers are 665 and 116, if we

---

[107] F. Lea, *John Middleton Murry* (1959), 27. *Rhythm: Art, Music, Literature*, a quarterly journal edited by Murry and Katherine Mansfield, ran to fourteen numbers, 1911–13; its contributors included Rupert Brooke, Frank Harris, James Stephens, Walter de la Mare, Paul Cézanne, H. Gaudier Brzeska, and Pablo Picasso. For Carco (i.e. F. Carcopino–Tusoli), see S. S. Weiner, *Francis Carco: The Career of a Literary Bohemian* (1952). For Radice's prize-winning target at 1,000 yards—still unbeaten—see A. C. M. Croome (ed.), *Fifty Years of Sport* (1913), ii (1913), 208, diagram.

[108] F. Goodyear (founder 1907); C. M. Pope (elected 1909); J. G. Reid and D. R. Brandt (elected 1910); A. F. Willmer (elected 1909); E. H. Crooke (President, Trinity term 1911); S. E. L. Gordon and H. W. Yeomans (elected 1912).

[109] *Brazen Nose*, ii. 210–11. 'Willmer's death', Fox wrote to Stallybrass, 'is a terrible blow . . . It's becoming unbearable' (ibid., iv. 159).

[110] *Frederic Goodyear: Letters and Reviews, 1887–1917*, ed. F. W. Leith Ross (1920), 93–4: 25 June 1915.

[111] Ibid. 100: 5 Jan. 1916 and 134: 14 May 1917.

include German nationals, notably Baron von Dalwig, a Rhodes Scholar of 1910–12, who died in Flanders in November 1915, 'pro patria sua'.[112] Such a proportion is not unusual for Oxford. But by this time BNC was no longer one of the biggest colleges; in fact by modern standards its scale seems almost familial. The impact of these losses must have been traumatic and the death toll among the youngest particularly cruel. Of the thirty-six school-boys who came up in October 1913, four out of eleven scholars or exhibitioners were killed; and six out of twenty-two commoners (excluding from the total intake two Germans and a Japanese).[113] In other words a death rate approaching one in three. Of those actually in residence in the summer of 1914, thirty-three never came back. By 1918 there were only eight undergraduates living in college, the lowest number since 1644. And when we focus on particular groups, the statistics become more telling still. Of the 1914 crew of the second Eight, as many as six—five oars plus the cox—failed to return from the battlefield. And of the dozen Phoenix men who dined in college with the Prince of Wales on 4 March 1913, exactly half became fatal casualties of war.

The last summer before the war had not been a vintage year for Brasenose oarsmen. But they made up in courage whatever they lacked in skill. Of the first Eight of 1914—they went down, alas, four places from 9 to 13—three men did not come back: E. H. Baillie, who rowed at bow, killed in action on Hill 70, near Loos, in 1915; G. H. Bailey, no. 4, who survived Gallipoli only to die at Morval in 1917; and H. H. Jackson, no. 6, who won an MC in 1917 and hung on to the very end only to die in November 1918. Another boat was even less lucky. 'The [first] Torpid of 1914', reported the chaplain in May that year, 'was bad…colleges which are not good at rowing are not much use at anything else.'[114] Well, the crew showed their pluck in other ways: E. W. R. Jacques, at bow, killed in action in 1916 at High Wood, Foureaux; J. H. Spencer, no. 3, a survivor of Gallipoli, who died of wounds at Limburg in 1918; the stroke, F. E. Marriott, killed in action at Hooge in 1915; and the cox, D. C. Johnston, who died of wounds at Rouen in 1918. The second Torpid that year (pl. 72) was equally unlucky, losing no fewer than five of its crew: J. H. van den Bergh, no. 3, killed at Vimy Ridge; C. R. Blackett, no. 5, killed at Zonnebeke; H. F. Miles, no. 6, killed at Falfemont Farm; F. G. Buckley, stroke, killed at Poelcappelle; and S. E. L. Gordon, cox, killed at Ypres. Five out of

[112] Full list: E. S. Craig and W. M. Simpson (eds.), *Brasenose College Roll of Service* (Oxford, 1920); photographic Roll of Honour: MEM 2L1/2/4. The Baron—son of a cavalry officer—lived in some style in III, 3; these rooms were previously occupied by his fellow countryman Count Schaffgotsch. The list of dead includes two Fellows: D. R. Brandt and R. H. Hutchison.

[113] A. L. A. M. von Marx, Baron F. von Schorlemer, and S. On-Kya. For wartime numbers in residence, see *Brazen Nose*, ii. 470.

[114] Ibid., i. 382.

nine; their photographic portraits exude a curious calm. These young men seem somehow detached; they gaze out fixedly at the camera, in sepia and grey, their tweeds a little rumpled, their faces still unlined.

Apart from rowing, 1914 had in fact been a summer of success. There were four Firsts in classical Mods, and an FRS for A. E. Boycott, a former Fellow in physics. And there was a bump supper too. For the second year running the college ran away with the athletics cup, led on to glory by its Olympic gold medallist and record holder Arnold Strode Jackson. Guinness for lunch, burgundy for dinner, Jacker—'the fabulous Jacker'—could train like a gentleman and race like a demon. There was 'a splendid "Bonner", that year', recorded the *Brazen Nose*, 'to which Principal [Heberden] applied the initial Lucifer'.[115] The magazine proudly illustrated photos of its four University captains: H. B. Moore (rugby), F. H. Knott (cricket), R. S. M. White (football), and of course the fleet-footed Jackson (athletics). 'A wonderful thing [for] one small college', noted the editor, and they are 'a good-looking lot of men' too—adding cautiously—'but not too good'.[116] Ominously that year 'the University O.T.C. was represented at Olympia in the Artillery Driving by four Brasenose men (out of a total of seven), in Tent-Pegging by two (out of a total of four), and in the Tug-of-war (oh! typical Brasenose "beef"!) by four (out of a total of ten) . . . we walk with our heads in the air'.[117] That was May 1914. Four years later, 'Jacker'—the hero of the college; the youngest brigadier-general in the British army—limped home in triumph with a rather different set of medals, a fistful of awards for 'conspicuous gallantry and brilliant leadership'.[118] Seventeen medals in all, including (unbelievably) a DSO and three bars (pl. 80).

The names are a little dusty now, on the tablet near the chapel door. But their bravery still makes one weep. Lancelot Vidal, President of the JCR, sportsman and botanist, killed at Givenchy on 25 September 1915, the fourth Bible Clerk to die in the war: 'A radiant personality, as clear and strong as the sunshine . . . he conquered examinations by sheer pluck.'[119] Or Alfred Allies, a

---

[115] Ibid. i. 385.

[116] Ibid., i. 359.

[117] Ibid.

[118] DSO 4 June 1917, 18 July 1917, 13 May 1918, and 2 Dec. 1918. He won the 1500 metres in the Stockholm Olympics of 1912, in 3 minutes 56.8 seconds, and the mile against Cambridge in 1912, 1913, and 1914. His 'gorgeous running' at Stockholm sent the 20,000 crowd 'into hysterics' (*The Times*, 19 July 1912, 15). In later life, as 'King of Eno's', he became a corporate executive in America; he died in Oxford at Norham End, Norham Road, in 1972. See F. A. M. Webster et al., *Success in Athletics, and how to Obtain it* (1919), illus. opp. p. 40; *Brazen Nose*, xv. 269–71; *ODNB* and obit, *The Times*, 28 Nov. 1972 (Philip Noel-Baker). 'Jacker' in IX, 1 and 'the Baron' (von Dalwig), in III, 3 had once been fellow members of the Octagon.

[119] *Oxford Mag.* 25 Jan. 1916, 215.

big man with a laugh like Falstaff: 'he was no athlete, but...he hit a cricket ball hard.'[120] Or dashing Jack Greenall, heir to a brewing fortune: 'handsome, merry, lovable...unflinching'.[121] Or Herbert Bolton, 'little Bolton', a theology student, destined for the Church. He died on 3 May 1915 after lying out wounded for several days. 'He was so marvellously good and patient', wrote one hospital nurse; 'he was a sweet boy, and so good.'[122] Or lastly Alfred Benn, a pint-sized soldier with the heart of a lion. 'Those who came through the dressing station reported... "he's wounded, Sir, but going fine. He won't come away". He never came away...'[123]

It is so hard now, a century later, to read the minds of these young men— 2,000 in August and September 1914 alone—who rushed to apply for commissions in that 'dingy little room in Alfred Street'.[124] They felt duty of course: to King and country, Church and state; and loyalty: to school and neighbourhood, to family and friends; but most of all pride: in their people, in themselves. Duty, loyalty, pride: for that generation of Brasenose men, all these emotions were focused fiercely on the college itself; on its grand new buildings; on its symbols and customs; on the curious circle of scholars who maintained its arcane rituals; and on that Brasenose man who somehow, through mud and blood, was leading to victory the biggest army in British history.

Just before he died, on 2 September 1918, a lieutenant in the Tank Corps—H. B. Spencer, BA—wrote his last letter home, with instructions for the education of his 6-year-old son. His words echo faintly now, across a veritable gulf of change: 'bring him up as a *man*, a *gentleman,* and a *sportsman*; and...send him to B.N.C.'[125]

---

[120] Ibid. 3 Mar. 1916, 231.
[121] 'Newspaper Gleanings', B.4a3, p. 80.
[122] *Oxford Mag.* 18 May 1917, 254.
[123] Ibid. 9 Feb.1917, 145.
[124] *Oxford University Roll of Service* (1920), introd. The OTC was based at 9 Alfred Street.
[125] *Oxford Mag.* 22 Nov. 1918; *Brazen Nose*, ii. 433.

7

1918–1948

Brideshead Suspended:
The Legacy of Stallybrass

'Oxford in the future', observed Falconer Madan in 1923, 'cannot be like it was in the past.' He was referring to three fundamental changes: the abolition of compulsory Greek; the admission of women to degrees; and the acceptance for the first time of a regular government grant. These three changes—all implemented soon after the end of the first World War—embodied a triple revolution. In one year, 1919–20, 700 years of history had been overturned. Academically, socially, financially, Oxford would never again 'be like it was in the past'. But wise old Madan was not too dejected. 'It may', he noted, 'be better, perhaps.'[1]

It would be too easy to see these changes as mere consequences of the Great War. The stranglehold of classical languages could scarcely have been maintained much longer; nor could the formal exclusion of women; nor could—though this is rather more debatable—the University's financial autonomy. But it was the conflict with Germany that brought all three arguments to a head. The debate over Greek, and the battle for women's equality, harked back to mid-Victorian disputes. The debate about funding, however, was essentially new. It was the product of two factors whose conjunction was indeed novel: monetary inflation and the growth of scientific research. Both had been accelerated by the conditions of war.

The election of Lord Curzon as Chancellor in 1907 proved to be the immediate catalyst of change. Curzon's objective was to forestall the appointment of yet another Royal Commission—at least until the Liberals were no longer in power—by opening up a programme of conservative

---

[1] F. Madan, *Oxford Outside the Guide-Books* (Oxford, 1923), 33; *Oxford Mag.* 28 May 1920, 362–3. The requirement for compulsory Greek was modified for scientists in 1911, and abolished in 1920. For Greek as an educational discipline, see E. A. Freeman, 'Greek in Universities', *Contemporary Rev.* 60 (1891), 663–71; for Greek as 'mumbo jumbo', see J. Perry, 'Oxford and Science', *Nature*, 69 (1903), 211–13.

change.[2] He began by publishing an agenda for renewal entitled *Principles and Methods of University Reform* (1909). He was only just in time. In July 1907 a debate in the House of Lords had already been initiated by one radical Oxonian, Charles Gore, Bishop of Birmingham. He accused Oxford of being 'a playground for the sons of the wealthier classes ... not in any serious sense a place of study at all'. His argument ran as follows. Oxford existed to educate the governing class; the governing class had expanded thanks to parliamentary reform; therefore Oxford's basis of recruitment must be commensurately enlarged.[3] And Gore was not alone. His plea for a new Royal Commission was taken up by the *Westminster Gazette*. So Curzon's little 'Red Book' set out to spike these radical guns by proposing a whole raft of pre-emptive reforms: streamlining the University's administration; eliminating compulsory Greek from Responsions;[4] equalizing women's status at degree level; and recruiting undergraduates from a wider social spectrum. The last of these proved to be very much the trickiest.

By the first Royal Commission, Oxford had been rationalized rather than democratized. It had been opened up to talent rather than disadvantage. The Commissioners, explained Curzon, had been 'more concerned in helping real ability than ... in compensating real poverty'. And therein lay the problem: how to pursue equality without capitulating to mediocrity. 'In opening the University to the poor', he continued, 'we do not wish to close it to the rich ... Oxford ... has never been, a purely eleemosynary institution. It exists ... [to give a] broad and liberal education ... to rich and poor alike.' Hence its unique potential for a universal 'training in citizenship'. But the key mechanism in this process—'the real secret of Oxford's spell'— was the practice of collegiate living.[5] And how could a poor man afford to enjoy this particular brand of magic? The cost of three years at Oxford was at least £400. By 1909 there were, in fact, about fifty students at Oxford holding county or borough council scholarships; plus 328 more—scattered over all three years—in receipt of some form of means-tested college endowment.[6] Collegiate endowments, however, were often hedged about by limiting

---

[2] 'A Commission would destroy the Oxford that we know, and the curriculum, finance, government and colleges would go in one sweep. I am appalled at the prospect and yet ... the status quo is impossible' (Curzon to P. Matheson, 11 May 1911, quoted in Earl of Ronaldshay (ed.), *Life of Lord Curzon* (1928), iii. 106–7).

[3] *Parl. Debates: Lords*, 4th ser. 158, 11–24 July 1907. What Curzon called 'the party of "thorough"' was led by Gore and Hastings Rashdall. See also the 'Reformers' Letter', *The Times*, 24 July 1907, 10, signed by two Brasenose Fellows: A. J. Evans and F. J. Haverfield.

[4] 'A travesty of learning ... an insult to the tongue of Thucydides and Aeschylus and Homer' (Curzon, *Principles and Methods of University Reform* (Oxford, 1909), 101, 104–5).

[5] Ibid., 43, 51, 54.

[6] Ibid., 67 n. 1, 70, 81. Out of a total of 734 scholarships or exhibitions.

regulations; and they were subject to competition. Their rewards seldom went to the poorest: they went to the better educated. That was the problem Curzon began to address in 1909. He was convinced that there had to be more provision for 'the lower middle classes'. But that would mean fewer Pass men; 'and without the Pass man, Oxford would not be able to pay its way'. 'I do not feel much sympathy', he noted, 'with the argument that the Pass man ought to be effaced in order to tap new social strata; for I see no reason why all these strata should not exist side by side'; in fact, 'it is in their co-existence or juxtaposition...that the service of Oxford resides'. No doubt that was true; but might not their numbers benefit from occasional culling? In 1901–6, one in seven candidates for Pass Mods and law Prelims failed at least twice; and one in eight of those for the Final Pass Schools.[7] There was surely something to be said for tightening up the system.

Among Curzon's allies in this debate was the Vice-Chancellor elect, Dr Heberden of Brasenose.[8] He had for some time been attempting to introduce into BNC just a little of the Balliol ethos. Among the doubters, however—those who saw much merit in a less puritanical regime—was the college's youngest Fellow, W. T. S. Sonnenschein (pl. 65).

Sonnenschein's background was academic and cosmopolitan. On his father's side he was Moravian and Jewish; on his mother's side French Huguenot. His grandfather—Abraham Sonnenschein—had been a schoolteacher who supported the Hungarian patriot Louis Kossuth, then fled to England in 1848 and married the daughter of a Congregationalist clergyman, a missionary to Siberia named Edward Stallybrass. Abraham (now calling himself Adolf) had several sons. One of these, E. A. Sonnenschein, eventually went to Oxford, took Firsts in Mods and Greats at Univ. and became Professor of Greek and Latin at Birmingham. He was a comparative grammarian, and a great talker. Another, W. S. Sonnenschein, founded a publishing house—Swan Sonnenschein Ltd.— later part of George Allen and Unwin. In 1917 he and his son Teulon—by now a Fellow of Brasenose, rejoicing in the nickname 'Sonners'—decided to change the family surname to Stallybrass. And so the future Principal of BNC emerged as a nominal Anglican, with an impeccably English provenance: Westminster, Christ Church, and the Inner Temple.[9]

---

[7] For BNC Pass men, see Asquith Commn., vol. ii. 1922, appendices, p. 184.

[8] Other supporters of reform included Gilbert Murray, Arthur Sidgwick, and A. L. Smith. One of those who later argued for redistributing college resources through a common fund was A. J. Jenkinson of BNC (Asquith Commn., vol. ii, appendices, p. 31).

[9] *ODNB*; F. A. Munby and F. H. W. Stallybrass, *From Swan Sonnenschein to George Allen and Unwin Ltd.* (1953). E. A. Sonnenschein was best known for his edition of Plautus; W. S. Sonnenschein produced many handbooks and dictionaries under the pseudonym of 'W. S. W. Anson'.

Sonners, as we must now call him, was already committed to sport. As an undergraduate he won a half-blue for cross-country running. As a schoolboy he actually touched the great W. G. Grace. As a Fellow he acted as treasurer of the OUCC for over thirty years, and played cricket at club level himself for more than a quarter of a century. His physical vitality—*mens sana in corpore sano*—was probably the reason Heberden chose him in the first place: he was appointed at short notice after the mental breakdown of R. W. Leage (pl. 67).[10]

Sonners's personal involvement in sport is so revealing of the man himself that it deserves a moment's pause. As soon as the Great War was over, he set up the Brasenose Wanderers' cricket tour, and captained the side until 1923. The idea was to bring together several different Brasenose generations. Fixtures were arranged each July in Kent, Surrey, and Sussex. The standard was fairly high—mostly BNC first Eleven versus serious club and school sides—and the tour was conducted with style. See them now, at the Imperial Hotel, Eastbourne (pl. 79): crammed into open tourers, Lanchesters, Vauxhalls, Lagondas; or lined up for the photographer in striped blazers and silk cravats, Sonners perched on one side of the tableau, the founder of the feast. As the tour became established it developed into a kind of 'village Olympiad', with several teams taking part and various forms of athletics. Sonners bowled regularly, at a fast medium pace. In 1921 he took 8 for 25 against East Grinstead, including a notable hat trick. In 1922 he took 27 wickets inside one month, at an average of 16.88.[11] Not bad for a hard-drinking don of nearly 35. Then there were the Authentics' tours—mostly composed of near blues—for which he acted as manager and treasurer. After 1923 he confined his own sporting activities to golf at Frilford Heath, or Tenby, and to less strenuous cricket matches with the Limpsfield Strollers. The Strollers were a light-hearted group of friends, who toured half a dozen Devon villages during a fortnight each September. Mornings began with pints of Worthington; evenings ended with bottles of port. In between there was Red Leicester cheese to be consumed at lunch, and endless innings on village greens, prolonged uproariously late into dusk. Sonners' stamina was remarkable. On one occasion he drove down to Devon from an Authentics' tour in Scotland and sat up talking till 4 a.m.; next day he bowled for nearly three hours on the run. As captain, he would regularly open the bowling, and he was still taking wickets as he neared the age of 50. Of course the standard was not exactly high. But he could still bowl straight. Between 1923 and 1934 he took 382 wickets at an average of 15.14. Twice he took 9 wickets in an

[10] S. G. Owen of Christ Church first alerted Madan in March 1911: 'There is something rather distinguished about [Sonnenschein's] mind, a bit above the common.' References from the Inner Temple—where he had topped the bar Finals list—followed in May (Sonnenschein file).

[11] *The Cricketer*, 27 July 1922; *Brazen Nose*, iii. 163, 235–6; PRI 25 I 1/1/1 (1921).

innings, three times he took 8; and twice he achieved a hat trick, once in 1931 and once in 1934. All this from a man with, effectively, one eye and an increasingly expansive girth. After dinner the fun would begin in earnest, with Sonners performing his favourite party trick. He could run backwards for 50 yards along the sea front at Seaton faster than his young friends could race 100 yards. After 1935 he retired as captain: he was after all Principal elect by then. In 1947—as Vice-Chancellor no less—he was still accompanying the touring party, though now with the title of 'Chaperon'.[12]

From his arrival at BNC in 1911 until his death in 1948 Stallybrass believed fervently in the amateur code: sport as a vehicle of leadership; sport as a school of courage; sport as a model of corporate action; sport indeed as a paradigm of virtue, part of some great moral dialectic, competitive and cooperative, disciplined and free. At college level, he regarded organized games as integral to the process of growing up; a key to the endless reciprocity of existence. 'Oxford's greatest gift of all', he wrote in 1918, 'is her social life'; its essence depends on 'the intangible, indefinable influence of the College, immanent in the souls of all her members'. 'To some of us', he explained, 'the living symbol of this College corporateness is the Sunday evening service in the College Chapel.'[13] To others, he might have added—and in this he should certainly have included himself—it lay less in the symbolism of chapel than in the rough-and-tumble of the playing field.

In all this, Sonners' views matched closely the views of Cecil Rhodes. From the start of the Rhodes foundation, he made sure—in partnership with Frank Aydelotte and Sir Francis Wylie—that Brasenose played a part in selecting and placing a long series of Rhodes Scholars. In the twenty-three years between 1918 and 1944, BNC took 92 men under the Rhodes scheme, an average of 4 per year. There were 12 Canadians, 38 from Southern Africa, and a sprinkling from the West Indies, Germany, and the Antipodes; the rest were all Americans. And very Brasenose they became. Most read law or PPE, a few read science or engineering. Directly or indirectly, nearly all of them read sport. Aydelotte, himself a Rhodes Scholar at BNC in 1905, put it like this:

Sport... [is part of] the great Anglo-Saxon tradition... [At Oxford it is essentially amateur,] a great deal more play and a great deal less practice, than in American

---

[12] COL 1/A1: W. E. P. Estridge, 'The Strollers Cricket Club', typescript, 1923–49 [c.1950]. The Strollers' colours were green, black and gold. The Authentics were founded in 1883 by undergraduates who had been schoolboys at Limpsfield, Surrey. They wore brown, blue, and gold. For a cartoon of Sonners in cricket gear see *Isis*, 10 May 1922, 10. His chief lieutenant on later tours was A. J. F. ('Doulers') Doulton. See *The Times*, 21 Aug. 1996, 17: photo, and *Brazen Nose*, xxx. 51–2 (P. T. C. Croker).

[13] W. T. Swan Sonnenschein, 'Social Life at Oxford after the War', *American Oxonian*, 5 (1918), 1–4.

institutions. English college Rugby teams play two or three matches a week, and almost never practice. The result is athletic sports at their very best; no spectators, no gate fees, no hint of professionalism or of the gladiatorial arena; instead, unlimited fun of playing for everybody and the highest possible level of sportsmanlike conduct.[14]

But for Aydelotte—for Stallybrass too; and this fact has to be emphasized— sport was only a means to an end, seldom an end in itself. That was a lesson Sonners learned at first hand from Heberden. Priority had to be given, first and foremost, to 'the intellectual life of the College'.[15] But that was only one half of the equation. The life of the mind, alone, would never create a college in the fullest sense. Sport therefore had its place: it was creative as well as simply recreative. It was through the mechanism of collegiate sport that Stallybrass set out to rebuild Brasenose in the years after the First World War.

The Great War had introduced Brasenose to a rather different world. Few undergraduates; little or no fee income; reduced salaries; shrinking reserves: the future of the college seemed bleak. Who could foretell the future? There had been Belgian students in the Old Quad and Serbian refugees in the New; there had been wounded Fusiliers sleeping on mattresses beneath Stocker's own quarters, in lecture room XI. On staircase IX Flying Corps officers had set up camp in the JCR. There was a barrack room in lecture room VII. There had even been 100 cadets from Manchester University, staying for a fortnight at 2*s.* per day.[16] And the end of war did not mean the immediate end of rationing. In 1917–18, BNC's 'coal allowance' was still limited by 'the local controller'.[17] Stocker was reduced to working out menus for non-residents and 'meatless dinners', in accordance with 'a national system of compulsory rationing'.[18] Immediately after the Armistice there were actually married officers, newly discharged, living as Brasenose undergraduates—though

---

[14] Aydelotte, in *American Oxonian*, 12 (1925), 5–6. Aydelotte was later President of Swarthmore College and Director of the Institute of Advanced Study at Princeton. In 1937 he became an Hon. Fellow of BNC, the first American to hold such an honour at Oxford. In 1953 he was made Hon. KBE for his work as American secretary to the Rhodes Trustees (*Brazen Nose*, x. 266–71).

[15] Stallybrass on Heberden—'universally loved . . . selfless . . . the only true Saint I have ever known'—in *Brazen Nose*, ix. 324, 352.

[16] V-P's Reg. 16 Oct. 1914, fo. 55; 10 Feb. 1915, fo. 62; 16 Mar. 1916, fo. 84; 16 May 1916, fo. 185; 28 Sept. 1916, fos. 89–90; Room Book, 1914–19. When air raids threatened in October 1917, the following direction was pinned up in the Lodge: 'In case of Air Raids, the basement of no. XII is recommended both for safety and for warmth' (Bras. Misc. IV, 66). See also E. Boardman, in *Brazen Nose*, xxxix. 117–25.

[17] V-P's Reg. 7 Dec. 1918, fo. 132; 18 June 1919, fo. 148.

[18] V-P's Reg. 7 Mar. 1918, fo. 118. Even if 'butcher's meat' had been available 'only at dinner', there had at least been 'porridge . . . at breakfast', 'soup . . . at lunch', and 'bacon or fish or eggs . . . at one other meal' (V-P's Reg. 17 Feb. 1917, fo. 98). One economy was the introduction, in 1916, of breakfast and luncheon in hall (Stallybrass, in *Oxford*, 6 (1939), 2).

admittedly they were living out of college. No wonder there was talk, once again, of having to amalgamate with Lincoln.[19] In terms of numbers, the two colleges were at this point almost equal (BNC, 141; Lincoln, 136). But BNC's net revenue (£18,057 p.a.) was three times that of Lincoln. No longer was Brasenose one of the richest colleges in the University; but at number 7 in the league table of income, it was comfortably in the top third.[20] Amalgamation was not—from BNC's point of view—a pressing necessity. And by December 1918, normal day-to-day living had more or less returned. 'Common breakfasts' were now mostly taken not in private rooms but in hall; and 'common lunches' in the JCR. But at least the Fellows were once again dining formally in black tie; and the Union flag, presented by Earl Haig himself, was proudly flying from the old tower.[21]

How did Sonners—an OBE now, for his work in munitions—envisage the future? As a young man he was very far from being a cynic. He believed that the horrors of the Great War must surely give way to a new union of nationalities, a federation of free states subject to the rule of law. In November 1918 he published a booklet entitled *A Society of States*. It was a plea of faith, in effect a call for the creation of a League of Nations. In this of course he was very far from being alone. But Stallybrass spoke more convincingly than most. He based his plan on a simple conviction: there was 'no alternative which holds out any hope for the future of civilisation'.[22] He dedicated it 'to the Principal of Brasenose [i.e. Heberden] and all those other Brasenose men who are fighting or working for the security of the British Commonwealth within a League of Nations'. He claimed to see no incompatibility between nationalism and internationalism: they were as interdependent as liberty and law. 'The goal to which history is painfully making its way is the reconciliation of cosmopolitanism with patriotism.' Ultimately, 'war will be recognised as justified only when it is used by the common purpose of the Society of Nations to prevent and punish the aggressor against international law and order'.[23] As an ideal this programme derived naively from Rousseau's solution to Hobbes's portrayal of man in a state of nature: a solution 'by which each one uniting with all obeys only himself, and remains as free as he

---

[19] 'Co-operation' seemed possible; but 'full amalgamation' was deemed 'inopportune' (V-P's Reg. 30 Apr. 1918, fo. 143). During the war Brasenose and Lincoln dons had messed together in BNC's SCR (R. W. Jeffery, 'A College Betting Book', *Oxford Mag.* 31 Jan. 1919, 141). For married undergraduates, see V-P's Reg. 11 May 1918, fo. 120.

[20] Asquith Commn., vol. ii, appendices, pp. 103, 183.

[21] V-P's Reg. 23 Sept. 1919, fo. 151; 21 Dec. 1918; 22 Jan. 1919, fo. 134. By Jan. 1919 the college had been 'entirely vacated' by the military (Bursar's Home Letter Book, 20 Jan. 1919).

[22] W. T. S. Stallybrass, *A Society of States* (1918), 6.

[23] Ibid. 124–5.

was before'.[24] Unfortunately, translating Rousseau's social contract into a system of international law required not only the consent of every state but the creation of an overarching, supranational force. Neither was forthcoming in the years after Versailles. The whole conceptual house of cards—the dream of Stallybrass' generation—collapsed within two decades.

As an academic lawyer, Sonners did not at this point give up international law. Nor did he forget his Latin. His speech as Senior Proctor in 1926 would shame many a modern classicist.[25] But after the failure of the League of Nations he turned increasingly to the teaching of criminal and civil law. A university legal education, he believed, was essentially a matter of training in law, not training for the law. That threw back on the teacher the responsibility for expanding the subject's theoretical base. In 1930 he published a dissertation that justified his claim to a DCL. This took the form of a comparison between the penal code of Alfredo Rocco and the principles of criminal law in England. As a Lecturer in Law at Brasenose, Lincoln, and Oriel, and then as University Reader in Criminal Law and Evidence (1923–39), he was in a strong position to produce a lasting academic memorial of his own. This now took the form of a seventh (1928), eighth (1934), ninth (1936), and tenth (1945) edition of Sir John Salmond's massive handbook *The Law of Torts: A Treatise on the English Law of Liability for Civil Injuries*. Textbooks of law make dry reading. But there is no doubting the usefulness of his revisions: look up the sections on 'Fair Comment', 'Contributory Negligence', or 'Trade Unions'. The Stallybrass additions to the original text were numerous: 373 additional cases in 1928, 489 in 1945; and their presentation is a model of clarity and concision. When R. F. V. Heuston produced the eleventh edition of Salmond in 1953, he paid tribute to his predecessor's 'deep learning, sound judgement, and clarity of expression'; also his skill in guiding the great work through four consecutive editions 'with a measure of success which is universally acknowledged throughout the common law world'.[26]

---

[24] 'The doctrine of the Social Contract as an account of the historical genesis of the State is palpably false; its logical truth as an explanation of the State in being is not thereby impugned' (ibid. 121). In general Stallybrass followed the natural law tradition of Grotius, as expounded in J. Lorimer, *Institutes of Law* (1872; 1880), rather than the theories of J. L. Austin and the Analytic School of Jurisprudence ('H.G.' in *Oxford Mag.* 37 (1918–19), 247–8). Austin's positivist theories were later developed by H. L. A. Hart of Brasenose, and would be questioned in turn by R. Dworkin.

[25] Printed in full in *OU Gazette*, 19 Mar. 1926, 484–8.

[26] J. Salmond, *The Law of Torts* (11th edn. 1953, ed. R. F. V. Heuston), p. vii. For Stallybrass in academic mode, see his chapter on 'Public Mischief' in *The Modern Approach to Criminal Law* (English Studies in Criminal Science 4, ed. L. Radzinowicz and J. W. C. Turner, 1945), 66–76. He was the first academic lawyer to be made an Hon. Bencher of the Inner Temple, in 1938, when he also became a member of the Lord Chancellor's Law Revision Committee.

At college level, Sonners's vision of Oxford after the Great War now seems surprisingly prescient:

After the war [some] ... may wish to enforce the ascetic life on Oxford ... I do not believe that they will succeed; but certain changes there must be ... [for example, a certain] simplification of our life ... In the past lack of means has made it difficult for the poor man to get all that is to be got out of Oxford life. The war has ... shown that the working man appreciates the value and importance of education as much as, if not more than, any other class of society. In the future we shall have many more poor men at Oxford proportionately than in the past. The Oxford undergraduate has long been democratic in spirit, but in the future it is probable that the poor man will to a larger extent set the fashion.... [Though] the forms of Oxford life may change, the spirit of Oxford cannot change.... [Long may] the old College wine clubs ... continue to cause anxiety to the College authorities![27]

A worthy sentiment no doubt. But spreading the benefits of Oxford education involved hard financial thinking; and that thinking, sooner or later, would have to grapple with the dilemmas of public funding.

'The question of State-aid to Universities', Sir Michael Hicks-Beach reminded Joseph Chamberlain in 1899, 'is a very large and thorny one.'[28] Just how thorny the next century would amply demonstrate. Scottish universities had been receiving regular state grants since 1707; their civic counterparts in England and Wales since 1889. The first grants to Oxford and Cambridge came only in 1912–13: to the Department of Engineering at Oxford and the Department of Medicine at Cambridge.[29] These were not annual subventions, nor even block grants. They were ad hoc capital awards bestowed by the Board of Education. Their purposes were limited and specific, prompted by the pressures of incipient war. Even so, their acceptance exposed the first material chink in the armour of Oxbridge autonomy.

As soon as the war ended—within weeks of the Armistice in fact—Oxford and Cambridge took a fateful step. They were beguiled into joining with the 'modern universities' in applying to the Board of Education for a regular parliamentary grant. The temptation was great. Wartime inflation had eroded investment income; the value of agricultural endowments had been falling for a generation; science departments were hungry for funds. The time seemed ripe for a new form of dialogue between government and University.

[27] Sonnenschein, 'Social Life at Oxford', 1–4.

[28] Quoted in K. Vernon, *Universities and the State in England, 1850–1939* (2004), 140. See also C. H. Shinn, *Paying the Piper: The Development of the University Grants Committee, 1919–46* (1986); R. O. Berdahl, *British Universities and the State* (Cambridge, 1959); B. Salter and T. Tapper, *The State and Higher Education* (1994).

[29] Asquith Commn., vol. ii, appendices, p. 218; H. C. Dent, *Universities in Transition* (1961), 51 *et seq.* A government Department of Scientific and Industrial Research had been set up in 1915.

It was H. A. L. Fisher, the future Warden of New College—at that time President of the Board of Education—who acted as broker between Oxford's Vice-Chancellor and the Chancellor of the Exchequer. It was he who, in November 1918, decided it was 'desirable' for Oxford and Cambridge to be drawn into discussions with the Department of Education.[30] He had already set in motion a national system of Higher Certificate examinations and state scholarship funding for students. Now it was the turn of University finance. As a first step, the ancient universities were in 1919 awarded emergency grants of £30,000 p.a. each, administered by a new institution: the University Grants Committee. In this way 'arm's-length' funding was born, notionally free of Prussian bureaucracy and Gallic *dirigisme*. A congeries of ad hoc 'Grants from Public Funds' had thus been translated into a monitored system of 'Parliamentary Grants'.

There was ambivalence in this new arrangement, an ambivalence that in the long run would prove unsustainable. Even as the tap of government largesse was turned on, its stream was constrained by the tourniquet of political control. It was partly to deconstruct this conundrum that a fourth Royal Commission, chaired by the Earl of Oxford and Asquith, was set up. It began sitting in 1919 and it reported in 1922. On the whole, its recommendations were conservative. The only radical proposal was the abolition of life Fellowships. Even that was not to be retrospective: at Brasenose, Stocker would be safe on staircase XI for another three decades. The focus of the Commission was limited to the University's financial administration. In effect, Asquith had been constituted as a guarantee of public trust. The Commission suggested £90,000 p.a. for Oxford plus £10,000 for libraries, plus £4,000 for women's colleges. In reply, the Treasury bid low: Oxford had to settle for £30,000 in addition to the existing £30,000 emergency fund, plus a special grant for pensions.

Note: these grants were directed to the University. The colleges received nothing. In this way Fisher tried to sidestep the eternal dilemma of autonomy versus control. Even so, the trap had now been set. Oxford was in receipt of two channels of public funding. On one hand there were quinquennial grants to the University; on the other hand state scholarships and local education grants awarded directly to students and thus indirectly to colleges. Asquith had indeed recommended state aid, but only as 'a stop-gap'; 'the minimum necessary to prevent immediate decline'. In the long run, the Commission assumed that the bulk of funding would still come from private sources: 'here

---

[30] Asquith Commn., vol. ii, appendices, pp. 217–23. Oxford's Vice-Chancellor, H. E. D. Blakiston, pleaded 'the magnificent lead given by Oxford men, young and old, in every direction during the War, and especially . . . the acknowledged services rendered by the Oxford Laboratories and their staffs' (Blakiston to Fisher, 19 Nov. 1918, ibid. 218).

lies the real hope of prosperity and development'.[31] But that assumption turned out to be wishful thinking. In 1923–4 the interim grant of £30,000 p.a. had to be doubled. By the mid-1930s Oxford and Cambridge were receiving 20 per cent of moneys awarded by the UGC to all universities in England and Wales[32]. The terms of engagement had thus been radically changed. The bulk of Oxbridge undergraduates, of course, were still privately paid for; and the conventions of arm's-length funding were still honourably observed. But between the upper and nether millstones of central and local funding, academic freedom would one day be ground, and ground very fine indeed.

And was the money really necessary? In 1920 college incomes amounted to £613,000; expenditure was only £579,000. In the same year, University income amounted to £210,000; expenditure was only £195,000.[33] On the face of it, all seemed well. But these figures disguise the true picture. Without the government's emergency funding, the University would have been in deficit. The colleges were secure enough. It was the University—in particular, the science departments—which needed taxpayers' support. And therein lay the temptation. Instead of lobbying for changes in the tax regime—for charitable funding along North American lines—it was easier to ask, and ask again, for direct parliamentary aid. Still, in its first decades, such funding never equalled the level of private donations. In the 1930s Rockefeller and Nuffield proved more generous than the Treasury. And even in the years immediately after the Second World War the danger of political influence remained reassuringly remote.

By becoming more and more a pensioner of the state, Oxford risked losing its natural lien on the generosity of alumni. In the long run it was also in danger of losing its immemorial control over admissions and appointments. These changes would not happen over night. But the signs were there, as early as 1919–23. In the debates over the establishment of the Asquith Commission in 1919 and over the Oxford and Cambridge Act in 1923, arguments were set out which would reverberate into the twenty-first century.

Asquith's conclusion had been clear enough.

If help is not forthcoming, from outside, the Universities will be forced to *raise their fees* to an excessive degree that must exclude many students not only of the artisan but of the professional class.... [But] it is important that the Universities should be permitted to maintain their own standards of intellectual tests... [For] to admit to the Universities poor students of lower intellectual calibre only because they are poor, would be, if it were ever proposed, as fatal as to permit a revival of the 'idle rich' student, or to encourage the undergraduate whose claim to residence is based

---

[31] Asquith Commn. (*PP* (1922), x) 81–3 (pp. 53–6). For a breakdown of the £30,000 emergency grant to Oxford in 1920–1, see Asquith Commn., vol. ii, appendices, p. 347.

[32] Vernon, *Universities and the State*, 198; J. P. D. Dunbabin, in *HUO* viii. 644.

[33] C. E. Mallet, *A History of the University of Oxford*, iii (1927), 492.

65. W. T. S. Sonnenschein ['Sonners'; later Stallybrass].
Vice-Principal, 1914–36; Principal, 1936–48; Vice-Chancellor, 1947–48.
Photographed as Pro-Proctor in 1915, aged 31.

66. The Ingoldsby Club, 1898.

STANDING: John Buchan, F. Bradley Birt, H.C. de J. du Vallon, W.M. Bouch, B.Consitt Boulter, Ellis Jones.

SITTING: P. J. Macdonell, J. D. Rolleston, John Foster Carr, Arthur J. Sargent, J. N. P. Mackie. [F. G. Williams: 'present in spirit']

The Ingoldsby was a book club and debating society. John Buchan stands on the far left.

67. The Fellows, June 1907.

STANDING: F. Madan, H. C. Wace, R. W. Leage, A. J. Jenkinson, H. F. Fox, G.H. Wakeling.

SITTING: W. N. Stocker, F. W. Bussell, C. B. Heberden, A. J. Butler, C. H. Sampson.

During Heberden's Principalship, B.N.C. began to move out of the gymnasium and into the academy.

68. Brasenose J.C.R., circa 1892.

Later the Shackleton Room (IX, 3–4).

Note the three trophies by the chimney piece: the Henley Visitors' and Steward's Cups, and the Head of the River Cup. The B.N.C.–Trinity Challenge Cup stands on the windowsill.

When the J.C.R. moved to the New Lodgings' kitchen in 1938 (later the Stallybrass Law Library), this room was occupied first by Stanley Cohn in 1938–39, and then by Robert Shackleton in 1948–79.

69. Brasenose Hall in 1891.

The 'fancy' portrait of King Alfred (1769, by Edward Penny) hangs in the centre, before the opening up of the entrance from Lecture Room VII in 1901. The floor is paved in black and white marble (1763), before the insertion of oak flooring in 1909. The tables, benches and panelling date from 1684; the chimney piece from 1748; the barrel-vaulted plaster ceiling from 1752. The hanging lights date from the installation of gas in 1840, prior to the arrival of electricity in 1892. 'Floodlighting' followed in 1933. The chairs at High Table, dating from 1828, were replaced in 1959, and eventually moved to IV, 4.

70. **Thomas Graham Jackson, later Sir Graham Jackson: design for a new High Street front, with 'Crowned Spire'.**
Drawing exhibited at the Royal Academy, 1887 (R.A. no. 1689).
William Morris warned the Bursar that such a tower would be 'a mistake'.

71. **Thomas Graham Jackson, later Sir Graham Jackson: The New Quadrangle.**
Drawing exhibited at the Royal Academy, 1890 (R.A. no. 1794).
Maurice Bowra later christened it 'The Anglo-Jackson style'. At the time, critics called it
'Advanced Jacobean'.

72. The 2nd Torpid, Hilary Term, 1914.

Bow: C. G. Gilbert; no.2: C. I. Parkin; no. 3: *J.H. Van den Bergh*; no. 4.: G. Alchin; no.5.: *C. R. Blackett*; no. 6: H. F. Miles; no. 7: C.H.N. Symon; Stroke: *F.G. Buckley*; Cox: *S.E.L. Gordon* [on windowsill].

Italicised names: killed in World War I.

73. **Officer Training Corps, B.N.C. section, 1915.**

STANDING: T.S. Griffiths, F.G. Rednal, R. B. Harrison, J. I. Moseley, R. H. Peck, C.M. Johnston, C. G. Gilbert, A. R. Jacobs.

SITTING: *R. Rodakowski*, A.G.F. Gibbs, W.T.S. Sonnenschein [later Stallybrass], W. L. Hoskins, *H.F. Bolton.*

Italicised names: killed in World War I.

'Sonners' – centre, front row – sports a military moustache.

74. **The Pater Society, 1911.**

BACK ROW: (?) ; C.H. Smith; (?) ; *C.M. Pope*, (?) .

MIDDLE ROW: P. A. Landon; L. G. Duke; *E. H. Crooke*; E. M. Gawne; (?) .

FRONT ROW: *J. G. Reid*; *A. F. Willmer.*

Italicised names: killed in World War I.

Founded in 1907 as a counter to the muscular ethos of the college.

75. The Phoenix, Trinity Term 1914.

?F. C. Verner   F.E. Hill

E.A. Shaw   *H.H. Jackson*   H.B. Moore

J.A. Paton   *G.H. Bailey*   F. H. Nott   A.N. Strode Jackson

M.H. O'Rorke   A. C. Williamson.

Italicised names: killed in World War I.

Of the dozen Phoenix men who dined with the Prince of Wales in 1913, half did not return from the war.

76. Eights Week, 1901.
    Not a good year. B.N.C. went down from 4th to 10th.
    The Barge dates from 1882.

77. Eights Week, 1931.

A very good year: Head of the River for the fourth time running.

The Barge dates from 1926.

Bow C. F. Williams, no.2 J. G. Guest, no.3 V.C. Fairfax, no. 4 *R.W.G. Holdsworth*, no.5 R. Poole, no.6 G. Smith, no. 7 C.M. Johnston, Stroke J. de R. Kent, Cox G.L. Phillips.
Italicised name: killed in World War II.

78. Bump Supper in Hall, 1922.

The 1st Eight goes Head of the River again, with five bumps.

Vice-Principal Stallybrass sits at the far left of High Table. Principal Sampson stands in the centre. The cox and future philosophy don, Jimmy McKie, sits four places to Sonners' right.

'The enthusiasm throughout the College was immense'.

79. The Wanderers at the Imperial Hotel, Eastbourne, 1924.
Wandering cricketers in Sussex. Sonners' motor car is third from the right:
the Vice-Principal at the wheel.

80. Arnold Strode Jackson (d. 1972).

'The fabulous Jacker': wounded, and home from the war.

Photographed by Stallybrass, *c.*1918, outside the V.–P.'s rooms, IV, 4.

In 1912, Jackson had won the 1500 metres Gold Medal at the Stockholm Olympics, with a display of 'gorgeous running' that threw the 20,000 crowd 'into hysterics'. By 1918 he was the youngest Brigadier General in the British Army; with seventeen medals, including 4 D.S.O.s for 'conspicuous gallantry and brilliant leadership'.

on his athletic qualifications. Wealth, poverty and athletic distinction are all equally welcome at Oxford and Cambridge, but no one of them must ever be taken as a substitute for intellectual fitness in deciding on the question of admittance.[34]

However, that did not satisfy certain elements in the Labour Party. In a submission to Asquith in 1922 the party made its intentions as regards Oxford and Cambridge crystal clear: 'The Labour Party wishes to establish the control of the Colleges by the Universities, and the control of the Universities by the nation.' In other words, it aimed to create an overarching system of 'continuous administrative control by the State'.[35] When in 1923 the Tory government proposed funding legislation, the opposition therefore put down two amendments tying future grants to equal status for women, and to the widening of access for 'poorer students'. The first of these was defeated by the Cambridge lobby; Oxford had, in any case, already jumped that particular hurdle. But the second amendment slipped through, almost unnoticed.

We are all in favour of freedom [announced Col. Wedgwood, MP,] But ... with public money must go some degree of control ... [After all] we are discussing the vital question of the education of the English master-class ... [And control by private benefactors would be] infinitely more dangerous [than control by the state] ... Education should be of public utility and should be made a public charge ... [That way will come a true] equality of opportunity.[36]

Fisher tried to sooth the backbenchers: 'I do not think that the ancient universities have anything to fear.'[37] But James Chuter Ede, MP—grocer's son turned schoolmaster; later first Baron Chuter-Ede; co-author of the Butler Education Act of 1944—took a rather different view. He did not beat about the bush:

I am not at all sure that it would be a bad thing if certain poor men's sons were admitted simply because they were the sons of poor men. .... [i.e. those] who show aptitude rather than attainment ... What the universities educate is not attainment but aptitude.[38]

---

[34] Asquith Commn. (*PP* (1922), x), 81, 84 (pp. 53, 56).

[35] Asquith Commn., vol. ii, appendices, p. 61.

[36] *Parl. Debates: Commons,* clxv, cols. 1882–3, 1886, 2766, 2774; 22 June 1923.

[37] Ibid., col. 1898: 22 June 1923. His optimism was later endorsed by his biographer: 'It is an interesting fact that the grant to the universities is one of the few items of State expenditure which has survived unscathed from successive agitations for economy; more important, and here the influence of Fisher counted for much, acceptance of the grant has never yet entailed any sacrifice of intellectual independence, as it has so often done on the continent. This is one of the few surviving relics of Gladstonian Liberalism' (D. Ogg, *Herbert Fisher* (1947), 82). See also H. Judge, 'H. A. L. Fisher', *Oxford Review of Education*, 32 (2006), no. i, 5–21.

[38] *Parl. Debates: Commons,* clxv, col. 1900: 22 June 1923.

In carrying this amendment—with its hints of remedial studies and the comprehensive university—the Labour Party had put down a very significant marker for the future. Such things did not escape the notice of W. T. S. Stallybrass (pls. 65, 81).

Between the two world wars—in its ethos, in its reputation—BNC *was* Stallybrass. It was as Vice-Principal (1914–36)—and, quintessentially, as Senior Proctor (1925–26)—that Stallybrass reached his peak. As Principal, 'good old Sammy' was simply there to keep the ship on an even keel. Now Sampson (pl. 67) was a devoted churchman, he was also a scholar; he had Firsts in classics as well as maths. But his shyness, his stammer, his inhibiting myopia, ruled him out as a public figure. Dinner in the Lodgings must have been quite an ordeal. 'Mrs. Sampson is rather a terror', noted one undergraduate in 1929. 'She is very large and fat with an aggressively homely... face and sits bolt upright at one end of the table carving the joint while Mr. Sampson curls about in his seat at the other.'[39] So the dynamic of the college remained with Sonners. His rooms in Old Quad, IV, 4, became the engine room of BNC, fuelled by alcohol and fired by a powerful sense of collegiate pride. Generations of undergraduates came somehow to accept that their stern mentor of the morning was actually their drinking partner of the night before. In theory he was a senior don. In practice he was an *Isis* Idol, an undergraduate at heart: part of an immemorial college hierarchy in which social barriers played no part. To scouts and porters he seemed omnipotent. And Brasenose at this time was lucky to enjoy the ministrations of a devoted generation of servants. John Stone, for instance, undershoeblack, second hallman, and bedmaker from 1898 to 1938; Harry Timms, Sonners' man on staircase IV; Henry Bustin, Platnauer's scout on staircase VI; and tiny Bill Drake who arrived as a scout's boy 'sometime before 1899' and died in 1956 after a lifetime of service, cleaning silver in the buttery. Their lives were hard but not entirely miserable. Bert King recalled that, in the 1920s at any rate, their arrival at 6 a.m. was usually sweetened with a gallon of beer; 'it had mostly gone by lunchtime'.

BNC between the wars was very much a masculine, almost aggressively homosocial, society. Sonners smiled particularly on athletes who were good-looking and blond. His misogyny was part instinct, part pose, but always integral to his image as a 'character'. In the jargon of the day, he was a big man, with no side to him. As one of his tutors at Christ Church put it, he had 'the gift of

---

[39] MPP 228. A1. Diary of Edgar Parsons, 3 Nov. 1929. See also Accession 276: L. Lethbridge to B. Nicholas, 22 May 1998; and Accession 129: G. H. S. Wild to B. Harrison, 30 Nov. 1988 and 5 Jan. 1989. Sampson's salary was £1,500 plus £324 income tax allowance. After his death the contents of the Lodgings were sold, even the Turkey stair carpet (Sampson file).

popularity'. 'His dinners were wonderful', recalled H. N. Spalding; 'from eight to four the joyous hours sped on'. And he had a genius for friendship. Picture him before breakfast, barrelling across two quadrangles in dressing gown and slippers, on his way to a morning bath at the bottom of staircase XII. His young companions of the early hours can scarcely believe their bleary eyes:

> ...passing a figure in the quad,
> Be-dressing-gown'd and bedroom-shod,
> Who greeted me with cheery smile
> (Strange! 'twas a figure which erstwhile
> Haunted my dream in robes Proctorial!)...[40]

There was a line, and it could be drawn firmly. When the young C. S. Lewis, then a wartime cadet at Keble, attended a Schools supper at Brasenose in June 1917, he got so 'royally drunk' that he thought he was on the other side of Brasenose Lane, in Exeter.

I am afraid [he wrote ruefully next morning] I must have given myself away rather as I went round imploring everyone to let me whip them for the sum of 1 shilling a lash! All this happened...in the rooms [Amsterdam 2] of an Indian called [M. D. M. Gokuldas]: but as I was not the only person in that condition, the Dean [i.e. Stallybrass] got fed up with the row and sent round a notice that Mr. [Gokuldas's] guests must leave the College at once...

Years later, during the Second World War, it was at Brasenose that Lewis— escaping from an unwelcome sermon—noticed a strange, double-sided ward-robe, converted out of the Principal's private entrance to the antechapel. Here was a trigger for imagination: here the kingdom of Narnia was born. Lewis and Stallybrass were never particularly close, though they were both—like Maurice Platnauer—habitués of Parson's Pleasure. But they shared a commitment— alcohol fuelled and classics oriented—to the camaraderie of college living. Undergraduates were their companions, their audience, their inspiration.[41]

[40] G.P.H., Ale Verse, *Brazen Nose*, iv. 74; Spalding, ibid., ix. 21; H. W. Blunt in Stallybrass file: 10 May 1911. For a photo of IV, 4, taken at 11 a.m. on 16 Nov. 1915, see PRI 25 H 1/2 /A 443. As Proctor 'he meets as many as he can among the criminal classes' (*Isis*, 21 May 1925, 21–2: photo). Leif Egeland, Fellow in Law 1927–30, marvelled at Sonners' 'constitution of iron which enabled him to combine sustained carousals with an incredible capacity for hard work and clear thinking' (L. Egeland, *Bridges of Understanding* (Cape Town, 1977), 43–5). His scout on IV, 4 in 1914 was Harry Timms (photo PR1 25 H3/1/3/A/115). For other scouts at this time, see *Brazen Nose*, x. 150–1 and 200–1.

[41] For the drunken party at Brasenose, see C. S. Lewis, *Collected Letters*, i (2000), 319: 10 June 1917, to Arthur Greeves. Gokuldas [later Muraji] was a Hindu, the son of a Bombay mill-owner. He was one of the very few to continue at BNC—together with his favourite black cat—throughout the First World War. He may have come to BNC initially through a family friendship with the Indian cricketer Ranjitsinhji. The wardrobe episode in *The Lion, the Witch and the Wardrobe* (written 1948; published 1949) echoes a short story by E. Nesbit, 'The Aunt

Sonners knows their faces, and he knows their names: from the time he leads each batch of freshmen into the Divinity School at matriculation to the time he congratulates them at a graduates' lunch in hall. By this date Brasenose had settled into a middling position in the table of colleges, that is in terms of numbers and wealth. In 1920, for example, it ranked seventh in terms of gross income (£24,246 p.a.) and ninth in terms of numbers (180 undergraduates). Of those 180, there were 95 in college, 85 in lodgings. Sonners made it his business to know them all. In June 1936 the following wager appeared in the SCR Betting Book: 'The Vice-Principal bets Mr. Ker one bottle of port that he can state correctly the initials of at least 90% of the members of the college. Lost by the Vice-Principal who failed over 44 names; ie scored 80%. Paid 12 June 1936'.

As Vice-Principal, it fell to Sonners to administer the ritual of morning roll-call for those not attending chapel. He made no secret of his own lack of piety. He read the lessons in chapel; but he had no time for those with closed systems of belief: 'those dreadful God people'. His own religion was a common-sense code of honour, reinforced for public purposes by legal formulae and scriptural allegory. Every morning he would sit, with darkened countenance, in lecture room VII, as undergraduates in gowns signed the roll-call book after their visit to the bath house and before their breakfast in hall. Until the rules were eased after the First World War, every undergraduate had to keep 18 roll-calls in the morning, at 7.55 in winter and 7.25 in summer—or 18 morning chapels: 'holy rollers'—as well as 18 evening chapels (including Sunday chapel, always a more crowded occasion). After 1919 morning chapel was no longer compulsory for those living out. Nevertheless any form of religious sanction must have been irksome to Sonners. In 1932 his voice seems to have been influential in abandoning compulsion altogether. That year, in fact, marked something of a watershed in the social life of BNC. Compulsory chapel; 'knocking in fines' between 9 and 11 p.m.; the ancient provision of commons—a daily portion of bread and butter consumed with cheese at lunchtime—all these were abolished in 1932.[42]

---

and Annabel', with which he regaled evacuee children at The Kilns, Headington Quarry, Oxford. For background, see G. Sayer, *Jack: C. S. Lewis and his Times* (1988). The story of the chapel wardrobe was recalled by A. N. Wilson on Radio 4 in 2006. For Parson's Pleasure, see Lewis, *Collected Letters*, i. 304 n., 563, 934.

[42] For chapel-going, lunching, and breakfasting at this period, see Accession 129: G. H. S. Wild to B. Harrison, 30 Nov. 1988 and 5 Jan. 1989; *Brazen Nose*, ix. 354 and xl. 115; V-P's Reg. 21 Jan. 1914, fo. 41, 25 Jan. 1919, fo. 136, and 23 Sept. 1919, fo. 151. When compulsory chapel went—partly as a result of agitation by one particularly pious freshman, D. F. Walker—Sonners pressed in vain for the abolition of the Bible Clerkship (V-P's Reg. 19 Oct. 1932, fo. 134). For the abolition of 'knocking in' fines, see V-P's Reg. 1 Oct. 1932. As regards college finance in general, see comparative numbers and endowments in 1920, in Asquith Commn., vol. ii, appendices, p. 325.

The buttery disappeared, becoming merely a pantry for the hall; and with it went the keeping of Buttery Books, records of daily living since 1612. One more novelty: a link was established with Gonville and Caius College, Cambridge. Or rather a second link; the first was Joyce Frankland.

Now skip forward a decade or so. The remaking of BNC begins to take on definitive form with Sonners' election as Principal in 1936. Architecturally, few changes have been made. Apart from staircases XIV (1929) and XV (1931), plus rearrangements in the Lodgings (1936–7), improvements to the kitchen's buttery area (1934), and a Gothic window in the old gate lodge (1936), the college remains physically unaltered. These alterations were all concessions to comfort rather than statements of taste. Sonners is more concerned with the morale of the place. From the date of his election he of course presides in hall; but he also presides in common room, not ex officio but simply by sovereignty of nature. The Fellowship—still less than twenty—he has largely recreated, and recreated in his own image. Over the appointment of two professors he has had little or no control. The Professor of Engineering Science (R. V. Southwell, FRS) will cause him little trouble. But the Camden Professor of Ancient History (H. M. Last) will prove to be his nemesis. All that will come later. Meanwhile he can rely on most of the Fellows.

It is worth pondering, for a moment, the team Sonners has assembled. First, there is the Vice-Principal (Maurice Platnauer) (pls. 92, 93, 95), epicure and scholar; then the Senior Tutor and Senior Dean (Michael Holroyd), a genial dilettante; then the Bursar (Andy Grant, 'the tweeded sloth'), a rugger blue disguised as an estate manager: he succeeded Wace in 1929. Then there is Wace's successor as chaplain (Reggie Owen), rowing blue, headmaster, and future archbishop; and the Tutor in Law (Humphrey Waldock), a hockey blue and future Professor at All Souls: *Isis* Idol turned academic, tipped by Sonners one day to succeed him. Then there is the Tutor in Philosophy (Jimmy McKie) (pl. 92), a whimsical Scotsman with a cox's guile; and Idwal Griffith, a golf-playing mathematician and physicist whom Sonners has 'seduced from St John's'. Outside the Fellowship is R. E. B. Maxse, a Lecturer in German and French between 1932 and 1945. He speaks six languages fluently and jogs along in another four. He has even been tutor to the sons of the Tsar. And then there is Tommy Taylor, Lecturer in Chemistry and Sonners' co-executor, a future Vice-Chancellor in the West Indies; plus a classical philosopher imported from London, K. J. Spalding: his pipe-smoking is so fierce that his pupils avoid it by sitting on the floor; he is Sonners' steadfast ally.[43] Last but not least there are the two history dons

---

[43] K. J. Spalding (1880–1962) exchanged a chair at King's (later Queen Elizabeth) College London for a Research Fellowship at BNC in 1928. His *Desire and Reason* (1922) was 'strongly Spinozistic', and he was 'totally out of sympathy' with modern Oxford philosophy (*The Times*,

(Stanley Cohn and Eric Collieu), opposing minds, opposing temperaments, locked in uneasy partnership.

To all these we will return. They form the supporting cast in the collegiate drama that is now about to unfold. But first, Cohn and Collieu: they deserve more than a parenthesis at this point. Edgar Stanley Cohn (pl. 91) arrived in 1933. He had been nine years at Oriel, and was notoriously at odds with that college's high Anglican tradition. Against all convention, Sonners managed to poach him from across the High, at exactly the moment BNC abandoned compulsory chapel.[44] In one sense they were soul-mates: indulgent, icono-clastic, misogynistic. In another way they were polar opposites. Sonners had extraordinary drive; he revelled in company. Cohn was solitary by instinct, procrastinating by temperament; and his lassitude increased with age. He had once been the most brilliant medievalist of his generation. After taking the top First of his year at Balliol in 1921, he progressed to Magdalen as Senior Demy, and began work on an important project: an edition of the letters of Peter of Blois. In 1923 he was elected Fellow of Oriel. There was one dissentient voice, that of the Regius Professor of Modern History, C. H. Firth. The Regius prophesied that young Cohn would do no research. And he was right. By the time of his transfer to Brasenose, Cohn was already a man with a fine future behind him. Apart from a short note in the *English Historical Review*, and a pseudonymous novel entitled *The Fools*, he had written nothing. Teaching occasionally amused him: he liked pupils with a touch of 'malice'. To these he could be quixotically kind. But for years he refused to hold

24 Jan. 1962, p. 15). He was an underwriting member of Lloyd's. See Platnauer's kindly obit, *Brazen Nose*, xiii. 101–3. His brother H. N. Spalding (1877–1953) had known Sonners since their days in Munitions: in 1917 they holidayed together on the Wye, bathing 'tous nus' (MPP 56 c1; PR 1.25 H3/1/1: photos); and both belonged to a coterie called the Survivors' Club. 'H. N.' retired from the Admiralty to the BNC Common Room in 1919, aged only 42. At Oxford he established the Spalding Professorship of Eastern Religions and Ethics (*The Times*, 7 Sept. 1953, 8). With a Thamesside house at Henley—The Hurst—he was a lavish patron of BNC Boat Club. Appropriately, much of the family fortune came from the manufacture of sports equipment (*Oxford Mag.* 21 Jan. 1954, 144–5).

[44] Sonners denounced such transfers, except under 'exceptional circumstances', as 'a violation of the comity of colleges' (*American Oxonian*, 35 (1948), 20). BNC's dropping of compulsory chapel coincided with Congregation's abolition of 'Divvers' (Responsions in Holy Scripture). Cohn was given six years' seniority on appointment, and moved into XII, 5 before transferring to IX, 3 and 4 in 1938–9. In October 1940 he moved into IV, 4 (V-P's Reg. 1 Feb. 1933, fo. 140; Room Book *passim*). He was succeeded at Oriel by W. A. Pantin. Cohn's pseudonym was Edgar Stanley. For Collieu's obituary of Cohn see *The Times*, 23 Mar. 1963, 10 and *Brazen Nose*, xiii. 172–3: tutorial photo by D. Lomax. For a sympathetic appreciation, see R. W. Southern in *Brazen Nose*, xxxix. 67–9. For Cohn in wartime (squadron leader, RAFVR), see R. A. Jenkinson, ibid., xxx. 37. For memories of a Cohn tutorial, see K. Shearwood, *Pegasus* (1975), 5.

college office, or even to examine. 'You don't', he used to say, 'put race horses between shafts.' He was a very donly don. He left his rooms just once a year, for a summer holiday at Modbury in Devon: his scout would charter two taxis for the station, the second containing suitcases. In college his routine became metronomic, his style—in speech and dress—increasingly mannered. After floating through the 1930s on a sea of epigrams and alcohol, he must almost have welcomed the Second World War as a blessed release. Certainly he took his war service seriously—flight control operations in Malta and Burma—and he felt most deeply the fate of his fellow Jews. In 1945 he returned to Brasenose rejuvenated: doubly acerbic, doubly sybaritic, and doubly determined to shake off the palsied regime of Dr Stallybrass. In this he had the support of his junior colleague, Eric Collieu.

Collieu had been appointed in 1935 from an unusually strong field. He beat Max Beloff and A. J. P. Taylor.[45] Thereafter he became the very model of an Oxford moral tutor. Kindly, dignified, punctilious; he treated his pupils as part of a supra-generational family, linked together in personal and collegiate loyalty. But even before the outbreak of the Second World War, somehow the spark had gone. His intellectual pleasure in history became wholly vicarious, filtered through the achievements of his pupils. As for his relationship with Cohn, it oscillated between hostility and indifference. When Cohn eventually overdosed on alcohol, Collieu's epitaph on his colleague was bleak: 'a life of unmitigated selfishness'. On one thing only had they been in full agreement: somehow, sooner or later, Sonners had to go.

Meanwhile there was Stocker (pl. 67)—or rather, still there was Stocker—the only Fellow appointed before the start of the Stallybrass regime. Unbelievably, he had been made a Fellow as long ago as 1877. He returned to BNC in 1901, after twenty years as Professor of Physics at the Royal Engineering College, Cooper's Hill. Back at Brasenose he discovered his true destiny as Curator of Common Room from 1908 onwards. Stocker stayed on as Curator—with a short stint as Home Bursar, 1920–5, sharing office with Wace as Estates Bursar—for thirty-seven years. Food, wine, conversation, decorum: these were almost his only responsibilities. He once admitted that he had lost interest in physics after examining in Schools in 1904. Once he enjoyed playing the piano—Bach mostly—but that habit disappeared in the 1930s. So how on earth did he spend his later days? Each

---

[45] V-P's Reg. 28 June 1935, fo. 180. For photos by Stallybrass, see PRI 25 H 1–2, A 1056–8, PRI 25 H 1/3, 3068–70, and PRI 25 H1/3, 3489–90. For R. Shackleton's funeral address on Collieu, see *Brazen Nose*, xvi. 35–8. A. J. P. Taylor had been a pupil of Cohn at Oriel, along with Geoffrey Barraclough. Cohn called them 'two vipers'. Collieu was a pupil of Sir Keith Feiling of Christ Church, who described him as 'one of the nicest of human beings', though lacking the powers of a 'creative' historian (MEM, 2J1: Collieu EG: 25 Mar. 1935).

morning his scout, Charlie Southorn, brought him a large breakfast on a tray. Then there were the papers to read. For lunch he would eat an apple or perhaps a piece of cheese. Every afternoon he would walk, and walk. As a young man he had explored the Celtic fringe. In old age he limited himself to Oxfordshire. There can have been few local villages he did not perambulate. His pedestrian feats were prodigious. In fifty years, 1876 to 1925, he clocked up just 150,000 miles. Week in, week out, he maintained an average of eight miles per day. Starting from a low point of 951 miles in 1876, he rapidly rose to more than 2,000 a year in 1880. After 1887 he seldom dropped below 3,000 miles per annum. Plodding on steadily between the 1880s and the 1920s, he hit a high point of more than 5,000 miles in 1904, cruising happily home through his fifth pedestrian decade at more than 3,000 miles a year. Thereafter his expeditions were more moderate. But he never relinquished the miniature barometer—kept in his waistcoat pocket—by which he measured the exact heights and contours of his route. The distances had always been worked out by means of a pedometer and careful study of Ordnance Survey maps. His speed, incidentally, was a steady 3.5 m.p.h., neither more nor less.

It was not until December 1945 that Stocker retired as Curator. After suffering a stroke in 1947, he was confined to his rooms on the first floor of staircase XI, the rooms he enjoyed for forty-five years. Now he could only walk, or rather stagger, from bedroom to sitting room, and back again. He died at the age of 98 in 1949, only a few months after Stallybrass. He had been a Fellow for seventy-two years, the last life Fellow in the University of Oxford. Appropriately, all his estate, which was considerable, went to BNC.[46]

Stocker was reputed never to leave college overnight except on the occasion of a bump supper. Between the wars there were a good many such events.

> What's the use of worrying? Come to Brasenose.
> Bump supper guaranteed at least once a term.

One photograph survives as a record (pl. 78). The occasion is the supper of 31 May 1922. This was the first for twenty-two years, and it celebrated a record five bumps by the first Eight. The night is hot; the hall is crowded to capacity; bread rolls litter the floor; and the photographer catches the moment when the tables are cleared, speeches commence, and the port

---

[46] *Brazen Nose*, viii. 15 and ix. 47–53 (M. Holroyd and F. Wylie); *The Times*, 3 Aug. 1949, 7; *Oxford Mag.* 20 Oct. 1949, 38–41 (M. Holroyd); pencil portrait by Powys Evans, 1927. He was elected on Rucker's recommendation. Madan thought him 'collected, and a little cold, but not unpleasant...[a] striking...Experimentalist, [though] not so good a mathematician' (B4 b9, i. 2: 2 Feb. 1877). For a photograph by Stallybrass in 1914, see PRI 25 H1/2, A 114. For tables of his pedestrian feats see *Brazen Nose*, iv. 195. For his piano duet with Heberden in Eights Week, 1919, see *Oxford Mag.* 6 June 1919, 346. He left the college £15,000.

begins to circulate. Sonners watches quizzically from the far end of high table. 'Good old Sammy', white haired and speechless, nominally presides in the centre. Jimmy McKie, cox and future philosophy don, turns shyly to face the camera, not far from Sonners' right.

We were probably faster [that day] than any other boat on the river.... The enthusiasm throughout the College was immense and 144 persons sat in the Hall on the great night.... [though] the limit was supposed to be 120. Need we say it *was* hot. The supper proceeded with merriment throughout, and when the speeches came every sally was met with uproarious applause... speech after speech, including one from practically every member of the crew... the Vice-Principal [Stallybrass], Prof. Stuart Jones [Camden Professor] and Mr. Alchin [Senior Hulme Scholar]. One of the wittiest speeches of all came from Mr. H. N. Spalding [patron of the Boat Club]... After the supper the old time jollification took place, and once again, no doubt to the delight of Walter Pater's ghost, the wonderful spire of St. Mary's, was brought into view on a splendid summer night by the glancing flames of a bonfire...[47]

The twenty years 1920–39 were not exactly triumphant in the history of Oxford rowing. Cambridge won the Boat Race during this period on all but three occasions: 1923, 1937, and 1938. The fact that three Brasenose men rowed in 1923, two in 1937, and four in 1938, plus the fact that the victorious crews of 1937 and 1938 included Conrad Cherry (pl. 87) of Brasenose—the greatest oarsman of his generation—may tell us something about BNC's contribution to Oxford rowing between the wars. More relevant, however, is the fact that the number of Brasenose blues was third only to Christ Church and Magdalen: bigger colleges, both of them, with legions of rowing Etonians. Finally, and in Oxford terms conclusively, over the same period BNC produced more presidents of the OUBC than any other college.[48]

In the annual battle for head of the river, the Brasenose story between the wars was a saga of upward mobility. Towards the end of Heberden's time, the college had sunk—unprecedentedly—to twenty-second place; bottom of the second division. Stallybrass and Wace made it a point of honour to obliterate that shame. In 1922 there were five bumps; in 1923, five more; in 1924, five again; in 1925 yet another five: twenty bumps in four years, taking the College from twenty-second to second. Then there was a pause: 1926 and 1927 were spent vainly pursuing Christ Church. And then, in 1928, on the first night of racing, Brasenose went head for the first time in thirty-seven years.

---

[47] *Isis*, 28 Feb. 1923, 3.; S L 7 C5/9; *Brazen Nose*, iv. 211.
[48] G. J. Mower-White (1924), H. C. Morphett (1928), A. Graham (1929), C. M. Johnston (1931), and J. C. Cherry (1937)—'A fine heavyweight of impeccable style' (G. C. Drinkwater, *The Boat Race* (1939), 133). For tabulated lists of BNC rowing blues, see R. D. Burrell, *The Oxford and Cambridge Boat Race, 1829–1953* (1954), 136.

Last June again that place was won
Which last was held in '91;
For, strongly rowing, our Eight sped
Onward and upward to the Head . . . [49]

At the bump supper, Wace (pl. 67) concluded his speech with a heartfelt prayer: 'Nunc Dimittis'. Or was it 'Bump Dimittis'? The record is uncertain. Anyway, he had done his work. The following year he retired to a property near Crowcombe in Somerset; appropriately its name was Paradise. Brasenose stayed head of the river for a record four years: 1928, 1929, 1930, 1931.

That final Eight in 1931—the last time Brasenose was to be head of the river—deserves a moment's scrutiny. The cox is a scholar, G. L. Phillips; after a First in Greats he will end as chaplain to London University. At nos. 2 and 3 there are two Australians from Geelong Grammar School.—J. C. Guest and V. C. Fairfax—both reading law. Both have a big future in business, Guest in mining, Fairfax in publishing.[50] Stroke is J. de R. Kent, son of C. W. Kent who stroked the Eight in its last period of great success, 1889–90. At bow is C. F. Williams, reading PPE, a future schoolmaster at Haileybury. And then there are four blues, at nos. 4, 5, 6, and 7: R. W. G. Holdsworth, the star of Brasenose (of whom more later); Robert Poole, an Etonian; Gordon Smith, a Wykehamist and cousin of Michael Holroyd; and Carruthers Melvill ('Monkey') Johnston, a glamorous Heath Harrison Exhibitioner from Sherborne, who will end up as CMG in the Coronation Honours List of 1953: scant reward for helping to clear up the Mau Mau troubles in Kenya.[51] Five of these men belong, or will belong, to Vincent's and the Phoenix. See them now, in a photograph (pl. 77) taken at the moment of triumph, that final night in 1931. Brasenose supporters swim out from the bank carrying bottles of champagne. The BNC barge is crammed with female spectators. After that, Brasenose rowing will never again achieve quite such success. By 1934 the first Eight will have sunk to sixth on the river. But its stroke will be a future Prime Minister of Australia, John Gorton.[52]

[49] Ale Verse (1928). For photos see: the triumphant Eight, *Isis*, 31 May 1928, 23; the Stroke, 'Bosher' Graham, *Isis*, 27 Jan. 1929, p. 7 and 23 May 1929, 23; and the no. 7, 'Turtle' Morphett, *Isis*, 13 Mar. 1929, 7 and 23 May 1929, 27.

[50] Guest was a prisoner of war in 1941–5, and later Manager and Director of Broken Hill Associates; Fairfax (CMG 1960) headed the family firm of J. Fairfax and Sons Ltd., publishers of the *Sydney Morning Herald*.

[51] He died in a car crash. Obit, *Brazen Nose*, xv. 151–2. 'If you can have an earthly saint, there was one' (Sir W. Coutts in *The Times*, 19 Nov. 1970, 13). For 'C.M.J.' as *Isis* Idol and President of OUBC—'a truly democratic spirit'—see *Isis*, 21 May 1931, 7: photo. In 1928–9 he was in VI, 3, paying £21 per term, next to Platnauer.

[52] Obit, *The Times*, 21 May 2002. For the victorious Eight of 1931, see SL8 B9/2/13.

On the rugby and cricket fields, BNC was equally powerful, and its power was longer lasting. Between 1919 and 1938, twenty-one Brasenose rugby men played thirty-one times against Cambridge. Two at least are now legendary figures: Alexander Obolensky, 'the Flying Prince', and Ian Smith, 'the Flying Scotsman'.[53] Others deserve almost equal fame. 'Knoppie' Neser, for example, who in 1920 switched at the last minute from hooker to stand-off half, and won the game for Oxford: 'Neser's Match'. He was also a cricket blue, a Rhodes Scholar, and a First in law; later he became a judge in the Supreme Court of South Africa.[54] Perhaps the strongest Oxford teams of this period were those of 1923 and 1924, with their mighty Brasenose combination of Norman Strong at scrum-half and Ian Smith, ever electric, out on a distant wing. But from a strictly BNC perspective the college team of 1931–2 must take some beating. Picture them in a photograph at the end of the season, triumphant cup winners.[55] Three of them will die in the Second World War: Gerry Chalk, J. H. Becher, and Mike Peacock. Five of them are blues: C. A. L. Richards, the captain; Sean Waide, an Irish international even before he played for Oxford;[56] F. L. Hovde, a strapping Rhodes Scholar from Devil's Lake HS, South Dakota: he can throw the ball 'one-handed...like a torpedo';[57] Mike Peacock, a future war hero; and Bill Roberts, the giant half-back from Cardiff HS, a Welsh international, four times a blue: at moments in 1929 he seemed almost to outplay the Fenland enemy 'single-handed... weaving and swaying his way through the Cambridge defence...Roberts kicking, Roberts charging with venomous ferocity...Roberts [ending with a drop goal to] send the ball flying between the posts'.[58]

This run of success was clearly Sonners' doing. And so—indirectly—was the parallel revival of Brasenose soccer. Here Sonners' agent was 'Blue-eyed Johnnie' Haslewood. He came up from Shrewsbury as a Heath Harrison major in 1929, and ended as captain of the Oxford team, 'unquestionably the finest all-round athlete in the university'.[59] BNC soccer was never quite the

---

[53] *Brazen Nose*, xv. 271–3; *Isis*, 22 May 1924, 22: photo. Smith played in thirty-five consecutive matches for Scotland, leading his country to the Triple Crown in 1932–3.

[54] *Isis*, 1 Dec.1920, 5–6: photo. 'There can never have been a more powerful stand-off half' (H. Marshall, *Oxford v Cambridge* (1951), 148).

[55] S L 8 D 3/4.

[56] Richards was destined for a long career in the Colonial Service in Uganda. Injury kept Waide out of the Colonial Service; he went into Shell-Mex and BP.

[57] *Isis*, 2 Dec. 1931, 24: photo; Marshall, *Oxford v Cambridge*, 193. Later President of Purdue University and a Trustee of the Carnegie Foundation.

[58] *Isis*, 20 Jan. 1932; photo; Marshall, *Oxford v Cambridge*, 195. Later a captain in the Welsh Guards, a journalist, and breeder of pedigree Welsh sows.

[59] *Isis*, 19 Oct. 1932, 18: photo. Nicknamed 'Sparrow' because of his diminutive size, he played for Oxford in six different sports: soccer, golf, Eton fives, rugby fives, cricket, and lawn tennis (*The Times*, 23 Nov. 1999; *Brazen Nose*, xxxiii. 48–9). Sonners considered him his 'greatest friend'(MEM 2J1: Boobbyer, B: Stallybrass to J. F. Wolfenden, 18 Mar. 1947).

same after he went down, with a creditable Second in law, in 1932. But Brasenose rugby went from strength to strength. In fact it was only in the twilight of Sonners' regime—the immediate post-war seasons—that BNC rugger reached its peak. The 1946 Oxford side—mostly ex-servicemen—led by 'Gullie' Wilson, was phenomenally strong: Brasenose dominated the scrum. And from 1947 to 1951 the roll-call of Brasenose names—Boobbyer in particular, exploding through the centre 'like a cork out of a bottle'— endowed the Stallybrass era with a kind of posthumous glory. In 1946 there were five Brasenose men in the Oxford side; in 1947 four; and in 1948 five again. One newspaper described the BNC pack of 1946 as resembling 'a human herd of buffalo which will be impossible to tame'.[60] One of the backs in that undefeated team—the future Lord Moore—would live to be private secretary to the Queen. Sonners would have relished the idea.

Now for cricket. In the 1920s BNC was strong; in the 1930s very strong. Between 1919 and 1930, thirteen Brasenose men played twenty-three times against Cambridge, Three of them as captain—C. H. Knott (son of F. H. Knott, also captain of a pre-war Oxford eleven);[61] G. B. ('Ginger') Legge, later a fine England batsman; and G. T. S. Stevens, for many years the best amateur all-rounder in the country. Greville Stevens' career began almost as a story out of the *Boy's Own Paper*. In 1919, while still a sixth-former at UCS London, he was picked for the Gentlemen v. Players match and proceeded to smite England's best bowler, Cecil Parkin, straight into the Lord's pavilion for six. Tall—6 ft 3 in in immaculate flannels—and strikingly handsome, he was soon playing for Middlesex at the top of the table, and for England when the Australians were at last defeated in 1926 in the Ashes clincher at the Oval. In 1923 alone, he scored 182 for Oxford against the West Indies, and 115 against MCC. In the same year, with devilish googlies, he took 47 wickets for the University at an average of 17.12. Stevens was 'a complex and highly intelligent man', recalled I. A. R. Peebles; with 'a sharp wit' and a talent for 'calculated effrontery'.[62] It was in 1929 that Peebles himself came up to BNC from Glasgow Academy. In 1930 he had the mortifying experience of taking

---

[60] *Isis*, 27 Oct 1946, 24. 'Boobbyer sells [his dummy] with whole-hearted joy' (*Isis*, 4 Nov. 1949, 17). For Boobbyer's life and faith, see his memoirs, *Like a Cork out of a Bottle* (Arundel, 2004). For this 'golden age' of BNC rugby, see *Brazen Nose*, xxvii. 49–50. One of the 1948/9 team (P. W. Kininmonth) went on to captain Scotland (obit, *Daily Telegraph*, 11 Oct. 2007, 27).

[61] *Isis*, 30 May 1923, 3: photo.

[62] I. A. R. Peebles in *The Cricketer Winter Annual*, 1970–1. 'His one extravagance is in the matter of dress...such a figure as his must be the joy of the tailor...Whether in flannels, dinner jacket or dressing gown, his appearance is the pride of his College. His one vice is an all-consuming passion for ginger beer and ices' (*Isis*, 25 May 1921, 5–6: photo). He later did well in the City and eventually retired to Scotland. Obits, *Brazen Nose*, xv. 148–51 and *The Times*, 22 Sept. 1970, 12. For his sixteen appearances in the annual Gents v. Players match, see P. Warner, *Gentlemen versus Players, 1806–1949* (1950).

7 for 75 and 6 for 162 against Cambridge, and still seeing Oxford lose. But for both Middlesex and England his left-arm googly bowling was guaranteed to mystify most opponents: he got Bradman out for 14 at Old Trafford in 1930. Sadly, his career ended abruptly. He lost an eye in the Second World War, and he had to reinvent himself as a cricket journalist. There his only rival proved to be Sir Neville Cardus.[63]

In the 1930s BNC cricket had its greatest run since the 1870s. Between 1931 and 1939, eighteen Brasenose men played forty-three times against Cambridge, five of them in the role of captain. In 1934 there were six BNC men in the Oxford team at Lord's, in 1935 seven, and in 1937 six again. By comparison, 1936 and 1938 were failures: in those years there were only five. Some of the batting performances at this time were memorable. Chalk's century in 1934: 64 of his runs in boundaries; Grover's century in 1937: majestic as Maclaren; Kimpton's half-century in 1937: *Wisden* compared him to Macartney; and a whole run of innings by 'Mandy' Mitchell-Innes: in 1934–7 he piled up 3,319 runs for Oxford at an average of 47.41.[64]

Not all BNC's stars had been schoolboy prodigies. Sandy Singleton, for example, improved only very gradually, but in 1937 he took over 100 wickets and scored over 1,000 runs for Oxford.[65] And not all these heroes came from traditionally prestigious academies. Hart came from Strathallan, Evans from St Asaph, Kimpton from Melbourne GS, Young from KCS Wimbledon, Van der Bijl from the Diocesan College, Rondesbosch. The majority, however, did hail from predictable public schools: Winchester, Malvern, Shrewsbury, Uppingham, Charterhouse, Sedbergh, Cheltenham. They were not materially ambitious: quite a number became schoolmasters. Commercial pressures and media-driven sports events would soon make their altruism redundant. But for the moment they were almost the last of the gilded amateurs, lucky to play their matches before the outbreak of the Second World War—Desmond Eagar, for example. In 1938 he hit a glorious century in the Parks against the combined might of the Australians. At his death forty years later, after a lifetime in cricket administration, John Arlott published a wry valediction that might almost stand as an obituary for this entire BNC

---

[63] *Brazen Nose*, xvii., 126–8 (S. E. A. Green) and 234–5. For his BNC days—ploughing law Prelims—see Peebles's autobiography, *Spinner's Yarn* (1977), 60. In the summer of 1930 he set a record for an Oxford bowler: 70 wickets at an average of 18.15. See *Isis*, 15 Oct. 1930, 4: photo.

[64] *Isis*, 4 May 1938, 7: photo (J. N. Grover); 1 May 1935, 7: photo (N. S. Mitchell-Innes); 19 May 1938, 14: photo (R. C. M. Kimpton). Mitchell-Innes played for Somerset in 1931, aged 16, while still a schoolboy at Sedbergh; and for England against South Africa in 1935, while an undergraduate of 20 at BNC. From 1937 to 1954 he worked with the Sudan Civil Service ('blues ruling blacks'). See obit, *Daily Telegraph*, 30 Dec. 2006; *The Times*, 7 Feb. 2007.

[65] His tutor, Stanley Cohn, seems to have thought he had academic ability: he unsuccessfully bet Sonners £1 that Singleton would end up with a First or a Second (Betting Book, 15 Dec. 1936).

generation: 'he was . . . a happy, healthy, honest, selfless and utterly enthusiastic anachronism.'[66] Time was certainly running out. Sonners had managed to outplay Cradock. But some celestial umpire was about to remove the bails.

One last bump supper of the old type deserves to be recorded here. The date is 28 May 1930, and the diarist is Edgar Parsons, cox of the first Torpid.

> Great enthusiasm after the race. All the B.N.C. boys jumped in and swam to the boat, some with Champagne and Beer, and all shouting themselves hoarse. The crowd on the bank cheered enormously too [but] none were so happy as we! Head of the River—'Hoorah'. And imagine my relief [as cox]—no more starvation this term! There was a Bump Supper of course. At the photo almost the only sober fellows were the crew! We dined with the dons on a dais, not exactly serene, and looking down on a Hall that was one medley of shouting and drinking and food-throwing: never was such pandemonium. I enjoyed the dinner immensely: good Champagne, good Port, general hilarity and complimentary speeches etc. Afterwards a glorious bonfire went roaring up to heaven, and the college danced round it intoxicated, Dons and all. I . . . finally got to bed . . . almost completely sober at 2 o'clock. My bedclothes etc. had been carted down to help feed the bonfire, but I scraped some things together and slept soundly: no unpleasant effects this time. What a night!'[67]

On such occasions it is tempting to assume that the Pass men came into their own. The average number of Pass candidates in Oxford on the eve of the First World War was seldom far short of 400. In 1912–13 more than 20 per cent of Brasenose men were still 'aiming at a Pass Degree'; in 1913–14 more than 30 per cent. These were very high figures. Pass men had been almost eliminated by that date at Balliol, Corpus, New College, and St John's. But BNC was by no means alone. At Oriel, Merton, and Christ Church the numbers were equally high; and at Wadham and Keble the figures were higher still. After the end of the war the percentage of Pass men in the University as a whole began to decline, and continued to decline. The figures slide from 20 per cent in 1900 to 1909, to 10 per cent in 1930–5; or, on a different basis of calculation, from 7.6 per cent in 1925–9 to 3 per cent in 1935–9. Some candidates had simply been squeezed out by economic pressures; others migrated from the Pass Schools to the lower slopes of law Mods, PPE, and forestry. By 1945 the number of Pass candidates in the University was only 0.5 per cent of the total: that is 1 in 200.[68] A Pass degree was now

[66] Quoted from *The Guardian* in *Brazen Nose*, xvi/3. 34–5. See also *Isis*, 15 Feb. 1939, 7, 'Pinhead' Eagar: 'in 1936 Desmond abandoned the unequal contest [School Certificate] and entered B.N.C., to read Law Mods and Pass groups, or rather to study cricket, poker and golf: his future success is assured.'

[67] MPP 228 A1: Parsons Diary, 28 May 1930. There were no more bonfires after 1936.

[68] Mallet, *History of the University*, iii. 483 n. 2; Harrison (ed.), *HUO* viii. 57, 92, 116, 521. The figures for women are slightly lower: 5% (1900–09) and 1% (1930–5). For numbers of Pass men at BNC in 1912–13 see Asquith Commn., vol. ii, 1922, appendices, p. 184.

popularly assumed to be a mere fig-leaf for sport. BNC was unusual in continuing to recruit quite a number of Pass men even after the Second World War.

But mention of Pass men involves several caveats. Most of the leading sportsmen at BNC between the wars did in fact read for an Honours degree, even if they scarcely read very hard. And the link between Pass degrees and sport was never absolute. Not all Brasenose Pass men, for example, played rugby. And not all rugger men read Pass degrees. Quite a number of BNC rugger blues between the wars—Neser, Peacock, and Obolensky come to mind—followed Honours courses and to good effect. But Oxford rugby did depend on a steady stream of players who were as professional in their commitment—and as international in their standards—as amateurs could possibly be. A good many of these gravitated towards Brasenose. In thirty years, 1919–49, there were twenty-five official rugby Varsity matches, and BNC produced thirty-five blues, many of whom played on several occasions. They were certainly not 'reading men'. To a certain extent the same held true for cricket and soccer. Each year the profiles of BNC's *Isis* Idols indicated their heroes' order of priorities. James Richardson (rugby three-quarter), 'toying with…Law…in his spare moments'; Norman Strong (rugby scrum-half): 'his zeal for study can be imagined by the fact that he took Responsions time and time again.'[69] 'Uncle' Harlow (soccer goalie): 'he immediately asserted his superiority by almost defeating Law Prelims and Divinity Mods on several occasions'.[70] Or 'Ginger' Legge (captain of cricket in Brasenose and the University): 'He passed Mods after very few attempts. The shock unhinged him…His 30/98 Vauxhall is the terror of the roads.'[71] Or finally—last of this group of reluctant students—'Sandy' Singleton, a freshman cricket blue: 'His first attack on Schools was repulsed by the Moderators, but he counter-attacked and routed them without needing to retire to consolidate his forces.'[72] As the 1920s gave way to the 1930s, such levity becomes rarer. The approach of another world war seems to have concentrated minds wonderfully. Even BNC began to buckle down to study. 'Throughout Oxford', noted *Isis* in May 1938, 'may be heard the high-pitched whine of brazen noses applied firmly to the grindstone.'[73]

Did this change of emphasis in the University—an increasing seriousness as the 1930s progressed—have much effect on BNC? Compare two snapshots: Brasenose in 1923 and Brasenose in 1937.

---

[69] *Isis*, 15 Oct. 1924, 7–8: photo; ibid. 21 Jan. 1925, 9–10: photo.
[70] Ibid. 25 Nov. 1925, 7: photo.
[71] Ibid. 28 Apr. 1926, 25: photo.
[72] Ibid. 6 May 1936, 7: photo.
[73] Ibid. 4 May 1938, 9.

The intake for 1923 comprised 17 scholars or exhibitioners (including 4 Rhodes Scholars) and 30 commoners (including 3 from abroad). All the UK entrants—except for 5 Hulme Scholars—came from well-established public schools. And the results were much as one might expect: roughly half the scholars or exhibitioners got Firsts; a quarter of the commoners were blues or near blues. Over the next fifteen years these proportions did not vary greatly. But by the end of the 1930s we can spot a few shifts of emphasis.

In October 1937—taking this time a four-year snapshot of members 'on the books'—there were 27 graduates, mostly older lawyers and medics, including 6 Senior Hulme Scholars. There were 201 undergraduates, that is 74 scholars or exhibitioners and 127 commoners. The scholars and exhibitioners included 8 Rhodes Scholars; 7 Somerset Scholars, all but one from Manchester Grammar School; 16 Hulme Exhibitioners, mostly from unfashionable northern schools; 6 sporting Heath Harrison Exhibitioners (3 from Winchester, one each from Charterhouse, Rugby, and Shrewsbury); and 27 open scholars: 4 of these had already achieved Firsts and several more would soon do so, including a future Principal (Barry Nicholas) and a future Fellow of All Souls (Peter Fraser). The commoners were a more varied group. They included an Estonian, 2 Russians, 4 Americans, a Lebanese, 5 Australians, 5 Indians, a Chinese, a German, 2 South Africans, an Argentinian, 2 Egyptians, a Serbian, and a New Zealander. Sonners' network of schoolmasters was clearly extensive. But in another way it was markedly restrictive. Among the 127 commoners in the 1937 list, there were only 2 Etonians and 2 Wykehamists, and scarcely half a dozen grammar schoolboys. The vast bulk of this four-year intake of commoners came from well-established but unglamorous public schools: Uppingham, Marlborough, Lancing, Malvern, for example. Among the 74 scholars and exhibitioners there was slightly more variation: the Heath Harrison Exhibitions guaranteed a sprinkling from top public schools, and the open scholarships ensured a leavening intake from provincial grammar schools and independent London day schools. But all in all, recruitment was distinctly uniform. Brasenose remained neither aristocratic nor proletarian, but essentially middle class. In this, Brasenose was little different from the majority of colleges. On the outbreak of the Second World War, 62 per cent of male undergraduates in Oxford came from independent schools. That was not surprising: the cost of a degree was still about £250 p.a.[74]

Such homogeneity obviously made the creation of a collegiate ethos a good deal easier. But then BNC had long been known for its sense of unity. Unlike

[74] Harrison, in *HUO* viii. 91, 94. For Sir Heath Harrison, Bt.—a Liverpool shipowner—and the Heath Harrison Scholarships and Exhibitions, see *Oxford Mag.* 24 May 1934, 750 (C.H.S.) and *The Times*, 17 May 1934, p. 18 (Stallybrass).

Trinity, for example, it recruited across national and racial boundaries. Among the freshmen lawyers of 1929 was Mohammad Khattak, one of the future leaders of Pakistan. One of three law Firsts in 1930 was an Afghan, a future ambassador: Abbas Khaleeli. Nor was there a total division between hearties and reading men. Scholars and commoners did not—as in some colleges— dine at separate tables. Breakfast now tended to be eaten collectively, in hall. There was no tradition of sconcing: surprising in such a noisy place. And if there was bullying it tended to be reserved for 'aesthetic' interlopers from other colleges. BNC was big enough to encompass all sorts of people—in the 1920s, for example, T. G. Cowling, a Baptist boy from Walthamstow Grammar. He would end up as a Royal Society astrophysicist. Or in the 1930s Paul Dehn, campest of film critics, son of a Jewish cotton merchant from Manchester: he would live to write the screenplay for *Goldfinger*. Partly through sporting tradition, partly through accidents of personality, inter-war Brasenose managed to maintain a characteristic spirit, reinforced—in Sonners's memorable phrase—by 'an overmastering power of assimilation'. Of course this process had a distinctly boarding-school flavour. But in the years after the First World War its assimilative power was particularly necessary: in 1919, 85 per cent of Oxford undergraduates were ex-servicemen.[75]

One of those who came up after service in the Great War was a young Welsh novelist named Charles Morgan. His presence reminds us that BNC was not entirely hearty. His father, a successful civil engineer, had sent him to Osborne and Dartmouth as preparation for a career in the Royal Navy. As a captured officer he spent much of the war interned in the Castle of Rosendaal in the Netherlands. Conditions were civilized. There were books in the library and lakes in the park. There was cosmopolitan company, and there was 'infinite time': 'freedom', he recalled, 'such as I had never known before'.[76] Morgan entered Rosendaal as a prisoner of war; he emerged a prisoner of his own conscience. Back in England on parole, he threw himself—emotionally at least—into the cause of conscientious objection. 'What *are* we fighting for?' he writes to a Quaker friend in November 1917; 'not for freedom, surely, not for peace. All that has been forgotten... Now it's revenge, and a little money, and a little territory.' British patriotism, he came to believe, was being used not as a guarantee of liberty but as an

---

[75] *Brazen Nose*, ix. 323. Recalling 1919, Charles Groves noted that 'silly young aesthetes were well and truly de-bagged—a practise I regret to hear only Brasenose has the good sense to continue'. 'Cubist Trousers' were a particular object of derision (*Isis*, 24 Nov. 1926, 5). For Cowling and Dehn, see *ODNB*. A brief memoir by Cowling deals with Oxford maths in the 1920s (*Brazen Nose*, xxvii. 51–2).

[76] *Selected Letters of Charles Morgan*, ed. E. Lewis (1967), 9.

instrument of collective self-interest. And he sensed that the system in which
he had been brought up was integral to this process of moral corruption.
'Once I thought that with patience we might break up the public school
system and educate men out of their stiff collars. But there comes a time
when education is useless. You can't train a mad dog. You can only kill
him. . . . By tradition and upbringing I am a Tory: I care enormously for peace:
I hate the idea of adding the suffering of revolution to the suffering of war.
But . . . if no constitutional and peaceful means can rid us of this yoke, then—
cost what it may—we must save our children's children.'[77]

It was during this period of frustration—unable to help the war or hinder
it—that Morgan wrote his first, and most explosive novel: *The Gunroom*
(1919). Its exposé of brutality below decks caused official embarrassment,
and it was quietly withdrawn by the publishers. Its appearance, however,
coincided exactly with its author's arrival at BNC. And it did his Oxford
career no harm at all. With charm and good looks, and a gift for histrionics,
he cut a dash at the Union. 'The rivers of imagination', he once announced,
'are choked with the wreckage of old men's illusions.' Posing in flamboyant
hat and cape, he found an obvious niche as President of OUDS. In his first
year he produced Hardy's epic play *The Dynasts*. It had a cast of 104. Then
came *As You Like It* and *Antony and Cleopatra*. By February 1921 he was an *Isis*
Idol. And he revelled in controversy: 'our Idol is never really happy unless he
is heckled.'[78] By 1922 he was reviewing plays for *The Times*. His future was
assured.

On the face of it, Morgan was an aesthete. When a younger Brasenose
man, Vernon Barlow, revived the Ingoldsby Club to talk *inter alia* about
'Beauty and Culture', it was all too much for the hearties. They threatened
to break up the first meeting. Morgan 'organised a bodyguard of like-minded
friends, who quietly took their places round the room and showed the
opposition that they too meant business. When Barlow thanked him,
[Morgan] replied briefly, "I always fight for liberty. If we can't get it at
Oxford, what's the use of anything?" '[79] Not for nothing was he a member of
Oxford's New Reform Club. And there were other distractions too.

---

[77] *Selected Letters of Charles Morgan*, ed. E. Lewis (1967), 46–7: to Mrs Robert Mennell, 15
Nov. 1917. When it came to the Second World War, Morgan had no doubts: '[there must be]
no compromise on the war. However great the losses, we can face them' (ibid. 154: to H. Morgan, 9
Oct. 1940). Morgan thought of himself as 'a revolutionary conservative'; never a socialist (ibid.
175: to R. Hart-Davis, 29 Mar. 1946 and 177: to J. Greaves, 23 Nov. 1946). His study of history
at Oxford convinced him that 'England was never a better or a happier place than in the early
years of Charles I' (ibid. 189: to L. Bonnerot, 28 Dec. 1948).
[78] *Isis*, 10 Feb. 1921, 3–4: photo. Morgan's rooms were II, 3 in 1919–20. His Brasenose friend
Gordon Alchin was also a figure in OUDS (ibid. 18: photo). He followed him on to *The Times*.
[79] *Letters of Charles Morgan*, ed. Lewis, 12–13.

A passionate engagement to Mary Mond—heiress to a chemical fortune—was at this time begun and broken off. He did not achieve his expected First in history; and his second novel, *My Name is Legion* (1925), mostly written while still a student, turned out to be chaotic: the product of 'profound personal bliss and misery'.[80]

But unlike most Oxford aesthetes in the 1920s, Morgan was by instinct a professional. 'As an undergraduate', noted Carola Oman, he had all the marks of 'a naval officer—organisation first class'. And that conflicted with his reputation as a theatrical boulevardier. His later novels did well. *The Fountain* (1932) sold 144,000 copies. But his high-flown diction came to be more appreciated in France than in England. He was in fact a passionate Francophile. France, he believed, is 'the heart that pumps the blood of civilisation'. In 1949 he was elected Membre de l'Institut de France. In England, however, he was never more than Galsworthy on stilts. Since his death in 1958 his celebrity has faded. But for those with an ear for elegance and an eye for the intuitive phrase, Morgan's writing retains a perennial charm.[81]

Of course, Morgan was by no means typical. In 1919 there was an unspoken agreement among most undergraduates to shake off the war and start afresh. Maurice Bowra, for example, back from the Western Front, found common cause with younger men straight from school: 'we wished to forget the war, [and] they did not wish to hear about it.' The result was a new escapism, an unprecedented cult of indulgence.[82] And the extravagance of the 'Roaring Twenties' lasted well into the 1930s. During the Slump, Oxford finances were not too badly hit. The holdings of most colleges were in land or gilts rather than equities. The Great Crash was only a minor inconvenience. The University's official *Report* for 1931–2, put it like this:

Contrary to general expectation . . . the economic crisis and the departure of Great Britain from the gold standard . . . did not materially affect the number of under-graduates in residence . . . But economic pressure left its mark . . . the consumption of

---

[80] Ibid. 96: to L. Bonnerot, 1 Mar. 1932.

[81] *ODNB*; *Who Was Who*; *Brazen Nose*, xi. 88–91; *Times Lit. Supp.* 1 Jan. 1960, 8, reviewing H. C. Duffin, *The Novels and Plays of Charles Morgan* (1959). Virginia Woolf disliked his 'damnable pretence of fine writing', and threw *The Fountain* 'out of the window half read' (*Letters*, ed. N. Nicolson, v (1979), no. 2537 to Hugh Walpole, 28 Feb. [1932], 25). She thought him 'a well meaning cultivated egoist', and mocked his writing routine: 'Bed at 2, after the play. Breakfast at 9 in bed; writes novels from 4 to 7. So it goes on, & The Fountain is the result' (*Diary*, iv (1931–5), ed. A. O. Bell and A. McNeillie (1983), 293: 30 Mar. 1935). Morgan's first play, *The Flashing Stream* (1938), was written as a starring role for his great amour, Margaret Rawlings (*ODNB*). He left over £100,000. He was twice blackballed at the Athenaeum.

[82] M. Bowra, *Memories, 1898–1939* (1966), 93. 'I do not suppose that there has ever been a time in Oxford's history when its undergraduates were so wholly indifferent about their degrees' (C. Hollis, *Along the Road to Frome* (1958), 65).

beer and spirits fell [by] about half... and the only drink to be found in the normal undergraduate's room was sherry... But the most obvious effect of the crisis... was the absence in 1932 of College balls and dances and bump-suppers.[83]

All true: even Brasenose cancelled its summer ball. But the University as a whole carried on well enough. The pound stayed strong. Dons lived comfortably on £600 to £1,000 p.a.[84] And the immediate post-war generation of undergraduates took full advantage of their luck. None more so than one particular undergraduate, a fey young man at Brasenose named Alastair Hugh Graham.

It was probably in the summer of 1923 that the affair between Evelyn Waugh and Alastair Graham began.[85] At that time Waugh was in his second year at Hertford College, reading history. He had visited Brasenose before. He had been there, for example, the previous May.

I went the other day to coffee with some men in B.N.C. to hear an American revivalist of great transatlantic fame. I thought he was dangerously near converting me to righteousness but like Pharaoh, I steeled my heart. There were a queer lot there—pretty typical of Oxford. A logical and fierce conventionalist from Worcester, a delightful Indian [M. Sirdar] with great wondering faun eyes full of superstition and simplicity from B.N.C., a well bred Roman Catholic and a few deep-thinking, pipe-sucking Christians.[86]

Alastair Graham was rather different. His father was a baronet, a Graham of Netherby. His mother had been born Jessie Low, daughter of a merchant who emigrated from Scotland to Savannah, Georgia, and there made a fortune out of cotton. That fortune—three-quarters of a million pounds, no less—was currently in process of dissipation by Jessie's brother Willie. Dissipation proved to be the operative word: it was through Willie Low that Alastair and Evelyn would eventually enter the glamorous demi-monde of Rosa Lewis' Cavendish Hotel in London.

As a Brasenose freshman, Alastair Graham must have been a lonely figure. At 15 he left Wellington under a cloud; at 17 he lost his father; at 18 he escaped from his dominant mother, and arrived at Oxford bookish, dreamy, sensual, and rich.

[83] *OU Report for the Year,* 1931–32, 44. All colleges agreed to a 'temporary abolition' of balls and bump suppers (V-P's Reg. 20 Jan. 1932, fo. 126).

[84] When first appointed to a Lectureship in Law in 1911, Stallybrass received £100 p.a. (V-P's Reg. 7 July 1911, fo. 246). To this, of course, should be added his stipend and privileges as Fellow. In 1923 he valued his possessions, for insurance purposes, as follows: 'Books £850; Furniture £160; Clothes £75; Silver £30; Pictures £20... Say £1,150' (Stallybrass file: 21 Dec. 1923).

[85] Graham spent Christmas 1923 with the Waughs at Underhill, Hampstead (S. Hastings, *Evelyn Waugh* (1994), 107). Thereafter Waugh was a frequent visitor to the grander Graham household at Barford, Warwicks. In 1923 both Graham and Waugh were members of the Railway Club (H. Lloyd-Jones (ed.), *Maurice Bowra: A Celebration* (1974), 120–1: 28 Nov. 1923).

[86] Waugh to Dudley Carew, [31 May 1922], *Letters of Evelyn Waugh,* ed. M. Amory (1980), 11.

Waugh found him irresistible. In Alastair Graham he identified his own Sebastian.[87] He was 'the friend of my heart', he later recalled; 'for two or three years we were inseparable'.[88] Now at Brasenose any aesthete learned quickly to keep a low profile. John Betjeman used to affect a limp whenever he entered the college, hoping in this way to arouse the pity of the hearties. Nevertheless, it was in Brasenose, in the very citadel of muscularity, that aestheticism achieved its definitive literary image. Alastair Graham never had rooms in college. He lodged at 22 the High, next door to All Saints Church.[89]. There he could evade the Bollinger Club—Waugh's combination of the Phoenix and the Strollers[90]—and enjoy without restriction the peripheral world of the *jeunesse dorée*. His relationship with BNC was thus semi-detached. But Brasenose was his official designation: there *Brideshead Revisited* was born.

Sometime in May 1923—that at least is the probable date—Waugh received the following letter from Graham, accompanied by a photograph of the sender *au naturel*.

I have found the ideal way to drink Burgundy. You must take a peach and peel it, and put it in a finger bowl, and pour the Burgundy over it. The flavour is exquisite. And the peach seems to exaggerate that delightful happy seraglio contentedness that old wine evokes.... An old French lady taught it to me, who has a wonderful cellar at Lavalles.

Soon afterwards came a more specific invitation: 'Will you come and drink with me somewhere on Saturday? If it is a nice day we might carry some bottles into a wood or some bucolic place, and drink like Horace...'[91]

---

[87] In the MS of *Brideshead*, Waugh occasionally substitutes the name Alastair for Sebastian (Hastings, *Waugh*, 108 n. 16). Graham took little part in University life, except as a member of OUDS. By 1924 there were a dozen Brasenose members of OUDS. In 1925 W. S. Adams and R. van den Bergh played minor parts in Ibsen's *Peer Gynt*, as did N. Ker Lindsay in Mrs Patrick Campbell's *The Fantasticks*; C. T. Plumb translated *The Two Pierrots* for its first public performance in England in dresses of the 'Watteau' style (*Oxford Mag.* 12 Feb. 1925, 271–3 and 18 June 1925, 558–9).

[88] E. Waugh, *A Little Learning* (1964), 192.

[89] He paid £2 per week for a bedroom and shared sitting room; 1*s.* per day for baths; 3*s.* per week for lighting; 12*s.* per week for a dozen scuttles of coal; and 2*s.* per day for breakfast. Lunch, tea, and dinner were to be taken in college (MEM 2J1: Graham, A. H.: Jessie Low to Wace, 7 Oct. 1922).

[90] Around 1884 the Authentics—cricket-playing pupils of a crammer named Bell of Limpsfield—asked permission to adopt the name 'Bollinger'. This was refused, though the firm presented the applicants with two dozen bottles as a gesture of goodwill. Stallybrass was not unacquainted with the locality: his mother was the daughter of W. H. Teulon of Limpsfield. From 1923 onwards the Limpsfield Strollers—captained by Sonners in 1924–35—revived the amateur spirit of the original 'Tics. The name 'Limpsfield' was dropped in 1933. 'The Bollinger' thus became the ultimate ancestor of 'The Strollers' (PRI 25, I 3/2: W. T. S. Stallybrass, *The Oxford Colleges and the Oxford Authentics, no 1, B.N.C.* (Oxford, 1926), 6–9; Col. 1/A 1: Estridge, 'The Strollers', [*c.*1950], 1).

[91] BL, Add. MS 81057, fos. 128–9 and fo. 130 (photo): Graham to Waugh [n.d., probably May 1923]; 81057, fos. 132–3 [1925]; fos. 134–6 [1925]. See also Hastings, *Waugh*, 108.

In Oxford bags and polo jumpers; in silks from Sulka and hats from Hall's; motoring across the countryside, to Cotswold churchyards and village hostelries, Alastair and Evelyn contrived to create a private world within a private world. Not for them the tutorial grind and Boat Club ritual, the Charleston and the Boston Two-Step. At the Hypocrites Club—with Harold Acton and Robert Byron—they parodied proctorial edicts: 'Gentlemen may prance but not dance.' At the George—the 'Georgeoisie' of John Betjeman and Maurice Bowra, of Brian Howard and Cyril Connolly—they dined to the throb of 'Blackbird' tunes and toyed with goblets of crème de menthe.

It was not a phase that lasted long. Alastair ploughed Mods, and went down at the start of his second year.[92] Evelyn did manage a Third in history, then woke to find himself penniless. But from various refuges, in schools, in clubs, in country houses, they continued their alcoholic odyssey for several years.

Oh Nina, what a lot of parties...Masked parties, Savage parties, Victorian parties, Greek parties, Wild West parties, Russian parties, Circus parties, parties where one had to dress as somebody else, almost naked parties in St. John's Wood, parties in flats and studios and houses and ships and hotels and night clubs, in windmills and swimming-baths, tea parties at school where one ate muffins and meringues and tinned crab, parties at Oxford where one drank brown sherry and smoked Turkish cigarettes, dull dances in London and comic dances in Scotland and disgusting dances in Paris—all that succession and repetition of massed humanity...Those vile bodies...[93]

No wonder Alastair became reclusive; no wonder Evelyn destroyed his Oxford diary.

Behind the posing, beyond the ferocious drinking, both men seem to have been lonely and uncertain. Alastair went over to Rome in 1924, Evelyn in 1930.[94] Evelyn married, then married again; finding his destiny in writing. Alastair preferred to travel the world. He especially enjoyed Athens in May 1926, the very month of the British General Strike. 'Most of [the Greek boys] are mad', he wrote to Claude Cockburn, 'and the rest are homosexual nymphomaniacs, but they all have a certain amount of charm.'[95] By 1928

[92] His mother had trusted that her son would 'fit in well and be a credit' to BNC. After he was sent down, she vainly hoped to see him 'settling down and working' at the Bartlett School of Architecture, London (Graham File: Jessie Low to Wace, 6 Nov. 1923). Any comments by his tutor, Michael Holroyd, do not seem to have survived.

[93] E. Waugh, *Vile Bodies* (1930), ch. viii. Permission to film the opening sequences of *Decline and Fall* at BNC was later refused (V-P's Reg. 11 Aug. 1965, fo. 65).

[94] Hastings, *Waugh*, 114, 223–30.

[95] Quoted in J. Knox, *Robert Byron* (2004), 101. In August 1926 he visited Mount Athos with Robert Byron and David Talbot-Rice. His great-grandfather, the 14th Duke of Somerset, had travelled the Levant in the 1840s, with a shotgun under one arm and a copy of Homer under the other (ibid.).

he was in Athens again, as an unpaid attaché at the English Embassy; the following year he transferred to Cairo; three years later his appointment was terminated.[96] That was the end of his career. For the next half-century he rusticated in Wales, an exiled Sebastian on the coast of Cardiganshire.[97] When *Brideshead* eventually appeared in 1945, its Brasenose origins had been wholly forgotten. And Brasenose itself, like the 'modern Arcadia' that Waugh set out to chronicle, was spinning fast towards irreversible change.

It was fun while it lasted: 'luncheons, luncheons all the way...'[98] Brian Howard's memoirs catch the moment only too well. Breakfast in Beaumont Street with Robert Byron, 'enshrined in a storm of Victorian whatnots'; coffee and epigrams with Maurice Bowra 'in his gay white rooms at Wadham'; a pre-prandial drink with Harold Acton: 'that sculptured voice, the apotheosis of style'; and then a long, slow lunch at Christ Church—the serious business of the day—hosted by William Acton.

From the soup, agog with every condiment (that extraordinary, bloodlike, soup heavy with eggs, and, sometimes magical potions) to the cigars, one could ask for no more splendid entertainment. Linens embroidered in Russia clothed the table, over which marched an army of glasses, of every size, shape and colour. On the bursting sideboard a hundred bottles displayed their invitations in as many languages. The fainting scout, supported by half-a-dozen distracted boys, tottered in and out with flagon after platter. Once... the company was so great that the Lobster Newburg had to be conveyed in a dustbin. At another time a small hipbath was utilised as a punch-bowl. In a brocaded corner, a gramophone would be singing a blues. Deployed over the walls in painted lanterns, electricity would supplement the light of day, since the number of guests would often shut out the sun...[99]

'Silly young man', snorted 'Colonel' Kolkhorst, 'he's been gilding our dreaming spires.'[100]

Behind all this guilt and gingerbread lay a very different Oxford: an Oxford of scholarship and plain endeavour; a place where books were studied rather than displayed.

[96] *Foreign Office List* (1928–31). For Graham in Cairo and Alexandria ('Gomorrah-on-Sea'), see BL Add. MS 71614, fos. 1, 14–16, 26, 42–54.

[97] At Wern Newydd, New Quay, Cardiganshire; after his mother's death in 1934 (BL Add. MS 71614, fo. 49: Graham to [Lady Harrod], 7 Apr. 1934). It was Graham who printed and published Waugh's first separate publication, *The Pre-Raphaelite Brotherhood* (1926).

[98] J. Betjeman, *Summoned by Bells* (1960; 1976), 33.

[99] B. Howard, in *Cherwell*, 25 June 1927; reprinted in M.-J. Lancaster (ed.), *Brian Howard: Portrait of a Failure* (1968), 186–7.

[100] Quoted ibid. 201. George Kolkhorst was University Lecturer in Spanish. Compare Harold Acton's *Memoirs of an Aesthete* (1948) with one contemporary polemic, T. Greenidge's *Degenerate Oxford?* (1930), and two parodies of Oxford in the 1920s: Beverley Nicholls's *Patchwork* (1921) and Cyril Connolly's *Where Engels Fears to Tread* [*c*.1923].

The testimony of one other Brasenose undergraduate—an exact contemporary of Alastair Graham—certainly suggests a different picture. The student's name was Edward Atiyah, father of the future Sir Michael Atiyah, President of the Royal Society.

Edward Atiyah was a Syrian Christian, born in the Lebanon and educated in Egypt. He arrived in Oxford in October 1923. One of his schoolfellows from Alexandria—an Egyptian Muslim called Amin Osman—was already at BNC: he was secretary of the soccer club. No doubt that gave young Atiyah an advantage. But then, unlike Trinity, Brasenose had never been an all-white college. In any case Atiyah brought with him a recommendation from Lord Allenby, the High Commissioner for Egypt.[101] And he was clearly a precocious student. Since childhood, he recalled, 'the name of Oxford [had been] for me a symbol of culture and refinement'. Now, 'after long years of waiting and yearning and dreaming the pilgrim had arrived at the shrine of his gods'. His first stop had been Westminster Abbey, there to muse on the ashes of the great. Then Oxford itself: the Mecca of western culture, 'its grey walls clothed in the dignity of centuries'. But first, there was one last hurdle: Responsions. Atiyah's French presented no problem; he even assisted the other two candidates. But at the viva he had to be tactically modest: he knew all about the English love of understatement. 'Well, Mr. A... A... Atiyah', stuttered Principal Sampson (pl. 67), 'wwwwwwww we aaaaaaa... cccc... cept you wwwwwww... without any h... h... hhhhhesitation.' 'In an exhultation of fulfilment long delayed I walked about the college looking proprietorially at the grey walls, at the grey October sky. The grey sky was the sky of England; the grey walls the walls of an Oxford College, and I was there, among those walls and under that sky, for at least three years, to take my share in the cultural heritage of the West.'[102]

Three days later term began, and this diminutive Arab boy encountered his fellow students for the first time. 'There was a rush of taxis in the High, and the Lodge was crowded with trunks and young men in plus-fours... These undergraduates were mostly giants. I had never before been thrown into such a massed company of six-footers. I felt like a hack among race horses.'[103] On his first night in hall, he sat next to a physicist, 'a very shy, pink-faced but good looking boy with intelligent but timid blue eyes, who wore a scholar's gown. His name was Michael de Selincourt and he was the son of Ernest de Selincourt, the well-known critic and Professor of Poetry... Yes, this was

[101] E. Atiyah, *An Arab Tells his Story* (1946), 83. As Sir Amin Osman Pasha, 'Os' later became a key figure in the Egyptian government and architect of the 1937 Anglo-Egyptian Treaty. He was assassinated in Cairo on 6 Jan. 1946 (*The Times*, 7 Jan. 1946, 4, 7). For Trinity's policy on recruitment, see C. Hopkins, *Trinity* (2005), 344.

[102] Atiyah, *An Arab Tells his Story*, 90–1.

[103] Ibid. 92.

Oxford life: the charm of intellectual companionship ... the midnight glow of friendly fires. The dignity of learning ... ' And then came his first sight of the Oxford Union, 'that august Parliament of youth'. The Union's most gifted orator turned out to be 'an Indian called Bandaranaike'. That gave Atiyah confidence. In due course he spoke out himself, and spoke well. Before long he was quite at home. Within months of his arrival he was visiting Florence with a Brasenose scholar from Manchester Grammar School. His new friend's name was John Scragg, and he was reading PPE.

Atiyah had a little money, Scragg had none at all. But with £10 from a kindly uncle Atiyah was able to pay for both their rail fares, third class. His own annual allowance—apart from a college scholarship—was £250.[104] For the first two terms he endured dismal lodgings in St John Street. Then he moved into a pair of attic rooms—'the cheapest set ... in College'—on staircase VII. These he managed to redecorate with souvenirs from Florence.

I had the walls repapered and the furniture re-covered. I bought an extra chair and lampshades, and I succeeded in wheedling a new rug out of the Bursar. From home I had brought with me a leopard skin which I spread over my book case, and on that was installed a small bust of Dante imported from Florence. My Michelangelo and Leonardo prints were then suitably arranged round the walls; and in the towering shadow of the Radcliffe Camera I sat for the first time in a room of my creation, and found it good. It was a small room, and when the fire blazed in front of the settee throwing its glow on the near walls, it looked very warm and cosy and friendly ... I loved the English winter.[105]

Scragg introduced Atiyah to the Pater Society; and at his very first meeting the visiting speaker was a real Brasenose author, Charles Morgan. Before long BNC's shy Arab not only felt at home; he had fallen in love with a girl called Jean Levens, sister of a Balliol friend who lodged not far away in Observatory Street. She would soon become Mrs Atiyah.

Meanwhile, there was the little matter of History Schools. Atiyah's tutor, G. H. Wakeling (pl. 67)—'dear old Wakkers'—had been kind to him from the start. 'When the first lecture was over he waited for me in the [hall] passage, and asked me if I had been able to follow comfortably (I had), if he had been slow enough for me (he had).' But three years later, in the Examination Schools, there came the day of reckoning.

---

[104] Ibid. 99, 126. That meant he was comfortably off. Like Osman, Atiyah had to pay a higher rate of Caution Money (£40; as against Scragg's £5). See A 3. 18: Caution Money Repayments. His battels in spring 1924 were running at more than £58 per term (University Dues £1 10s.; Room Charge £10; Tuition Fees £10; Establishment Charge £6; Subscriptions £2 14s. 8d.; Buttery £1 16s. 2d.; Kitchen £9 13s. 3d.; Stores £8 12s. 3d.; Coals 2s. 7d.; Laundress £1 13s. 10d.; Gate Fines 17s.; Damage 3s.). See B.F. 13 D 1/5: Pupils Battels. All these sums were no more than average, according to Asquith Commn., vol. ii, appendices, pp. 29, 190.

[105] Atiyah, *An Arab Tells his Story*, 104, 107.

I walked down the 'High' with hundreds of others in cap and gown and white tie. . . . We walked into the judgement hall, sat down and wrote feverishly, came out and walked in again. And so 'Schools' week rushed past, crammed with the history of the ages. For seven days three hundred young men and women sat there writing eagerly, anxiously, with the shades of Alfred and Aristotle, and Nelson and Napoleon, and the endless Edwards and Henrys, and the Whigs and Tories, and the Burghers of London and the Sansculottes, and Lord Beaconsfield bringing back peace with honour, and George the Third's mother saying 'George be a king' and Queen Victoria unamused, and Mr. Dunning attacking the Crown and Burke declaiming on America, and Lord Palmerston shaking Europe to protect a Portuguese gentleman in Greece, and a thousand other minor ghosts all stalking invisibly along the silent corridors in a confused and confusing pageant . . . My viva, when it came, proved a very perfunctory affair . . . Two days later the results were announced on the board. Jean and I went down to see them. We elbowed our way through the seething crowd. My name with a big bold A. headed the Second Class. On our way out we met [Wakeling] striding in. 'Well?' he asked. I told him. He gave me a comforting pat on the back. 'My fault', he said, 'not yours'.[106]

That last remark was probably true. BNC's examination record between the two world wars—with the notable exception of law—can only be described as dismal.

Between 1894 and 1924 results in Schools had been by no means contemptible. In Finals the scores were: twenty-five Firsts in Lit. Hum.; twelve in modern history; twelve more in jurisprudence and BCL; nine in maths, four each in chemistry and physics, three in engineering, two in physiology, and one each in English and zoology. That was well behind Balliol and Corpus, New College and Queen's; but it was a respectable middle-of-the-table performance. In 1925 Brasenose did better still: six Firsts in classical Mods—equalling New College and outscoring Balliol—as well as two in maths Mods, plus the Junior and Senior Mathematical Prizes, and a Prize Fellowship in Law at All Souls. Not at all bad for a sporting college with perhaps a quarter of its members reading Pass degrees. The real decline came after that. From 1926 to 1932 there were never more than four Firsts a year in Finals, in all subjects; and over the same six years, never more than four in Mods. This at a time when leading colleges were regularly clocking up four or five times that number. During the same period the number of blues rose steadily: from 15 in 1928–9 to 26 in 1929–30; from 24 in 1930–1 to 30 in 1931–2 and 32 in 1932–3.[107] The culture of BNC at this time can hardly have been favourable to study. Private coaching had largely disappeared; but

---

[106] Atiyah, *An Arab Tells his Story*, 92, 117. Atiyah died in 1964, while debating Arab–Israeli relations at the Oxford Union. See *The Times*, 29 Oct. 1964, p. 15; *Brazen Nose*, xiv/1. 38–40.
[107] *Brazen Nose*, iv. 9 and x. 149.

private reading must have been equally rare. 'Sporting one's Oak', recalled R. H. Lloyd-Jones, 'would have been considered eccentric at Brasenose.'[108]

The next six years, 1933–9, were nearly as bad: never more than six Firsts in Finals in any one year, and never more than five in Mods. Only the results in law lent an air of plausibility to the record. Under Stallybrass and Waldock, teaching in law was clearly effective. At its peak, in 1937–9, seven out of thirteen Firsts in the Law School came from BNC, and three out of nine in BCL. Between the two world wars, in fact, Brasenose collected about one-sixth of all Firsts in jurisprudence and BCL. And several of these—for example V. H. Neser in 1920; R. W. G. Holdsworth (pl. 85) in 1934—more than fulfilled the BNC ideal, by combining athletic skill with academic excellence.

> Three years of Brasenose Beer had built the stamina
> That bore them past the beetle-browed examiner.[109]

And before damning Brasenose results as a whole, it is worth noting that in 1949—right at the end of the Stallybrass era—BNC's tally of only two Firsts, though very much worse than Balliol, Magdalen, or New College, was no worse than Pembroke, Trinity, or Worcester, and actually better than Hertford, Keble, and Merton.

In sciences the number of candidates—as in most other colleges—was still very small. The first holders of the new chair in Engineering Science—Frewin Jenkin, FRS, and R. V. Southwell, FRS—brought personal lustre to the SCR.[110] But their impact on college teaching cannot have been great. In maths there was a limited, but regular, stream of candidates. Between 1925 and 1939, the majority of years could show a Brasenose First in maths Finals; in 1939 there were no less than three in Mods. Such successes, however, seem to have been won in spite of, rather than because of, tuition by I. O. Griffith.[111] And in modern history BNC's

---

[108] Accession 129: R. H. Lloyd-Jones to B. Harrison, May 1981. For the rarity of private coaching at this date, see Asquith Commn., vol. ii, appendices, p. 196.

[109] Ale Verse, 1939 (*Brazen Nose*, vi. 425). Waldock succeeded Leif Egeland as Fellow in Law in 1930 (Egeland, *Bridges of Understanding*, 43–4). In 1947 he succeeded J. L. Brierly, another BNC lawyer, as Chichele Professor of International Law (*Brazen Nose*, xvii. 218–21). Styler noted his 'considerable gifts and limited vision' (Styler Tapes).

[110] For Jenkin see *Brazen Nose*, v. 67 and vii. 69–70. For Southwell, see *Oxford Mag.* 4 Dec. 1958, 158–9 and *BMFRS* 18 (1972). He had been involved in the design of Airship R101 (*Brazen Nose*, v. 7). Stallybrass credited A. J. Jenkinson with securing the chair for BNC (ibid, iv. 349).

[111] I. O. Griffith was a kindly tutor—'too kindly'—but spent overlong on the golf course and in committee (B. Williams to J. M. Crook, 11 Mar. 2005); Accession 129: F. W. Dillistone to B. Harrison, 14 Jan. 1989 and 28 Feb. 1989; obituary by Stallybrass in *Brazen Nose*, vii. 165–9). One mathematician from this period, Peter Twinn, while working at Bletchley Park in the Second World War, became the first British cryptographer to break the German Enigma coding machine (*The Times*, 24 Nov. 2004).

record was dire. Over a period of nineteen years, 1921–39, there were only four Firsts. During the same period Christ Church achieved thirty-three and New College thirty-one. Nor did the gloomy tale end there. There were two 'wartime' modern history Firsts in 1940 and 1947; otherwise nothing until 1958, and nothing again until 1969. Statistically, PPE was even worse: only two Firsts in thirty years, in 1926 and 1955. But PPE was a new subject, with comparatively few candidates. Modern history was very much more popular. And yet the college achieved only eight Firsts in nearly half a century.[112]

Such things do not happen by accident. Wakeling and Jeffery were conscientious tutors but intellectually uninspiring. Each of them lectured regularly in hall. In Michaelmas term 1924, for example, a diligent student might hear Jeffery on 'Outlines of European History, 800–1789' on Tuesdays and Thursdays at 10.00; Wakeling on Hobbes and Rousseau, on Mondays, Wednesdays, and Fridays at 12.00. At other times Wakeling also covered large swathes of English history. Jeffery (pl. 83A) was essentially an antiquarian, an angular Yorkshireman with an eclectic knowledge of the early history of Brasenose. He was a devoted college man, who waited years for promotion from Lecturer to Fellow. 'Jeffery was a dear', recalled one pupil from the early 1920s; 'he taught me a love of sources, which I have never lost. He also had a marvellous memory, but his books are dull reading. He lived at Great Rollright and stayed in College during the week. He had a daughter who could not walk . . . paralysed from the waist down . . . and I can see him pushing her wheelchair about College.' He drank heavily; in later years he had a nervous breakdown; and he died eventually in the Warneford Hospital.[113] Jeffers' lecture audience must largely have consisted of his own pupils. But Wakkers had a following well beyond Brasenose. For many years he filled not only the hall but lecture room VII as well; and he could be heard unseen in both places simultaneously, thanks to the pitch of his voice and the clarity of his enunciation.[114] He spoke at dictation speed and spiked his delivery with

[112] One of these (N. F. Hall, BA 1924) became eventually Principal of the College; another (J. M. Crook, BA 1958) eventually became its historian. Vincent Harlow, a future Beit Professor, was awarded a Second in 1921.

[113] Accession 129: E. Atkinson to B. Harrison, 7 Apr. 1989. Jeffery graduated with a Second in history in 1899 and immediately began tutoring; but he was only appointed Hulme Lecturer in 1910 (at £100 p.a.) and Fellow in 1922 (*OU Gazette*, 8 Feb. 1922). He was very close to Stallybrass (correspondence 1916–17 and 1931: MPP 56 c1). He edited the *Brazen Nose* from 1919 to 1934, and was librarian from 1929 to 1934; he died in 1956 (*Brazen Nose*, x. 15, 162–6).

[114] Stallybrass, in *Oxford Mag.* 29 Oct. 1936, 82. The post was first offered to Grant Robertson (V-P's Reg. 14 Nov. 1894, fo. 72). Hawksworth of Queen's and Lord St Cyres of Christ Church were also considered. Wakeling had the advantage of sporting interests: 'it is a curious fact that one member of Vincent's (Wakeling) succeeds another (Lodge) as History Tutor at Brasenose' (*Oxford Mag.* 8 May 1895, 326). Madan would have preferred to advertise: 'our private enquiries have failed, and Wakeling is not obviously good enough' (B4 b10: 25 Jan. 1895).

epigrams. In 1911 the future Lawrence of Arabia found Wakkers' lectures on Hobbes 'very useful' for Schools, 'and amusing too'. No doubt these performances suited generations of sportsmen with their eye on the clock. But they can scarcely have nourished potential Firsts. In any case BNC recruited very few of the latter. Every year during the 1920s and 1930s a selection of schoolmasters was invited to dinner. But they were quizzed about likely athletes rather than budding scholars. The destination of Brasenose men during this period was most likely to be the Colonial Service (pl. 83B). In 1923 the College supplied no fewer than seven out of twenty-one successful candidates nationwide.[115]

Quite a number of BNC's future colonial servants read modern history; but not, it has to be admitted, to any great effect. When Wakeling and Jeffery were replaced in 1933 and 1935, the results did not improve. If anything things got worse. Ironically it was their successors—Cohn and Collieu—who eventually led the revolt against Stallybrass in pursuit of higher academic standards.

BNC's performance in classics during this period was very much better. And that was due chiefly to Maurice Platnauer (pls. 92, 93, 95). Before he arrived at Brasenose in 1923, Platnauer had enjoyed a sparkling career at Shrewsbury and New College; he had survived the slaughter of the Somme; and he had taught classics at Winchester. His performance in Mods—fourteen leading alphas—was legendary.[116] He was known for his knowledge of food and wine, his economy of phrase, his early capacity for long-distance walking and canoeing, and his preference for the company of handsome young scholars. He was Housman without the malice; Pater without the affectation. With Michael Holroyd—a cultured if rather less impressive figure—he shared the teaching of Mods and Greats for the whole inter-war period.

Holroyd's undergraduate career had been broken by the Great War: he was badly wounded at Ypres. In 1919, without taking Schools, he was elected Fellow and moved straight into Bussell's old rooms on XII, 5. Thereafter he seems never to have settled to active research. But he was a mainstay of BNC life, hospitable and bonhomous. His taste was fastidious, and his sympathies liberal. After marrying in 1932, he lived first at no. 1 Holywell, and then at

[115] *Brazen Nose*, vi. 91. For Lawrence, see his *Letters*, ed. D. Garnett (1938), 110: 8 June 1911, to W. A. Lawrence.

[116] His tutor, H. E. Butler, was characteristically pedantic: 'May I congratulate you on a *very* good first, one of the first six, I think . . . The most creditable ever got by a commoner. . . . and beaten by few scholars at New College' (Platnauer scrap book, 127). Oliver Franks scored the same number of alphas in 1924. Platnauer was appointed to a Fellowship, with five years' credit for military service, at £588 p.a., subject to 'five years' marriage restriction' (V-P's Reg. 15 Mar. 1922, fo. 217). He was not a sportsman. Even so, in 1923 he walked from Oxford to Winchester in a day (Betting Book, 21 June 1923).

Foxwood on Boar's Hill, where he would entertain undergraduates to endless tea and talk. Holroyd had a background in the arts: his father had been Director, successively, of the Tate Gallery and the National Gallery. And his teaching of ancient history was infused with wide artistic knowledge: he inspired at least one star pupil, Eric Birley, the future archaeologist of Roman Britain. With Sonners he drove sportsmen from matches to lodgings in an open Vauxhall tourer. With Platnauer he enlivened innumerable meetings of the Pater. Indeed he seems to have acted as an ebullient foil to Platnauer's defensive calm.[117]

Different again was the third member of the Lit. Hum. team, a Liverpudlian named Jimmy McKie (pls. 92, 93). With twinkling eyes and a mystifying admiration for Hegel, McKie had coxed the BNC eight when it made five triumphant bumps in 1922. That certainly did him no harm in the eyes of Sonners. But McKie must bear at least some of the responsibility for BNC's lamentable record in PPE. Geoffrey Warnock remembered him as 'a man of inexhaustible kindness of heart, unstoppable garrulity of tongue, and inextricable confusion of mind'. In his early days, he seems to have been effective. R. H. Lloyd-Jones went to him in 1930 for a special subject on 'French Rationalist Thought' as part of the modern languages course.

Lying face downwards on the sofa, his head in a cushion, [McKie] appeared oblivious to what I was reading, but when I had finished it was clear that he had not only heard every word but had carefully considered every word of my essay. The lively and incisive mind of this young don enabled him to teach me my subject in detail and at the same time introduce me to philosophical principles in general.[118]

[117] For photos by Stallybrass, see PR 1 25 H3 /3/ 26, nos. A 1114–16 and PR 1 25 H3/3/ 29, nos. A 1238–9. For Holroyd's appointment—defeating P. W. Dodd and F. W. Ogilvie— see *Oxford Mag.* 6 June 1919, 334 and V-P's Reg. 30 May 1919, fo. 145. In 1919 Robert Dundas predicted that he 'would never be . . . a merely learned hermit-tutor' (MEM 2J1: Holroyd, M., 6 May 1919). When he died in 1953—while actually marking essays for Collections—he had been a Fellow for thirty-four years (*Brazen Nose*, ix. 387–90; *Oxford Mag.* 28 Jan. 1954, 166–8; *The Times*, 14 Oct. 1953, 10, and 19 Oct. 1953, 11). Once he walked from Oxford to Hadrian's Wall in six days (Betting Book, 10 May 1928). For Holroyd caricatured as a jovial Nero, see *Isis*, 30 Oct. 1951, 12. For Freda Holroyd see *Brazen Nose*, xviii. 35–6.

[118] Accession 129: R. H. Lloyd-Jones to B. Harrison, May 1981. See *Brazen Nose*, xiii/ 1. 25–8. For Warnock's memories, see *Brazen Nose*, xxv. 41. When applying for the Fellowship vacated by Jenkinson in 1928—he was supported by Joachim of New College—McKie admitted his lack of interest in 'research': 'I do not see myself ever editing a single text, ancient or modern . . . [such work] is not philosophy.' He found modern Oxford philosophy 'uncongenial'. He followed the Realist school of Cook Wilson and Jenkinson. See his 'Note upon Time and Cause', *Proceedings of the Aristotelian Society*, NS 26 (1935), 39–60. But he preferred 'to allow his ideas to ripen in solitude' (John Laird of Aberdeen, MEM 2J1: McKie, J; obit, *The Times*, 4 Oct. 1960, 15).

When it came to modern philosophy, however, McKie seems to have been rather less useful. If the Brasenose performance in classics held up at all well between the wars—and occasionally it did—then the credit must go primarily to Platnauer.

The diary of Edgar Parsons, an open scholar from King's School, Worcester, explains a little of the Platnauer mystique. Parsons moved into rooms at the top of new staircase XV in Michaelmas, 1929. He was perfectly happy with his new quarters. The walls were 'cheery yellow'; the curtains 'cherry red'. He was less happy with his tutor. 'I didn't like Platnauer at first', he wrote; 'looks as if he drinks. All the same, he seemed to know his job and was perfectly sensible and businesslike. Musical too: the room had a piano [actually a pianola] and there were scores and other musical books about.' That was 11 October. By 1 November 'Plat's' famous charm was beginning to operate. 'Maurice (that's Platnauer) is an extremely nice fellow. My suspicions that he drinks are now quite confirmed—but what of that? He's never drunk anyway. He [is] certainly extraordinarily pleasant to us...at tutorials. He must have pots of money too, judging by his room.' That last remark was certainly true. Platnauer was said to be descended from a Jewish sailor of that name who fought with Nelson at Trafalgar. Whatever the truth of the legend, his family seems to have prospered in Yorkshire and South Africa. One of his cousins was to have come to BNC as a Rhodes Scholar in 1914, but died in the First World War. From this accident stemmed at least part of Plat's inheritance. Over the years, he would become one of the greatest benefactors in Brasenose history. Soon young Parsons was accepting tickets for concerts, and dining to music in those legendary quarters on staircase VI. He still kept up a steady rate of six hours' reading per day. And after Collections in hall on 21 June 1930—'Don Rag' they called it in those days—he noted: 'Maurice expects me to get a first.' That proved to be over-optimistic. But there must have been some delicious moments, listening with Maurice to records of Brahms's First Symphony, and delighting in renditions of 'the [C?] sharp minor Chopin Scherzo on the pianola'. 'One little incident I must put down', he adds; 'because it illustrates Maurice's Epicurean tastes so well. He keeps some special crystals to put on the fire to make it turn blue: could a studious determination to enjoy life go further?' The décor, of course—on the full Paterian principle—was brightened by shades of similar gemlike flames. And on one shelf—to make the image complete—stood a blue-bound copy of *Marius the Epicurean*.[119]

[119] Parsons Diary, 25 Nov. 1930. Platnauer bequeathed *Marius* (2 vols., 1907) to Brasenose library. Parsons describes a typical Sunday lunch for six in winter: 'Crab in a delicious sauce, Jugged Hare, custard cream (real cream), and savoury with hot claret cup: delicious! And afterwards...coffee and cigarettes talking till 4 o'clock' (ibid. 25 Jan. 1931). For Platnauer's ancestry, see *Brazen Nose*, xxviii. 29 (L. Harris). In the 1920s his scout was Henry Bustin.

It is worth emphasizing that several major works did emerge from the classics side of Brasenose in the 1920s and 1930s—Platnauer's editions of Claudian (1922) and Euripides (1938); Sir Arthur Evans's *Palace of Minos at Knossos* (1922–36); and Sir Henry Stuart-Jones's ninth edition of Liddell and Scott's *Greek Lexicon* (1925–36). All three rank high in any table of scholarship. In fact the last two might be described as masterly. But only Platnauer was a Tutorial Fellow. Evans was an academic colossus—PSA, FRS, FBA—but his field of operations as Professor of Prehistoric Archaeology and Keeper of the Ashmolean was far removed from mundane college teaching. Henry Stuart-Jones, FBA, played a greater part in college life—he was an inveterate after-dinner speaker—but his head was in the Greek Lexicon, and his heart was in the hills: he ended as Vice-Chancellor of the University of Wales. Little of his learning can have filtered down to undergraduate level.

Apart from Eric Birley, there were in fact few emerging classical stars among Brasenose undergraduates between the wars. Platnauer—"plump, peach-coloured and port-fed"[120]–rode a very loose rein. When Edmund Atkinson went up in 1921 he was quite alarmed. 'I was only 18 years old', he recalled, 'and I was immediately struck by the amount of drink consumed, and the amount of drunkenness it caused...Sonners...held a lot of parties in his rooms...and made people drunk. I was never invited because he knew I didn't drink!'[121] Eight years later Edgar Parsons was appalled. On almost his first night at Oxford, he noted in his diary: 'two [undergraduates] (B.N.C. I fear) have just gone by [in the High Street], rolling tight and stopping at intervals to lie down in the gutter—repulsive sight!' But within weeks he seems to have adapted well.

The Dons gave the 1st Togger a dinner [last night], so I had to dress—my debut in evening clothes. It was a fine dinner. Champagne throughout which soon overcame our shyness, and I was arguing with Michael Holroyd about Macbeth and then about Homer. Before long my head was swinging, and it was difficult keeping up coherent—not to say intelligent conversation—with McKie. After a bit—about four rounds of the bottle—we went to the Senior Common Room, I holding carefully to the railings upstairs, and there had coffee but it had no clearing effect. By the end I felt as if I should like to crawl under the table. I believe we looked at *Punch*, discussed the humour of back numbers. I think I said some fairly intelligent things, but now I have a horrid feeling that I probably said them six or seven times, which rather spoils the effect.[122]

If there was a world elsewhere, it can hardly have been noticed. May 1926, for example, marked two events: the end of Sonners' proctorial tenure and

---

[120] H. Trevor-Roper, quoted in A. Danchev, *Oliver Franks* (Oxford, 1993), 152: 10 Feb. 1960.
[121] Accession 129: E. Atkinson to B. Harrison, 7 Apr. 1989.
[122] Parsons Diary, 11 Oct. 1929, 15 Feb. 1930.

the onset of the General Strike. When the strike began, Vice-Principal Stallybrass called a meeting of junior members and college employees, to explain the implications of the situation. Day by day the Fellows kept in touch with the drama outside: they listened to 'a splendid wireless set' owned by one particularly rich cricketer, 'Ginger' Legge. And when it was all over, as if to celebrate England's return to parliamentary rule, the college treated itself to a brand new barge.

During the six days of the Strike, Sonners reported, Brasenose supplied

not only relatively but absolutely, more volunteers than any other College. In the whole College there were only eight undergraduates who did not offer their services, and almost all showed a willingness not only to help but to face hard work (a thing new to some of them), great discomfort, and personal danger in order to hold society together. There was no distinction of race or colour or party politics—some members of the labour party were at work maintaining supplies for the Government before some extreme anti-socialists had even offered their services ... Brasenose may well be proud of the men in residence in Trinity Term 1926.[123]

There is no doubt that Vice-Principal Stallybrass had his own methods of blocking out distractions. He kept the world at bay with copious supplies of alcohol. At Saturday dinners on staircase IV generations of undergraduates learned to match him drink for drink, as the cigar smoke swirled about them and the glasses rattled late into the night. On 20 June 1930 the Earl of Birkenhead—no mean toper himself—dined at BNC with a group of chosen oarsmen. Parsons, still a freshman, noted his own intake: '2 glasses of sauternes, 1 glass of champagne, 2 glasses of port, 2 glasses of brandy, 1/2 glass of chartreuse ... 3 pints of beer ... bed at 2.30 ... after a speech from Lord Birkenhead. Sonners getting more and more tight like ourselves.'[124] The long-term results of such experience were sometimes unexpected: within three years young Parsons had joined the Communist Party.

Drinking with Sonners—or dining with Platnauer—was certainly not to everybody's taste. One who seems to have reacted strongly against so much indulgence was the future Nobel Prizewinner William Golding. Now Golding had gone up to Oxford in 1930, intending to become a scientist: 'some sort of botanist—a microscopist'. That, at least, had been his father's wish. Golding sen. had been a schoolmaster, an atheist and socialist of Cornish stock, who taught science for many years at Marlborough Grammar School.

[123] *Brazen Nose*, iv. 154. For the Commem. Ball, on 21 June, Stallybrass, Holroyd, and Waldock were all on the committee. Between foxtrots—Sonners was not averse to dancing—the Vice-Principal presumably enjoyed his favourite dessert, 'Chartreuse B.N.C.' (Menu and Programme, Bras. Misc. IV, 82). For his consumption of liqueurs, see Common Room Book, 1935–8, *passim*.

[124] Parsons Diary, 20 June 1930. For Parsons' obit, see *Brazen Nose*, xxviii. 47–8.

Golding Jun. found science dry and factual. It told him nothing about the human spirit; nothing about that other world he longed to penetrate, the world of dark unreason. After two years he switched to English literature. But in his five years as an undergraduate—partly spent living in rooms directly above Sonners—he seems to have cut himself off from mainstream college society. In fact we would today know next to nothing about his Oxford career were it not for the survival of Edgar Parsons' diary. There we encounter a rather surprising figure called 'Bill' Golding. In November 1932, we find him present at the BNC Music Society, debating with Michael Holroyd and Leslie Scarman the motion 'That Opera is a Bastard Art'. We even discover him playing a rather rudimentary game of rugger for the second Fifteen. More important, there he is in IV, 6, in the summer of 1933, reading out his own poems to a select group of friends, each clutching a glass of crème de menthe. To the college at large the future Nobel Laureate must have been something of a mystery. Notices reminding him of uncollected mail remained unnoticed, pinned to the college gate for weeks.[125] Years later, in conversation with John Carey, he could hardly recall his tutors' names:

Do you remember any of the tutors or lecturers?
No, I don't in fact ... C. L. Wrenn, was he ... ?
An Anglo-Saxonist, wasn't he?
Yes (*gloomily*) he was an immense scholar. . . .
Tolkien was not there then?
I think he may have been, but I don't remember him. . . . I don't remember any of them.[126]

After service in the Royal Navy—he was present on D-Day in 1944—Golding followed his father into teaching, at Bishop Wordsworth's School, Salisbury. Whether he knew of the Wordsworth connection with BNC seems doubtful. But it was there—and presumably through his father—that he learned to fear the innate barbarity of the young, so memorable in *Lord of the Flies* (1954). That novel, which made him world famous, was rejected by twenty-one publishers before acceptance by Faber and Faber. It sold ten million copies. It took him only three or four months to write. At Oxford, Golding had in fact published a few of his poems. But the University was for him the very opposite of inspirational. Brasenose seemed to him unreal. Not

[125] N. Hidden to J. M. Crook: 19 July 2003. For entries on Golding in Parsons' Diary, see *Brazen Nose*, xxiii. 49–50. Golding's moral tutor was T. W. J. Taylor.

[126] Golding, in interview with J. Carey, in Carey (ed.), *William Golding, the Man and his Books* (1986), 178. In fact he must have shown his *Poems* (1934) to one of his out-of-college tutors. In the copy presented to a BNC friend, Adam Bittleston, he wrote in 1988: 'Rett Switt my Tutor merely remarked of this collection that I was "rather unfair to Pope"' (Christie's London, 8 June 2005, lot 238).

so the Navy. There he found only too much reality: 'One had one's nose rubbed in the face of the human condition.'

Before the second world war [he wrote in 1965] I believed in the perfectibility of social man ... after the war I did not. . . . I must say that anyone who moved through those years without understanding that man produces evil as a bee produces honey must have been blind or wrong in the head.[127]

Ever afterwards he remained 'bitterly left of centre'.[128] And always there stayed with him the consciousness of original sin: not dressed up as a metaphysical proposition, but simply existing as brute psychological fact. At Brasenose—despite the crème de menthe—he had felt essentially alone. He belonged, for example, to a different world from that of his near contemporary Jack Profumo. And something of that undergraduate loneliness—high up on staircase IV—seems to have haunted him ever after: '... through an alley, across another road, a quadrangle. . . . bare wooden stairs. . . . a fire and all the bells of Oxford. . . . "I am so alone".'[129] In that sense, Brasenose was Golding's preparation for war.

Unlike 1914, the year 1939 did not inaugurate an effective closure of the University. Oxford carried on, though operating at half-pressure. Science received a major boost: the number of staff and students in the Clarendon Laboratory tripled in five years. Most of those still reading for degrees had a particular reason for being there: scientists, medics, linguists, mathematicians. There were still undergraduates registered at BNC, but they were living in Meadow Buildings at Christ Church. One of these was the future Sir John Mortimer, creator of Rumpole of the Bailey. His memories of BNC in exile are perhaps a little over-spiced. He dismisses Platnauer as a 'bald gastronome' in carpet slippers; Stallybrass appears as 'a mountainous old man who ... peered at me through glasses thick as ginger-beer bottles, and was for ever veering away from Justinian's views on Riparian ownership to Catullus's celebration of oral sex'. But Mortimer does manage to catch the curious, twilight world of wartime Oxford.

The Oxford of the twenties and thirties was still there, like college claret, but it was rationed, on coupons, and there was not very much of it left. The famous characters still behaved as though they lingered in the pages of *Decline and Fall*. They were famous for being nothing except Oxford characters ... but even then, in rationed,

---

[127] Golding, 'Fable' (1965), quoted in *ODNB*.
[128] J. I. Biles, *Talk: Conversation with William Golding* (New York, 1970), 33, 49. See also S. Metcalf, reviewing P. Crawford, *Politics and History in William Golding* (Columbia, Mo., 2003), in *Times Lit. Supp.* 16 May 2003, 23.
[129] Golding, *Pincher Martin* (1956), 181. His room was IV, 6 in 1931–2. He became an Hon. Fellow of BNC in 1966, and was knighted in 1988.

blacked-out Oxford, there were limitless hours for talking, drinking, staying up all night, going for walks with a friend.[130]

Tutorials and lectures continued, though on a reduced scale. Sports too: with BNC and Christ Church fielding united teams. These arrangements seem to have worked well. Brasenose and House men dined at separate tables; each contingent had their own scouts; rations—yes, rations—were pooled; the Christ Church JCR was shared. Sonners and Platnauer—and of course the immovable Stocker—stayed on in their old quarters at BNC, surrounded latterly by trainee officers and female nursing personnel (FANYs). Pulling strings in the Lord Chancellor's Office, Sonners at first hoped to keep the college as a reserve location for the Royal Courts of Justice. But increasingly BNC was given over to service purposes. There was even a Nissen hut in the Deer Park. Still, the SCR survived. As in 1914, Lincoln dons dined happily there; and in 1944—as before in 1917—proposals for merger were once more tentatively discussed.[131] It was Sonners' conviction, however, that Brasenose would survive this second German war; and of course he was right. But the cost was terribly high.

BNC's losses in the Second World War were crushing. In all, 123 men did not return; or 124 if we include J. C. von Ruperti (pl. 88), a German Rhodes Scholar killed on the Russian front in 1943.[132] That figure represents—most unusually—a higher total than the list of those who fell in the First World War. The reason is cruelly simple. The ethos of Brasenose—athletic, loyal, light-hearted, physically courageous—matched only too well the ethos of the Royal Air Force. As pilot officers, flight lieutenants, and squadron leaders, Sonners' men held the fort against Nazism in 1940, and they paid a heavy price. The college was bigger than it had been, of course; so the numbers

---

[130] J. Mortimer, *Clinging to the Wreckage* (1982), 54–7. Mortimer left under a cloud in 1941. For this episode, see V. Grove, *A Voyage around John Mortimer* (2007).

[131] V-P's Reg. 26 Apr. 1944, fo. 51. FANYs were members of the First Aid Nursing Yeomanry.

[132] He was the son of the Provincial Governor of Allenstein in East Prussia (photo (pl. 88) in Von Ruperti file). In 1936–7, while instructing soldiers on Luneburg Heath, he was still reading *The Times*, and wishing he was back in England. 'It would be silly to deny that I did not enjoy myself [during four years' training] in the army...The army...is one of the few institutions in this country, which are not so intensely affected by politics as most things are....As regards politics I feel [as though] I am sitting in a big 'bus...with not the least chance of influencing the course which the driver takes...' (*Brazen Nose*, vi. 213–14, 218). Sonners noted: 'Our four German members in this country were interned [in 1940], but we are glad to say are all now released and doing the best which they are allowed to do to defeat Hitlerism'—i.e. H. A. Mammelmann, K. H. Stein, G. Kochmann, and H. K. G. Gottstein. See *Brazen Nose*, vii. 147. It was Barry Nicholas who was chiefly responsible for commemorating Ruperti's death. The Association of German Rhodes Scholars thanked BNC for its 'chivalrous and noble act' (V-P's Reg. 27 May 1950, 16 Mar. 1954, 29 July 1955).

killed were proportionately less severe. But the calibre of losses must have been devastating. Appropriately, the first to fall was a sportsman who was already a national celebrity: Pilot Officer Prince Alexander Obolensky.

Obolensky was the son of Prince Sergey Obolensky, lord of an estate the size of Yorkshire; captain in the Tsar's Imperial Horse Guards. He escaped from the Bolsheviks in 1919; he was educated in England at Trent College, Nottinghamshire; he arrived at Brasenose in 1934. By that date he was already a star: in one season as a sixth-form rugby winger, he scored forty-nine tries. He was the fastest player in England: he could run 100 yards in 10.2 seconds. Immediately capped for Oxford and England, he became immortal with a single match, England's first victory over New Zealand on 4 January 1936. Now Obolensky was a sprinter with extraordinary acceleration. But he was also a devout evangelical Christian. That very year, he published an essay in a volume entitled *Be Still and Know: Oxford in Search of God*. And he was a patriot: he publicly criticized the 1933 Oxford Union motion declining to 'Fight for King and Country'. But whatever he did, he did with style. Before a big match he would lunch in St James's Square on oysters and champagne. With dazzling footwork, his 'fair hair streaming in the wind', he was indeed a 'Flying Prince'. That wintry afternoon in 1936 much was expected of him. Just before kick-off, the Prince of Wales—soon to be Edward VIII—rudely asked him what qualification he had to play for England. Back came the icy reply: 'I am a student of Oxford University... *sir.*' Within an hour he was the toast of Twickenham. Roared on by a crowd of 70,000, he jinked his way through the All Black scrum, and ran at an angle from right to left—covering three-quarters of the pitch—to score his second try and clinch the game: 'Obolensky's Match'. Four years later he was dead. His plane crash-landed on a training run at Martlesham in Suffolk on 29 March 1940. He was just 24 years of age.[133]

Brasenose losses in the air that year were grievous. Like Obolensky, numbers of sportsmen had already joined the University Air Squadron. They moved immediately to the RAF Volunteer Reserve and the Fleet Air Arm. They were first in line when the Battle of Britain began. With easy banter, and RAF slang; nonchalantly smoking cigarettes; all battledress blue and wavy hair; they smile into Sonners' camera as they visit Oxford on their last leave home. John Body: 'fearless and happy-go-lucky... He had an immense zest for life but was not afraid to die.'[134] Tony Tisdall (pl. 86):

---

[133] *ODNB*; *Isis*, 22 Jan. 1936, 7: photo, and 5 Feb. 1936, 5: caricature; *The Times*, 1 Apr. 1940, 3; *Brazen Nose*, vii. 80–1; R. McWhirter and A. Noble, *OURFC* (Oxford, 1969), appendix. For Obolensky's Match, see *The Times*, 6 Jan. 1936, 5. He took a Fourth in PPE in 1938. After his death, the college wrote off his unpaid battels (V-P's Reg. 30 April 1941, fo. 18).

[134] *Brazen Nose*, vii. 70–2; *The Times*, 17 Aug. 1940, 9.

'one of those gallant and cheerful pilots whose exploits have won the admiration of the world'.[135] Mike Peacock, DFC, wittiest of after-dinner speakers; acrobatic pilot, star of 601 Squadron; 'Valhalla-bound' most surely, 'if Valhalla there be'; for 'in the air, on the rugby field...he did not know what fear was'.[136] Brian Black: ten times capped for England, a mighty forward with 'no frills about him'; the very 'embodiment of life'.[137] Casualties, all of them—among the best of the few—that blinding summer in 1940.

Others too. 'Ginger' Legge, rich and bold; a test cricketer at war.[138] Max Scott, strong and stocky; 'a very gallant little man'; Michael Worthington: 'straight as a die'.[139] Jimmy Halstead (pl. 84): handsome, eager, brave, the very spirit of BNC[140]. Peter Beane: 'quite unconscious of his own good looks...In spite of his great strength...the gentlest of men.'[141] Alan Bulmer, with his ready smile and 'merry laugh';[142] and his best friend Ken Millar—a veritable 'blithe spirit'—shot down both of them, within days of each other (pl. 89).[143] Then there was David Warburton: 'a trier who never gave up'.[144] Ronnie Barlow, a man with 'the supreme gift of being able to laugh at himself'.[145] Peter Landale, DFC, quietest of leaders;[146] Tony Ward, 'good through and through';[147] Hector Pilling, a generous spirit;[148] David Walker, a cricketing Christian, 'able, simple and gentle'.[149] All these were sportsmen who flew for England. Pilots all of them, fighters or bombers. Several were Heath Harrison Scholars. Most of them read law. All were Sonners' men. They shared the qualities he most admired: 'manliness...humanity...

---

[135] *Brazen Nose*, vii. 77–8.

[136] Ibid. 75–7; *The Times*, 27 Aug. 1940, 7 (G. D. Roberts) and 28 Aug. 1940, 7 ('a great young Englishman': C.R.J.P.). Three times he was reported missing, but somehow returned. 'He was a wild and dangerous man; but all his wildness was not just skin-deep bravado, but Mike Peacock right through' (Hector Pilling, himself lost over Mannheim in 1942, in *Brazen Nose*, vii. 266). For photos of Peacock by Stallybrass on the Strollers Tour of 1932, see Col. I B 3.

[137] *Brazen Nose*, vii. 79–80.

[138] Ibid. 108–11; *The Times*, 30 Nov. 1940, 7 (W. T. S. Stallybrass).

[139] *Brazen Nose*, vii. 111–12; ibid. 112–13.

[140] 'He loved beautiful women...beautiful music and writing, and the country and flowers... Seldom has so much courage and so much kindness been taken from us in one life' (*Brazen Nose*, vii. 216–18). He played the cello and drove a 1927 Alvis. See also PRI 25 H1/ 3 and PRI 25 H1/3, 3087–8.

[141] *Brazen Nose*, vii. 114–16.

[142] Ibid. 116–18.

[143] Ibid. 121–2. 'In [Millar's] room the lambs of the College Boat Club [lay] down with the Lions of the Greats school.' For a photo by Stallybrass of Bulmer and Millar together on 10 Oct. 1940, see PRI 25 H1/3, 3032 (pl. 89).

[144] *Brazen Nose*, vii. 122–3.   [145] Ibid. 258–9.   [146] Ibid. 264.

[147] Ibid. 270.   [148] Ibid. 265–7.   [149] Ibid. 268 –70; *The Times*, 8 Sept. 1942, 6.

purpose'.[150] Normally they would have gone on to the bar or into the Colonial Service. As it was, they went down in flames, one after another, in the early phases of the war. It was Sonners who wrote their obituaries.

Somehow, there was a glorious simplicity about this part of the Second World War: a last-ditch fight against manifest evil. And BNC produced the right heroes at the right time. A man like John Anderson, for example; hockey star, tennis star, 'happy, simple and good'. His Lancaster was shot down over France in May 1942. He personified 'the very chivalry of games'.[151] Or Gerry Chalk—daring cricketer, daring pilot—shot down in his Spitfire over northern France in 1943.[152] Or Charles Elgar, handsome and popular, 'staunch, direct and true...one of those...whose virtue is the... pride of the College'.[153] Or Tom Rushton, DFC, a Yorkshire landowner who found himself—the *mot juste* perhaps—with 107 Squadron, flying Bostons through a hail of shrapnel in daylight raids over the Netherlands.[154]

Of course BNC had its heroes in the other forces, outside the RAF. Kenneth Rhodes, for instance, who served in both wars and died in the second. He was the college's first Heath Harrison Exhibitioner, and by no means the least.[155] Or Ian Lawrie, bespectacled and smiling, a brave tank commander: 'only the examiners could defeat him.'[156] Or Rae Duncan, captain of the rugby cuppers team in 1938–9: he died in France in May 1940. As a soldier, 'his hair became shorter and his bearing more military. ... But we in Brasenose shall always have a picture [of him] in our minds. ... inspiring his forwards by his dash as he led them, with his long hair streaming over his eyes.'[157]

And many of the best did manage to survive. H. A. S. Johnston, for example, who won his DFC in Malta. Or Robert Runcie—the future Archbishop of Canterbury—who won his MC in a tank battle in the Netherlands.[158] Or the legendary Captain Pieter Van der Bijl, MC, the giant South African test cricketer. At Brasenose he had been a Rhodes Scholar and a heavyweight boxing blue. His injunction to his men, facing enemy bombardment in

---

[150] *Brazen Nose*, vii. 125. 'Academic aptitude is not the only test of ability' (ibid. 109).

[151] Ibid. 298–300.

[152] The wreckage of his plane, and his body, were only recovered in 1948 (ibid. 364 and xxiv. 68).

[153] Ibid., vii. 309–10.

[154] Ibid., 362–3 (R. E. B. Maxse); *The Times*, 10 Aug. 1943, and 20 Aug. 1943, 8.

[155] *Brazen Nose*, vii. 124–5.

[156] 'His sight was poor but it was a thrilling spectacle to see him dashing fearless for the line at rugby, speeding down the wing at hockey or scudding across the field at cover point... Educational reformers may say that Oxford has no place for such as he, but [if so] Oxford will be the poorer' (ibid. 175–6).

[157] Ibid. 73–4.

[158] *The Times*, 13 July 2000, 25.

Abyssinia, still echoes down the years. When the shells fell short, he told them not to worry: 'Never mind the long-hops, chaps; it's the full tosses that count.'[159]

But the charismatic figures, the ones the gods love best, seem almost to have been singled out by the enemy. Michael Fisher—tall, handsome, 'all that was best in Oxford'—killed in the battle of Flanders, 1940; leading his men 'under the most intense shell and mortar fire', among the woods surrounding Nieuport.[160] Or gallant Desmond Magill: 'bubbling over with vitality'; he survived Dunkirk only to die the following year.[161] Or Conrad Cherry (pl. 87)—'Uncle Con' to his contemporaries—captain of Leander, stroke of the Brasenose Eight, President of OUBC—the finest heavyweight oarsman of his generation. His winning Oxford boat was the best for a quarter of a century. In his BNC days, his rough-worn tweeds, his air of easy calm, his jaunty cap, even his temporary moustache, were trademarks of a man at ease. He was 'a grand chap...large of frame, large of heart...the right stuff all through...he never let down a friend'. In 1940 he was at Dunkirk. In 1943 he was killed instantly when his ship was hit by a torpedo.

It makes one think a bit at sea [he wrote to his parents some time before his death] and it makes one say things that probably I ought to have said long ago. One thing I want to do is to thank you both for sending me to a good school and a good college. Whatever happens now, I have had a grand time, thanks to you. I don't want to die a bit; but I can't help thinking that death is not so important as it seems. So try not to worry about me. Anyhow, I would not have missed this thing for anything. For the first time I feel I am doing something for others.[162]

Fifteen years after the end of war his photograph, faded and dusty, still hung on the wall in his scout's old pantry at the top of staircase I.

> ...Now drink to...Uncle Con
> With wild and woolly trousers on,
> His pink and Blue, and fine moustache
> And chequered cap, *un peu apache*...[163]

---

[159] *Brazen Nose*, vii. 323; *Isis*, 11 Mar. 1931, 7: photo. Once, after dinner with Sonners, he bent a steel poker in half; the Vice-Principal was annoyed, so he bent it back again, and left it 'resembling a corkscrew' (*Brazen Nose*, xv. 276).

[160] *Brazen Nose*, vii. 118–19.

[161] Ibid. 120–1; *The Times*, 16 Sept. 1940, 6 (C. A. Alington) and 24 Sept. 1940, 7 (W. T. S. Stallybrass).

[162] Quoted anonymously by Reggie Owen in his war commemoration address, 16 Mar. 1946 (bound into *Brazen Nose*, viii, n.p.).

[163] P. C. W. D.[isney], Ale Verse (1937), *Brazen Nose*, vi. 212, 340–1; ibid., vii. 301–3; *Isis*, 3 June 1936, 7, and 26 Jan. 1938, 18: photos; *The Times*, 10 Feb 1942, 7 (G. O. Nickalls) and 4 Mar. 1943, 7. Photo as oarsman: PR1 25 H3/3/24, tipped in. His scout was Bert King, himself wounded in the First World War.

Conrad Cherry was a loss. Dick Holdsworth (pl. 85) was a catastrophe. They were always close friends, and they died within a year of each other. In fact Cherry was Holdsworth's best man; another wartime marriage tragically cut short. Holdsworth raised the concept of 'all-rounder' to astonishing heights. He was the son of the great legal historian Sir William Holdsworth. But his nickname, 'the Prof.', was something he earned for himself. Three times he was in the Brasenose eight: it was head of the river in 1931. Three times he rowed for Oxford, and twice he rowed as stroke: 1933 will always be known as 'Holdsworth's Race'. He was secretary of the Phoenix, President of the Ellesmere, President of the JCR, President of the Vampires; he achieved a First in law in 1933, and he was elected to a Fellowship at Univ. in 1936. From Lincoln's Inn to All Souls, he was a man whose presence could light up a room. Today he has his own fragment of immortality as one of the brave young pilots in Richard Hillary's *The Last Enemy* (1942). But his loss in April 1942 was a Brasenose tragedy. 'Some eight years ago', noted Stallybrass, 'it was a common topic of speculative discussion...whether Dick [Holdsworth] or Michael Peacock or Leslie Scarman would go furthest at the Bar or on the Bench. Now thanks to the ravages of war Squadron Leader Scarman remains alone.'[164] Scarman went on to be a Lord of Appeal. Peacock and Holdsworth are now just names on a tablet in Brasenose cloister.

As the war progressed, Oxford, Brasenose, and Sonners in particular seemed to BNC men in uniform the very symbols of what they were fighting for. During the First War he had acted as an indefatigable editor of the *Oxford Magazine*. During the Second War he wrote endless letters—literally hundreds of them—to BNC servicemen around the world. And the burden of his message was always the same: that Oxford did not change. Not in spirit, anyway.

Men can still walk and talk freely; [he noted in dark days of 1941] the present order of things can still be frankly challenged; youthful enthusiasms are not damped, nor heresies persecuted; the passion for truth still prevails. And as young men talk to each other of poetry and art and politics and love and God, those intimate friendships are still made which are Oxford's most precious gift.... So long as these things be, even though our streets be darkened at night and crowded by day with uniforms

---

[164] *Brazen Nose*, vii. 221–5; *Oxford Mag.* 28 May 1942, 326–7; *Isis*, 18 May 1933, 5: photo; *The Times*, 5 May 1942, 6 (Sir William Beveridge) and 8 May 1942, 7 (H. G. Hanbury). For Stallybrass's obituary of Sir William Holdsworth, see *Law Quarterly Rev.* 60 (1944), 138–59. Holdsworth's year (1933) was particularly badly hit by war. Besides Holdsworth and Peacock, there was J. H. Becher, President of the Pater Society, and three cricket stars: F. G. H. Chalk, D. F. Walker, and J. A. Brittain.

and refugees from hard-pressed London, we can say that in no essentials has the war changed life at Oxford.[165]

But if the spirit of Oxford survived—and it survived not one world war but two—its personnel had certainly begun to change. 'Was there perhaps a new race of Englishmen arising out of this war', wondered Richard Hillary in 1942; 'a race of men bred by the war, a . . . synthesis of the governing class and the great rest of England; that synthesis of disparate backgrounds and upbringings to be seen at its most obvious best in R.A.F. Squadrons?' Would they be the 'true representatives of the new England?'[166] And was Oxford capable of absorbing this fundamental change?

The change itself was rooted in finance. The Education Act of 1944 had one basic aim: 'to throw open the gates of educational opportunity to all on equal terms'.[167] In the university sphere that meant increasing the number, and size, of central and local grants. The pool of potential recruits was thus dramatically enlarged. Between the wars eighteen leading schools—nine boarding, nine day—had supplied 40 per cent of all scholarships and exhibitions to Oxford. Only five of these had been grammar schools. Suddenly that latter figure multiplied. From 1946 onwards state scholarships and local education authority awards not only expanded in number; they increased in value—subject to means testing—so as to cover the full rate of maintenance at university. At Oxford and Cambridge, open college awards were similarly supplemented. The change was fundamental. Oxford was now accessible, as of right, to state-educated pupils without means. In 1938, 62 per cent of male undergraduates came from independent schools; in 1948 only 45 per cent. And the huge influx of ex-servicemen—90 per cent of the 1946–7 intake—underlined this diversification of recruitment. For the first time, competition for places (as opposed to scholarships) became intense. Here was clear evidence of a social revolution, even if—for another generation at least—its nature would be disguised by the cultural filter of grammar-school selection. From his office in the Clarendon Building, Vice-Chancellor Stallybrass looked out over an educational landscape fundamentally and irreversibly different. He was not entirely pleased. He had no objection to state-educated pupils. He enjoyed, for example, the 'winning personality' of John Rowe, a grammar-school boy from Cornwall who scored a

---

[165] Stallybrass, 'Oxford in War-Time', *American Oxonian*, 28 (1941), 101 (reprinted from *Britain Today* no. 39; partly reprinted in R. A. Scott-James (ed.), *Education in Britain* (1945), 25–34). In 1947, some 250 ex-servicemen presented him with a silver loving cup by George Hart of Chipping Campden (*Brazen Nose*, viii. 201, ill.).

[166] R. Hillary, *The Last Enemy* (1942), 174–5.

[167] *The Times*, 8 Apr. 1944, 5. The principles of the Education Act (1944) had been sketched out in the White Paper on 'Educational Reconstruction' (1943). Funding provision as regards University access (Education Act, 1944, clause 76) was left vague (*Parl. Debates: Commons*, cccxcvi, cols. 470–1: 20 Jan. 1944 and *Lords*, cxxxii, cols. 515–22: 28 June 1944).

rare First in history in 1940. But in matters of recruitment he thought instinctively in terms of familiar networks and old alliances. And he was alarmed at the prospect of state-controlled tertiary education. As a member of the Committee of Vice-Chancellors and Principals; as a member of the University Grants Committee, he was witnessing at close quarters the transformation of universities into instruments of the welfare state. In 1945 the Labour government doubled Oxford's annual grant for recurrent expenditure, and earmarked sums for capital spending that were quite unprecedented in scale. The UGC pondered its future: 'The question cannot be avoided whether the greatly increased dependence of the universities on Government grants may carry with it a threat to their continued existence as free institutions.'[168]

At his installation as Vice-Chancellor in October 1947, Sonners announced himself 'an unrepentant believer in the college system'.[169] At its best, he believed, the collegiate ethos was academically diverse, socially pluralist, and ideologically tolerant. 'Traditions and memories', he emphasized, 'are bound up within the College walls, not in the Laboratories, the Bodleian or the Examination Schools... The College system is something rare and precious and, like most such things, very expensive.'[170]

With the benefit of hindsight we can now see that the threats to this self-contained, collegial world were threefold: financial, social, and political. Financially, there was the threat of inflation, that is the erosion of college endowments and their replacement by centrally distributed grants. Socially, there was the perennial problem of marriage—'Holy Deadlock' Sonners called it—that increasingly drew Fellows away from corporate life. And politically there was the greatest threat of all: the emergence in government of an egalitarian philosophy of education, which would denounce selection as elitist. Of these, only the first two were present realities for Sonners' generation. In the 1920s and 1930s his centrifugal views appeared to be perfectly plausible. Until 1939, for example, college JCRs still rejected the creation of a central Student Representative Council. Nor was Sonners against cooperation between colleges. Coordinated teaching, particularly in new and scientific subjects, was an obvious good. But cooperation was not the same thing as federation. The danger as he saw it was the emergence of the over-mighty Faculty: recruiting students, appointing staff, and supplementing its finances with government grants channelled and controlled by an expanding University executive. In short, he saw the growth of Big Science—employing lecturers, apportioning block grants—as the greatest threat to collegiate autonomy. 'The unfettered right of each College to choose

[168] *University Development from 1935 to 1947* (Report of the UGC., 1948), 11, 77. For recruitment figures, see K. Thomas, in *HUO* viii. 195, 385–6.

[169] *Isis*, 15 Oct. 1947, 9.

[170] Stallybrass, 'The Oxford College System and its Preservation', *American Oxonian*, 35 (1948), 23.

its own members', he explained, 'whether senior or junior, is perhaps the most important right of all.... Each College has its own ethos.' The continental system—professorial teaching, Faculty control, government finance—seemed to pose ever-increasing dangers. The threat of universities being subject to political pressure, he warned—Germany was the obvious precedent—'is always present, and the danger of it [is] not imaginary'. 'No such pressure', he added, 'can be brought upon the Colleges. Only new legislation can weaken their position.'[171]

Those words would turn out to be rather too sanguine. But much to Sonners' relief, the Labour government of 1945 showed little inclination to take the egalitarian route towards a state-funded comprehensive university.[172] That might come later. The more immediate threat to Sonners' own position came from much closer to home; from the junior members in his own Common Room.

It was just after the end of the Second World War that the balance of the Brasenose Fellowship swung away from Stallybrass. A clutch of new appointments brought in a different generation with a different set of priorities. In 1946–8, no less than eight new men joined the Governing Body (pls. 92, 93): Robert Shackleton (modern languages), George Gordon (physiology), John Barltrop (chemistry), Ron Maudsley and Barry Nicholas (law), Nicholas Kurti (physics), Norman Leyland (economics), and Leslie Styler (chaplain).[173] Maudsley and Nicholas owed professional and personal loyalty to Sonners. Styler (pl. 94)—a kindly priest who liked his ale—instinctively chose a middle way. But the others—particularly Gordon and Shackleton—took up arms against the old regime. They wanted a different college, a college more academically oriented, a college in tune with post-war thinking. In this they were led on by two dissentient voices within the pre-war Fellowship: Cohn and Collieu. Tempers grew strained. The scene was set for confrontation. And the rebels now had a leader: the Camden Professor of Ancient History, Hugh Last.

Last had been a solitary undergraduate at Lincoln during the First World War. As a rising star in the field of Roman history, he was quickly elected to a Fellowship at St John's in 1919. Olympian in the lecture room, sardonic in

---

[171] Ibid. 21. For centralizing tendencies, see Harrison (ed.), *HUO*. viii. 683–95.

[172] As Vice-Chancellor, Stallybrass pledged at least one of his two votes to Mr Attlee (*Isis*, 18 Feb. 1948, 8: photo of Attlee and Sonners).

[173] V-P's Reg. 13 July 1946, fo. 84 (Shackleton); 11 Dec. 1946 fo. and 28 May 1947 fo. 103 (Barltrop); 30 Apr. 1947, fo. 101 (Gordon); 14 May 1947, fo. 102 (Maudsley, Nicholas, Styler); 23 June 1947, fo. 106 (Leyland). R. A. Hull had been elected Fellow in Physics in 1944; he fell to his death on Mont Blanc in 1949 (*Oxford Mag.*, 20 Oct. 1949, 38).

conversation, trenchant in committee, he was soon both revered and feared. 'Tall, dark, and heavily built', recalled Peter Fraser, he was a man who walked 'with a deliberate gait, and always dressed with the greatest care, his Homburg hat, his pipe, his walking stick, and the grey woollen scarf thrown back over his shoulder'.[174] His health had never been robust; but he managed to fabricate an aura of power. His manner was a skilful construct; a worldly image of international scholar and man of affairs. In reality he was a parochial figure, a pedant with ice in his veins. Typically, he produced no full-scale books of his own. He specialized in hypercritical reviews. His long-running feud, for example, with the future Sir Ronald Syme would mar relations within the post-war Brasenose Common Room.[175] Meanwhile, newly arrived at Brasenose in 1936, he brought with him formidable skills as a college politician. These he used to devastating effect in the declining days of Stallybrass.

The Principal was vulnerable on two accounts. First, by controlling the selection of commoners and closed scholars, he laid himself open to accusations of partiality. Before 1907 there had been no entrance examination except for open scholars. After that date admissions were formally made by the Principal, on the advice of Tutorial Fellows. But first as Vice-Principal then as Principal, Stallybrass managed to turn this informal system into an expression of his own preferences. Sport came to occupy a privileged position in the process of recruitment; and at meetings of the Governing Body the principalian vote was used with relish. By 1938 Cohn was already demanding change. By 1948 the old system was clearly unsupportable.[176] In the second place, through his dominance of two successive Bursars—Wace and Grant—Stallybrass invited suspicions of extravagance and financial negligence. His personal entertainment allowance had been fixed at £300 p.a. in 1936.[177] But that was only the beginning. Brasenose had been insulated too long by the resilience of the Hulmeian Trust. During the later inter-war years college funds tended to languish in equities instead of

[174] He lacked "the most important qualities of a historian—a lively historical imagination and a lasting creative vein" (*ODNB*). For kinder notices, see *Gnomon,* 1958 (F. E. Adcock) and *Brazen Nose*, xxvii. 54–5 (S. Scott).

[175] For this dispute, see G. W. Bowerstock and P. A. Brunt in *Brazen Nose*, xxix. 59–61 and xxx. 43–4. Last 'lacked creative power'; as a committee man he took no trouble to avoid 'asperities' or 'barbed language' (Nicholas, ibid., xi. 14–19).

[176] 'I cannot, as you know, cease to be disturbed by the trend of your policy in the matter of admissions' (MEM 2J/1: Cohn, E. S.: Cohn to Stallybrass, 23 Apr. 1938). 'The question of admissions has always been in the hands of the Principal' (ibid., Stallybrass to Cohn, 25 Apr. 1938). Stallybrass regularly used his second vote in Governing Body, unlike Last (Styler Tapes, recorded in conversation with Harry Judge, 1982).

[177] V-P's Reg. 5 Dec. 1936, fo. 203. The Principal's butler, Albert Thomas, published his own memoirs: *Wait and See* (1944); 'the most stately butler in Oxford' (*Evening News*, 1 Mar. 1944). It seems that he made himself too familiar with Sonners' cellar. Stallybrass left £23,062, mostly to BNC (*The Times*, 10 Feb. 1946, 6).

thriving in real estate. Even Sonners admitted that Wace's speciality as Bursar was not saving but spending. Not for nothing did he occupy the choicest rooms himself: VI, 4 as chaplain and Old Lodge 4–5 as Bursar. But these were merely the formal grounds of complaint. In essence, what Brasenose now witnessed was a clash of generations. Wace had gone, but Stallybrass was very much still there. As the years went by, alcohol and nicotine had taken their toll (pl. 81). The deaths of so many young friends must have hit him hard. By his early sixties, Sonners seemed already an old man, and his attitudes had dated.

He still believed in Oxford. He still believed in Brasenose. University and college, college and University: their roles were necessarily contradictory and complementary. But he remained convinced that true education—the interchange of life and learning—was still just possible, a product of Oxford's uneasy equilibrium. Hence his search for balance; a balance of academic and personal development. 'If Oxford's greatest lesson', he concluded, 'is to teach her sons to live in company, another of her lessons is to give men the resources for the self-sufficient life.'[178] The secret lay in the alchemy of college living. And in Brasenose that meant more than the examination syllabus. Socially, it meant tolerance, loyalty, integrity. Academically, it meant mental stamina, intellectual curiosity. Ultimately, it meant a feeling for life in the round; a code of libertarian values; a sense of the absurd. He liked to quote Andrew Marvell on the execution of King Charles I: 'He nothing common did or mean.'[179] Such virtues, Sonners believed, had to be fostered consciously, then handed down from generation to generation. 'The College is greater than any of its members. The College is perpetual... [for] death cannot sever the links which bind the members of Brasenose one to another.'[180]

It was not a vision the younger Fellows could easily share. They talked a different language. They began to laugh behind his back. One scrap of Common Room banter says it all. In 1936, Eric Collieu, then a newly elected Fellow, noted in his diary a conversation on the abdication of Edward VIII.

> Sonners: 'I've seen it before; it's the yellow streak,
> when a man won't fall on the ball.'[181]

There was nothing yellow about Stallybrass. But the younger Fellows were looking for a different sort of resolution.

As so often in Common Room matters, it was an apparently trivial issue which crystallized discontent. In November 1940—yes, November

---

[178] Stallybrass, 'Oxford in Peace and War', in Scott-James, *Education in Britain*, 33 and *American Oxonian*, 28 (1941), 100.
[179] Stallybrass at the Tweedsmuir Dinner, 9 July 1935 (*Brazen Nose*, vi. 92).
[180] Stallybrass on the death of Principal Sampson, 8 Nov. 1936 (ibid. 164).
[181] In conversation with the author.

1940—Stanley Cohn refused to dress for dinner. 'Dress to be worn at dinner', he informed the Principal, should 'be left to individual discretion for the duration of the war.' Sonners was outraged. Stocker refused to change the rules. Cohn withdrew from high table to his bunker in IV, 4. There, he told Sonners, 'I propose to continue to adjust my dining clothes to my own notions of propriety.'[182] Within weeks he had left Brasenose for the war. It was only with the return of peace that real hostilities—the SCR's clash of generations—could once again be resumed.

October 1947 marked the inauguration of BNC's first Vice-Chancellor since Heberden. On 25 May 1948 Princess Elizabeth, soon to be Queen Elizabeth II, visited Brasenose and lunched on high table. Beaming proudly, the Principal guided Her Royal Highness round the college. The President of the JCR Robert Runcie—the future Archbishop—was there to greet her at the Lodge. But the dissident Fellows were already sharpening their claws. In April 1948 responsibility for admissions had at last been wrested from the Principal's control. Cohn engineered the appointment of Leslie Styler as Oxford's first Tutor for Admissions.[183] And on 13 October 1948, Hugh Last put up a new and deadly proposal: that steps be taken to investigate the relative decline in college finances 'since 1922', that is since the fourth Commission and the departure of the saintly Heberden.[184] In effect this was a motion of no confidence in the entire career of W. T. S. Stallybrass. Tension in the Governing Body was electric. Sonners, enraged by the effrontery of a mere professorial Fellow, ended the meeting with a curse: 'Damn you, Last!'[185]

That was 13 October. The motion was to be debated at the next meeting. After dinner on 26 October, Sonners and Styler sat up late into the night. They talked till 3 a.m.; nominally about admissions, actually about 'the succession'.[186] Next morning the Principal set out for London, for a meeting of the University Grants Committee. Then he dined at the Inner Temple. That night his body was found on the railway line between Langley and Iver stations. It was the anniversary of the death of William Hulme.

Curiously, it had happened before. There was a precedent, not noticed at the subsequent inquest. In 1927 Canon R. W. Porter, Rector of Steeple

---

[182] MEM 2J/1: Cohn, E. S.: Cohn to Stallybrass, 22 Nov. 1940.

[183] V-P's Reg. 10 Mar. 1948, fo. 119 and 28 Apr. 1948, fo. 121; Styler Tapes. Styler continued as chaplain, having succeeded Owen in 1947. Richard Hull had tried to diminish the Principal's control over admissions before the war. For Styler's appointment as Fellow—partly as the result of a mistake: he was at first confused with his brother—see Styler Tapes. For Owen see P. Jessel, *Owen of Uppingham: Primate of New Zealand* (1965).

[184] V-P's Reg. 13 Oct. 1948, fo. 129.

[185] Styler Tapes.

[186] Styler Tapes. Stallybrass was at this time only 64; the retirement age was 70.

Aston, had fallen to his death from the Calais boat train at the entrance to the tunnel at Boulogne. Now Steeple Aston was a Brasenose living, and the Canon was a Brasenose man, a double First in classics no less, with a distinguished clerical career behind him. Apparently, he had 'turned the handle of the door at the end of the coach opening onto the line, in mistake for the door of the lavatory'.[187] Or so it was suggested. The Canon had been appointed to Steeple Aston only a year before the accident. It must certainly have been Common Room gossip. Sonners cannot have forgotten it. And the teasing ambiguity of such a case—open to three contradictory explanations: accident, murder, or suicide—cannot have escaped him.

The news came through to Platnauer in the early hours of the morning of 28 October. He called an emergency meeting of the Governing Body. There was only one item on the agenda. As Vice-Principal, Platnauer took the chair; then there were Sonners' old allies, Spalding, McKie, and Grant, all in a state of shock; then Cohn and Collieu, sensing their time had come; and then the younger Fellows. Last was conspicuously absent; Shackleton too. 'Death of the Principal', notes the Register curtly. 'The Principal died as the result of an accident in the early hours of this morning. It was decided to express the wishes of the College to the University as follows: the College wishes the time and date of the funeral to be the afternoon of Monday November 1st—assuming no legal difficulties—and the place of the service to be St. Mary's Church. It was agreed to hold a Memorial Service for Brasenose men only in Chapel on November 3rd, Wednesday, at 3 pm.'[188]

That is all. Not a word of regret; not a mention of thirty-five years' service to the college; not a hint of his standing in the University—he was after all Vice-Chancellor—nor of his reputation in the world of law and sport. Sonners died on the Feast of St Jude: patron saint of 'causes despaired of'. For years afterwards Cohn and Collieu would raise their glasses in anniversary triumph: 'Thanks be to St. Jude!'[189]

The inquest was held at 10.30 a.m., on 11 November, in Slough Police Station. The Vice-Chancellor's secretary testified that Sonners was 'practically blind at night'. Tommy Taylor recalled in a letter that the Principal had once tried to get out of a stationary train at Paddington by opening the door on the wrong side. The coroner—clearly a BNC sympathizer—told the jury firmly that Sonners 'was the last sort of man in the world who would commit suicide'. The jury obediently returned a verdict of 'Death by misadventure'.[190]

---

[187] MPP 56 F 4/1: newspaper report 30 Sept. 1927, tipped in.

[188] V-P's Reg. 28 Oct. 1948, fo. 129.

[189] In conversation with the author.

[190] Stallybrass file; *Oxford Times* and *Oxford Mail*, 11 Nov. 1948, 3; *The Times*, 11 Nov. 1948, 2. The coroner was P. Nickeson. The train left Paddington at 12.15; as it passed through Iver at

Leslie Styler, alone of the Brasenose Fellows, attended the inquest. As chaplain, he had already conducted the funeral at St Mary's, and the memorial service at BNC. Stanley Cohn was conspicuously absent from both. It fell to Styler to dispose of the Principal's ashes. He placed them next to the altar, beneath a small stone engraved with familiar initials: W. T. S. S. Cohn is reported to have danced upon the spot.[191]

On the night of the memorial service, Cohn, McKie, and Styler sat talking in Common Room after dinner. Cohn seized the moment to settle the succession. McKie was for Waldock: that, after all had been Sonners' last wish, as Styler knew very well. Cohn was unequivocally for Last. He had already prevented Waldock becoming Junior Proctor, by nominating John Barltrop. Now he moved quickly to block Waldock's chances once more. He led his two colleagues straight away to the Vice-Principal's rooms on staircase VI. As expected, Platnauer declined to stand. More reluctantly, he also withdrew his preference for Waldock. Next morning Cohn called on Bursar Grant. Within two days unanimity had been secured. A telegram was then dispatched to Last. He replied with a warning from the physician in Plato's *Republic*: 'The bridle of Theages forbids.' George Gordon—the only Fellow with any medical knowledge—persuaded him to go back to his doctor for a second opinion. This time he was given seven years to live. On 27 November, Last was elected Principal.[192]

Tributes to Stallybrass poured in from all over the world.[193] There was a general sense that Oxford had changed, irrevocably. Certainly BNC would never be the same again. Even the Oxford Union suspended its proceedings for one minute's silence. Lord Lindsay, Master of Balliol, called him 'a great Vice-Chancellor . . . the fairest and justest man I ever knew . . . a great lawyer . . .

12.30 a carriage door was seen to be open; an emergency stop signal was sent on to Slough East; and the body was located soon afterwards. The carriage door had swung open on the off side; the sliding door to the corridor was also wide open; and the corridor itself, running along the near side, was well lit. Both locks had a similar mechanism. The train had been travelling on a famously fast, straight stretch, at 60 to 65 m.p.h. This GWR line had been the first to institute corridors throughout its length, in 1892. For the earlier incident at Paddington, see PR1 25 L1/1: T. Taylor to M. Platnauer, 1 Nov. 1948. Historically, Iver was part of the Somerset bequest of 1679. The record of this benefaction was the last entry in Principal Yate's monumental 'Schedula & Abstracta' (1668); and in the end its location marked the death of Stallybrass.

[191] Barry Nicholas, who—like David Stockton—confirmed this story, seems to have been unaware of the initialled stone (*Brazen Nose*, xxxi. 27; PR1 25 L1/1). The inscription on the memorial in the antechapel was composed by Platnauer.

[192] V-P's Reg. 27 Nov. 1948, fo. 131; Styler Tapes. In the event, Last survived in office for seven years seven months, and died sixteen months after that in Oct. 1957. The fateful telegram originally read: 'The Bridle of The Ages Forbids'. Apparently it was McKie who solved the riddle.

[193] PRI 25 L1/1–3: letters to Platnauer, and Grant, and Spalding.

a great Englishman'.[194] Maurice Bowra—who might have been seen as a rival—paid him a sensitive tribute.

I was very fond of Sonners... He was so modest that he dissimulated his taste for the arts [though his knowledge of music was] great and genuine. And of course he had that wonderful gift of making a community happy. It had been his job at Brasenose for years, but he was beginning to transfer his gift to the whole University with uncommon success. Meetings of boards became a pleasure with him! It is all nonsense to say he had prejudices. He had convictions and ideals... We shall all miss him terribly and I cannot bear to think of Oxford without him.[195]

So many attended the service at BNC that it had to be relayed by loudspeaker to the overflow congregation in hall.

Frank Aydelotte, Sonners' partner over many years in the selection of Rhodes Scholars, wrote the best obituary. It ended with words by Robert Louis Stevenson. They deserve to be expanded here.

It is better to lose health like a spendthrift than to waste it like a miser. It is better to live and be done with it, than to die daily in the sickroom... and does not life go down with a better grace, foaming in full body over a precipice, than miserably struggling to an end in sandy deltas? When the Greeks made their fine saying that those whom the gods love die young, I cannot help believing they had this sort of death also in their eye. For surely, at whatever age it overtakes the man, this is to die young... In the hot-fit of life, a-tip-toe on the highest point of being, he passes at a bound on to the other side. The noise of the mallet and chisel is scarcely quenched, the trumpets are hardly done blowing, when, trailing with him clouds of glory, this happy-starred, full-blooded spirit shoots into the spiritual land.

In that sense, Aydelotte observed, 'Sonners died young... We only have to comfort us the reflection that he went before his time, not after it.'[196]

The circumstances of those final hours remained mysterious—sufficiently mysterious to preserve the good name of the college. 'Death by misadventure' covered a multitude of suppositions. And down the years the story has been told and retold. Dinner with old friends at the Inner Temple, the taxi ride to Paddington and the midnight train for Birkenhead; a solitary first-class carriage; the drowsy rhythm of the rails; stumbling feet, unsteady hands; and then the sudden smash of air: '...Damn you, Last!'

---

[194] *Oxford Mail*, 29 Oct. 1948, 2. For undergraduate praise, see *Isis*, 3 Nov. 1948, 7. For Holroyd's affectionate tribute, see *Oxford Mag.* 11 Nov. 1948, 126–7.

[195] PRI 25 L1/13: Bowra to K. N. Spalding, 13 Nov. 1948 (from Cambridge, Mass.). The University Registrar, Sir Douglas Veale, agreed: Sonners gave 'marvellous advice. He was always right' (PRI 25 L1 /2).

[196] R. L. Stevenson, 'Aes Triplex', in *Works*, xiii (1900), 104–5; F. Aydelotte, 'Sonners', *American Oxonian*, 36 (1949), 1–3. In 1924 Aydelotte had transplanted ivy from BNC to Swarthmore College's Worth dormitory (F. Blanshard, *Frank Aydelotte* (Middletown, Conn., 1970), 202).

8

1948 onwards

All Change: Towards a Global Elite

'As the social structure of England changed', noted Jan Morris in 1978, 'so Oxford increasingly debated how best to reform its own entry, still predominantly upper-crust. Everybody but a lunatic core wished to see the University open to people from all social backgrounds; a more intractable problem concerned someone we may call, borrowing the name from Ronald Knox, Carruthers—the agreeable, stalwart, dependable, salt-of-the-earth young English gentleman who was not, as it happened, very clever. Was there a place for him in a truly competitive University?' After all, 'Carruthers survived at Oxford until the Second World War, which he won.'[1] But did Carruthers have a future?

As in some ways the prime representative of the Carruthers tradition—Carruthers' *alma mater* perhaps—Brasenose had to face up to this question seriously. And BNC's problem was Oxford's too. How were the leaders of the future to be selected? Was the process to be a product or a precondition of the higher educational system? How realistic in practice was the whole notion of an accessible elite? Would it ever be possible to universalize privilege; to reconcile equality and talent? Were the higher forms of civility—what Matthew Arnold called true culture—ultimately compatible with the democratic impulse? Or was this multiple conundrum in the end insoluble?

The close of the Sonners era found Brasenose financially under pressure. Between 1930–2 and 1951–3 its average net external revenue—vis-à-vis that of other colleges—declined from third position to eleventh. During the same period, the national cost-of-living index more than doubled. At the Betty Morley dinner in 1952 Fellows even had to pay for their own wine.[2] Like all colleges, BNC was still subject to rationing. Students surrendered their ration books each term to the Bursar. Dons depended on the resources of a

---

[1] J. Morris, *The Oxford Book of Oxford* (1978), 378–80. Carruthers featured in Ronald Knox's parody *Let Dons Delight* (1939).

[2] V-P's Reg. 17 Oct. 151, fo. 68. For costs of living, see *Oxford Mag.* 20 Oct.1955, 25.

dwindling cellar. But thanks to the post-war increase in undergraduate numbers—and thanks to Principal Last's regime of economy—deficits were gradually reduced. By 1952–3 the Bursar was able to report a small surplus. By 1957, net external income was double that of 1938. And by 1958–9 the wealth of the college could be counted comfortably within the University's first division: eighth in fact, behind Christ Church, Magdalen, New College, Queen's, Balliol, St John's, and Merton.[3] At £104,000, its income was admittedly less than two-thirds that of Magdalen; but it was nearly double that of Pembroke and nearly three times that of Hertford.

When it came to 'College Entertainments', however, the BNC Common Room was well ahead of most. In 1959 it ranked third in fact, with £76 p.a., per Fellow (more than three times Merton; more than fifteen times Wadham). Its feasts were now almost as lavish as before the war; its ale consumption legendary. By 1968 its 'entertainment' ranking was still sixth, with a total of £3,410; nearly nine times that of Wadham and Hertford. On the other hand, BNC's 'staff–student ratio'—that is, its proportion of teachers to taught—was one of the least generous in Oxford. In 1948–9 it stood at a miserly 1 to 32; in 1958–9 at 1 to 20; in 1964–5 at 1 to 23. These figures represented scarcely half the ratio available at Magdalen.[4] In 1962 the total number of Tutorial Fellows was still only fifteen: again less than half the total for Magdalen. The Fellows of Brasenose ate well, and perhaps they smoked and drank too well. But they were scarcely overpaid. In 1958–9, for example, Tutorial Fellows received a stipend that rose from £600 (aged 22) to £1,475 (aged 50), plus an entertainment allowance of £20 p.a. Married Fellows living out of college received an extra £60 p.a. for each child, plus a housing allowance of £50 p.a. These men taught hard, and talked very hard. It was part of their ideal of Fellowship. First and foremost, they were scholars. But they saw their role only partly in terms of research. Their concern was primarily educative. In Last's defiant phrase, their job was 'the education of the intellectual aristocracy of the country'.[5] In terms of 'contact hours' they certainly earned their keep. And the strain told. Right into the 1980s, not a single Tutorial Fellow lived to retirement age. This had been almost a tradition at BNC since the First World War; and it continued until the retirement of George Gordon, Fellow in Physiology, in 1987. Fellows of

---

[3] Compare V-P's Reg. 29 May 1957, fo. 58 and 13 Nov. 1968, fo. 10. See also tables in *Oxford Gazette*, 29 Jan. 1960 and *Oxford Mag.* 18 Feb. 1960, 194, 196. 'Entertainments' for 1959 stood at £1,270. But the cost-of-living index rose from a base of 100 to 268 over the period 1959–68. All Souls and Nuffield, of course, were not undergraduate colleges.

[4] Compare Franks Report ii, table 24. Compare *Oxford Mag.* 1 Feb. 1962, 160–1; 8 Feb. 1962, 176; 15 Mar. 1962, 258–9.

[5] *Oxford Mag.* 10 Mar. 1955, 266. For salaries, see V-P's Reg. 30 Apr. 1958, fo. 110, and 27 May 1959, fo. 158.

Brasenose, for most of the twentieth century, died young. Their lives were bibulous, bookish, and short. Whether the college's allocation of expenditure—its balance of scholarship versus gastronomy—was responsible for this state of affairs is rather a nice question.

Who were these Fellows—who talked so hard, and died so comparatively young—on whom the future of the college rested? As the 1960s gave way to the 1970s, Fellows of long standing became increasingly rare. Financial pressures, and the international market, multiplied the rate of turnover. The number of transitory Fellows grew larger; and not all of them can be mentioned here. A key group, however, stayed on. They became part of BNC's collective memory.

At their head, after Platnauer's retirement in 1960, was Sir Noel Hall (pl. 95).[6] Now Hall had been a rare First in history at BNC in the 1920s; he had also played hooker in the rugby Fifteen. He began with a meteoric early career. In London and Princeton he had been regarded in the 1930s as a rising star in economics, an 'economist impatient of theory'. As Professor of Political Economy at University College London, at a precociously early age, he recruited Hugh Gaitskell to his department and was about to recruit the young Harold Wilson when the Second War broke out. Then off he went to Washington with the Ministry for Economic Warfare. Officially, he was a Minister in the Diplomatic Service. Unofficially, he was known as 'the young man with an encyclopaedic mind': 'Know-all Hall'. After the war he went first to West Africa, then to India, and then to Henley, as first Director of the Administrative Staff College. In effect this was Britain's first business school, and it was largely Hall's creation. In each of these roles he displayed a wary bonhomie and a worldly sense of the possible. However he came to the Principalship of Brasenose *faute de mieux*. Sir Oliver Franks had been first choice; but he was distracted by the lure of the University Chancellorship. At BNC Hall proved adept in public relations, and resilient in troubled times. But the Common Room came in the end to doubt the wisdom of its selection. In committee he turned out to be incorrigibly vague. Sometimes this created situations that were positively surreal. He seems to have believed that two Fellows—Graham and Bernard Richards—were actually one; and that another Fellow, Leighton Reynolds, possessed a name that somehow belonged to two different people. On one occasion he was famously caught off guard, perhaps because the Bursar had recently taken to wearing a toupee. 'I don't think we've met', muttered Hall, playing for time. 'But I am the Bursar', came the reply. 'Really?' mused the Principal: 'Which college?' At high table he was a glorious name-dropper. 'As Maynard said to me', he loved to say; 'Noel you've hit the nail on the head.' But with students—and especially with old members—he was genuinely popular.

[6] Obits, *Brazen Nose*, xviii. 1 (D. Stockton), 32–4 (Lord Roll). Portrait (1971) by John Ulbricht.

During his regime, the Governing Body grew by two-thirds; and the SCR was both distinguished and content. Perhaps too content. The changing context of University affairs would find quite a few of the Fellowship unprepared.

Not, however, in law. BNC's strongest suit continued to operate efficiently throughout the 1960s and 1970s, under the direction of an unlikely duo: Ron Maudsley and Barry Nicholas. Both owed their recruitment to Stallybrass. Maudsley came to Oxford via Birmingham, and he never forsook his Midlands roots. In fact he continued to captain the Warwickshire cricket team—admittedly in vacations—while actually holding office as Tutorial Fellow. Very much a man in the Sonners mould—a triple blue as well as a First in BCL—Maudsley was a worldly figure, in some ways too big for BNC. But to Brasenose he brought valuable transatlantic teaching experience: from Harvard, Miami, Chicago, New York, San Diego. And it was in America that he died, too young, in 1981.[7] Fortunately for Brasenose he was succeeded by another Midlander who had already turned the teaching of law into an art form: J. W. Davies.[8] The combination of Davies and Nicholas—supplemented during the 1970s and early 1980s by Peter Birks—guaranteed that the stream of able BNC lawyers would continue undiminished. Birks, who eventually became Regius Professor of Civil Law at All Souls, was a charismatic tutor; a scholar who could range at will over swathes of Roman, English and German law. College life he loved. 'Brasenose', he recalled, 'was a wonderful place to be and to be a lawyer.'[9] His intensity neatly complemented Davies's cooler approach. And both of them worked in easy harness with the imperturbable Barry Nicholas. Meanwhile, in his rooms on Heberden staircase—cavernous, book-bound—Harry Lawson talked and talked: the first Professor of Comparative Law; the founder of his own discipline. His successor talked a little less, but with greater powers of persuasion. He was the redoubtable Sir Otto Kahn-Freund, master of trade union legislation.[10]

Nicholas (pl. 93) was almost the polar opposite of Maudsley. He brought to the study of Roman law all the precision of a top civil service mind. Lucid as a lecturer, genial as a tutor, tenacious in committee, he must have trained

---

[7] Obit., ibid., xvii. 214–15. His books included *Land Law* (1967), *Trusts and Trustees* (1973), and *The Modern Law of Perpetuities* (1979).

[8] *Brazen Nose*, xxxv. 49–50 (N. Withington).

[9] Obit., ibid., xxxviii. 144–8; *The Times*, 9 July 2004, 34. He wrote *An Introduction to the Law of Restitution* (1985); and edited *English Private Law* (2000), *English Public Law* (2004).

[10] For both Lawson and Kahn-Freund see *ODNB* (B. Nicholas). Lawson's works include *A Common Lawyer Looks at the Civil Law* (1955), *The Rational Strength of English Law* (1951), and *Introduction to the Law of Property* (1958). Kahn-Freund, besides his mastery of European and labour law, was the editor of the sixth to ninth editions of *Dicey*. For his notion of 'collective laissez-faire', see M. Ginsberg (ed.), *Law and Opinion in the 20th Century* (1959).

more future judges than any law Fellow in Oxford. His *Introduction to Roman Law* (1962)—to say nothing of his third edition of Jolowicz's *Historical Introduction to the Study of Roman Law* (1972)—dominated the teaching of the subject for a generation. His *French Law of Contract* (1982) even satisfied the French: in 1987 he received an honorary doctorate from the University of Paris. From his arrival as a classical scholar in 1937 to his retirement as Principal in 1989—and from then on to his death in 2002—he represented the best of BNC. He lived to make it 'a dutiful and profoundly decent community'. Throughout his life, in Peter Fraser's words, he was 'above all, loyal to three things...the College, the Law and the Catholic Church'.[11] Indeed, he was to become the first practising Roman Catholic Principal of any Oxford or Cambridge college since the Reformation.

By this time Leslie Styler (pls. 92, 93, 94)—first schoolmaster, then chaplain, and finally administrator—was moving into the third phase of his career. But his primary loyalty remained fixed on BNC. 'Clubbable...good-natured, kindly, ebullient, full of fun, a born talker': Styler was destined for Common Room life. More particularly, he was born to be cellarius at Brasenose.[12] Such qualities became increasingly rare in the 1970s, as Oxford turned itself into a more strictly academic society. Luckily for BNC, two elections in the 1950s and 1960s guaranteed the survival of older priorities. David Stockton's enthusiasm for ancient history could never exclude 'cakes and ale'. 'An archetypal Oxford tutor', wrote one of his pupils; 'a preservation order (Grade One) should be clapped on him immediately' (pl. 93).[13] In Michael Woods he found a more than agreeable teaching partner. Woods' passion for ancient philosophy was tempered by a twitchy eccentricity, as genuine as it was endearing. Not just odd socks, but odd shoes too: on occasion one black, one brown. His scholarly giggle—cut short by untimely illness—was almost a throwback to the age of Bussell. And in the person of John Ackrill—Woods' own tutor in all things Aristotelian—both Woods and Stockton found their perfect foil (pl. 93).[14]

Platnauer's successor as Mods tutor was Leighton Reynolds. Before his premature death—soon after retirement in 1997—he had established himself as the still, calm centre of BNC. Bursar Barltrop used to say that 'he only had to spend a few minutes in Leighton's company to feel his blood pressure

[11] *Brazen Nose*, xxiii. 29; xxxvi. 36–8; *Proceedings of the British Academy*, 124 (2004), 219–39 (P. Birks); portrait in hall by Mark Wickam.

[12] *Brazen Nose*, xxv. 57 (D. Stockton).

[13] Ibid., xxvi. 7. His works include *Cicero: A Political Biography* (1971), *The Gracchi* (1979), and *The Classical Athenian Democracy* (1990).

[14] For Woods, see *Brazen Nose*, xxvii. 1–2 (D. Stockton), 44–5: his *Eudemian Ethics* (1982; 1992) is 'a book that will be used and valued as long as Aristotle is studied' (J. Ackrill). For Ackrill, see *The Times*, 20 Dec. 2007, p. 5.

going down'. No wonder some of his best work was done in collaboration: *Scribes and Scholars: A Guide to the Transmission of Greek and Latin* (1968) and *Texts and Transmission: A Survey of the Latin Classics* (1983). Fellow, Dean, Vice-Principal, twice Acting Principal, Reynolds bridged in his own career the world of private scholarship and the world of competitive assessment. With his passing, the Brasenose of Maurice Platnauer vanished for good.[15]

But before that there was Norman Leyland (pl. 92): jazz fan; stock market magician; as Lancashire as his surname; twice Bursar, indeed 'one of the great building Bursars' of Brasenose.[16] His early days at Manchester Grammar had been hard; but his middle years—he died before retirement—were filled with good fortune. Although a Tutor in Economics, Leyland was never a theoretician. He was a hands-on administrator with an instinct for making money. As investment manager he had remarkable success: he doubled the value of the Platnauer benefaction in ten years. Appropriately, in 1965, he became Director of the Oxford Centre for Management Studies (later Templeton College).

It was during the 1950s and 1960s that English literature first developed its teaching strength at Brasenose. First Ian Jack, then Alastair Fowler—both future FBAs—made it a discipline to reckon with. In different ways both broke new ground: Jack on the Romantics, Fowler on the Elizabethans. And each knew the secret of communicating his own enthusiasm to a lecture audience. So too, for twenty years, did Bernard Richards: keeper of the Paterian flame. But not Brian Miller. Under various titles—Hulme Lecturer in English Philology, Lecturer in English Language, or just plain Fellow in English—he taught Anglo-Saxon intermittently at BNC from 1953 to 1992, between spells in Oriel and Singapore. 'Intermittent', however, gives quite the wrong impression. He taught intensively, with almost manic precision. He spoke in sentences, and thought in paragraphs. He tutored in chapters, and he lectured—to empty halls—in veritable volumes. His language was obstinately Latinate; his delivery camp to the point of caricature. Once, when someone left a pair of highly coloured gloves in his room, he demanded: 'To whom does this polychromatic handwear belong?' Gaunt, pale, etiolated, he once informed a candidate for admission: 'This University is not a place of education but of learning.'[17] In some of his utterances, he resembled Robert Shackleton. But it was Shackleton without the twinkle.

By the early 1960s Shackleton (pls. 92, 93) had emerged as 'the Doyen of Montesquieu scholars'.[18] He would go on to be Bodley's librarian and Marshal Foch Professor of French at All Souls. His origins had been humble.

---

[15] *Proceedings of the British Academy*, 111 (2000), 659–76 (M. Winterbottom). *Brazen Nose*, xxxiv. 46–50, 70–1 (J. Hopkin, G. Richards, M. Reeve).

[16] Obit, *Brazen Nose*, xvii. 302–10 (B. Nicholas, G. Cross, J. Wain).

[17] Ibid., xxxv. 77 (B. Richards).

[18] Obit, *The Times*, 11 Sept. 1986, 18; *Daily Telegraph*, 11 Sept. 1986. *Brazen Nose*, xxi. 76–88.

He was the son of a Yorkshire shoemaker. Or perhaps Lancashire: he came from Todmorden on the very boundary of Lancashire and Yorkshire. But although he was poor his deprivation was certainly not scholastic. As a keen sixth-former he was able to study in the Rylands Library at Manchester. Two of his contemporaries at Todmorden Secondary School went on to be Nobel Prizewinners. That tells us something about the vitality of state education in the 1930s. Even so, young Shackleton was certainly brought up in provincial obscurity, and he remained something of an outsider all his life. Non-conformist by upbringing; agnostic by conviction; Liberal in politics; obliquely combative in manner: he was a curious combination of austerity and greed. Something of all this was audible in his manner of speech. He stored up words with miserly precision, then enunciated their syllables with relish. The accents of both his native counties—overlaid with French, Italian, and Oxford English—seemed to struggle for mastery with a nasal twang which was positively adenoidal. It did his career no harm. Committees he managed. Lecture audiences he learned to control. But he was fundamentally solitary. Books he loved; their paper, their bindings; the feel and smell of them. 'The physical objects we call books', he wrote, 'are the bone structure of literature ... [indeed] bibliography and literary history are inseparable disciplines.'[19]

As BNC's librarian and Senior Dean (1954–61), Shackleton lived up to his reputation as a 'character'. His angular gestures, his capacity for food and wine, his peculiarities of speech, made him the butt of endless anecdotes. In his own words, he was much 'given, ah yus, to affirmative iteration'. His movements were curiously distinctive: in Richard Cobb's phrase, he walked 'like a procession of one'. 'Shackles' must have been BNC's most parodied, and best-loved, bachelor don since Bussell. When one undergraduate-errant surreptitiously concealed his after-hours girl friend in a dustbin, he was roundly condemned: not for 'moral turpitude'—'ah, yus'—but for a striking 'lack of chivalry'. On such occasions, penalties were distributed with panache. His Junior Dean, John Ackrill (pl. 93), had a drier touch. After a successful shooting trip in 1955, one freshman hung from his window a bleeding brace of duck. Ackrill crisply invoked the categorical imperative: 'What if everybody did that?' Shackleton preferred a lighter rein. When in 1959 a group of undergraduates—led by a future Lord of Appeal—hijacked several candidates for admission and subjected them to a series of mock interviews, the Senior Dean was unconcerned: 'It did, ah yus, no appreciable damage to the college fabric.' One night a notorious inebriate revenged himself on a less than popular Fellow, Dr Desmond Bagguley. With copious weedkiller he wrote upon the New Quad lawn: 'Balls to Bagguley'. Next morning the culprit found himself carpeted on staircase IX. 'I see you have written—ah, yus—"Balls to

---

[19] Quoted in *Proceedings of the British Academy*, 73 (1987), 657–84 (G. Barber).

Bagguley"', mused Shackleton. 'That is a serious offence; ah, yus, a serious offence; though it is a sentiment from which I cannot wholly—ah, yus—dissociate myself.' The subsequent fine was accompanied by a glass of Chianti. As a gourmet, Shackleton was not quite in the same league as Platnauer. But his appetite, at least before the onset of illness, was robust. His last words—at Ravello, near Naples—were touchingly appropriate: 'Prosciutto, per favore'. In the end it was A. L. Rowse who got him absolutely right. On the flyleaf of his copy of Richard Cobb's Shackletonian address, he noted simply: 'Good Man. Good Friend. Odd Accent.'[20]

Shackleton failed in only one ambition. He never became Principal. That honour would go first to Herbert Hart and then to Barry Nicholas. To both we will return. Hart's election he accepted. He was obviously the right man at the right time. But the election of Barry Nicholas was difficult for him. Nicholas was a tutor of dedication and skill. But Shackleton was a scholar's scholar, the very spirit of Bodley. And among the humanities Fellows of post-war Brasenose, there was only one man to whose learning he deferred: Professor Sir Ronald Syme, OM.

Syme merits more than a moment's pause. A prodigy in New Zealand; a rising star at Oriel: pure alpha in Roman history in 1927; a popular tutor at Trinity, and a wartime intelligence officer in Belgrade and Istanbul; then back again to Oxford, and quick promotion to the Camden chair: on the face of it Syme's progress was dazzling. Apart from some quibbling by Arnaldo Momigliano, his first great book, *The Roman Revolution* (1939), earned widespread acceptance for its mastery of prosopographical technique. His *Tacitus*—both in style and substance—won resounding acclaim. Reading 'Syme on Tacitus', wrote one reviewer, 'is like reading Tacitus on Tacitus...[He even] thinks like a Roman...[He stands] in the triumvirate of modern masters of Roman history beside Gibbon and Mommsen.'[21] And yet Syme's period at Brasenose was not exactly happy. It was marred from the start by a feud—there is no other word for it—a poisonous feud with Principal Last.

When Syme was elected to the British Academy in 1944, Last—as current holder of the Camden chair and a notable non-Academician—was not exactly pleased. On 21 September he wrote to Syme to say that he had heard 'the news that you [have] joined that Academy of theirs...Well, well. My respect for you is such as to survive even heavier blows than that. But the thing does become more futile with the years, and the publications of its

[20] Farewell epistle by Bernard Richards, *Brazen Nose*, xvii/1. 46; *Memorial Addresses of All Souls College, Oxford* (privately printed, 1989), 215. Portraits by Sir William Coldstream (Bodleian), Bob Tulloch, and Margaret Foreman (BNC).
[21] T. W. Africa, in *American Hist. Rev.* (June 1971), 753.

members which discredit British scholarship more numerous.' A few months later, in February 1945, he added: 'British Academy—All right: I put it down to an altruistic addiction to slumming on your part.'[22] Three years after that, in 1948, open hostilities broke out. A discussion article by Syme appeared in the *Journal of Roman Studies*, dissecting a new edition of Tacitus recently published in Switzerland. Syme's review took up a position that was textually conservative. 'The historical writings of Tacitus', he began, 'are a prosopographical jungle'; a jungle, he implied, best avoided by the uninitiated. As for Tacitean style its peculiarity, he suggested, defied regularization. Better to accept its idiosyncrasy; its 'rapidity, acerbity, and abruptness'. Wilful emendations ran the risk of leaving the master 'purged and debilitated'. There have been 'too many changes', he concludes; 'glosses and interpolations have had their day'; such techniques represent 'an outworn tradition of scholarship'.[23]

That was scarcely calculated to please the pundits. Last nursed his displeasure for a full three years, watching with manifest distaste Syme's appointment to the Camden chair after his own election to Brasenose. Then in December 1951 he unleashed a minor thunderbolt. Still smarting from Syme's review of 1948, he threatened to resign from the *Journal*'s editorial committee: 'my attitude to bad scholarship and lowered standards is as remorseless as ever.' At this Syme diplomatically backed down—he had in any case completed his term as President of the Society for the Promotion of Roman Studies—and was replaced by Momigliano. It was a Pyrrhic victory for Last. Such disputes, he informed Syme, should be considered 'irrelevant to our relations as members of a College'.[24] That was asking too much. The rift had become too wide. Last retreated to the Lodgings, the marks of death already on him. He resigned the Principalship in 1956, and died in 1957.[25]

---

[22] Quoted by G. W. Bowerstock from Bodl. Syme MSS, in *Proceedings of the British Academy*, 84 (1993), 539–63.

[23] *Jnl. of Roman Studies*, 38 (1948), 122–31.

[24] Bowerstock, in *Proceedings of the British Academy*, 84 (1993), 539–63 and *Brazen Nose*, xxix. 48–67. P. A. Brunt suggested that Last's attitude to Syme 'was in fact actuated by something resembling *odium theologicum*' (*Brazen Nose*, xxx. 44).

[25] He seems to have believed—and he apparently convinced Hugh Trevor-Roper—that he was 'the only civilised man' at BNC; struggling to reverse 'a swollen flood-tide of total philistinism' (Trevor-Roper to Bernard Berenson, 5 Feb. 1950: *ex inf.* Richard Davenport-Hines). Last's notice of resignation is a curiosity: 'This letter will probably not be thought genuine unless it contains some outrageous remarks before its end. I do not propose to defend or apologise for what has happened in College since 1948. We seem to me to have regained some ground that had been lost, and I have no doubt that if we are to retain it and regain more, the College will need a Principal with his wits more actively about him.' The letter was merely 'acknowledged' by the Governing Body (V-P's Reg. 26 May 1956, fo. 18). In 1966 Shackleton's proposal that a memorial tablet be placed in the antechapel was rejected (V-P's Reg. 9 Nov. 1966, fo. 12).

Syme worked on in his book-lined rooms—Stocker's old quarters—ensconced on staircase XI. In 1958 his two-volume *Tacitus* appeared to international applause. A knighthood followed in 1959; and the Order of Merit in
1976. He was hailed—not least by his staunch friend Sir Isaiah Berlin—as the
greatest living English historian. In the end he clocked up some twenty
academic honours. At BNC however things went rather less well. With
younger Fellows, Vernon Bogdanor for instance, he could mix agreeably.
But sometimes he must have felt like a titan among minnows.[26]

Succeeding Syme cannot have been easy. But as Camden Professor, 1970–
82, Peter Brunt more than established his own reputation. His *Italian Man-
power 225 B.C.—A.D. 14* (1971) was magisterial. His *Social Conflicts in the Late
Republic*, published in the same year, could be said to have educated a whole
generation of classicists. Brunt's manner was intimidating. Some said his
name must have been a conflation of 'brusque' and 'blunt'. He did have a
kindly side. But in University affairs he was a hard fighter. He once admitted
that he regarded the demolition of error as his most important contribution
to scholarship. That could hardly have been the motto of his immediate
successor, Fergus Millar. The sweep of Millar's writings—from the crowd in
republican Rome to the Jewish people in the time of Christ—confirms a
rather more panoramic vision.[27] Still, Brunt's acerbity earned the approval of
at least one of his Brasenose colleagues: Philip Jones. Appointed as a
replacement—and a contrast—to Stanley Cohn, Jones was a man who
concealed a wry interior behind a very wry exterior. Geoffrey Holmes recalls
his presence: 'Tall, spare, scholarly... [with] probing, deep-set, dark brown
eyes... [and] sandy hair; a long grey overcoat... And [extraordinary] eyebrows... tawny and grey, extravagantly exuberant, wiry, virile... devastat-
ingly grotesque... projecting almost beyond the top of the nose.' When
Barry Nicholas once remarked to the Governing Body that he was looking
for a handsome, personable Fellow to look after some significant visitor,
Jones was heard to growl, 'Why pick on me?' The more somnolent aspects
of BNC life were viewed by him with sardonic affection. 'History is a

---

[26] See F. Millar in *Brazen Nose*, xxiv. 77–80 and *ODNB*; *The Times*, 4 Apr. 183, photo p. 7: 'a
world scholar at the top of the first division... the noblest Roman of them all' (M. Howard).
Last declined to take part in Syme's election as Camden Professor. Syme, for his part, tried in
vain to have his chair transferred to Trinity (V-P's Reg. 27 May 1949, fs. 113, 137). He took
particular exception to the cost of his accommodation: £20 per term for XII, 7 in 1949–53;
£30 per term for XI, 3 in 1953–70 (Room Books *passim*). On his retirement in 1970, Sir Isaiah
Berlin found him a strategic niche in Wolfson College. He died in 1989 worth over £1,000,000.

[27] *Brazen Nose*, xl. 164–6. Brunt's collected essays appeared as *The Fall of the Roman Republic*
(1988), *Roman Imperial Themes* (1990), and *Studies in Greek History and Thought* (1993). Millar's
works include *The Emperor in the Roman World* (1977; 1992); *Rome, the Greek World and the East*, 3
vols. (2002–6); and *The Roman Republic in Political Thought* (2002).

nightmare', he used to say, 'from which even Brasenose must wake.' In his own gruff way he was a real college man. And he knew more about medieval Italy than any Italian historian.[28]

What of the science Fellows? Here three names stand out: Barltrop, Birch, and Kurti. 'Black Jack' Barltrop began as a legendary Tutor in Organic Chemistry, and ended as a Bursar with a masterful capacity for organization.[29] Both sides of his career would be echoed in the next generation by one of his ablest pupils, the future Bursar Robert Gasser. Bryan Birch played a smaller part in college affairs. But as Professor of Arithmetic (1985–98) he built up a formidable name. In all its mathematical mystery, the Birch and Swinnerton-Dyer conjecture still stands. As for Nicholas Kurti, his reputation survives on at least two levels. He began as one of the Breslau cohort of low-temperature physicists recruited to the Clarendon Laboratory in 1933 by Frederick Lindemann. There he became a key player in Lindemann's top-secret programme for nuclear fission. In the 1940s he was associated with the darkest mysteries of the atom bomb. Later on he held the world record for the lowest temperature ever achieved in a laboratory. After the war he stayed on to develop the Clarendon's high magnetic field laboratory. He was elected a Research Fellow at Brasenose in 1947 thanks to Richard Hull (briefly Fellow in Physics; killed in a fall on Mont Blanc in 1949 at the age of 38, and succeeded by Desmond Bagguley). To the world at large, Kurti was a heavyweight physicist: Vice-President of the Royal Society. But at BNC he will be remembered as a Common Room legend: genial, omniscient, master of exotic cuisine ('gastrophysics'). He delighted in the camaraderie of the SCR. One night he wagered and won a bottle of claret by eating two large cream crackers inside sixty seconds. At one Fellows' Christmas dinner he arranged for the table to be laid with hypodermic syringes: for injecting brandy into mince pies. 'The discovery of a new dish', he wrote, 'could be just as rewarding intellectually and just as beneficial to mankind as the discovery of a new inter-atomic force, or of a new low temperature phenomenon, or a new elementary particle, or of a new star.' By the time of his death, at the age of 90, he represented almost a vanished generation: Oxford's last link with 'the heroic era of 20th century physics'.[30]

---

[28] *Brazen Nose*, xxiv. 8–9 (T. Dean); xvi/4. 9. The first volume of his *magnum opus*, *The Italian City-State*, appeared to great applause in 1997 (*Times Lit. Supp.* 31 Oct. 1977, p. 16). Curiously, he proposed that the SCR should include provision for table tennis (V-P's Reg. 29 Apr. 1970, fo. 129; 27 May 1970, fo. 135).

[29] *Brazen Nose*, xxiv. 6–7.

[30] Ibid., 5–6; xxxii. 10, 60–1; xxxiii. 40–1 (J. Peach). See also G. Thomson, 'F. A. Lindemann, Viscount Cherwell', *B.M.F.R.S.* 4 (1958); R. F. Harrod, *The Prof.* (1959); F. W. F. Smith, *The Prof. in Two Worlds* (1961). For Kurti and nuclear fission, see R. V. Jones, *Most Secret War* (1978). For Bagguley, see *Brazen Nose*, xxxix. 160–2 (J. Peach).

In two respects, these post-war Fellows of Brasenose remained strikingly traditional. In the first place, over a period of thirty years—1935–65—one-third of all those elected to the Governing Body (17 out of 51) were themselves originally Brasenose undergraduates. BNC men recruited BNC men. In the second place, a similar proportion of Fellows—as many as 13 out of 33 in 1966—remained bachelor dons, living and working in college. That was not so unusual in post-war Oxford, perhaps 10 per cent higher than the average. But BNC enjoyed its bachelor image, and that made for a certain conservatism. In 1968 the dons still entered hall in order of seniority; their placement at dinner was dictated by their date of election. Nevertheless the SCR as a whole was by no means reactionary. In 1961, for example, under-graduate reviews of lectures were published for the first time in *Isis*. The very fact of publication—students assessing dons—produced something of a sensation. The Vice-Chancellor and Proctors issued peremptory bans. Four-teen Fellows of BNC signed a public letter supporting the students. Shackle-ton signed twice.[31] Perhaps that was absent-mindedness. But if Shackleton had a vein of conservatism in his make-up, it extended only so far as his daily living arrangements. There, of course, he was against all change. When a certain Frenchwoman—a rich Frenchwoman—dared to look upon him with matrimonial eyes, he beat a tactical retreat: 'in spite of the attractions of her chateau, ah yus, I demurred.'[32]

The years 1966–8, however, marked a turning point at Brasenose. During this time no fewer than eight Fellows were appointed. Here was a new wave of younger scholars; mostly of progressive inclination—four in particular. Firstly there was Laszlo Solymar, Fellow in Engineering, 1966–86: he went on to be Professor of Applied Electromagnetism and FRS. Second, there was Vernon Bogdanor, BNC's first Fellow in Politics; he would become Professor of Government and FBA, and constitutional adviser to half a dozen governments worldwide. Third, there was Robert Evans: he would become Regius Professor of Modern History, and FBA at the remarkably early age of 41. And fourth, there was Graham Richards: he would end as Oxford's Chairman of Chem-istry, managing one of the biggest chemistry departments in the world.

So much for the dons, or rather the Fellows of longest standing. Now for the students. The immediate post-war intake at BNC was large. In 1938 there had been 89 freshmen. That was the highest number in any Oxford college. By 1949 there were as many as 104. For Brasenose this was an unprecedented

---

[31] *Oxford Mag.*, 9 Feb. 1961, 209. In 1955 Shackleton carried a motion in Governing Body that candidates for admission should not be required to state their religion (V-P's Reg. 16 Feb. 1955, fo. 156).

[32] *Brazen Nose*, xxxiv. 44 (D. Cooper).

figure: second in fact among the twenty-three men's colleges. Afterwards matriculations fell back. By 1950 they had dropped to 82. Even so, this put BNC in fourth place among colleges in terms of numbers. In terms of examination results, however, the figures look rather different.[33] In that same year, 1950, the college slumped to eighteenth in the inter-college table, with a mere two Firsts from more than one hundred candidates. The reputation of the place was still decidedly hearty. When in 1950 a fire broke out in OL 7–9, J. L. Leckie found himself trapped on the top floor. 'Throw down any valuable possessions', shouted the firemen. Into Radcliffe Square sailed one well-scuffed pair of rugby boots. A year later Alex Jones gained a different sort of immortality: he was the last man to climb the Radcliffe Camera, and live. But there were quite a few students of rather different stamp—John Brademas for one: a future President of New York University. George Bull, for another: a Shackleton protégé; translator, journalist, and man of letters. But they represented a minority. 'Brasenose is still the same', noted *Isis* in 1952, 'in spite of . . . George Bull.'[34]

The same journal's account of one particular episode around this time can be dismissed as over-coloured. But it must have worried the SCR.

A screaming horde of drink-sodden rugger players ran riot and severely damaged college and private property . . . Following an old Rugger Club custom, about thirty of them gathered in the cosy beer cellar and got themselves systematically intoxicated. At closing time they unsteadily tottered out to assault and wreck the rooms on staircase xiv and xv, called the Arab Quarter after some of its post-war inhabitants . . . It was met by a fierce defence. Lights flickered on and off as the attackers seized control of the fuse-box and used it to confuse the defenders. Water was poured over the mob, china thrown, a window broken . . . Fire-extinguishers were let off by both sides and banisters smashed. . . . An uneasy quiet now broods over B.N.C. Each side is quarrelling with the Bursar . . . [35]

That gives an unjust impression, no doubt. The majority of students were rather more serious. The Pater Society, to give one counter-example, was flourishing at this time as a centre of intellectual debate. And in any case there was rowdiness in other colleges too. But academic results in the early 1950s hardly reflected the stern regime of Principal Last. During the years 1951–4 there was an average of no more than six Firsts per year; half the totals achieved by Balliol, Magdalen, Queen's, and New College. Not until 1955 did the tide turn. In that year there were 13 Firsts in schools: 4 in Greats, 3 in law, 2 in English, and 1 each in PPE, physics, chemistry, and zoology. And in maths

[33] Final Schools tables in *Oxford Mag.* 12 Oct. 1951, 6; 16 Oct. 1952, 4; 22 Oct. 1953, 28–9; 17 Oct. 1957, 14; 7 Nov. 1957, 81–2; 16 Oct. 1958, 12–13; 15 Oct. 1959, 4, 6; 13 Oct. 1960.
[34] *Isis*, 11 June 1952, 11; *Brazen Nose*, ix and xxxv. 62–3.
[35] *Isis*, 14 Nov. 1951, 20.

Mods there were actually three more. Brasenose was now running a close third to Balliol and Magdalen, and the results were hailed in the *Brazen Nose* as 'the best in the history of the college'. That may even have been true. Particularly notable was the quartet of Firsts in Greats: Colin Leach, Geoffrey Rickman, David Wiggins, and Keith Workman.[36] Leach's collection of prizes was unprecedented. Understandably, the Fellowship rejoiced. The revolution of 1948, it seemed, had belatedly born fruit. Nor was it a narrow academic success. Wiggins—later Wykeham Professor of Logic—also won a half-blue for fencing. And Ian Boyd—the only physicist among the legendary thirteen—ran in the Bannister–Landy 'Mile of the Century' at Vancouver in 1954. He even reached the 1500 metres final of the 1956 Melbourne Olympics. But this moment of triumph turned out to be short lived. The college reverted to type. In the nine years 1956–64 there was again an average of only half a dozen Firsts per year. That at a time when Balliol, New College, and Magdalen were regularly scoring nearly three times as many. Perhaps Sonners' ghost could be heard to mutter: 'I told you so.' On the face of it, little had changed. Compare the schools results over two twenty-year spans. Between 1920 and 1939, BNC ended up in the top half of what would eventually be known as the Norrington Table on six occasions. Between 1951 and 1970 the corresponding figure was no more than four.[37] Brasenose, it seemed, had cast off its sporting glory without achieving compensating scholastic distinction.

That at least is one possible conclusion. The statistics, however, tell a rather more complicated tale.[38] Several caveats need to be made. Between the 1920s and the 1950s the total number of blues in the University rose very little; but the number of students increased considerably. At the same time the number

Year	Blues	Firsts
1928–9	15	4
1929–30	26	3
1930–1	24	2
1931–2	30	1
1932–3	32	6
1950–1	29	6
1951–2	28	9
1952–3	30	6
1953–4	25	4
1954–5	24	13

[36] *Brazen Nose*, x. 53, 104; *Oxford Mag.* 26 Jan. 1956, 210–12.
[37] D. J. Wenden, in *HUO* viii (1994) 528.
[38] Tables in *Brazen Nose*, x. 149.

81. **Principal Stallybrass (1883–1948).**

Photographed by J. L. Halstead, 28 January 1940.

'Sonners' in the snow, aged 56. During the war years he wrote hundreds of letters to B.N.C. servicemen – and prisoners of war – and recorded their home visits in scores of photos.

82. Albert Thomas, *c*.1944.
The Principal's Butler: 'the most stately butler in Oxford'.
'To me the mere planning of a dinner is a joy'.

(opposite)

83. A. Christopher William Dawson, C.M.G.
Installation as Chief Secretary and Officer Administering the Government of the Colony of Sarawak, 1946.
A very B.N.C. career: Dulwich, Brasenose, India, Malaya, Singapore, Sarawak, Midhurst.

B. Reginald Jeffery (1876–1956) and Ursula Jeffery.
At tea on 11 May 1916, outside staircase I before alteration. The empty chair is that of the photographer, Vice-Principal Sonnenschein.

84. Jimmy Halstead (d. 1941)
'He loved beautiful women … beautiful music and writing, and the
country and flowers… He played the cello and drove a 1927 Alvis.'
Lost in 1941 during air operations over the North Sea.

85. Dick Holdsworth (d. 1942)
A triple rowing Blue, a First in Law, a Fellow of University College.
'The Prof.'; 'the star of Brasenose'.
Shot down, April 1942.

86. Tony Tisdall (d. 1940)

Photographed by Stallybrass in 1940.

'One of those gallant and cheerful pilots whose exploits have won the admiration of the world'.

Shot down a few weeks later.

87. Conrad Cherry (d. 1943)
'Uncle Con.' Photographed by Stallybrass in the year of Dunkirk.
The finest oarsman of his generation.
Torpedoed at sea, 1943.

88. Carl Von Ruperti (d. 1943)

German Rhodes Scholar, killed on the Russian Front in 1943.

'The army', he assured Stallybrass, 'is one of the few institutions in [Germany] not so intensely affected by politics'.

The Association of German Rhodes Scholars thanked B.N.C. for its 'chivalrous and noble act' in commemorating Ruperti in Chapel.

89. Alan Bulmer (d. 1940) and Ken Millar (d. 1940).
Photographed by Stallybrass outside staircase XI, on 10 October 1940.
Best friends: 'the Co-Pilots'; a 'merry laugh' and a 'blithe spirit'.
Shot down within days of each other, a few weeks later.

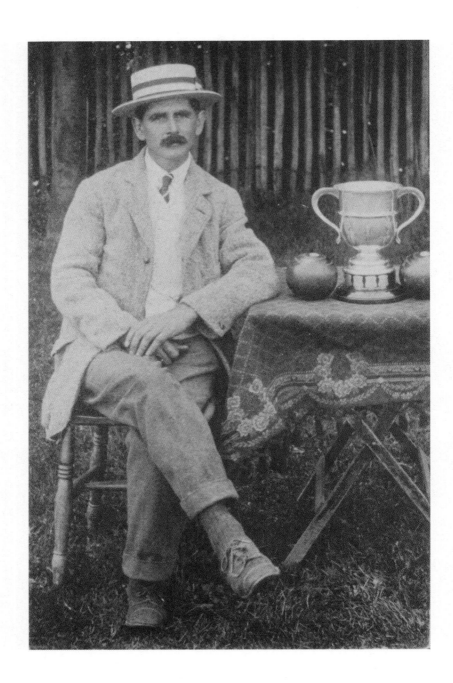

90. Edmund King (1872–1963).
College Groundsman, 1895–1959.
Photographed in 1918, as the local bowls champion.
'Not a little of Brasenose itself died with Edmund King'.

91. Edgar Stanley Cohn (1899–1963).
Photographed in 1960 by David Lomax during a tutorial in IV, 4.
'I think you may safely consign that essay to the flames'.

92. Dinner in Hall, Trinity Term 1958.

Clockwise, left to right:

HIGH TABLE: Ronald Hope, Trevor Harvey, Maurice Platnauer, Leslie Styler, Robert Shackleton, K. Sorten, Norman Leyland, Jimmy McKie.

CENTRE TABLE: John Edwards [C.M.G.], William Tucker [R.A.], John Burn [tennis Blue], Graeme Williams [Q.C.], Paul Barker [editor of *New Society*].

93. Collections in Hall, Trinity Term 1958.

Left to right: Robert Shackleton, Leighton Reynolds, John Ackrill, David Stockton, Maurice Platnauer, Jimmy McKie, Leslie Styler, Barry Nicholas.

The victim is C. H. Clark.

94. Revd. Leslie Styler (1908–90).

Chaplain Fellow and Oxford's first Tutor for Admissions.

'Candidates are considered without respect of persons or origin; and we should like more candidates to come forward. No-one should be frightened off'.

95. Three Principals, 1972.

Sir Noel Hall, 1960–73; Maurice Platnauer, 1956–60; Herbert Hart, 1973–78.

Photographed by Leslie Styler at a party to celebrate the golden anniversary of Platnauer's election to a Fellowship.

96. Lord Windlesham (1932–).
Principal 1989–2002.
The first Principal of BNC to have held Cabinet office.

of Firsts remained more or less constant: 132 in 1931–3 and 135 in 1953–5. In other words, the proportion of Firsts to successful candidates—University-wide—fell sharply, from 11 or 12 per cent to 7 per cent. But the corresponding proportion in Brasenose rose from 6.5 per cent to 9.5 per cent. That small percentage is significant. BNC had made huge efforts to escape its sporting reputation; all in return for a First-class dividend of just 3 per cent. The revolution of 1948 did pay off. But the process proved predictably unglamorous, and the rewards themselves turned out to be statistically marginal.

By 1956 there were other revolutions to think about. To say that Brasenose was convulsed by Suez and Hungary would be rather an exaggeration. Still, there was no ignoring the storm outside. 'For the first time in years', noted *Isis*, 'Oxford has thrown off its legendary apathy.'[39] When the Royal Navy steamed out to reclaim the Suez Canal, a majority of Brasenose Fellows signalled public dissent. When Hungarian refugee students began to arrive in England, one of them (A. J. Sandor) was given residence in college and a Hulmeian grant of £100 per term.[40] But BNC was not exactly in the forefront of protest. At one Oxford demonstration against Prime Minister Eden, *Isis* noticed that 'a group, mainly from Brasenose, sang "Rule Britannia" . . . their substitute for thought'.[41] They probably represented a majority view. So when the same team of loyalists raised a toast in hall, a handful of lefties retaliated by letting off a smoke bomb. 'Don't know about this', observed one scout; 'I'm all for the wogs meself.' 'Ah', replied another, 'but you ain't educated.' BNC was trying hard to escape its former reputation. But it was still uncertain of its image. And when, in 1958, *Isis* triggered off a wave of concern in Oxford about the dangers of nuclear holocaust, there were few campaigners at Brasenose. Oxford's collegiate structure—polycentric, centripetal—was invariably an insurance against concerted agitation. Ten years later, when agitation was again an issue, BNC came down firmly on the side of order. That did not imply mere lack of conscience. In 1968, the JCR sponsored a Czech refugee student (P. Kysel) to the tune of £345 p.a. But Brasenose was a very collegial college. And 'in a collegiate university', as *Isis* admitted early in 1968, 'student power is a dead duck'.[42]

Brasenose had never been a very political college. In the '50s it was still more interested in sport. During the fifteen years 1950–65, the college had sixteen men in the Oxford rugby fifteen:

---

[39] *Isis*, 7 Nov. 1956, 7.

[40] V-P's Reg. 5 Dec. 1956, fo. 38; 29 May 1957, fo. 60; 16 Oct. 1957, fo. 67.

[41] *Isis*, 7 Nov. 1956, 10.

[42] Ibid. 24 Jan. 1968, 3; V-P's Reg. 4 Oct. 1968, fo. 3. In 1958 BNC did have one or two radicals. One of the compilers of the *Isis* 'H. Bomb' issue of 26 Feb. was the future William Tucker, RA (pl. 92); another contributor of articles on 'art and class' was the future Michael Horovitz, OBE, poet-founder of *New Departures*. Bruce Kent of C. N. D. had been up in 1949. Kysel was elected to the Phoenix in 1970, the same year as T.S. Mangwazu, a native of Malawi.

B. Boobyer, N. A. H. Creese, E. J. Wimperis, D. J. Skipper, K. M. Spence, A. W. Ramsay, J. H. ('Chic') Henderson, J. P. ('Pom-Pom') Fellows-Smith, V. W. Jones, M. G. Allison, H. R. Moore, R. W. Wilson, P. M. Dawkins, N. T. Slater, C. S. Wates, and A. K. Morgan.

Two of these—Spence and Ramsay—were captains of the University side. But only the last four names belonged to the 1960s. Brasenose rugby was by then a waning force. In the five years 1950–4 the college dominated rugby cuppers. But after that, for the next fifteen years—with the grand exception of 1961—leadership passed almost exclusively to St Edmund Hall. And no BNC man played rugby for Oxford against Cambridge between 1965 and 1975. The following decade would have been equally barren, had it not been for T. P. Enevoldson's record run of six consecutive blues—and a First in medicine—in 1975–81. Still, in the 1950s, at least, in Spence and Dawkins—quicksilver and power—Brasenose possessed two players of electrifying presence. Pete Dawkins had been an All American Footballer: the Cambridge backs were mesmerized by his one-armed torpedo throw-ins. And his triple blue in 1959–61 rescued BNC from some embarrassment: the season of 1957–8 had been the first since 1902 in which the college could boast no representative in the Varsity team. Ken Spence was cast in a more traditional mould. He was almost the last of a long line of Brasenose sportsmen from Loretto. As a scrum-half his 'passing, tackling and defensive kicking were almost perfect'. Years later he was asked what it felt like to play at Twickenham in one's very first Varsity match:

Empty, nervous, strangely tired, almost breathless, before the game when we sat in the changing room like pet mice at a children's party. You could feel the excitement outside, and the shock of the noise when we appeared was considerable; deafening, continuous, no impression of individual shouts. It was elating, carried you long past the normal checks of fatigue, but made communications between us on the pitch very difficult. The speed, intensity and effort was far greater than in an International and more satisfying, more fun. It is still a vivid memory and remains a wonderful privilege.[43]

Brasenose cricket at this time also had a story to tell. In twenty-two years, 1950 to 1972, the college notched up sixteen blues:

P. D. S. Blake, B. Boobbyer, A. D. Jose, M. C. Cowdrey, J. P. Fellows-Smith, J. C. Marshall, G. H. McKinna, I. Gibson, R. W. Wilson, A.C. Smith, D. M. Sayer, D. M. Green, F. W. Neate, D. R. Walsh, D. F. Allison, and B. May.

Cricket cuppers had been abandoned after 1922—supposedly because of BNC's dominance; actually because of timetabling problems—and the

---

[43] Quoted in R. McWhirter and A. Noble, *O.U. Rugby Football Club* (Oxford, 1969), 181, 190. For a fine obit of Spence, by J. A. Cuddon, see *Brazen Nose*, xxxiv. 73–6.

competition was not revived until forty-four years later in a new, limited-overs format. But when that time came, in 1966, Brasenose triumphed again—as if there had been no interruption—and a 'Stump Supper' was held in hall, with the coveted cup agleam on high. In his speech of congratulation, Noel Hall was able to announce that the victory coincided with Colin Cowdrey's appointment as captain of England.[44] But thereafter there was less to cheer. Between 1972 (B. May) and 1989 (E. D. Hester), not a single Brasenose man played cricket against Cambridge.

Cowdrey's career—MCC at BNC; Sir Colin; Baron Cowdrey of Tonbridge (pl. 55)—reads today like a tale from a distant age. As a schoolboy prodigy, he had been coached by another celebrated Brasenose blue, 'John' Knott. Coming up in October 1951, he read geography in a desultory way as a Heath Harrison Exhibitioner (£60 p.a.); he won blues for cricket and rackets; then went down without a degree in 1954—down under in fact—to join the Ashes-winning team in Australia.

I found Oxford a calm, happy place … Like the wise owl, the more I thought, the less I spoke. [I remember] warm days … net practices … good wickets, good fellowship—a simple, uncomplicated life … breakfast, nets, the match, a beer or two, dinner at Vincents … leather armchairs … tankards of ale, and laughter … [45]

He even helped Brasenose win soccer cuppers in 1953 by scoring both goals in the final match. His subsequent career in international sport and sport administration was to become the stuff of legend. Few can have helped and entertained so many; and surely none made fewer enemies in the process.

The decline of BNC rowing, however, during this period was precipitate. Before the First War, recalled one Rhodes Scholar, 'the idea that Brasenose might end in the Second Division seemed comparable to the Fall of Constantinople in 1453'.[46] But in 1950–2 Brasenose could boast not a single Oxford oarsman. The following year 'Ginty' Hammond—a beer-drinking Welsh Buddhist—actually made it to the blue boat. And E. V. Vine—a Phoenix athlete from Geelong—did the same in 1954. There were good years for boating in 1955, 1960, and 1967. But on the whole the college Eight sank steadily lower: from fourth to eleventh in 1950; from fourteenth in 1954 to sixteenth in 1964. Despite the construction of a new boathouse—designed

[44] *Brazen Nose*, xiv. 78–9.
[45] C. Cowdrey, *M.C.C.: The Autobiography of a Cricketer* (1976), 47–9; *Brazen Nose*, xxxv. 66–7. For an early profile, see *Isis*, 10 June 1954, 17, photo: 'his chief hobbies are eating oranges and sleep.' His rooms were in Frewin Hall. For Cowdrey on Knott, see *The Times*, 22 June 1988, 14. When he retired in 1975, he had scored 42,719 first-class runs at an average of 42.89, including 107 centuries; and he had taken 638 catches, 120 of them for England.
[46] F. F. Russell in *Brazen Nose*, xi. 93.

by Peter Shepheard in 1958[47]—the decline continued. By 1965–6, the Torpid had fallen to its lowest position in the history of Brasenose rowing. By the end of the 1960s, it seemed unlikely that the first Eight would ever again recapture its position in the First Division. Few freshmen were now recruited with any experience of rowing at school; and by the time they were fit and trained they were already under the eye of the examiners. Ironically, it took the arrival of women in 1974–5 to recapture the Boat Club's honour. In that year Jane Reid-Kay coxed home the First Eight to a total of six bumps and a bump supper. It seemed a symbolic moment. But in 1976 BNC sank back again to twentieth and the very future of college rowing seemed in doubt. Only the vigour of Brasenose women held out any prospect of improvement. But recovery did eventually arrive. In 1992 the women's first Eight came within a length of catching Somerville—at that point still an all-female college—as the women's head of the river. Not to be outdone, the men's first Torpid came within a canvas of becoming the first BNC boat to go head in fifty years. The following year Brasenose actually achieved a rowing blue (Richard Manners); and the cox of the *Isis* boat was the same Brasenose woman who coxed the women's blue boat the year before: Samantha Benham.[48]

It is worth noting at this stage that—by comparison with the Stallybrass era—BNC's sporting results were already declining long before the arrival of women in October 1974. Fewer men from boarding schools; fewer enthusiasts to create a team-building critical mass. The focus necessarily shifted from college to University teams. In any case, the culture of the college had changed. Extra-curricular feats were no longer applauded: Stephen Proctor was the last man, in 1957, to chip a golf ball over the Camera and into All Souls. The intake of the college had been democratized. Its range of catchment schools had widened. And its ethos was about to be feminized. Restrictions on 'lady visitors' had already been made more liberal. By 1964 there were women in college until 11.30 p.m. By 1971 the JCR was even agitating for twenty-four-hour visiting privileges.

> There are women in the Buttery
> And women in the Hall.
> There are women in the J.C.R.
> Why have a Summer Ball?[49]

---

[47] V-P's Reg. 28 July 1954, fo. 140; *Architectural Rev.* 127 (1960), 53; *Brazen Nose*, xi. 73: illus.; *Isis*, 22 May 1957, 14 (P. Thompson). Estimate: *c.* £10,000. (V-P's Reg. 16 Oct. 1957, fo. 74).

[48] Third Year, Experimental Psychology (*Country Life*, 25 Mar. 1993, frontispiece photo by Derry Moore).

[49] Ale Verse, 1964: *Brazen Nose*, xiii. 266; V-P's Reg. 15 Oct. 1969, fo. 81. The Governing Body asked the JCR 'how in their view [twenty-four hour visiting] could be implemented while preventing "lodgers" in College' (V-P's Reg. 1 Dec. 1971, fo. 97).

Given the nature of 1960s student life, it had become impossible to defend segregation. Popular culture—what the communicators were beginning to call media-based discourse—had fundamentally altered the nature of the place.

Pop culture did occasionally have its compensations. For one brief moment BNC seemed almost to have its name in lights. It was on 5 March 1964 that Jeffery Archer—then a Dip. Ed. student noted chiefly for his talent as a sprinter—arranged for the Beatles to visit the Lodgings as the climax to a fund-raising appeal for Oxfam. One memorable photograph survives, showing the 'Fab Four' sharing a joke with Sir Noel Hall, watched over by David Stockton and the future Lord Archer himself. Another shows the irrepressible Archer again, this time with Chancellor Macmillan, holding aloft a cheque in favour of Oxfam, for £500,000.[50] Money, and publicity, were beginning to loom increasingly large in the daily thinking of the college.

Since the 1920s Brasenose undergraduates had expected to spend at least one of their years in lodgings. That remained the case until the 1960s. But rising rents, and the gradual disappearance of the Oxford landlady, forced colleges to expand their own accommodation. For BNC that meant two building programmes: the Platnauer Building (1959–61) and the extensions to Frewin Hall (1975–81; 1996–7). These enabled the college to stabilize its annual intake at about 100 undergraduates, with the figure for postgraduates running initially at around a quarter of that number. By the time both projects were complete—and by the time they were supplemented by the St Cross building of 1996—Brasenose was in a position to house the great majority of its student population. That was a considerable achievement. Sadly, the process of financial rearrangement also involved the disposal of one crucial item in the college's property portfolio: the site, and development potential, of Grandpont House.[51]

It was Robert Shackleton in August 1955 who first formally proposed the construction of a new range of accommodation within the envelope of the central college site. Seven months later, architects were approached. And a

---

[50] *Isis*, 7 Nov. 1964, 23–4. In 1975 Dr Mary Archer, then attached to the Royal Institution, taught physical chemistry during W. G. Richards's absence on sabbatical (V-P's Reg. 30 Apr. 1975, fo. 35). In 1966 she had been married to Jeffery Archer by Leslie Styler in St Mary's Church.

[51] Grandpont House had been built next to Folly Bridge in 1785, by William Ellis Taunton, Clerk of Accounts at Brasenose from 1779 to 1796 (*Brazen Nose*, vi. 56). Bought by the college in 1847, it was sold for £12,000 in 1958 to the Revd J. Crozier of Opus Dei (V-P's Reg. 15 Oct. 1958, fo. 127; *The Times*, 6 Feb. 1961, 10; *Oxford Mag.* 4 Mar. 1965, 258–9; *Quat. Mon.* VI, 45). That represented little more than the price of a house on Boar's Hill (V-P's Reg. 29 May 1957, fo. 55), or the cost of BNC's new boathouse (V-P's Reg. 16 Oct. 1957, fo. 74). The sale overturned the recommendation of the Estates Bursar (V-P's Reg. 16 Oct. 1957, fo. 68).

year after that, estimates were approved. A committee was set up to 'advise the Bursar on aesthetic matters'; a self-styled 'Committee of Aesthetics' no less.[52] Bursar Leyland needed little prompting. He had already decided on a statement of modernity. As architects, he chose Powell and Moya, the firm responsible for the Skylon at the Festival of Britain in 1951. The critics were enthusiastic. John Summerson looked forward to a real specimen of 'modern architecture' in Oxford; some buildings at last with 'a serious intellectual basis'.[53] Stephen Gardiner anticipated a rare synthesis of 'severity'; 'toughness', and 'humanity'. It did not turn out quite like that. Still, Powell and Moya's use of space was ingenious. The traditional system of staircase access was compressed, almost to the point of suffocation. Philip Powell explained just how they set about it.

The B.N.C. extension started off in an entirely mundane way, a series of mathematical and intellectual problems [on] an absurd site . . . [But] before you could say it was absurd there was the intellectual exercise in light angles and views to cope with, rather than just the appearance of the building . . . and then you suddenly found there were possibilities—you found you *could* see the Radcliffe Camera dome, there were views of the Church; and what seemed a rather squalid little site was actually rather pleasant. But you make up all these things afterwards, you don't analyse all the clever or sentimental reasons at the time.[54]

Seeking to explain such things to old members, the *Brazen Nose* described the new building as 'the architectural equivalent of a century in bad light on a turning wicket'.[55] The site was the last available space in college: the strip of land between New Quad and Lincoln to which T. G. Jackson had consigned the college lavatories, bath house, and bicycle shed. Within a budget of £76,000, Powell and Moya managed to squeeze in thirty-two bed-sitting rooms distributed between a five-storey tower (XVII–XVIII) and two one-storey 'pavilions'. The reviewers rejoiced. John Pinsent extolled 'the lightness of the glass bridges . . . the monumental, Mycenaean quality of the "quadlets" '.[56] Gardiner was entranced: 'The form, the planning, the materials . . . [arise] logically from the shape and nature of the site . . . The play of Portland stone, cantilevered concrete, and large expanses of glass in thin frames, shows in a magical way the vitality and sharpness one material can give to another . . . [This is] *real* modern architecture [not something] dressed up to

[52] V-P's Reg. 18 June 1958, fo. 121. Its members were Platnauer, Cohn, and Nicholas. For the first proposals, see ibid. 5 Aug. 1955, fo. 175; 12 Oct. 1955, fo. 3; 18 Jan. 1956, fo. 10; 15 Feb. 1956, fo. 14.

[53] Summerson lecture: *Isis*, 1959, 300–1 ('The truth is that *things which do not clash dilute*').

[54] *Isis*, June 1967, 31–2.

[55] *Brazen Nose*, xiii/1. 6. For plans and perspectives, see ibid., xi. 79–80.

[56] *Oxford Mag.* 30 May 1963, 338. This comment was neatly dismissed by Hugh Plommer as simply 'sound without sense' (ibid. 13 June 1963, 363).

look modern...There is always [a] feeling of inevitability about a good building...There is something heroic about...Brasenose'.[57]

That was not quite how it would seem in years to come. Even by 1963 the project was being damned for its 'brutality': 'a mere trunk-maker's cleverness in three-dimensional packing, with sunken "barbican" terraces reduced to rathole size'.[58] By 1967 the college was complaining to the RIBA about damp and subsidence. The architects confessed themselves 'extremely sorry', and handed back £1,050. Such confessions are rare. But if there was an element of heroism about this building it was largely conceptual: a heroism of abstract form. It was not the heroism of utility. Its modernity was essentially formalistic: not the verities of use but the poetry of reductive shapes. The building's sculptural qualities may well have been echoed by Henry Moore's bronze statue: *Reclining Figure on Pedestal* (1963). Its abstract linearity may actually have been improved by Unger Schulze's 'mosaic in rough marble' (1972). And as a place of vertical residence the tower block may even be counted a success. But the lower levels lived up to their nickname of 'the bunker'. The title 'Platnauer' somehow never caught on. The stairs are narrow; the fittings spartan; the plumbing vestigial; the ambience unrelenting. The Portland stone cladding has stained and splintered, and the joys of abstract geometry on such a meagre site have staled and withered with the years. Better perhaps to have aimed at the genius of the place, and gone for a distillation of Jackson's notion of the Picturesque. By contrast it was those very qualities of discretion in design—adapting building to site, and site to use—that made the modest development of the Frewin–New Inn Hall area such a striking success.[59]

Between the mid-1960s and the mid-1970s, Brasenose found itself ineluctably drawn into the changes overtaking Oxford. Leslie Styler (pl. 94)—Admissions Tutor, 1948–62—became secretary to the University Admissions Office, integrating from 1965 onwards all Oxford colleges within the framework of the Universities Central Council for Admissions (UCCA). Robert Shackleton (pls. 92, 93) joined the Kneale Committee set up to review the University's examination structure. Soon he would chair the committee charged with ironing out the heterogeneity of Oxford's libraries.[60] And two

---

[57] *Oxford Mag.*, 4 May 1961, 322 (Stephen Gardiner); *Isis*, 25 Nov. 1962, 15.

[58] Plommer, in *Oxford Mag.*, 21 Feb. 1963, 196–8.

[59] *Brazen Nose*, xvi/2. 3–4; xvi/4. 14–16; xvii. 185–6; xxx. 12 illus. (Architects Design Partnership). The cost of the whole project in its several phases, residential and commercial, was not modest: over £3 million in fact. Ten years later Fellows were thinking of building 'public rooms beneath the lawn in the New Quad' (V-P's Reg. 26 Apr. 1972, fo. 124; 14 June 1972, fo. 141). For faults in the Platnauer Building, and Powell and Moya's contractual liability, see V-P's Reg. 26 Apr. 1967, fo. 41; 24 May 1967, fo. 46; 6 Dec. 1967, fo. 81.

[60] For its recommendations, see *Oxford Mag.*, 1966, Mich. no. 7, 117–18, 136–9.

successive Principals, Herbert Hart (pl. 95) and Barry Nicholas (pl. 93), found themselves in the front line of political action. Hart would become almost an official trouble-shooter for the University establishment. His celebrated Report of 1969 poured quantities of liberal oil on the troubled waters of 1968; most notoriously the 'siege' of All Souls. As for Barry Nicholas, he served on the committee of inquiry dealing with postgraduate studies. Then he presided over the Disciplinary Court, set up in the wake of the Hart Report and first brought into action to deal with the 'riots' of 1974: disturbances in which the Indian Institute was stormed by a posse of students bent on establishing 'a real Students' Union'. This was not the first time that Nicholas had faced student troubles. In 1970 he cut his teeth on an earlier incident, the six-day occupation of the Clarendon Building. The object of the rioters on that occasion was quite spurious: the recovery of mythical secret files. But at the time it all seemed serious enough. One of the ringleaders sent down afterwards was a Brasenose man: S. P. Bolchover, late of Manchester Grammar School. Eric Collieu spoke up for him on Governing Body. John Davies acted as his defence counsel.[61]

All these incidents were portents of change. Within the college itself a brand new category of visitors had actually been sighted several years before, dining in hall—even at high table—during term time. These were the first female guests—not members, of course; just guests—and the date of their arrival was 14 February 1964: the feast of St Valentine.[62] Change indeed. And in the same year the SCR moved radically towards a lunchtime cafeteria system; priced at 4 shillings per head in the Eckersley Room. The food was simple, and 'joints of meat' were forbidden: they were held to be too 'expensive'; they might even lead to 'uncontrollable consumption'. There

---

[61] For Bolchover etc., see V-P's Reg. 6, 27 May 1970, fos. 130–1; *The Times*, 24 Apr. 1970, p. 2; *Isis*, 2 Mar. 1970, 3, 9 Mar. 1970, pp. 10–11 and 11 Oct. 1970, 16–17. The Clarendon Building was occupied from 24 Feb. to 1 Mar. 1970. In November 1973 the Examination Schools were occupied for a week. The Indian Institute was briefly occupied on 13 February 1974; eighteen students were rusticated after a hearing lasting fifteen days (*The Times*, 30 Mar. 1974, 1; 5 Apr. 1974, 5; 8 Apr. 1974, 15). See also B. Harrison in *HUO* viii (1994), 704–7, 744–6.

[62] V-P's Reg. 13 Nov. 1963, fo. 38, 4 Dec. 1963, fo. 42, 27 May 1964, fo. 65, 2 Dec. 1964, fo. 84, 6 May 1970, fo. 130; *Brazen Nose*, xiii. 212. 'Women in hall' was by no means wholly popular with the JCR; voting on the issue was inconclusive. Opponents staged a famous jape, during which the unicorn above high table was most improperly decorated. On the orders of Principal Hall it was therefore rendered detumescent. Not until a quarter of a century later was the creature privily repaired under the direction of Bursar Gasser. As early as 1950 permission had been given for ladies to dine as guests of undergraduates on Saturdays, provided they left the premises by 9.30. At Shackleton's insistence, the Saturday high table was therefore transferred to Common Room (V-P's Reg. 8 Nov. 1950, fo. 34). In 1959, however, he agreed to Ackrill's proposal to allow lady guests at high table, in hall, on one stated night in each vacation (V-P's Reg. 18 Feb. 1959, fo. 144).

was a new egalitarianism in the air, a new puritanism too; and a new determination to forget the past. In 1967 the Vampires—hell-raisers to the last—were indefinitely suspended by decanal sanction. In the same year, as we have already seen, the memorial tablet in the gate lodge to 'Earl Haig and all other Brasenose men' who served in the Great War was removed to make way for 'additional notice-boards'.[63]

So many changes. And yet it took the death of a single college servant to make clear the speed of the revolution that was now overtaking Oxford. Edmund King (pl. 90), the Brasenose College groundsman since 1895, died, aged 91, on 7 August 1963. King had been born and bred a groundsman, and he spent his final days in the same college house at Grandpont where he had lived for half a century. His father, Sam King I, was University groundsman from 1878 to 1918. Three of his brothers were groundsmen too: Herbert, forty-six years at Balliol; Percy, forty-eight years at New College; and Sam II, forty-four years at Merton. At 12 years of age Edmund was 'fagging for cricket balls' at Oriel. At 20 he was cutting grass at Radley. When BNC moved to Grandpont in 1895 from the University Playing Fields at Cowley Marsh, Edmund King came too; and he brought his own horse with him. In 1914 he was rather too old for war service. In any case, by 1917 he had lost a foot in an accident. That hardly affected his activity as local bowls champion, still less his competence as a cricket umpire. And his memory remained pretty clear. As the generations came and went, he would tell old tales of half-forgotten times. The King brothers' pretty sister, for example: she was much admired by the boys of the locality. One of her suitors had been young 'Billy Morris', the future millionaire Lord Nuffield. Nothing came of it. King's family thought him not 'good enough for our girl'. As the years went by, two of Edmund's own sons became groundsmen as well. But one of them went on to be a headmaster.

> They used to watch him on his mower
> Lapping the ground, and liked to joke
> That he would mow off into the river
>
> One day. Now he is quite blind
> They do not predict now. For the sake
> Of his health they prescribe one round
>
> Of his cricket field. The boundary
> Is clearly marked. Where he can stump
> As though seeing. . . .
> Stumping footsteps along the boundary.

[63] V-P's Reg. 26 Apr. 1967, fo. 41. The Vampires survived, unofficially, until at least 1969 (minutes SL 9 A1/1: 1960–9). Photos SL 9 A2, SL 7 C5/1, 4–8; SL 9 A2/1 (1885); SL 9 –A2/2 (1886).

When the end came in the summer of 1963, 'not a little of Brasenose itself died with Edmund King'.[64]

In a sense the cultural hierarchy of the college had been inverted. To the new wave of boys produced by the welfare state, groundsman King became simply 'Mr.' King. BNC's first entrant from a comprehensive school—Paul Barker, later editor of *New Society*—arrived in 1955.[65] To Shackleton he became a kind of academic godson. This new generation was impatient with many of the conventions of its predecessors. When Maurice Platnauer spoke on 'Punctuation' at a meeting of the Pater Society in 1957, Barker dismissed his use of semicolons as 'fascistic'. 'Bit of a rough diamond, Barker', murmured the Principal. But Plat's niceties of syntax did now seem a little irrelevant. Social conscience kept getting in the way of scholarship. And social conventions began to feel even more constricting than grammatical codes. The proportion of male to female undergraduates in Oxford was a desperate 8 to 1. But fraternizing with local women—to use a term familiar to national servicemen—was certainly not encouraged. In the mid-1950s the Proctors still monitored public dances at the Forum on the High Street. But etiquette was changing fast. By the late 1960s, when Platnauer sent out his customary invitations to drinks, he was often mortified to receive no reply at all. And then there was the problem of team sports. By the early 1960s, fielding a rugger team or raising and training a rowing eight had become—in societal terms—decidedly problematic.

> For now the Nose can scarcely raise a side
> Of fifteen men to uphold the College pride ...
> Where are the men who once turned out to play
> For first, for second, All Stars every day?
> They all wear spectacles, they all are weak;
> They cannot run, they cannot walk, [indeed] they scarcely speak.[66]

Even organizing literary societies, with the old paraphernalia of elections, minutes, and uniform symbols—the names that link; the ties that bind—was fast becoming politically suspect. Students now had less time for generalized debate. They preferred to concentrate on the syllabus. Still, competition was forcing up productivity. The Fourth class had gone; the Third was going. Firsts were no longer impossibly rare. Course work had taken hold. By 1969 students were complaining that the library shut at midnight.[67]

[64] Poem by H. R. Moore, in *Brazen Nose*, xiii. 193. Appreciation by D. L. Stockton, ibid. 252. See also *Isis*, 1 Mar. 1951, 27: photo.

[65] From Calder High School, Mytholmroyd, Yorkshire. In Dec. 1952 Barker was the first person to gain entry to either Oxford or Cambridge from a comprehensive school.

[66] Ale Verses, 1962: *Brazen Nose*, xiii. 1923.

[67] *Brazen Nose*, xv/1 (1969), 5.

As early as 1956, the *Oxford Magazine* was wondering plaintively: 'Why have dons and undergraduates drifted apart?'[68] At that date the difficulty could still be explained by differences of age: after the rigours of military service, men in their middle twenties could hardly be expected to take easily to donnish dominion. Ten years later a more subtle analysis was required. The post-national service generation not only rejected academic authority. They rejected its culture too.

Here the argument trembles on shifting sand. All ages are transitional. But the 1960s changed faster than most. What happened—in shorthand terms—was the disruption of those shared assumptions and values on which inter-war Oxbridge culture was based. And this reflected changes at large. First came the collapse of classical education; then the withering of Christian verities; then the erosion of bourgeois capital. The unravelling of all three exposed the frailty—the real unity and illusory equality—of relations between JCR and SCR during the inter-war period. When Noel Annan regretted the disappearance of 'Our Age'; when Maurice Bowra bemoaned the death of Sonners, they were lamenting the loss of their own youthful milieu. The terms of reference had changed. The old jokes had begun to fall flat. As Bowra remarked to Anthony Powell, students in the early 1960s seemed to think in a different language: 'I don't understand them at all nowadays.'[69]

This 1960s cohort, with its grammarian ethos, had been intensively schooled; individualized by competition; trained above all to pass exams. They saw themselves as future professionals, not hereditary amateurs. And they spurned their predecessors' ordered memories of playing field and parade ground. Chapel too: by the end of the 1960s BNC was fast becoming a secular place. That was true for Oxford as a whole. By 1964 only 30 out of 586 Oxford Fellows were still in holy orders. At Brasenose only the chaplain (Leslie Styler) and his deputies (Richard Askew, for example) fell into that diminishing category. The influence of chapel was now ceremonial rather than sacramental. Its remit had become inclusive rather than confessional: in 1968 a Catholic mass was actually celebrated there, the first in college since the Reformation.[70] There would still be chaplains who would leave their mark: James Bell, Jeffrey John. But the role of the chaplain had become pastoral rather than pietistic. Perhaps it had been for years. Still this accelerating decline in religious observance

---

[68] 'J.J.W.', in *Oxford Mag.*, 3 May 1956, 376.

[69] Noel Annan and Anthony Powell, in H. Lloyd-Jones (ed.), *Maurice Bowra: A Celebration* (1974), 83, 103.

[70] V-P's Reg. 1 May 1968, fo. 108, 2 Nov. 1970, fo. 12 (visit of Fr. Borelli). 'Series III' (1965) was adopted for holy communion in 1967 (V-P's Reg. 18 Oct. 1967, fo. 71). But the Book of Common Prayer (1662) remained the liturgy for college prayers. For the declining number of clerical Fellows, see V. H. H. Green, *Religion at Oxford and Cambridge* (1964), 365. In 1845 there had been 325 out of 470.

involved—at the very least—a traumatic literary loss. It was part of a pervasive amnesia that came to characterize the counter-culture of the 1960s. Here was a generation which thought itself intellectually self-sufficient. It shrugged off the correctives of inherited civility. When national service ended in 1960, Oxford did return once more to the age profile of its pre-war years. But by that time the revolution had already begun. The age of cavalry twill was nearly over. Jeans were first worn at BNC in 1958. Ten years later they were *de rigueur*, and speech patterns followed suit. Undergraduate slang gave way to the cult of vernacular.

All this did not happen overnight. As late as 1959, the gossip columnist of *Parson's Pleasure* could still report: 'As I entered Brasenose, I heard the baying of the bloodies.'[71] But change was already manifest. And the process accelerated in the 1960s. The generation of the 1970s—comprehensive now rather than grammar—experienced a cultural shift of growing momentum. Dons were getting older, appointed after doctoral training, and students seemed correspondingly younger still. Arriving straight from school—without a third year in the sixth form; without the ordered socializing of two or three years' military discipline—they out-narcissized their inter-war predecessors. Since 1969 the age of majority had been 18, not 21. Colleges no longer stood *in loco parentis*. And there was another, irreversible difference. For role models now the new generation looked to the media rather than to the Senior Common Room. Gresham's Law had moved into the cultural market. In 1963 the first television set arrived at Brasenose.[72] Within a generation, the internet would complete what television began. Information, if not knowledge, had been democratized. Universalized too: collegiate cohesion now took second place to generational conformity. BNC men—still men of course until 1974–5— were students now rather than undergraduates.

The fact that Brasenose felt the impact of these changes rather less than most colleges suggests the existence of some 'inner harmony'. And there may be some truth in that. Student troubles found little or no place at BNC. The early 1960s in fact, with Michael Palin and Robert Hewison to the fore, were a vintage period for student creativity. 'Perhaps no College', noted Eric Collieu in 1974, not long before his death, 'has allowed itself to be less affected . . . by the disorders recently prevailing in the University at large.'[73] Dons and students remained on friendly terms; their amity underpinned by the loyalty of almost the last generation of traditional college servants—Jack

---

[71] The party, in lecture room VII, was given by Peter Rawley, Sir Jonathan Backhouse, and Simon Matthews.

[72] In the JCR's New Buttery (V-P's Reg. 20 Feb. 1963, fo. 15). A television had been installed in lecture room VII in 1953 for the Coronation (V-P's Reg. 12 Nov. 1952, fo. 99). In the early 1950s even radios were uncommon.

[73] *Brazen Nose*, xv. 323. 'Good relations [between senior and junior members] are the keystone of college discipline' (V-P's Reg. 18 June 1969, fo. 68).

Markham, for instance; the presiding spirit of the beer cellar. Or Jock Wallace, Head Hallman; the very heart of B. N. C. From the Black Watch in the Second World War, to a pub in deepest Jericho, to his definitive role at Brasenose, Jock brought with him dignity, pride, and unsinkable good humour. For not far short of thirty years—that means at least 3,000 undergraduates—he was, almost literally, the centre of college life. Barry Nicholas and David Stockton remembered him in 1957:

a dashing and youthful man, with black hair and black eyebrows over piercing eyes. A genius who was equally good at managing the crowds at lunch or dinner on an ordinary day or setting the scene for some great occasion and presiding over it with magisterial dignity in his tailcoat . . . with all the panache of Sir Henry Wood at the Proms . . . He had a great eye for the beauty of a well set table, with silver . . . shining against dark wood . . . As the years passed the black hair turned to grey but the presence remained and . . . . the humour. Jock's Hall was a happy one—and that was not always easy in the troublous times [of 1968 to 1974] . . . [We] shall always remember Jock's great laugh coming across the quadrangle from the Buttery.[74]

Day after day; night after night; seven days a week; two full sittings for every dinner in hall. The strain must have been immense. He died of a heart attack within eight months of his retirement in 1985.

At root, many of these changes were economic. Financial provision by the state in the years immediately after the Second World War had done much to trigger a broader range of recruitment. Eighty-two per cent of undergraduates at Oxford were receiving public money in 1950–1.[75] The social spectrum did narrow with the passing of the ex-army bulge: the state-assisted figure for 1951–2 was only 71.7 per cent.[76] But in the later 1950s it began to rise again. That did not mean any dramatic or immediate reduction in recruitment from independent schools. In April 1961 the number of undergraduates at Brasenose from maintained and direct grant schools stood at 47.6 per cent; independent schools supplied 52.4 per cent. Gradually, the balance seemed to be moving towards a 50/50 split. Comparisons with other colleges at this point are revealing. BNC's intake from the private sector in 1960–1 exactly matched the intercollegiate average. Compared, for example, with Trinity (80.6 per cent independent) and Christ Church (70 per cent independent), Brasenose had come to seem decidedly *déclassé*. On the other hand BNC's recruitment of direct grant schoolboys (20.7 per cent) was rather above the

---

[74] *Brazen Nose*, xx. 1 and xxi. 54–5 (conflated).

[75] That is 6,021 out of 7,322: i.e. 1,500 on ex-army grants, 2,000 funded by the Ministry of Education; 2,521 by local education authorities (Ministry of Education figures quoted in *Cherwell*, 30 Oct. 1951, 13).

[76] UGC Report (Cmd. 8875), quoted in *Oxford Mag.* 15 Oct. 1953, 4.

average (in 1965–6 it was the highest in Oxford); and recruitment from the state or wholly maintained sector (26.9 per cent) was rather below the average (in 1965–6 it was almost as low as that of Christ Church). In other words, Brasenose was still playing to its traditional strengths: second-order public schools, particularly in the west; and urban grammar or direct grant schools, notably in the north. In the early 1960s a typical BNC man might still be assumed to be a commoner from Wellington or a scholar from Manchester Grammar. Socially and academically, Brasenose occupied an almost exactly median position in the inter-college league: twelfth in terms of public school recruitment; fourteenth in terms of examination results.[77] These figures, of course, represent the nature of the applicant as much as the preference of the college. In 1964, Leslie Styler summed up official policy as follows:

We should put it clearly on record that the candidates that present themselves are considered without respect of persons or origin; and that what we should like is that more candidates should come forward, and that no-one should be frightened off either by the thought that the examination is too hard, or that the dice are loaded against him, or that he would be out of his element if he came here.[78]

Well, perhaps. There is no doubting Styler's inclusive vision. But such good intentions disguised a structural problem. The traditional scholarship system—an additional entrance examination, usually taken after nearly three years in the sixth form—attracted candidates chiefly from the independent sector. By 1964 the number of successful applicants from independent schools had in fact declined somewhat: to 45 per cent.[79] But to the public at large it still seemed suspiciously high. During the previous decade, calls for abolition of both open and closed scholarships—and for the integration of Oxford and Cambridge colleges within a national university entrance system—had grown more and more insistent.[80] In 1964 Brasenose had 46

---

[77] *Oxford Mag.*, 27 Apr. 1961, 306–7. Compare Franks Report, ii, table 46. An alternative calculation, based on two years, 1920 + 1949, suggests a total of 8% Clarendon School and 3% working-class freshmen; placing BNC in eighth position in terms of class, out of twenty-one colleges (J. A. Soares, *The Decline of Privilege: The Modernisation of Oxford University* (Stanford, Calif., 1999), 89, table 3).

[78] *Oxford Mag.*, 12 Mar. 1964, 255.

[79] Ibid. 4 Hilary 1966, 254 n. 3.

[80] In 1949 a Working Party on University Awards suggested a central clearing house for all applications (*Oxford Mag.*, 29 Apr. 1954, 280). In 1953–4 the CVCP, prompted by the Chancellor of the Exchequer, set in motion an inquiry under Prof. D. V. Glass into the whole process of University admissions (*Oxford Mag.* 19 Nov. 1953, 89). The Anderson Report of 1960 aroused fears that the abolition of parental means testing—automatic grant aid based on some sort of 18 plus examination system—would eliminate collegiate control over admissions altogether (*The Times*, 13 Oct. 1960, 15). For further discussion of autonomy, see Earl Russell, *Academic Freedom* (1993).

scholarship holders and 64 exhibitioners: some 110 in all. Only Balliol, Queen's, Christ Church, and Jesus had more. And BNC's closed awards could be relied on to attract numbers of well-drilled pupils from the greater grammar schools of the north. But such traditional local loyalties had begun to seem parochial. They scarcely fitted the emerging parameters of state-financed higher education. In 1963 came a crucial change: responsibility for University funding was transferred from the Treasury to the Department of Education. Oxford found itself drawn irreversibly into a nationalized education industry. Entrance and scholarship exams were combined after 1962; closed scholarships were phased out during the 1970s; open entrance awards went in 1984. And while public attention was focused on the provenance of undergraduates, another change—ultimately much more fundamental—was already taking place. The growth of postgraduate recruitment between the 1960s and 1980s had begun to transform the whole balance of the University. By 1962 BNC could boast a Middle Common Room of its own; by 1968 an established tutor for graduates.

Of course, the replacement of college entrance and scholarship examinations by simple A level scores did little to solve the problem of admissions. If anything it made it worse. The change coincided with the switch to non-selective state secondary schools in the 1960s and 1970s. It was in 1969 that Oxford reached its 'egalitarian' high-water mark: 62 per cent of the undergraduates in that year were from state schools. 'The meritocracy', noted Harry Judge, 'has triumphed. Dons prowl the countryside like medieval friars searching for brains.'[81] Britain seemed at last to be matching the selective educational systems of its European competitors: France, Germany, Italy. But the moment passed. The goal of an expanding meritocracy in tertiary education—based on needs-blind academic selection—was compromised at secondary level by the comprehensive revolution. By 1980 Oxford's state school intake had dropped to 56 per cent. By 2003 it had fallen to 53 per cent.

The reason was fairly straightforward. Selective private schools—reinforced after 1976 by direct grant and grammar schools deprived of state funding—simply produced better A level results in core subjects of importance. Attempts by government to 'equalize' the syllabus and examination system merely produced a spurious register of A level distinctions. The separation between 'progressive' teaching in state schools and 'traditional' teaching in private schools remained, accentuated by the abolition of 'assisted places' in 1997. By that date admissions tutors found themselves faced with a set of impossible choices, based on qualifications and predictions of identical excellence. In 2007, for example, more than one-quarter of all A level scripts received an A grade award. Admission decisions based on such nebulous

[81] Quoted in *The Times*, 24 Feb., 13 Aug. 2003 (T. Luckhurst).

evidence—actual or predictive—cried out for the wisdom of Solomon. 'We need to know the top 5%', protested Bill Swadling, BNC's admissions tutor; '20% is useless. We don't have the places.' So during the later 1990s, entrance exams began to return—supplementing interviews—at least for subjects in which competition was fiercest. But even these could never guarantee an objectively level playing field. By 2005–7, compared with state schools, private schools were scoring twice as many A grade A levels per pupil (50 per cent to 25 per cent); up to 60 per cent of the A grades achieved in A level modern languages; and between 46 per cent and 48 per cent of the A grades at A level in maths, physics, and chemistry. And these figures were replicated at GCSE level. At that stage, in 2007, independent school pupils achieved A grades in 60 per cent of papers taken; the figure for state schools was 19 per cent.[82]

So what was the result? 'Exclusion based on economic property', noted one transatlantic observer in 1999, had been 'replaced by a new type of exclusion based on cultural competency'. And that had unforeseen results. 'A pure meritocracy, funded by taxpayers, benefits individual members of the middle class more than it enhances either social equity or institutional self-reliance.' Oxford became socially narrower as well as financially weaker: in a tax-based state system, the legacy pool inevitably shrinks. The University emerged politically as well as financially exposed; because 'a state university that defies the existing government's will must either have constitutional guarantees backed by high courts or [else the support of] electoral opinion'. Oxford seemed in danger of abandoning its political constituency just as it lost its financial stability. 'It was as though Oxford was suspended in a social vacuum, and the myths [the *Brideshead* image] moved in to fill the abandoned space.'[83] Egalitarians to the left, philistines to the right: was there a future for academic excellence? Oxford entered the twenty-first century with its portals

---

[82] *The Times*, 19 Jan. 2006, 28 July 2007, 7, 25 Aug. 2007, 3, 1 Sept. 2007, 25; *Daily Telegraph*, 10 May 2005, 1; *Sunday Telegraph* and *Sunday Times*, 10 Oct. 2004 (M. Beloff); *Sunday Telegraph*, 26 Aug. 2007, 13; *Sunday Times*, 26 Aug. 2007, 10 (C. Woodhead) and 6 Jan. 2008, pp. 1–2. By 2007 languages were compulsory in only 17% of state schools (*The Times*, 5 May 2007). For the lowering of A level standards—a slippage of two grades over twenty years, 1987–2007—see *Sunday Telegraph*, 22 Jan., 22 Sept. 2002, p. 24 (J. Clare); *Sunday Times*, 22 Aug. 2004, 19 Aug. 2007, 16, 30 Sept. 2007, 11 (C. Woodhead); *Sunday Telegraph*, 22 Aug. 2004; *Daily Telegraph*, 10 May 2005; *The Times*, 17 Aug. 2007, 14. For the value of entrance exams, see *Oxford Mag.* 27 Oct. 1967, 24–6 and *The Times*, 20 Aug. 2003, 17 (H. Judge); *Sunday Times*, 17 Aug. 2003, 17 (C. Woodhead). For the declining content of state school teaching, see *Sunday Times*, 3 Apr. 2005, 11 (C. Woodhead), and R. Whelan (ed.), *The Corruption of the Curriculum* (Civitas, 2007). In the decade to 2007 private schools saw a 16.3% increase in A grades at A level compared with 5% in state schools (*The Times*, 18 Aug. 2007, 2); over the same period the number of pupils gaining three A grades at A levels in private schools almost doubled to 28%, as against 6.8% in state schools (*Daily Telegraph*, 13 Oct. 2007, 8).

[83] Soares, *Decline of Privilege*, 268, 276–7.

open to talent. But there was no universally acceptable definition of that particular attribute. Nor could there ever be. And a solution to the conundrum of equalized opportunity seemed as far away as ever. What remained was conceptual confusion—the blurring of 'elite' and 'elitist'—nullifying the validity of the meritocratic message.[84]

Back again to finance. The maintenance grant for state scholarships to Oxford in 1959 stood at £325 p.a.—means tested according to parental income—plus £30 vacation grant, plus a contribution for approved college fees (say £110 p.a.).[85] In 1946 the figure had been £205; in 1949 £265. These figures represented a fairly comfortable stipend for a student at that time, usually still living at home for nearly half the year. The average charge for Oxford lodgings in 1949 was little more than £3 per week for bed and breakfast. But the cost of living was rising fast: up 25 per cent, for example, between 1946 and 1949. The golden age of student finance would turn out to be brief. It was eventually killed by the great inflation of the 1970s. 'Almost everyone', it was noted as early as 1951, 'goes down in debt.'[86] Here lay the roots of endless funding problems in the future. Meanwhile, what would become of means-tested grants? Such things are seldom sustainable for long in a taxpaying democracy. By 1957, it was officially reckoned that 80 per cent of all Oxford undergraduates were receiving some form of financial assistance from the state. But the bulk of these—73 per cent of the men; 85 per cent of the women—still came from 'professional and managerial families'.[87] On the face of it, sectional advantage was being funded from general taxation. Sooner or later comprehensive taxation would demand comprehensive admission and with it remedial teaching.

The state funding of the post-war period went in large part not to the colleges but to the University. For this reason the CUF lectureship system had been designed as a method of channelling taxpayers' money more directly back to those who bore the brunt of teaching. But colleges—BNC in particular—were nervous of accepting any further funding from government, even when it was filtered through the mechanisms of the CUF. They

[84] For early Oxford debates on the merits of open meritocracy versus competitive handicapping, see S. Watson in *Oxford*, Dec. 1960 and *Oxford Mag.* 2 Feb. 1961, 184–5; [K. V. Thomas] in *Oxford Mag.* 19 Jan. 1961, 143 and 2 Feb. 1961, 185; W. F. R. Hardie in *Oxford Mag.* 23 Feb. 1961, 240–3. For the dangers built into the apparent fairness of an open elite, see Robbins Report, para. 222. In a way, the conundrum of admissions remains quasi-metaphysical: 'the point at which the egalitarianism of democracy and the aristocracy of merit become one' (Earl of Bessborough, *Hansard: Lords*, 11 Dec. 1963, col. 1248).

[85] *Oxford Mag.* 29 Jan. 1959, 198.

[86] *Isis*, 23 Feb. 1949, 7; 30 Oct. 1951, 13, 28.

[87] *Applications for Admission to Universities*, table 16; quoted by C. Clark in *Oxford Mag.* 7 Nov. 1957, 88.

preferred to enlarge student numbers in order to maximize housekeeping revenue. In this way teaching margins were eroded and collegiate amenity undermined. Meanwhile tension between University and state grew more acute. Nor had the age-old tension between college and University been resolved. 'Sometime in the near future', predicted the *Oxford Magazine* in 1959, 'the educational rulers of the country will have to make up their minds about the college system: whether to treat it as an untidy relic of the past, an administrative nuisance, or as an institution to be cherished.'[88] As Eric Collieu would have said, 'Yes, indeed. Yes indeed!'

Between the Asquith Commission and the Franks Commission, Oxford changed fundamentally. In roughly forty years—say 1922–1964—the number of undergraduates doubled; the number of teachers trebled; and the number of postgraduates quintupled. Over the same period, however, Oxford's share of Britain's student population as a whole did not alter very much: it went down from 9.7 per cent to 7.1 per cent.[89] The revolution in that respect would come later. What did change dramatically in this period was the rate of government funding, and with it the proportionate relationship—within the University—between arts and science. Oxford's endowment income rose, over these four decades, from £454,000 to £1,994,000. Over the same period, recurrent state funding (excluding capital grants) rose from £30,000 to £4,233,000.[90] The bulk of this vast increase went to science. And with it swung—irreversibly—the preponderant balance of the University. The University waxed potent, and the colleges waned. The science departments emerged almost as autonomous fiefdoms; the arts faculties, though comparatively poorer, marshalled their governance into supra-collegiate entities. Either way, by the 1970s it was clear that the autonomy of colleges had diminished vis-à-vis the power of the coordinating General Board. After decades of growth, 1946–70, it fell to the General Board to husband Oxford's dwindling resources during the colder, leaner years from 1971 onwards. At college level, economies in living arrangements were seldom more than small scale. The idea of a Brasenose–Lincoln alliance, for example, reared its head once more in 1970.[91] But the economies of the early 1980s—freezing appointments, restructuring salaries—were more fundamental. They were implemented not by the colleges but by the administrators of Wellington Square. By 1987, when the Thatcher government replaced the University Grants Commission (UGC) with the University Funding Council (UFC), the colleges of Oxford had

---

[88] [Ed.], 'The Economy of the University', *Oxford Mag.* 28 Nov. 1957, 145. In 1954 BNC expressed disquiet over state involvement in anything 'which touches the foundations of the independence and finance of the colleges' (J. P. D. Dunbabin, in *HUO* viii. 654).

[89] Franks Report, i, paras. 70–1.

[90] Ibid., para. 74.

[91] V-P's Reg. 11 Mar. 1970, fo. 121; 17 June 1970, fos. 140–1.

become—administratively speaking—poor relations of the University. By 1998, when the Blair government introduced draconian control of tuition fees, they were on the brink of relegation to the level of picturesque sideshows.

These are just some of the factors—the ominous background music—against which the progress of Brasenose between the 1970s and the 1990s must be measured.

When Herbert Hart (pl. 95) was pre-elected Principal in 1972—the first non-Brasenose Principalian election in the history of the college—he was teased by intellectual friends for selling out to the hearties. He had apparently joined a college crammed, as he put it, with 'old Turks and young fogies'. In fact the Brasenose for which he was now responsible was worlds away from the BNC of W. T. S. Stallybrass. For a start, the Fellowship was academically outstanding. Simon Schama's election in 1976 could be seen as symbolic: a media polymath replaced the last of the pre-war Fellows, Eric Collieu. And of those senior members in post during Hart's brief tenure (1973–8), no less than eleven were, or would become, Fellows of the British Academy: Hart himself, Robert Shackleton, Barry Nicholas, John Ackrill, Leighton Reynolds, Philip Jones, Vernon Bogdanor, Robert Evans, Peter Brunt, Robert Auty, and Peter Birks. At the same time, four more Fellows of that period were already, or would soon become, Fellows of the Royal Society: Laszlo Solymar, Nicholas Kurti, Douglas Holder, and Bryan Birch. With a rare quintet of Academicians emeritus and supernumerary still active in college as well—Boris Unbegaun, F. H. Lawson, Sir Ronald Syme, Sir Otto Kahn-Freund, and Colin Clark—BNC's high table in the 1970s could well be described as a formidably cerebral place. Twenty honorands in all: never before had Brasenose known a Senior Common Room so blessed with academic laurels. There were even Visiting Fellows in Creative Arts: Howard Hodgkin and John Wain.[92]

Distinction among the Fellowship was one thing, however. Translating it into examination success was quite another. Between 1964 and 1968, BNC had fallen from sixth to twenty-first in the Norrington Table.

> In Oxford's fair city,
> Where the Dons are so witty,
> I first set my eyes on Sir Noel Hall;
> As his vision grew misty,
> While he sank back his whisky,
> Crying 'Brasenose, Oh Brasenose, the best of them all'.
>   The best of them all,

[92] Kahn-Freund (*Brazen Nose*, xvii/1. 25–9); Auty (ibid., xvi/4. 29–33); Holder (ibid., xvi/3. 24–6); Unbegaun (ibid., xv. 266–9); Lawson (*Proceedings of the British Academy*, 76 (1990), 473–85). For John Wain see *ODNB* (B. Richards). Occasional tutors: Jonathan Culler and George Landow.

> The best of them all,
> Though your chance of a first is exceedingly small ... [93]

In 1963 the SCR announced a crackdown on 'continued and conspicuous idleness'. In 1970, and again in 1974, the Governing Body established committees to explore ways of raising the quality of admissions and the level of examination success. In the mid-1970s a scheme was set up by Peter Birks and Harry Judge to encourage candidates from comprehensive schools in Cheshire.[94] Improvements, however, came slowly. In 1975, the college was lying twenty-sixth out of twenty-eight in the Norrington Table; in 1978, twenty-first; in 1980, twenty-seventh. Thereafter results showed a degree of progression. But other colleges seemed to advance at a faster rate.

Perhaps it was too much to expect Herbert Hart to cure this malaise in a mere five years. But the presence of 'an intellectual giant'—'the outstanding British legal philosopher of the 20th century'—did much to galvanize an SCR demoralized by declining results. Here was a philosopher who began as an Oxford realist in the tradition of Cook Wilson, and Prichard; who started as an admirer of G. E. Moore; who then switched schools to join the linguistic brigade under the influence of Ryle and Hampshire, Austin and Waismann. With a trajectory like that, he was more than well placed to apply the techniques of linguistic analysis to problems in the philosophy of law. The time was right too. His best-known work, *The Concept of Law*, sold more than 150,000 copies in thirty-three years. 'There had been nothing to compare with it', noted Honoré 'since Hobbes' *Leviathan* and Bentham's *Of Laws in General*.'[95] By bridging the worlds of philosophy and law; by grappling publicly with the crudities of student politics; by infusing even the platitudes of administration with the fervour of his own liberalism—in all these ways Hart raised BNC's academic game in a manner inconceivable during the reign of Principal Hall. The Hart Report itself—produced in response to the troubles of 1968—settled the question of student representation for a generation.[96] Hart's openness to

---

[93] Ale Verse, 1971 (*Brazen Nose*, xv. 166).

[94] V-P's Reg. 23 Jan. 1963, fo. 11; 11 Nov. 1970, fo. 21; 2 Dec. 1970, fo. 28; 16 Oct. 1974, fo. 11; 13 Nov. 1974, fo. 15; *Brazen Nose*, xvi. 9.

[95] T. Honoré, in *Proceedings of the British Academy*, 84 (1993), 312. See also *Brazen Nose*, xxvi. 46–7 and *ODNB* (Honoré). Portrait (1978) by Derek Hill. His wife, Jennifer Hart, wrote a revealing autobiography, *Ask Me No More* (1998).

[96] 'A university in which the existence and exercise of authority creates among its students a sense that the university is divided into "Them" and "Us" is a howling wilderness where no academic purposes can prosper' (Hart, *Report of the Committee on relations with junior members* 1969, para. 34). Don't 'take Hart', replied Christopher Hitchens and Tariq Ali; 'take the Clarendon Building' (*Isis*, 9 Oct. 1968, 13; 16 Oct. 1968, 13). But by recommending 'participatory representation' rather than 'direct democracy', Hart effectively spiked most of the radical guns. 'The Hart Report settles deep amid the dust it was supposed to stir' (*Isis*, 28 May 1969, 3). For its composition and recommendations, see *Isis*, 22 Jan. 1969, 9 and 14 May 1969,

ideas, his Jewish wit, his sheer intellectual horse-power, made him in some ways an ideal head of house. In other ways he remained an outsider. He rarely used the Lodgings. He never accepted the college's fondness for 'Lucullan' feasts. But he did eventually come to understand the spirit of the place. After all, at Bradford Grammar School he had once been a contemporary of Leslie Styler.

Hart's attitude to reform was pragmatic. As an undergraduate he had himself taken part in protests, but on issues of personal liberation, not in the cause of political combat. Oxford, he believed to the end, was first and foremost a place of education not an instrument of revolution.

> You know, it's a hellish job [he told *Isis* in October 1968] trying to devise anything to fit a complex, federal university like Oxford . . . I don't want the University sacrificed for some 'visionary view' of society. But don't think I'm not in favour of social reform. I agree with the militants that society is hell . . . But I don't agree to destroying something very precious, liberal university education, from which the real hope of social reform comes . . . I can't swallow the dogmas of the New Left . . . Anyway, why is bourgeois liberty a fraud? Marcuse doesn't tell us . . . But as far as university reform is concerned, [the New Left] won't take YES for an answer . . .[97]

True enough. But in smaller matters he remained a root-and-branch reformer. Within a year or two of his arrival, most male scouts at BNC were replaced by part-time female domestics. Students were given closer access to the Governing Body's decision-making process; but now they were also expected to clean and tidy their own rooms. Sometimes they were even seen serving in hall. By 1974 a washing machine had actually been installed on staircase XIII.[98] The world of Maurice Platnauer (pl. 95)—'the golden age of the don, 1945–75'— was almost over. At one point during the early 1970s the college decided to dispose of one particular item in its property portfolio: Stow Wood. That meant Fellows would no longer receive Christmas trees. Hart did not repine. 'The feudal age', he announced, '*had* to come to an end sometime.'[99]

One development at Brasenose with which Hart was wholly in sympathy was the decision to admit women. Moves in this direction had begun in 1966–7. On 24 May 1967, the Governing Body had come to a historic decision: it voted, by a wide margin (17 to 3), that it would be willing to amend college

---

3–4; *Oxford Mag.* 24 Oct. 1969, 21–2. Its essence is contained in an Appendix: 'Student Radicalism in Oxford'. For an amusing commentary, see [H. R. Trevor-Roper], *The Letters of Mercurius* (1970), 23–7, 78–82.

[97] *Isis*, 9 Oct. 1968, 9.

[98] V-P's Reg. 21 Feb. 1973, fo. 31; 14 Nov. 1973, fo. 69; 20 Feb. 1974, fo. 92; 19 June 1974, fo. 112.

[99] *Brazen Nose*, xxvii. 6; N. Annan, *Our Age: English Intellectuals between the World Wars* (1990), 377. For the disappearance of scouts, see C. Platt, *The Most Obliging Man in Europe: The Life and Times of the Oxford Scout* (1986).

statutes so as to remove all barriers of gender.[100] In this it was, by some years, ahead of every other college in Oxford or Cambridge. In 1964, New College had already given signs of proceeding along similar lines. But its reformers made the mistake—prior to a definitive vote—of advertising their intention to bring the matter before Congregation.[101] That produced stalemate. The reformers at BNC were more subtle. They brought up the proposition obliquely: it emerged during a discussion relating to the redevelopment of New Inn Hall Street. In effect, the possibility of co-residence—first for women graduates, then for women at all levels—was built into the specification for planning and plumbing.

Now the suggestion that any of the men's colleges might admit women was strongly resisted at this time by the women's colleges themselves. They feared a creaming off of talent, and a narrowing of career opportunities for women. And it was this view that steered the Franks Commission away from the issue altogether.[102] The reformers, however, were persistent. Graham Richards for one: he spoke boldly for co-residence at the Pater Society in 1969.[103] The proposal came up again at BNC on Governing Body in 1970 and 1971.[104] By that time, a real momentum for change had emerged. Even Cambridge was beginning to accept the notion of integration. Segregated learning seemed about to become Oxford's last lost cause. It was in the summer of 1971, at its meeting in the eighth week of Trinity term, that the Governing Body of BNC voted by a three to one majority (24 to 8) in favour of removing the prohibiting statute: that is statute I, clause 2: 'No woman may become a member of the College.'[105] One year later, in 1972, Brasenose, Hertford, Jesus, St Catherine's, and Wadham—'the five IQ-grabbing men's colleges'—defied the continuing opposition of all the women's colleges, and made a definitive move towards co-residence.[106] The first female candidates

[100] V-P's Reg. 24 May 1967, fo. 50. By a less decisive vote (14 to 11), the Governing Body agreed 'to envisage the accommodation of women within the present curtilage of the College'. In effect these decisions accepted the recommendations of a subcommittee on which W. G. Richards was the activating force (V-P's Reg. 20 Mar. 1966, fo. 14).

[101] *Oxford Mag.* 15 Oct. 1964, 4–7 (G. E. M. de Ste. Croix), 138–40 (P. Ady), and 312–13 (M. Hubbard), 321–2 (A. Pirie).

[102] V-P's Reg. 21 Feb. 1968, fo. 98; 1 May 1968, fo. 112; *Oxford Mag.* 11 Mar. 1965, 269. For Franks's view, see his letter to the Warden of New College in *OU Gazette*, 18 Mar. 1965, criticized in *Isis*, 28 Apr. 1965, 8.

[103] B1 a 46 (2), 11 Mar. 1969.

[104] V-P's Reg. 20 Jan. 1970, fo. 2; 14 Oct. 1970, fo. 2; 11 Nov. 1970, fo. 13; 20 Jan. 1971, fo. 37.

[105] V-P's Reg. 14 Oct. 1970, fo. 2 and 20 Jan. 1971, fo. 37. See also *Brazen Nose*, xv. 130 and xxviii. 26–8 (W. G. Richards). Corpus admitted ten female postgraduates in 1970, the year in which King's College, Cambridge, decided to admit women as undergraduates (*Isis*, 9 Mar. 1970, 5). For arguments in favour (D. Stockton) and against (M. Warnock), see *Oxford Mag.* 89 (1972), ii. 4–6.

[106] *Isis*, 19 May 1972, 3; V-P's Reg. 26 Apr. 1972, fo. 124.

for admission appeared at BNC in December 1973; the first matriculands in October 1974; the first graduates in July 1977. By October 1977 there were 131 women at Brasenose, as against 294 men. Twenty years later the figures approached parity. But it was only in 1981–2 that the first women Fellows entered the SCR: Mary Stokes (Tutor in Jurisprudence) and Rosa Bedding-ton (Platnauer Fellow in Physiology; later FRS).[107] The results of the revolution were slow to materialize. Not until twenty-five years after the admission of women could BNC hail its first female judge, Belinda van Heerden of South Africa. Twenty-seven years were to pass before the election of a female Honorary Fellow: Julie Mellor of the Equal Opportunities Commission. And for thirty years after their appearance, women at BNC lagged behind men in the annual league table of Firsts. But there were other considerations. Co-residence turned out to be a civilizing process. There could be no going back. Oxford had changed, and Brasenose too.

So what were they like, these Brasenose men—and women—of the last quarter of the twentieth century? And was their college still recognizably the same? On the face of it not much had altered. There were fewer scouts now of course. And fewer blues. And—proportionately—not many more Firsts, at least not until the later 1980s. But the rituals of the academic year still marked out the stepping stones of innumerable careers: matriculation photo, Schools dinner, graduation lunch. Several of the distinctive marks of BNC tradition were still very much in place: the Ale Verses on Shrove Tuesday; Ivy Ale on Ascension Day; Collections in hall; septennial gaudies for returning members; Latin Grace; Sunday evening chapel; the Summer Ball; the Betty Morley at the end of Hilary term; and of course tutorials, gowns, books, and beer. The plumbing was better. Christian names replaced surnames. Parents were no longer invisible. Counsellors replaced moral tutors. The old hierarchy of open and closed scholarships had almost disappeared, and with it many of the traditional links with particular schools. And there would be two further changes of fundamental importance. First, University departments would play an increasing role in appointments and admissions policy, particularly as regards postgraduates. That had long been the case in science. It was now increasingly so in arts and social sciences too. Second, new patterns of recruitment were beginning to work their way through the system. The social composition of the college was becoming very different. There were new opportunities now; new hopes, new ambitions. Compare for a moment the matriculation lists for 1955, 1965, and 1975.

---

[107] V-P's Reg. 27 May 1981 and 20 Jan. 1982. Jeannie Lawson was the first BNC woman to get a First in classical Mods; Rosa Beddington the first to get a First in schools (*Brazen Nose*, xxxv. 55–6). Janet Dyson was a Lecturer in Maths in 1973–4; Susan Treggiari a Visiting Fellow in 1976–7 (V-P's Reg. 28 Apr. 1976). The Sex Discrimination Act was passed by Parliament in 1975.

A breakdown of the list for Michaelmas 1955 shows first the impact of post-war state subsidy and, second, the persistence of traditional catchment areas.[108] Of the 108 entrants, 31 still came from British public schools (6 from Wellington alone). But all the remainder—minus 17 entrants from abroad, including 6 from white southern Africa—now emerged from the state sector: direct grant, grammar, or maintained. Of these no fewer than 13 were still from the Manchester region. So the balance overall had become predominantly state educated. But this was still a state system selective in its intake and consciously academic in its programme. The culture of the college—indeed of Oxford as a whole—remained scholastically traditional, even if its social provenance had shifted radically from upper middle class to lower middle class. As for Pass men, in Oxford they were now so rare as to be 'almost fabulous'.[109] But they still existed at BNC. And of course there were no women.

Now take the intake for 1965. This time there are 105 names on the list. No change there. And many of the old close scholarships and exhibitions are still visible: from Manchester and Bury, from Shrewsbury, Marlborough, and Sherborne. There are no Pass men: that rare species has disappeared with the last years of Platnauer's Principalship. By 1968 the gentleman's Fourth will vanish into history. The number of postgraduates, however, and the number of undergraduates arriving from abroad, is noticeably higher: perhaps one-quarter of the total. The intake from public schools accounts, as before, for about one-third. The number from BNC's traditional north-western heartland remains much the same. And there are still no women.

Now look at the intake for 1975. There are 120 names on the list, a significant increase. But, *mirabile dictu*, 27 of them are women. Public schools now provide only a quarter of the intake; grammar schools perhaps half; and—for the first time—comprehensive schools supply a significant handful of entrants. The greatest change in the list—apart of course from the matter of gender—lies in the number of postgraduates, mostly from abroad. They make up at least one-sixth of the total.

Two things are striking about all three lists. First, there is the element of continuity in recruitment. Brasenose retained an identifiable link with the north-west until well into the 1970s. Second—and conversely—there is the growth of the postgraduate intake, particularly from abroad. Over the next quarter of a century—the final quincentennial decades—these tendencies would significantly diverge. There would be fewer recruits from Lancashire and Cheshire; and many more—often paying premium fees—from Europe, Asia, Africa, and North America. Brasenose, like Oxford in general, would soon become part of a worldwide market in talent, a globalized academic elite.

---

[108] *Brazen Nose*, x. 153–4.
[109] R. B. McCallum in *Oxford Mag.* 24 Oct. 1957, 38.

The internationalizing of BNC proceeded slowly after the Second World War. Between 1947 and 1962 undergraduates coming from abroad averaged scarcely 10 per cent of the annual intake, despite unusually high numbers from old Commonwealth countries in the 1950s. That was one of the lowest percentages in Oxford. Thereafter the figures begin to climb. And this increase was reflected in miniature in the make-up of the Brasenose SCR. Three refugees of formidable distinction became Fellows: Kurti, Unbegaun, and Kahn-Freund. Each had travelled a difficult road: Unbegaun was actually a graduate of Buchenwald. All three were warmly encouraged, not least by Robert Auty, who succeeded Unbegaun as Professor of Slavonic Languages in 1965. Auty was a Yorkshireman by birth, but a refugee by instinct. In 1938–9 he had been instrumental in securing the release of numerous Jews from Nazi concentration camps. And he kept in touch with them. On one occasion in the later 1960s he introduced three guests at dinner. Apologizing for the excessive number, he added, 'You see, it is the first time we have seen each other since Buchenwald.' Those years of course were exceptional. But the number of imported scholars at Brasenose continued to rise as the academic market expanded. By 2005, up to one-third of both current Fellows and current Lecturers had come to BNC from abroad. In 2002 alone, no fewer than four Fellows from Germany were elected simultaneously: a philosopher (Thomas Sattig), a physicist (Laura Herz), and two lawyers (Thomas Krebs and Stefan Vogenauer).

The arrival of women in 1975 coincided with the deaths of Eric Collieu and Maurice Platnauer. Collieu had come to accept the change. Not so Platnauer. The last tranche of his fortune never found its way to BNC. Perhaps if he had lived a little longer he might have changed his mind. For the admission of women turned out in some ways to be a non-event. Manners improved. The quadrangles were quieter, the libraries more full. There were fewer lectures in any case now, and rather more seminars. More generally, the college became socially self-sufficient; and—paradoxically—security became for the first time an issue of importance. Locks were placed on bed-sitting room doors. Previously no student had ever possessed a key. Otherwise, changes were minimal. Examination results did not improve overnight. The Phoenix and the Octagon continued to imbibe. The takings of the Beer Cellar showed little or no diminution. The Pater and the Ellesmere continued to confabulate. And—as gloomily predicted—team sports continued to decline. By 1981 the rugby Fifteen had sunk to Division III for the first time ever. But the real revolution was taking place behind the scenes: the steady, ultimately dramatic growth in the numbers of postgraduates. The figures are worth repeating. In the half-century after the Second World War, the number of postgraduates at Oxford rose from about 400 (mostly scientists) to over 4,000 (nearly one-third of the student body). And they would go on rising. At

BNC—with its small scientific intake—the growth in the percentage of postgraduates was comparable, though on a lower scale: 16.5 per cent in 1948–9; 11.6 per cent in 1958–9; 21.1 per cent in 1963–4; 22.7 per cent in 1964–5. As the proportion rose, the international range of these students became more and more striking. In the Brasenose intake of 1992–3, for example, graduate students came from Australia, China, Eire, France, Germany, Hong Kong, Hungary, India, Italy, Japan, Korea, Malaysia, Russia, Sweden, Thailand, the USA, and Vietnam. And when they arrived, this particular cohort found that the following countries were already represented: Canada, Greece, Pakistan, South Africa, and Venezuela.[110]

All this was the product of a much wider movement: the emergence of a mass system of higher education during the half-century following the Robbins Report of 1963.

Expansion at Oxford had certainly been fast. In Trinity term 1939 there had been 4,589 students in residence; in 1953, 6,878; in 1956, 7,346. At that point the Vice-Chancellor hazarded a guess that numbers could rise to 8,000 without much risk to 'traditions and standards'.[111] That optimism would be tested almost to destruction during the next quarter of a century. In forty years, 1923–63, the student population of Oxford more than doubled; the proportion of undergraduates dropped from nine-tenths to four-fifths; and the proportion reading arts and social studies from four-fifths to two-thirds.[112] But all this was as nothing to the expansion of student numbers nationwide. In 1957 there were already fears that Oxford and Cambridge would be overwhelmed. 'The pernicious doctrine of parity of esteem' seemed to dictate that all universities in the United Kingdom would ultimately be financed by the state on an equal basis.[113] 'Oxford is doomed', announced John Wain; 'splitting apart under the hammering blows of the 20th century.' Kingsley Amis spoke for many: 'More will mean Worse.'[114] But in 1960 there were still plenty of voices calling for altruistic expansion: 'not to a meagre 175,000 by the mid-sixties, but to at least half a million.' 'Oh God', gasped the editor of the *Oxford Magazine*; 'who is going to teach this half

---

[110] *Brazen Nose*, xxvii. 4. [D. Stockton]; Franks Report, ii, table 22. For students from EU countries, see *The Times*, 28 Dec. 2005.

[111] *Oxford Mag.*, 25 Oct. 1956, 44. 'The bulge is here' (ibid. 1 Nov. 1956, 57).

[112] Halsey, in *HUO* viii. 722.

[113] *Oxford Mag.*, 30 May 1957, 473.

[114] J. Wain, *Sprightly Running* (1962), 99; Amis, in *Encounter*, 15 (1960), 8–9 denouncing Lord Esher's plea for open access: i.e. that 'desire rather than any archaic nonsense about capacity, should be an adequate entrance qualification' (*The Times*, 12 May 1960, p. 4). See also Henry Fairlie's comments in *Daily Mail*, quoted in *Oxford Mag.* 6 June 1957, 498. For the results of expansion, see R. Stevens, *University to Uni: The Politics of Higher Education in England since 1944* (2003).

million?"[115] By early 1963 Labour was calling for 700,000, distributed among eighty universities. Then came Robbins. This threw down the gauntlet of open-ended expansion; that is expansion geared to keep up with any possible number of willing and qualified applicants. For Oxford that meant serious change: a degree of change—in attitudes as much as in institutions—commensurate with the advent of mass education at tertiary level. At the time, Robbins's call for a target of one-sixth of the relevant age group to be given access to higher education—60 per cent of them in universities—seemed almost utopian. Forty years later, the call would go out for 50 per cent; yes, 50 per cent by the year 2010, and all to be educated in universities. In forty years, 1964–2004, the UK university student population would multiply from *c.*340,000 to *c.*2,000,000. By 2007 the total number of students at Oxford would top 20,000. Such would be the momentum of change. Meanwhile, Robbins had challenged Oxford and Cambridge to reform or be reformed: to streamline their administrative and policy-making procedures; to clarify their financial machinery and systems of recruitment, or else face up to the bleak imperatives of governmental diktat. It was a threat endorsed with some vigour by the Labour Party.[116] So Oxford went for a pre-emptive strike. It decided to put its own house in order.[117] And it took care to start the process before the impending General Election of 1964. Thus was born the commission of inquiry presided over by Lord Franks.

The Franks Commission was the most scrupulous investigation ever carried out into the workings of any university. Its proposals, though limited, were radical. 'Franks', explained Steven Watson, 'is like 1787; previously the states [i.e. colleges] were autonomous units of a confederation, now they are members of a federal union.' The plan was for a stronger Hebdomadal Council to direct the General Board of Faculties; with—or so it was

---

[115] [Mary Warnock], *Oxford Mag.* 20 Oct. 1960, replying to K. Hill's call for half a million students in *The Times*, 14 Oct. 1960, 15; P. A. Brunt in *Oxford Mag.* 9 May 1963, 276 quoting *The Years of Crisis* (Transport House), 47.

[116] Robbins Report, para. 678; Harold Wilson, quoted in *Oxford Mag.* 25 Feb. 1965, 238. This reversed Attlee's earlier reliance on 'trust' and Dalton's still earlier protection of a free-floating UGC (*Hansard: Lords*, 22 May 1957, cols. 1125–6; 12 Dec. 1963, cols. 1265, 1392–3, 1400–2). By 1963, Labour thinking was already moving towards ministerial control: the replacing of the University Grants Committee with a different sort of 'buffer', a University Grants Commission (*Hansard: Lords*, 11 Dec. 1963, cols. 1225–6, 1261, 1267–8, 1295–6). Lord Robbins himself believed that increasing numbers of students did not necessarily mean increasing state control. Although his Report sought 'to dissolve artificial hierarchy' in educational institutions, he assumed that a large sector of higher education would remain outside the university system (*Hansard: Lords*, 11 Dec. 1963, col. 1262; L. Robbins, *The University in the Modern World*, 1966). In both respects, he underestimated the built-in *dirigisme* of expansion (*Times Lit. Supp.* 19 May 1966, 417–19).

[117] For Cambridge's response, see N. Annan, in *Universities Qtly.* 20 (1965–6).

hoped—a new Council of Colleges giving voice at last to the intercollegiate will. More women; more science; more postgraduates; more inter-college taxation. And, overall, more recruitment of students from a wider social range, to be expedited by the phased abolition of collegiate scholarships. Much of this came to pass. But the problem of coordinating the collectivity of colleges remained unresolved. It would stay unresolved even after another inquiry, the North Report of 1997. And then there was the bigger picture. For all its merits, Franks ignored its wider remit: to 'inquire into the part which Oxford should play in the future of the system of higher education in the United Kingdom'.[118]

Franks had been partly prompted by Robbins. And Robbins, in turn, had been prompted by the pressure for expansion in the early 1960s. But neither report had the status of a Royal Commission. Despite the reforming investigations of the mid-nineteenth century; despite the huge expansion of the university system in the mid-twentieth century—doubling numbers between 1939 and 1959; multiplying government grants during the same period by a factor of 18—there had never been a Royal Commission on Higher Education. In 1953 the Labour Party's programme—'Challenge to Britain'—had demanded 'a Royal Commission to carry out a full investigation of the whole problem [i.e.] the relation between the Universities and the needs of society'.[119] Nothing came of it. Labour's next call for a Royal Commission in 1958 was kicked into touch by the 1959 General Election.[120] Instead there appeared a sober Fabian pamphlet, floating among other ideas the suggestion that Oxford might become a graduate institution on the lines of ANU, Canberra.[121] In 1963, Lord Robbins suggested a separate inquiry of Royal Commission stature, simply to deal with Oxford and Cambridge.[122] As before, the issue was mothballed. Or rather, it was forestalled by Franks. Instead of radical rethinking—from both sides of the political spectrum— came a series of expansionist expedients, culminating in the Tory decision in 1992 to turn polytechnics into universities overnight. By the turn of the century, the United Kingdom emerged with not far short of 200 institutions licensed to award diplomas, degrees, higher degrees, and honorary degrees.

All that separated these institutions, in official eyes, was their varying capacity for research; a capacity henceforward to be measured by the yardstick of central assessment exercises. It was a blunt instrument, but to a

---

[118] *The Times*, 12 May 1966, 1, 13; *Isis*, 11 May 1966, 1–4, 20.

[119] *Isis*, 22 Oct. 1953, 25.

[120] *The Times*, 11 June 1958, 18. Trevor Lloyd prophetically called for a petrol tax to fund university expansion.

[121] G. C. Moodie, *The Universities: A Royal Commission?* (Fabian Society, 1959). Its approach has little of the resentment of Oxford and Cambridge to be found in 'Bruce Truscott', pseud. [E. A. Peers], *Redbrick University* (1943; 1945; 1951).

[122] J. Carswell, *Government and the Universities in Britain* (Cambridge, 1985), 31.

certain extent it worked. By 2003 the top fifteen universities were in receipt of 60–70 per cent of all government research funding. Of course there was a snag. Such largesse came at a price. Without the shelter of UGC mediation—replaced from 1993 by the pressures of Research Council provision—the tertiary system was exposed for the first time to tighter political control. The balance of power had changed. The paymaster was calling the piper's tune. And yet the results of this great shift in cultural influence had yet to be worked out. 'The quantity, quality, and content of British higher education', Sir Eric Ashby announced in 1963, 'are designed for an elite selected by examination; the assumption that only an elite needs higher education is obsolete.' Well, yes. But that begged an obvious question: what exactly was to be the nature of this mass-produced higher education? And how much of it was appropriate to a university?[123] Fundamental questions—the scale of participation; the balance between vocational and non-vocational learning; the dilemmas of a mixed economy in the tertiary system; the dangers of politicized expansion and 'quality control'; the actual mechanisms of central-ized funding; the very purpose of a university education—all these, sooner or later, would have to be reassessed. But Oxford grappled with such twenty-first-century problems reluctantly. Instead of broadening outwards, debate turned inwards: to the technicalities of governance and the dismal decimals of finance.

It was of course on finance that the future of Oxford and its constituent colleges turned. Between the 1960s and the 1990s, under governments of left and right, higher education was dramatically expanded while its funding, in real terms, was drastically reduced. 'The unit of resource'—that is the cost per student to the taxpayer—was relentlessly driven down. State funding per UK student fell, in real terms, by 20 per cent between 1976 and 1989; by 38 per cent between 1989 and 2002. And the collapse in the value of academic salaries followed a similar trajectory. As far as Oxford was concerned, successive governments seemed to be trying to run a world-class university on the back of a third-world salary structure.

As early as 1963, John Vaizey was already prophesying the choice that lay ahead: 'Oxford is a great international university. If the Government denies it money, either we shall as a nation no longer have an outstanding university—or we shall have to do what Harvard has done.'[124] In other words, privatize or perish. Vaizey's words would be echoed repeatedly over the following

---

[123] Ashby, *Financial Times*, 11 Feb. 1963, 40–1. 'The intellect ... the intellect ... the intellect. *That* is what universities exist for. Everything else is secondary' (Noel Annan, in *Encounter* 20 (1963), 7).

[124] *Oxford Mag.*, 7 Nov. 1963, 63. For funding figures, see *Times Higher Ed. Supp.* 21 Aug. 1998, 12; *Sunday Times*, 31 Mar. 2002, 20. For salaries, see *The Times*, 14 May 2003.

half-century. But whether they ever represented a realistic choice must always have seemed rather doubtful.[125]

Meanwhile, recruitment figures for Brasenose had begun to reflect the emerging pressures of a globalized intake. In the first five years of the twenty-first century undergraduate recruitment averaged around 110 p.a., with men and women sharing places almost equally. The proportion of independent to non-independent schools varied from year to year, but came out roughly at 56 to 44. That was rather different from the proportionate intake for the University as a whole, which stood at 53.7 per cent from state schools in 2005–6. Brasenose had remained loyal to its former direct grant constituency. Perhaps too loyal: quite a number of its catchment schools now found themselves effectively privatized by the withdrawal of state funding. In any case recruitment varied from subject to subject. The most popular fields at BNC (economics and management, law, medicine, and PPE) recorded at least five applications for every place. Their tariff for entry was therefore appropriately high. Interestingly, the total figures for undergraduate admission at Brasenose, though clearly a product of intense competition, were not hugely different from the figures recorded half a century before. The numbers from state schools, however, had indeed fallen significantly over the years, despite all the efforts of a special Target schools programme from 1984 onwards. That reflected first the transfer of direct grant schools and grammar schools to the independent sector in the 1970s and, second, the limited teaching of core subjects—maths, science, languages—available in comprehensive sixth forms from the 1980s onwards. By 2007 nearly one-quarter of English sixth-formers—and 45 per cent of those achieving A grade passes in A-level maths—were being educated in independent schools. And 93 per cent of those taking an A-level in media studies came from comprehensives.

These were all significant factors. But what had changed most of all was not the origin of undergraduates but the proportion of postgraduates. By 2001–2 the student body at Brasenose totalled 527, made up of 385 reading for first degrees and 142 for graduate courses. By 2006–7 the figures were 537, 379, and 158. That year BNC's new intake stood at 104 undergraduates to 90 postgraduates, the majority coming from abroad or from other British universities. Brasenose itself was very far from being the most postgraduate of Oxford colleges. But its high proportion of graduate students reflected

---

[125] A. H. Halsey, *Decline of Donnish Dominion: The British Academic Profession in the Twentieth Century* (Oxford, 1992); A. Kenny, *Oxford Mag.*, 8th week, Trinity 2007, 20–3. In 1950 it was calculated that £17 million would be needed to secure independence; in 1965 at least £20 million. In 1971 an appeal to Oxford's business alumni aroused little interest (Soares, *Decline of Privilege*, 196–7, 202). In 1997 it was estimated that £2 billion of additional endowment would be needed to replace £85 million p.a. funding from the taxpayer; and that this might take a century to raise (North Report (1997), 220–1).

only too clearly the changing emphasis of University studies. By 1995–6, 30 per cent of Oxford students were postgraduates, as against 14 per cent in the UK. By 2006–7 Oxford had 12,106 undergraduates to 7,380 postgraduates. And of those postgraduates, over 60 per cent came from abroad. Less than ten years into the twenty-first century, the University was more than half-way to becoming a postgraduate institution significantly financed by students from outside the U.K. That had by no means been the intention. Oxford's commitment to undergraduate teaching remained unshaken. But numerically the change was dramatic. And the training of these older students—so many and so demanding—presented Oxford with an intellectual and administrative challenge of the first order.[126]

Every Oxford college entered the last quarter of the twentieth century with its finances stretched to the limit. The Blair government's phased withdrawal of tuition fee funding from 1998 onwards certainly cost the colleges dear. The process was painful and protracted. First, government funding via college tuition fees was reduced. Then part of the funding stream was supplemented, in effect, by a graduate tax in the form of top-up fees. But this time the money came with strings attached. And the strings—backed by the threat of financial sanctions—were now to be controlled by a quango with a truly Orwellian acronym: the Office for Fair Access (OFFA; aka 'Off Toff').[127]

During the 1980s, however, Brasenose had acquired one tactical advantage. Robert Gasser, Bursar from 1982 to 2000, managed to improve its financial position significantly. As Vice-Chairman of the General Board, 1978–80, Gasser had been a big wheel in University administration. Now he turned his attention to the regeneration of BNC. In round terms he increased the college endowment from £10 million to £70 million. In the 1960s, Norman Leyland had multiplied the college's capital base. But in the following decade inflation seriously eroded reserves. Land held its value; equities shrank. The Frewin scheme had run way over budget, and there were regular revenue deficits.

---

[126] For postgraduate figures, see *OU Gazette*, 25 July 2007, 1403–16. Compare North Report, i. 12–13, 16. For the sixth-form figures quoted above, see *Daily Telegraph*, 7 Mar. 2007; *The Times*, 4 May 2007, 20 (Independent Schools Council); *Sunday Times*, 6 Jan. 2008, pp. 1–2.

[127] For the finances of the debate on college fees, see *Times Higher Ed. Supp.* 25 July, 8 Aug. 1997; 3, 24 July 1998; 21 Aug. 1998; 11 Sept. 1998. See also *Oxford Mag.* 149 (1998); *Higher Education Qtly.*, Apr. 1998; *Hansard: Lords*, 12 Nov. 1997, 583, cols. 155–212; N. Annan, *The Dons: Mentors, Eccentrics and Geniuses* (1999), 298–303. Not the least serious aspect of this loss of fee income was the arbitrary manner of its implementation: in effect a 'nationalisation of the Colleges' (A.W. F. Edwards, *Times Higher Ed. Supp.* 3 July 1998, 15; T. Tapper and D. Palfreyman, *Oxford and the Decline of the Collegiate Tradition* (2000), 169). For the political implications of the top-up fee debate, see *The Times*, 25 Sept. 2003 and 15 Jan. 2004, 22 (A. Keletsky); 9 Jan. 2004, 30 (C. Cavendish); 26 Jan. 2004, 16 and 16 Feb. 2004, 16 (W. Rees-Mogg); *Daily Telegraph*, 22 Jan. 2003 (J. Daley).

Gasser set out to restock the reserves. Domestic staff levels were reduced; conference programmes increased; tourists encouraged; and film revenues maximized. Those were the years of 'Inspector Morse'. But it was the redevelopment of the old Oxford City football ground at Grandpont that transformed the situation. It proved to be the biggest financial coup in the history of the college.[128] A new trading company was set up—Richard Sutton Development Ltd.—with Bernard Rudden (Barry Nicholas's successor as Professor of Comparative Law) in the chair. Planning permission for housing was secured. Pegasus Retirement Homes Ltd. acted as joint developer. And Gasser guided the whole project home. Capital values, of course, will vary from year to year. But by 1997–8, Brasenose ranked thirteenth out of thirty-six in the Oxford league table of gross endowment income, with £1,770,000 from a capital endowment of £44 million. Its annual income from all sources was nearly £4 million.[129] As a result, the building of more college rooms became financially feasible. First the St Cross Building, finished in 1996; then the final Frewin extension in 1997. At last BNC could accommodate any undergraduate, and the majority of postgraduates, who opted to live in college.

It was too good to last. By 2002–3, stock market fluctuations had reduced the college endowment—investments, land, property—to £57 million. Still, by 2003–4 the figure was up again to £62 million, and rising. That meant an annual endowment income of £2 million, plus £1.7 million from 'hotel' charges; supplemented by a sizeable £1.6 million in tuition fee income—tapering down each year, of course—deriving ultimately from the taxpayer's pocket. When all expenses were taken into account, the budget for 2003–4 showed a surplus of £334,630—about 6 per cent of income—after payment of intercollege taxation. That was by no means luxurious, taking fabric depreciation and progressive loss of fee income into account. Still, it was a basis for the future.[130]

This recovery of college finances coincided with a welcome academic renaissance. The election in 1989 of Lord Windlesham (pl. 96) as Principal—the first peer in that office, and the first Principal to have been a cabinet minister—added yet another to BNC's long list of legal luminaries. His political experience also chimed in well with the expansion of a subject now rivalling law as BNC's strongest suit: PPE. In the 1980s 'modern Greats' prospered exceedingly, under the direction of Vernon Bogdanor, Peter Sinclair, Michael Woods, John Foster, and Tony Courakis. Politics was a comparatively new subject at Brasenose; and for many years Bogdanor—'the

---

[128] *Brazen Nose*, xxxv. 41–7 (R. Gasser).
[129] Tapper and Palfreyman, *Decline of the Collegiate Tradition*, 158, table 7.1. This represented one-quarter of St John's endowment and half that of Queen's.
[130] *Brazen Nose*, xxxviii. 69–72 (J. Knowland).

Bagehot of Brasenose'—had to shoulder the bulk of its teaching while simultaneously keeping up an outstanding public profile.[131] But in economics, R. G. L. McCrone and Colin Clark—truly a statistician extraordinary— had already created a tradition of high-pressure tuition, a tradition vigorously maintained by Peter Sinclair.[132] Between 1983 and 1989 there were no fewer than twenty PPE Firsts, plus another nine in associated, joint-honours schools. Classics still scored well. And law by no means lagged behind: in 1993 Nicholas McBride won a Prize Fellowship at All Souls. But recruitment in PPE was setting the pace. Students were becoming strikingly international: 'from Canada, Cyprus, France, Germany, Greece, Hong Kong, India, the Ivory Coast, Malawi, the Netherlands, Singapore, South Africa, Sweden and as many as fifteen different American states'. During the 1990s Bogdanor's seminars became almost national events. Guest speakers included two Prime Ministers, two Home Secretaries, the heads of MI5 and MI6, and no fewer than four Cabinet Secretaries.

Here was the making of a revolution. The college was open to the world, and its placement of PPE graduates, in particular, became correspondingly wide:

in Parliament; the Foreign Office, the Treasury, and other departments of State; the B.B.C., I.T.N. and Channel 4; the Bank of England, the merchant banks, and other financial institutions; in accountancy, management consultancy, economic and political research, film-making, publicity, the financial press, the law, commerce and industry; running pension funds, whisky distilling, farming, writing books; teaching in schools and universities. There are Brasenose economists...on the faculty of Berkeley, Edinburgh, Harvard, M.I.T., N.S.W., Penn State, South Carolina, Tasmania and Williams, and Oxford too...[133]

Several of this generation of PPE stars turned out to be names to conjure with: Sir Robin (later Lord) Janvrin, private secretary to HM the Queen; Kate Allen, Director of Amnesty International; 'Cappy' Hill, President of Vassar; Diane Coyle and Camilla Cavendish, columnists on *The Economist* and *The Times*; and the Rt. Hon. David Cameron, MP, Leader of the Conservative Party.

So often in college histories, academic and sporting successes go hand in hand. In the later 1990s, BNC scored well in both spheres; drawing strength from the college's stronger financial base. Cricket and rugby cuppers were each won twice running in 1995–6 and in 1999–2000, with Chris Townsend, Peter Nicholas, and William Rubie all achieving blues. In 1997 Andrew

---

[131] His works include: *The People and the Party System* (1981), *Multi-Party Politics and the Constitution* (1983), *The Monarchy and the Constitution* (1995), *Devolution in the United Kingdom* (1999), and *The British Constitution in the 20th Century* (2003).

[132] *Brazen Nose*, xxiv. 68–70 (R. G. L. McCrone).

[133] Ibid. 21 (P. J. N. Sinclair).

Lindsay and Roberto Blanda rowed in the winning blue boat. In 2002 Dan Perkins rowed no. 4 in an epic victory over Cambridge. By 1998 Lindsay had been elected President of the University Boat Club, and James Fulton captain of the University Cricket Club. And by 1999 Lindsay had multiplied his list of battle honours with a First in geography and a Gold Medal in the Sydney Olympics. Most striking of all, in 2001 Brasenose chalked up no fewer than thirty Firsts in a single year, a record figure that earned the college third place in the Norrington Table. Lord Windlesham's period as Principal was ending in a warm glow of success. The Brasenose ideal of all-round excellence—so long pursued; so seldom achieved—at last seemed almost in reach. The Tanner Lectures, the Platnauer Concerts, the chapel choir, the annual student Arts Week: all these were evidence of established and continuing vitality. So was the creation of two new categories of Fellow. Together the Kurti Fellows and Golding Fellows had begun to attract outstanding scholars unattached to other colleges; at the same time they supplied a series of fruitful links between Senior and Middle Common Rooms. Brasenose was adapting to its new constituency. In the University at large, issues of governance were endlessly debated. But BNC still managed to hit the right buttons. In 2001–3 the college once again renewed its claims to excellence in law: Birke Häcker and Philip Woolfe were elected to Prize Fellowships at All Souls. 'Colleges', noted the *Brazen Nose*, 'are bastions of stable continuous improvement rather than revolution, and amongst Oxford colleges few are more stable and happy than Brasenose.'[134]

Of course changes continued to occur. By 2003 the college was taking as many medics as lawyers. As postgraduate numbers increased so did the intake of science students, and with it the proportion of science dons. The proportion of science tutors and lecturers at Brasenose moved up from 29 per cent in 1964, to 38 per cent in 1974, to 45 per cent in 1989. In 1964 only four colleges had recorded a lower percentage; by 1989, only one college boasted a higher figure.[135] Appropriately, in 2003 BNC chose its first scientist Principal: Professor Roger Cashmore, FRS, a particle physicist of world standing, from Cambridge, Balliol, and Geneva. The election was not easy. And no doubt it was thought there would be difficulties. Major building improvements were pending. The urgent need for more student bursaries, for better academic housing and salaries, for extra library and conference space, for better postgraduate provision, for larger capital endowment: all these would be problems for the twenty-first century. But the auguries were good. The spirit was there. As the college moved forward to its second 500 years, it could look to the future with a degree of optimism.

---

[134] *Brazen Nose*, xxxiv. 11 (W. G. Richards).
[135] Soares, *Decline of Privilege*, 118, table 10.

Courage, my brothers! Troubles past forget!
On to fresh deeds! The gods love Brasenose yet![136]

Oxford may be ancient: as antique as Magna Carta. But it never really grows old. It renews itself each autumn with a fresh infusion of youth. In the same way, Brasenose—the essential BNC—is curiously ageless. Its buildings are physically reborn, piece by piece, generation after generation. Its people come and go. Its manners mutate. Its educative functions evolve. But its style—in Syme's memorable phrase—abides. In that sense, this story of an Oxford college must stand as history unfinished, a biography without end.

[136] R. E. E. F.[rampton], Ale Verse, 1886.

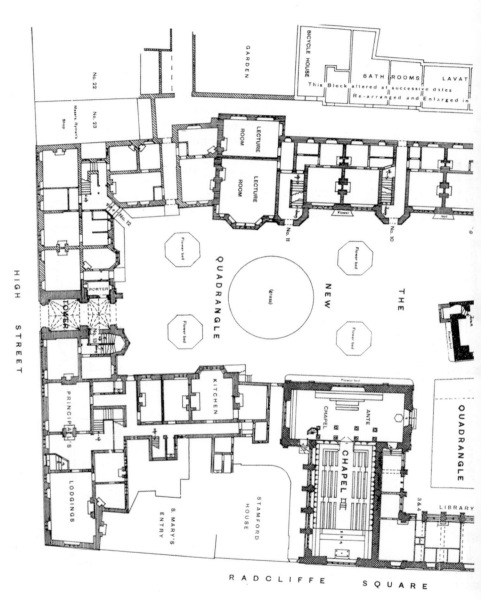

Plan of Brasenose College in 1909

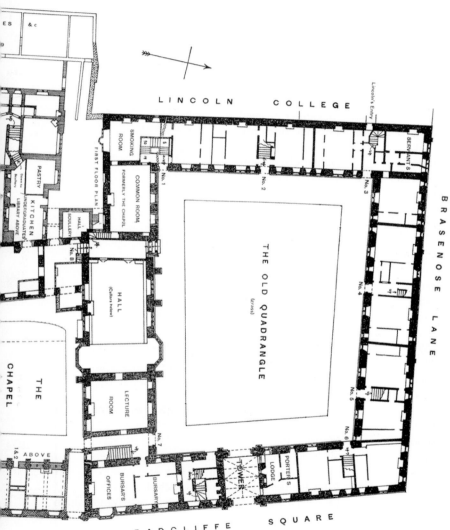

APPENDIX A
List of Principals

1512–1548	Matthew Smyth
1548–1565	John Hawarden
1565–1574	Thomas Blanchard
1574–1595	Richard Harris
1595	Alexander Nowell
1595–1614	Thomas Singleton
1614–1648	Samuel Radcliffe
1648–1660	Daniel Greenwood
1648 and 1660–1681	Thomas Yate
1681–1710	John Meare
1710–1745	Robert Shippen
1745–1770	Francis Yarborough
1770	William Gwyn
1770–1777	Ralph Cawley
1777–1785	Thomas Barker
1785–1809	William Cleaver
1809–1822	Frodsham Hodson
1822–1842	Ashurst Turner Gilbert
1842–1853	Richard Harington
1853–1886	Edward Hartopp Cradock [formerly Grove]
1886–1889	Albert Watson
1889–1920	Charles Buller Heberden
1920–1936	Charles Henry Sampson
1936–1948	William Teulon Swan Stallybrass [formerly Sonnenschein]
1948–1956	Hugh Macilwain Last
1956–1960	Maurice Platnauer
1960–1973	Sir Noel Frederick Hall
1973–1978	Herbert Lionel Adolphus Hart
1978–1989	John Keiran Barry Moylan Nicholas
1989–2002	David James George Hennessy, Lord Windlesham
2003–	Roger John Cashmore

APPENDIX B
List of Major Benefactors

(with dates of bequests, and commemorations in chapel; plus commemorative Sundays in term: Michaelmas, Hilary, and Trinity; excluding living donors).

1508	William Smith (3 January) (M1)
1508	Sir Richard Sutton (1st Sunday after Michaelmas) (M1)
1508	Edmund Croston
c.1511	Hugh Oldham
1515	Elizabeth Morley (26 January) (H3)
1518	John Coxe (30 October) (M3)
1520	John Williamson
1522	Sir John Port, Kt. I
1528	John Elton, alias Baker (30 November)
1531	William Porter (5 November) (M4)
1538	Edward Darbie (4 May) (T4)
1538	William Clifton (19 April)
1538	John Claymond (30 November)
1543	Humphrey Ogle (1st Sunday after Epiphany) (H2)
1547	John Booth
1549	Brian Higden (19 April)
1555, 1560	Sir John Port, Kt. II (6 June) (T6)
1557	Matthew Smyth (6 February) (H4)
1562, 1678, 1730	Henry Fisher
1565	Alexander Nowell (13 February) (T8)
1571	John, 2nd Baron Mordaunt (19 April) (T3)
1572	Richard Harpur (30 November) (M6)
1586	Joyce Frankland (5 September) (M5)
1587	Richard Barnes
1593	Charles Langford
1593	George Philpotts
1607	James Binks, alias Stoddard
1609	George Palin
1613	Richard Taylor
1620	William Smith
1620	Henry Mason

1637	Thomas Allen
1628	John Barneston
1640	Samuel Radcliffe (26 June) (H1)
1647	William Hutchins
1654	John Milward
1657	William Brock
1663 etc.	John (24 June) and Ursula Cartwright (26 June) (T7)
1666	John Newton
1675	Michael Woodward
1675	Anne Walker
1675	Hugh Henley
1675	Daniel Greenwood
1676	Richard Reed
1676 etc.	Thomas Church (19 February) (H6)
1679	Sarah Alston, Dowager Duchess of Somerset (17 February) (M8)
1679	Ralph Eaton
1677, 1680 etc.	Sir John Egerton, 3rd Bt.
1680	Thomas Yate (22 April) (H1)
1683	Thomas Weston
1691	William Hulme (28 October) (T1)
1698	Robert Jones (5 November) (M4)
1701	Sir Francis Bridgeman, Kt. (21 December) (M3)
1702	James Hamer
1708	Hon. Francis Powlet
1708	John Blackburne
1725	William Grimbaldson MD (24 June) (T8)
1726	Richard Atherton
1727	George Clarke
1731	Benjamin Swete
1731	Thomas Lee Dummer
1733	Sir Darcy Lever
1737	Sir John Cheshyre, Kt. (15 May) (T4)
1741	Thomas Brown
1747	Henry Wilbraham
1748	Assheton Curzon
1749	William Drake
1750	William Cartwright
1751	John Davie
1751	Sir Henry Harpur, 5th Bt.
1752 etc	Francis Yarborough
1753	James Parker

1752	Henry Currer
1752	Richard Heber
1752	James Dansie
1753	Sir Peter Leicester (formerly Byrne), 4th Bt.
1759	Roger Mather
1761	James Parr
1761	Robert Philips
1763	Thomas Cartwright
1763	William Strode
1763	Lucy Knightley
1763 etc.	Ralph Cawley
1767	Thomas Noel, 2nd Viscount Wentworth
1767	Sir Frank Standish, 3rd Bt.
1769	James Smith Barry, 5th Earl of Barrymore
1772	Edward Foley and Andrew Foley
1774	Herbert Mayo
1774	Richard Brooke
1775	Richard Beaumont
1781	Thomas Barker
1788	Samuel Malbon
1792	Samuel Jackson (10 March) (H7)
1795	John Holmes
1814	Sir Ellis Gosling
1833	John Lingard
1842	Elizabeth, Lucy, and Susannah Colquitt (H8)
1860	Thomas Poynder
1863 etc.	George Hornby
1875	Jane Ann Robinson (née Watson) (H8)
1887	John Wordsworth
1892, 1902	Charles Buller Heberden (T5)
1899, 1904	Albert Watson (T5)
1905, 1973	Robert Arthur Germaine
1908, 1925	Sir Heath Harrison, 1st Bt. (H5)
1909	Henry Rothwell Bently
1909 etc.	Francis Law Latham
1910	Luke Owen Pike
1910, 1925, 1949	William Nelson Stocker (M7)
1910	Frederick George Rucker
1911	Charles Edward Harris-St John
1915	Thomas Farmer Collins
1916	Horace Evelyn Clayton
1916, 1937, 1978	Frederick William Bussell

1917	David Leopold Lewis
1927	John Ambrose Jupp (H5)
1933	John Hubert Ware
1935	Nathaniel ffarington Eckersley
1939	Charlotte Gertrude Faithful Collins
1940	Albert Profumo
1948 etc.	W. T. S. Stallybrass (formerly Sonnenschein) (28 October) (M2)
1950, 1964	Alice and Edith Humphreys
1954, 1960, 1971	Maurice Platnauer (T2)
1956	Reginald W. Jeffery
1956	W. A. P. Waters
1957, 1986	Hugh Macilwain Last
1961, 1978	John Alexander Sutton
1962, 1985	Kenneth Jay Spalding
1963	Edgar Stanley Cohn
1963, 1986	Alice Constance Scott
1967	W. A. Fiddian
1968, 1977	W. L. Antrobus
1968	Claude Geoffrey Holt Thompson
1969	Cyril John Gadd
1975	Sir Val Duncan
1978	C. A. W. Manning
1984	Sir John Smith (The Manifold Trust)
1987	Robert Shackleton
1987	Sir Reginald Verdon-Smith
1988	Joyce Duncan (née Pilling)
1989	Brian Miller
1989	Eric Birley
1990	B. E. Lippincott
1990	Leslie Styler
1990, 1996	The Wolfson Foundation
1990	S. J. Batchelor
1991	L. A. Bardsley
1992	Peter Brunt
1993	The Baring Foundation
1993	A. W. Sedgwick
1994	Gertrude McKie
1996	R. N. J. Bedford
1997	C. B. Dix
1997	P. V. Curran
1998	S. M. Kimpton

2000	Richard Whitfield Harding
2000	Arthur Gould Thomas
2001	Ursula Monica Casswell
2001	Raymond Lucas
2002	John Prichard Burton
2002	Sir Kenneth Butt
2004	Roger Niell Ponsonby Radice
2004	Roger Thomas
2004	The Victoria Park Trust
2005	Doris Eileen Mason [W. T. Beynon]
2005	Robert Bruce Chalmers
2006	Captain F. H. Thomas
2007	John Wemyss Seamer

APPENDIX C

Members of the Phoenix Common Room

[* = blue]
[+=original member]

1782–6
+J. Alderson
+R. Hesketh
+J. Pemberton (Fellow of BNC, 1786)
+G. Powell (Fellow of Balliol, 1786)
+F. H. Rodd (Fellow of All Souls, 1787)
+R. W. Blencowe
+G. Terry
+R. Crowther
+R. Symonds (Fellow of Oriel, 1791)
+W. H. Heron
+W. Bagshaw
+C. Mainwaring
+J. Mayo (Fellow of Oriel, 1784)
+J. Latham (Pres. Royal Coll. Physicians)
+G. Hulme

1787
J. L. Bennett
J. H. Hindley
J. W. Master
D. Ashley
F. Hodson (Fellow of BNC, 1794; Principal 1809–22)
Hon. G. Annesley (later Visc. Valentia)

1788
H. J. Langford

1789
C. Mytton
T. Leigh (later Trafford Trafford)

J. Bate
J. C. Cockle (Fellow of BNC, 1793)

1790
J. H. Mallory
Mark Sykes (later Sir Mark Sykes, MP)
R. Darke
G. E. Leigh
H. Cholmondeley (Fellow of BNC, 1796; Dean of Chester)
J. W. Roberts

1791
W. Feilden (later Sir W. Feilden, MP)
J. Huish (Fellow of BNC, 1795)
H. Wise
T. Howard
B. Bromhead

1792
H. Case
R. Crockett
T. Apperley

1793
C. M. Wentworth
C. Madely
V. Isham
R. Marriott
A. R. Sidebottom
R. Farrer (Fellow of BNC, 1799)

1794
J. J. Cleaver
T. Whalley
N. P. Williams
R. Vernon

1795
W. Nicholson
E. S. Radcliffe

1796
R. Hill
J. Cleaver
B. Port (hero of R. Heber's *Whippiad*)
H. C. Isham
R. Caldwell
T. Kenyon
W. Yates

1797
W. J. Palmer
E. Lloyd
W. Grant
W. W. Drake
J. Boswell (son of Dr Johnson's biographer)

1798
C. W. Finch
T. Ponton
J. Dickin
R. Egerton

1799
J. Markland
J. Clavering
F. Popham
E. H. Jodrell (Fellow of BNC, 1802)

1800
J. Drake
W. Praed (or Pread)
B. Penny
H. Williams (Fellow of Merton, 1803)
H. Fortescue (1st Visc. Ebrington and Earl Fortescue; Ld. Lt. of Ireland 1839–41; KG, FRS).
S. J. Porten
R. H. Johnson

1801
T. Fane
W. Egerton (MP)

B. Grey
R. Heber (Fellow of All Souls, 1805; Bp. of Calcutta, 1822)
T. Dorrien
Hon. C. H. Coote
T. T. Drake
J. F. Parker

1802
E. T. S. Hornby (Fellow of All Souls, 1803)
E. Ravenshaw
T. Winfield
J. Poulett (Visc. Hinton).
R. Heber (MP)
T. W. Egerton

1803
J. Pollard
T. C. Heber (Fellow of BNC, 1807)
C. W. Golding
C. Shipley (Fellow of All Souls, 1806)
J. Hanmer
W. G. Orrett
S. G. Newport
J. E. Tarleton (Fellow of All Souls, 1803)
Sir O. Mosley, Bt. (MP)

1804
J. W. Farrer
J. Loveday
O. Farrer
H. Grey
J. Whalley (later Sir. J. W. S. Gardiner, Bt.)
R. Gumbleton

1805
G. R. Cross (Counsel to the University, 1821)
C. Warde
Lord George N. Grenville (1st. Baron Nugent)
G. W. Bampfylde
W. H. Campion
Sir J. M. Stronge, Bt.

H. D. Roundell
W. Hulton

1806
J. P. Ross
T. Daniell
J. B. Bingham
J. Latham (Fellow of All Souls, 1806)
C. T. Johnson
W. Assheton
D. H. C. Poole
G. ['Squire'] Osbaldeston
A. Dawson (Fellow of BNC, 1812)
T. C. Hincks
H. G. Liddell

1807
J. King
T. Farrer
W. L. Farrer
R. T. Garden
Hon. J. Somers Cocks
C. Cator

1808
C. T. Drake
W. Gregson
R. W. Eyton
J. W. Spicer
G. B. Lyon
G. A. Maddock
W. Currie
E. Ashton
R. Franco (MP) [later Lopes]
Sir C. Farnaby, Bt.
Le G. Starkie

1809
P. Broughton
G. Winstanley
J. O. Crewe
J. T. Drake

1810
A. H. Buchanan
W. Codrington
J. H. Poole
G. Camplin
Hon. W. J. F. Vane (later 3rd Duke of Cleveland)
J. Clark
T. Blackburne
G. J. West, Earl Delawarr

1811
H. F. Luttrell (MP)
J. Doyne
R. Winter
E. J. Walhouse (later Baron Hatherton MP)
C. P. Shakerley
H. H. Aston
E. Mainwaring

1812
J. Coulthurst
P. L. Brooke
G. Chetwode
T. Cator
T. Lewes
Hon. E. Wingfield
Hon. W. H. Yelverton (MP)

1813
W. Cookson
E. Wyvill
J. Smith Barry
C. W. St John Mildmay (Fellow of Merton, 1816)
J. S. Menteath
G. T. Drake
E. H. Dawkins (Fellow of All Souls, 1815)

1814
R. Burke
J. Hordern
H. Porter
J. A. Partridge
R. Burdett
G. Rumbold

1815
F. Sullivan (Fellow of All Souls, 1818)
E. A. Sanford (MP)
A. I. Aston (Envoy at Madrid, 1840)
C. Leycester
C. C. Cholmondeley
P. Lewes

1816
J. Smith Barry
A. Chichester
R. Fayle
T. Hill

1817
H. Cholmondeley
H. Mallory
W. L. Maberley
T. Gronow
F. Shaw
C. D. Beckford (Fellow of All Souls, 1821)
J. Buchanan
H. W. Buckley (Fellow of Merton, 1821)

1818
A. Clive
P. Hordern
F. K. Bouverie

1819
H. Perceval
J. C. Girardot
Hon. H. A. Rous
G. W. C. Stapylton
R. Biddulph (MP)

1820
S. G. Gunning
J. Lodge
W. Harvey
W. de C. Brooke
Le G. N. Starkie

1821
G. C. R. Dering
Hon. A. Thellusson
Hon. A. Waldegrave
E. Duncombe
R. F. Jenner
G. Brooke

1822
E. Willes
R. Harington (Fellow of BNC, 1822; Principal 1842–53)
T. P. Meade (Fellow of All Souls, 1825)
J. W. Knightley
J. Brooke

1823
R. J. Price
W. W. Congreve
C. K. Mainwaring
J. L. Philipps
J. Hargreaves

1824
T. Denman
S. V. Dashwood
T. Ince
J. E. Verner
C. B. D. Garrard
R. Cox
W. Chaloner

1825
O. J. A. Fuller-Meyrick
A. L. Lister-Kaye
J. C. Clarke
J. C. Whalley
A. Fawkes

1826
J. Proctor
M. J. Taylor (present at the Centenary Dinner, 1886)
G. T. Forester

T. W. Booth
Hon. S. G. Osborne ('S.G.O.' in *The Times*)

1827
T. Mainwaring
J. D. Shafto

1828
E. A. Waller
R. C. Windham
T. J. Ormerod

1829
J. Bailey
C. Turnor
W. P. Pigott
E. Golding
J. Greenfield

1830
Hon. H. Toler
J. B. Monck
C. Hill
H. P. M. Cox

1831
S. S. Bankart
T. D. Shafto
M. E. Archdale

1832
J. Drake
J. M. Steele
J. B. Conolly

1833
T. Hanmer
J. H. Brooks

1834
G. Day
J. Smith Barry
T. H. Lloyd

1835
J. H. Borrer

1836
L. E. G. Clarke
A. Brown

1837
T. C. Powell
R. C. Legh

1838
J. Penrice
W. H. Cooper

1839
W. Worthington
J. Hughes

1840
J. J. T. Somers Cocks
G. Worley
[J. Woodhouse]

1841
J. T. Drake
R. Barton
A. R. Kenyon
S. R. Hole (President at the Centenary Dinner, 1886; Dean of
    Rochester, 1887)

1842
G. Gordon
W. B. Glegg
T. H. G. Puleston
G. S. Master

1843
Hon. H. R. Pakenham

1844
G. H. Littledale
G. L. Hall

1845
C. W. P. Crawfurd
J. E. Severne (MP)
T. R. C. Dimsdale
H. V. Packe

1846
W. H. Midgley
R. Smith
J. Allgood
J. W. C. Perring

1847
J. A. Dawkins
J. H. Milne

1848
N. C. Curzon
G. W. Gunning

1849
J. G. Johnson
J. B. Currey

1850
A. G. Onslow
H. H. Bradshaw

1851
J. L. Errington
E. P. Nicholl
A. H. Minor

1852
R. A. Hole
J. Gott (Bp. of Truro)

1853
L. E. Traherne
G. Mallory
H. P. Lance

1854
R. Calvert

1855
W. H. Davey
R. Battye

1856
T. B. Shaw-Hellier
*J. E. Codrington
H. B. L. Puxley
T. B. Ferguson
*T. G. Edmondson

1857
J. G. P. Hughes
G. H. G. Haigh
W. I. Allgood

1858
P. H. Lee
*J. W. Morley

1859
J. B. Orme
J. B. White
A. Henry

1860
J. H. Gumbleton
P. Arden
J. Dunn
F. G. Farquhar

1861
S. Phillips
*W. H. Erskine (later 11th Earl of Mar and Kellie)
*W. E. Heap
H. Garnett

1862
P. A. Latham
S. E. Illingworth

1863
C. E. Harris
A. W. Grant
W. H. Dunn
A. C. Plowden (founder of the Vampires; later a Metropolitan Police
    Magistrate)
L. Garnett

1864
G. C. Fisher
*T. M. Colmore
Hon. R. T. O'Neill (MP)

1865
J. P. Law
*E. L. Fellowes
E. P. Garnett

1866
*F. Crowder
*W. Evetts

1867
H. Francklin

1868
*E. Mathews
C. Entwisle
Hon. B. E. B. Fitz-Patrick (later 2nd Lord Castletown)
*B. Pauncefote
C. A. Hopwood

1869
*C. Marriott
A. D. Neeld
A. Nicolson

1870
E. Wilson
*W. H. Hadow
E. E. Venables
*C. K. Francis

1871
E. F. Alexander
H. P. Hornby
C. E. Thornycroft
*W. Law

1872
E. P. Rawnsley
C. H. Thomas

1873
H. A. Anderson
*E. R. Still
W. W. Whitmore
T. M. F. Parkyns
E. F. S. Stanhope (later 10th Earl of Chesterfield)
*P. H. Coxe

1874
A. J. Edwards
F. D. Hunt
A. E. Leigh
R. Pryor

1875
*M. J. Brooks

1876
T. R. Ker
*T. C. Edwards-Moss (MP)
*V. P. F. A. Royle
A. C. Miles
E. F. Sandeman

1877
C. C. Rogers (MP)
H. D. Daunt
A. G. Weguelin
L. S. B. Tristram
*H. F. Blaine

1878
M. C. Pike
W. A. Sandeman
J. R. Story
W. J. M. Hughes
A. R. H. Harter
*P. J. M. Rogers
F. J. Ridgway

1879
J. C. Page
T. G. Gardiner
H. A. N. Smith
E. H. Hulse
W. Stirling

1880
J. G. Menzies
F. W. Hayes
B. H. Barton
R. W. Byass
A. R. Cuninghame
T. S. G. H. Robertson-Aikman
J. I. Blencowe
H. E. Phillips
W. M. Low

1881
*E. L. Puxley
D. H. Barry
*D. Haig (later Field Marshal Earl Haig)
G. F. Farnham

1882
H. S. Barton
F. W. L. Popham
R. H. Rawson
W. M. Pike
*T. Hitchcock
*A. G. G. Asher

1883
W. Scott
P. Y. Gowlland
W. J. Barry
*S. E. R. Lane
C. Child

1884
H. H. Dobinson
*H. T. Arnall-Thompson
*A. S. Blair
*C. W. Berry

1885
*H. H. Castens

1886
J. Methuen
E. F. Macpherson
*J. D. Boswell
*H. R. Parker
G. E. Rhodes

1887
F. Routledge
*A. Pearson
*W. F. C. Holland
R. H. Tilney

1888
*F. G. Barker
C. S. Currie
W. A. Leith
W. M. Crowdy

1889
*C. W. Kent
C. A. Spottiswoode
G. P. Bancroft
*W. H. Parkin
G. E. Barker

1890
H. S. Persse
R. E. Leigh
C. H. R. Horwood
*R. G. T. Coventry
J. F. Anderson

1891
E. Edwards
E. Johnson
W. H. Rhodes
R. P. Burra

1892
W. A. Dewhurst
J. S. Porter
*W. B. Stewart
W. G. Pennyman
H. C. Haldane

1893
E. F. Cockcroft
*R. B. Pearson (later Sir Robert Pearson)
T. O. Lloyd

1894
A. B. Nutter
*W. P. Donaldson
J. D. Graham
E. D. Sidgwick
J. L. Rushton
H. S. Chinnock
H. A. M. Barbour

1895
*J. C. Hartley
*J. K. Murphy
C. E. Jenkins
C. C. Eley

1896
C. J. Astbury
*H. R. K. Pechell

J. H. Preston
R. E. P. Gorringe
H. F. Chamberlayne
F. M. May
W. J. Thomson
C. H. Style

1897
J. Taylor
E. T. Lyon
C. Toogood
J. R. Torrens

1898
S. U. Meerza (Prince Meerza)
*L. W. B. Martin
H. G. Baker-Cresswell
R. Ralston-Patrick
R. Brown
T. R. Thomson
G. B. Eaton
G. J. L. Batchelor

1899
H. C. Brocklehurst
J. G. Heath
B. E. Bucknall
A. Neill
G. W. P. Swinburn
P. A. R. Pritchard
W. M. Bouch

1900
E. N. Trappes-Lomax
R. S. Ker
P. P. Leschallas
F. P. Murphy

1901
W. A. T. Bowly
R. L. Macdonald
H. B. Spencer

*J. R. Cleave
C. H. Arnhold

1902
J. E. Lord
C. R. Maude
F. C. Thompson

1903
*J. L. Humphreys
C. B. Greenhill

1904
L. G. P. Eiffe
R. N. Reid (later Sir Robert Reid)
*P. C. Underhill
E. C. M. Phillips
J. A. Hammond-Chambers-Borgnis

1905
R. C. Courtney
C. A. E. Williams
*R. S. Wix
T. Aubertin

1906
M. H. Ravenhill

1907
H. P. Egleston
E. F. Chinnery
R. A. Heath
R. J. Hunter
P. J. S. Pearson-Gregory
*Hon. D. G. Finch-Hatton
J. H. Knox

1908
Hon. A. V. Agar-Roberts
T. P. Fenwicke-Clennell
*G. F. Rogers

G. R. Frere
*C. V. L. Hooman

1909
C. Gordon
C. R. Huggins
V. H. M. Egleston
J. E. Greenall
C. H. Newton

1910
*C. Howard Smith
E. R. Kewley
*F. N. Tuff
M. E. Coxhead
L. P. Millar

1911
J. C. Dixey
A. K. S. Cunninghame
G. H. Bailey
H. Hall Jackson
A. W. Strickland

1912
P. R. Frere
*F. H. Knott
C. Whadcoat
D. C. Lindsay
E. A. Shaw
*A. N. Strode Jackson

1913
H. B. Moore
J. A. Paton
H. A. Gartside Neville

1914
F. E. Hill
A. C. Williamson
H. C. Wace (Chaplain and Fellow, BNC, 1898)

F. C. Verner
H. O'Rorke

1920
G. A. Keay
*V. H. Neser
T. G. L. Ashwell
P. Liesching
J. H. Thompson
*C. H. Evans
E. N. Mylius
C. L. J. Bowen
V. St J. Killery
H. D. Badger

1921
J. M. Pritchard
A. D. Grant (Bursar and Fellow, BNC, 1929)
N. H. Brewis
*C. V. Hill
*H. M. Watt
*G. T. S. Stevens
R. A. Marriott

1922
*C. H. Knott
E. A. Ree
F. W. Rhodes

1923
*P. R. Wace
R. Bagwell
*F. H. Barnard
P. F. Saunders
*G. J. Mower-White
*W. P. Mellen
*W. H. Robertson-Aikman
*H. W. Standring

1924
A. D. Jupp
*J. L. Guise

*J. V. Richardson
O. C. Sewall
D. C. Bennett
*I. S. Smith

1925
*G. B. Legge
P. E. H. Marsh
*A. C. J. German
*C. H. M. Waldock
*W. I. N. Strong
*F. K. R. Coldstream

1926
*E. C. G. Harlow
*G. H. Crawford
*G. O. M. Taylor
*L. R. Serrurier
J. S. Smith
*J. W. Greenstock
T. B. Bovell Jones

1927
H. L. Mullins
J. H. White Thompson
*E. Snell
*E. A. Sweatman
J. T. Bush
*J. H. F. Edmiston
M. W. Harris

1928
*A. L. Novis
*H. C. Morphett
*B. H. Black
*A. S. Bradshaw
C. H. Thornley (later Sir Colin Thornley)
*P. S. Snow
*A. Graham

1929
*G. S. Gee
*W. T. Taylor

R. W. Parr
L. F. C. R. Balding

1930
*P. F. Garthwaite
*C. M. Johnston
*W. Roberts
*R. A. J. Poole
*H. S. Townend
*P. G. V. Van der Bijl
D. A. Hodgkinson
G. G. Baker (later Sir George Baker)

1931
*T. L. Jones
*G. M. L. Smith

1932
L. E. C. Davies
*J. S. O. Haslewood
J. E. Nicholls
*R. W. G. Holdsworth (Fellow of Univ., 1937)
*T. J. R. Dashwood
*F. G. H. Chalk
*R. G. Stainton
*D. M. Borland

1933
*E. A. Barlow
*R. G. Raw
*M. F. Peacock
J. C Hickingbotham
J. C. Guest

1934
A. M. Lee
*W. F. Moss
S. M. Kimpton
*D. F. Walker
*J. W. Seamer
A. L. Warr
*J. H. Ingham

1935
J. S. Owen
*H. A. S. Johnston
*J. G. S. Ker
H. C. Lumb
R. F. Harding
*A. P. Singleton

1936
*J. C. Cherry
*E. O. W. Hunt
*N. S. Mitchell-Innes
*W. A. Hay-Cooper
*J. D. Anderson

1937
*J. N. Grover
*R. C. M. Kimpton
*J. C. Lawrie
D. O. Hay
J. C. Stratford
*R. F. H. Darwall-Smith

1938
*Prince A. Obolensky
*H. A. Davies
*A. W. Selwyn
*H. A. S. Disney
*E. D. R. Eagar
H. J. L. Marriott
*N. M. Beyts

1939
*F. V. Scopes
P. R. Crompton

1948
*N. C. F. Bloy
M. Platnauer (Fellow of BNC, 1923; Principal 1956–60)
*G. P. Jackson
*G. A. Wilson
M. Lee

*A. W. H. Mallett
*J. D. P. Tanner
D. I. Darling
*P. W. Kininmonth

1949
C. J. Studdert-Kennedy
*D. A. Emms
*K. A. Shearwood
*G. H. Chesterton
S. M. Duff
*C. R. G. Neville
*R. H. Maudsley (Fellow of BNC, 1947)
B. H. Gale
J. M. Dean

1950
*P. D. S. Blake
G. L. Powell
M. H. Fairbank
N. A. H. Creese

1951
V. H. Bailey
D. S. Kemp
*J. C. Marshall
E. J. Wimperis
J. A. B. Cudden
*N. Micklem

1952
*E. C. B. Hammond
*K. M. Spence
*J. Clegg
*G. H. McKinna
R. I. Ingram
R. M. Charlesworth

1953
*O. R. S. Bull
*M. C. Cowdrey (later Sir Colin; Baron Cowdrey)
P. F. S. Kittermaster

*M. T. Robinson
E. R. C. Marriott

1954
*E. V. Vine
*J. P. Fellows-Smith
B. K. Workman
A. G. MacIntyre
*C. J. S. Hill
R. N. Bowes
P. A. R. Greenstreet

1955
D. G. Blakeley
*D. G. Harrison
*H. R. Moore
M. I. Ross
*T. H. Douglas
*M. G. Allison
M. O. Kinkead-Weekes

1956
R. E. A. Steward
R. S. Levy
E. C. Mumford

1957
*S. K. Proctor
*M. C. Grint
D. P. Henry
A. F. Raikes
*N. G. Rennie
D. Stuart
J. Summerscale

1958
J. Drysdale
J. T. Meek
M. S. Stegman
D. W. Baldock
R. Murray
*J. M. Costeloe

C. F. Phelps
*J. R. E. Kent

1959
L. G. N. Bruford
C. Penn
C. R. Knight
C. M. Edwards
A. W. Gemmill
D. L. Stockton (Fellow of BNC, 1954)
J. Blair
*A. C. Smith
*J. O. B. Sewall
P. J. Hamilton
C. M. Smith

1960
*D. H. Veit
A. P. K. Osmond
*J. H. C. Mellen
D. C. Bennett
M. B. Connell (later Sir Michael Connell)
*M. J. Theobald
*J. W. Flecker
J. C. Marlas
M. A. P. S. Downham

1961
C. I. C. Harrison-Wallace
*P. M. Dawkins
H. G. Owen-Hughes
*J. S. Grinalds
D. R. Hayes
*G. P. Harrison
*R. J. S. Hawes
*W. C. C. Guest
*M. J. Gillette
*F. W. Neate

1962
S. R. Brown
M. Blackwell

J. A. Dodds
R. B. M. Nicholas
W. G. Richards (Fellow of BNC, 1966)
W. M. Wardell
C. J. Tobin
R. J. O'Neill
J. P. Cobb
L. Badgett
A. D. Latimer

1963
*D. A. Cuthbertson
*J. J. Penn
J. R. Sanders
P. R. Dawson-Bowling
D. T. Evans
A. H. Bernstein

1964
J. K. Ledlie
M. F. Roetter
*M. F. Baker
*T. M. Swan
E. R. Woods
J. R. Beale
T. C. Grey

1965
D. R. Witcher
M. G. Darling
*C. C. T. Durrant
P. J. Lloyd
R. S. Stewart
C. N. Wain

1966
*R. A. Chick
F. W. Meier
D. M. Lloyd
P. M. A. Richardson
C. W. Bellamy
J. P. McClure

*J. K. Antill
A. N. T. McKenna

1967
S. A. R. Disney
J. R. Linn
W. A. McKean
G. L. Stephens
T. W. Pearce
J. R. Loasby
R. B. Janvrin (later Sir Robin; Baron Janvrin)
*R. E. S. Early
B. A. B. Bikales

1968
V. J. Cunningham
J. M. Kirchberg
M. I. Whitehead
P. H. Marsh
D. N. Farrow
D. T. Greenland
J. M. Moss
W. G. Verdon-Smith
A. M. Dart

1969
A. F. Tredwell
D. E. Eardal
J. L. Pearce

1970
P. Kysel
T. S. Mangwazu
R. M. Moss
R. L. Trope
I. D. Murdoch
N. C. Pitt
D. Bradbury
J. B. Macpherson
A. G. Mursell
W. J. Jenkinson

1971
M. A. Timmis
D. A. Hurndall
S. M. Raper
P. C. Rogers
C. D. Brims

1972
N. C. J. Dennys
N. J. Brown
D. O. Clark
C. P. A. Norman
P. M. Thomas

1973
M. J. H. Miller
D. D. Johnston
R. S. Laura
P. Koronka
S. T. I. Carr
C. A. M. Lowndes
J. K. Hilton
P. G. D. Kaufmann
F. V. Bee
C. A. W. Gibson

1974
C. D. O. Barrie
A. J. H. Reed

1975
J. D. Kelleher
G. J. Craig
A. J. O. Martin

1976
H. A. S. Crawford
J. E. Flynn
C. P. J. Fitzgibbon
D. J. Hertzell
R. H. Rosa

A. N. Tyler
E. C. Stenton
D. C. Pusinelli
M. H. Walton
N. R. Withington

1977
J. R. Childs
*D. G. Westcott
M. Prinsley
C. D. St Joseph
K. J. Monserrat
T. J. Pashley

1978
J. P. C. Bailey
A. S. Burrows
D. N. J. Hart
J. R. Monroe
S. J. B. Ring
C. H. Scott

1979
M. P. Tree
G. D. Vinter
M. D. E. Conder
R. J. D. Brown
*T. P. Enevoldson
N. C. Thum
H. C. H. Williams
C. I. Nicholls

1980
J. P. Rountree
M. D. Williams
M. D. Peters

1981
C. J. Coles
N. J. P. Fox
*N. J. A. Langman

W. H. M. Gibson
A. D. Gardner
J. J. Legge
*K. M. Campbell

1982
D. M. Millar
I. G. Hilditch
J. N. Jee
N. H. Jones
R. M. Dixon

1983
D. J. Schofield
G. Turner
D. A. Wallace
C. I. O. Brooks

1984
R. W. Turner
J. G. Byam-Shaw
M. A. Skipper
K. D. O'Connor
M. C. Walton

1985
P. R. F. D. Aylott
D. J. Cellan-Jones
*D. S. Barton
*A. D. Booth

1986
R. J. Borg
M. M. R. Chick
P. J. C. Cowan

1987
D. Davidson
P. L. Gauci
*T. M. Harrison
S. R. C. De H. Mee

1988
*G. M. Cullity
D. C. B. Rogers

1989
R. A. Hadfield
N. Simmonds
C. L. Wilkes
I. J. Popplewell
M. N. Bouette

1990
*R. E. Clayton
T. C. J. Elbrick
C. D. Jones
R. J. Baugh

1991
*J. P. Ralph
*St J. K. H. Anderson

1992
*A. A. F. Laird
E. Boni

1993
T. J. Attenborough
A. J. Hampel
G. R. Wilson
S. L. Goldstone

1994
F. C. Muennich
*S. W. Howe
*R. J. Turnill

1995
G. S. Baldwin
*R. D. M. Edwards
J. A. Oram
*D. J. Trunkfield
*J. P. Willcocks

1996
M. A. Tindall
*B. Cope
G. D. I. Williams
G. A. Noel-Clark

1997
J. M. Fletcher
F. F. R. Ingham
H. J. Fyson
G. A. R. Kemp

1998
*A. J. R. Lindsay
G. R. McPherson
R. J. Way
S. M. Chirnside

1999
G. D. Cook
*E. G. W. W. Whitworth

2000
W. Stockley

2001
*A. E. Selby
E. M. Bridgeland
F. P. K. Neave
B. T. Long
A. M. B. Mavor

2002
P. T. Wrigley
S. A. Fickling
J. T. Waddilove
C. J. Von der Heyden

2003
J. Went
*T. Bowden
B. J. Mclean

F. E. F. Barnfield
B. P. Lewsley

2004
R. P. Martin
E. Mitropoulos
*A. Holbourn

2005
*T. D. Profumo
F. G. M. Young

2006
J. A. Cope
F. G. D. Ciardi
W. F. Trevelyan-Thomas
A. S. Feld

2007
E. M. Donadoni
A. C. de Haes
K. L. Von Bismark

2008
D. Holland
A. P. Lomas
M. T. Rothkopf
C. Nordby

APPENDIX D
List of Rhodes Scholars

*=blue

Matriculation or scholarship	Name	Subject	Nationality
1904	Brooks, Robert	Modern History	American
1904	Bush, Charles	Jurisprudence	American
1904	Kendall, William	BCL	American
1904	*Schutt, Warren	Jurisprudence	American
1905	Aydelotte, Frank	B.Litt.	American
1905	Foster, Carol	Eng. Literature	American
1905	Papineau, Talbot	Jurisprudence	Canadian
1906	Bray, Harry	Modern History	Canadian
1906	Juett, Alexander	Physiology	Australian
1907	Gilbert, Joseph	Jurisprudence	Bermudan
1907	*Hull, Lawrence	BCL	American
1908	Horan, John	Physiology	Australian
1908	Mandt, Harold	Economics	German
1908	Newton, Charles	[Resigned]	Rhodesian
1910	von Dalwig, Baron George	Economics	German
1910	*Robertson, William	Jurisprudence	Bermudan
1910	*Thomas, Walter	Jurisprudence	Rhodesian
1911	*Russell, Franklin	Jurisprudence	American
1911	Rehmke, Hans	Economics	German
1911	*Savage, John	Physiology	Australian
1912	*Melle, Basil	Medicine	South African
1912	van Campe, Carl	Economics	German
1913	*Boor, Alaric	Medicine	Australian
1913	*Pearse, Gerald	Engineering	South African
1913	Simpson, Richard	History	American
1914	Jackson, E. B.	Physics	American
1914	*Row, A. W. L.	Physiology	Australian
1916	Binns, J. H. S.	BCL	American
1918	*Neser, V. H.	BCL	South African
1919	Little, Joseph	BCL	American
1919	Manning, C. A. W.	Jurisprudence	South African

Matriculation or scholarship	Name	Subject	Nationality
1920	Evans, E.	BCL	American
1920	Hudson, William	Physics	South African
1920	McGowan, F. P.	Jurisprudence	American
1920	*Mennie, J. H.	B.Sc.	Canadian
1921	Moe, H. A.	BCL	American
1921	Newton, Carl	BCL	American
1922	Ellsworth, Paul	PPE	American
1922	Fourie, I. S.	PPE	South African
1923	Grieveson, J. A.	Engineering	South African
1923	Hynes, W. S.	BCL	American
1923	McGregor, J. G.	Physiology	South African
1923	Tucker, V. K.	BCL	South African
1924	Bradley, H.	Jurisprudence	American
1924	*Fiddian-Green, W. B.	Physiology	South African
1924	*Johnson, Arthur	Jurisprudence	Canadian
1924	*Livingstone, G. S.	Economics	Canadian
1924	* Serrurier, Louis	BCL	South African
1925	Duff, Colin	Forestry	Rhodesian
1925	Mais, Norman	Jurisprudence	Jamaican
1925	*Campbell Rodger, I. M.	Engineering	South African
1925	Shaffner, F. I.	B.Litt.	American
1926	Forder, C. P.	BCL	South African
1926	Hennessy, P. K.	Jurisprudence	American
1926	Keet, Raymond	Eng. Literature	South African
1926	Legendre, Morris	[Resigned]	American
1926	*Pfann, George	Jurisprudence	American
1926	Stephens, Robert	Forestry	South African
1927	Burrus, J. De M.	Jurisprudence	American
1927	Farquharson, G. A. R.	Engineering	Jamaican
1927	Horowitz, Charles	Jurisprudence	American
1927	Parr, R. W.	Modern History	South African
1928	MacPherson, Ian	Jurisprudence	South African
1928	*McHendrie, Douglas	Jurisprudence	American
1928	Orselli, Alfred	[Resigned]	American
1928	*Van der Bijl, P. G. V.	Modern History	South African
1929	Boothe, Armistead	Jurisprudence	American
1929	*Hovde, F. L.	Natural Science	American
1929	*MacIntyre, Malcolm	BCL	American
1929	Tolmie, John	BCL	Canadian

Matriculation or scholarship	Name	Subject	Nationality
1929	*Woods, F. K. S.	PPE	South African
1930	*Deiter, G. H.	Physics	American
1930	*Poole, William	BCL	American
1930	*Little, Charles	Mod. Languages	Canadian
1930	*Gratias, Orvald	D.Phil.	Canadian
1931	Holden, G. R.	B.Litt.	American
1931	Hickingbotham, J. C.	BCL	American
1931	MacDonald, James	BCL	Rhodesian
1931	Rangeley, W. H. J.	Anthropology	South African
1932	Bean, Atherton	PPE	American
1932	Bekker, Pieter	Jurisprudence	South African
1932	Drake, E. F.	B.Litt.	American
1932	Milliner, J. H. S.	Engineering	Jamaican
1932	*Nadeau, J. E.	Jurisprudence	Canadian
1933	Brown, Arthur	Mathematics	American
1933	Franks, Frank	Engineering	South African
1933	Lumb, Harold	Jurisprudence	American
1933	*Norval, I. P.	Botany	South African
1933	von Ruperti, J. C.	Economics	German
1934	Acock, A. M.	D.Phil.	South African
1934	Hopkins, H. J.	Engineering	South African
1934	Macpherson, James	PPE	South African
1935	Gray, Michael	Jurisprudence	South African
1935	*Hammelmann, H. A.	D.Phil.	German
1935	Moller, Lester	BCL	New Zealander
1935	Olver, John	Geography	Rhodesian
1935	Plumb, H. J.	Geology	South African
1936	Ballard, Marshall	PPE	American
1936	Farmer, Guy	Jurisprudence	American
1936	Findlay, A. C.	BCL	Canadian
1936	Marriott, Henry	Clinical Medicine	Bermudan
1936	*Spies, Emerson	BCL	American
1937	*Davoud, John	D.Phil.	Canadian
1937	*Duffie, William	BCL	Canadian
1937	*Tucker, Eugene	Physiology	South African
1937	Wellman, Harvey	Jurisprudence	American
1938	*Brown, Gerald	PPE	South African
1938	Chalmers, John	PPE	American
1938	*Franklin, B. L. S.	Jurisprudence	South African
1938	Gardner, James	Jurisprudence	American
1938	Hoch, Peter	Physiology	American
1939	Pelz, Edward	[resigned]	American

Matriculation or scholarship	Name	Subject	Nationality
1940	*Martin, R. B.	Natural Science	Jamaican
1945	Dreyer, Eric	Engineering	South African
1945	Newham, Walter	Jurisprudence	Rhodesian
1945	Henwood, Desmond	Geography	South African
1945	*Harcourt, Arthur	BCL	South African
1945	*Rumbold, Jack	BCL	New Zealander
1946	*Williams, Lloyd	D.Phil.	Australian
1946	Misick, Michael	Modern History	Bermudan
1946	Kinkead-Weekes, Noel	BCL	South African
1946	Hill, Gordon	D.Phil.	Australian
1946	Beck, Charles	Jurisprudence	South African
1946	*Woodward, William	Medicine	Australian
1947	*Henrick, Keith	PPE	Canadian
1947	*Jepsen, Charles	PPE	American
1947	*Jordan, Amos	PPE	American
1947	*Merdinger, Charles	D.Phil.	American
1948	Ball, John	Forestry	Rhodesian
1948	*Barnard, Ronald	Jurisprudence	Bermudan
1948	*Jacobson, Raymond	PPE	American
1948	*Blumberg, Nathaniel	D.Phil.	American
1948	*Powell, George	B.Litt.	American
1949	Clower, Robert	B.Litt.	American
1949	*Shaw, Michael	Jurisprudence	East African
1949	*Jose, Anthony	Physiology	Australian
1949	*Murad, Aslam	Engineering Science	Pakistani
1949	*Strain, Milton	PPE	American
1950	*Hatherley, Colin	Jurisprudence	South African
1950	Brademas, John	D.Phil.	American
1950	*Hamilton, Charles	Modern History	American
1951	Evans, Lloyd	D.Phil.	New Zealander
1951	Kinkead-Weekes, Marcus	English Lit.	South African
1952	Gilbert, David	Modern History	Bermudan
1952	*Duby, John	Natural Science	Canadian
1952	Goodman, George	B.Litt.	American
1953	Wells, Frank	Jurisprudence	American
1953	Bogle, Donald	Modern History	Jamaican
1953	Horsley, David	B.Litt.	New Zealander
1953	Acheson, Robert	PPE	Rhodesian
1953	Rabinowitz, Benjamin	Jurisprudence	South African
1953	*Jones, Vincent	Jurisprudence	American
1954	Lochtenberg, Bernard	D.Phil.	Australian

Matriculation or scholarship	Name	Subject	Nationality
1954	Lamb, Karl	D.Phil.	American
1954	Garms, Michael	PPE	South African
1955	Nelson, Everard	Physics	Jamaican
1956	*Sadler, John	D.Phil.	American
1956	Ball, Robert	Jurisprudence	American
1956	Anderson, B.	PPE	American
1957	Fleissner, Erwin	PPE	American
1958	Jordan, Stuart	Mathematics	American
1958	Feldman, Daniel	Physics	American
1958	*Sewall, John	PPE	American
1959	*Dawkins, Peter	PPE	American
1959	*Ellis, Jeremy	Engineering	Australian
1959	*Gillette, Michael	PPE	American
1960	*Swinburn, Malcolm	Clinical Medicine	Australian
1960	*Grinalds, John	Geography	American
1961	Tobin, Christopher	BCL	New Zealander
1961	Sterling, William	PPE	American
1961	O'Neill, Robert	PPE	Australian
1961	Badgett, Lee	PPE	American
1962	*Cuthbertson, David	B.Litt.	Canadian
1962	Lines, Roland	Physics	Bermudan
1963	*McAllister, Ronald	D.Phil.	Canadian
1963	*Schantz, Mark	PPE	American
1963	*Chumir, Sheldon	B.Litt.	Canadian
1963	Van Huyssteen, Matthys	B.Litt.	South African
1964	Hutchinson, Daniel	Mod. Languages	South African
1964	*Puxley, Peter	Geography	Canadian
1964	Rowe, William	Jurisprudence	Canadian
1965	Nehring, Richard	PPE	American
1965	Disney, Shaun	Mathematics	Australian
1965	*Antill, John	Zoology	Australian
1966	*Early, Stewart	B.Phil.	American
1966	*Dawes, Ian	D.Phil.	Australian
1966	Boldt, Stuart	PPE	New Zealander
1967	Kirchberg, Jerome	Geography	American
1968	Adam, Rudolf	D.Phil.	German
1969	*May, Barry	M.Phil.	Rhodesian
1969	Gass, David	D.Phil.	Canadian
1970	Blignault, Andries	PPE	South African
1970	Mehlman, Maxwell	PPE	American
1971	*Bogan, Willie	PPE	American
1971	Brewer, Thomas	Jurisprudence	American

Matriculation or scholarship	Name	Subject	Nationality
1971	Robertson, Graeme	D.Phil.	Australian
1972	Doggett, Wayne	B.Phil.	Canadian
1972	Robinson, Kenneth	Jurisprudence	Bermudan
1973	*Kalis, Peter	PPE	American
1974	Craig, Graham	PPE	South African
1975	Hunter, Charles	Mod. Languages	Canadian
1975	Goldstein, Joel	B.Phil.	American
1976	Hart, Derek	D.Phil.	New Zealander
1976	Mitchell, Solace	D.Phil.	American
1977	Halpern, Sue	B.Phil.	American
1977	Koehn, Daryl	PPE	American
1977	*Pressley, Lynne	D.Phil.	Australian
1977	Devitt, Carol	Politics	Australian
1978	*Baudot, Nadine	PPE	Canadian
1978	*Seitz, Virginia	PPE	American
1978	Turnbull, Malcolm	BCL	Australian
1978	Harding, Jane	D.Phil.	New Zealander
1979	Hefty, Elaine	[resigned]	American
1979	Lord, Sara	PPE	American
1980	Downer, William	Jurisprudence	South African
1980	Welch, Jillian	PPE	Canadian
1980	Roe, Betsy	Law	American
1981	Fondas, Nanette	PPE	American
1981	Johnson, Michelle	PPE	American
1982	*Pint, Ellen	PPE	American
1982	Van Heerden, Belinda	Law	South African
1982	Tilton, Douglas	PPE	American
1983	Hoexter, Cora	Law	South African
1983	*Telgarsky, Jeffrey	PPE	Canadian
1984	Barton, Dominic	Economics	Canadian
1984	Pohl, Dietrich	Oriental Studies	German
1985	Wear, Eric	History of Art	American
1985	Myers, David	Law	Trinidadian
1986	Mallick, Robert	Economics	Australian
1986	Bobroff, Kenneth	Sociology	American
1986	Whaley, Anthony	Law	Bermudan
1987	Stobart, Andrew	Management	Zimbabwean
1987	Cockrell, Alfred	Law	South African
1987	*Dow, Robert	Politics	American
1987	*Cleaver, Anthony C.	Law	South African
1987	Welch, Kelly	PPE	American
1987	Stid, Daniel	PPE	American

Matriculation or scholarship	Name	Subject	Nationality
1988	Fraley, Douglas	PPE	American
1988	Elias, Michael	Economics	Australian
1989	*Buchanan, Michael	Economics	Australian
1990	Wayland, Stephen	PPE	South African
1990	Wong, Alfred	Materials	Hong Kong
1990	Weeks, Kelvin	Law	Australian
1991	Fox, Justin	English	South African
1991	Cassius De Linvel, Robert	PPE	Canadian
1991	Thomas, Graham	PPE	South African
1991	Prather, Darcy	PPE	American
1992	Tudor, John	PPE	South African
1992	Hanson, Craig	PPE	American
1993	Norton, Anthony	Law	South African
1993	Panikowski, Stanley	PPE	American
1993	Gunasekaran, Ganesh	Int. Relns.	American
1993	Cloud, John	Politics	American
1993	*Edwards, Rhys	Social Studies	Australian
1994	Chabbuck, Katharine	English	American
1994	Amm, David	PPE	South African
1995	Blomerus, Paul	Advanced Degrees	South African
1995	*Tindall, Mark	Advanced Degrees	South African
1995	Archer, James [formerly Paquin]	Law	Canadian
1996	Banerjee, Subho	PPE	Australian
1996	Brown, Brenton	PPE	South African
1996	Chye, Eleanor	Geography	Singaporean
1997	Olver, Aaron	PPE	American
1997	Byrne, Darragh	Philosophy	Irish
1998	Koch, Andre	Econ. and Management	South African
1998	*McArthur, John	Economics	Canadian
1999	Van Der Heyden, Constantin	Geography	South African
1999	Pedynowski, Dena	Geography	American
1999	Polkinghorn, William	PPE	American
1999	Nel, Marthinus	PPE	South African
1999	Thigpen, Samuel	PPE	American
1999	Van Der Colff, William	Law	South African
1999	Garland, Ross	Law	South African
2000	Dodman, David	Geography	Jamaican
2000	Lanham, Michael	Maths, Biology	American

Matriculation or scholarship	Name	Subject	Nationality
2000	Vos, Wiesner	Statistics	South African
2001	Moller, Carl	Law	Australian
2002	Raychaudhuri, Arjun	Econ. Management	Indian
2002	Walshe, Rachel	English	American
2003	Herring, Fiona	Management	Bermudan
2004	Kuhn, Christina	Ancient History	German
2004	Marquis, Chenoa	English	American
2004	Bonnici, Francois	Management	South African
2005	Shell, Jason	International Relations	American
2006	Mayne, Elizbeth	Physiology	American
2006	Cherneski, JanaLee	Political History	Canadian
2007	Shipley, Andrew	Sociology	New Zealand
2007	Wilner, Daniel	PPE	Canadian

APPENDIX E

Presidents of the Brasenose Society

1937–9	John Buchan, Lord Tweedsmuir (probably until his death in February 1940)
1940	Sir Robert Pearson
1948	Sir Allan Ellis
1948–50	R. H. Peck
1951–2	H. M. Last
1952–4	Sir Guy Nott-Bower
1954–5	D. Drysdale
1955–7	M. Platnauer
1957–9	C. H. M. Waldock (later Sir Humphrey Waldock)
1959–60	A. D. Grant
1960–1	M. Platnauer
1963–4	P. R. Frere
1964–6	Sir George Baker
1966–8	Sir Ronald Bodley Scott
1968–70	A. J. F. Doulton
1970–2	Sir Reginald Verdon-Smith
1972–4	Sir Leslie Scarman (later Lord Scarman)
1974–6	Sir Val Duncan
1976–7	Sir Colin Thornley
1977–8	J. S. O. Haslewood
1978–9	Sir Edward Eveleigh
1979–80	R. A. K. Runcie (later Abp. of Canterbury)
1980–1	G. Rippon (later Lord Rippon)
1981–2	Sir Lindsay Alexander
1982–3	R. F. Brown
1983–4	Professor J. K. B. M. Nicholas
1984–5	A. T. Whitehead
1985–6	R. K. Ingram
1986–7	D. A. Emms
1987–8	J. R. Moss
1988–9	Sir Robert Reid
1989–90	Sir Ralph Gibson
1990–1	D. L. Stockton

1991–2	N. A. Ward-Jones
1992–3	Sir Colin Cole
1993–4	G. A. Wilson
1994–5	P. R. Dawson-Bowling
1995–6	R. D. Gill
1996–7	Professor Graham Richards
1997–8	Lord Cowdrey of Tonbridge
1998–9	Sir Roger Bell
1999–2000	A. C. Smith
2000–1	F. W. Neate
2001–2	C. Penn
2002–3	Sir Scott Baker (later Lord Baker)
2003–4	Sir Iain Vallance
2004–5	Sir Robin Janvrin (later Lord Janvrin)
2005–6	L. B. Smith
2006–7	J. J. McMullen
2007–8	Alexandra Marks
2008–9	Lord Saville of Newdigate
2009–10	Professor J. Mordaunt Crook

APPENDIX F
College Grace

Ante cibum (prandium)

Oculi omnium spectant in te, Deus. Tu das illis escas tempore opportuno. Aperis manum tuam et imples omne animal tua benedictione.

Mensae caelestis nos participes facias, Deus, rex aeternae gloriae.

Post cibum (prandium)

Qui nos creavit, redemit et pavit, sit benedictus in aeternum. Deus, exaudi orationem nostram. Agimus tibi gratias, Pater caelestis, pro Gulielmo Smith episcopo, et Ricardo Sutton milite, Fundatoribus nostris; pro Alexandro Nowell, Jocosa Frankland, Gulielmo Hulme, Elizabetha Morley, Mauritio Platnauer, aliisque benefectoribus nostris; humiliter te precantes ut eorum numerum benignissime adaugeas.

Ecclesiam Catholicam, et populum Christianum custodi. Haereses et errores omnes extirpa. Elizabetham Reginam nostram et subditos eius defende. Pacem da et conserva, per Christum Dominum nostrum.

[1] *Ante cibum (coenam)*

Omnipotens et sempiterne Deus, sine quo nihil est dulce, nihil odoriferum, misericordiam tuam humiliter imploramus, ut nos coenamque nostram benedicas; ut corda nostra exhilares; ut quae suscepturi sumus alimenta, tuo honori, tuaeque beneficentiae accepta referamus, per Christum Dominum nostrum.

[2] *Post cibum (coenam)*

Quod corpora nostra, Deus optime maxime, cibo potuque abunde refecisti, agimus tibi gratias, quantas possumus maximas; simulque precamur, ut animas nostras verbo et spiritu deinde pascas; ut omnia mala fugiamus; ut quae sint tibi placitura perfecte intelligamus, diligenter meditemur, et ad ea praestanda toto impetu feramur, per Christum Dominum nostrum.

---

[1] Said on Shrove Tuesday (Ale Verses) and on 1 June (laying of foundation stone).
[2] As n. 1.

INDEX OF NAMES

Members of Brasenose College are listed with their date of Oxford matriculation or incorporation in brackets. Figures in bold type refer to plates and captions.

Abbot, Charles; 1st Baron Colchester, 180
Aboudanak, Rabbi, 88
Acheson, Robert (1953), 480
Ackermann, Rudolph, **frontispiece,** 168
Ackrill, John (1940), **93,** 389, 391, 406, 417
Acock, A. M. (1934), 479
Acton, Sir Harold, 356–7
Acton, William, 357
Adam, Rudolph (1968), 481
Adams, Peter (1647), 60
Adams, Richard (1647), 64, 84, 85
Adams, Thomas (1652), 4, 83
Adams, W.W.S. (1923), 355
Addington, Henry; 1st Viscount Sidmouth
    (1774), 3, 5, 109, 184
Agar-Roberts, Hon. A. V. (1906), 460
Agas, Radulph, 17
Agutter, W., 173
Alchin, Gordon (1913), **72,** 343, 352
Alcock, Thomas (1728), 121
Alcocke, Anthony (1624), 123
Aldersey, William (1629), 49
Alderson, E. H. (1884), **59**
Alderson, Joseph, Snr., 153
Alderson, Joseph (1779), 153, 187–8, 442
Aldrich, Henry, 137, 207
Alexander II, Tsar, 203
Alexander VII, Pope, 204
Alexander, E. F. (1870), 455
Alexander, Sir Lindsay (1939), 485
Alford, Thomas (1721), 101–2
Alfred, King, **69,** 6, 7, 9, 11, 129, 151–2,
    360
Ali, Tariq, 418
Allen, Kate (1974), 431
Allen, Thomas (1589), 20, 438

Allenby, Edmund; 1st Viscount, 358
Allestree, Richard, 54
Allfrey, Edward Wilfred, 79
Allgood, J. (1845), 452
Allgood, William (1856), **48,** 256, 266, 453
Allibone, Samuel, 192
Allies, A. E. (1910), 322
Allison, D. F. (1967), 400
Allison, M.G. (1953), 400, 467
Alston, Edward, 118
Amery, E. V., 205
Amhurst, Nicholas, 109
Amis, Kingsley, 424
Amm, David (1994), 483
Anderson, B. (1956), 481
Anderson, H. A. (1870), 455
Anderson, J. D. (1934), 372, 465
Anderson, J. F. (1889), 458
Anderson, St. J. K. H. (1990), 474
Anderson, Robert, 215
Anderton, Matthew (1602), 44
Anderton, Robert (1578), 34
Andrews, Edward (1608), 47
Andrews, John, 132
Andrews, Robert (1807), 200
Andrewes, Bp. Lancelot, 215
Annan, Noel; Baron, 409, 427
Annesley, Hon. G.; Viscount Valentia
    (1787), 442
Ansley, Edmund (1552), 32, 33, 35
Antill, J. K. (1965), 470, 481
Antrobus, Ralph (1596), 36
Antrobus, Samuel (1774), 108
Antrobus, W. L. (1925), 440
Appach, A. R. (1884), **59**
Apperley, Thomas (1792), 443

Archdale, Mervyn (1830), 189, 450
Archer, James [formerly Paquin] (1995), 483
Archer, Jeffrey; Baron (1963), 4, 403
Archer, Lady (née Mary Weeden), 403
Arden, P. (1858), **48,** 453
Arkle, A. W. (1874), **58**
Arlott, Sir John, 347
Arnall-Thompson, H. T. (1883), **59,** 457
Arnold, C. H. (1900), 460
Arnold, Matthew, 224, 249, 262, 277, 283, 385
Arnold, Thomas, xviii, 229, 277
Arran, Charles (Butler), Earl of, 123, 128, 130–31, 143
Arundel, Philip (Howard), 13th Earl of, 42
Ashbroke, John (1549), 32, 33
Ashby, Sir Eric, 427
Asher, A. G. G. (1881), 299, 456
Ashley, Daniel (1786), 442
Ashmole, Elias (1644), 4, 5, 13, 54, 87
Ashton, Ellis (1807), 446
Ashton, Sir Thomas, 1st. Bt. (1616), 52, 53
Ashton, Thomas (1647), 64, 66
Ashwell, T. G. L. (1919), 462
Ashworth, Abraham (1776), 120
Askew, Richard (1955), 409
Askwith, George; 1st Baron (1880), **58,** 296, 498
Aspinall, Alexander (1566), 38
Aspinwall, Peter (1642), 85
Assheton, Richard (1712), 146, 147
Assheton, Richard (1744), 147
Assheton, William (1658), 124
Assheton, William (1775), 108
Assheton, William (1805), 446
Astbury, Charles (1854), 236
Astbury, C. J. (1892), 458
Aston, A. I. (1814), 448
Aston, H. H. (1810), 447
Aston, John (1648), 60
Aston, Sir Thomas (1617), 54
Asquith, Herbert Henry; 1st Earl of Oxford and Asquith, 318, 333
Atherton, Richard (1672), 438
Atiyah, Edward (1923), 358–60
Atiyah, Mrs. Jean (née Levens), 359
Atiyah, Sir Michael, 358

Atkinson, Edmund, 366
Attenborough, T. J. (1991), 474
Atterbury, Bp. Francis, 142, 143
Attlee, Clement; 1st Earl, 378, 425
Aubertin, Thomas (1903), 460
Austen, Jane, 156
Austen, Joseph (1854), 236, 242
Austin, J. L., 331, 418
Auty, Robert (1965), 417, 423
Awsiter, (of Brighton), 154
Aydelotte, Frank (1905), 312, 328–9, 384, 477
Aylott, P.R.F.D. (1984), 473

Bach, J. S., 314
Bachelor, Humphrey, **I**
Backhouse, Sir Jonathon (1958), 410
Backshaw (battelling), 55
Bacon, John, 174
Bacon, Friar Roger, 7
Badeley, Edward (1820), 223
Badger, H. D. (1919), 462
Badgett, Lee (1961), 469, 481
Bagguley, Desmond (1943), 391, 395
Bagshaw, John Charles (1840), 218
Bagshaw, Edward (1640), 53
Bagshaw, Samuel (1774), 108
Bagshaw, William (1783), 188, 442
Bagwell, R. (1920), 462
Bailey, G. H. (1910), **75,** 321, 461
Bailey, Joseph (1828), 450
Bailey, J.P.C. (1976), 472
Bailey, V. H. (1949), 466
Baillie, E. H. (1911), 321
Baillie, Robert (1879), **58,** 296
Baker, Sir George (1927), 55, 464, 485
Baker, John [alias Elton], 23, 437
Baker, M. F. (1962), 469
Baker, Richard (1801), 171
Baker, T. Scott; Baron (1957), 486
Baker, Thomas, 102
Baker-Cresswell, H. G. (1896), 459
Balding, L. F. C. R. (1926), 464
Baldock, D. N. (1954), 467
Baldwin, G. S. (1994), 474
Baldwin Brown, Gerard (1869), 261, 287, 312
Balindon, Simon de, 8

Ball, John (1600), 43
Ball, John (1948), 480
Ball, Robert (1956), 481
Ball, Thomas (1716), 133
Ballard, Marshall (1936), 479
Ballanchi, Paniattotti, 151
Bampfylde, G. W. (1804), 445
Bancroft, G. P. (1888), 457
Bancroft, Bp. Richard, 41
Bandaranaike, Salomon, 359
Banerjee, Subho (1996), 483
Bankart, S. S. (1828), 450
Banks, Mrs. G. Linnaeus (née Isabella
    Varley), 120
Banner, T. B., 48
Barbet, Jean, 79
Barbour, Harold (1893), 310, 458
Barham, Richard Harris (1807), 199–200
Bardsley, L. A. (1949), 440
Barère de Vieujac, Bertrand, 175
Baring, Henry, 175
Baring, Thomas, 287
Baring-Gould, Sabine, 305
Barker, Frederick (1886), 302, 457
Barker, G. E. (1888), 457
Barker, Paul (1955), **92,** 4, 408
Barker, Thomas (1745), 95, 157, 161,
    436, 439
Barlow, Bp. Thomas, 49
Barlow, E. A. (1931), 464
Barlow, Joseph Wagstaff (1841), 205, 228
Barlow, R. W. (1934), 372
Barlow, V. H. (1919), 352
Barltrop, John (1938), 378, 383, 387,
    389, 395
Barnard, F. H. (1921), 462
Barnard, Ronald (1948), 480
Barnes, Barnabe (1586), 41
Barnes, Bp. Richard (1552), 32, 437
Barneston, John (1581), 438
Barnfield, F. E. F. (2002), 476
Barnfield, Richard (1589), 41
Barraclough, Geoffrey, 341
Barratt, Alfred (1862), 287, 304
Barrett, Richard (1565), 35
Barrie, C. D. O. (1972), 471
Barrie, James, 313
Barron, Caroline, v

Barry, Douglas (1880), 296, 456
Barry, G. J. (1864), **42B,** 264
Barry, William (1882), **59,** 296, 457
Barrymore, (Smith Barry), 4th
    Earl of, 151
Barrymore, James (Smith Barry;
    Visc.Buttevant), 5th Earl of, 151, 439
Barrymore, Richard (Smith Barry), 7th
    Earl of, 151
Barton, B. H. (1877), 456
Barton, Dominic (1984), 473, 482
Barton, Henry (1880), **58,** 296, 298, 456
Barton, James (1763), 151
Barton, Richard (1840), 217, 451
Batchelor, G. J. L. (1897), 459
Batchelor, S. J., 440
Bate, John (1788), 443
Bateson, James (1554), 39
Bathe, Anthony (1867), 274
Bathurst, Richard, 68, 73
Battye, R. (1853), 453
Baudot, Nadine (1978), 482
Baugh, R. J. (1987), 474
Bavand, Robert (1689), 126
Baxter, Henry Fleming (1857), 268, 284
Bayne, T. V., 212
Bazely, Henry (1861), 261
Bazely, Thomas (1826), 201, 217, 261
Beale, J. R. (1962), 469
Bean, Atherton (1932), 479
Beane, Peter (1938), 372
Beatles, The, 403
Beaufort, Charles (Somerset), 4th Duke
    of, 129
Beaufort, Henry (Somerset), 3rd Duke
    of, 129
Beaufort, Henry (Somerset), 5th Duke of,
    150, 153
Beaufort, Lady Margaret, **I,** 11, 12, 15
Beaumont, Richard (1767), 155, 439
Bebb, Llewellyn (1881), 306, 315
Becher, J. H. (1931), 345, 375
Beck, Charles (1946), 480
Beckford, Charles (1816), 186, 448
Beckford, William, 195
Beddington, Rosa (1974), 421
'Bede, Cuthbert', see Bradley, Edward
Bedford, A. E. R. (1884), **59**

Bedford, R. N. J. (1946), 440
Bee, F. V. (1968), 471
Bekker, Pieter (1932), 479
Bell, Gertrude, 301
Bell, James (1972), 409
Bell, Sir Roger (1959), 486
Bell [of Limpsfield], 355
Bellamy, C. W. (1964), 469
Beloff, Max; Baron, 341
Bembo, Pietro; Cardinal, 134
Bengal, Nawab of, 309
Benham, Samantha (1990), 402
Benn, Alfred (1913), 323
Bennett, Arnold, 313
Bennett, D. C. (1922), 463, 465
Bennett, Thomas (1710), 96
Bennett, J. L. (1787), 442
Benson, Arthur Charles, 275, 281
Bentham, Edward, 179
Bentham, Jeremy, 418
Bently, Henry Rothwell (1877), 439
Bereblock, John, 17
Berenson, Bernard, 246, 276
Berkly, William (1856), 237, 242
Berlin, Sir Isaiah, 394
Bernard, John Augustine (1681), 92–4
Bernstein, A. H. (1961), 469
Berry, C. W. (1883), 299, 457
Berry, Richard (1651), 62
Bessborough, Frederick (Ponsonby);
    10th Earl of, 415
Bethell, Samuel (1774), 109, 191
Betjeman, Sir John, 291, 356
Beynon, W. T. (1930), 441
Beyts, N. M. (1935), 465
Biddulph, R. (1818), 448
Bikales, B. A. B. (1966), 470
Billingsley, Richard (1581), 26
Bingham, John (1630), 51
Bingham, J. B. (1805), 446
Binks, James [alias Stoddard], 437
Binney, John (1854), 236
Binns, J. H. S. (1916), 477
Birch, Bryan (1966), 395, 417
Birch, Samuel (?1657), 85
Birkenhead, F. E. (Smith); 1st Earl of, 367
Birks, Peter (1961), 388, 417–8
Birley, Eric (1924), 364, 366, 440

Bispham, Thomas, 55
Bittleston, Adam (1933), 368
Black, Brian (1926), 372, 463
Blackborne, John (1640), 61, 62,
    63, 70
Blackburne, F.G. (1857), **56**
Blackburne, John (1668), 438
Blackburne, John (1805), 165
Blackburne, Thomas (1776), 147
Blackburne, Thomas (1809), 447
Blackett, C. R. (1913), **72,** 321
Blackleech, Nicholas (1587), 41
Blackstone, Sir William, 157, 302
Blackwell, M. (1960), 468
Blacow, Richard (1741), 143
Blaine, H. F. (1876), 455
Blair, A. S. (1883), **59,** 299, 457
Blair, Abbot Sir David Oswald Hunter,
    Bt., 257
Blair, J. W. (1957), 468
Blair, W. J. (1973), v
Blake, P.D. S. (1948), 400, 466
Blakeley, D. G. (1952), 467
Blakeny, E. H., 241
Blakiston, H. E. D., 333
Blanc, Louis, 216
Blanchard, Thomas (1539), 29, 436
Blanda, Roberto (1996), 432
Blandford, Bp. Walter, 74
Blandy, Mary, 100
Blencowe, J. I. (1879), **58,** 456
Blencowe, Robert Willis (1784), 188, 442
Blignault, Andries (1970), 481
Blixen, Karen (née Dinesen), 319
Blois, Peter of, 340
Blomerus, Paul (1995), 483
Blount, Thomas (1623), 51
Blow, Matthew (1774), 109
Bloy, N. C. F. (1945), 465
Blumberg, Nathaniel (1948), 480
Blyth, P. H (1884), 299
Boada, Sarah, v
Boardman, Elizabeth, v
Bobart, Jacob, 128
Bobruff, Kenneth (1986), 482
Bodley Scott, Sir Ronald (1934), 485
Body, John (1932), 371
Bogan, Willie (1971), 481

Bogdanor, Vernon (1961), v, 394, 396, 417, 430
Bogle, Donald (1953), 480
Bolchover, Stephen (1965), 406
Boldt, Stuart (1966), 481
Bolton, Edmund (1724), 101–2
Bolton, Herbert (1913), **73,** 323
Bolton, Robert (1592), 43
Bolton, Robert (1684), 53, 95
Boni, E. (1992), 474
Bonner, Bp. Edmund, 31, 32
Bonnici, Francois (2004), 484
Boobyer, Brian (1948), 4, 346, 400
Boor, Alaric (1913), 477
Booth, A. D. (1984), 473
Booth, Sir George, 63, 87
Booth, John (1615), 20, 437
Booth, T. W. (1824), 450
Boothe, Armistead (1929), 478
Borg, R. J. (1985), 473
Borland, D. M. (1930), 464
Borelli, Fr. 409
Borrer, J. H. (Hamilton) (1835), 451
Bosanquet, Sir John, 185
Bossum, John, **40, 41,** 205, 250–51, 265
Bostock, Nathaniel (1616), 47
Boswell, James (1797), 179, 184–5, 444
Boswell, John (1885), **59,** 299, 302–3, 457
Boteler, Sir Allen, 86
Boteler, Lady (née Bartlett), 86
Bouch, William (1896), **66,** 312, 459
Bouette, M. N. (1988), 474
Boulter, Benjamin Consitt (1895), **66,** 309
Bourne-Taylor, Carole (née Rodier), v
Bourne-Taylor, Geoffrey, v
Bouverie, Francis Kenelm (1816), 448
Bovell Jones, T. B. (1924), 463
Bowden, T. (2001), 475
Bowden (battelling), 55
Bowdler, Stephen (1691), 95
Bowen, C. L. J. (1919), 462
Bowen, George Ferguson (1840), 232, 243
Bower, J., 158
Bowes, R. N. (1952), 467
Bowker, Margaret, 12
Bowles, Joseph (1957),
Bowly, W. A. T. (1898), 459
Bowra, Sir Maurice, **71,** 291, 353, 356, 384, 409

Bowyer, Thomas, 40
Boycott, Arthur (1894), 322
Boyd, Ian H. (1952), 398
Boyle, Robert, 68, 73
Boyse, Nathaniel, 92
Bradbury, D. (1968), 470
Brademas, John (1950), 397, 480
Bradley, Edward, 251
Bradley, Herbert (1924), 319, 478
Bradley Birt, Frank Bradley (1893), **66,** 310–11
Bradman, Sir Donald, 347
Bradshaigh, Thomas (1701), 143
Bradshaw, A. S. (1926), 463
Bradshaw, Frederick (1896), 307
Bradshaw, H. H. (1847), 452
Bradshaw, James (1630), 51, 53, 85
Brahms, Johannes, 365
Brandt, D. R. (1906), 321
Brandt, Francis (1858), **48,** 269
Brassey, Mrs. Albert (née Bingham), 302
Bray, Harry (1906), 319, 477
Bray, Sir Reginald, 12
Breithweite, Thomas (1765), 120
Brent, Nathaniel, 56, 59
Brereton, William (1626), 51, 52
Brerewood, Edward (1581), 38, 47
Brerewood, Robert, 48
Brewer, Thomas (1971), 481
Brewer, William (1648), 60
Brewis, N. H. (1919), 462
Brewster, Samuel, 127
Brideoake, Ralph (1630), 53
Bridgeland, E. M. (1999), 475
Bridgeman, Sir Francis, 97, 438
Bridgewater, John (1552), 32, 33, 35
Brierly, James (1900), 307, 361
Brims, C. D. (1969), 471
Brindley, James, 180
Briscall, Samuel (1797), 178
Brittain, J. A. (1932), 375
Broadhurst, Ephraim, 79
Brock, William (1610), 438
Brocklehurst, H. C. (1896), 459
Brodie, Sir Benjamin, 2nd Bt. 235
Brodrick, George, 228
Bromhead, B. (1790), 443
Brooke, G. (1820), 449

Brooke, Henry (1627), 51
Brooke, Henry, 146
Brooke, John (1821), 449
Brooke, Leigh (1696), 99
Brooke, P. L. (1811), 447
Brooke, Richard (1771), 155, 439
Brooke, Rupert, 320
Brooke, Stopford, 215
Brooke, W. de C. (1819), 448
Brookes, Joshua (1774), 109, 120
Brooks, C. I. O. (1982), 473
Brooks, Joseph (1831), 250, 450
Brooks, Hon. Marshall (1873), 272,
    285, 455
Brooks, Robert (1904), 477
Brooksbanke, Joseph (1633), 53
Broome, William (1774), 107, 108
Broster, John (1646), 60
Broughton, Peter (1807), 446
Brown, Alexander (1834), 451
Brown, Arthur (1933), 479
Brown, Brenton (1996), 483
Brown, Gerald (1938), 479
Brown, John, I, 266
Brown, John, II, 266
Brown, John (1858), 264
Brown, N. J. (1970), 471
Brown, Robert, 9
Brown, Robert (1895), 459
Brown, R. F. (1931), 485
Brown, R. J. D. (1977), 472
Brown, S. R. (1959), 468
Brown, Thomas (1703), 438
Browne, Gerard (1632), 53
Browning, Oscar, 283
Browning, Robert, 200
Bruce, Robert, **43**
Bruch, Atherton (1614), 44
Bruch, George (1529), 27
Brucker, James, 112
Brudenell, Sir Thomas, 21
Bruen, Samuel (1647), 64, 68, 71
Bruford, L.G. N. (1957), 468
Brunel, Isambard Kingdom, 231
Brunt, Peter (1935), 393–4, 417, 440
Brzeska, H. Gaudier, 320
Buccleugh, Charles (Montague-Douglas-
    Scott); 4th Duke of, 236

Buchan, John; 1st Baron Tweedsmuir
    (1895), **III, 66,** 1, 2, 4, 191, 200, 299,
    307–14, 485
Buchanan, A. H. (1808), 447
Buchanan, J. (1816), 448
Buchanan, Michael (1989), 483
Buckingham, George (Villiers) 1st Duke
    of, 55, 135, 139
Buckingham, George (Nugent-Temple-
    Grenville); 1st Marquess of, **I,** 161
Buckingham, Katherine
    (MacDonnell; née Manners);
    Duchess of, 54
Buckingham and Chandos, Richard
    (Temple-Nugent-Brydges-Chandos;
    Earl Temple); 1st Duke of (1791),
    I, 162, 174
Buckler, John Chessel, **46, 54,** 6, 18, 80,
    81, 168, 204, 222, 239, 298
Buckley, F. G. (1912), **72,** 321
Buckley, Henry (1816), 186, 448
Bucknall, B. E. (1897), 459
Bull, George (1949), 397
Bull, O. R. S. (1951), 466
Bulmer, Alan (1938), **89,** 372
Bulteel, Henry Bellenden (1818), 223
Bunbury, J. W. McClintock (1870), 288
Burdett, Sir Robert, 6th Bt. (1813), 447
Burdon, R., 223
Burges, William (1642), 60
Burges, W. T. (1859), **56, 57**
Burgess, Henry (1868), 285
Burke, Edmund, 360
Burke, Robert (1812), 447
Burn, John (1955), **92**
Burne-Jones, Sir Edward, 237–40, 277
Burra, R. P. (1891), 458
Burrows, A. S. (1975), 472
Burrows, Montagu, 302
Burrus, J. De M. (1927), 478
Burscough, John (1648), 64, 71
Burton, John Prichard (1941), 441
Burton, Robert (1593), **14,** 4,
    41, 152
Bury, Edward, 21
Bush, Charles (1904), 477
Bush, J. T. (1925), 463
Buss, R. W. (1955), 222

Bussell, Frederick William (1881), **II, III, 60, 67,** 4, 247, 275, 304–7, 309, 316, 319–20, 363, 391, 439
Bussell, Mrs. Mary (née Dibdin), 306
Bustin, Henry, 336, 365
Bute, John (Chrichton-Stuart), 3rd Marquess of, 274
Butler, Alfred (1869), **67,** 295, 303, 309, 315–6, 319
Butler, Bp. Joseph, 208, 209, 210
Butler, H. E., 363
Butler, Samuel (1869), 269, 271
Butt, Sir Kenneth (1927) 441
Byam-Shaw, J. G. (1982), 473
Byass, R. W. (1879), 456
Byrne, Darragh (1997), 483
Byrom, John, 121–2, 145
Byrom, Ralph (1629), 47, 60, 62
Byron, Arabella (née Milbanke), Lady, 216
Byron, George, 6th Baron, 200
Byron, Robert, 356–7
Bywater, Ingram, 275

Calamy, Edward, 65
Calcott, Anthony (1576), 39
Caldwell, Richard (1533), 30
Caldwell, R. (1795), 444
Calley, Thomas (1771), 151
Calvert, Reginald (1852), 453
Camden, William, 6, 78, 89
Cameron, David (1985), 4, 431
Campbell, K. M. (1980), 473
Campbell, Mrs. Patrick (Beatrice Tanner), 455
Campbell Roger, I. M. (1925), 478
Campion, St. Edmund, 42
Campion, Edward, 55
Campion, Sir William, 55
Campion, W. H. (1803), 445
Camplin, George (1808), 188, 447
Canning, George, 177
Capes, W. W., 304
Carco, Francis, 320
Cardus, Sir Neville, 347
Cardwell, Edward (1806), 169, 174, 187, 191, 243
Carey, John, 368
Carlyle, Thomas, xviii, 73, 216, 238

Carpenter, John (1645), 64
Carr, John Foster (1895), **66**
Carr, Morgan (1553), 29
Carr, S.T. I. (1971), 471
Carte, Thomas (1698), 142–3
Carter, George (1894), 307
Cartwright, John (1627), 51, 74, 266, 438
Cartwright, Thomas (1753), 100, 439
Cartwright, William (1721), 438
Cartwright, Ursula, 438
Cary, Christopher (1551), 29
Case, Henry (1791), 443
Case, Thomas (1863), 287, 304
Cashmore, Roger (1965), v, 432, 436
Cassius de Linvel, Robert (1991), 483
Castens, H. H. (1884), 457
Castlemaine, Roger (Palmer), Earl of, 89
Castletown, Bernard (Fitzpatrick); 2nd Baron, 263
Caswall, Edward (1832), 207, 223
Casswell, Ursula Monica, 441
Catell, Thomas (1707), 146–7
Cator, Charles (1805), 446
Cator, Thomas (1810), 447
Catto, Jeremy, v, 8
Cave, John, 63
Cave, Sir Richard, 86
Cavendish, Camilla (1989), 431
Cawley, Mrs. Ann, 113, 156
Cawley, Ralph (1738), 95, 112, 115, 141, 151, 153, 156, 436, 439
Cawston, Arthur, 274
Caxton, William, 196
Cecil, Sir Robert, 41
Cecil, Sir William, 30
Cecil, Lord Robert, 230
Cellan-Jones, D. J. (1984), 473
Cezanne, Paul, 230
Chabbuck, Katharine (1994), 483
Chaffers, Thomas (1831), 243–5
Chalk, F. G. H. (1934), 375, 464
Chalk, Gerry (1930), 345, 347, 373
Chalmers, John (1938), 479
Chalmers, Robert Bruce (1948), 441
Chalmers, Thomas, 214
Chaloner, James (1616), 51, 57
Chaloner, Thomas, 57
Chaloner, Sir Thomas, 57

Chaloner, William (1823), 449
Chamberlain, Joseph, 332
Chamberlain, Thomas, 273
Chamberlayne, H. F. (1893), 459
Champneys, Weldon (1858), **44, 57,** 222, 262, 265, 266, 268, 285
Chandler, Arthur (1878), 303, 306–7
Channing, W. E., 214
Chantrey, Sir Francis, 177
Charles I, King, 45, 51, 54, 57, 75, 139, 142, 229, 352, 380
Charles II, King, 68, 229
Charles Edward Stuart [Charles III; the Young Pretender], 143, 147, 152
Charlesworth, R. M. (1949), 446
Charlett, Arthur, 90, 94, 98
Charlwood, Harry, **41,** 251
Charnock, Hugh (1532), 35
Chatham, John (Pitt); 2nd Earl of, 176
Chaucer, Geoffrey, 237, 239, 277
Cheere, John, 139
Cheeseman, Thomas, 188
Cherneski, JanaLee (2006), 484
Cherry, Conrad (1933), **87,** 343, 374–5, 465
Cheshyre, Sir John, 438
Chesterton, G. H. (1946), 466
Chetwode, G. (1809), 447
Cheynell, Francis, 59
Chichester, A. (1815), 448
Chichester, Francis (Lea); Earl of (1613), 155
Chick, M. M. R. (1985), 473
Chick, R. A. (1965), 469
Child, Coles (1882), 457
Child, Harold (1888), 303
'Child of Hale', see Middleton, J.
Childs, J. R. (1975), 472
Chillingworth, William, 63
Chilver, Henry, 55
Chinnery, E. F. (1906), 460
Chinnock, H. S. (1894), 458
Chirnside, S. M. (1997), 475
Cholmondeley, C. C. (1814), 448
Cholmondeley, Hugh (1790), 175–7, 178, 443
Cholmondeley, Hugh (1815), 448
Cholmondeley, Mary, 194–5

Cholmondeley, Robert (1669),
Cholmondeley, Thomas, 176
Chopin, Frederic, 365
Christopher, A. M. W., 261
Chumir, Sheldon (1963), 481
Church, Richard (1610), 54
Church, Thomas (1634), 60, 62, 70, 71, 74, 438
Churchill, Mrs. (of High Street), 132
Churton, Ralph (1772), 1, 2, 31, 160, 174, 179–80, 181, 182–4, 192
Churton, Thomas (1817), 201, 204, 210, 213, 217, 243, 275
Churton, Whitaker (1828), 201, 212, 217, 222, 243
Chuter-Ede, James (Chuter Ede), 1st Baron, 335
Chye, Eleanor (1996), 483
Ciardi, F. G. D. (2005), 476
Cibber, Colley, 128
Clack, Thomas (1763), 108
Clare, Lady Elizabeth (Halles; née Vere), Countess of, 83
Clarence, Duke of, 190
Clarendon, Henry (Hyde), 2nd Earl of, 84, 302
Clark, Andrew, 37
Clark, Colin (1924), 417, 431
Clark, C. H. (1956), **93**
Clark, David Owen (1970), 471
Clark, John (1808), 447
Clarke, George (1675), 87, 88, 135, 136–8, 298, 438
Clarke, J. C. (1823), 449
Clarke, L. E. G. (1835), 451
Claughton, Thomas, 221
Clavering, J. (1797), 444
Claymond, John, 15, 23, 437
Clayton, Thomas 56
Clayton, John (1727), 5, 121–2, 144–9
Clayton, R. E. (1986), 474
Clayton, Horace Evelyn (1871), 439
Clayton and Bell, (stainer glaziers), 212, 289, 295
Cleave, J. R. (1900), 460
Cleaver, Anthony C. (1987), 482
Cleaver, Abp. Euseby, 161
Cleaver, John (1795), 444

Cleaver, J. J. (1793), 443
Cleaver, Bp. William (1757), **24,** 31, 99,
   113, 153, 156, 158, 160–62, 164,
   165–6, 170, 172, 436
Cleaver, Mrs. (née Ashton), 161
Clegg, J. (1950), 466
Clerk, Samuel, 90
Cleveland, John, 54
Clifford, Isaac (1653), 85
Clifton, William, 13, 155, 437
Clinch, (print seller), **1**
Clive, Archer (1817), 186–7, 448
Cloud, John (1993), 483
Clough, Arthur Hugh, 242
Clower, Robert (1949), 480
Cobb, J. P. (1959), 469
Cobb, John Wolstenholme (1847), 205
Cobb, Richard, 391
Cobbe, William, 59
Cobden, F. C., 271
Cockburn, Claude, 356
Cockle, J. C. (1788), 443
Cockman, Thomas, 128–30
Cockrell, Alfred (1987), 482
Cockroft, E. F. (1889), 458
Cocks, Hon. J. Somers (1806), 213, 219,
   446
Cocks, J. J. T. Somers (1839), 451
Codrington, John (1852), 268, 453
Codrington, W. (1808), 447
Cohn, Edgar Stanley (1918), **68, 91,**
   340–41, 347, 363, 378–9, 381–3,
   394, 404, 440
Coke, Thomas, 55
Coldstream, Sir William, 392
Coldstream, F. K. R. (1922), 463
Cole, Sir Colin (1941), 486
Coleraine, Henry (Hare), 2nd Baron, 118
Coleraine, Henry (Hare), 3rd Baron, 118
Coles, C. J. (1979), 472
Collet, John (1774), 108
Colley, Jonathan (1694), 145
Collieu, Eric George (1929), 152,
   340–41, 363, 378, 380, 382, 406,
   410, 416–7, 423
Collins, Charlotte Gertrude Faithful, 440
Collins, Thomas Farmer (1855), 439
Colmore, Clement (1566), 40

Colmore, Thomas (1863), 258–9,
   454
Colquitt, Elizabeth, 439
Colquitt, Lucy, 439
Colquitt, Susannah, 439
Colton, Ralph (1590), 20
Colvin, Sir Howard, 79
Colvin, Sidney, 280
Comte, Auguste, 250
Comyns-Carr, Philip (1893), 310
Conder, M. D. E. (1977), 472
Congreve, W. W. (1822), 449
Connell, Sir Michael (1958), 468
Conolly, Cyril, 356
Conolly, John (1832), 188, 450
Constable, Sir Robert, 28
Constable, William (1537), 28
Conybeare, W. J., 242
Cook, G. D. (1998), 475
Cook, John Earley (1840), 217
Cook, Thomas (1614), 44, 47
Cook Wilson, John, 364, 418
Cooke, George, 138
Cookco, Will (1696), 107
Cookson, Thomas, 138
Cookson, W. (1811), 447
Cooper, Richard (1965), v
Cooper, Thomas, 9
Cooper, W. H. (1837), 451
Coote, C. H. (1800), 445
Cope, B, (1995), 475
Cope, J. A. (2004), 476
Copleston, Edward, 194
Coppock, Thomas (1739), 145, 147–8
Cornbury, Henry (Hyde); 1st
   Viscount, 185
Cornish, Basil (1837), 303
Costeloe, J. M. (1956), 467
Cottam, John (1566), 4, 38
Cottam, Thomas (1569), 34, 35
Cotton, Charles, 63
Cotton, Robert (1527), 27
Coulthurst, J. (1810), 447
Courakis, Tony (1969), 430
Courtenay, William; 1st Viscount, 108
Courtney, R. C. (1904), 460
Coventry, R. G. T. (1888), 458
Cowan, P. J. C. (1985), 473

Cowdrey, Colin; Baron (1951), **55,** 4, 400,
    401, 466, 486
Cowley, A. E., 190
Cowley, Hannah, 102
Cowling, T. G. (1924), 351
Cox, George, 164,172
Cox, H. P. M. (1830), 450
Cox, John, 13, 23
Cox, R. (1823), 449
Coxe, John (1545), 32, 437
Coxe, P. H. (1872), 455
Coxe, Seymour (1860), **56,** 258, 262
Coxe, William (1648), 64
Coxhead, M. E. (1908), 461
Coxhill, W. T. (1944), 103
Coyle, Diane (1978), 431
Cradock, Edward Hartopp (formerly
    Grove) (1827), **36, 53A,** 232, 242–3,
    247–9, 253–4, 261, 269, 275,
    277, 278, 286, 290, 292, 295, 299,
    301–2, 348, 436
Cradock, Mrs. Harriet (née Lister), 204,
    248, 254
Cradock and Joy (publishers), 173
Craig, Graham (1974), 471, 482
Crakanthorp, Richard, 47
Cranmer, Abp. Thomas, 29, 33
Crawford, G. H. (1922), 463
Crawford, H. A. S. (1974), 471
Crawfurd, C. W. P. (1844), 452
Crawshaw, Thomas (Brooks); 1st
    Baron, 272
Crawshay, Lionel (1895), 310
Creese, N. A. H. (1948), 400, 466
Creighton, Mrs. Louise (née van
    Glehn), 278
Crewe, J. O. (1808), 446
Cripps, Reginald (1887), 303
Crockett, R. (1791), 443
Crofts, William (1864), 241, 268, 285
Croker, P. T. C. (1955), 328
Crompton, P. R. (1936), 465
Crompton, Thomas (1627), 85
Crompton, William (1617), 43
Cromwell, Oliver, 57, 65, 69, 70, 72
Crook, J. Mordaunt (1955), 362, 486
Crooke, E. H. (1909), **74,** 320
Cross, G. R. (1803), 445

Cross, John, 59
Crosse, Andrew (1802), 163
Croston, Edmund, 11, 20, 437
Crouchley, John (1730), 146
Crowder, Frederick (1864), 268, 454
Crowdy, W. M. (1885), 457
Crowe, William, **I**
Crowther, Robert (1786), 188, 442
Croxton, Thomas (1620), 51
Crozier, J., 403
Cruikshank, Robert, 199
Crumpton, Thomas (1650), 85
Cudden, J. A. B. (1949), 466
Culler, Jonathan, 417
Cullity, G. M. (1987), 474
Cumberland, Ernest, Duke of, 262
Cunningham, V. J. (1963), 470
Cunninghame, A. K. S. (1909), 461
Cunninghame, A. W. R. (1878), 456
Curran, P. V., 440
Currer, Henry (1748), 439
Currer, Mary Richardson, 191
Currey, J. B. (1848), 452
Currie, C. S. (1885), 457
Currie, William (1807), 446
Curthoys, M., 261
Curzon, Assheton (Curzon), 1st Viscount
    (1747), 117, 155, 438
Curzon, George Nathaniel; Marquess
    Curzon of Keddleston, 324–5
Curzon, N. C. (1847), 452
Curzon, Penn (1774), 108
Cuthbertson, David (1962), 469, 481

Dalgairns, J. D., 211
Dalton, Hugh; Baron, 425
Dalton, James (1587), 26, 39
Dalton, Richard (1578),
Dalwig, Baron Georg von (1910), 321
Daniel, Jim, v
Daniell, T. (1804), 446
Dansie, James (1734), 439
Darbie, Edward, 23, 155, 437
Darboy, Abp. Georges, 225–6
Darke, R. (1789), 443
Darling, D. I. (1945), 466
Darling, M. G. (1964), 469
Darlington, Joseph (1869), 249, 283

Dart, A. M. (1966), 470
Darwall, John (1752), 120
Darwall-Smith, R. F. H., (1934), 465
Darwall-Smith, Robin, v
Darwin, Charles, 279
Dashwood, Sir Francis, 1st Bt., 187–8
Dashwood, Sir Henry, 3rd Bt. (1763), 188
Dashwood, S. V. (1823), 449
Dashwood, T. J. R. (1929), 464
Daubeny, C., 210
Daubuz, John (1861), 265
Daunt, H. D. (1874), 455
Davenport, John (1858), 247
Davey, W. H. (1853), 453
Davidson, D. (1985), 473
Davie, John (1728), 438
Davies, H. A. (1936), 465
Davies, Hugh, 10
Davies, John W. (1954), v, 388, 406
Davies, L. E. C. (1928), 464
Davoud, John (1937), 479
Dawber, Sir Guy, 135, 292
Dawes, Ian (1966), 481
Dawkins, E. H. (1812), 447
Dawkins, James Annesley (1846), 205, 452
Dawkins, Peter (1959), 400, 468, 481
Dawson, Ambrose (1805), 446
Dawson, Christopher William (1919), **83B**
Dawson-Bowling, P. R. (1961), 469, 486
Day, George (1833), 450
Deacon, Thomas, 145, 148
Dean, Frank (1859), 257
Dean, John (1791), 185
Dean, J. M. (1947), 466
Dean, William (1659), 88
Deane, Thomas (1648), 64, 92
De Haes, A. C. (2006), 476
Dehn, Paul (1931), 351
Deiter, G. H. (1930), 479
Delafield, W. H. (1957), v
Delamotte, William, 188
Delane, John, 241
Denison, William, 128–30
Denman, Thomas; 2nd Baron (1823), 449
Dennys, N. C. J. (1970), 471
Dent, John, 196
De Quincey, Thomas, 162
Derby, Edward (Stanley), 14th Earl of, 169

Derby, Henry (Stanley), 4th Earl of, 39
Derby, James (Stanley), 7th Earl of, 53
De Villiers, Evangeline, Lady, 1
Dering, G. C. R. (1819), 449
Devis, Arthur William, **27,** 149
Devitt, Carol (1977), 482
Dewhurst, W. A. (1890), 458
Dibdin, Sir Robert, 306
Dibdin, Thomas Frognall, 191, 193–4, 196
Dicey, Albert, 316–7
Dickens, Charles, 214, 241, 295
Dickenson, William (1774), 108
Dickin, Joseph (1796), 444
Dighton, Robert, **24,** 161
Dimsdale, T. R. C. (1844), 452
Dirg (battelling), 55
Disney, H. A. S. (1936), 465
Disney, S. A. R. (1965), 470, 481
Disraeli, Benjamin; 1st Earl of
        Beaconsfield, xviii, 199, 305, 360
Dix, C. B. (1931), 440
Dixey, J. C. (1908), 461
Dixon, R. M. (1981), 473
Dixon, R. W., 237
Dobinson, Henry Hughes (1882), 299, 457
Dod, John (1698), 135
Dod, Thomas (1700), 127, 142
Dodd, P. W., 364
Dodds, J. A. (1960), 469
Dodman, David (2000), 483
Doggett, Wayne (1972), 482
Dolben, Sir William, 185
Dollinger, Ignaz von, 225
Domville, Randle (1621), 60
Donadoni, E. M. (2001), 476
Donaldson, W. P. (1891), 458
Dorrien, Thomas (1801), 445
Dorset, Bennett (1752), 151
Doughtie, John (1613), 44, 54
Douglas, T. H. (1954), 467
Doulton, A. J. F. (1934), 328, 485
Dow, Robert (1987), 482
Downer, Arthur Cleveland (1866), 264
Downer, William (1980), 482
Downham, M. A. P. S. (1958), 468
Doyne, J. (1808), 447
Drake, Bill, 336
Drake, Charles (1774), 108

Drake, C. T. (1806), 446
Drake, E. F. (1932), 479
Drake, G. T. (1812), 447
Drake, John (1798), 444
Drake, John Dean (1829), 450
Drake, J. T. (1808), 446
Drake, J. T. (1840), 217–8, 220, 451
Drake, T. T. (1801), 445
Drake, William (1739), 438
Drake, W. W. (1796), 444
Dreyer, Eric (1945), 480
Driffield, George Townshend (1835), 213
Drury, Henry, 191
Dryden, John, 130
Drysdale, D. (1925), 485
Drysdale, J. (1956), 467
Duby, John (1952), 480
Duckworth, Richard (1648), 64, 68, 71, 90
Du Croz, P. F. (1878), **58**
Duff, Colin (1925), 478
Duff, S. M. (1946), 466
Duffie, William (1937), 479
Duke, L. G. (1909), **74**
Dun, J. A. (1882), **59**
Dummer, Thomas Lee (1728), 438
Dunbar, Thomas (1801), 198
Duncan, Joyce (née Pilling), 440
Duncan, Rae (1936), 373
Duncan, Sir Val (1932), 440, 485
Duncombe, Edward (1820), 449
Duncombe, William Duncombe
    (1851), 204
Dundas, Robert, 364
Dunn, James (1859), **48,** 453
Dunn, William (1861), 266, 454
Dunning, John; 1st Baron Ashburton, 360
Duppa, Brian, 44
Durrant, C. C. T (1963), 469
Dutton, Henry (1641), 60
Du Vallon, H. C. de J. (1896), **66**
Durham, Hercules (1769), 151
Durham, James, Snr., 151
Dworkin, Ronald, 331
Dymocke, Robert (1553), 32, 33
Dyson, Janet, 421

Eagar, Desmond (1936), 347–8, 465
Earbury, William (1620), 56

Eardal, D.E. (1966), 470
Early, Stewart (1966), 470, 481
East, David, **41**, 251
Eastwick, Contance, 107
Eaton, Byrom (1633), 62, 63
Eaton, George Biddulph (1895),
    310–11, 459
Eaton, Ralph (1652), 65, 88, 438
Eaton, Robert (1577), 38, 39, 64, 71
Eaton, Robert (1643), 60
Eaude, Richard (1636), 60, 61, 62, 63
Eccles, Allan (1757), 151
Eckersley, Nathaniel ffarington (1875),
    440
Eden, Anthony; 1st Earl of Avon, 399
Eden, C. P., 227
Edmiston, J. H. F. (1925), 463
Edmondson, Thomas Grassyard (1854),
    236, 453
Edmundson, George (1867), 286
Edward, III, King, 9
Edwards, A. J. (1872), 455
Edwards, C. M. (1957), 468
Edwards, Evan (1889), 458
Edwards, John (1955), **92**
Edwards, R. D. M. (1993), 474
Edwards, Rhys (1993), 483
Edwards-Moss, Ian Cottingham (1874),
    269, 272, 289, 455
Egeland, Leif (1924), 337, 361
Egerton, Brooke de Malpas (1864),
    47A, 267
Egerton, George Henry (1840), 217–8
Egerton, Sir Holland, 4th Bt. (1704), 80,
    89, 135
Egerton, Sir John, 3rd Bt., 438
Egerton, Philip (1712), 107
Egerton, Rowland (later Warburton)
    (1798), 444
Egerton, T. W. (1802), 445
Egerton, Wilbraham (later Egerton-
    Tatton) (1800), 444
Eginton (glassmakers), 155, 164
Egleston, Harold (1904), 319, 460
Egleston, Vivian (1907), 319, 461
Eiffe, L G. P. (1902), 460
Elbrick, T. C. J. (1989), 474
Eldon, John (Scott), 1st Lord, 159

Eley, Charles (1892), 458
Eley, Humphrey (1552), 32, 33
Eley, William (1546), 29, 32, 33
Elgar, Charles (1930), 373
Elias, Michael (1988), 483
Eliot, George [Marian Evans], 172, 280
Eliot, T. S., 317
Elizabeth I, Queen, 17, 19, 23, 29, 31, 35, 40, 41
Elizabeth II, Queen, 381
Ellesmere, Thomas (Egerton); 1st Baron (1556), 3, 42, 44
Elliott, Wallace (1903), 317
Ellis, Sir Allan (1910), 485
Ellis, Jeremy (1959), 481
Ellis, William Webb (1825), 5, 219
Ellsworth, Paul (1922), 478
Elton, John, see Baker, John
Elton, Thomas (1589), 41, 155
Emms, D. A. (1947), 466, 485
Emden, A. B., 2
Enevoldson, T. P. (1975), 472
Engels, Friedrick, 238
Entwisle, Cecil (1867), 264, 454
Entwistle, Robert, 141
Erdeswick, Sampson (1553), 32, 33
Errington, J. L. (1847), 452
Erskine, Walter Henry; 11th Earl of Mar and 13th Earl of Kellie (1859), **48**, 265, 266, 453
Esher, Lionel (Brett), 4th Viscount, 424
Estwick, Sampson, 123
Evans, Arthur (1840), 218, 243
Evans, Sir Arthur (1870), 4, 9, 243, 261, 312, 315, 325, 366
Evans, C. H. (1917), 462
Evans, D. T. (1961), 469
Evans, E. (1920), 478
Evans, F. G. D. (1931), 347
Evans, Sir John (1903), 9
Evans, Lloyd (1951), 480
Evans, Margaret (née Freeman), 261
Evans, Powys, 342
Evans, R. J. W. (1969), v, 396, 417
Evanson, Thomas (1765), 151
Eveleigh, Sir Edward (1938), 485
Evelyn, John, 68, 91
Everard, Charles (1865), **47A**, 267

Evetts, William (1865), 270, 454
Eyton, R. W. (1807), 446

Fairbank, M. H. (1947), 466
Fairfax, Thomas; 3rd Lord Fairfax of Cameron, 57
Fairfax, V. C. (1929), **77**, 344
Fairlie, Henry, 424
Fallows, I. D., v, 119, 162, 165
Fane, Thomas (1552), 32
Fane, Thomas (1800), 444
Farington, Joseph, 163
Farington, Robert (1777), 163,168, 179
Farmer, Guy (1936), 479
Farmer and Brindley, (marbling), 294
Farnaby, Sir Charles, Bt. (1807), 446
Farnham, G. F. (1878), **58**, 456
Farquhar, Francis (1858), **48**, 264, 453
Farquharson, G. A. R. (1927), 478
Farrand, Richard (1650), 64
Farrell, J. G. (1953), 4
Farrer, J. W. (1802), 445
Farrer, Oliver (1802), 445
Farrer, Richard (1793), 443
Farrer, Thomas (1805), 165, 186, 446
Farrer, William (1805), 186, 446
Farrow, D. N. (1966), 470
Faulkner, C. J., 237–40
Fausset, Godfrey, 231
Fawkes, Ayscough (1824), 449
Fayle, Richard (1815), 448
Fazakerley, John (1774), 108
Fazakerley, Nicholas (1702), 144
Featly, John (1605), 107, 132–3
Feilden, Sir William (1790), 443
Feiling, Sir Keith, 341
Feld, A. S. (2004), 476
Feldman, Daniel (1958), 481
Fell, Samuel, 59, 64
Fellows, Edward Lyon (1864), 265, 270, 454
Fellows-Smith, J. P. (1952), 400, 467
Fenwicke, John (1780), 120
Fenwicke-Clennell, T. P. E. (1905), 460
Ferguson, T. B. (1855), 453
Fergusson, Robert, 130
Fermor, William, 20

Fernel, Jean, 47
Ferrand, Richard (1650), 85
Fickling, S. A. (2001), 475
Fiddian, W. A. (1899), 440
Fiddian-Green, W. B. (1924), 478
'Field, Michael' [Katherine Bradley and Edith Cooper], 276
Finch, C. W. (1797), 444
Finch-Hatton, Hon. Denys (1907), 319, 460
Findlay, A. C. (1936), 479
Firth, Sir Charles, 340
Fisher, Edward (1627), 52
Fisher, G. C. (1863), 454
Fisher, Henry (1559), 437
Fisher, Herbert, **43**
Fisher, H. A. L., 300, 333
Fisher, St. John; Bp., 12
Fisher, Michael (1935), 374
Fitzclarence, Lord Augustus (1824), 190
Fitzgibbon, C. P. J. (1974), 471
Fitz-Patrick, Hon. B. E. B.; 2nd Lord Castletown (1867), 454
Flaubert, Gustave, 275
Flecker, J. W. (1958), 468
Fleissner, Erwin (1957), 481
Fletcher, J. M. (1996), 475
Fletcher, Stephen (1742), 154
Flynn, J. E. (1974), 471
Fogg, John (1638), 85
Foley, Andrew (1768), 439
Foley, Edward (1764), 439
Foley, John (1760), 108
Fondas, Nanette (1981), 482
Forbes, Alexander Penrose (1840), 4, 217–8, 222–6, 236
Ford, John (1805), 165
Forder, C. P. (1926), 478
Foreman, Margaret, 392
Forester, G. T. (1824), 449
Forrest, Robert (1788), 100
Fortescue, Hugh (Ebrington); 2nd Earl (1800), 444
Foster, Carol (1905), 477
Foster, John (1561), 22
Foster, John (1960), 430
Fourie, I. S. (1922), 478
Fourier, Francis, 216

Fowler, Alastair (1952), 390
Fowler, Thomas, 299
Fox, Herbert (1877), **67**, 309, 315, 317–8, 320
Fox, Justin (1991), 483
Fox, N. J. P. (1979), 472
Fox, Bp. Richard, 16
Foxe, John (1532), 4, 11, 20, 29, 30, 31, 50
Foxley, Thomas (1730), 121–2, 146
Fraley, Douglas (1988), 483
Francis, Charles (1768), 151
Francis, Charles King (1869), **55**, 271, 454
Franckland, Thomas (1649), 66
Francklin, Henry (1866), 454
Franco, R. [later Sir Ralph Lopes, 2nd Bt.] (1807), 185, 200, 446
Frankland, Mrs. Joyce (née Trappes), **10**, 23, 24, 77, 155, 202, 437
Franklin, B. L. S. (1938), 479
Franks, Frank (1933), 479
Franks, Oliver; Baron, 363, 387, 425–6
Fraser, P. M. (1937), 350, 379, 389
Freake, Robert (1610), 52
Frederick William III; King of Prussia, 165
Freeman, Edward Augustus, 6, 80, 261
Freeman, George (1682), 99, 124
Frere, G. R. (1907), 461
Frere, Laurie (1885), 303
Frere, P. R. (1910), 461, 485
Frewin, Richard, 141
Frogley, Arthur, 82
Froude, Hurrell, 210
Fry, C. B., **45**, 270
Fry, Roger, 246
Fulford, William, 237–40
Fuller, Isaac, **15**
Fuller-Meyrick, O. J. A. (1822), 449
Fulton, James (1966), 432
Funcker, Elizabeth (née Woods), 62
Furnivall, Richard (1646), 60
Fyson, H. J. (1996), 475

Gadd, Cyril John (1912), 440
Gaitskell, Hugh, 387
Gale, B. H. (1948), 466
Galsworthy, John, 353
Gamul, Thomas (1587), 54
Garbett, Edward (1837), 213–4

Garbett, James (1819), 211, 214, 229
Garden, Robert (1806), 169, 446
Gardiner, Bp. James, 94
Gardiner, Stephen, 404
Gardiner, T. G. (1877), 456
Gardner, A. D. (1980), 473
Gardner, James (1938), 479
Garland, Ross (1999), 483
Garms, Michael (1954), 481
Garnett, E. P. (1864), 454
Garnett, H. (1861), 453
Garnett, Lionel (1862), 266, 454
Garnett, William (1835), 219
Garrard, C. B. D. (1823), 449
Garside, Charles (1837), 212, 223
Garthwaite, P. F. (1928), 464
Gartside Neville, H. A. (1911), 461
Gass, David (1969), 481
Gasser, Robert (1953), 395, 406, 429–30
Gauci, P. L. (1986), 473
Gawne, E. M. (1908), **74**
Gee, G. S. (1926), 463
Gemmill, A. W. (1956), 468
Gennys, John (1769),
George I, King, 128, 145
George II, King, 147
George III, King, 152, 182, 360
Gerard, Charles (1649), 64
Gerard, Ratcliffe (1639), 52
German, A. C. J. (1924), 463
Germaine, Robert Arthur (1874), 439
Giambologna, **19**, 138–40
Gibbes, James Alban (1673), 87
Gibbon, Edward, 114, 302, 392
Gibbon, John (1866), 270
Gibbons, Grinling, **22**, 118
Gibbs, A. G. F. (1913), **73**
Gibbs, James, 141
Gibson, C. A. W. (1972), 471
Gibson, Bp. Edmund, 133
Gibson, Ian (1954), 400
Gibson, Sir Ralph (1941), 485
Gibson, Thomas, **22**, 118
Gibson, W. H. M. (1980), 473
Gilbert, Bp. Ashurst Turner (1805), **34,** 156, 187, 202–3, 208, 210–12, 222, 436
Gilbert, C. G. (1913), **72, 73**
Gilbert, David (1952), 480

Gilbert, Elizabeth, 212
Gilbert, Joseph (1907), 477
Gildart, Thomas (1774), 108
Gill, Eric, 299
Gill, John (1771), 120
Gill, R. D. (1946), 486
Gillette, Michael (1959), 468, 481
Gillray, James, **I**, 181
Gilman, John (1649), 64
Girardot, J. C. (1817), 448
Gladstone, William Ewart, 223, 226, 230
Glass, D. V., 412
Glasse, George, 180
Glasse, Samuel, 180
Glegg, W. B. (1841), 451
Glendole, John (1650), 64, 91
Glover, George (1797), 163
Glyn, Richard (1804), 200
Glynne, Sir John, 72
Godby, C. V., 285
Gokuldas (later Muraji), M. D. M. (1915), 337
Golding, Alec, 367
Golding, C. W. (1802), 445
Golding, E. (1828), 450
Golding, Sir William (1930), 4, 367–9
Goldsmith, Jonathan (1712), 107
Goldstein, Joel (1975), 482
Goldstone, S. L. (1993), 474
Golightly, Charles, 231
Goodman, Christopher (1536), 30
Goodman, George (1952), 480
Goodyear, Frederick (1905), 305, 318–20
Gordon, Cameron (1907), 461
Gordon, George (1841), 451
Gordon, George (1938), 378, 383, 386
Gordon, S. E. L. (1911), **72,** 320–21
Gore, Bp. Charles, 325
Gorges, Sir Richard, 1st Bt.; later Meredyth (1752), 105
Gorham, George, 212, 223
Gorringe, Peter (1863), **47A**, 267
Gorringe, R. E. P. (1893), 459
Gorton, John (1932), 4, 344
Gosling, Sir Ellis, 439
Gosse, Edmund, 246
Gott, Bp. John (1849), 452
Gottstein, H. K. G. (1936), 370

Gough, Robert (1860), 307
Gowing, J., 274
Gowlland, P. Y. (1881), **58**, 457
Grace, W. G., 327
Grafton, George (Fitzroy), 4th Duke of, 182
Graham, Alastair (1926), 343–4, 463
Graham, Alastair Hugh ['Sebastian'] (1923), 4, 354–7
Graham, J. D. (1892), 458
Graham, Mrs. Jessie (nee Low), 354, 356
Grant, Arthur (1862), 266, 454
Grant, A. D. (1919), 339, 379, 382–3, 462, 485
Grant, William (1796), 444
Grasty, Samuel (1649), 85
Gratias, Orwald (1930), 479
Gray, Michael (1935), 479
Green, Mrs. Alice (née Stopford), 278
Green, Mrs. Charlotte (née Symonds), 278
Green, D. M. (1958), 400
Green, J. R., 261, 275, 276
Green, S. E. A. (1962), v, 347
Green, Thomas, **41**, 251
Green, T. H., 275
Greenall, Jack (1907), 323, 461
Greenall, Richard (1848), 268
Greene, Anne, 67
Greene, Edward (1723), 100, 101–2, 108
Greene, Robert, 7
Greenfield, James (1828), 450
Greenhill, C. B. (1899), 460
Greenland, D. T. (1966), 470
Greenstock, J. W. (1924), 463
Greenstreet, P. A. R. (1952), 467
Greenwood, Daniel (1624), 47, 59, 61, 62, 63, 65, 68, 70, 71, 74, 80, 86, 91, 436
Greenwood, Daniel (1645), 63, 65, 438
Greenwood, Moses (1659), 87
Greenwood, Nathaniel (1653), 63, 65, 86
Gregson, William (1806), 170, 446
Grenville, Lord George; 1st Baron Nugent (1804), 162, 163, 185, 186, 445
Grenville, William (Wyndham), 1st Baron, **I**, 169, 173, 181–2
Gresley, Sir Thomas, 175
Greville, William, 21
Grey, Booth (1800), 445

Grey, Sir Charles, 196
Grey, Harry (1802), 445
Grey, Roger, 8
Grey, T. C. (1963), 469
Grieveson, J. A. (1923), 478
Griffith, Idwal O. (1898), 339, 361
Griffith, Matthew (1615), 53
Griffiths, T. S. (1914), **73**
Grimald, Nicholas, 30
Grimbald, of St. Bertin, 6, 7
Grimbaldson, William, 168, 438
Grimshaw, Samuel (1827), 223
Grimston, George (1649), 118
Grinalds, John (1960), 468, 481
Grint, M. C. (1954), 467
Grissell, Hartwell (1859), **42A–B, 48, 51,** 257, 264
Grissell, Thomas, 257
Gronow, Thomas (1816), 448
Grosvenor, Sir Robert, 6th Bt. (1712), 107
Grosvenor, Sir Thomas, 5th Bt. (1712), 107
Grove, Sir William (1829), 4, 313
Grover, J. N. (1934), 347, 465
Groves, Charles, 351
Groves, Peter (1989), v
Grundy, George (1888), 299, 302, 303
Grundy, James, 119
Guest, J. G. (1930), **77**, 344, 464
Guest, W. C. C. (1956), 468
Guettée, Francis (later Vladimir), 226
Guise, J. L. (1922), 462
Gumbleton, John (1859), **48**, 257, 453
Gumbleton, Richard (1803), 445
Gunasekaran, Ganesh (1993), 483
Gunning, G. W. (1847), 452
Gunning, S. G. (1818), 448
Gwyer, Samuel Keate (1869), 263
Gwyn, William (1751), 95, 154, 156, 436

Häcker, Birke (1997), 432
Haddon, Giles (1752), 151
Hadfield, R. A. (1987), 474
Hadow, Walter (1868), **55**, 271, 454
Haig, Douglas; 1st Earl (1880), **58**, 3, 295–8, 302, 308, 313–4, 323, 330, 407, 456

Haigh, Gordon (1856), 256, 453
Hakewill, Henry, 81, 168
Halcomb, Thomas (1852), 239
Haldane, H. C. (1890), 458
Hall, G. L. (1844), 451
Hall, Henry, 143
Hall, Sir Noel (1921), **95**, 119, 362, 387–8,
    403, 406, 436
Hall, Samuel (1806), 169, 204
Hallam, Henry, 302
Halliwell, Henry (1783), **26**, 163,
    179, 197–8
Halpern, Sue (1977), 482
Halstead, George (1638), 60
Halstead, J. L. (1936), **81, 84**, 372
Hamer, James (1649), 438
Hamilton, Charles (1950), 480
Hamilton, P. J. (1958), 468
Hamilton, Sir William, 230
Hammelmann, H. A. (1935), 479
Hammond, E. C. B. (1949), 401, 466
Hammond, George (1710), 134
Hammond-Chambers-Borgnis, J. A.
    (1903), 460
Hampden, John, 53
Hampden, Renn Dixon, 202–3, 209, 210
Hampel, A. J. (1992), 474
Hampshire, Stuart, 418
Hanbury, H. G., 311
Hanmer, John (1801), 445
Hanmer, Thomas (1831), 450
Hanson, Craig (1992), 483
Harcourt, Arthur (1945), 480
Harcourt, Simon; 1st Viscount, 131, 143
Harding, Jane (1978), 482
Harding, R. F. (1933), 465
Harding, Richard Whitfield (1947), 441
Hardinge, William Money, 281
Hardman, John, 204
Hardwick, Philip, **20B**, 79, 155, 167
Hardy, Thomas, 273, 352
Hare, Augustus, 20
Hargreaves, John (1822), 449
Harington, Mrs. Cecilia, 230
Harington, Richard (1818), **35**, 186, 188,
    190, 203–5, 208, 210, 222, 229,
    230–32, 236, 242, 436, 449
Harington, Sir Richard, 11th Bt., 204

Harlow, E.D.G. (1923), 463
Harlow, Vincent (1919), 349, 362
Harper, George (1779), 179, 191
Harpur, Sir Henry, 5th Bt. (1725), 438
Harpur, Richard, 15, 23, 437
Harries, John (1774), 108
Harris, Charles; later Harris-St. John
    (1861), **42A**, 264–5, 266, 439, 454
Harris, Frank, 282–3, 320
Harris, James Parker (1841), 205
Harris, M. W. A. (1925), 463
Harris, Richard (1559), 29, 39, 40, 436
Harris, Robert, 59
Harris, W. C. (1860), **56, 57**
Harris, George; 5th Baron, 271
Harrison, D. G. (1953), 467
Harrison, Frederick, 215
Harrison, G. P. (1958), 468
Harrison, Hamlett (1783), 163
Harrison, Sir Heath, 1st Bt. (1876),
    350, 439
Harrison, R. B. (1913), **73**
Harrison, T. M. (1985), 473
Harrison-Wallace, C. I. C. (1958), 468
Hart, Derek (1976), 472, 482
Hart, George, 376
Hart, H. L. A. (1936), **95**, 331, 392, 406,
    417–9, 436
Hart, Mrs. Jenifer (née Williams), 418
Hart, T. M. (1930), 347
Harter, A. R. H. (1876) 456,
Hartley, J. C. (1893), 458
Hartlib, Samuel, 67
Hartopp, Sir Edmund Cradock, 1st
    Bt. (formerly Bunney), 247
Hartshorne, Charles, 193, 195
Harvey, Christopher (1613), 39
Harvey, John (1625), 85
Harvey, Trevor (1930), **92**
Harvey, William (1819), 448
Haslewood, J. S. O. (1929), 345, 464, 485
Haslewood, Joseph, 194
Haster, John (c. 1510), 20
Hatch, Edwin, 237
Hatchard, Thomas Goodwin (1837),
    213, 214
Hatherley, Colin (1950), 480
Haverfield, Francis John (1879), 4, 325

Hawarden, John (1515), 27, 28, 29, 436
Hawarden, Thomas (1530), 27, 33
Hawes, R. J. S. (1959), 468
Hawkins, John, **41**, 250–51
Hawksworth, C. E. M., 362
Hawksmoor, Nicholas, **18**, 137–8
Hay, D. O. (1935), 465
Hay-Cooper, W. A. (1933), 465
Hayes, Thomas (1657), 91
Hayes, D. R. (1960), 468
Hayes, F. W. (1878), 456
Hayhurst, Joseph (1637), 85
Hayward, Richard, 139
Haywood, Thomas, 55
Head, Sir E., 206
Heap, William (1861), 265, 266, 453
Hearn, John ['J.C.R. Spider'], **49**
Hearne, Thomas, 67, 96, 98, 114, 123,
    126, 127, 132, 133, 138
Heath, Arthur (1875), 271, 299
Heath, James, 89
Heath, J. G. (1898), 459
Heath, R. A. (1905), 460
Heath, Thomas, 55
Heathcote, Sir W., 248
Heber, Reginald, Snr., 174, 180
Heber, Bp. Reginald (1800), **30**, 4, 164,
    171, 174, 177, 183, 188, 193, 196–8,
    284, 309, 445
Heber, Richard (1746), 439
Heber, Richard (1790), 4, 173–5, 177,
    179–85, 191–6, 445
Heber, Thomas (1802), 174, 445
Heber-Percy, Algernon, v
Heberden, Charles Buller (1868), **67**, 1,
    191, 275, 286, 292, 295, 300–2,
    304, 306, 309, 311–12, 315–6, 322,
    326–7, 329, 342, 381, 436, 439
Hedges, John, **41**, 251
Heerden, Belinda van (1982), 421
Hefelé, Carl Joseph von, 225
Hefty, Elaine (1979), 482
Henderson, J. H. (1952), 400
Henley, Hugh, 438
Hennessy, P. K. (1926), 478
Henrick, Keith (1947), 480
Henry, VII, King, 11, 12
Henry, VIII, King, 11, 13

Henry, Prince, 39
Henry, Arthur (1858), **48**, 453
Henry, D. P. (1955), 467
Henshall, Samuel (1782), 120
Henshaw, Henry (1543), 32
Henwood, Desmond (1945), 480
Herbert, George, 55
Heron, William (1786), 188, 442
Herring, Fiona (2003), 484
Hertzell, D. J. (1974), 471
Herz, Laura (2002), 423
Hesketh, Robert (1781), 188, 442
Heskins, Samuel (1648), 64
Hester, Edmund (1985), 401
Heuston, R. V. F., 331
Hewison, Robert (1962), 410
Heyes (battelling), 55
Heylin, Peter, 89, 93
Heywood, Robert (1628), 47
Hibbert, George, 196
Hickingbotham, J. C. (1931), 464, 479
Hicks-Beach, Sir Michael, 332
Hidden, Nicholas (1935), 368
Higden, Brian, 23, 155, 437
Higgins, Edward (1576), 39
Higginson, Thomas (1645), 64
Highfield, Edmund (1632), 62, 63
Hilditch, I. G. (1980), 473
Hill, C. J. S. (1952), 467
Hill, Charles (1829), 450
Hill, C. B. (1976), 431
Hill, C. V. (1919), 462
Hill, F. E. (1911), **75**, 461
Hill, Gordon (1946), 480
Hill, K., 425
Hill, Richard (1607), 44, 46, 62
Hill, Rowland (1794), 444
Hill, Thomas (1815), 448
Hillary, Richard, 375–6
Hilton, J. K. (1970), 471
Hincks, T. C. (1805), 446
Hinde, Thomas (1659), 82
Hindley, John Haddon (1784),
    191, 442
Hinton, John, Viscount; later 5th Earl
    Poulett (1801), 445
Hinton, John, **41**, 251
Hitchens, Christopher, 418

Hitchcock, Thomas (1880), **58**, 296, 456

Hobbes, Thomas, 67, 89, 271, 330, 362–3, 418

Hobhouse, Benjamin (1774), 108

Hobhouse, Henry (1758),

Hobhouse, Henry (1793), 175

Hoch, Peter (1938), 479

Hodgkin, Howard, 417

Hodgkinson, D. A. (1928), 464

Hodgkinson, Joseph (1792), 185

Hodgson, John (1545), 29

Hodson, Frodsham (1787), **I, 25,** 146, 164–5, 168–9, 170, 172–4, 180–85, 188, 194, 197, 228, 231, 240, 261, 290, 436, 442

Hodson, George (1757), 120

Hodson, Grenville Heber Frodsham (1839), 164

Hoexter, Cora (1983), 482

Holbourn, A. (2003), 476

Holborne, Robert (1613), 53

Holden, G. R. (1931), 479

Holder, Douglas (1962), 417

Holdsworth, R. W. G. (1930), **77, 85,** 344, 361, 375, 464

Holdsworth, Sir William, 375

Hole, R. A. (1850), 452

Hole, Samuel Reynolds (1840), 217–22, 451

Holland, Claude (1886), 289

Holland, D. (2006), 476

Holland, W. F. C. (1886), 303, 457

Holmes, Sir Charles (1887), **39B**, 303, 305

Holmes, Geoffrey, 394

Holmes, John (1763), 125, 439

Holmes, Robert (1532), 27

Holroyd, Mrs. Winifred (née Colwill), 364

Holroyd, Michael (1911), 339, 344, 356, 363–4, 366–8, 384

Holt, Sir John, 96

Holt, William (1565), 35

Honoré, A. M., 418

Hood, Paul, 56

Hooman, C. V.L. (1907), 461

Hope, A. J. B. Beresford, 223, 225, 236

Hope, Ronald (1939), **92**

Hopkins, Gerard Manley, 276–7

Hopkins, H. J. (1934), 479

Hopwood, C. A. (1866), 454

Horan, John (1908), 477

Hordern, Joseph (1813), 447

Hordern, Peter (1816), 448

Hornby, E. T. S. (1800), 445

Hornby, George (1808), 12, 161, 172, 181, 439

Hornby, Henry, 12

Hornby, H. P. (1868), 445

Hornby, J. J. (1845), 247–8, 268

Hornby, William (1870), 264

Horne, Bp. Robert, 29

Hornsby, Arabella, 198

Hornsby, Thomas, 198

Horowitz, Charles (1927), 478

Horovitz, Michael (1954), 399, 478

Horsley, David (1953), 480

Horwood, C. H. R. (1888), 458

Hoskins, W. L. (1913), **73**

Houghton, John (1625), 47, 49, 60, 62, 64–5, 70, 77, 84

Houghton, Thomas, 121

Houghton, William (1847), 268

Housman, A. E., 363

Hovde, H. L. (1929), 345, 478

Howard, Brian, 356–7

Howard, Thomas (1790), 443

Howard Smith, C. (1907), 461

Howe, John (1648), 65

Howe, S. W. (1993), 474

Hoyle, Nathaniel (1650), 64

Huddesford, Mrs., 113

Huddesford, George, 132

Huddesford, William, 132

Hudson, George, 231

Hudson, William (1920), 478

Hugeloot, John, 83

Huggins, C. R. (1905), 461

Hughes, J. G. P. (1856), 453

Hughes, John (1838), 451

Hughes, W. J. M. (1876), 456

Huish, John (1790), 443

Hull, Laurence (1907), 477

Hull, R. A. (1929), 378, 381, 395

Hulme, Banastre, 119

Hulme, George (1781), 442

Hulme, John (1625), 119

Hulme, Samuel (1632), 119
Hulme, Thomas (1586), 119
Hulme, William (1648), 95, 118–9, 262, 381, 438
Hulse, E. H. (1877), 456
Hulton, Ralph (1646), 60
Hulton, William (1804), 178, 446
Humphreys, Alice, 440
Humphreys, Edith, 440
Humphreys, J. C. (1900), 460
Hunt, E. O. W. (1934), 465
Hunt, F. D. (1871), 455
Hunter, Charles (1975), 482
Hunter, R. J. (1906), 460
Huntingdon, Ferdinando (Hastings); 6th Earl of, 228
Huntingdon, Henry (Hastings), 3rd Earl of, 78
Hurndall, D. A. (1969), 471
Hussey, John; Baron, 28
Hutchins, Edward (1576), 49
Hutchins, William (1602), 46, 438
Hutchinson, Charles (1873), 283
Hutchinson, Daniel (1964), 481
Hutchison, R. H. (1909), 321
Huxley, Aldous, 277
Huxley, Charles (1716), 134
Huyshe, F. J. (1860), **56**
Hyde, John (1688), 124
Hynes, W. S. (1923), 478

Illingworth, Stonehewer (1861), 256, 266, 453
Ince, Peter (1630), 51, 85
Ince, Townsend (1823), 449
Inge, Theodore (1729), 115
Ingham, F. R. (1995), 475
Ingham, J. H. (1933), 464
Ingleby, Charles (1662), 84
Ingleby, Francis (1562), 35
Ingram, Arthur (1904), 319
Ingram (of Rivel), 142
Ingram, Charles (1898), 310
Ingram, R. I. (1947), 466
Ingram, R. K. (1949), 485
Irby, Hon. Llewellyn (1840), 217
Irwin, Rich (Ingram), 5th Viscount, 142
Isham, Sir Charles, 10th Bt. (1840), 4, 217

Isham, Henry Charles (1795), 444
Isham, Vere (1792), 443
Isherwood, Francis (1870), 271

Jack, Ian (1947), 390
Jackson, A. N. Strode (1910), **75, 80,** 5, 322, 461
Jackson, E. B. (1914), 477
Jackson, Gilbert, **11, 14,** 24, 41
Jackson, G. P. (1946), 465
Jackson, H. Hall (1910), **75,** 321, 461
Jackson, John (surveyor), 77–8, 80
Jackson, John (1774), 108
Jackson, John (artist), 162
Jackson, Richard, 273
Jackson, Samuel (1726), 439
Jackson, Thomas (1646), 60
Jackson, Sir Thomas Graham, **70, 71,** 135, 164, 290–5, 404
Jacobs, A. R. (1914), **73**
Jacobson, Raymond (1948), 480
Jacques, E. W. R. (1913), 321
Jacques, William Baldwin (1882), 299
James I, King, 44, 75
James II, King, 68, 91–95, 97, 130, 230
James III (Old Pretender), 93–4, 142–3
James, Alfred (1864), **47A,** 267
James, Henry, 276
James, Rolfe Scott (1897), 310
Janion, Richard (1809), 185
Janion, Joseph, 185
Janvrin, Robin; Baron (1966), 431, 470, 486
Jee, J. N. (1981), 473
Jeffery, R. W. (1895), **83B,** 141, 362–3, 440
Jeffery, Mrs. Ursula, **83B**
Jelf, W. E., 208
Jenkin, Frewin (1908), 361
Jenkins, C. E. (1894), 458
Jenkinson, Alfred (1896), 315
Jenkinson, A. J. (1900), **67,** 316–7, 326, 361, 364
Jenkinson, W. J. (1968), 470
Jenner, Charles (1724), 143
Jenner, R. F. (1820), 449
Jepsen, Charles (1947), 480
Jephson, William (1624), 51
Jersey, Earl of, 185
Jeune, Francis, 230, 248

Jeune, Mrs. Margaret (née
    Symons), 230
Joachim, H. H., 364
Jodrell, Edmund (1798), 178, 444
John, Jeffrey (1972), 409
Johnson, Arthur (1924), 478
Johnson, Ben, 41
Johnson, Charles Henry, 181
Johnson, C. T. (1804), 446
Johnson, Ernest (1888), 303, 458
Johnson, J. G. (1848), 452
Johnson, Lawrence [*alias* Richardson]
    (1570), 34, 36
Johnson, Lionel, 260
Johnson, Michelle (1981), 482
Johnson, R. H. (1799), 444
Johnson, Samuel, 149, 249
Johnston, A. A. (1932), 373
Johnston, C. M. (1913), **73**
Johnston, Carruthers Melville (1928), **77,**
    343–4, 464
Johnston, D. C. (1913), 321
Johnston, D. D. (1970), 471
Johnston, H.A. S. (1932), 465
Jones, A. O. (1948), 397
Jones, C. D. (1989), 474
Jones, Ellis (1894), **66**
Jones, Ernest, 262
Jones, Inigo, 38, 137
Jones, Llewellyn; later Atherley-Jones
    (1869), 262–3, 285
Jones, N. H. (1980), 473
Jones, Philip (1940), 394–5, 417
Jones, Robert (1642), 62, 64, 438
Jones, Theophilus (1842), 203
Jones, T. L. (1929), 464
Jones, Vincent (1953), 400, 480
Jordan, Amos (1947), 480
Jordan, Mrs. Dorothy (née Phillips), 190
Jordan, Stuart (1958), 481
Jose, Anthony (1949), 400, 480
Jowett, Benjamin, 215, 235, 242, 246, 254,
    259, 276, 281–2
Judge, Harry (1948), v, 379, 413, 418
Juett, Alexander (1906), 477
Jupp, A. D. (1921), 462
Jupp, John Ambrose, 440
Jussell, Jeffry, 8

Kahn-Freund, Sir Otto (1964), 388,
    417, 423
Kalis, Peter (1973), 482
Kaufmann, P. G. D. (1971), 471
Keay, G. A. (1916), 462
Keble, John, 203, 211, 215, 223–4
Keet, Raymond (1926), 478
Kelleher, J. D. (1972), 471
Kelsey, Thomas, 62
Kemble, J. M., 120
Kemp, D. S. (1949), 466
Kemp, G. A. R. (1998), 475
Kemp, Thomas Reade, 215
Kempe, Charles Eamer, **54,** 80, 204,
    289, 295
Kendall, William (1904), 477
Kenrick, John (1750), 116
Kennett, Bp. White, 127
Kent, J. de R. (1928), **77,** 344
Kent, J. R. E. (1956), 468
Kent, Samuel (1774), 109
Kent, William (1886), 303, 344, 457
Kenyon, A. R. (1839), 451
Kenyon, George (1750), 116
Kenyon, Lloyd; 1st Baron, 116
Kenyon, Robert, 141
Kenyon, T. (1795), 444
Keppel, Sir Henry, **43**
Ker, A. (1923), 338
Ker, Gervas (1775), 151
Ker, J. G. S. (1933), 465
Ker, R. S. (1889), 459
Ker, T. R. (1873), 455
Kershaw, John (1645), 64
Kettle, Tilly, **28,** 154
Kewley, E. R. (1907), 461
Key, K. J., 285
Keynes, John Maynard; Baron, 67, 387
Khaleeli, Abbas (1927), 351
Khattak, Mohammad (1929), 351
Killery, V. St. J. (1919), 462
Kimpton, R. C. M. (1934), 347, 465
Kimpton, S. M. (1932), 440, 464
Kinderton, Baron, 55
King, Bert, 336, 374
King, Bryan (1831), 261
King, Edmund, **90,** 407–8
King, Herbert, 407

King, John (1804), 446
King, Percy, 407
King, Robert (1629), 59–62
King, Sam Snr., 407
King, Sam Jnr., 407
King, William, 103
Kingsley, Charles, 238, 241, 259, 265
Kingsmill, Andrew, 39
Kininmonth, Peter (1946), 346, 466
Kinkead-Weekes, Marcus (1951), 467, 480
Kinkead-Weekes, Noel (1946), 480
Kipling, Rudyard, 4, 237, 241
Kirchberg, Jerome (1967), 470, 481
Kittermaster, P. F. S. (1951), 466
Knight, C. R. (1957), 468
Knight, Richard Payne, 198
Knightley, J. W. (1821), 449
Knightley, Lucy (1760), 439
Knollys, Erskine William (1861),
 42A–B, 264
Knott, C. H. (1920), 346, 401, 462
Knott, F. H. (1910), **75**, 322, 346, 461
Knott, J. W. (1840), **38**, 222, 247, 261
Knox, John, 30
Knox, J. H. (1905), 460
Knox, Ronald, 385
Knox, Vicesimus, 159, 223
Koch, Andre (1998), 483
Kochmann, G. (1936), 370
Koehn, Daryl (1977), 482
Kolkhorst, George, 357
Koronka, P. (1972), 471
Kossuth, Louis, 326
Krebs, Thomas (2002), 423
Kuhn, Christina (2004), 484
Kurti, Nicholas (1945), 378, 395, 417, 423
Kynaston, John (1746), 99–100
Kysel, P. (1968), 399, 470

Lach-Szyrma, Wladyslaw (1859), 257
Laird, A. A. F. (1991), 474
Laird, John, 364
Lake, Edward, 54
Lake, W. C., 235
Lamb, Karl (1959), 481
Lambert, Brooke (1854), 237, 242
Lamerie, Paul de, 105
Lance, H. P. (1852), 452

Landale, David (1860), **57**, 256
Landale, Peter (1934), 372
Landon, Philip (1906), **74**, 319
Landow, George, 417
Lane, S. E. R. (1882), 457
Langford, Charles, 437
Langford, H. J. (1788), 442
Langman, N. J.A. (1980), 472
Lanham, Michael (2000), 483
Larcom, Sir Thomas, 68
Larking, Lambert Blackwell (1816), 190
Lascelles, Hon. Henry, 183
Last, Hugh Machilwain (1914), 339, 378–9,
 381–3, 386, 392–4, 397, 436, 440, 485
Latham, Francis Law (1856), 237,
 241–2, 439
Latham, John (1778), 188, 442
Latham, John (1803), 446
Latham, P. A. (1861), 265–6, 453
Lathbury, Daniel (1850), 239
Latimer, A. (1961), 469
Latimer, Bp. Hugh, 11, 38
Laud, Abp. William, 42, 44–5, 53, 59, 75,
 84–5, 93
Laura, R. S. (1972), 471
Law, J. P. (1863), 454
Law, William, 145
Law, William (1870), 271, 455
Lawes, Sir John (1833), 313
Lawrence (non-juror), 127
Lawrence, T. E., 363
Lawrie, Ian (1929), 373
Lawrie, J. C. (1935), 465
Lawson, Charles, 146
Lawson, F. H. (1915), 388, 417
Lawson, Jeannie (1974), 421
Lea, Edward (1581), 41
Leach, Colin (1951), 398
Leach, R. Burton (1855), **48, 56, 57**, 266
Leach, Thomas (1901), 319
Leadam, Isaac Saunders (1867), 13, 15,
 287, 304
Leage, R. W., **67**, 316–7, 327
Leche, John (1528), 27
Leckie, J. L. (1948), 397
Ledlie, J. K. (1960), 469
Lee, A. M. (1932), 464
Lee, Frederick George, 226

Lee, M. (1946), 465
Lee, P. H. (1858), **48**, 453
Lee, Vernon [Violet Paget], 274, 282
Leech, Humphrey (1590), 35–6, 39
Leech, John, 221
Legendre, Morris (1926), 478
Legge, G. B. (1922), 346, 349, 367, 372, 463
Legge, J. J. (1979), 473
Legh, Calverley (1702), 126
Legh, John, 8
Legh, Sir Peter, 66
Legh, R. C. (1837), 451
Legh, Thomas (1608), 47
Leicester, Peter (1629), 52
Leicester, Sir Peter, 4th Bt. (formerly
    Byrne) (1750), 155, 439
Leicester, Robert (Dudley), Earl of, 34
Leigh, A. E. (1873), 455
Leigh, Edmund (1600), 46
Leigh, G. E. (1790), 443
Leigh, R. E. (1887), 458
Leigh, Thomas (1631), 52
Leigh, Trafford; later Trafford Trafford
    (1789), 442
Leigh, William (1571), 38–9
Leigh, William (1819), 223
Leith, Alexander (1888), 303
Leith, W. A. (1888), 457
Le Long, Jacques, 191
Le Mesurier, John (1805), 165
Le Neve, Sir William, 54
Lennox-Boyd, Hon. C. A., v
Lenthal, William (1723), 108
Leschallas, P. P. (1898), 459
Lever, Sir Darcy (1722), 147, 438
Lewsley, B. P. (2002), 476
Levy, R. S. (1954), 467
Lewes, Pryce (1814), 448
Lewes, Thomas (1811), 447
Lewis, C. S., **32**, 4, 337
Lewis, David Leopold, 440
Lewis, Rosa, 354
Leybourne, Robert (1711), 131–2
Leycester, Charles (1814), 448
Leycester, Sir Peter, 1st Bt. (1629), 79
Leycester, Phillip (1635), 62, 64
Leyland, Norman (1940), **92**, 378, 390,
    404, 429

Liddell, H. G. (1805), 446
Liddell, Henry, 209, 301, 307
Liddon, Henry, 273, 276
Liesching, P. (1914), 462
Lightfoot, J. P., 247
Lightfoot, H. Le B., **III**
Linacre, Thomas, 36
Lindemann, Frederick, 395
Lindsay, Alexander; 1st Baron, 383–4
Lindsay, Andrew (1996), 431, 475
Lindsay, D. C. M. (1911), 461
Lindsay, N. Ker (1923), 355
Lines, Roland (1962), 481
Lingard, John, 439
Lingham, James, 75
Linn, J. R. (1965), 470
Lippincott, B. E. (1925), 440
Lipscomb, Arthur (1859), 257
Lisle, Ambrose Phillipps de, 226
Lister, Thomas (1577), 35
Lister-Kaye, A. L. (1824), 449
Litler, Joseph (1853), 244
Little, Charles (1930), 479
Little, Joseph (1919), 477
Littledale, G. H. (1843), 451
Littleton, Edward (1616), 52
Littleton, Edward, Baron, 55
Liverpool, Robert (Jenkinson), 2nd Earl
    of, 164
Livingstone, G. S. (1924), 478
Lloyd, D. M. (1963), 469
Lloyd, Edward, 55
Lloyd, Edward (1796), 444
Lloyd, P. J. (1964), 469
Lloyd, Trevor, 426
Lloyd, T. H. (1833), 450
Lloyd, Thomas (1892), 310, 458
Lloyd, William (1750), 105
Lloyd-George, David; 1st Earl of
    Dwyfor, 318
Lloyd-Jones, H. R. (1927), 361, 363
Loasby, J. R. (1965), 470
Lochtenberg, Bernard (1954), 480
Lodge, Eleanor, 300
Lodge (later Ellerton), John (1818), 448
Lodge, Sir Oliver, 300
Lodge, Sir Richard (1874), 191, 275, 287,
    300–301, 304, 307, 309, 362

Loggan, David, **7**, 77, 135
Lomas, A. D. (2006), 476
Lomas, Holland (1841), 218
Lomax, David (1958), **91**, 340
Lomenie de Brienne, E. C.; Cardinal, 191
Long, Basil (1897), 307
Long, B. T. (2000), 475
Longford, John (1774), 108
Longland, Bp. John, 11, 27–8
Longspee, Stephen de, 228
Lonsdale, William (Lowther), 2nd Earl
   of, 303
Looker (butler), 186
Lopes, Sir Manasseh, 185
Lord, J. E. (1900), 460
Lord, Sara (1979), 482
Lorimer, J., 331
Louis XVIII, King of France, 164
Lovat, Simon (Fraser), 11th Lord, 130
Loveday, John (1802), 445
Low, Willie, 354
Low, W. M. (1880), 456
Lowe, James Jackson (1810), 191
Lowndes, C. A. M. (1972), 471
Lucas, John, 158
Lucas, Raymond (1950), 441
Lumb, Harold (1933), 465, 479
Luttrell, Henry (1809), 447
Lydford, William, 89
Lyon, E. T. (1894), 459
Lyon, G. B. (1806), 446
Lyttleton, R. H., 271

Maber, William (1859), 257
Maberley, W. L. (1815), 448
McAllister, Ronald (1963), 481
McArthur, John (1998), 483
Macartney, C. A., 347
McBride, Nicholas (1988), 431
McClure, J. P. (1964), 469
McCrone, R. G. L. (1965), 431
MacDonald, Sir Archibald, 185
Macdonald, H. J., 237
MacDonald, James (1931), 479
Macdonald, R. L. (1900), 459
Macdonnell, P. J. (1890), **66**
Mackarness, John, 280
Mackay, R. W. (1821), 172

Mackenzie, A. O. M. (1878), **58**, 299
Mackey, Bryan (1788), 100
Mackie, J. N. P. (1893), **66**
McGowan, F. P. (1920), 478
McGregor, J. G. (1923), 478
McHendrie, Douglas (1928), 478
MacIntyre, A. G. (1951), 467
MacIntyre, Malcolm (1929), 478
Mackay, R. W. (1821), 172
McKean, W. A. (1965), 470
McKenna, A. N. T. (1963), 470
McKie, Mrs. Gertrude, 440
McKie, J. L. (1918), **78, 92, 93,** 339, 343,
   364–6, 382–3
McKinna, G. H. (1949), 400, 466
Mackonnochie, Alexander Heriot, 274
Maclaren, (gymnasium owner), 237
Maclaren, Archie, 347
McLean, B. J. (2002), 475
Macmillan, Harold; 1st Earl of
   Stockton, 403
McMullen, J. J. (1968), 486
Macpherson, E. F. (1883), **59**, 457
McPherson, G. R. (1996), 475
MacPherson, Ian (1928), 478
Macpherson, James (1934), 479
Macpherson, J. B. (1969) 470
McQueen, J. R., 246
Madan, Falconer (1870), **52B, 67,** 1–2,
   82, 191, 204–5, 286–7, 294,
   298–9, 307, 309, 315–6, 318,
   324, 327, 362
Maddock, G. A. (1807), 446
Maddock, Henry William (1823), 228
Maddock, Matthew (1738), 100
Maddock, Thomas (1731), 121
Madely, Clement (1792), 443
Maestlin, Michael, 47
Magill, Desmond (1934), 374
Magliabecchi, Antonio, 191
Mainwaring, Charles (1786), 188, 442
Mainwaring, C. K. (1821), 449
Mainwaring, Edward (1810), 447
Mainwaring, Townshend (1825), 450
Mais, Norman (1925), 478
Malbon, Samuel, 439
Malcolm, Dougall, 308
Mallett, A W. H. (1946), 466

Mallet, Sir Charles, 1, 14
Mallick, Robert (1986), 482
Mallock, W. H., 283
Mallory, G. (1851), 452
Mallory, H. (1815), 448
Mallory, J. H. (1789), 443
Mammelmann, H. A. (1935), 370
Manchester, Robert (Montagu), 3rd Duke of, 100
Mandt, Harold (1908), 477
Mangwazu, T. S. (1969), 399, 470
Manly, (battelling), 55
Manners, Richard (1992), 402
Manning, C. A. W. (1919), 440, 477
Mansfield, Katherine, 317, 320
Manwaring, Sir Henry (1599), 54
Manwaring, Sir Thomas, Bt. (1594), 54
Mapleton, James (1864), 284
Mare, Walter de la, 320
Markham, Jack, 411
Markham, Robert (1748), 151
Marckland, Richard, 22
Markland, John (1797), 444
Marlas, J. C. (1959), 468
Marks, Alexandra (1977), 486
Marlborough, George (Spencer Churchill), 5th Duke of, 181
Marlborough, John (Spencer-Churchill); 7th Duke of, 196
Marlborough, Sarah (née Jenyns), Duchess of, 136
Marquis, Chenoa (2004), 484
Marriott, Charles (1867), 271, 454
Marriott, E. R. C. (1951), 467
Marriott, F. E. (1912), 321
Marriott, George (1875), 271, 285
Marriott, Henry (1873), 269, 285
Marriott, Henry (1936), 465, 479
Marriott, Robert (1792), 443
Marriott, R. A. (1919), 462
Marsden, Gamaliel (1651), 85
Marsh, P. E. H. (1922), 463
Marsh, P. H. (1966), 470
Marshall, R., 29
Marshall, Frederick (1839), 217
Marshall, James (1857), 242, 261
Marshall, John (1841), 217
Marshall, J. C. (1949), 400, 466

Marston, John (1592), 41
Marten, Henry, 57
Martin, A. J. O. (1973), 471
Martin, L. W. B. (1897), 459
Martin, R. B. (1940), 480
Martin, R. P. (2002), 476
Martindale, Thomas, 85
Martineau, James, 214
Martyr, Peter, 30
Marvell, Andrew, 380
Mary I, Queen, 28–9
Mary, Queen of Scots, 33
Mary II, Queen, 94
Marx, A. L. A. M. von (1913), 321
Marx, Karl, 238
Maskelyne, N. S., 210
Mason, Doris Eileen, 441
Mason, Henry (1593), 20, 43, 54, 437
Mason, James (1609), 49
Massey, William (1573), 38
Master, G. S. (1841), 451
Master, J. W. (1786), 442
Mather, Cotton, 85
Mather, Increase, 85
Mather, Richard (1618), 85
Mayher, Roger (1735), 116, 439
Matthew, Tobie, 39, 40
Mathews, Ernest (1866), 270, 454
Matthews, Simon (1958), 410
Maude, C. R. (1900), 460
Maude, Richard, 76
Maudsley, Ron (1946), 378, 388, 466
Maurice, Frederick Denison, 238
Mavor, A. M. B. (2000), 475
Mawton, John (1635), 85
Maxse, R. E. B. (1932), 339
May, Barry (1969), 400, 401, 481
May, F. M. (1893), 459
Mayne, Elizabeth (2006), 484
Mayo, Herbert (1739), 439
Mayo, John (1778), 442
Mayor, John Bickersteth, 282
Mayor, Susan, v
Meade, T. P. (1821), 449
Meare, Elizabeth, 98
Meare, John (1665), 95, 98, 124, 230, 436
Meare, John II (1698), 98
Meare, Peggy, 98

Meare, Thomas (1698), 98
Mee, S. R. C. De M. (1986), 473
Meek, J. T. (1956), 467
Meerza, Prince Synd Ulee (1894), **II**, 309, 459
Mehlman, Maxwell (1970), 481
Meier, F. W. (1965), 469
Melbourne, William (Lamb), 2nd Viscount, 202
Melle, Basil (1912), 477
Mellen, J. H. C. (1957), 468
Mellen, W. P. (1921), 462
Mellor, Dame Julie (1975), 421
Melvill, Henry, 214
Melville, Harry, 283
Mennie, J. H. (1920), 478
Menteath, J. S. (1812), 447
Menzies, Frederick (1833), **38**, 239, 247
Menzies, J. G. (1879), 307, 456
Merdinger, Charles (1947), 480
Meredith, William George (1821), 199
Methuen, J. (1882), **59,** 457
Meynell, Godfrey (1838), 219
Meyrick, Edward (1774), 108
Meyrick, Jasper, 55
Micklem, N. (1949), 466
Middleton, John ['The Child of Hale'], 48
Middleton, J. H., 299
Midgley, W. H. (1845), 452
Mildmay C. W. St. John (1812), 447
Miles, A. C. (1874), 455
Miles, H. F. (1913), **72**, 321
Miles, John (1636), 85
Mill, John, 92
Millar, D. M. (1979), 473
Millar, Fergus (1955), 394
Millar, Ken (1937), **89**, 372
Millar, L. P. (1908), 461
Miller, Brian (1942), 390, 440
Miller, Douglas (1896), 310
Miller, James, 109
Miller, M. J. H. (1970), 471
Miller, William Henry, 196
Milliner, J. H. S. (1932), 479
Millington, Thomas (1673), 87
Mills (marbler), 295
Milman, Henry Hart (1810), **31,** 4, 170, 302
Milne, John Haworth (1846), 205, 452

Milne, Richard (1864), 267
Milner, Alfred; Viscount, 282, 313
Milward, John (1654), 438
Minor, A. H. (1849), 452
Minton, (tiler), 239
Misick, Michael (1946), 480
Mitchell, Solace (1976), 482
Mitchell-Innes, N. S. (1932), 347, 465
Mitropoulos, E. (2002), 476
Mocket, Richard (1696), 43–44
Moe, H. A. (1921), 478
Moke, G. E. (1879), **58**, 296
Moller, Carl (2001), 484
Moller, Lester (1935), 479
Mollet, John William (1854), 240
Molyneaux, John, **41,** 252
Momigliano, Arnoldo, 292
Monck, George (1868), 283
Monck, J. B. (1829), 450
Monkton, Lionel, 319
Mond, Mary, 353
Monmouth, Charles (Middleton), 1st Earl of Monmouth, 130
Monroe, J. R. (1974), 472
Monserrat, K. J. (1976), 472
Moore, G. E., 418
Moore, Henry, 405
Moore, H. B. (1886), **75,** 322
Moore, H. B. (1911), 461
Moore, H. R. (1953), 400, 467
Moore, H. Wilkinson, 294
Moore, P. B. C.; Baron (1945), 346
Mordaunt, John; 2nd Baron, **11,** 23–24, 77, 152, 155, 437
More, Robert (1529), 27
More, St. Thomas, 16
Morgan, A. K. (1961), 400
Morgan, Charles (1919), 4, 351–3, 359
Morgan, G. O., 207
Morley, Mrs. Elizabeth (née Sutton), 13, 23–24, 437
Morley, George, 45
Morley, John (1857), 258, 269, 453
Morphet, H. C. (1926), 343–4, 463
Morres, Robert (1774), 109
Morris, Jan [James], 385
Morris, Marcus (1933), 4
Morris, William, **70,** 237–40, 277–8

Morrison, George, 269
Morshead, Walter (1853), 242
Mortimer, J. H., 289
Mortimer, Sir John (1940), 4, 369
Moseley, Edward (1612),
Moseley, J. I. (1914), **73**
Mosely, Oswald, 147
Mosely, Sir Oswald, 1st Bt. (1691), 147
Mosley, Sir Oswald, 2nd Bt. (1802), 445
Moss, J. M. (1967), 470
Moss, J. R. (1938), 485
Moss, R. M. (1968), 470
Moss, W. F. (1932), 464
Moss, Thomas (1731), 146
Mower-White, G. J. (1921), 343, 462
Mozley, J. B., 231
Muckleston, William (1774), 108, 151
Muennich, F. C. (1993), 474
Muir-Mackenzie, Montague (1866), 285
Mules, Sir John, 86
Mules, Lady (née Yate); formerly Lady
    de Sylva, 86
Muller, Mrs. Georgiana (née Grenfell),
    278
Müller, Max, 229, 278
Mullins, George (1855), 237, 242
Mullins, H. L. (1924), 463
Mumford, E. C. (1954), 467
Munson, George (1534), 27
Murad, Aslem (1949), 480
Murdoch, I. D. (1969), 470
Murphy, F. P. (1898), 459
Murphy, J. K. (1892), 458
Murray, Gilbert, 309, 326
Murry, J. Middleton (1908), 4, 317–20
Murray, Roger (1956), 467
Murphy, H. D. (1900), 306
Mursell, A. G. (1967), 470
Myddelton, Sir Richard, 3rd Bt. (1670), 89
Myers, David (1985), 482
Mylius, E. N. (1916), 462
Mytton, Charles (later Thornycroft)
    (1788), 442

Nadeau, J. E. (1932), 479
Napier, Wyndham (1723), 101–2, 108
Napleton, John (1755), **27,** 99, 151,
    158–160

Napoleon, I, 360
Napper, William (1564), 16
Nash, Alexander (1864), **47A**, 267
Nash, John, 165
Neale, John Mason, 211
Neate, F. W. (1958), 400, 468, 486
Neave, F. P. K. (2000), 475
Neeld, A. D. (1867), 454
Nehring, Richard (1965), 481
Neill, A. (1896), 459
Nel, Marthinus (1999), 483
Nelson, Everard (1955), 481
Nelson, Horatio; Viscount, 360, 365
Nelson, Thomas, 313
Nelson-Ward, H. H. E. (1882), **59**
Nesbit, Edith [Bland], 337
Neser, V. H. (1919), 345, 349, 361, 462, 477
Nettleship, Henry, 279
Neville, C. R. G. (1942), 466
Newcastle, Henry (Clinton); 2nd Duke
    of, 146
Newcome, Henry (1696), 124, 131
Newdigate, Sir Richard, 185
Newham, Walter (1945), 480
Newman, E., 204, 251
Newman, Francis (1631), 53
Newman, John Henry; Cardinal, 203, 208,
    210, 214, 221, 223–4, 226, 259, 275
Newport, S. G. (1802), 445
Newton, Carl (1921), 478
Newton, Charles (1908), 461, 477
Newton, George (1669), 96
Newton, Sir Isaac, 115
Newton, John (1622), 47, 59–62,
    70–71, 438
Nicholas, Peter (1997), 431
Nicholl, Sir John, 183–5
Nicholas I, Emperor of Russia, 165
Nicholas, J. K. B. M. (1937), **93,** 350,
    370, 378, 383, 388–9, 392, 394,
    404, 406, 410, 417, 436, 485
Nicholas, R. B. M. (1960), 469
Nicholl, E. P. (1850), 452
Nicholls, C. I. (1975), 472
Nicholls, John (1570), 36
Nicholls, J. E. (1929), 464
Nichols, George (1564), 35
Nicholson, William (1794), 443

Nickeson, P., 382
Nicolson, Arthur (1868), 454
Noel-Clark, G. A. (1995), 475
Norfolk, Thomas (Howard); 4th Duke of, 31
Nollekens, Joseph, 181
Nordby, C. (2007), 476
Norman, C. P. A. (1970), 471
North, Frederick; 2nd Earl of Guilford (Lord North), 152
North, P. M., 426
Norton, Anthony (1993), 483
Norton, Richard (1631), 53, 84
Norval, I. P. (1933), 479
Nott, F. H. (1904), **75**
Nott-Bower, Sir Guy (1909), 485
Novis, A. L. (1925), 463
Nowell, Alexander (1536), **9**, 1, 5, 18, 23–4, 30–1, 40, 77, 135, 436–7
Nowell, Alexander (of Underley), 42
Nowell, Mrs. Elizabeth [Bowyer], 40
Nowell, Robert, 38
Nowell, William (1730), 149
Nuffield, William (Morris), Viscount, 334, 407
Nugée, F., 274
Nutter, A. B. (1889), 458
Nye, Philip (1615), 56

Oakley, John (1852), 236, 239
Obolensky, Prince Alexander (1934), 4, 345, 349, 371, 465
Obolensky, Prince Sergey, 345
O'Connor, K. D. (1983), 473
Ogilvie, F. W., 364
Ogle, Humphrey, 13, 23, 437
Oldham, Bp. Hugh, 15–16, 20, 437
Oldham, Col. Sir H., 266
Oliphant, Mrs. Margaret (née Wilson), 280
Olver, Aaron (1997), 483
Olver, John (1935), 479
Oman, Carola, 353
O'Neill, Revd. Baron, 259
O'Neill, Hon. Robert (1864), 259, 454
O'Neil, Robert (1961), 469, 481
On-Kya, S. (1913), 321
Onslow, A. G. (1848), 452
Oram, J. A. (1993), 474

Orme, James (1858), **48**, 257, 453
Ormerod, George (1803), 100
Ormerod, John Aderne (1832), **38**, 229–30, 233–4, 247
Ormerod, Thomas (1826), 201, 450
Ormond, Lady, 63
Ormonde, James (Butler); 2nd Duke of, 142, 144
O'Rorke, M. H. (1913), **75**, 462
Orrett, W. G. (1802), 445
Orpen, Sir William, 314
Osbaldeston, George ['Squire'] (1805), **55**, 4, 185–6, 446
Osbaldeston, William, 55
Osborne, Hon. S. G. (1824), 450
Orselli, Alfred (1928), 478
Osman, Sir Amin (1920), 358–9
Osmond, A. P. K. (1958), 4, 468
Ottaway, Cuthbert John (1869), **45, 55,** 4, 270–71, 299
Owen, Adam, **41**, 251
Owen, John, 57, 72
Owen, J. S. (1932), 465
Owen, Bp. Reggie (1906), 339, 374, 381
Owen, S. G., 327
Owen, Thomas (1635), 52
Owen-Hughes, H. G. (1957), 468
Oxford, Edward (Harley); 2nd Earl of, 124

Packe, H. V. (1843), 452
Page, Francis, 185
Page, J. C. (1877), 456
Page, Philip Pryce (1905), 310
Paget, (battelling), 55
Pakenham, Hon. H. R. (1841), 451
Paley, William, 207
Palin, George, 23, 437
Palin, Michael (1962), 4, 410
Palladio, Andrea, 137, 138
Palmer, William, 4, 313
Palmer, Thomas (1553), 32, 33
Palmer, William (1796), 180, 444
Palmerston, Henry (Temple); 3rd Viscount, 232, 360
Panikowski, Stanley (1993), 483
Pantin, William Abel, 340
Papineau, Talbot (1905), 477

Paravacini, Frank, 285
Parker, Henry (1885), **59,** 303, 457
Parker, James (1719), 438
Parker, J. F. (1801), 445
Parker, Abp. Matthew, 29
Parker, Thomas, 176
Parker, William (1732), 121–2
Parkes, Richard (1577), 43
Parkin, Cecil, 346
Parkin, Charles (1857), **57,** 258
Parkin, C. L. (1912), **72,** 302
Parkin, William Hugh (1889), 303, 457
Parks, Chrysostom, 76
Parkyns, T. M. F. (1872), 455
Parr, James (1720), 439
Parr, R. W. (1927), 464, 478
Parsons, Edgar (1929), 336, 348, 365–8
Parsons, John (1776), 179
Partridge, J. A. (1813), 447
Pashley, T. J. (1974), 472
Pate, John (1613), 52
Pater, Clara, 278
Pater, Walter Horatio (1858), **37, 39B, 49,**
    61, 4, 246–7, 250, 254, 258, 260,
    271–84, 286, 288–9, 292–3, 299,
    303–6, 343, 365
Paton, J. A. (1912), **75,** 461
Patten, Thomas (1730), 143, 149
Pattison, Mark, 165, 168, 199, 204, 286
Pattison, Mark James (1805), 199
Pauncefote, Bernard (1867), 264,
    270–71, 454
Payton, Mris., 55
Peacock, Michael (1930), 345, 349, 372,
    375, 464
Peacock, Thomas (1589), 43
Peacock, Thomas Love, 7
Pearce, J. L. (1968), 470
Pearce, T. W. (1966), 470
Pearce, Gerald (1913), 477
Pearson, Alexander (1884), **59,** 457
Pearson, J., 289
Pearson, Sir Robert (1891), 458, 485
Pearson-Gregory, P. J. S. (1906), 460
Peberdy, Robert, v
Pechell, H. R. K. (1894), 458
Peck, R. H. (1912), **73,** 485
Pedynowski, Dena (1999), 483

Peebles, Ian (1929), **55,** 346–7
Peel, Sir Robert, 164, 202, 211
Pelham, Henry (1865), 312, 315
Pelz, Edward (1939), 479
Pemberton, Goddard (1631), 52
Pemberton, James (1781), 188, 191, 442
Pembroke, Philip, 4th Earl of, 58
Pendleton, Henry (1538), 32
Penn, C. (1957), 468, 486
Penn, J. J. (1960), 469
Penny, Benjamin (1798), 444
Penny, Edward, **69,** 152
Pennyman, W. G. (1890), 458
Penrice, John (1837), 451
Pepper, W., Snr., 216
Peploe, Bp. Samuel, 145, 147–8
Peploe, Samuel, Jnr., 147–8
Pepys, Samuel, 48, 67
Perceval, Henry (1817), 186, 448
Percevale, John, 88
Percival, Francis (1863), **47A,** 267
Perkins, Dan (2001), 432
Perring, J. W. C. (1845), 452
Persse, Henry (1889), 302, 458
Peterborough, Henry (Mordaunt); 2nd
    Earl of, 93
Peters, M. D. (1978), 472
Peters, C. M. D. (1929),
Petty, Sir William (1649), **15,** 64, 66–9,
    73, 87
Pfann, George (1926), 478
Phelps, C. F. (1953), 468
Philip IV, King of Spain, 139
Philipps, J. L. (1818), 449
Philips, Robert, 439
Phillips, E. C. M. (1902), 460
Phillips, G. L. (1930), **77,** 344
Phillips, H. E. (1879), **58,** 456
Phillips, Robert, 174
Phillips, Sidney (1859), 266, 453
Phillips, Thomas, **25, 30,** 211
Philpotts, George, 437
Philpotts, Bp. Henry, 223
Phippes, Christopher (1610), 36
Picasso, Pablo, 320
Pickering, Edward (1840), 218
Pickering, John (1587), 39
Piercy, George (1895), 310

Pigot, John Taylour (1840), 218
Pigott, W. P. (1828), 450
Piggot, Thomas, 20,
Pike, Luke Owen (1853), 240, 439
Pike, M. C. (1875), 456
Pike, W. M. (1880), **58**, 456
Pilling, Hector (1931), 372
Pincocke, William (1668), 95
Pinsent, John, 404
Pint, Ellen (1982), 482
Pitra, J. - B., Cardinal, 225–6
Pitt, Anne, 282
Pitt, N. C. (1968), 470
Pitt, William, 176, 180, 184
Pitts, Arthur (1566), 35
Pitts, Robert (1559), 35
Plant, Samuel (1840), 218
Platnauer, L. M. (1915), 365
Platnauer, Maurice (1906), **92, 93, 95,** 5, 9,
    119, 304, 337, 339–40, 344, 363,
    365–7, 369–70, 382–3, 390, 392, 404,
    408, 419, 423, 436, 440, 465, 485
Platt, Hugh, 286
Plommer, Hugh, 404–5
Plowden, Alfred (1862), **42A,** 259–60,
    264–7, 454
Plumb, C. T. (1924), 355
Plumb, H. J. (1935), 479
Plumptre, E. H. (1840), 224
Plumptre, F. C., 248
Pocklington, Duncan (1860), **55,** 262, 265,
    268, 289
Pohl, Dietrich (1984), 482
Pole, Abp. Reginald; Cardinal, 28, 29
Polkinghorn, William (1999), 483
Pollard, John (1801), 445
Ponton, Thomas (1797), 444
Poole, D. H. C. (1805), 446
Poole, J. H. (1808), 447
Poole, Robert (1928), **77,** 344, 464
Poole, William (1930), 479
Pope, Alexander, 368
Pope, Cyril (1907), **74**
Popham, Francis (1798), 180, 444
Popham, F. W. L. (1881), 456
Popham, H. F. A. L. (1882), **59**
Popplewell, I. J. (1988), 474
Porson, William, 191

Port, Bernard (1794), 197, 444
Port, Sir John (1524), 21, 23, 437
Port, Sir John II, 169, 175, 228, 437
Porten, S. J. (1798), 444
Porter, Henry (1811), 447
Porter, John (1644), 60
Porter, J. S. (1890), 458
Porter, Roger (1629), 47, 50
Porter, R. W. (1890), 381–2
Porter, William, 13, 23, 437
Potter, Christopher, 44
Potter, Abp. John, 157
Poulett, John (Hinton); 5th Earl
    (1801), 445
Powell, Anthony, 409
Powell, George (1781), 188, 442
Powell, George (1948), 466, 480
Powell, James, 164, 289
Powell, Philip, and Moya, Hidalgo, 404
Powell, T. C. (1834), 451
Powlet, Hon. Francis (1704), 135, 438
Poynder, Thomas (1832), 439
Praed, William (1798), 444
Prather, Darcy, (1991), 483
Prees, Ann (alias Crotchley), 189
Prescot, Kenrick (1848), 268
Pressley, Lynne (1977), 482
Preston, J. H. (1893), 459
Prestwich, Sir Thomas (1642), 52
Price, Cormell (1854), 237–41
Price, R. J. (1822), 449
Prichard, Charles (1864), 284
Prichard, H. A., 418
Prickett, John (1717), 107
Prideaux, John, 45
Prime, John, 39
Prince, D., 100
Prinsley, M. (1975), 472
Prior, John, **41,** 251
Pritchard, J. M. (1913), 462
Pritchard, P. A. R. (1897), 459
Proctor, John (1825), 449
Proctor, Stephen (1955), 402, 467
Profumo, Albert, 440
Profumo, John D. (1932), 4, 369
Profumo, T. D. (2004), 476
Prothero, G. W., 300
Proust, Marcel, 246

Prower, Mervyn (1866), **47A**, 264
Prynne, William, 59
Pryor, Roderick (1874), 455
Pryse, J. P., 153
Pugin, Augustus Charles, **frontispiece**
Puleston, T. H. G. (1841), 451
Purchas, John, **34**, 211
Purefoy, James (1649), 64
Pusey, Edward Bouverie, 203, 212, 215, 221, 224, 226, 231, 259
Pusinelli, D. C. (1974), 472
Puxley, Edward (1880), 298, 456
Puxley, H. B. L. (1854), 236, 453
Puxley, J. L. (1880), **58**
Puxley, Peter (1964), 481
Pym, John, 53
Pyne, J. B., 244, 265

Quirk, John (1901), 307

Rabinowitz, Benjamin (1953), 480
Rodakowski, R. (1914), **73**
Radcliffe, Sir Alexander (1587), 52
Radcliffe, E. S. (1794), 443
Radcliffe, Houstonne (1758), 158, 188
Radcliffe, Houstonne (1825), 189
Radcliffe, John, 79
Radcliffe, Samuel (1597), **12**,10, 42, 45, 49, 54, 56, 58, 61, 65, 71, 74, 76–7, 152, 436, 438
Radclyffe, Edward (1702), 98–9
Radice, Fulke (1907), 319
Radice, R. N. P. (1943), 441
Radley, C. E. (1879), 298
Raffalowitch, A., 281
Raikes, A. F. (1955), 391, 467
Rainolds, John, 39
Ralph, J. P. (1989), 474
Ralston-Patrick, Robert (1895), 310, 459
Ramsay, A. W. (1951), 400
Rangeley, W. H. T. (1931), 479
Ranjitsinhji, Vibhaji ['Ranji'], Maharaja, 337
Raper, S. M. (1969), 471
Rashdall, Hastings, 14, 325
Rashleigh, William (1885), **59**, 302–3
Ratcliffe, William (1633), 52
Ravenhill, Montgu (1904), 319, 460

Ravenscroft, Thomas (1615), 52
Ravenshaw, Edward (1800), 445
Raw, R. G. (1931), 464
Rawdon, James (1854), 236, 242
Rawley, Peter (1958), 410
Rawlings, Margaret [Lady Barlow], 353
Rawlinson, George, 304
Rawnsley, E. P. (1870), 455
Rawson, Ralph (1634), 60–3, 70–1, 74, 87, 136, 250
Rawson, R. H. (1881), 456
Raychaudhuri, Arjun (2002), 484
Raymond, Sir Robert, 129
Readinge, Thomas (1647), 60
Redford, Robert, 319
Redhead, William, 78
Rednall, F. G. (1912), **73**
Ree, E. A. (1920), 462
Reed, A. J. H. (1971), 471
Reed, Richard (1630), 438
Regent, Prince; later King George IV, 165
Rehmke, Hans (1911), 477
Reid, J. G. (1919), **74**
Reid, Sir Robert (1902), 460, 485
Reid-Kay, Jane (1974), 402
Reilly, Anthony Adams (1855), 240
Reinold, Arnold (1863), 312
Rennie, N. G. (1955), 467
Reynolds, Leighton (1954), **93**, 387, 389–90, 417
Reynolds, Samuel Harvey (1850), **38**, 191, 249–50, 255, 260–61, 285
Reynolds, Thomas, 28, 188
Rhodes, Cecil, 268, 328
Rhodes, F. W. (1920), 462
Rhodes, George (1884), **59**, 303, 457
Rhodes, Kenneth (1908), 373
Rhodes, W. H. (1890), 458
Ribblesdale, Thomas (Lister); 1st Baron (1769), 109
Ribblesdale, Thomas (Lister); 3rd Baron, 248
Ribblesdale, Thomas (Lister); 4th Baron, 248
Ricardo, David, 67, 175
Richards, Arthur (1862), 265
Richards, Henry, 161
Richards, Bernard (1959), v, 387, 390

Richards, C. A. L. (1929), 345
Richards, Graham (1958), 387, 396, 403, 420, 469, 486
Richardson, Gabriel (1602), 46–7
Richardson, James V. (1922), 349, 463
Richardson, Joshua (1634), 85
Richardson, P. M. A. (1963), 469
Richardson, Ralph (1601), 46
Richardson, Richard (1774), 108
Rickman, Geoffrey (1951), 398
Ridgway, F. J. (1876), 456
Ridgway, Robert (1649), 64, 71
Rilston, Edward (1578), 38–9
Ring, S. J. B. (1976), 472
Rippon, Geoffrey; Baron (1941), 485
Rishton, Edward (1568), 35–6
Robbins, Lionel; Baron, 425–6
Roberts, J. W. (1790), 443
Roberts, Richard (1634), 62, 70
Roberts, Thomas (1769), 151
Roberts, William (1928), 345, 464
Robertson, Frederick William (1837), 4, 214–7, 236, 243
Robertson, Graeme (1971), 482
Robertson, Sir Grant, 362
Robertson, William (1910), 477
Robertson-Aikman, T. S. G. H. (1879), 456
Robertson-Aikman, W. H. (1922), 462
Robespierre, Maximilien de, 175
Robinson, Henry Crabb, 195
Robinson, Jane Anne (née Watson), 439
Robinson, Bp. John, 127
Robinson, Kenneth (1972), 482
Robinson, Matthew (1730), 150
Robinson, M. T. (1950), 467
Rockefeller, J. D., 334
Rodakowski, R. J. P. (1914), **73**
Rodd, Francis Hearle (1784), 188, 442
Rodwell, Warwick, 19
Roe, Betsy (1980), 482
Roetter, M. F. (1961), 469
Rogers, C. Coltman (1873), 264, 455
Rogers, D. C. B. (1986), 474
Rogers, G. F. (1905), 460
Rogers, P. C. R. C. (1970), 471
Rogers, P. J. M. (1876), 456
Rolleston, J. D. (1891), 66
Romney, George, 149

Rosa, R. H. (1974), 471
Rosebery, Archibald (Primrose); 5th Earl of, 250
Ross, J. P. (1804), 446
Ross, M. I. (1953), 467
Ross, William, 68
Rossetti, Dante Gabriel, 239
Rothenstein, Sir William, **60, 61**
Rothkopf, M. T. (2006), 476
Rothschild, Nathan Meyer de, 175
Rothwell, Richard Rainshaw I (1792), 163
Roundell, C. S., 235, 262
Roundell, H. D. (1804), 446
Rountree, J. P. (1977), 472
Rous, Hon. H. A. (1818), 448
Routledge, Arthur, 186
Routledge, F. (1885), **59,** 457
Row, A. W. L. (1914), 477
Rowe, John (1935), 376–7
Rowe, William (1964), 481
Rowlandson, Thomas, **IV, 26,** 167
Rowse, A. L., 392
Roxburghe, James (Innes-Ker); 7th Duke of,
Royds, Edward (1837), 219–20
Royle, Vernon (1873), **55,** 271, 455
Rubie, William (1999), 431
Rucker, Arthur William (1867), 287, 321, 342
Rucker, Frederick George (1874), 439
Rudden, Bernard (1965), 430
Rumbold, George (1813), 447
Rumbold, Jack (1945), 480
Rumsey, Robert (1862), 285
Runcie, Abp. Robert; Baron (1941), 3, 4, 373, 381, 485
Rundell and Bridge, (silversmiths) 162
Rushton, J. L. (1892), 310, 458
Rushton, T. J. L. (1932), 373
Ruskin, John, 80, 216, 238, 246, 283
Russell, Conrad; Earl, 412
Russell, Franklin (1911), 401, 477
Russell, John (1710), 141
Russell, Lord John, 203, 226, 242
Ryle, Sir Gilbert, 418

Sacheverell, Henry, 125
Sacheverell, Patrick (1552), 29, 123

Sadler, James, **I,** 181
Sadler, John (1956), 481
Sagar, Stephen (1688), 95
St. Cyres, Viscount, 362
St. George, Sir Henry, 55
St. Joseph, C. D. (1976), 472
Saintsbury, George, 249, 275
Sala, George Augustus, 256
Salmon, Matthew (1730), 149
Salmon, Richard (1774), 108, 151
Salmond, Sir John, 331
Salvin, Anthony, 192
Salway, Humphrey (1590), 51
Sampson, Charles Henry (1878), **67, 78,**
    301, 316, 343, 358, 380, 436
Sampson, Mrs. Margaret (née Bolckow),
    316, 336
Sandars, T. C., 265
Sandeman, E. F. (1874), 455
Sandeman, W. A. (1876), 456
Sanders, J. R. (1962), 469
Sanderson, Ellis (1585), 38
Sanderson, Robert, 88
Sandor, A. J. (1957), 399
Sanford, E. A. (1813), 448
Sankey, Sir Jerome, 68
Sargent, Arthur J. (1891), **66**
Sargent, John Singer, 248
Sattig, Thomas (2002), 423
Saunders, P. F. (1920), 462
Savage, Sir Edward, 55
Savage, John (1911), 477
Savile, Sir George, 63
Savile, Henry (1561), 37
Saville, Mark; Baron (1956), 391, 486
Sayer, D. M. (1957), 400
Sayers, Tom, 258
Scarman, Leslie; Baron (1930), 368,
    375, 485
Schaffgotsch, Count J. U. G. M. E.
    J. Bedburg (1909), 321
Schama, Simon (1976), 417
Schantz, Mark (1963), 481
Schofield, D. J. (1982), 473
Schulze, Unger, 405
Schutt, Warren (1904), 477
Scoles, Jasper (1648), 60
Sconce, Robert Knox (1836), 223

Scopes, F. V. (1936), 465
Scott, Alice Constance, 440
Scott, C. H. (1976), 472
Scott, Max (1930), 372
Scott, R., 234
Scott, Sir Walter, 174–5, 195, 196
Scott, Sir William, 180
Scott, William (1881), 457
Scotus, Duns, 7, 15–16, 312
Scotus Erigena, John, 6–7, 312
Scragg, John (1921), 359
Scudamore, Rowland (1630), 47, 53
Seamer, John Wemyss (1932), 441, 464
'Sebastian', see Graham, A. H.,
Sedgwick, A. W. (1951), 440
Seitz, Virginia (1978), 482
Selbie, William (1882), 303
Selby, A. E. (2000), 475
Selden, John, 249
Selincourt, Ernest de, 358
Selincourt, Michael de (1922), 358
Selwyn, A. W. (1935), 456
Serrurier, Louis (1924), 463, 478
Severne, J. E. (1844), 452
Sewall, John (1958), 468, 481
Sewall, O. C. (1922), 463
Seyer (schoolmaster), 163
Shackleton, Robert (1937), **68, 92, 93,** 341,
    378, 382, 390–93, 396, 403, 405–6,
    417, 440
Shadwell, C. L., 274, 276
Shaffner, F. I. (1925), 478
Shafto, J. D. (1826), 450
Shafto, T. D. (later Eden) (1830), 189, 450
Shakerley, C. P. (1810), 447
Shakerley, Sir Geoffrey (1638), 52, 101, 135
Shakerley, George (1698), 101
Shakerley, Jane, 101
Shakerley, Peter (1667), 101
Shakespeare, William, 38, 237, 273, 306,
    352, 366
Shand, Thomas (1845), **38,** 247, 260–61,
    263, 285
Shaw, E. A. (1911), **75,** 461
Shaw, Sir Frederick, 3rd Bt. (1816),
    186, 448
Shaw, John (1628), 53
Shaw, Michael (1949), 480

Shaw-Hellier, T. B. (1855), 453
Shearwood, K. A. (1947), 466
Sheldon, Gilbert, 44, 61, 84
Shell, Jason (2005), 484
Shepheard, Peter, 402
Shepherd, Augustus (1857), 237
Shepherd, Robert (1859), **56, 57,** 265, 268
Shepherd, Thomas (1774), 108
Shepherd, Thomas, 244–5
Sherington, Gilbert (1670), 70
Sherson, (of London), 42
Shert, John (1564), 34–5
Shipley, Andrew (2007), 484
Shipley, Charles (1802), 445
Shippary, Edward (1707), 107, 133
Shippen, Edward (1687), 123
Shippen, Mrs. Frances (Lady Clarke; née
    Legh), 126, 133
Shippen, Mrs. Margaret (née Stote), 132
Shippen, Robert (1693), **17,** 95, 99,
    123–41, 157, 436
Shippen, William Sen., 134
Shippen, William (1687), 123, 131, 141, 143
Short, Thomas, 245
Shovel, Sir Cloudesley, 103
Shrewsbury, Charles (Talbot); 19th Earl
    of, 212
Shrigley, William (1721), 146–7
Shrimpton, A. T., **33, 39A,** 247–8,
    255, 305–6
Shuttleworth, William (1641) 51
Sibthorp, Charles (1801), 178
Sidebottom, A. R. (1793), 443
Sidgwick, Arthur, 326
Sidgwick, E. D. (1891), 458
Sidney, Sir Philip, 89
Simmons, J. S. G., 307
Simmonds, N. A. (1987), 474
Simpson, Richard (1913), 477
Simpson (cook), 133
Sinclair, Peter (1964), 430–31
Singleton, A. P. (1932), 347, 349, 465
Singleton, Thomas (1573), 39, 41–3,
    75, 436
Sirdar, M. (1921), 354
Sixsmith, Thomas (1616), 47, 60–3, 87
Skipper, D. J. (1950), 400
Skipper, M. A. (1982), 400, 473

Slade, Thomas (1689), 124
Slater, N. T. (1959), 400
Slatterly, Sally, 305
Smail, Richard (1976), v, 165
Small, E. H. T. F. (1882), **59**
Smethurst, James (1690), 123
Smith, Adam, 67
Smith, A. C. (1957), **55,** 400, 468, 486
Smith, A. L., 326
Smith, C. H. (1907), **74**
Smith, C. M. (1957), 468
Smith, Goldwin, 13, 209, 229, 235, 248, 254
Smith, Gordon (1928), **77,** 344, 464
Smith, H. A. N. (1876), 456
Smith, Ian (1922), 345, 463
Smith, James (1809), 169, 201
Smith, John (1730), 121–2
Smith, Sir John, 440
Smith, J. S. (1924), 463
Smith, L. B. (1963), 486
Smith, L. Pearsall, 309
Smith, Matthew (1532), 30
Smith, Bp. Miles (1568), 36
Smith, Rowland (1845), 452
Smith, Sydney, 175
Smith, Thomas (1669), 101
Smith [Smyth], Bp. William, **2,** 1, 10–14,
    19–22, 76, 135, 138, 152, 156, 164,
    202, 437
Smith, William, 437
Smith, William (1774), 109
Smith Barry, J. H. (1767), 151
Smith Barry, John (1811), 153, 447
Smith Barry, James (1815), 153, 448
Smith Barry, James (1833), 450
Smyth, Matthew (1509), 10, 19, 27–8,
    436–7
Smyth, Thomas Scott (1794), 172,
    175, 179
Snell, E. (1925), 463
Snow, P. S. (1926), 463
Sneyd, John (1752), 105
Sneyd, Walter (1769),
Soane, Sir John, **20A, 21A–B, 63,**166–7
Solomon, Simeon, 283
Solymar, Laszlo (1966), 396, 417
Somerset, Algernon (Seymour); 14th
    Duke of, 356

Somerset, John (Seymour); 4th Duke of, 118

Somerset, Sarah (Alston), Duchess of Somerset, **22**, 95, 117–8, 152, 155, 438

Sonnenschein, Abraham [later Adolf], 326

Sonnenschein, E. A., 326

Sonnenschein, alias 'W.S.W. Anson'; (later Stallybrass), W. S., 326

Sonnenschein (later Stallybrass; 'Sonners'), William Teulon Swan (1906), **65, 73, 78, 80, 81, 83A, 86, 87, 88, 89**, 304, 307, 319, 326–32, 336–51, 354, 366–84, 398, 417, 436, 440

Sorocold, Thomas (1580), 39

Sorten, K., **92**

Southey, Robert, 175

Southorn, Charlie, 342

Southwell, Sir Robert, 88

Southwell, Sir R. V. (1929), 339, 361

Spalding, H. N. (1896), 337, 340, 343

Spalding, K. J. (1898), 339, 382, 440

Spelman, Sir John (1641), 6, 55

Spence, K. M. (1950), 400, 466

Spencer, George; 2nd Earl, 196

Spencer, Henry (1899), 323, 459

Spencer, J. H. (1913), 321

Spicer, John (1807), 188, 446

Spiers, (of the High), 265

Spies, Emerson (1936), 479

Spinckes, Bp. Nathaniel, 96

Spottiswoode, C. A. (1886), 457

Spottiswoode, John, 89

Stahl, Daniel, 88

Stainer, Sir John, 221

Stainton, R. G. (1930), 464

Stallybrass, Edward, 326

Stallybrass family in general; see Sonnenschein

Standish, Sir Frank, 3rd Bt. (1763), 439

Standley, Thomas (1574), 25

Standring, H. W. (1920), 462

Stanhope, E. F. S.; 10th Earl of Chesterfield (1872), 455

Stanley, 1st Baron, 228

Stanley, Arthur Penrhyn, 214–5, 235, 242

Stanley, Edward (1579), 22

Stanley, Thomas (1693), 124

Stapylton, G. W. C. (1818), 448

Starkey, Simon (1509), 27

Starkie, Le G. (1808), 446

Starkie, Le G. N. (1817), 448

Starkie, Piers (1704), 135

Steel-Maitland, A. H. D., 308

Steele, J. M. (1829), 450

Stein, K. H. (1937), 370

Stegmann, M. S. (1957), 467

Stenton, E. C. (1973), 472

Stephen, Henry, 20

Stephens, G. L. (1964), 470

Stephens, James, 320

Stephens, Richard (1802),

Stephens, Robert (1926), 162, 478

Stephenson, Robert, 231

Sterling, William (1961), 481

Stevens, Greville T. S. (1920), 346, 462

Stevenson, Robert Louis, 384

Steward, R. E. A. (1954), 467

Stewart, R. S. (1964), 469

Stewart, William (1891), 310, 458

Stid, Daniel (1987), 482

Still, E. R. (1871), 455

Stirling, William (1878), 456

Stobart, Andrew (1987), 482

Stock, William (1547), 32–3

Stocker, William Nelson (1869), **67**, 287, 292, 316, 329, 333, 341–2, 370, 381, 394, 439

Stockley, W. (1998), 475

Stockton, David (1946), **93**, 383, 389, 403, 410, 420, 468, 485

Stodart, W. W., 209

Stokes, Mary (1959), 421

Stonard, John (1789), 175, 180, 184

Stone, Charles (1855), 240

Stone, John, 336

Stonhouse, William (1857), 254

Storr, Paul, 165

Story, J. R. (1875), 456

Stote, Sir Richard, 132

Stradling, Sir Edward, 2nd Bt. (1615), 52

Strafford, Thomas (Wentworth); 1st Earl of, 84, 305

Strain, Milton (1949), 480

Stratford, J. C. (1935), 465

Stratford, William, 123, 129–30
Street, George Edmund, 204
Strickland, A. W. (1910), 461
Strickland, H. E., 229
Strode, James (1765), 151
Strode, William (1755), 439
Strong, W. I. N. (1923), 345, 349, 463
Stronge, Sir James; 1st Bt. (1769), 151
Stronge, Sir James, 2nd Bt. (1803), 445
Stronge, James (1868), 263
Strype, John, 32
Stuart-Jones, Sir Henry (1886), 343, 366
Stuart, Duncan (1953), 467
Stubbs, Bp. William, 261
Studdert-Kennedy, C. J. (1946), 466
Stukeley, William, 118
Style, C. H. (1895), 459
Styler, Leslie (1926), **92, 93, 94, 95,** 361,
    378, 381, 383, 389, 403, 405, 409,
    412, 440
Sullivan, Frederick (1814), 448
Summerscale, Jeremy (1955), 467
Summerson, Sir John, 404
Sunderland, Langdale (1639), 52
Sussex, Duke of, 190
Sutton, John Alexander, 440
Sutton, Sir Richard, **3,** 1, 10, 12–16, 22–3,
    76, 135, 138, 152, 164, 437
Sutton, Thomas (1773), 120
Sutton, William (1521), 8, 27
Swadling, William (1997), 414
Swan, T. M. (1961), 469
Sweatman, E. A. (1924), 463
Swete, Benjamin, 438
Swift, Johnathan, 107
Switt, Rett, 368
Swinburn, G. W. P. (1895), 459
Swinburn, Malcolm (1960), 481
Swinburne, Algernon Charles, 239
Swinnerton-Dyer, Sir Peter; 16th Bt., 395
Sykes, John Henry (1841), 218
Sykes, Sir Mark Masterman; 3rd Bt. (1788),
    191, 196, 443
Sykes, Sir Tatton (1788), 4, 163
Sylva, Sir Francis de, 86
Syme, Sir Ronald (1925), 4, 379, 392–4,
    417, 433
Symon, C. H. N. (1912), **72**

Symons, Arthur, 273
Symonds, John Addington, 280
Symonds, Robert (1786), 188, 442

Talbot-Rice, David, 356
Tanner, J. D. P. (1945), 466
Tarleton, Sir Banastre, 109
Tarleton, J. E. (1802), 445
Taunton, William Ellis, 403
Taverner, Harvey (1864), 267
Taylor, A. J. P., 341
Taylor, D., 137
Taylor, G. O. M. (1923), 463
Taylor, Henry (1859), 257
Taylor, Jeremy (1626), 4, 53, 150, 274
Taylor, John (1893), 459
Taylor, M. J. (1824), 449
Taylor, Richard (1583), 39, 437
Taylor, Richard (1664), 66
Taylor, Sir Robert, **17,** 141
Taylor, T. W. J. (1913), 368, 382
Taylor, W. T. (1927), 339
Tegg, Thomas, **IV**
Telgarsky, Jeffrey (1983), 482
Temple, Frederick, 206, 227
Tench, John (1783), 172
Tennyson, Alfred, Lord, 197, 216, 221, 240
Terry, George (1785), 188, 442
Teulon, W. H., 355
Thackeray, William Makepeace, 4, 221, 295
Thellusson, Hon. Arthur (1820), 449
Theobald, M. J. (1958), 468
Thigpen, Samuel (1999), 483
Thom, Alexander, 138
Thomas, Albert, **82,** 379
Thomas, Arthur Gould (1951), 441
Thomas, C. H. (1870), 455
Thomas, F. H., 441
Thomas, Graham (1991), 483
Thomas, P. M. (1970), 471
Thomas, Roger, 441
Thomas, Walter (1910), 477
Thomas, William (1609), 86
Thompson, Benjamin, 86
Thompson, Claude Geoffrey Holt
    (1925), 440
Thompson, F. C., (1902), 460
Thompson, J. H. (1919), 462

Thompson, 'Sugary', 256
Thompson, T. R. (1896), 459
Thompson, William (1686), 124–5
Thomson, William (1895), 310, 459
Thornley, Sir Colin (1926), 463, 485
Thornton, Richard, 171
Thornycroft, C. E. (1868), 455
Thoyts, John (1789), 178
Thum, N. C. (1978), 472
Thyer, Robert (1727), 121–2, 145, 149
Tilney, Robert (1885), 302, 457
Tilton, Douglas (1982), 482
Timmis, M. A. (1969), 471
Timms, Harry, 336–7
Tindall, Mark (1995), 475, 483
Tisdall, Tony (1937), **86**, 371
Titchener, Edward (1885), 303
Tobin, Christopher (1961), 469, 481
Toler, Hector; 3rd Earl of Norbury
        (1829), 450
Tolkein, J. R. R., 368
Tolmie, John (1929), 478
Tombs, W. H., 251
Tomlins, Richard, 68
Tomlins, Mrs., (publican), 131
Tompson, Ralph (1565), 40
Tonge, Israel, 134
Toogood, Clifford (1894), 459
Torrens, J. R. (1896), 459
Tout, Thomas Frederick, 300
Townend, H. S. (1928), 464
Townsend, Christopher (1991), 431
Townshend, William (1868), 271
Tracey, John (1881), **59**
Trafford, Edward Leigh (1832), 189, 213
Trafford, John (1610), 47
Trafford, Trafford, 189
Traherne, L. E. (1852), 452
Traherne, Thomas (1653), 4, 73
Trappes, Robert, 23–4
Trappes-Lomax, E. N. (1898), 459
Tredwell, A. F. (1967), 470
Tree, M. P. (1977), 472
Treggiari, Susan (nee Franklin) (1958), 421
Trenchard, Hugh; 1st Viscount, 314
Trevelyan, George Macaulay, 277
Trevelyan-Thomas, W. F. (2005), 476
Trevor-Roper, Hugh; Baron Dacre, 393

Tristram, L. S. B. (1876), 455
Trope, R. L. (1969), 470
Trumbull, Sir William, 93–4, 98
Trunkfield, D. J. (1993), 474
Tucker, Eugene (1937), 479
Tucker, V. K. (1923), 478
Tucker, William (1955), **92**, 399
Tuckwell, William, 198
Tudor, John (1992), 483
Tuff, F. N. (1908), 461
Tulloch, Bob, 392
Tunstall, Cuthbert, 36
Turnbull, Malcolm (1978), 482
Turnbull, Ralph, 86
Turner, Edward Tindall (1840), **33**, 217,
        237, 247, 253, 261, 263–4, 275, 287
Turner, G. (1982), 473
Turner, J. M. W., 135
Turner, R. W. (1983), 473
Turnill, R. J. (1992), 474
Turnor, Cecil (1828), 450
Turton, Edmund (1876), 264
Turton, William (1653), 86
Twopenny, Rev., 42
Twinn, Peter (1935), 361
Tylecote, E. F. S., 285
Tyler, A. N. (1974), 472

Ulbricht, John, 387
Unbegaun, Boris (1953), 417, 423
Underhill, P. C. (1902), 460

Vaizey, John; Baron, 427
Vallance, Sir Iain (1962), 486
Van Campe, Carl (1912), 477
Van den Bergh, J. H. (1913), **72**, 321, 355
Van der Bijl, Pieter (1928), 347, 373,
        464, 478
Van Der Colff, William (1999), 483
Van Der Heyden, Constantin (1999), 483
Van Dyck, Sir Anthony, 54
Van Heerden, Belinda (1982), 482
Van Huyssteen, Matthys (1963), 481
Van Nost, John, Jnr., **19**,138–9
Vane, William; 3rd Duke of Cleveland
        (1809), 200, 447
Vaughan, H. Halford, 210, 233, 248
Vaux, Lawrence (1551), 32–3

Vawdrey, L. B. (1863), **47A**
Veale, Sir Douglas, 384
Veit, D. H. (1957), 468
Venables, E. E. (1868), 454
Venables, Peter (1618), 52, 55
Verdon-Smith, Sir Reginald (1932),
    404, 485
Verdon-Smith, W. G. (1967), 470
Vergil, Polydore, 10, 12
Verner, F. C. (1911), **75**, 462
Verner, J. E. (1823), 449
Vernon, George (1654), 86
Vernon, Ralph (1794), 443
Vernon, Robert, 55
Victoria, Queen, 360
Vidal, Lancelot (1906), 322
Vine, E. V. (1953), 401, 467
Vinter, G. D. (1975), 472
Vogenauer, Stefan (2002), 423
Von Bismark, K. L. (2006), 476
Von Dalwig, Baron George (1910), 477
Von de Heydem, C. J. (1999), 475
Von Marx, A. L. A. M. (1913), 321
Von Ruperti, J. C. (1933), **88**, 370, 479
Von Schorlemer, Baron Fritz (1913), 321
Vos, Wiesner (2000), 483
Voyle, William (1609), 86

Wace, Henry (1856), 241–2
Wace, Henry Charles (1886), **67**, 241,
    315–6, 319, 339, 341, 343–4,
    379–80, 461
Wace, P. R. (1920), 462
Waddilove, J. T. (2000), 475
Waddington, Samuel (1862), 259
Waddington, William (1854), 240
Wagner, A. D., 211
Waide, Sean (1931), 345
Wailes (of Newcastle), 204–5, 216
Wain, John (1943), 417, 424
Wain, C. N. (1964), 469
Waismann, Friedrick, 418
Wake, Abp. William, 94, 124
Wakeling, George (1887), **67**, 273, 307,
    317, 359–60, 362–3
Waldegrave, Hon. Augustus (1820), 449
Waldock, Sir Humphrey (1922), 339, 361,
    367, 383, 463, 485

Wales, Edward, Prince of; later King
    Edward VII, **43**, 263, 270
Wales, Albert Edward, Prince of Wales,
    later King Edward VIII, 371, 380
Walhouse, E. J. (later Littleton); Baron
    Hatherton (1809), 447
Walker, Anne, 23, 438
Walker, David (1932), 332, 372, 375, 464
Walker, Frank, 251
Walker, Ithiel (1649), 64
Walker, James (1734), 120
Walker, John (1837), 212
Walker, Joseph, 201, 231, 243
Walker, M. L. (1923), 1
Walker, Obadiah, 92–3, 134
Walker, Russell (1860), **55**, 270
Wall, Martin, 158
Wallace, D. A. (1980), 473
Wallace, Jock, 410
Waller, E.A. (1825), 450
Waller, Edmund (1846), 205
Wallis, John, 67, 73
Wallroth, Conrad (1870), 271
Walls, Richard (1837), 219
Walmesley, Henry (1573), 42
Walpole, Horace, 144
Walsh, D. R. (1965), 400
Walshe, Rachel (2002), 484
Walsingham, Sir Francis, 34
Walton, Izaak, 43, 89
Walton, M. C. (1982), 473
Walton, M. H. (1974), 472
Warburton, David (1938), 372
Warburton, Bp. William, 150
Ward, George ('Jolly'), 128–30
Ward, Mary (Mrs. Humphry Ward, née
    Arnold), 274–5, 277–9
Ward, Thomas Humphry (1864), 263,
    277–9, 281, 290
Ward, Tony (1939), 372
Ward, W. G. ('Ideal'), 223, 226
Warde, Charles (1804), 445
Wardell, W. M. (1959), 469
Ward-Jones, N. A. (1946), 486
Ware, John Hubert (1882), **59**, 303, 440
Warmstrey, Thomas (1628), 53
Warnock, Mary (née Wilson);
    Baroness, 420

Warr, A. L. (1932), 464
Warren, T. H., 275
Washington, George, 56
Washington, Laurence (1619), 4, 56
Waters, W. A. P. (1888), 440
Wates, C. S. (1959), 400
Watson, Albert (1847), **38, 39A, 50,** 191, 234, 242, 247, 263, 275, 281, 285, 292, 295, 299, 436, 439
Watson, J. Steven, 425
Watt, H. M. (1919), 462
Watteau, Antoine, 277, 282, 355
Waugh, Evelyn, 153, 354–7
Way, John (1869), 268
Way, R. J. (1997), 475
Wayland, Stephen (1990), 483
Waynflete, Bp. William, 21
Weatherly, Frederick Edward (1867), 4, 284–5
Wear, Eric (1985), 482
Webb, Matthew ['Capt. Webb'], 258
Wedgwood, Josiah; 1st Baron, 335
Weeks, Kelvin (1990), 483
Weguelin, A. G. (1876), 455
Weigall, Albert (1858), 242
Welch, Jillian (1980), 482
Welch, Kelly (1987), 482
Wellington, Arthur (Wellesley); 1st Duke of, 169, 178, 231
Wellington, Arthur (Wellesley); 2nd Duke of, 263
Wellman, Harvey (1937), 479
Wells, Frank (1953), 480
Wells, Thomas, **41,** 252, 296
Welton, Richard, 126–8, 134
Welton, Richard Jnr. (1724), 134
Went, John (2001), 475
Wentworth, Sir Charles, 2nd Bt. (1792), 443
Wentworth, Thomas (Noel); 2nd Viscount (1763), 439
Wesley, Charles, 115, 144, 150
Wesley, Emily, 131
Wesley, John, 121, 144, 149–50, 157
West, G. J.; 5th Earl Delawar (1810), 447
Westby, family, 153
Westcott, D. G. (1976), 472
Weston, Thomas (1646), 64, 438

Whadcoat, C. C. (1909), 461
Whaley, Anthony (1986), 482
Whalley, James (later Sir James Smythe-Gardiner, 3rd Bt.) (1804), 445
Whalley, J. C. (1824), 449
Whalley, Thomas (1793), 168, 443
Wheatley, William (1806), 165
Wheaton, Henry, 302
White, Bp. John, 29
White, J. B. (1858), 453
White, R. S. M. (1912), 322
White, Simon, 77
Whitefield, George, 149
Whitehead, A. T. (1946), 485
Whitehead, M. I. (1966), 470
Whitehead, Robert (1694), 96
White Thompson, J. H. (1924), 463
Whitinge, John, 55
Whitmore, W. W. (1872), 455
Whitney, Walter (1647), 60
Whittingham, William (1540), 30
Whittington, Richard (1860), **56, 57,** 265
Whittington, (stainer glazier), 289
Whittlesey, (engraver), **6**
Whittuck, Charles (1868), 281, 286, 298, 306
Whitworth, E. G. W. W. (1997), 475
Whyte, William, v
Wickham, Samuel (1632), 86
Wiggins, David (1951), 398
Wilberforce, Samuel, 215
Wilbraham, Henry (1719), 438
Wilbraham, Roger, 191
Wilbraham, Sir Thomas, 2nd Bt. (1618), 74
Wild, John, 77
Wilde, James (1650), 120
Wilde, Oscar, 246, 257, 268, 276, 280, 283, 288
Wildgoss, Thomas, 138
Wilkes, C. L. (1988), 474
Wilkes, John, 153
Wilkins, John, 67, 73
Willcocks, J. P. (1994), 474
Willes, Edward (1821), 449
William III, King [William of Orange], 94–5, 98, 130, 203

Williams, C. A. E. (1903), 460
Williams, C. F. (1923), **77**, 344
Williams, F. G. (1896), **66**
Williams, Geoffrey (1894), 312
Williams, Graeme (1955), **92**
Williams, G. D. I. (1995), 475
Williams, Henry (1797), 444
Williams, H. C. H. (1978), 472
Williams, Isaac, 211
Williams, John, 189
Williams, Bp. John, 44–5, 49
Williams, Lloyd (1946), 480
Williams, M. D. (1978), 472
Williams, N. P. (1793), 443
Williams, Robert, 285
Williamson, A. C. (1911), **75**, 461
Williamson, John, 23, 155, 437
Williamson, William (1648), 64
Willis, Browne, 134
Willis, Francis (1734), 5
Willis, John (1769), 151
Willis, Thomas (1703), 135
Willmer, A. F. (1909), **74**, 319–20
Wilner, Daniel (2007), 484
Wilson, A. N., 338
Wilson, Edward (1868), 454
Wilson, G. A. (1946), 346, 465, 486
Wilson, G. R. (1992), 474
Wilson, Harold; Baron, 387
Wilson, John (1651), 86
Wilson, J. M., 248, 250
Wilson, R. S. (1849), **38**, 247
Wilson, R. W. (1955), 400
Wilton, Thomas (Egerton); 1st Earl of,
    165
Wimperis, E. J. (1948), 400, 466
Winchelsea, Henry (Finch-Hatton); 13th
    Earl of, 319
Winder, Thomas (1726), 114–5
Windham, R. C. (1827), 450
Windlesham, David (Hennessey); 3rd
    Baron (1951), **96**, v, 430, 432, 436
Winfield, Thomas (1800), 445
Wingfield, Hon. Edward (1811), 447
Winniffe, Bp.Thomas, 62
Winstanley, George (1807), 446
Winter, George Robert (1845), 205,
    244, 256

Winter, Roger (1808), 447
Wise, (mercer), 100
Wise, Henry (1791), 443
Witcher, D. R. (1962), 469
Withington, N. R. (1975), 472
Witt, Joanne de, 191
Wittock, N., 168
Witton, Joshua (1631), 86
Wix, Randolph (1904), 460
Wodenoth, Arthur, 55
Wodhull, Michael (1758), 108
Wolsey, Thomas; Cardinal, 19, 22
Wong, Alfred (1990), 483
Wood [à Wood], Anthony, 17, 19–20,
    26–7, 39, 50, 58, 64–6, 69, 72, 85–6,
    90–1, 93–4, 134
Wood, C. J. (1849), **38**, 247
Wood, Sir Henry, 410
Wood, James (1763), 151, 157–8
Woodcock, James (1763), 151
Woodforde, James ['Parson'], 107–8, 121,
    151, 157–9
Woodgate, Walter Bradford (1859), **44,
    57,** 4, 244, 254–9, 266, 268, 285,
    287–9
Woodhouse, John (1837), 212–13, 451
Woods, E. R. (1962), 469
Woods, F. K. S. (1929), 479
Woods, Michael (1952), 389, 430
Woodward, Michael, 438
Woodward, William (1946), 480
Woolf, Virginia, 317, 353
Woolfe, Philip (2001), 432
Worde, Wynken de, 13
Wordsworth, Bp. John (1861), 263,
    280–81, 285, 287, 294, 304, 439
Wordsworth, William, 248
Workman, Keith (1951), 398, 467
Worley, George (1840), 451
Worsley, Thomas, 139
Worthington, Michael (1932), 372
Worthington, Thomas (1570), 35–6
Worthington, William (1838), 451
Wren, Sir Christopher, 73, 130
Wrenn, C. L., 368
Wright, John (1638), 86
Wright, William (1714), 133
Wrighte, Nathan (1696), 135

Wrigley, P. T. (1999), 475
Wroe, Richard, 146
Wroe, Robert (1774), 108, 157
Wroe, Thomas (1719), 146
Wurm, Stanilas, 319
Wyatt, George, 168, 240
Wyatt, James, 155, 165
Wyatt, Sir Thomas, 32
Wylie, Sir Francis (1884), 301, 328
Wynn, C. W. Williams, 197
Wynne, O., 93
Wyvill, Edward (1811), 447

Yarborough, Francis (1713), **28,** 95, 115,
    154–5, 436, 438
Yardley, (cricketer), 271
Yate, Mrs. Elizabeth (née
    Bartlett); formerly Lady
    Cave, 71, 86

Yate, Jeremiah (1677), 86, 161
Yate, Samuel (1639), 70, 86
Yate, Thomas (1619), **13,** 61–3,
    70–1, 74, 77, 83, 86, 383,
    436, 438
Yate, Thomas (1665), 86
Yate, Thomas (1685), 86
Yate, William (1662), 86
Yates, William (1795), 444
Yates, William (1849), **38,** 247, 261
Yeates, W. B., 247
Yeld, George (1863), 284
Yelverton, Hon. William
    (1810), 447
Yeomans, H. W. (1911), 320
Young, F. G. M. (2004), 476
Young, James (1885), 303
Young, J. M. (1938), 347
York, Duke of, 177

EPITOME

"Epitomes [are] the moths of just history; they eat out the poetry of it" (Shelley, *A Defence of Poetry* [1822] Camelot edn., 1886, 9).

FABRIC

Site

site before College buildings (1509), 8–9
site plan (1909): showing stages of building, 434–5

Buildings

Earliest College Buildings:
   intended building of College first
      mentioned (1508), 10–11
   first College buildings (1509–21),
      17–21
   foundation stone laid (1509), 17
   materials used in construction, 18
   survival of elements from Brasenose
      Hall (in Kitchen and Old
      Lodgings), 19, 75
   few documents relating to early
      buildings, 17
   survey of College buildings in
      Bereblock's woodcut (1566), 17
   view of, in Agas's map (1578), **6**, 17
   sculpted heads of Alfred and Scotus
      (1509), 6–7
   Lecture room VII, and VII, 2 (first
      gentlemen scholars), 22
   Dog, or Dagg, lane (1609), 76
   sculpted heads of Smith and Sutton
      (1635), 10–11
   extensions to College buildings: attics,
      dormers etc. (1604 onwards;
      1635–7), 45, 75–6
   further extensions to College buildings:
      chapel, library, cloister
      (1656–66), 74–80

improvements to College buildings: hall,
      lodgings, common room etc.
      (1670s–80s), 18, 81–3
   Radcliffe's schemes for extensions, 75
Tower:
   construction (c1510–20), 18–19
   porter's lodge; gates, 18, 155, 339
   provisions stored in, during Civil
      War, 54
   sash windows inserted in
      (c.1730), 135
   timber mullions substituted by
      H. Hakewill (1817), 18, 81, 168
   original work a model for Gothic
      revivalists (1823), 18
   statuary and stone mullions replaced by
      J. C. Buckler (1861–3), **46**, 168
   Haig memorial, 314–5, 407
   Tower Bursary; Treasury, 18, 168
Chapel and its furnishings:
   temporary chapel (pre 1520), 19
   first chapel (1520–1666; later SCR),
      19–20, 50
      Bp. Smith's bequest to (1513),
         19, 56
      vestments, plate etc., 41, 56, 79
      forms of service in, 19–20, 55, 59
      converted into college rooms
         (1667), 81
   second chapel (1656–66), 74–80
      foundation stone laid (1656), 74,
         76, 78
      building accounts, 77–8
      progress of building, 76–78

both sides in Civil War contribute to cost, 74

consecration of (1666), 74

vaulting; roof above from old St. Mary's Coll., 79–80

eclectic style, 79–80

windows; old tracery removed to Denton House, Oxon. (1844–5), 79

seating arrangements in, 80, 295

forms of service, 74, 84, 275, 409

eagle lectern (1708; 1731; 1860), 222

chandeliers (1749; 1887), 222

candles (in 1843), 222

organ (1876; 1892), 295, 311

decoration by J.C. Buckler (1859–61), 80, 239

redecoration by C. E. Kempe (1895), 80, 295

refurbishment (1951; 1980), 80

reredos (1733; 1860;1902; 1980), 222, 295

'glory' (on reredos of 1733; 1819), 222

stained glass in, 156, 204–5, 216, 289, 295

antechapel, **32**

burials in, 124, 125–6, 141, 156, 174, 177, 200, 204, 232, 383

memorials in, 141, 174, 177

cloister (1657–63), 79

burials in, 71, 74, 86, 125, 161

converted into rooms by J. Soane (1807), **63**, 166

burials elsewhere, 71, 74, 87, 91, 154, 161, 198, 212, 275

Common Rooms:

first SCR (c.1682; later II, 3), 81, 135

second SCR (I, 4; 1707 onwards), 135, 181

pictures in, 12, 54–5, 107

coats of arms in, 135

chairs in, 135

smoking room, adjoining (1899; 1936; 1965), 135, 292

first JCR (IX, 3; later Shackleton Room), 292

modelled on Glastonbury Court House, 292

second JCR (1937; previously part of Principal's New Lodgings; later Stallybrass Law Library), 339

third JCR (1958: previously Principal's entrance hall), 292–3

first HCR (1962; previously cloister), 166

second HCR (2008; previously III,3), 166

Hall:

construction (c1520), 20–21

reconstruction (1683–4), 82–3

unicorn (1684), 83, 406

ceiling (1751–2), 82

alterations (1748; 1751–54; 1763), 155

seating arrangements in, 21

furniture in 82–3

portraits in, **2, 3, 9, 10, 11, 12, 13, 22, 25, 28**, 12, 13, 41, 77, 118, 152, 174, 211

Hulme's memorial brass in, 119

stained glass in, 9, 12–13, 155, 164

chandeliers in (1772), 155

gas lighting in (1839), 155

brazen nose, placed in (1890), 9–10

lectures in, 362–3

Library:

first library (c1520 onwards; later IV, 4), 20, 82

second library (1657–63), 76–7

chained volumes in, until 1779, 155

new ceiling and columns by J. Wyatt (1779–82), 155

tracery renewed by P. Hardwick (1845), 155

old tracery removed to Denton House (1844–5), 155

opened to undergraduates (1879), 315–6

windows re-opened on west side (1954), 155

Stallybrass Law Library (previously part of New Lodgings), 339

Principal's Lodgings:
    first, in tower (c1520–1771), 18
      improved by Radcliffe (c1635), 76
      further improvements (1690s), 18
      converted into college rooms (1771),
        155–6
    second, in High Street (1771–1887), 156
    third, in High Street (1887–90), 292–3
      partly converted into JCR, Stallybrass
        Law Library, etc. (1937; 1958),
        339
    fourth (1956 onwards; previously
      VI, 1–6), 174–5
Old Quad:
    first buildings (c1509–20), 17–19
    cocklofts, dormers etc. (1604–37), 18,
      45, 75–6
    Hawksmoor's plans for (1719–20),
      18, 137
    sundial in (1719), 138
    statue of 'Cain and Abel' in (1727;
      removed 1881), **19**, 138–9
    sash windows in (c1730), 135
    Soane's plan for attic additions
      (1804), **20A**
    two oriels, on N. and E. sides, inserted
      by J. C. Buckler (1861–3), **23,
      47B**, 168, 244
Chapel Quad ('Deer Park'):
    stages in building (1657–66), 75–81
    cloisters in (1657–66), 76–7, 79
      converted into college rooms
        (1807), 167
      re-converted into HCR (1962) and
        library (2010), 166
    staircase VIII (17th–18th c.), 292
Back Quad (site of New Quad):
    New Buildings: Old Staircase 10
      (1809; dem. 1887), 167, 290
    Garden Buildings: Old Staircase 9 (1740;
      1810; dem. 1883), 167, 290
    New Quad: plans by N. Hawksmoor
      (1712–13; 1723; 1734), **18**,
      137–8
      plans by J. Wyatt (1800), 165
      plans by J. Nash (1800), 165–6

      plans by J. Soane (1804–8), **20A,
      21A, 21B**, 166
      plans by P. Hardwick (1809), **20B**, 167
    High Street frontage purchased (1715,
      1724, 1727, 1736), 135, 156, 290
    Plans and buildings by T. G. Jackson
      (1881–1911), 290–95
    rejected plans for new tower (1887),
      70, 293–4
Peripheral College Buildings:
    All Saints Entry, 301
    St. Mary's Entry (1887–9), **52B**, 294
    Platnauer Building [staircases xvii–xviii]
      (1959–61), 403–5
    Frewin Hall (1887–94; 1975–81;
      1996–97), **43**, 78, 294, 430
    Grandpont House (1785; sold 1958), 403
    Cricket pavilion (1894–6), 309
    St. Cross Building (1996), 430
Gardens:
    Old Quad: maze or garden in,
      7, 135–6
    Principal's garden (south of chapel),
      82, 248
    Fellows' garden (site of New Quad), 19,
      138–9
    'Deer Park', in chapel quad, 76–7, 82
Particular Staircases:
    staircases I to VII (c1509–20), 17–19
      cocklofts and dormers (1604–37), 18,
      45, 76
      lecture room VII, 21–2, 329, 338,
      362, 410
    new staircases IX to XIII (1881–1911),
      291–93
      Beer Cellar and New Buttery
      ['Gertie's'], (staircase X), 410,
      423
      Broadgates and Amsterdam
      (1909–11), 293
      lecture room XI, 329
    Staircases XIV (1929) and XV (1931)
      ['Arab Quarter'], 339, 365, 397
    Heberden Staircase [former
      Lodgings], 388
    Stamford House (1895), 317

Particular Rooms:

Atiyah's rooms (VII, 4), 359

Buchan's rooms (VIII, 1; I, 7; VI, 3), 309

Bussell's rooms (VII, 2; XII, 5), 340, 365

Chaffers' rooms (IV, 4), 20, 244–5

Churton's rooms (VI, 4), 213

Cohn's rooms (IV, 4), 20, 381

Collieu's rooms (II, 3), 81–2

Cowdrey's rooms (Frewin Hall), 401

Dalwig's rooms (III, 3), 322

Daubuz's rooms (II, 3), 81–2, 265

Downer's [Evangelicals] rooms
(old X), 264

Finch-Hatton's rooms (117 High
St.), 319

Fitzpatrick's [pet python] rooms (II, 2),

Gokuldas's rooms (Amsterdam 2), 337

Golding's rooms (IV, 6), 368–9

Graham's ['Sebastian's'] rooms (22
High Street), 355

Haig's rooms (IV, 2), 295

Heap's [Vincent's] rooms (III, 3), 295–6

Heber's rooms (VI, 3), 174–5, 196

Hole's rooms (IV, 6), 218

Holroyd's rooms (XII, 5), 363

Jackson's rooms (IX, 1), 322

Johnston's rooms (VI, 3), 344

Jones's rooms (old X, 8), 263

Larking's rooms [Freemasons] (O.L.4),
190

Lawson's rooms (Heberden 1), 388

Leckie's rooms (O. L. 7–9), 397

Meredith's rooms (IV, 5), 199

Morgan's rooms (II, 3), 81–2, 352

Pater's rooms (O. L. 4–5; later
O. L. 2–3), 258, 272–3, 283, 288

Platnauer's rooms (VI, 4), 76, 365

Price's [Pre-Raphaelites] rooms (VI, 6),
237

Prichard's rooms (VI, 3), 284

Radcliffe's rooms (old IX, 9), 189

Schaffgotsch's rooms (III, 3), 321

Shackleton's rooms (IX, 3–4), 340, 391

Shand's rooms (VII, 2), 260

Stallybrass's rooms (IV, 4), 20,
336–7, 367

Stocker's rooms (XI, 3), 292, 341–2

Styler's rooms (VII, 2), 389

Syme's rooms (XI, 3), 394

Tower Bursary, 18–19, 76

Trafford's rooms (III, 3), 189

Turner's rooms (VI, 4), 76

Waddington's rooms (VI, 5), 259

Weatherley's rooms (old X, 7; III, 6), 284

Webb Ellis's rooms (I, 8), 219

'White Room' [Ward's rooms], (III, 4),
62, 277

Woodgate's rooms (V, 4), 266

Woodhouse's rooms (III, 5), 213

Outbuildings; Buttery, Kitchen,
Brew-house, Stables:

Buttery, construction (c 1510–20),
17, 19
ceases to serve commons (1932), 338

Kitchen, construction and retention of
(15th c.), 75

Brew-house, old (1696 onwards), 82
new (1826 onwards), 292

Stable: old (Glassyn Hall), 75,
140–41
new (Holywell St.), 141

Lighting:

gas lighting in rooms (1854),

electric lighting in rooms (1893),

Plumbing:

old privies or 'bogg house'
(Back Quad), 81

chamber pots, cold water hip-baths
(pre-1910), 243, 251, 291

lavatories and bath house (1862; 1909),
291

bathrooms (staircase XII), first
(1909–11), 291, 293, 337

'en suite' plumbing, first (1960
onwards), 291

ESTABLISHMENT

Brasenose Hall
site of, 7–9
expansion of, 8
teaching at, 8–9

Brasenose College
Founders (1509), 10–14
Aims and ideals, 14–16

Brasenose College (Cont.)
　Charter (1512), 11
　Statutes (1514), 13
　Statutes (1522), 13–4, 16
　Reforming Ordinances (1855–57), 13,

Finance

College Income:
　Brasenose income doubles
　　between 1514 and 1535, 23
　and nearly doubles between 1535
　　and 1547, 23
　college endowments
　　significantly increase: 28
　　major benefactors
　　1509–1609, 23
　but college debts accumulate, 1588–92, 49
　and college seriously in debt by 1643, 49
　however college income recovers
　　by 1649, 69
　and continues to increase in 1660s and
　　1670s, 81
　college deficits recorded in 1761, 1791
　　and 1801, 103–4
　but college enjoys a surplus in 1771 and
　　1781, 103–4
　'the best endowed College in the
　　University' (Farington, 1794),
　　163
　college income doubles between 1790
　　and 1810, 163
　and increases by half between 1810 and
　　1860, 163, 205
　benign effect of College Estates
　　Acts (1858; 1860), 205
　ratio of internal and external income in
　　1871, 252
　income from urban rents in
　　1880s–1890s more than
　　compensates for agricultural
　　losses in 1870s, 252
　net external income rises by a third,
　　1871–1903, 315
　and gross income rises by more than a
　　third, 1879–1916, 315
　Brasenose settles into upper third sector
　　in table of college incomes,
　　1918, 330

Slump 1931–2: only minor effects
　　of, 353–4
but BNC slips from third to eleventh in
　　college-income table between
　　1930–32 and 1951–3, 385
yet by 1957 net external income is
　　double that of 1938, 386
college endowment multiplies in 1960s
　　and shrinks in 1970s, 429
capital endowment increases sevenfold,
　　1982–2000, 429
by 1997–8, BNC ranks thirteenth out of
　　thirty six in Oxford's inter-
　　college table of gross
　　endowment income, 430

Individual College Benefactors:
Allen, 20
Baker, 23
Binks (Stoddard), 437
Booth, 20
Brudenall, 21
Bury, 21
Church, 438
Claymond, 15, 23
Clifton, 13, 23
Colquitt, 439
Colton, 20
Cox, 13, 23
Croston, 10–11, 20
Darbie, 23
Elizabeth I, 23
Fermor, 20
Frankland, 23–4
Greville, 21
Grimbaldson, 168
Harpur, 15, 23
Haster, 20
Heath Harrison, 350
Henley, 438
Higden, 23
Hulme, 118–20
Mason, 20
Mordaunt, 23–4
Morley, 13, 23–4
Nowell, 18, 23–4
Ogle, 13, 23
Oldham, 20

Palin, 23
Pigott, 20
Platnauer, 365, 423
Port, 21, 23
Porter, 23
Smith, 11–12, 22–23
Somerset (Iver and Thornhill), 117–8
Stallybrass, 379
Sutton, 12–15, 22
Walker, 23
Williamson, 23
Yate, 438

Particular College Estates:
Ashton-under-Lyne, Lancs., 119
Denton, Lancs., 119
Didsbury, Lancs., 107
Harwood, Lancs., 119
Heaton Norris, Lancs., 119
Iver, Bucks., 118
London: 39–53, Kensington High
    Street, 23–24
Prescot, Lancs., 14, 33, 38, 48, 154, 164
Prestbury, Cheshire, 14, 48
Redditch, Lancs., 119
Stow Wood, Oxon., 419
Thornhill, Wilts., 118
Wootton Rivers, Wilts., 118

Particular College Livings:
Catworth Magna, Hants., 100
Clayton, Sussex, 198
Cottingham, Northants., 63, 98
Didcot, Oxon., 125, 131
East Ham, London (St. Mary
    Magdalen), 249
Great Billing, Northants., 125–6, 131
Great Rollright, Oxon., 71, 87, 98, 172,
    250, 362
Great Shefford, Cambs., 256
Middleton Cheney, Oxon., 63, 70,
    86, 98, 125
Northolt, Middx., 306
Steeple Aston, Oxon., 29, 45, 63, 65, 71,
    74, 90, 125, 382
Stepney, London (St. George in the
    East), 126, 131, 244
Stoke Bruerne, Northants., 258

Whitechapel, London (St. Mary
    Matfelon), 127–8, 131, 134

The College Community

Principal and Fellows:
original 'Scholar Fellows' to be chosen
    from Lancashire and Cheshire;
    in particular from Prestbury and
    Prescot (1512; 1522), 13–14
their stipends (1512; 1522), 14
the cost of their commons (16th c.), 26
origins of Fellows during 17th c.: 43%
    plebeians or paupers; 1% titled
    families, 46
their stipends and allowances
    still meagre (1634), 46–7
and their emoluments slow to rise
    (1649), 69–70
the Fellowship continues to be drawn
    predominantly from Lancashire
    and Cheshire (1710; 1770), 99
strong links among Fellowship
    with Manchester Grammar
    School, 99
e.g. 18 Fellows (1738–73), 117
and 7 successive Vice-Principals
    (1770s–80s), 120
Senior Fellowships rise to £200 p.a.;
    Junior to £140 p.a. (1794), 163
despite efforts of Frodsham Hodson,
    Close Fellowships remain
    unreformed (1819), 169
composition of Fellowship (1835),
    201–2
elections to Fellowships on the basis of
    remote kinship continue
    (Maddock, 1827; Ormerod,
    1838; Barlow, 1846), 228, 230
belated abolition of Close Fellowships
    (1855), 232–3
no elections to Fellowship between
    1855 and 1863, 242
Fellows now elected by open
    examination (1855–81), or
    at least after public
    advertisement (1881–5),
    287, 304

The College Community (Cont.)

Fellows in 1861 (group photo), **38**, 247–50

relative salaries of Principal and Fellows (1871), 205, 252–3

relative earnings of married and unmarried Fellows (Ward and Pater; early 1870s), 278

Fellows of BNC and Lincoln compared (1877–8), 286

Fellows in 1907 (group photo), **67**, 315–7

two Fellows killed in World War I (Brandt and Hutchison), 321

Fellows between World War I and II, 339–42

Fellows during World War II, 369–70, 375–6

changing balance of Fellowship: 8 elections in 2 years (1946–48), 378–81

Fellows in 1950s and 1960s, 387–96
   Arts, 387–92
   Sciences, 395

continuing strength of Law, 360–61, 388–9

feuding in the SCR (Last *versus* Syme, 1948–55), 392–4

changing balance of Fellowship: eight elections in two years (1966–68), 396

academic distinction of SCR during mid 1970s: 16 FBAs; 4FRSs, 417

growing strength of Politics, Philosophy and Economics in 1980s–90s, 430–31

first female Fellows elected (Stokes and Beddington, 1981–2), 421

Servants, Scouts, Porters:
   very few college employees in 16th c.; eg. manciple, cook, porter, clerks, 38
   their wages, 38–9

laundress (1552), 26

equivocal status of butler, cook, steward (17th–18th c.), 107, 161

   one steward a brother of Principal Yate (late 17th c.), 161

one butler a brother of Principal Barker (mid 18th c.), 161

Principal's patronage: servants and tradesmen (1706), 133–4, 141

Principal's servants (1720s), 126

barber (1774–1816), 186

common room man transported for theft (Brucker, 1788), 112

servitors cease to wait in Hall (1799), 199

frugal pension of under-butler (1825), 186

shoeblack's duties (1819; 1861), 186, 252

bedmaker's duties (1820), 199

servants' wages and perquisites (1861), 250–52

scouts' foibles, parodied in *Verdant Green* (1853), 219, 251

daily gallon of beer for scouts (King, 1920s), 336

scouts transfer to Ch. Ch. in World War II, 370

scouts' reaction to Suez (1956), 399

retirement of last generation of scouts; few replaced (1970s), 419

male scouts give way to female domestics (1980s onwards), 419

Individual scouts, porters etc.:
   group photo (1861), **41**, 250–52

Bossum (Head Porter, 1860), **40**, 205, 250

Brookings (Cohn's scout, 1950s), 341

Bustin (Platnauer's scout, 1920s), 336

Charlwood (Pater's first scout, 1860s), **41**, 251

Drake (silver cleaner, c. 1899–1956), 336

Hawkins (head porter, 1861–66), 251

'old Job' (Ch. Ch.; 1686), 92

King (college groundsman, 1895–1963), **90**, 407–8

Markham (beer cellar manager, 1950s), 410–11

Newman (common room man, 1886), 204

Prior (butler, 1861), **41**

Southern (Stocker's scout, 1930s–40s), 342

Stone (undershoeblack, second
hallman, bedmaker
1898–1938), 336
Thomas (Principal's butler, 1944), **82**
Timms (Sonners' scout, 1930s), 336–7
Tombs (Pater's underscout, 1880s), 251
Walker (Pater's second scout, 1880s),
251
Wallace (head hallman,
1957–85), 411

SOCIETY

Living

Accommodation in College:
shared rooms (16th– early
17th c.), 17–18
rooms for gentlemen scholars
(staircase VII), 21–2
'rooms not answerable for families'
(Elizabeth I, 1561), 40
record numbers crammed into
limited space (early 17th c.),
24–5
improved accommodation
(later 17th c.), 81–2
rooms for boisterous living (1725),
101–2, 121–2
Hawksmoor's unbuilt apartments
(1734), 140
'Gentlemen's lodgings' planned in
High St. (1770), 156
college 'superabundantly full' (1800),
170
rooms planned for Hulme
exhibitioners (1795–1810),
165–7
'temporary' buildings (1740;
1809–10), 167
homes fit for gentry (1790; 1801),
171, 174–5
primitive plumbing (old
New Buildings; staircase I,
1837–40), 243
cocklofts "small but snug"
(IV, 6; 1840), 218
attics 'a veritable nest of poets' (VI, 6;
1857), 239

a 'set' of undergraduates: for
breakfast and lunch (II,3;
1862–4), 265
Pater paints his panelling;
first primrose, then green
(O.L. 4–5; 1864 onwards), 272
Ward paints his panelling white
(1870), 277
'my own furniture, my own pictures,
my own piano' (Weatherley in
III,6; 1869), 284
rooms planned picturesquely
by Anglo-Jackson (1881
onwards), 291–2
Atiyah decorates 'the cheapest set in
College' (attic on staircase VII;
1924), 359
'cheery yellow' and 'cherry red'
(Parsons' rooms on staircase
XV; 1929), 365
'bare wooden stairs, a fire and all the
bells of Oxford' (Golding in IV,
6; 1931–2), 369
Syme reluctantly pays £30 per term
for XI, 3 (1953–70), 394
'heroic brutalism' of rooms
in Platnauer Building
(1959–61), 405
Accommodation out of College:
smart lodgings in Catte St. (1862),
42A-B, 264
poor lodgings in St. John St. (1923),
359
Graham ['Sebastian'] at 22 High St.
(1923–4), 355
Finch-Hatton at 117 High St.
(1908–9), 319
Fellows' Houses:
Butler (13 Crick Rd.; 1882), 315
Holroyd (1, Holywell; 1932), 363
'Foxwood', Boar's Hill, 364
Lodge (23 Norham Rd.), 301
Brasenose House, All Saints Entry
(c.1886), 301
37 St. Margaret's Rd. (1887), 301
Madan (St. Mary's Entry c. 1886), 294
Pater (2, Bradmore Rd.), 278

Living (*Cont.*)
12, Earl's Terrace, London, 278
64, St. Giles, 278
Spalding ('The Hurst', Henley), 340
Wace ('Paradise', Crowcombe,
Somerset), 344
Ward (5, later 17, Bradmore
Rd.), 279
Entertainment:
'tipling, dicing, carding, talking' (1582),
26
Parson Woodforde plays cards for
money in SCR (1774–5), 157–8
dangers of gaming (1838), 212
'Russy' Walker teaches Prince of Wales
to play cards (1860), 258
whist and 'vingt-et- un' popular
(1802–4), 265
Haig refuses roulette (1881), 297
Finch-Hatton's midnight roulette
parties at 117 High St. (1909),
319
Music:
Early chapel organs (16th c.), 19
Heberden's organ (1892–3), 295
rebuilt by Collins (1972–3), 295
renewed by Bower (2001), 295
hymns by Heber, **30**, 197
anthems by Caswall, 207
songs and lyrics by Weatherley, 284
Bussell collecting folk-tunes
('Widecombe Fair', 1890s), 305
Bussell's incidental music for
Shakespeare and Aristophanes
(1890s), 306
Piano recitals by Heberden and Stocker
(1919), 342
Stocker playing Bach on piano (1920s),
341
Platnauer playing Brahms on
gramophone (1930), 365
Platnauer playing Chopin on pianola
(1930), 365
Sonners' knowledge of music 'great and
genuine' (Bowra, 1948), 384
The Beatles, visit of (1964), 403
Platnauer Concerts (1970s onwards), 432

Theatre:
Grimald's *Christus Redivivus* performed
in hall (1542), 30
Cottam, Shakespeare's tutor (1590s), 38
The Act [predecessor of
Encaenia], 90
a Brasenose *terrae filius* (1665; 1669), 91
Brasenose satirised (1704; 1779), 102–3
theatricals outside college; imported
actresses (1847), 256
first college theatricals in Oxford, at
BNC (1858–9), 256
continued in 1861–63,
256–9
banned by proctors (1871); revived,
with imported amateur actresses
(1883), 257
continued in 1890s (fancy dress), **II,
III**, 306
Morgan as President of OUDS
(1920–21), 352
Graham ['Sebastian'] as a member of
OUDS (1924), 355
BNC prominent in OUDS (1925), 355
Arts Week (1980s onwards), 432
Club Life:
Alfred Lodge (1769), 150–153
Apollo Lodge (1819), 190–191, 264–5,
266, 268
Authentics ['Tics] (1883), 327–8, 355
'The Bollinger', 355
Brasenose Society (1937), 485–6
The Bullingdon [Ch. Ch.], 208
Chess Club (1810), 198
The Club [O.U.] (1790), 191
Crocodile Club (1896), 310
Daubuz's circle (1861–63), 265
Ellesmere Society (c.1933), 423
The Gridiron [O.U.], (1884), 267
Hulme Common Room (1962), 413
Hypocrites Club [O.U.], 356
Ingoldsby Essay Club (1879), **66**, 303,
352
The Isis [Ch. Ch.], 208
Junior Common Room (1887), **68**, 377
Loder's [Ch. Ch.], 267
Music Society (1932), 368

New Reform Club (O. U.), 352
The Octagon (1866), **47A**, 267,
      322, 423
The Owls (1850s), 240
Pater Society (1907), **74**, 319–20,
      397, 423
Phoenix Common Room (1782), **48, 75,**
      153, 187–9, 213, 240, 298, 321, 423
Price's [Pre-Raphaelite] circle
      (1854–58), 237–40
The Quintain [Ch. Ch.], 208
Railway Club [O.U.], 354
Rouser's [Ch. Ch.], 267
Roxburghe Club, 193–4, 247
[Limpsfield] Strollers (1923), 327–8
The Survivors, 340
Sutton Society, 312
The Tome (1862), 267
The Vampires (1865), **58, 59**, 267
Vincent's (1863), **52A**, 266–7
The Wanderers (1919), **79**, 327

Learning

Teaching and Examinations:
   earliest college lectureships
         (1522 onwards), 14–16, 23
   early role of the college tutor
         (1522 onwards), 21–22
   Tutor first becomes one of the Fellows
         (1576), 22
   four Fellows usually acting as
         Tutors (early 17th c.), 22
   genesis of tutorial system; duties of
         Tutor, financial, disciplinary
         and didactic (early 17th c.),
         22, 66, 88–9
   Andrews 'a special good tutor' (1622),
         47
   decline of University lectures (late 16th–
         early 17th c.), 37
   unreformed system of University
         examinations (mid 18th c.),
         159–60
   Napleton of Brasenose initiates change
         (1773), 159
   programme of examination reform
         (1773–1809), 160, 171
   outstanding results under Frodsham
         Hodson (1801 onwards),
         169–71
   teaching improvements at BNC (1809),
         168–9
      Collections in Hall (1809), 168
      Declamation in ante-chapel (1809),
         168
   but Hodson prevented from opening up
         elections to Fellowships (1819),
         169
   Richard Heber's vacation reading
         (1793), 179
   Smythe's revision reading for Oriel
         (1800) 179–80
   Clive's criticism of BNC teaching
         (1817), 186–7
   but scholars no longer regarded as
         'charity boys' (1830), 199
   inadequate separation of Pass and
         Honours teaching (1830), 206–7
   lack of matriculation exam prior to entry
         (1840s), 209
   but BNC unusual in teaching Maths
         seriously (1840s), 209
   Responsions instituted at BNC (1850),
         209
   reform of University Final Honours
         (1850), 209
   teaching, inadequate at BNC (1856),
         241–2
   respectable results in 1860s, despite
         emphasis on sport, 260–61
   though much depends on private
         coaching (1860s), 285
   decline in numbers reading for Honours
         (1871–75), 262
   research versus administration (1878),
         286
   Heberden and Lodge aim to raise
         intellectual level (1890s),
         300–301
   Pass men: gradually declining numbers
         (1880s; 1890s; 1912–60), 302,
         348–9
   BNC institutes an entrance examination
         (1901), 301

Learning (Cont.)
  examination results improving
    (1894–1925), 307. 360
  increasing numbers of Firsts
    (1901–1910), 307
  examination results in decline, except in
    Law (1926–32; 1933–1939),
    360–61
  rarity of Firsts at BNC (1919–1969), 361–2
  scarcely improving (1946–54), 397
  but record results in 1955, 397–8
  results in 1930s and 1950s compared,
    398–9
  tutorials: meagre staff-student ratio, in
    1948, 1958 and 1964, 386
  CUF lectureships (1954), 415
  attempts to improve lack-lustre results,
    1960s–70s, 417–8
  PPE prospers in 1980s and 1990s, 430–31
  record results in 2001, 432

Individual Studies and Texts:
  Aeschylus, 179, 187, 208, 32–6
  Aldrich, Henry, 207
  Aldrovandi, Ulisse, 20
  Ambrose, St., 15
  Andrewes, Lancelot, 215
  Aristophanes, 165, 208, 306
  Aristotle, 16, 36–7, 47, 187, 208–9,
    360, 389
  Augustine, St., 15
  Bacon, Sir Francis, 249–50
  Banez, Domingo, 47
  Bellarmine, St. Robert, 20
  Bentivoglio, Guido, 89
  Boethius, Anicius, 36
  Buridad, Jean, 47
  Catullus, 369
  Cicero, Marcus Tullius, 16, 36, 115
  Claudian, 191–2, 366
  Dante, 225, 274, 359
  Demosthenes, 179
  Descartes, René, 67
  Erasmus, Desidarius, 16, 78
  Euclid, 36, 169, 207, 301
  Euripides, 179, 187, 207, 300, 366
  Ezekiel, 138
  Fagius, Paulus, 20

  Florus, Lucius, 88
  Frisius, Gemma, 36
  Gassendi, Pierre, 67
  Grote, George, 209
  Grotius, Hugo, 115, 331
  Hartlib, Samuel, 67
  Hebricus, 179
  Hegel, 364
  Herodotus, 179, 187, 207–8
  Hobbes, Thomas, 67
  Homer, 295, 325–6, 356, 366
  Hooker, 215
  Horace, 116, 187, 192, 207–8
  Isendoorn, Gisbert ab, 88
  Jerome, St., 15
  Justinian, 302
  Juvenal, 115, 179, 208
  Keckermann, Bartholomew, 47
  Lingard, John, 302
  Livy, 187, 207–8
  Locke, John, 115, 210, 271
  Lombard, Peter, 15
  Lucan, 191
  Malory, 237, 239
  Medina, Bartolomé de, 47
  Melancthon, Philipp, 16
  Mendoza, Pedro (Gonzales de), 47
  Milton, John, 89
  Mommsen, Theodore, 392
  Niebuhr, Reinold, 209
  Origen, 15
  Ovid, 192
  Paley, 207
  Pascal, Blaise, 274
  Persius, 192
  Piccolomini, Alessandro, 47
  Plato, 116, 208, 274, 383
  Plautus, 326
  Pliny, 20
  Politian, 191
  Porphyry, 36
  Ptolemy, 36
  Ramus, Petrus [de la Ramée], 37
  Ranke, Leopold von, 302
  Rocco, Alfredo, 331
  Rousseau, Jean Jacques, 330, 362
  Ruvio, Anthanius, 47
  Sacrabosco, Joannes de, 47

Sannazarius, 191
Silius Italicus, 191–2
Smiglecius [Smiglecki] Marcin, 47
Raleigh, Sir Walter, 89
Socrates, 165
Solomon, 138
Sophocles, 115, 179, 208
Spigelius, Adrianus, 47
Tacitus, 208, 392–4
Terence, 134
Thucydides, 179, 187, 208, 325–6
Virgil, 36, 187, 192, 208, 277
Vida, 191
Vitruvius, 138
Wollebius, Joannes, 88
Xenophon, 116, 179
Zabarella, Count Giacomo, the elder, 47
Zanchi, Hieronymus, 39

Private Life

Celibacy:
    Elizabeth I's policy on academic
        marriage (1561), 40
    Dons 'sigh for a living or a wife' (1780),
        114
    Chaffers 'ruined by the old celibate
        Common Room life' (1840s),
        244
    Ward resigns Fellowship but remains a
        Tutor on marriage to Mary
        Arnold (1872), 277
    Fellows permitted to marry, subject to a
        two-thirds majority vote among
        Fellowship (1878), 234
    Stallybrass on 'Holy Deadlock', 377
    female guests of students first
        permitted in Hall on Saturdays
        (1950), 406
        but Fellows dine in Common Room,
        406
    female guests of Fellows admitted to
        High Table one night in each
        vacation (1959), 406
    female guests first permitted to dine at
        High Table during term (14 Feb.
        1964), 406
        despite protest by male students
        against 'women in Hall', 406

BNC's resident bachelor Fellows still
    10% above Oxford average
    (1966), 396
first female students matriculate (1974),
    420–21
    benign influence of, 421
first female Fellows elected (1981–2),
    421

Dress:
    regulated clothing (early 16th c.), 25
    gentlemen commoners' finery (1720s),
        101
    hierarchy of dress (mid 18th c.), 105
    dress of gentlemen commoners (1720s),
        101
    Phoenix dine in claret and brown
        (1823), 188
    hunting dress (1840), 218
    servants' dress, graded (1861), 250–51
    dress of dons' wives in North Oxford
        (1870s), 277–8
    Pater as an aesthetic young man (1860s),
        272
    Bussell as dandy (1890s), 306
    'Sebastian' and the 'Georgeoisie' (1924),
        355–6
    'Cubist Trousers' debagged (1926), 351
    jeans: dressing by the left (1958), 410

Eating, Drinking and Dancing:
    dinner menu (1597), 26
    'in eating [Houghton] has no fellow'
        (1638), 47
    increasingly elaborate 'way of
        entertaining' (1650s), 72
    'heroic' eating on Oak Apple Day (29
        May, 1693), 89–90
    gargantuan drinking at Proctorial
        Dinner (1669), 90
    disorderly drinking by Gentlemen
        Commoners (1725), 101–2
    formidable menu at St. Thomas's Day
        feast (1771), 113–4
    elaborate dishes at Betty Morley
        and Shrove Tuesday feasts
        (mid 18th c.), 112
    weighty fare at Gaudies (1762; 1771),
        110–11

Private Life (Cont.)
    considerable quantities of ale consumed
        (1762–3), 109–10
    picnics and travel fare (1731), 121–2
    dinner in SCR (1774), 157
    Shrove Tuesday feasts (1775–6), 158
    'beastly' dinners for Commoners (1801),
        171–2
    'cold collation' for Louis XVIII (1808),
        164
    banquet for the Allied Sovereigns
        (1814), 165
    wartime economies at table (1812;
        1817), 178
    triumphant election dinners (1821),
        184–5
    midnight drinking in Old Quad (1822),
        199
    'Fancy Dress and Polka Ball' (1845), 208
    'breakfasts' and 'wines' (1850s), 240
    punch and tobacco with the Pre-
        Raphaelites (1854–8), 237
    devilled oranges with the Owls (1854),
        240
    oysters, lobsters, dressed crab, grilled
        bones, poached eggs and punch
        or mulled ale at undergraduate
        suppers (1859–60), 256, 264
    Masonic Balls (1863–5), 268
    Masonic Fetes (1863–5), 268
    Show Sunday (1860s–70s), 267–8
    Procession of Boats and Nuneham
        Picnics (1860s–93), 267–8
    Pater at Snow's Restaurant, Piccadilly
        (1880s), 282
    'The Bollinger' (1884), 355
    Freshman's Wine (1904), 317
    Bussell's 'Paternal dinner' for the Pater
        Soc. (1909), 319
    heavy drinking at all levels (1921; 1929;
        1930), 366–7
    Graham ('Sebastian') at Cavendish
        Hotel, St. James's (1924), 354
    Sonners' dinners (1920s–30s), 337
    Sonners' dancing (1926), 323
    Platnauer's luncheons (1931), 365
    Quartercentenary Ball (1909), 319
    wartime rationing (1917), 329

    post-war rationing (1946), 385
    proctorial monitoring of dances at the
        Forum (1950s), 408
    expenditure on 'entertainment' (1959;
        1968), 386
    Commems. and Summer Balls, (1908,
        1926), 319, 367, 421
    Schools' Dinners (1980s onwards), 421
Etiquette:
    changing meal-times (18th c.), 110
    ritual toasting at feasts (1771–3), 112
    college graces at dinner and supper,
        Appendix F
    seating in hall (1520; 1786), 20–21, 100
    seating in chapel (1666), 80
    last of the Gentlemen Commoners
        (1840), 213
        honorific revival of the title (1908), 213
    seating at High Table (before 1968), 396
    'capping' (early 18th c.), 105
    'general change of manners' (1818), 198
    parties (in 1920s), 356–7
    parties (in 1950s), 410
    loosening manners (in 1960s), 408
    influence of women (1970s onwards),
        420–21
    changing role of parents (1860s; 1980s),
        247, 421
Health and Disease:
    six outbreaks of plague (1550s–90s), 25
    Principal Meare's madness (1710),
        98, 124–5
    heavy smoking (1860s; 1930s), 262, 380
    Principal Last and 'the bridle of
        Theages' (1948), 383
    premature deaths of Tutorial Fellows
        (early and mid 20th c.), 386
Homosexuality:
    Richard Heber accused of
        (1826), 193–5
    cross-dressing among undergraduates
        (1845; 1860s; 1890), 208, 256,
        306
    Pater and 'the Balliol bugger' (1974),
        281–2
    Pater in louche company
        (1880s), 283

Hutchinson's *Boy Worship*
(1880), 283–4
C.S. Lewis at BNC whipping party
(1917), 337
Graham ('Sebastian') and
Waugh (1923–6), 354–7
Parson's Pleasure
(1920s), 337

Language:
use of Latin, 20, 25, 83, 118, 185
Vice-Principal's Register in Latin (until
1770s)
Accounts compiled using Roman
numerals (until 1773), 103
Accounts recorded in Latin (until 1835),
103
Turner 'put up first notice in English
about reassembling after the
Vacation' (1878), 287
Bussell's Ale Verses in Latin (1888)
Sonners' proctorial address in Latin
(1926), 331
Platnauer on punctuation
(1957), 408
vernacular culture (1960s
onwards), 410

Morality and Discipline:
Principal Grey (of Brasenose Hall),
charged with throwing a park-
keeper into the river (1438), 9
lecturer (Sutton) charged with lewd and
disorderly behaviour at Cold
Norton (1530), 27
fisticuffs between Fellows (1574), 40
Principal Harris publicly insults Dean of
Ch. Ch. in University Church
(1580), 39–40
'kissing Sixsmith' reads 'a virginitie
lecture' (1638), 47
Lord Littleton keeps a 'concubine' in
college (1644–5), 55
Principal Greenwood calls in soldiers to
control 'clamorous' scholars at
St. Mary's (1651), 65, 91
Baby found at night in bushes of
Old Quad (1671), 90

Principal Yate's nepotism (1661–76), 86
proctorial arrest of local girl for
'dancing in the Mitre Inn with
Brasenose men in boy's
apparel' (1683), 90
Principal Meare's nepotism
(1681–1710), 98–9
Meare's daughter secretly married to a
Fellow (1690s), 98
Principal Shippen, 'a most lecherous
man' (Hearne, 1732), 132
incidents in his regime (1710–45);
'truculent, dishonest,
interfering...sensual' (Jeffery,
1931), 123–35
Mrs. Shippen (Lady Clarke), 'given
much to drinking and gaming'
(Hearne, 1728), 126
undergraduates stealing bread from
Buttery 'window' (1760), 104
Kynaston loses Fellowship after
'disgusting' offence (1764), 100
Brucker (common-room man) sent to
Botany Bay for stealing 570
bottles of port (1788), 112
thefts from SCR by 'Charles the hall boy'
(1799), 176
episode of *The Whippiad* (1802), 197–8
prevalence of 'vice and immorality'
(1811), 185
prostitution; dangers of (1838), 212
'a comparatively quiet college ... we
did not fall foul of our dons as
in other colleges' (Woodgate,
1860s), 255
'abundant leisure and abundant
temptation' (Plowden, 1860s),
260
political bullying (Jones, 1870), 262–3
nocturnal roof-climbing (1869; 1871),
264
corruption in local politics
(1880), 296

Riot and Disorder:
bump supper riots (1881; 1891), 297–9,
306–7

Private Life (Cont.)
  hell-raising Vampires: Boswell
      and Rashleigh (1885–8), 302
  sportsmen demonstrate in Hall (1898),
      309–12
  bonfires (none after 1936), 297–9,
      306–7, 322
  attack on 'Arab Quarter' (1948), 397
  muted Suez demonstration (1956), 399
  student troubles: absence of protests at
      BNC (1974), 410

Sanctions:
  statutory regulation: provision for
      corporal punishment (1522), 14
  Broome's imposition: translating a
      sermon by Swift into Latin
      (1744), 107
  dinner in Hall compulsory during Ascot
      (1841), 208
  tolerance shown by dons
      (1880), 298
  penalties imposed on undergraduates
      for misconduct (1810; 1832;
      1842; 1876; 1880; 1885–6;
      1892), 189, 213, 298, 307
  Vampires dissolved by decanal fiat
      (1967), 407

Religious Life
  statutory role of Visitor (Bp. of
      Lincoln), 14
    Bp. Langland's conservative
        influence (1540s), 28
  College assents to University resolution
      repudiating papal supremacy
      (1534), 27
  Bible Clerk (1530s), 25
  Catholic conformists (1530s–50s),
      27–30
  Protestant reformers (1530s–1603),
      30–32, 38–39, 41–3
  Jesuits (1560s–80s), 33, 35
  Catholic martyrs (1580s), 34–5
  Catholic recusants (1550s–1688), 32–6,
      84, 91–4
  'Church puritans' (1603–41), 43–5,
      49–51

  Arminians (1630–41), 44, 51–3, 34–5
  Presbyterians (1646–52), 56–7, 59
  Independents (1652–8), 56–7
  Anglicans (1660 onwards) 83–5, 91–4
  ejected incumbents (1660), 84–5
  Non-jurors (1688), 95–6
  Catholic Jacobites (1715; 1745),
      145–6, 153
  Methodists (1729–51), 144–5, 149–50
  Freemasons (1769–82; 1817 onwards;
      1860s), **48**, 99, 150–53, 190,
      264–8
    Lodge premises (Alfred St.; Frewin
        Court; High St.; Banbury
        Road), 190
  attitudes to church patronage
      (1790s–1820s), 175–7
  'low temperature Anglicanism'
      (1830s–40s), 217
  Tractarians (Oxford Movement,
      1834–45), 202–3, 210–12
  Forbes's career (1840s onwards), 22–6
  Catholic converts (1845–50), 223
  Hole's career (1840–86), 218–22
  Robertson's career (1847–53), 214–6
  'free trade in religion' (1850s–60s), 264
  Evangelicals (1820s–60s; 1920s),
      210–11, 213–4, 218, 241, 261,
      264
  High Churchmen (1840s–60s), 218,
      222–6, 261
  'muscular Christians' (1850s–60s), 213,
      220, 265
  'middle-stump C. of E.' (1870s–90s),
      286
  Pater's career: doubt denied (1864–94),
      273–6, 279–81
  chapel services (first chapel,
      1520–1666):
    daily Mass (1520–49), 19–20
    1st and 2nd Prayer Book
        services (1549; 1552); Act
        of Uniformity (1549), 20, 28
    return of Mass (1556), 29
    return of Prayer Book
        (1559), 29
    imposition of 39 Articles (1562), 34

subscription to, a condition of matriculation (until 1803); of graduation (until 1854); and of MA status (until 1871), 96, 234

Holy Communion (Authorised Version 1611); attendance seven times p.a. (1615), 50, 55, 84

puritan services; morning and evening (Directory for Public Worship, 1648), 59

return of Authorised Version (1611); Act of Uniformity (1662); use of Prayer Book (1662), 83–4

chapel services (second chapel, 1666 onwards):

James II absolves Bernard from Easter attendance at chapel (1686), 92–3

Fellows' oaths confirmed: to college, university, church and crown (1688), 96

imposition of Easter and Whitsun communion confirmed (1774), 96

Barham too late for morning chapel (1807), 200

austere services, without music or sermons (1840), 221–2

increasing ritual; polychrome refurbishment (1860–63; 1894–6), 239, 274–5

over 50% of BNC men in 1850s and 1860s take Holy Orders, 261

compulsory chapel modified (1919), 338

and abolished (1932), 234, 338

first Muslims at BNC (1923), 358–60

Book of Common Prayer (1662) retained for College Prayers; Series III (1965) adopted for Holy Communion (1967), 409

first Catholic Mass at BNC since Reformation (1968), 409

decline in religious observance (1960s onwards), 409

changing role of chaplains (1970s onwards), 409

Associated Churches, etc.:

Amersham, Bucks., 131

Aynho, Northants., 100, 154

Brighton, St. Nicholas, 154

Trinity Chapel, 215–6

Caunton, Notts., 220

Chichester Cathedral, 211–2

Croydon, Bp.'s Palace, 51

Cuddesdon, Oxon., 71

Daylesford, Worcs., 205

East Bradenham, Norfolk, 205

Elsfield, Oxon, 308

Ewelme, Oxon, 126, 131

Farmington, Glos., 205

Gawsworth, Cheshire, 13, 134

Kelstern, Lincs., 94

Ledbury, Herefs., St. Katherine's Hospital, 159

Leeds, St. Saviour's, 261

Lincoln Cathedral, 11, 156

Little Gidding, 55

London:

All Saints, Margaret St., 226, 236

Margaret Street Chapel, 212, 223

St. Alban, Holborn, 274

St. Austin's Priory, Walworth, 274

St. Barnabas, King Square, 276

St. Leonard, Foster Lane, 24

St. Mildred, Bread St., 84

St. Paul's Cathedral (Old), 29, 31, 32, 43

St. Paul's Cathedral (New), 221

St. Paul, Walworth, 274

St. Philip, New Rd., [Newark St.], Stepney, 274

St. Thomas, Regent St., 274

Ludford Parva, Lincs., 94

Malpas, Cheshire, 174

Manchester:

Collegiate Church (later Cathedral), 33, 119, 146

St. John, Deansgate, 146

Trinity Chapel, 149

Oxwick, Norfolk, 188

Philadelphia, U.S.A., Christchurch, 128

Rotherfield Greys, Oxon., 62

St. Asaph, Bp.'s Palace, 162

Salford, Lancs., Trinity Chapel, 145

Religious Life (Cont.)
Sandon, Staffs., 33
Sefton, Lancs., 163
Sheviocke, Cornwall, 213
Sion, Middx., monastery, 13
Snave, Kent, 147
Stoke Edith, Herefs., 159
Sydney, Australia, St. Andrew, 223
Tarporley, Cheshire, 176
West Hampnett, Sussex, 212
Windsor, St. George's Chapel, 53
Worcester Cathedral, 41, 243

Scientific Life
Savile's career (1561–64), 36–7
Burton's career (1590s), **14**, 41
Sixsmith's teaching (1630s), 47–8
Ashmole's studies (1644–45), 87–8
Petty's career (1646–59), **15**, 67–9, 73
Traherne's interests (1653–6), 73
Maths teaching (1638; 1700; 1770), 47, 88, 115
examination reforms (1800–1809), 160
Maths teaching (1818; 1833), 169
Maths lectures by Tench ['Dr. Carp'] (1788–1812), 172
electro-chemistry (Grove in 1840s), 313
Maths and Physics teaching (1840s), 207, 243
Physical Sciences 'ignored in our Academical System' before 1849, 210
Agricultural science (Lawes in 1850s), 31
minimum of science teaching (1867), 301
physicists in Royal Society (Reinold and Rucker, 1880s), 312
Stocker gives up physics after 1904, 341
compulsory Greek abolished for scientists (1920), 324
Cowling a future astrophysicist (1920s), 351
first holders of chair in Engineering Science (Jenkins and Southwell), 361
Twinn a future Enigma cryptographer, 361
Science at BNC between World War I and II, 360–61

Big Science: a threat to collegiate autonomy (1940s onwards), 377–8
physics in 1940s (Kurti's career), 395
four Royal Society Fellows (1970s), 417
maths and science teaching in state schools declines (early 21st c.), 414, 428
increasing proportion of science Fellows (1964–89), 432
first election of a scientist as Principal: R. Cashmore (2003), 432

Sporting Life
early sports:
fives (16th c.), 26
hand ball (1608), 26
riding:
in the 16c., 26–7
horse-racing forbidden (1772), 121
ownership of horses restricted (1785), 121
hunting (1820s), 185
cost of hunting (1817), 186
pet dogs (1851; 1880), 255
point-to-point [or 'Grind'], (1840), 218–9
polo in 1881 (Haig), 293
cost of riding (1897), 310
boating:
BNC first Head of River (1815), 219
Cradock's enthusiasm for, 248–9, 254, 287–9
successes, 1840s–1860s, 219, 265, 268–9
college colours, black and gold (1858), 219
Woodgate's feats (1860s), 257–8
successes in the 1870s, 269
Procession of Boats (until 1893), 267–8
Head of River on 110 nights (1839–91), 285–6
Head in Torpids in 22 out of 62 years, 300
4 rowing trophies in a year (1890), 300

Head of the River (1889–91), 300
Head in Torpids (1886–94),
    300
bump-supper riots (1881; 1891),
    297–8, 307
bump-supper in 1922, **78**, 342–3
bump-supper in 1928, 343–4
bump-supper in 1930, 348
twenty bumps in four years
    (1922–25), 343
Head of the River, in 1928–31, 344
1ˢᵗ Eight (1931), **77**, 344
Cherry's career, **87**
Holdsworth's career, **85**, 375
BNC successes at Henley Regatta, **44**,
    220, 255, 268, 285, 300
    Weatherley and Woodgate invent
        coxwainless fours (1868), 285
first BNC Barge (1846), 219
second Barge (1882), **76**, 268
third Barge (1926), **77**
boathouse (1958), 401–2
training diet:
    in 1860s, 259, 269
    in 1906, 312
    in 1913, 269
30% of undergraduates row in Eights
    or Torpids (1890s), 307
decline in college rowing
    (1900–1914), 316
casualties among oarsmen in World
    War I, 321–2
serious decline of BNC rowing, 1950s
    onwards, 401–2
success of women's rowing (1974
    onwards), 402
Lindsay's international success
    (1999), 432
cricket:
    first BNC team (1835), 219
    Cradock's passion for, 269, 287
    great success in 1860s, 269–70
    triumphs of the 1870s, 270–71
    Ottaway's feats (1870s), **45**, 270–71
    'strong and manly' (1881), 296
    in the 1880s, 302, 309
    successes in 1920s, 346–7

triumphs in 1930s, 347–8
Stallybrass's enthusiasm for, 327–8,
    348
cricket Blues, 1950–72, 400–401
Cowdrey's career (1951–54), **55**, 401
decline of BNC cricket, 1972
    onwards, 401
cuppers' revival (1995–6), 431
first sports ground (Cowley Marsh),
    287
second sports ground (Grandpont),
    309
cricket pavilion (1894–6), 309
football:
    early games (16ᵗʰ c.), 26
    first formalised (1874; 1882), 299
    revival under Haslewood (1929
        onwards), 345–6
rugby:
    earliest games (1872), 299
    successes in 1880s, 299
    continuing success (1919–38), 345
    amateur spirit (1925), 328–9
    cuppers' triumph (1931–32), 345
    Obolensky's career (1934–6), 371
    unbeaten 'herd of buffalo' (1946–47),
        346
    rugby Blues, 1950–65, 399–400
    decline of college rugby (1965
        onwards), 400, 423
    cuppers' revival (1999–2000), 431
athletics:
    'Springy Colmore' (1866), 258–9
    Brooks's jumping feats
        (1876–7), 272
    Strode Jackson's running
        (1912), 322
    athletics bump supper (1914), 322
    Boyd's running feats (1954–6), 398
shooting:
    Radice's Bisley record, 319
    Barry's shooting diary (1880s), 296
walking:
    in Cotswolds (1731), 121–3
    in Oxfordshire (1880s), 304
    Stocker's feats (1876–1949),
        341–2

IMAGE

Name

first mention of 'Brasenose' (1279), 9
legends concerning, 7
confused with King's hall and chapel,
Woodstock, Oxon., 19
The Brazen Nose, or Knocker (12ᵗʰ c.),
9–10
removed to Stamford (1333), 9
returned to BNC (1890), 10
nose on Tower gateway (before 1534),
10
nose on 'Childe of Hale' (1ˢᵗ Eight,
1850s), **64**

Fame

a college of the North West (1509–1970s),
14, 25, 38–9, 48, 51–3, 97, 99,
108–9, 117–20, 121, 143–9, 217,
231, 236, 350, 412, 422
a Catholic college (1509–1570s), 14, 25,
27–30, 32–6
a Protestant college (1580s–1630s),
30–32, 40–45, 49–50
a Royalist college (1640–48), 50–63
a Parliamentary college (1648–60),
64–73
an Anglican college (1660–1688–1714),
83–6, 91–4
a Jacobite college (1714–45), 95–6, 99,
123–4, 141–54
tentatively reformist (1773; 1800–1809),
'59–60
socially glittering: an 'expensive' college
(1790s–1820s), 161–65, 185–7,
198–200
academically impressive: 'the leading
minds of Brasenose'(George
Eliot, 1809; 1820s–1830s),
168–9, 172
politically progressive: a Liberal Tory
college (1790s–1840s), 175,
181–4
Parliamentary elections for
O.U. (1806; 1821), 180–85
election of Chancellor
(1809), 181–2

financially prosperous: 'an unexampled
increase in members, revenue
and fame' (1809), 162
physically robust: 'rowdy and drinking'
(Mark Pattison, 1830), 185, 204
administratively cautious: a
Conservative college
(1830s–40s), 211, 229–30,
231–2
consciously sporting: 'not a reading
college' (1840s onwards), 208,
241–2, 287, 302
progressively inclined: a Liberal
college (1853 onwards), 232–6,
242–3, 249
'fast, but ... not sacrilegious' (1873), 266
Brasenose 'pluck' (1860s onwards),
253–4, 286, 308
an Imperial college (1880s–90s), 296, 308
'the Aborigines of Brasenose' (Logan
Pearsall Smith, 1881), 297–9,
303, 393
Liberal attitudes (1890s onwards), 311,
318, 328–9, 332, 380
'manly, upright, sportsmanlike' (1899),
307
'a college full of bloods' (Middleton
Murry, 1908), 311, 317
'never a dressy college' (Haig,
1917), 313
'sporting one's Oak eccentric at
Brasenose' (1920s), 361
patriotically apolitical (1926), 367
a college for law and sport (1920s–30s),
328–9, 343–9, 360–62
ideal of balanced education (Stallybrass,
1941), 332, 380
academically weighty; scholastically low-
key (1940s–70s), 388–9, 392–6,
397–9, 417
politically quiescent (1956), 399
socially exuberant: 'the baying of the
bloodies' (1959), 410
willingly meritocratic (1940s onwards),
376, 385, 412–5, 428
societally pluralistic (1950s onwards),
412–3, 428

athletically disinclined (1960s onwards),
        408
untroubled by student 'troubles'
        (1970s), 406, 410, 418–9
welcoming to the admission of
        women (1974), 419–21
increasingly postgraduate (1960s
        onwards), 413, 423–4
increasingly studious (1970s onwards),
        408, 430–32
increasingly international (1980s
        onwards), 423, 428–9, 431
ratio of state-school to
        independent-school
        pupils (1946–2009), 325,
        334–6, 350, 376–7, 385,
        411–5, 422–3, 428

Brasenose Abroad:
    Aix-la-Chapelle, 257
    Athens, 356–7
    Avranches, 205
    Cairo, 357
    Dinan, 205
    Douai Coll., 33, 35, 36
    Florence, 359
    Marienbad, 257
    Melbourne (Olympics, 1956), 398
    Menton, 219
    Sark, 250
    Spa, 257
    Stockholm (Olympics, 1912), 322
    Sydney (Olympics, 1999), 432

Brasenose Travellers:
    Reginald Heber in Northern
            and Eastern Europe
            (1806), 196–7
    Richard Heber in France and Holland
            (1820s), 192–3
    Pater in Italy (1865), 276

Brasenose and Foreign Wars:
    Brasenose 'puritans' to New England
            (1630s), 85
    Brasenose non-jurors to Philadelphia
            (1724), 128, 134
    Brasenose in American War
            of Independence (1776–83),
            109

Brasenose in French Revolutionary and
        Napoleonic Wars (1793–1815),
        177–9
Brasenose in Indian Mutiny
        (1857–8), 205
Brasenose in World War I (1914–18),
        313–4, 320–23
    BNC casualties, 320–23
    estimates of Haig, 313–4, 407
    Stallybrass and the League of Nations,
        330–31
Brasenose in World War II (1939–45),
        369–76
    BNC casualties, 370–75
    BNC undergraduates evacuated to
            Christ Church, 369–70
    BNC links with Buchenwald, 423
    BNC links with Bletchley Park, 361
BNC and Suez (1956), 399
BNC and Hungary (1956), 399
BNC and CND (1958), 399
BNC and Czechoslovakia
        (1968), 399

Brasenose and the British Empire:
    Reginald Heber in India (1823–6), 197
    Forbes in India (1830s), 222
    Pickering in South Africa
            (1840s), 218
    Knott in India (1869), 261
    Sconce in Australia (1850s), 223
    BNC supplies recruits for Colonial
            Service (1920s–1940s), **83A**,
            344, 345, 347, 363

Globalised Recruitment:
    Recruitment to BNC of students from
            the Commonwealth
            (1930s–50s), 422
    Rhodes Scholars (1904 onwards),
            328–9, 477–84 (Appendix D)
    international intake of students (1980s
            onwards), 424, 428–9, 431
    impact on composition of Fellowship
            (1990s onwards), 423

Networks and Structures
Relations with the Crown:
    choice of name (1509), 11
    receipt of Charter (1512), 11

Networks and Structures (Cont.)
  Royal Visitation (1535), 16
  Royal Visitation (1549), 28
  Marian Visitation (1556), 29, 37
  James I fails to secure
      Walmsley's election as
      Principal (1608), 42
  opposition to the Crown (Civil War),
      51–2
  loyalty to the Crown (Civil War), 50, 52–3
  Principal and Fellows reinstated by
      Royal Commissioners (1660),
      70–71, 83
    Oaths of Supremacy and Allegiance
      (1661), 83
    Act of Uniformity (1662), 83
  James II's Declaration of Indulgence
      (1686); effect in Brasenose, 91–4
  Glorious Revolution (1688);
      consequences of, 95–6
    Oath of Supremacy (1689), 96
    Oath of Allegiance (1689), 96
    Oath of Abjuration (1701), 96
  Brasenose support for Jacobites (1715;
      1745), 141–50
  a blackmailer of Brasenose Jacobites,
      whipped from Carfax to
      Eastgate (1721), 142
  Royal Visits:
    1st visit of Elizabeth I (1566), 17
    2nd visit of Elizabeth I (1592), 39
    visit of James I (1605), 76
    visit of the Duke of York, later James
      II (1683), 82
    visit of Louis XVIII (1808), 164
    Prince of Wales (later Edward VII) at
      Frewin Hall (1859–60), 253
    Prince of Wales (later Edward VIII)
      at Phoenix Dinner (1913), 321
    Visit of Princess Elizabeth (later
      Queen Elizabeth II) (1948), 381

Relations with Parliament:
  Brasenose under Parliamentary
      Visitations (1647–58), 56–64
  Fellowship purged (1648), 58–63
  oaths of loyalty to Parliament
      (1648–49), 60–61

  acceptance of Parliamentary settlement
      in Church and State (1660; 1688;
      1714), 95–96
  support for Jacobite opposition
      (1714–45), 123–49
  Liberal Tory views (1790s–1840s),
      59–60, 175, 180–85
  Conservative instincts regarding reform
      (1830s–52), 229–32
  Liberal attitudes (1853 onwards), 232
      et seq.
  1st Parliamentary Commission
      (1850–52), 226–36
    BNC refuses to co-operate
      (1851–52), 229–30
    but willingly accepts results (1854),
      232
  2nd Parliamentary Commission
      [Cleveland] (1872–77), 235
  3rd Parliamentary Commission
      [Selborne] (1877–82), 235
  4th Parliamentary Commission
      [Asquith] (1919–22), 324–6
    resulting government grants; first to
      be made by Board of Education
      to Oxford University (1912–13;
      1919), 332–4
  increasing state funding for Oxford
      (1922; 1945; 1964), 326, 377, 426
  Labour Party's aim: colleges weaker *vis á
      vis* University; University weaker
      vis á vis State (1922; 1953; 1958;
      1965), 334–6, 416–7, 425, 426
  Education Act (1944); influence of, on
      recruitment, 376–7
  University Grants Committee (later
      Commission); limited impact on
      Oxford's autonomy, 335, 377–8,
      412, 415–6, 425
  increasing numbers of Oxford students
      receiving state grants (1938;
      1948; 1950–52; 1957), 376,
      411, 415
  conflation of entrance and scholarship
      exams (1962), 412–13
  University funding transferred from
      Treasury to Dept. of Education
      (1963), 413

Robbins Report (1963), effect of, 424–5
Oxford's response: colleges and the
    Franks Report (1966), 425–6
admissions policy and practice (UCCA
    and BNC); 1965 onwards, 412–5
closed scholarships phased out (in
    1970s), 413
effects of comprehensive school
    reorganisation (1960s–1970s),
    413–15
  in particular on admissions based on
    A level teaching and syllabus,
    413–4
abolition of Assisted Places Scheme;
    effects of (1976), 413
entrance scholarships abolished (1984),
    413
proportion of state-school pupils at
    BNC drops slightly from 47%
    (1964) to 44% (2005), 411–12
  compared with Oxford's state-school
    intake; which falls from a high
    point of 62% in 1969 to 56% in
    1980, and to 53% in 2005, 413,
    423
'Unit of resource' (state funding per
    student), driven down in
    1976–89 and 1989–2002, 427
effects on colleges of Oxford's
    expansion in mid and later
    20th c., 416
  in particular, on growing
    power of General Board,
    vis á vis colleges
    (1970s–1980s), 416
BNC's near doubling of postgraduate
    recruitment (1948–65), 43, 413,
    423–4
  continues until undergraduate and
    postgraduate intakes approach
    parity (2006–7), 428
University Grants Commission (UGC)
    replaced by University Funding
    Council (UFC), in 1987, 416
Research Councils: effects of target-
    driven funding on research,
    teaching and recruitment (1993
    onwards), 426–9

governance: North Report (1997)
    and after, 426–7
tuition fees; government control of
    (1993), 417, 429
colleges and the Office for Fair Access
    (OFFA), 2004 onwards, 429
relative qualifications of state and
    independent school pupils at
    admission, in 2005–7, 414
plans to reverse drift towards
    dependence on government
    finance (1950; 1965; 1997;
    2007), 428–9

Relations with Other Oxford Colleges
    and O.U. Institutions:
All Souls Coll., 23, 43–4, 53, 57–8, 61,
    81, 86, 93, 135–7, 197, 274,
    307–8, 319, 339, 350, 360, 390,
    402, 406, 431–2
Ashmolean Museum, 128, 132, 257, 312
Balliol Coll., 23, 69, 93, 128, 143,
    208, 227, 231, 242, 248, 260,
    276, 279, 281, 287, 300–1, 318,
    326, 340, 348, 359, 361, 386,
    397–8, 407, 413
Beam Hall, Merton St., 54
Black Hall, 75, 84
Bodleian Library, 128, 279, 316
Brasenose Hall, 7–10, 12
Broadgates Hall, 8
Broad Walk (Ch. Ch. Meadows), 267
Christ Church, 22–4, 30, 41, 44–5,
    55, 59, 62, 69, 75, 81, 86,
    88, 92–6, 98, 121–2, 135,
    137, 144–5, 156–7, 160,
    162–3, 167, 170, 173–4,
    198, 205–6, 208, 231, 253,
    266–7, 276, 279–80, 301,
    326, 341, 343, 348, 362,
    369–70, 386, 411–2, 413
  rivalry with:
    in 1580s, 39–40
    in 1790s, 163
    in 1820s, 173
    in 1920s, 343
Clarendon Building, 376, 406, 418
Clarendon Laboratory, 312, 369, 395

Networks and Structures (Cont.)

Corpus Christi Coll., 14–15, 23, 29, 32, 81, 122, 231, 260, 290, 299, 348, 359

   rivalry with (1512; 1514), 16

   Claymond scholars attend Humanity and Greek lectures at (1538), 15

Cowley Marsh (old BNC/Ch. Ch. cricket ground), 287, 407

Examination Schools (New), 290, 294, 406

Exeter Coll., 22, 45–6, 50, 69, 85, 97, 161, 237, 244–5, 249, 337

Frewin Hall, 253, 294, 401, 405

Glazing (Glassyn) Hall, 75

Gloucester Hall, 33, 91

Grandpont (BNC cricket ground), 309, 407–8

Grandpont House, 403

Hart Hall, 125

Haberdasher Hall, 8

Hertford Coll., 290, 361, 386, 420

Ivy Hall, 8

Jesus Coll., 57, 69, 413, 420

Keble Coll., 267, 297, 337, 348, 361

Kettle Hall, 91

Lady Margaret Hall, 300

Lincoln Coll., 12, 16, 18, 23–4, 33, 46, 57, 69, 82, 150, 157, 286, 290, 330–1, 370, 404, 416

   proposals for merger with:

     in 1878, 286–7

     in 1918, 330

     in 1944, 370

     in 1970, 416

Little St. Edmund Hall, 8, 18, 76

Little University Hall, 8–10, 12

Magdalen Coll., 21–4, 31–2, 46, 58, 93–4, 140, 155, 232, 253, 276, 343, 361, 386, 397–8

Magdalen Hall, 58, 95–6, 98–9, 114, 205, 340

Merton Coll., 23, 29, 33, 37, 44, 57–9, 69, 81–2, 97, 205, 230, 240, 253, 255, 262, 348, 361, 386, 407

New Coll., 17, 23–4, 29, 35, 57, 69, 96, 98, 108, 121, 135, 205, 211, 230–1, 240, 253, 260, 268, 318, 359, 361–4, 386, 397–8, 407, 420

   Fellows at Shrove Tuesday feast (1775–6), 158

New Inn Hall, 64

Oriel Coll., 12, 46, 64, 69, 107, 141–2, 160, 170, 179, 206, 209, 227, 231, 253, 331, 340–1, 348, 390, 392

Pembroke Coll., 69, 91, 97, 237, 239, 361, 386

Queen's Coll., 23, 44, 69, 99, 122, 230–1, 246, 253, 260, 288, 315, 359, 362, 386, 397, 413, 430

Radcliffe Camera, 95, 140–41, 143, 165, 187, 271, 292, 297, 359, 397, 402, 404

Radcliffe Square, 137, 181, 184, 318, 397

St. Alban Hall, 71, 132

St. Aldate's, 261

St. Catherine's Coll., 420

St. Cross, 403, 430

St. Ebbe's, 215

St. Edmund Hall, 92, 115, 400

St. John's Coll., 22, 33–4, 44, 58, 69, 78, 185, 211, 231, 253, 268, 315, 339, 348, 378, 386, 430

St. Mary's Coll., New Inn Hall Street, 78–80, 82

St. Mary's Entry, **52B**, 8

St. Thomas's Hall, 8

Salissury Hall, 8, 76

Sheldonian Theatre, 99, 130, 196, 203, 217, 264

Shield Hall, 8

Somerville Coll., 290, 402

Staple Hall, 18, 70, 75

Templeton Coll. (Centre for Management Studies), 390

Trinity Coll., 58, 69, 82, 93, 232, 245, 251, 290, 361, 392, 411

Union Society, 236, 239, 359, 360, 371

University Church (St. Mary's), 7, 11, 15, 25, 39–41, 55–6, 61, 78, 87, 90–1, 98, 160, 204, 223, 273, 299, 403

University Coll., 6, 8, 22–3, 92–3, 95,
128–30, 134, 140, 255, 275
University Parks (cricket ground), 287
University Schools (Old), 7, 15
Wadham Coll., 46, 58, 69, 97, 255,
290–1, 348, 386, 420
Worcester Coll., 137, 268, 361

Relations with the City of Oxford and
St. Mary's Parish:
Alfred St., no. 9 (OTC), 323
All Saints [later Lincoln Coll. library],
153, 293, 404
Catherine Wheel (hostelry), 35
Clarendon Hotel, Cornmarket, 284, 317
Corn Exchange, 268
Floating Chapel, 224
Grandpont (City football ground), 430
High Street, 290, 293–4
Holywell, no. 1, 363
Holywell Music Room, 240
Holywell St., stables, garden, 141, 248
Holywell Mill, 91
King's Head, Cornmarket, 151
Long Wall Street, houses, 251
Maclaren's Gymnasium, Oriel St., 237
Mitre Inn, High St., 90
Mynchery Wood, Headington, 77
New Inn, 151
Oxford Castle (Bocardo or Prison), 112,
176
Phoenix Inn, 153
Port Meadow, 177, 296
St. Aloysius, 277
St. Cross [Holywell], churchyard, 74, 275
St. Mary's [University Church]
members of Brasenose buried in, 11,
41, 55, 71, 91, 189
St. Mary Magdalen, 78
burial of John Jackson in, 78
Star Hotel, Cornmarket, 190
St. Thomas's, 224, 273
Three Tons hostelry, 131
Warneford Hospital, 362

Relations with Colleges and Universities
elsewhere
Cambridge:
Christ's Coll., 16

Emmanuel Coll., 24
Gonville and Caius Coll., 24
King's Coll., 420
St. John's Coll., 12, 22, 42, 118
Canberra, A.N.U., 426
Carnegie Foundation, USA, 345
Dublin, Trinity Coll., 64
Edinburgh Univ., 300
Glasgow Univ., 222, 300, 309
Gresham Coll., London, 126
Harvard Univ., U.S.A., 427
Henley, Administrative Staff Coll.,
Berks., 387
London Institution, 282
London Univ., 312
Bartlett School of Architecture, 356
King's Coll., 241, 339
University Coll., 387
Purdue Univ., USA, 345
Princeton, Institute of Advanced Study,
USA, 329
Rothampstead, Herts., 313
Royal Institution, 403
Royal Engineering Coll., Cooper's Hill,
Surrey, 341
Swathmore Coll., U.S.A., Worth
dormitory, 384

Relations with Particular Schools:
Banbury G.S., 12
Bath Coll., 318
Birmingham, King Edward's
School, 238
Birmingham, Oratory, 208
Boston G. S., 150
Bradford G. S., 419
Bristol, The Fort, 163
Bury G. S., 119, 422
Calder H.S., Mytholmroyd, 408
Canterbury, King's School, 246, 257
Cardiff H.S., 345
Charlbury G. S., 65, 87
Charterhouse, 347, 350
Cheltenham Coll., 347
Clifton Coll., 271, 295
Dartmouth Naval Coll., 35
Devil's Lake H. S., South Dakota, 345
Edinburgh Academy, 222

Networks and Structures (Cont.)
Eton Coll., 37, 217, 263, 266, 271, 288–9, 296, 343–4, 350
Farnworth G. S., 12
Geelong G. S., 344, 401
Glasgow Academy, 346
Haileybury Coll., 217, 222, 344
Harrow School, 217, 263, 270–1, 296, 300, 311
Hartley Coll., Southampton, 240
Hereford Cathedral School, 231, 284
Horsham G. S., 317
Lancing Coll., 350
Leicester G. S., 12
St. Paul's School, 257
Loretto School, 299, 400
Macclesfield G. S., 12, 134
Malvern School, 347, 350
Manchester G. S., 38, 109, 117–120, 144, 146–7, 149, 163–4, 212, 217, 231, 244, 262, 303, 350, 359, 406, 412, 422
Marlborough Coll., 231, 257, 350, 422
Marlborough G. S., 367
Melbourne, G. S., 347
Middleton G. S., 23, 36, 45
Newark G. S., 217
Oldham G. S., 119
Osborne Naval Coll., 351
Oswestry G. S., 217
Oundle School, 257
Prescot G. S., Lancs., 12, 14
Radley Coll., 255, 257, 266, 407
Repton School, 299
Rondesbosch, Diocesan Coll., South Africa, 347
Rossall School, 257, 271
Rugby School, 217, 271, 287, 350
St. Asaph School, 347
Salford G. S., 149
Salisbury, Bp. Wordsworth's School, 368
Sedbergh School, 347
Sherborne Coll., 422
Shrewsbury School, 299, 345, 350, 363, 422
Steeple Aston G. S., 71

Stockport G. S., 123
Strathallan School, 347
Tarporley G. S., 96
Todmorden Secondary School, 391
Tonbridge School, 217, 401
Trent Coll., 371
United Services Coll., Westward Ho!, 241
Uppingham School, 237, 350
Wakefield G. S., 217
Walthamstow G. S., 351
Wellington Coll., 354, 412
Wimbledon, King's Coll. School, 347
Winchester Coll., 271, 303, 344, 350, 363
Worcester, King's School, 365

Associated Houses:
Airmyn Hall, Howden, Yorks., 180
Alloa House, Clackmannan., 265
Ancoats Hall, Manchester, 147
Appleton Manor, Berks., 126
Barrymore House, Wargrave, Berks., 152
Basing House, Hants., 84
Beckley Park, Oxon., 9
Belmont, Cheshire, 152
Beresford Hall, Derbys., 63
Birtsmorton Court, Oxon., 311
Blount's Court, 35
Boconnoc, Cornwall, 182
Boughton, Northants., 139
Buckden, Hunts., 11
Chatsworth, Derbys., 139
Chirk Castle, Denbighs., 89
Corfe Castle, Dorset, 51
Daylesford, Worcs., 205
Denton House, nr. Cuddesdon, Oxon., 79
Drayton House, Northants., 139
Dropmore, Bucks., 182
Earnwood, Buxton, Derbys., 223
Eshton House, Yorks., 191–2
Fota Island, co. Cork, 152
Gogerddan, Denbighshire, 153
Gresgarth Hall, Lancs., 236
Guiana Island, Antigua, 221
Gwersyllt, Denbighshire, 101

Hale Hall, Lancs., 48,
Harrowden Park, Northants., 139
Hawarden Castle, Flints., 52
Headington Quarry, 'The Kilns', 338
Heaton Hall, Lancs., 165
Hodnet Hall, Salop., 174, 178, 192, 194
Kellie Castle, Fife, 265
Killiow, Cornwall, 265
Kirtlington Priory, Oxon., 42
Knighton Park, Leics., 248
Knowsley Hall, Lancs., 38
Latham House, Lancs., 51
Lyddington, Rutland, 11
Lyme Hall, Cheshire, 66
Mallow Castle, co. Cork, 51
Maristow, Devon, 200
West Marton Hall, Yorkshire, 174, 180
Mowbreck Hall, Lancs., 153
Norbury Park, Surrey, 257
North Villa, Regent's Park, London, 270
Ordsall Hall, Lancs., 52
Piddington Grange, Northants., 76
Pimlico Lodge, London, 192
Queluz Palace, nr. Lisbon, 139
Ravenscragg, Ullswater,
        Westmoreland, 302
Read Hall, nr. Whalley, Lancs., 42
Rosendaal Castle, Holland, 351
St. Paul's Walden Bury, Herts., 139
Seaton Delaval, Northumberland, 139
Sedbury Park, Glos., 201
Shardeloes, Bucks., 217
Sharrow Bay, Ullswater, 302
Shenstone Park, Staffs., 248
Southgate House, Arno's Grove,
        Middx., 270
Southill, Beds., 139
Stansted Abbots, Herts, Rye House, 24
Tabley Hall, Cheshire, 79

Tackley Park, Oxon., 270
Underlay Hall, Westmoreland, 42
Wern Newydd, New Quay,
        Cardiganshire, 357
West Court, Finchampstead, 265
Whitbourne Hall, Herefs., 204
Whitfield House,
        Herefs, 187
Wicklewood, Norfolk, 192
Woodchester Park, Glos., 223

Relations with the Media and Public:
first permanent TV set in college
        (1963), 410
visit of the Beatles to BNC
        (1964), 403
student troubles and the media
        (1966; 1968; 1970; 1973; 1974),
        405, 409
    reception of the Hart Report (1969),
        406, 418–19
    assault on Clarendon Building
        (1970), 406
    occupation of Examination Schools
        (1973), 406
    attack on the Indian Institute
        (1974), 406
    administrative response: Disciplinary
        Court (1974), 406
cultural realignment: the process
        of democratising and
        feminising (1970s),
        402–3, 406–8, 410,
        419–21
cultural pressures and questions of
        access (1960s onwards), 385,
        410–15, 421–9
undergraduates become students
        (1970s onwards), 410